Praise for

THE GREATER JOURNEY

"An epic of ideas, as well as an exhilarating book of spells . . . This is history to be savored."

—Stacy Schiff, *The New York Times Book Review*

"From a dazzling beginning that captures the thrill of arriving in Paris in 1830 to the dawn of the 20th century, McCullough chronicles the generations that came, saw and were conquered by Paris. . . . It will entice a whole new generation of Francophiles, armchair travelers and those Americans lucky enough to go to Paris before they die."

—Bruce Watson, *The San Francisco Chronicle*

"There is not an uninteresting page here as one fascinating character after another is explored at a crucial stage of his development. . . . Wonderful, engaging writing full of delighting detail."

—John Barron, *Chicago Sun-Times*

"McCullough's skill as a storyteller is on full display. . . . The idea of telling the story of the French cultural contribution to America through the eyes of a generation of aspiring artists, writers and doctors is inspired. . . . a compelling and largely untold story in American history."

—Kevin J. Hamilton, *The Seattle Times*

"Few authors have done more to popularize American history than David McCullough. Not only has the historian-lecturer made it more accessible than ever, he has made it sing."

—Allen Pierleoni, *Sacramento Bee*

"A lively and entertaining panorama. . . . By the time he shows us the triumphant Exposition Universelle in 1889, witnessed through the eyes of such characters as painters John Singer Sargent and Robert Henri, we share McCullough's enthusiasm for the city and his affection for the many Americans who improved their lives, their talent and their nation by drinking at the fountain that was Paris."

—Michael Sims, *The Washington Post*

"For more than 40 years, David McCullough has brought the past to life in books distinguished by vigorous storytelling and vivid character-izations. . . . McCullough again finds a slighted subject in *The Greater Journey,* which chronicles the adventures of Americans in Paris. . . . Wonderfully atmospheric."

—Wendy Smith, *Los Angeles Times*

"[McCullough] deploys his paramount storytelling skills to create a thoroughly engaging historical montage."

—Rebecca Steinitz, *The Boston Globe*

"[McCullough] wants us to know more than just the dry facts of our country's history; he wants us to share the vivid emotional experience of those who inhabited it. Life is love and conflict and drama and change, not just names and dates. McCullough reminds us of that with each shimmering, resonant page he writes. . . . Exhilarating."

—Julia Keller, *Chicago Tribune*

"David McCullough [is] a man who can tell a riveting story. . . . It was Bostonian Thomas Gold Appleton who observed, 'When good Americans die they go to Paris.' Nothing so drastic is required for the delightful Paris stay of seven decades McCullough treats us to in this magnificent book."

—James R. Carroll, *The Courier-Journal*

"Luminous. . . . McCullough succeeds because he sees the greater significance of his work, and the care with which he writes reveals that greater purpose. He tells these stories so as to inspire the current generation of Americans to the pursuit of excellence: a virtue McCullough's work both encourages and exemplifies."

—Brian Bolduc, *National Review*

"McCullough is that rare phenomenon, a bestselling historian. . . . *The Greater Journey* makes clear why: He combines extensive, meticulous research and a scholar's skill at synthesis with an always engaging, clear prose style and deft narrative."

—Colette Bancroft, *St. Petersburg Times*

"A series of sketches by a masterful storyteller. . . . inviting us to celebrate a (perhaps more innocent) time when talented and ambitious Americans loved Paris, every moment of the year."

—Glenn C. Altschuler, *Pittsburgh Post-Gazette*

"Riveting. . . . Like all great entertainers, [McCullough] leaves his audience wanting more."

—Craig Seligman, *Mobile Register*

"[McCullough] tells his story well. . . . [His] description of the 1870–71 siege of Paris and the subsequent nightmare of the Paris Commune is masterly."

—*The Economist*

"[McCullough] has woven a scintillating account of young Americans, driven by wanderlust, setting out in search of greener Parisian pastures. . . . McCullough's superb writing style—an exquisite combination of crisp academic inclination with a light, whimsical storytelling component—brings these unique characters to life in a robust, exciting manner. . . . McCullough has added another impressive chapter to his legacy of writing books of vital historical importance with mass appeal."

—Michael Taube, *Christian Science Monitor*

"[A] sparkling gem of a book. . . . McCullough is a wonderful storyteller."

—Michael D. Langan, *Buffalo News*

"Captivating."

—Doug Childers, *Richmond Times-Dispatch*

"A rich and enjoyable literary experience. There are reminders on almost every page why Mr. McCullough is one of the nation's great popular historians."

—Claude R. Marx, *The Washington Times*

ALSO BY DAVID McCULLOUGH

The Pioneers

The American Spirit

The Wright Brothers

1776

John Adams

Truman

Brave Companions

Mornings on Horseback

The Path Between the Seas

The Great Bridge

The Johnstown Flood

THE GREATER JOURNEY

AMERICANS IN PARIS

David McCullough

Simon & Schuster Paperbacks

NEW YORK   LONDON   TORONTO   SYDNEY   NEW DELHI

SIMON & SCHUSTER PAPERBACKS
A Division of Simon & Schuster, Inc.
1230 Avenue of the Americas
New York, NY 10020

First Simon & Schuster trade paperback edition May 2012

SIMON & SCHUSTER PAPERBACKS and colophon are
registered trademarks of Simon & Schuster, Inc.

For information about special discounts for bulk purchases,
please contact Simon & Schuster Special Sales at
1-866-506-1949 or business@simonandschuster.com.

Designed by Amy Hill

Manufactured in the United States of America

15   17   19   20   18   16

The Library of Congress has cataloged the hardcover edition as follows:

McCullough, David G.
The greater journey : Americans in Paris /
David McCullough. —1st Simon & Schuster hardcover ed.
         p.   cm
Includes bibliographical references and index.
1. Americans—France—Paris—History—19th century.
2. Intellectuals—France—Paris—History—19th century.
3. Artists—France—Paris—History—19th century.
4. Authors, American—France—Paris—History—19th century.
5. Physicians—France—Paris—History—19th century.
6. Paris (France)—Intellectual life—19th century.
7. Americans—France—Paris—Biography   8. Paris (France)—Biography.
9. Paris (France)—Relations—United States.
10. United States—Relations—France—Paris.   I. Title.
DC718.A44M39   2011
920.009213044361—dc22   2010053001
ISBN 978-1-4165-7176-6
ISBN 978-1-4165-7177-3 (pbk)
ISBN 978-1-4165-7689-1 (ebook)

The illustration facing the title page is *Man at the Window* by Gustave
Caillebotte; on p. 1: the exterior of Notre-Dame; on p. 137: the Place
Vendôme; on p. 265: the Eiffel Tower under construction. The front
endpaper is the rue de Rivoli; the back endpaper is avenue de l'Opéra.
Pages 559-560 constitute an extension of the copyright page.

For Rosalee

For we constantly deal with practical problems, with moulders, contractors, derricks, stonemen, trucks, rubbish, plasterers, and what-not-else, all the while trying to soar into the blue.

—AUGUSTUS SAINT-GAUDENS

Contents

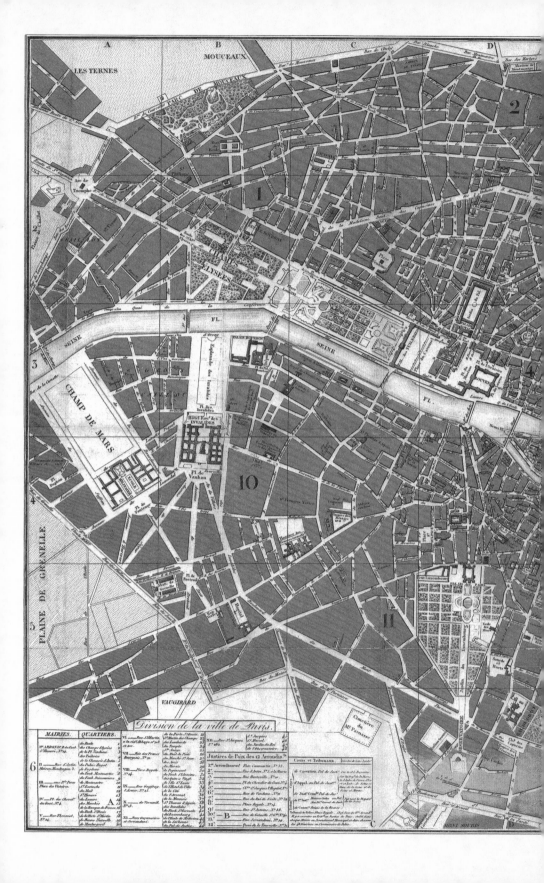

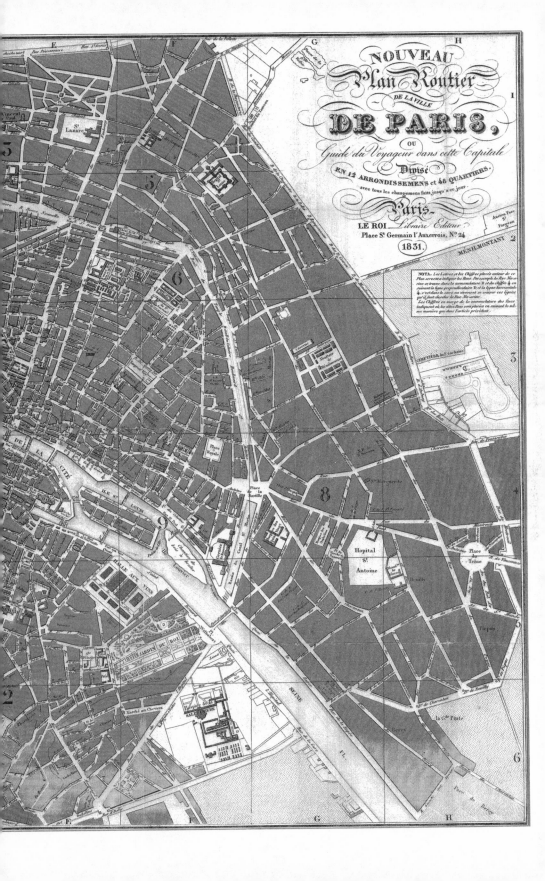

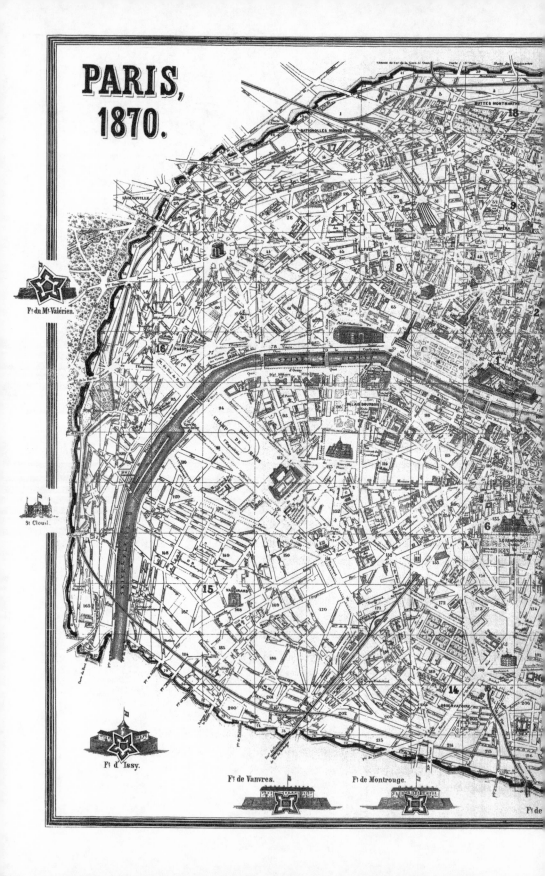

PARIS,
1870.

Ft de l'Est.

Ft d'Aubervilliers.

Ft Romainville.

Ft de Noisy.

Ft de Rosny.

Ft de Nogent.

Ft de Charenton.

Ft d'Ivry.

PART I

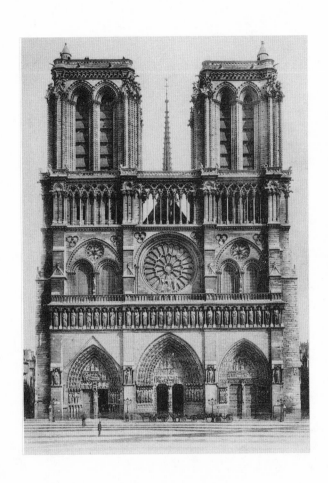

CHAPTER ONE

THE WAY OVER

The thought of going abroad makes my heart leap.

—CHARLES SUMNER

I

They spoke of it then as the dream of a lifetime, and for many, for all the difficulties and setbacks encountered, it was to be one of the best times ever.

They were the first wave of talented, aspiring Americans bound for Paris in what, by the 1830s, had become steadily increasing numbers. They were not embarking in any diplomatic or official capacity—not as had, say, Benjamin Franklin or John Adams or Thomas Jefferson, in earlier days. Neither were they in the employ of a manufacturer or mercantile concern. Only one, a young writer, appears to have been in anybody's pay, and in his case it was a stipend from a New York newspaper. They did not see themselves as refugees or self-imposed exiles from an unacceptable homeland. Nor should they be pictured as traveling for pleasure only, or in expectation of making some sort of social splash abroad.

They had other purposes—quite specific, serious pursuits in nearly every case. Their hopes were high. They were ambitious to excel in work that mattered greatly to them, and they saw time in Paris, the experience of Paris, as essential to achieving that dream—though, to be sure, as James Fenimore Cooper observed when giving his reasons for needing time in Paris, there was always the possibility of "a little pleasure concealed in the bottom of the cup."

They came from Boston, New York, Philadelphia, Ohio, North Carolina, Louisiana, nearly all of the twenty-four states that then constituted their country. With few exceptions, they were well educated and reasonably well off, or their parents were. Most, though not all, were single men in their twenties, and of a variety of shapes and sizes. Oliver Wendell Holmes, as an example, was a small, gentle, smiling Bostonian who looked even younger than his age, which was twenty-five. His height, as he acknowledged good-naturedly, was five feet three inches "when standing in a pair of substantial boots." By contrast, his friend Charles Sumner, who was two years younger, stood a gaunt six feet two, and with his sonorous voice and serious brow appeared beyond his twenties.

A few, a half dozen or so, were older than the rest by ten years or more, and they included three who had already attained considerable reputation. The works of James Fenimore Cooper, and especially *The Last of the Mohicans*, had made him the best-known American novelist ever. Samuel F. B. Morse was an accomplished portrait painter. Emma Willard, founder of Emma Willard's Troy Female Seminary, was the first woman to have taken a public stand for higher education for American women.

Importantly also, each of these three had played a prominent part in the triumphant return to the United States of the Marquis de Lafayette in 1824. Cooper had helped organize the stupendous welcome given Lafayette on his arrival in New York. Morse had painted Lafayette's portrait for the City of New York, and a visit to Emma Willard's school at Troy had been a high point of Lafayette's tour of the Hudson Valley. All three openly adored the old hero, and a desire to see him again had figured in each of their decisions to sail for France.

Cooper had departed well ahead of the others, in 1826, when he was thirty-seven, and had taken with him his wife and five children ranging in age from two to thirteen, as well as a sixteen-year-old nephew. For a whole family to brave the North Atlantic in that day was highly unusual, and especially with children so young. "My dear mother was rather alarmed at the idea," the oldest of them, Sue, would remember. According to Cooper, they were bound for Europe in the hope of improving his health—his stomach and spleen had "got entirely out of trim"—but also to benefit the children's education.

As their ship set sail from New York, a man on board a passing vessel, recognizing Cooper, called out, "How long do you mean to be absent?" "Five years," Cooper answered. "You will never come back," the man shouted. It was an exchange Cooper was never to forget.

Morse, who had suffered the sudden death of his wife, sailed alone late in 1829, at age thirty-eight, leaving his three young children in the care of relatives.

Emma Hart Willard, a widow in her late forties, was setting off in spite of the common understanding that the rigors of a voyage at sea were unsuitable for a woman of refinement, unless unavoidable, and certainly not without an appropriate companion. She, however, saw few limitations to what a woman could do and had built her career on the premise. Her doctor had urged the trip in response to a spell of poor health—sea air had long been understood to have great curative effect for almost anything that ailed one—but it would seem she needed little persuading.

In addition to establishing and running her school, Mrs. Willard had written textbooks on geography and history. Her *History of the United States, or Republic of America* had proven sufficiently profitable to make her financially independent. She was a statuesque woman of "classic features"—a Roman nose gave her a particularly strong profile—and in her role as a schoolmistress, she dressed invariably in the finest black silk or satin, her head crowned with a white turban. "She was a splendid looking woman, then in her prime, and fully realized my idea of a queen," remembered one of her students. "Do your best and your best will be growing better," Mrs. Willard was fond of telling them.

Leaving the school in the care of her sister, she boarded her ship for France accompanied by her twenty-year-old son John, ready to face whatever lay ahead. To see Europe at long last, to expand her knowledge that way, was her "life's wish," and she was determined to take in all she possibly could in the time allotted, to benefit not only herself and her students, but the women of her country.

Oliver Wendell Holmes—Wendell as he was known—was also going in serious pursuit of learning. A graduate of Harvard and a poet, he had already attained fame with his "Old Ironsides," a poetic tribute to the USS *Constitution* that had helped save the historic ship from the scrap heap:

> *Ay, tear her tattered ensign down!*
> *Long has it waved on high,*
> *And many an eye has danced to see*
> *That banner in the sky;*
> *Beneath it rung the battle shout,*
> *And burst the cannon's roar;—*
> *The meteor of the ocean air*
> *Shall sweep the clouds no more.*

He had "tasted the intoxicating pleasure of authorship," as he would write, but feeling unsuited for a literary life only, he had tried law school for a year, then switched to medicine. It was to complete his medical training that he, with several other young men from Boston, set off for Paris, then widely regarded as the world's leading center of medicine and medical training.

Among the others were James Jackson, Jr., and Jonathan Mason Warren, the sons of Boston's two most prominent physicians, James Jackson and John Collins Warren, who had founded the Massachusetts General Hospital. For both these young men, going to Paris was as much the heart's desire of their fathers as it was their own.

Wendell Holmes, on the other hand, had to overcome the strong misgivings of a preacher father for whom the expense of it all would require some sacrifice and who worried exceedingly over what might become of his son's morals in such a notoriously licentious place as Paris. But the young man had persisted. If he was to be "anything better than a rural dispenser of pills and powders," he said, he needed at least two years in the Paris hospitals. Besides, he craved relief from the "sameness" of his life and the weight of Calvinism at home. Recalling the upbringing he, his sisters, and his brother had received, Holmes later wrote, "We learned nominally that we were a set of little fallen wretches, exposed to the wrath of God by the fact of that existence which we could not help. I do not think we believed a word of it. . . ."

Charles Sumner had closed the door on a nascent Boston law practice and borrowed $3,000 from friends to pursue his scholarly ambitions on his own abroad. As a boy in school, he had shown little sign of a brilliant career. At Harvard he had been well-liked but far from distinguished as a scholar. Mathematics utterly bewildered him. (Once, when a professor besieged him with questions, Sumner pleaded no knowledge of mathematics. "Mathematics! Mathematics!" the professor exclaimed. "Don't you know the difference? This is not *mathematics*. This is *physics*.") But Sumner was an ardent reader, and in law school something changed. He became, as said, "an indefatigable and omnivorous student," his eyes "inflamed by late reading." And he had not slackened since. From boyhood he had longed to see Europe. He was determined to learn to speak French and to attend as many lectures as possible by the celebrated savants at the College of the Sorbonne.

Such ardent love of learning was also accompanied by the possibility of practical advantages. Only a few years earlier, Sumner's friend Henry Wadsworth Longfellow had returned from a sojourn in Europe with a sufficient proficiency in French, Spanish, Italian, and German to be offered, at age twenty-eight, a professorship of modern languages at Harvard, an opportunity that changed his life.

"The thought of going abroad makes my heart leap," Sumner wrote. "I feel, when I commune with myself about it, as when dwelling on the countenance and voice of a lovely girl. I am in love with *Europa*."

There were as well artists and writers headed for Paris who were no less ambitious to learn, to live and work in the company of others of like mind and aspiration, inspired by great teachers and in a vibrant atmosphere of culture far beyond anything available at home.

Even someone as accomplished as Samuel Morse deemed Paris essential. Morse had been painting since his college years at Yale and at the age of twenty-eight was commissioned to do a portrait of President James Monroe. In 1822 he had undertaken on his own to paint the House of Representatives in session, a subject never attempted before. When, in

1825, he was chosen to paint for the City of New York a full-length portrait of Lafayette during the general's visit, his career reached a new plateau. He had followed Lafayette to Washington, where Lafayette agreed to several sittings. Morse was exultant. But then without warning his world had collapsed. Word came of the death of his wife, Lucretia, three weeks after giving birth to their third child. Shattered, inconsolable, he felt as he never had before that his time was running short and that for the sake of his work he must get to Paris.

He needed Paris, he insisted. "My education as a painter is incomplete without it." He was weary of doing portraits and determined to move beyond that, to be a history painter in the tradition of such American masters as Benjamin West and John Trumbull. On his passport, lest there be any misunderstanding, he wrote in the space for occupation, "historical painter."

For a much younger, still struggling, and little known artist like George P. A. Healy of Boston, Paris was even more the promised land. While Morse longed to move beyond portraits, young Healy had his heart set on that alone. He was the oldest of the five children of a Catholic father and a Protestant mother. Because his father, a sea captain, had difficulty making ends meet, he had been his mother's "right hand man" through boyhood, helping every way he could. At some point, his father's portrait had been done by no one less than Gilbert Stuart, and his grandmother, his mother's mother, had painted "quite prettily" in watercolors. But not until he was sixteen had the boy picked up a brush. Once started, he had no wish to stop.

Small in stature, "terribly timid," as he said, and an unusually hard worker for someone his age, he had a way about him that was different from others and appealing, and for someone with no training, his talent was clearly exceptional.

When the friendly proprietor of a Boston bookstore agreed to put one of his early efforts in the window—a copy Healy had made of a print of *Ecce Homo* by the seventeenth-century Italian master Guido Reni—a Catholic priest bought it for $10, a fortune to the boy. At age eighteen, he received his first serious encouragement from an accomplished artist, Thomas Sully, who upon seeing some of his canvases told him he should make painting his profession. "Little Healy," as he was called, rented a studio and began doing portraits. He would paint anyone willing to sit for him. Mainly he painted his own portrait, again and again.

Most important, the beautiful Sally Foster Otis, the wife of Senator Harrison Gray Otis and the acknowledged "queen of Boston society," agreed to sit for her portrait after Healy, summoning all his courage, climbed the steps to her front door on Beacon Hill and stated his business.

"I told her that I was an artist, that my ambition was to paint a beautiful woman and that I begged her to sit for me." She agreed, and the resulting work led to further opportunities to do others of "the right set" in Boston. One small, especially lovely portrait left little doubt of Healy's ability and would be long treasured by one of Beacon Hill's most prominent families and their descendants. It was of young Frances ("Fanny") Appleton, who lived next door to Mrs. Otis.

But he knew how much he had still to learn to reach the level of skill to which he aspired, and made up his mind to go to Paris. As he would explain, "In those far-off days there were no art schools in America, no drawing classes, no collections of fine plaster casts and very few picture exhibitions." After scraping together money enough to take him to Europe and to help support his mother for a year or two, he proceeded with his plan.

> I knew no one in France, I was utterly ignorant of the language, I did not know what I should do when once there; but I was not yet one-and-twenty, and I had a great stock of courage, of inexperience—which is sometimes a great help—and a strong desire to be my very best.

Like Charles Sumner, Samuel Morse, Wendell Holmes, and others, Healy did not just wish to go to Paris, he was determined to go and "study hard."

Among the writers was Nathaniel Parker Willis, like Morse a graduate of Yale, who with his poems and magazine "sketches" had already, at twenty-five, attained a national reputation. It was Willis who was traveling as a correspondent of sorts, having been assigned by the *New-York Mirror* to provide a series of "letters" describing his travels abroad. He was a sociable, conspicuously handsome, even beautiful young man with flowing light brown locks, and a bit of a dandy. Wendell Holmes would later describe him as looking like an "anticipation of Oscar Wilde." Willis was, besides, immensely talented.

And so, too, was John Sanderson, a teacher in his fifties known at home in Philadelphia for his literary bent. He was going to Paris for reasons of health partly, but also to write about his observations in a series of letters, intending to "dress them up one day into some kind of shape for the public."

Except for Cooper and Morse, those embarking for France knew little at all about life outside their own country, or how very different it would prove to be. Hardly any had ever laid eyes on a foreign shore. None of the Bostonians had traveled more than five hundred miles from home. Though Cooper and his family spent a year in advance of their departure learning French, scarcely any of the rest had studied the language, and those who had, like Holmes and Sumner, had never tried actually speaking it.

The newspapers they read, in Boston or New York or Philadelphia, carried occasional items on the latest Paris fashions or abbreviated reports on politics or crime in France, along with periodic notices of newly arrived shipments of French wine or wallpaper or fine embroidery or gentlemen's gloves, but that was about the limit of their cognizance of things French. The Paris they pictured was largely a composite of the standard prints of famous bridges and palaces, and such views as to be found in old books or the penny magazines.

Many of them were familiar from childhood with the fables of La Fontaine. Or they had read Voltaire or Racine or Molière in English translations. But that was about the sum of any familiarity they had with French literature. And none, of course, could have known in advance that the 1830s and '40s in Paris were to mark the beginning of the great era of Victor Hugo, Balzac, George Sand, and Baudelaire, not to say anything of Delacroix in painting or Chopin and Liszt in music.

It may be assumed they knew the part played by the French army and navy and French money during the American Revolution. They appreciated Lafayette's importance and knew that with the deaths of Jefferson and Adams in 1826, he became the last living hero of the struggle for American independence. They knew about Napoleon and the French Revolution of 1789 and the horrors of the Terror. And fresh in mind was the latest violent upheaval, the July Revolution of 1830, the Paris revolt that had lasted just three days and resulted, at a cost of some 3,000 lives, in the new "Citizen King," Louis-Philippe.

Although born of the powerful Orléans family, the new ruler in his youth had supported the Revolution of 1789 and served bravely as an officer in the republican army before fleeing the Terror in 1793. For years he had been unable to return to France. Considered a moderate, Louis-Philippe was now king largely because of the support of the hugely popular Lafayette.

When news of the July Revolution reached America, it was cause for celebration. The tricolor was unfurled on the streets of American cities. The "Marseillaise" was sung in theaters. New Yorkers put on a parade two and a half miles long. Louis-Philippe, as Americans knew, had spent three years of his exile from France living in the United States and traveled far and wide over much of the country. Well-mannered, still in his twenties, and with little or no money, he had made a favorable impression everywhere he went. He had worked for a while as a waiter in a Boston oyster house. He had been a guest of George Washington's at Mount Vernon, and this, and the fact that he now had the approval of Lafayette, contributed greatly to how Americans responded to the new regime in Paris.

———

Again except for Cooper and Morse, few of those bound for Paris in the 1830s had ever been to sea, or even on board a seagoing ship, and the thought, given the realities of sea travel, was daunting, however glorious the prospects before them.

The choice was either to sail first to England, then cross the Channel, or sail directly to Le Havre, which was the favored route. Either way meant a sea voyage of 3,000 miles—as far as from New York to the coast of the Pacific—or more, depending on the inevitable vagaries of the winds. And there were no stops in between.

Steamboats by this time were becoming a familiar presence on the rivers and coastal waters of America, but not until 1838 did steam-powered ships cross the Atlantic. As it was, by sailing ship, the average time at sea was no better than it had been when Benjamin Franklin set off for France in 1776. One could hope to do it in as little as three weeks, perhaps less under ideal conditions, but a month to six weeks was more likely.

Nor were there regular passenger vessels as yet. One booked passage on a packet—a cargo ship that took passengers—and hoped for the best. But even the most expensive accommodations were far from luxurious. That there could be days, even weeks of violent seas with all the attendant pitching of decks, flying chinaware and furniture, seasickness and accidents, went without saying. Cramped quarters, little or no privacy, dismal food, a surplus of unrelieved monotony were all to be expected. Then, too, there was always the very real possibility of going to the bottom. Everyone knew the perils of the sea.

In 1822, the packet *Albion* out of New York, with 28 passengers on board, had been caught in a fearful gale and dashed on the rocks on the coast of Ireland. Of the passengers, several of whom had been bound for Paris, only two were saved. At the time when James Fenimore Cooper and his family sailed, in the spring of 1826, a London packet fittingly named *Crisis* had been missing nearly three months, and in fact would never be heard from again.

All who set sail for France were putting their lives in the hands of others, and to this could be added the prospect of being unimaginably far from friends, family, and home, entirely out of touch with familiar surroundings, virtually everything one knew and loved for months, possibly even years to come. In *The Sketch Book,* a work familiar to many of the outward-bound venturers, Washington Irving, describing his own first crossing of the Atlantic, made the point that in travel by land there was always a kind of "continuity of scene" that gave one a feeling of being connected still to home.

> But a wide sea voyage severs us at once. It makes us conscious
> of being cast loose from the secure anchorage of settled life,
> and sent adrift upon a doubtful world. It interposes a gulf not
> merely imaginary, but real, between us and our homes—a

gulf subjected to tempest and fear and uncertainty, rendering distance palpable, and return precarious.

Sailings were regularly listed in the newspapers, and it was important to choose a good ship. Most were brigs: two-masted square-riggers carrying cargo of various kinds. The most desirable berths, those having the least motion, were near the middle of the ship. Fare to Le Havre was expensive, approximately $140.

The last days before departure were filled with arranging the clothes needed for a long absence, selecting a stock of books to fill time at sea, and packing it all in large black trunks. Acquaintances who had made the trip before advised bringing an ample supply of one's own towels.

There were final calls to be made on friends, some of whom could be counted on to question the very thought of such a venture, whatever one's reasons. Hours were devoted to farewell letters, parting sentiments, and words to the wise set down for children or younger siblings. "I am very glad, my dear, to remember your cheerful countenance," wrote Charles Sumner to his ten-year-old sister from his room at the Astor House in New York the night before sailing. "I shall keep it in my mind as I travel over the sea and land. . . . Try never to cry. . . . If you find your temper mastering you, always stop till you can count *sixty*, before you say or do anything."

"Follow, my dear boy, an honorable calling, which shall engross your time and give you position and fame, and besides enable you to benefit your fellow man," Sumner lectured a younger brother in another letter. "Do not waste your time in driblets."

The mothers and fathers of the voyagers, for whom such partings could be profoundly painful—and who in many cases were paying for it all— had their own advice on spending money wisely and looking after one's health. With good reason, they worried much about health, and the terrifying threats of smallpox, typhoid, and cholera, not to mention syphilis, in highly populated foreign cities. What wrong turns might befall their beloved offspring untethered in such places? The young men were warned repeatedly of the perils of bad company. They must remember always who they were and return "untainted" by the affectations and immorality of the Old World.

The written "Instructions" of the eminent Boston physician John Collins Warren to his medical student son ran to forty pages and included everything from what he must study to how his notes should be organized, to what he should and should not eat and drink. Mason, as he was known, must choose his friends judiciously and avoid especially those "fond of theaters and dissipation."

Emotions ran high on the eve of departure. Melancholy and second thoughts interspersed with intense excitement were the common thing. "And a sad time it was, full of anxious thoughts and doubts, with mingled gleams of glorious anticipations," wrote Charles Sumner in his journal. Samuel Morse was so distraught about leaving his children and his country that he descended into "great depression, from which some have told me they feared for my health and even reason."

But once the voyagers were on board and under way, nearly all experienced a tremendous lift of spirits, even as, for many, the unfamiliar motion of the ship began to take effect. "We have left the wharf, and with a steamer [tug boat] by our side," Sumner wrote from on board the *Albany* departing from New York.

> A smacking breeze has sprung up, and we shall part this company soon; and then for the Atlantic! Farewell then, my friends, my pursuits, my home, my country! Each bellying wave on its rough crest carries me away. The rocking vessel impedes my pen. And now, as my head begins slightly to reel, my imagination entertains the glorious prospects before me. . . .

Nathaniel Willis, departing from Philadelphia, described the grand spectacle of ten or fifteen vessels lying in the roads waiting for the pilot boat.

> And as she came down the river, they all weighed anchor together and we got under way. It was a beautiful sight—so many sail in close company under a smart breeze . . .

"The dream of my lifetime was about to be realized," Willis wrote. "I was bound for France."

Not all pioneers went west.

II

They sailed from several different ports and in different years. When Samuel Morse embarked out of New York in November 1829, it was with what he thought "the fairest wind that ever blew." Emma Willard sailed in the fall of 1830; James Jackson, Jr., the medical student, in the spring of 1831; Nathaniel Willis that fall; and Wendell Holmes in 1833. George Healy, the aspiring young painter, made his crossing in 1834; John Sanderson, the Philadelphia teacher, in 1835. Charles Sumner set forth on his scholarly quest in 1837.

At this juncture, as it happens, a young French aristocrat, Alexis de Tocqueville, decided to brave the Atlantic in the opposite direction, sailing from Le Havre in 1831. He was twenty-five years old, short, and slightly built. Nothing about his appearance suggested any remarkable ability. His intention, he said, was to "inquire into everything" in America, "to see what a great republic is like." He had never spoken to an American in his life. He had never been to sea.

Samuel Morse had comparatively little comment about his crossing, beyond that it took twenty-six days, including five days and nights of gale winds, during which the motion of the ship was such that no one slept. Nathaniel Willis, who sailed on the nearly new brig *Pacific*, commanded by a French captain, enjoyed days of fair winds and smooth seas, but only after what to him was an exceedingly rough week when the one thing he had to smile about was the achievement of dinner.

"In rough weather, it is as much as one person can do to keep his place at the table at all; and to guard the dishes, bottles and castors from a general slide in the direction of the lurch, requires a sleight and coolness reserved only for a sailor," Willis wrote, in a picturesque account that was to delight readers of the *New-York Mirror*.

"Prenez garde!" shouts the captain as the sea strikes, and in
the twinkling of an eye everything is seized and held up to
wait for the lurch, in attitudes that would puzzle the pencil
of [Samuel] Johnson to exaggerate. With his plate of soup in
one hand, and the larboard end of the tureen in the other, the
claret bottle between his teeth, and the crook of his elbow
caught around the mounting corner of the table, the captain
maintains his seat upon the transom, and with a look of most
grave concern, keeps a wary eye on the shifting level of his
vermicelli. The old weather-beaten mate, with the alacrity of
a juggler, makes a long leg back to the cabin of panels at the
same moment, and with his breast against the table, takes
his own plate and the castors, and one or two of the smaller
dishes under his charge; and the steward, if he can keep
his legs, looks out for the vegetables, or if he fails, makes as
wide a lap as possible to intercept the violent articles in their
descent.

Once conditions improved, there was no happier man on board than
Willis. He gloried in the sea air and smooth sailing. "It is a day to make
one in love with life," he wrote one brilliant morning. "Hundreds of sea
birds are sailing around us . . . the sailors, barefoot and bareheaded, are
scattered over the rigging, doing 'fair-weather' work. . . ."

Willis was the sole passenger on board his ship, in contrast to Wendell
Holmes, who crossed on the packet *Philadelphia*, out of New York, with
thirty other passengers in cabin class and fifteen in steerage. The *Philadelphia* was considered top-of-the-line. ("The accommodations for passengers are very elegant and extensive," it was advertised. Beds, bedding,
wine, and "stores of the best quality" were always provided.) The cabin
passengers were mostly from Boston. Several were friends of Holmes's,
including a convivial fellow Harvard graduate, Thomas Gold Appleton,
one of the Beacon Hill Appletons (and brother of Fanny), who was trying
to make up his mind whether to become an artist or a writer, and having
a thoroughly fine time in the meanwhile.

They sailed in April and enjoyed gentle seas nearly the whole way, the

kind travelers dreamed of. As Appleton's journal attests, one unremark-
able day followed another:

> I felt nothing of that do-little drowsy *ennui* that I had ex-
> pected. I varied my amusements, and found them all de-
> lightful. I talked sentiment with Dr. Holmes; then flirted in
> bad French with Victorine [a maid accompanying one of the
> women passengers]; soon joined with Mr. Curtis and our two
> doctors in a cannonade of puns.

Everyone was in high spirits. One dinner was followed by a night of singing made especially memorable when a "voice in the steerage gave us a
succession of stirring ballads."

The morning after, however, "the still-life of the day previous had un-
dergone a sea change." Struggling to get out of his bunk, Appleton was
nearly pitched head-first through the window of his cabin. Having succeeded in dressing, "bruised and battered," he went aloft. The live chick-
ens and ducks on board were "chattering in terror," the captain shouting
"pithy orders" through a trumpet to sailors standing "at ridiculously acute
angles with the deck."

Few appeared for breakfast that morning, fewer still for dinner. But
peace returned soon enough, and Appleton, his desire to paint stirring,
studied the "deeply, darkly, beautifully blue" sea, "that blue which I had
heard of, but never saw before. The water hissed and simmered as we clove
its ridges, running off from the sides in long undulating sheets of foam,
with partial breaks of the most exquisite beryl tint."

"A most delightful evening," he began another of his journal entries.
"The moon showed but a lurid disk, and that was soon lost behind brown-
black volumes of a long curtain of hanging cloud. It was glimmering darkness, and our sole spectacle was the water. How magnificent that was!"

> What an odd, good-for-nothing life we lead! [he observed hap-
> pily several days later] A prolonged morning nap, jokes . . . a
> turn on deck, a sluggish conversation, a book held in the hand
> for an hour or two, another turn on deck; the bell sounds—we

dash to dinner; three courses, laughter, candles, tea, and the moon . . .

Only when, at dinner the following night, the captain mentioned the possibility of "vast islands of ice" did the mood change. "This all frightened us pretty considerably," Appleton wrote, "and I could not get to sleep for hearing, in fancy, the crushing of our ship on an iceberg. . . ." When, by morning, the danger had passed, life on board resumed its pleasant pattern.

So sweet and benign a crossing was the exception. For nearly all the rest of the voyagers came days of howling winds and monstrous seas when death seemed imminent. For Emma Willard, who sailed from New York on the *Charlemagne*, it was "a rough crossing" indeed. She had come aboard with her health much on her mind. What exactly her troubles were she never explained. There was repeated talk of weather. "Some of the older passengers play a covert game to frighten those who are fresh and timid," she wrote. She paid them no mind. Then heavy weather struck. Worse than the raging winds of day were the seas after the winds abated. "Then the waters rise up in unequal masses, sometimes lifting the vessel as if to the heavens, and again plunging her as if to the depths below; and sometimes they come foaming and dashing and breaking over the ship, striking the deck with a startling force." Most terrifying was a night of mountainous seas breaking over the ship.

> Thus with the raging element above, beneath, and around us; with nothing to divide us from it, but a bark whose masts were shaking, whose timbers were creaking and cracking, as they were about to divide; the feeling of the moment was, a ship was a vain thing for safety; that help was in God alone. Thoughts of ocean caverns—of what would be the consequence of one's death, naturally rise in the mind at such a time.

To Mrs. Willard's amazement, she was never seasick. Rather, the violence of the weather, "the rocking and rolling and tossing," the holding on for dear life to "some fixed object . . . to keep from being shot across the cabin, and grasping the side of my berth at night for fear of being rolled over the side," seemed to benefit her health.

All the same, she seriously contemplated whether, if she survived the voyage, it might be the better part of wisdom to remain in France.

Reflecting on his experience aboard ship, John Sanderson wrote, "If any lady of your village has a disobedient husband, or a son who has beaten his mother, bid her send him to sea."

So wretchedly sick was Charles Sumner during his first days out he could not bear even the thought of food, let alone drag himself to the dining table. "Literally 'cabined, cuffed and confined' in my berth, I ate nothing, did nothing. . . ." Until the fourth day, he was too weak even to hold a book. (To be unable to read was for Sumner the ultimate measure of wretchedness.) Then, astonishingly, his appetite returned "like a Bay of Fundy tide," and he was both back at the table and back to his books.

On Christmas Day in the English Channel, the long voyage nearly over, Sumner expressed in the privacy of his journal what so many felt.

> In going abroad at my present age, and situated as I am, I feel that I take a bold, almost rash step. . . . But I go for purposes of education, and to gratify longings that prey upon my mind and time. . . . The temptations of Europe I have been warned against . . . I can only pray that I may be able to pass through them in safety. . . . May I return with an undiminished love for my friends and country, with a heart and mind untainted by the immoralities of the Old World, manners untouched by its affectations, and a willingness to resume my labors with an unabated determination to devote myself faithfully to the duties of an American!

III

They would stand by the hour on deck, watching the emerging shapes and details on land growing slowly, steadily larger and more distinct. At home it was known as the Old World. To them it was all new.

Whether they arrived at Le Havre, the great port of Paris at the mouth of the Seine, or crossed from England to land at Calais or Boulogne-sur-Mer, the first hours ashore were such a mélange of feelings of relief and exhilaration, and inevitably, such confusion coping with so much that was new and unfamiliar, as to leave most of them extremely unsettled.

No sooner were they ashore than their American passports were taken by French authorities to be sent on to Paris. Their passports, they were told, would be returned to them in Paris in exchange for a ticket that they had to ask for at a nearby police office. In the meantime, swarms of pushing, shouting, unintelligible porters, coachmen, and draymen vied for attention, while trunks and bags were carried off to the Custom House to be gone through. All personal effects, except clothing, were subject to duties and delays. Any sealed letters in their possession were subject to fine. They themselves could be subjected to examination, if thought suspicious-looking. Many had difficulty acquiescing to the "impertinence" of authorities searching their bags or, worse, having their own person inspected. Desperate to shut off his porter's "cataract of French postulation," Nathaniel Willis, like others, wound up paying the man three times what he should have.

Even without the "impertinences," the whole requirement of passports—the cost, the "vexatious ceremony" of it all—was repugnant to the Americans. In conversation with an English-speaking Frenchman, John Sanderson mentioned that no one carried a passport in America, not even foreign visitors. The man wondered how there could be any personal security that way. To Sanderson this seemed only to illustrate that when one was used to seeing things done in a certain way, one found it hard to conceive the possibility of their being done any other way.

Having at last attended to all the requirements for entry into France, Sanderson went straightaway to the nearest church "to pay the Virgin Mary the pound of candles I owed for my preservation at sea."

Most of the travelers preferred to wait a day or more at Le Havre, to rest and look about before pushing on. Though nothing was like what they were accustomed to, what struck them most was how exceedingly old everything appeared. It was a look many did not like. Not at first. Charles Sumner was one of the exceptions. With his love of history, he responded immediately and enthusiastically to the sense of a long past all about him. "Everything was old. . . . Every building I passed seemed to have its history." He saw only one street with a sidewalk. Most streets were slick with mud and uncomfortable to the feet. Men and women clattered by in wooden shoes, no different from what their grandparents had worn. It was of no matter, he thought. Here whatever was long established was best, while at home nothing was "beyond the reach of change and experiment." At home there was "none of the prestige of age" about anything.

From Le Havre to Paris was a southeast journey of 110 miles, traveled by diligence, an immense cumbersome-looking vehicle—the equivalent of two and a half stagecoaches in one—which, as said, sacrificed beauty for convenience. It had room for fifteen passengers in three "apartments"—three in the front in the *coupe*, six in the *intérieur*, and six more in the *rotonde* in the rear. Each of these sections was separate from the others, thereby dividing the rich, the middling, and the poor. "If you feel very aristocratic," wrote John Sanderson, "you take the whole coupe to yourself, or yourself and lady, and you can be as private as you please." There were places as well for three more passengers "aloft," on top, where the baggage was piled and where the driver, the *conducteur*, maintained absolute command.

The huge lumbering affair, capable of carrying three tons of passengers and baggage, was pulled by five horses, three abreast in front, two abreast just behind them. On one of the pair a mounted *postillon* in high black boots cracked the whip. Top speed under way was seven miles an hour, which meant the trip to Paris, with stops en route, took about twenty-four hours.

Once under way, before dawn, the Americans found the roads unexpectedly good—wide, smooth, hard, free from stones—and their swaying conveyance surprisingly comfortable. With the onset of first light, most of them thoroughly enjoyed the passing scenery, as they rolled through level farm country along the valley of the Seine, the river in view much of the way, broad and winding—ever winding—and dotted with islands.

Just to be heading away from the sea, to be immersed in a beautiful landscape again, to hear the sound of crows, was such a welcome change, and all to be seen so very appealing, a land of peace and plenty, every field perfectly cultivated, hillsides bordering the river highlighted by white limestone cliffs, every village and distant château so indisputably ancient and picturesque.

> I looked at the constantly occurring ruins of the old priories, and the magnificent and still used churches [wrote Nathaniel Willis], and my blood tingled in my veins, as I saw in the stepping stones at their doors, cavities that the sandals of monks, and the iron-shod feet of knights in armor a thousand years ago, had trodden and helped to wear and the stone cross over the threshold that hundreds of generations had gazed upon and passed under.

Most memorable on the overland trip was a stop at Rouen, halfway to Paris, to see the great cathedral at the center of the town. The Americans had never beheld anything remotely comparable. It was their first encounter with a Gothic masterpiece, indeed with one of the glories of France, a structure built of limestone and far more monumental, not to say centuries older, than any they had ever seen.

The largest building in the United States at the time was the Capitol in Washington. Even the most venerable houses and churches at home, north or south, dated back only to the mid seventeenth century. So historic a landmark as Philadelphia's Independence Hall was not yet a hundred years old.

An iron spire added to the cathedral at Rouen in 1822 reached upward 440 feet, fully 300 feet higher than the Capitol in Washington, and the cathedral had its origins in the early thirteenth century—or more than two hundred years before Columbus set sail for America—and work on it had continued for three centuries.

The decorative carvings and innumerable statues framing the outside of the main doorways were, in themselves, an unprecedented experience. In all America at the time there were no stone sculptures adorning the exteriors of buildings old or new. Then within, the long nave soared more than 90 feet above the stone floor.

It was a first encounter with a great Catholic shrine, with its immense scale and elaborate evocations of sainthood and ancient sanctions, and for the Americans, virtually all of whom were Protestants, it was a surprisingly emotional experience. Filling pages of her journal, Emma Willard would struggle to find words equal to the "inexpressible magic," the "sublimity" she felt.

I had heard of fifty or a hundred years being spent in the erection of a building, and I had often wondered how it could be; but when I saw even the outside of this majestic and venerable temple, the doubt ceased. It was all of curious and elegantly carved stonework, now of a dark grey, like some ancient gravestone that you may see in our oldest graveyards. Thousands of saints and angels there stood in silence, with voiceless harps; or spread forever their moveless wings—half issuing in bold relief from mimic clouds of stone. But when I entered the interior, and saw by the yet dim and shadowy light, the long, long, aisles—the high raised vaults—the immense pillars which supported them . . . my mind was smitten with a feeling of sublimity almost too intense for mortality. I stood and gazed, and as the light increased, and my observation became more minute, a new creation seemed rising to my view—of saints and martyrs mimicked by the painter or sculptor—often clad in the solemn stole of the monk or nun, and sometimes in the habiliments of the grave. The infant Savior with his virgin mother—the crucified Redeemer—adoring angels, and martyred saints were all around—and unearthly lights gleaming from the many rainbow-colored windows, and brightening as the day advanced, gave a solemn inexpressible magic to the scene.

Charles Sumner could hardly contain his rapture. Never had a work of architecture had such powerful effect on him. The cathedral was "the great lion of the north of France . . . transcending all that my imagination had pictured." He had already read much of its history. Here, he knew, lay the remains of Rollo, the first Duke of Normandy, the bones of his son,

William Longsword, and even the heart of Cœur de Lion, the Lionheart himself.

> And here was I, an American, whose very hemisphere had been discovered long since the foundation of this church, whose country had been settled, in comparison with this foundation, but yesterday, introduced to these remains of past centuries, treading over the dust of archbishops and cardinals, and standing before the monuments of kings. . . .

How often he had wondered whether such men in history had, in truth, ever lived and did what was said they had. Such fancy was now exploded.

In an account of his own first stop at Rouen and the effect of the cathedral on him and the other Americans traveling with him, James Fenimore Cooper said the common feeling among them was that it had been worth crossing the Atlantic if only to see this.

With eighty miles still to go, most travelers chose to stop over at Rouen. Others, like Nathaniel Willis, eager to be in Paris, climbed aboard a night diligence and headed on.

Great as their journey had been by sea, a greater journey had begun, as they already sensed, and from it they were to learn more, and bring back more, of infinite value to themselves and to their country than they yet knew.

CHAPTER TWO

VOILÀ PARIS!

The origin of Paris and the character of its first inhabitants are necessarily involved in deep obscurity. According to historians whose opinions are generally received, an errant tribe obtained permission of the Senones, at a very remote period, to settle upon the banks of the Seine, near their territory. Upon the island now called Île de la Cité *they constructed huts, which served as a fortress for them to retreat with their flocks and effects when an attack from any of the neighboring tribes was apprehended. To their fortress they gave the name of* Lutèce, *and themselves assumed that of* Parisii, *which most probably was derived from their contiguity to the country of the Senones, the word* par *and* bar *being synonymous, and signifying* frontier. *According to this derivation the* Parisii *would be* dwellers on the frontier.

—*GALIGNANI'S NEW PARIS GUIDE*

I

The first impressions were often badly disappointing.

Much of Paris in the 1830s was still a medieval city. So after rolling smoothly along the broad, tree-lined final approach on the main road from Rouen, the American adventurers suddenly found themselves plunged into a dark labyrinth of narrow, filthy, foul-smelling streets running off every which way. Ancient stone buildings, some black with centuries of smoke and soot, crowded on all sides. Wagons and drays and shouting vendors with pushcarts clogged the way. People could be seen living in the most wretched squalor. To picture what the rat population might be took no great stretch of imagination.

"*Voilà Paris!*" the conductor would call from atop the diligence. "*Voilà Paris!*"

"And with my mind full of the splendid views of squares, and columns, and bridges, as I had seen them in prints, I could scarce believe I was in Paris," wrote Nathaniel Willis. "The streets run zig-zag and abut against each other as if they did not know which way to run," wrote John Sanderson. "As for the noise of the streets, I need not attempt to describe it.

> What idea can ears, used only to the ordinary and human noises, conceive of this unceasing racket—this rattling of cabs and other vehicles over the rough stones, this rumbling of the omnibuses. For the street cries—one might have relief from them by file and handsaw.

Even as the famous bridges on the Seine, the splendors of gardens and palaces and the gilded dome of the Invalides came into view, the close proximity of such appalling poverty and immeasurable riches was both startling and unsettling. After years of living in Paris, James Fenimore Cooper said he still struggled to adjust to a country comprised of "dirt and gilding . . . bedbugs and laces."

Many, like Emma Willard, arrived so utterly exhausted that under the circumstances little if anything could have pleased them. Gone was any trace of the "sublimity" she had felt at the cathedral in Rouen. "We were amidst dirt and disorder, fatigued . . . and strange eyes seemed to glare upon us."

But the famous allure and vitality of the great city won them over soon enough. Never in their lives had the Americans seen such parks and palaces, or such beautiful bridges or so many bridges. Or so many people of every kind. For those staying at the best hotels, such comforts and attentions as awaited them almost immediately, magically alleviated whatever initial disappointment they had felt.

To Nathaniel Willis the Hôtel des Étrangers on the rue Vivienne was everything the weary traveler longed for. Arriving in the rain at midmorning after a long night on the road, he was shown every courtesy, including his choice of several "quite pretty" rooms. The beds were surely the best in the world, he thought. "Five mattresses are successively piled on an elegant mahogany bedstead" to a thickness of eighteen inches. The pillow was "a masterpiece." There was simply no "opiate" like a French pillow. Then followed a breakfast that carried the day:

> There are few things bought with money that are more delightful than a French breakfast. If you take it at your room, it appears in the shape of two small vessels, one of coffee and one of hot milk, two kinds of bread, with a thin, printed slice of butter, and one or two of some thirty dishes from which you can choose, the latter flavored exquisitely enough to make one wish to be always at breakfast, but cooked and composed I know not how or of what. The coffee has an aroma peculiarly exquisite, something quite different than any I have ever tasted before; and the *petit pain*, a slender biscuit between bread and cake, is, when crisp and warm, a delightful accompaniment.

And the cost was a third that of steak and coffee at home and the civility of the service worth three times the money.

The location on the bustling rue Vivienne was ideal. The Palais Royal, with all its famous enticements, the Louvre, and the Garden of the Tuileries were only a little way down the street, southward toward the Seine. Up the street in the other direction was the Bourse, which with its grandiose Doric columns looked more like a palace or temple than what it was, a stock exchange.

Best of all, Galignani's, the English bookstore and reading room, a favorite gathering place, stood across the street from the hotel. There one could pass long, comfortable hours with a great array of English and even American newspapers. Parisians were as avid readers of newspapers as any people on earth. Some thirty-four daily papers were published in Paris, and many of these, too, were to be found spread across several large tables. The favorite English-language paper was Galignani's own *Messenger*, with morning and evening editions Monday through Friday. For the newly arrived Americans, after more than a month with no news of any kind, these and the American papers were pure gold.

Of the several circulating libraries in Paris, only Galignani's carried books in English, and indispensable was *Galignani's New Paris Guide* in English. Few Americans went without this thick little leather-bound volume, fully 839 pages of invaluable insights and information, plus maps.

Like Nathaniel Willis, schoolmistress Emma Willard delighted in her first breakfast at the fashionable Hôtel de l'Europe on the rue de Richelieu, and in the café au lait in particular. Nothing could exceed it, she wrote, adding, "the bread is fine and the butter exquisite." She was also much the better after a restorative night's sleep.

Breakfast concluded and accompanied by a young lady from New York traveling with her father, whom she had met on board ship and identified in her letters only as "Miss D," Mrs. Willard set forth full of expectations for a first walk in Paris, down the rue de Richelieu in the direction of the Seine and into the luxurious garden and arcades of the Palais Royal. The spectacle of the immense garden with its fountain playing was "brilliant and beautiful," and, enclosed as it was by the Palais, blessedly removed from the clamor of the streets. It was also, much to her approval, "promenaded by multitudes of the elegant and fashionable."

> We took the rounds under the arcades, upon the finely paved marble walk. . . . And surely we had never seen anything with which to compare the splendor of the shops. . . . You have not the least idea of the elegance of some of the painted porcelain; and then there are such quantities. . . . Jewelry, too, abounds in all its dazzling sheen . . . and hats of many fashions, with snowy plumes. . . .

Having purchased a few "wearable things," she and her companion returned to the hotel to announce they had found the Paris they had expected to see.

Samuel Morse had hardly unpacked at his hotel when he was handed an invitation to a soirée at the home of Lafayette. On his arrival, the warmth of his welcome from the general took Morse's breath away. "When I went in he instantly recognized me, took me by both hands, said he was expecting to see me in France, having read in the American papers that I had embarked."

In her turn, Mrs. Willard sent off a note to "apprise" General Lafayette that she had arrived, expecting to receive no answer for days, given his importance in the new government as commander of the army. But the following morning the general himself appeared to greet her with open affection. For nearly an hour they reminisced about his visit to her school, talked of their families, and discussed politics and the new government. "His heart seemed to expand as to a confidential sister," she wrote with boundless pride. No welcome to Paris could have pleased her more, and it was not to be her only time with him, as he had graciously assured her.

———

The Palais Royal, the Louvre, the Palace and Garden of the Tuileries, were all in the first of the twelve arrondissements, or districts, of Paris. It was the royal arrondissement par excellence. As Wendell Holmes wrote, in an effort to explain to his parents how things were arranged, the Palais Royal was the great center of the luxury and splendor of Paris.

He, however, had "fairly settled" in the quite different Sixth Arrondissement, across the Seine in the Pays Latin, the Latin Quarter, on the Rive Gauche, the Left Bank. The ancient College of the Sorbonne and the School of Law were there. So, too, were the École de Médecine and several major hospitals, and hence it was where the medical students lived in high, dingy old houses closely packed along narrow, unpaved streets with gutters down the middle and rarely a sidewalk. (Describing the choices this left to the pedestrian, Holmes wrote, "If he keeps near the wall his feet probably become victims of some animal or vegetable abomination. If on the other hand he keeps to the middle he is almost inevitably splashed by the horses with mud of an intensity that defies competition.") In this same crowded, compact neighborhood lived and worked the medical-book sellers, instrument makers, medical artists, preparers of natural and artificial skeletons, in addition to professors and lecturers of highest renown who were advancing the art and science of medicine as nowhere else in the world.

Holmes, like his fellow Bostonians James Jackson, Jr., and Mason Warren, found lodgings on the rue Monsieur-le-Prince, a street barely wide enough for two carts to pass. Consistent with his nature, Holmes had no complaints.

Those who, like Holmes or John Sanderson, arrived in late June or early July were delighted from the outset by the long summer days of northern Europe. In Paris, as they had to remind themselves, they were as far north as Newfoundland. And what pleasure to be out and about in daylight at ten at night! In December, as they would discover, it would still be pitch dark at eight in the morning, and night again by four in the afternoon. Winter, too, brought endless rain, mud, snow, and fog, often heavy fog. The penetrating cold of a Paris winter was commonly said to be worse even than in London.

Charles Sumner, who arrived in late December, took a room near the Sorbonne, intending to devote his time first to learning French, but was so distressed by the dank, bone-chilling weather he could hardly concentrate on anything. A blazing fire had little effect.

> The cold continues intolerable [he wrote in his journal], and my chamber, notwithstanding all my exertions, frigid beyond endurance. I go to bed tonight earlier than usual—the clock this moment striking midnight—in the hope of escaping the cold. My French grammar will be my companion.

In the morning he studied as close by the fire as he dared sit, bundled to the neck in an overcoat. "I freeze behind, and my hair is so cold that I hesitate to touch it with my hand."

Yet life had never been so exhilarating. To a friend at home Sumner wrote, "My voyage has already been compensated for—seasickness, time, money, and all—many times over."

———

They were in Paris! It was no longer something to read about at home, or talk about at sea. They were there—this was nearly always the first thought on awakening each morning. Paris was right there out the window, out the door, and the common impulse was to get out and walk, to get one's bearings, certainly, but also, as they discovered, Paris was a place where one wanted to walk, where to walk—*flâner*, as the French said—was practically a way of life. ("Ah! To wander over Paris!" wrote Honoré de Balzac. "What an adorable and delectable existence is that! *Flânerie* is a form of science, it is the gastronomy of the eye.")

In spirited letters and diary entries, the Americans described walking the uncommonly broad sidewalks of grand avenues and boulevards under "noble" chestnut trees, or venturing off into the "charming irregularities" of the endless side streets. A mile was nothing. Without realizing it, one could walk the whole day in an effort to see everything. Or to ward off homesickness, which often hit with surprising force. Interestingly, "Home, Sweet Home," a favorite song then throughout the English-speaking world, was written by an American in Paris. "Mid pleasures and palaces / Though we may roam," wrote John Howard Payne, "Be it ever so humble, / There's no place like home."

The French had a different idea about distances. A destination described as only "two steps away" could turn out to be a walk of several miles. Aching legs were common by day's end. The soles of good Boston (or New York or Philadelphia) shoes wore thin sooner than expected.

When the walking became too much, there were the famous Paris omnibuses, giant, horse-drawn public conveyances that went to all parts of the city and were available from eight in the morning until eleven at night, and that some of the Americans found an even better way to relieve spells of homesickness or melancholy. "If you get into melancholy," wrote John Sanderson, "an omnibus is the best remedy you can imagine.

Whether it is the queer shaking over the rough pavement, I
cannot say, but you have always an irresistible inclination to
laugh. . . . I often give six sous just for the comic effect of an
omnibus. Precipitate jolts against a neighbor one never saw,
as the ponderous vehicle rolls over the stones, gives agitation
to the blood and brains and sets one thinking.

But walk they did more often than not, and were amazed by the thousands of Parisians doing the same, and how friendly they were. *Galignani's
Guide* made a point of the "uniform politeness which pervades all classes,"
and it seemed true. "Indeed," wrote Holmes, "the only very disagreeable
people one meets are generally Englishmen."

Of the foreigners in the city, the Americans were but a tiny minority,
probably less than a thousand during the 1830s, a mere fraction compared
to the English in Paris, or the Germans and Italians.

It was also disconcerting for the Americans to find how little Parisians
knew about America, though over time this was to be remedied in good
measure by Baron Alexis de Tocqueville's *De la Démocratie en Amérique*,
or *Democracy in America*, as it would be titled in English. After a nine-
month visit to the United States, and more than a year at work in an attic
room in Paris, de Tocqueville had produced as clear-eyed and valuable a
study of America as any yet published, in which he wrote about the nature
of American politics, the evils of slavery, the American love of money, and
of how, from the beginning, "the originality of American civilization was
most clearly apparent in the provisions made for public education." Volume I appeared in 1835. A second volume followed in 1840.

Increasingly, with every passing day, the Americans were struck by
how entirely, unequivocally *French* Paris was. Every sign was in French,
the money was French, every overheard conversation was in French.
Hardly a soul spoke a word of English. All this they had been forewarned
about, but the difference between what one had been told and what one
came to understand firsthand was enormous.

Facing necessity, they began to learn a few words—that left was
gauche; right, *droite;* that a waiter was a *garçon;* a baker, a *boulanger;* and
that some words, like "façade" and "rat," were the same in both languages.

Even the more hesitant were surprised to find themselves saying *bonjour*, *très bien*, and *merci* quite naturally, even venturing a whole sentence— "*Excusez-moi, je ne comprends pas.*"

To find that every noun had a gender—that a hand was feminine, while a foot was masculine—and that one was expected to know which was which, seemed to some of the newcomers too much to cope with, and often illogical or even unfair. Why were all four seasons—*hiver, printemps, été,* and *automne*—masculine, for instance. Could not spring perhaps be feminine? And how a word looked on a printed page or menu and how it was pronounced could be worlds apart.

But then if one were clearly making an effort to learn the language, the French were nearly always ready to help. Indeed, so appealing was the attitude of nearly everyone the Americans encountered that there was seldom cause to complain. "You ask a man the way," wrote Holmes's friend Thomas Appleton, "and he will go to the end of the street to show you." The Americans soon found themselves adopting the same kind of civility.

The fashion for mustaches and beards among the French dandies, the Parisian "exquisites," had little or no appeal, however. "Don't you hate to see so many ninnies in mustaches?" wrote John Sanderson. Beards annoyed him still more. "One loves the women just because they have no beards on their faces." If a man was born a fool, Sanderson concluded, he could be a greater fool in Paris than anywhere on earth, such were the opportunities.

By the 1830s trousers had replaced britches as the fashion. Light tan trousers, a dark tight-fitting frock coat, a bright-colored vest coat, top hat, fine straw-colored or white kid gloves, laceless shoes or boots always highly polished, and a malacca cane or furled umbrella under the arm comprised the *à la mode* wardrobe of the gentleman *flâneur.* For women who dressed *à la dernière mode* it was the full, flounced skirt, puffed and banded sleeves, and large flowered hats that tied with a large ribbon beneath the chin.

Some years earlier, in 1826, nineteen-year-old Henry Longfellow had reported happily from Paris to his brother in New England how he had "decorated" himself with a claret-colored coat and linen pantaloons, and how on Sundays he added "the glory of a little French hat—glossy and brushed." Learning of this, his father wrote, "You should remember that you are an American, and as you are a visitor for a short time only in a place, you should retain your own national costume." But for Longfellow, Paris instilled what was to be a lifelong love of fine clothes, as it would, too, for young Mason Warren and Thomas Appleton.

Nathaniel Willis was delighted to find that in men's apparel shops only attractive young women greeted the prospective customer.

> No matter what is the article of trade—hats, boots, pictures, books, jewelry, anything or everything that gentlemen buy— you are waited upon by girls always handsome and always dressed in the height of the mode. They sit on damask-covered settees behind the counter; and when you enter, bow and rise to serve you with a grace and a smile of courtesy that would become a drawing room.

John Sanderson claimed to have been nearly "ruined" financially by one pretty sales clerk with a way of "caressing and caressing each of one's fingers, as she tries on a pair of gloves one doesn't want."

Though it seemed hard to believe, there were no drunks reeling about in the streets, as in cities at home. Nor did men chew tobacco and spit, and no one abused public property. Park benches showed no other marks than the natural wear of people sitting on them. White marble statues in public gardens remained as pristine as if inside a museum.

Surprising, too, was the presence of dogs everywhere and the way the French doted on them. No woman of fashion, it seemed, made an appearance except in the company of her dog, a *très petit chien* most often and with a step as stylish as her own. Amazingly also, the women of Paris could walk quite as fast as a man.

Especially appealing was the great quantity of glass everywhere—glass doors, huge plate-glass windows fronting shops and cafés. And mirrors, mirrors everywhere, mirrors large and small, great gilt-framed mirrors in hotel lobbies, entire walls of mirrors in cafés and restaurants that multiplied the size of rooms, multiplied the light of day no less than the glow of gaslight and candles after dark, and doubled or tripled the human presence.

The French seemed to take every meal in public, even breakfast, and whenever dining, showed not the slightest sign of hurry or impatience. It was as if they had nothing else to do but sit and chatter and savor what seemed to the Americans absurdly small portions. Or sip their wine ever so slowly.

"The French dine to gratify, we to appease appetite," observed John Sanderson. "We demolish dinner, they eat it."

The general misconception back home was that French food was highly seasoned, but not at all, wrote James Fenimore Cooper. The genius in French cookery was "in blending flavors and in arranging compounds in such a manner as to produce . . . the lightest and most agreeable food." The charm of a French dinner, like so much in French life, was the "effect."

> A dinner here does not oppress one. The wine neither intoxicates nor heats, and the frame of mind and body, in which one is left, is precisely that best suited to intellectual and social pleasures. I make no doubt that one of the chief causes of the French being so agreeable as companions is, in a considerable degree, owing to the admirable qualities of their table. A national character may emanate from a kitchen. Roast beef, bacon, pudding, and beer and port, will make a different man in time from *Château Margaux*, *côtelettes*, *consommés* and *soufflés*. The very name *vol-au-vent* is enough to make one walk on air!

Ralph Waldo Emerson, another of Wendell Holmes's Boston friends, turned up in Paris in 1833, the same year as Holmes, but a little later that summer and by way of Italy. Having concluded he no longer wished to be a minister of the gospel, Emerson was trying to decide at age thirty what to make of his life. Far from charmed by Paris, he found it, after the antiquity of Italy, a "loud modern New York of a place." Yet repent he did. In a matter of days he was calling it "the most hospitable of cities." Walking the boulevards in ideal weather, he was captivated by the human scenery and the multitude of ingenious ways some men made a living.

One vendor had live snakes crawling about him as he sold soaps. Another had an offering of books spread across the ground. Half a dozen more strutted up and down selling walking sticks and canes. Here a bootblack "brandished" his brush at every passing shoe; there a man sat cleaning old silver spoons.

> Then a person who cut profiles with scissors. "Shall be happy to take yours, sir." Then a table of card puppets. . . . Then a hand organ. . . . Then a flower merchant. Then a bird shop with 20 parrots, four swans, hawks, and nightingales. . . .

In stark contrast were the beggars—pitiful men without arms or legs, ancient, hunched women who pleaded mainly with their eyes, and ragged street boys singing mournfully in Italian. Nathaniel Willis kept seeing a woman who sat playing a violin while holding in her lap a sleeping child so still and pale that Willis wondered if it might be made of wax.

Henry Longfellow, who made a return visit to Paris in 1836, loved the crowds as much as anything about the city. When a friend from home, accompanying him on a walk, showed no interest in the passing parade, but insisted on talking about predestination and the depravity of human nature, it was more than Longfellow could bear.

Sundays brought out the greatest crowds, and for many Americans this took getting used to, in that no one seemed the least inclined to keep the Sabbath. The Bostonians found it especially difficult to accept. As said, Boston on Sunday remained "impatient of all levity." In Paris it was not only meant to be a day of enjoyment for everyone, but remarkably everyone seemed entirely at ease with enjoyment. *"Vivez joyeux"* was the old saying. "Live joyfully."

Church bells rang, but hardly more than on other mornings—the bells of the great cathedrals were as characteristic of the city as any sound—and most churches were filled through a succession of services that began at an early hour. But shops, cafés, and restaurants all did business as usual. The opera and theaters were open. The great public gardens were filled with tens of thousands of people, more people than some of the Americans had ever seen all in one place. It was on Sunday only that the Musée du Louvre was open to the public, and to the astonishment of the Americans, the enormous Sunday crowds at the museum included people from all walks of life, as though everyone cared about art.

On Sundays nearly every public garden had its elegant rotundas for dancing. (Happy the nation that once a week could forget its cares, the English author Laurence Sterne had once written of life in Paris.) There were public ballrooms in all parts of the city. John Sanderson hired a cabriolet and escorted a lady from New Orleans to half a dozen different public dances where they found everyone having a perfectly grand time. These Parisians had the right idea, he thought.

Perhaps as unfamiliar for the Americans as almost anything about their first weeks in Paris was the realization that they were foreigners— strangers, *les étrangers*, as the French said—something they had never been before.

"It is a queer feeling to find oneself a *foreigner*," wrote Nathaniel Willis.

———

As robust a walker as any of them was James Fenimore Cooper, who in earlier years had been known to walk from New York City all the way to his country home in Westchester County, a distance of twenty-five miles. No sooner had Cooper settled in Paris in 1826 than he decided to make the entire circumference of the city on foot, taking with him an old friend, a retired American naval captain with the memorable name of Melancthon T. Woolsey, under whom Cooper had once served at sea. The captain was a good-hearted but irritable man with a big voice and, like many Americans, inclined to speak even louder when trying to make himself understood in his outstandingly bad French. "He calls the Tuileries, 'Tullyrees,' the Jardin des Plantes, the 'Garden dis Plants,' the guillotine, 'gullyteen' and the garçons of the cafés, 'gassons,' " wrote Cooper with delight.

Starting at the Barrière de Clichy by the city's old toll wall, they had set off at eleven in the morning, moving at a steady clip. By noon they had covered four miles.

The captain commenced with great vigor, and for near two hours, as he expressed himself, he had me a little on his lee quarter, not more, however, he thought, than was due to his superior rank. . . . At the Barrière du Trône, we were compelled to diverge a little from the wall, in order to get across the river by the Pont d'Austerlitz. By this time I had ranged up abeam of the commodore, and I proposed that we should follow the river up as far as the wall again, in order to do our work honestly. But to this he objected that he had no wish to puzzle himself with spherical trigonometry, that plane sailing was his humor at the moment, and that he had, moreover, just discovered that one of his boots pinched his foot.

By three o'clock they were back where they started, having completed the entire circuit, eighteen miles, in something over four hours. Then to find a cab, they had to walk another two miles.

For his first overall view of Paris, Cooper had gone to the top of Montmartre, a high hill to the north, crowned by a picturesque village and windmills. Here was the best "look-out," and he purposely chose an overcast day, as the most favorable kind of light.

We were fortunate in our sky, which was well veiled in clouds, and occasionally darkened by mists. A bright sun may suit particular scenes, and particular moods of the mind, but every connoisseur in the beauties of nature will allow that, as a rule, clouds and very frequently obscurity, greatly aid a landscape. . . . I love to study a place teeming with historical recollections, under this light, leaving the sights of memorable scenes to issue, one by one, out of the gray mass of gloom, as time gives up its facts from the obscurity of ages. . . .

From Montmartre one could see the whole broad sweep of the city.

The domes sprung up through the mist, like starting balloons; and here and there the meandering stream threw back a gleam of silvery light. Enormous roofs denoted the sites of the palaces, churches, or theaters. The summits of columns, the crosses of the minor churches, and the pyramid of the pavilion-tops, seemed struggling to rear their heads from out of the plain edifices. A better idea of the vastness of the principal structures was obtained here in one hour than could be got from the streets in a twelve-month.

The Cathedral of Notre-Dame, miles in the distance, towered so above everything around it as to seem to stand on a ridge of its own.

Seeing the same view another day, from the same spot but in full sunshine, Cooper found the spell had vanished. All the details he loved, the "peculiarities" of so much history, were reduced to a "confused glittering."

Charles Sumner, for his part, chose to climb the four hundred steps to the top of Notre-Dame to see all of gigantic Paris beneath his feet—Paris, a city of nearly 800,000 people, or four times the size of New York; Paris, the capital of France and the cultural center of all Europe. The capital of his own country, which Sumner had seen on a trip a few years earlier, was a city of "great design" but of small population (a mere 25,000) and "streets without houses to adorn them or businesses to keep them lively." There was nothing natural about its growth, and this troubled him. "It only grows under the hot-bed culture of Congress," he had written.

The "great design" of Washington was the work of a Frenchman, the Paris-born engineer and architect Pierre-Charles L'Enfant. The new Capitol, which Sumner considered an "edifice worthy . . . of the greatest republic on earth," had only just been completed in 1829 under the direction of the American architect Charles Bulfinch, who during a visit to Paris in 1787 had toured the city's monuments with the American minister to France, Thomas Jefferson.

The view from the heights of Notre-Dame, like nearly everything about the ancient cathedral, had lately acquired unprecedented popular interest as a result of a new novel, *Notre-Dame de Paris*, by young Victor Hugo, who had set the story in the fifteenth century. It was his first novel, and a sensation. The first edition in English appeared in 1833, under the title *The Hunchback of Notre-Dame*, a title Hugo disliked but by which the book would be known ever after.

Hugo adored Gothic architecture for all its upward aspirations, its spires, steeples, and pointed arches, its dramatic use of light and dark, for the sense of the sublime in its stained glass, the grotesque in its gargoyles. He intended the book to be a summoning call for historic preservation. "We must, if it be possible, inspire the nation with a love of its national architecture," he wrote in the introduction. "That, its author here declares, is one of the chief aims of this book." He saw Notre-Dame in particular, and Gothic architecture overall, as history writ large in stone before the advent of the printing press.

Hugo loved especially the view from the top of the towers, and to this, the view as he imagined it to have been in the fifteenth century, he devoted one of the most appealing chapters in the book, inspiring thereby no one knows how many thousands of his readers, then and later, to undertake the climb to see for themselves.

The cornerstone of Notre-Dame had been laid in the year 1163 by Pope Alexander III on the eastern end of the Île-de-la-Cité in the Seine. The island was the precise historic center of Paris, since it was there in 52 B.C., under the Romans, that the city was born. It was called the Île-de-la-Cité because it once constituted all there was of Paris. As one learned in Victor Hugo's book, the shoreline of the Seine was its first city wall, the river its first moat.

At the opposite or western end of the island, where its sharp tip pointed downstream like a ship's prow, was the broad Pont Neuf, the New Bridge, which crossed the divided river in two sections and was, in fact, the oldest of the bridges of Paris and the largest. Built of heavy stone in 1604, it was the favorite bridge of the Parisians, a major promenade, and for the Americans it had an air of romance and a view without rival. On the Pont Neuf they felt they were truly in Paris. John Sanderson wrote that it was when he stepped out on the bridge that he began to breathe. "The atmosphere brightened, the prospect suddenly opened, and the noble river exhibited its twenty bridges, and its banks, turrets, towered and castellated, as far as the eye could pierce."

Emma Willard described for her students back in Troy the giant equestrian bronze of Henry IV, Henry of Navarre, "that most chivalrous, best-headed, and kindest-hearted of all the French kings," which commanded the bridge's midway point, where it was grounded on the end of the Île-de-la-Cité. She noted the long lines of bookstalls that reached down the river from the ends of the bridge and the great barges of the Seine, with their washlines hanging out. She wrote of the "delightful streets" called quays following the river's edge and of what splendid promenades they were. The river itself, however, was a disappointment compared to the Hudson, she wrote, adding in true schoolmistress spirit, "But you must make the best of it as it is."

The bridge immediately downstream, the slim, elegant Pont des Arts was her favorite, as it was for many. The first cast-iron structure in Paris, its wide wooden deck was for the convenience and pleasure of pedestrians only. Strolling over the Seine with her on the Pont des Arts, James Fenimore Cooper assured her there was no finer view in all Europe.

She had come to Paris "to see and learn." Suggesting in one of her letters that her students at home accompany her, in a manner of speaking, to the "very heart of Paris," she led them not to the Pont des Arts or to the shops of the Palais Royal, but to the Louvre, and few other Americans would have contested the choice. Like the cathedral at Rouen, the Louvre was a nearly overpowering reminder of the immense difference between the Old World and the New.

It was the world's greatest, richest, most renowned museum of art in what had formerly been a royal palace. Its history was long and complicated. A great part of it had been built for Catherine de Medici in the sixteenth century. Its famous Grande Galerie on the second floor was the longest room in the world, fully 1,330 feet, or more than a quarter of a mile, in length, its entire tessellated wood floor waxed like a table top. The collection of paintings numbered 1,224, and only masterpieces were included. It had been opened to the public, the admission free, by the government of the Revolution in 1793, the same year King Louis XVI and his wife, Marie Antoinette, were taken to the guillotine. Though the Parisian public was admitted only on Sunday, "*étrangers*" were welcome every day, much to the surprise of the Americans. They had only to show their passports.

He entered the Louvre "with a throb," wrote Charles Sumner. Ascending its magnificent marble stairway, he rejoiced to think that such a place was not something set apart for royalty only. So numerous and vast were the galleries that he spent four hours just walking through them.

"Holmes and I actually were at the Louvre this morning three hours instead of one, such is the seduction of the masters," recorded Thomas Appleton, who was in raptures. "O Rubens, emperor of glowing flesh and vermeil lips; Rembrandt, sullen lord of brown shades and lightning lights . . . O Titian, thou god of noble eyes and rich, warm life . . . O Veronese . . . when shall I repay you for all the high happiness of this day?"

Another day Appleton returned on his own to concentrate on Roman sculpture. Except for a solitary art student with his brushes and long loaf of bread, he had the gallery of sculpture to himself and took his time, catalogue in hand. Appleton could not get enough of the Louvre. On his fourth day he found himself so enthralled by a portrait of a boy by Raphael that he returned still again the next day with easel, paints, and brushes to try his hand at a copy.

Emma Willard loved seeing the many young women at work doing copies of paintings in the galleries. Women in France were not disassociated from art, or confined to the periphery. There were women artists in Paris whose works were "much esteemed and bear a high price," she was glad to report to her students.

That the female anatomy in its natural state was so conspicuously glorified on canvas and in sculpture posed a problem for Mrs. Willard. When it came to describing the charms of the nearby Garden of the Tuileries, she chose to omit altogether the marble statues which, as Cooper said, had "little or no drapery."

> No, my dear girls, I shall not take you to examine those statues. If your mothers were here, I would leave you sitting on these shaded benches, and conduct them through the walks, and they would return and bid you depart for our America, where the eye of modesty is not publicly affronted, and virgin delicacy can walk abroad without a blush.

Had she been aware of the randy side of "that most chivalrous" King Henry IV, she no doubt would have had less to say about his statue as well.

The French thought American visitors like Mrs. Willard absurdly squeamish, and some Americans found reactions such as hers embarrassing. Crossing the Garden of the Tuileries one day, Cooper watched a fellow countryman and two women burst into laughter as they passed close to a statue, then start running, and their "running and hiding their faces, and loud giggling left no one in ignorance of the cause of their extreme bashfulness."

John Sanderson, as devoted a teacher as Mrs. Willard, thought the statues in the Tuileries depicting classic mythology made a splendid gallery, its "silent lessons" improving public taste in the arts and "elegancies" of life. Sanderson loved all the gardens of Paris. "Who would live in this rank old Paris if it was not for its gardens?"

Designed by the great seventeenth-century landscape architect André Le Nôtre, the Garden of the Tuileries covered sixty-seven acres, all enclosed by an iron fence and everything—paths, statues, basins, fountains, flower beds, rows of trees—laid out in formal symmetry. A broad, smooth central path—the main avenue for strolling—ran its length, with huge ponds, the Bassin Rond and the Bassin Octagonal, at either end. Just beyond the eastern perimeter stretched the immense Palais des Tuileries, where King Louis-Philippe and Queen Marie-Amélie resided with their numerous family. Begun in the sixteenth century by Catherine de Medici, it was dominated by the central dome of the Pavillon de l'Horloge.

Framing the north side of the garden was a long row of handsome townhouses that lined the new rue de Rivoli, and from an elevated terrace running the length of the north side one could see the beautiful Place Vendôme with its immense, bronze column made of melted-down cannon taken by Napoleon's army at the battle of Austerlitz. To the west, past the octagonal pond, was the enormous Place Louis XV, or Place de la Concorde, where once the guillotine had stood, and beyond the long perspective of the Champs-Élysées extended upward to the giant, but still uncompleted Arc de Triomphe.

On the south rim of the garden another elevated terrace offered strollers an uninterrupted view of the Seine. On this same terrace Thomas Jefferson had settled himself day after day to watch construction of the domed Hôtel de Salm across the river, so "smitten" by its neoclassical elegance that he would later rebuild his own Monticello to achieve a similar look.

Galignani's Guide proclaimed the Garden of the Tuileries "the most fashionable promenade in Paris," and late afternoon was the time to see the show. Even the plump "Citizen King," Louis-Philippe himself, could occasionally be seen out for a stroll, looking very like the banker he once was, in top hat and black frock coat and carrying a green umbrella.

For many who frequented the garden, whether to walk or to linger comfortably on a shaded bench or hired chair, the children were the favorite part of the show, all happily laughing and running about, and all amazingly (to the Americans) chattering away in French, while watched over by immaculate, full-skirted Swiss maids. "I have been there repeatedly since I have been in Paris, and have seen nothing like the children," Nathaniel Willis reported to his readers in the *New-York Mirror*. "They move my heart always, more than anything under heaven." It was enough to make one forget Napoleon and his wars.

But then Paris was a continuing lesson in the enjoyment to be found in such simple, unhurried occupations as a walk in a garden or watching children at play or just sitting observing the human cavalcade. One learned to take time to savor life, much as one took time to savor a good meal or glass of wine. The French called it "*l'entente de la vie*," the harmony of life.

John Sanderson, watching the parade of fashionable women on the wide path of the Garden, said, "I never venture in here without saying that part of the Lord's Prayer about temptation. . . ."

Sanderson kept thinking how much city life at home could be improved by public spaces of such beauty. At home the value of city property was reckoned almost exclusively by what could be built on it. Independence Square, he had heard Philadelphians calculate, was worth a thousand dollars a foot, "every inch of it." Pride in new railroads and the like too often lead Americans to measure value by the capacity to answer some practical, physical need. "Utility with all her arithmetic very often miscalculates," he wrote.

Let us have gardens, then, and other public places where we may see our friends, and parade our vanities, if you will, before the eyes of the world. Did you ever know anyone who was not delighted with a garden?

Sooner or later all the newly arrived Americans crossed the Seine to walk the labyrinth of narrow streets in the Latin Quarter. Or to see the great inner courtyard of the Sorbonne, or the Luxembourg Palace and its magnificent gardens. Or take in the "curiosities" at the Jardin des Plantes, including the famous Zarafa, the only giraffe in all of France, which stood eleven and a half feet high, even higher when she stretched her neck.

The quantities of books to be browsed among in one little shop after another, and the low prices, even for rare books, were astonishing. A student could buy "a library on the street from a quarter of a mile of books at six sous a volume," reported an exuberant Sanderson. "I have just bought Rousseau in calf, octavo, at ten sous!"

Here, too, in the Latin Quarter were the poor. Compared to the Right Bank, it stood apart "as if the city of some other people."

To the west, on the same side of the river, was the fashionable Faubourg Saint-Germain, in the Seventh Arrondissement, the quiet neighborhood where Cooper and his family lived. Farther beyond stood the Hôtel des Invalides, the immense gold-domed barracks and military hospital built in the days of Louis XIV.

Père Lachaise, the city's largest, most famous cemetery, was a good walk back over the river to the northeast. There one could stroll among weeping willows and some 50,000 grave markers and the marble tombs of the eminent dead of France.

Or for those with the stomach for it, there was another popular attraction of which no mention was to be found in *Galignani's Guide.* At the Paris morgue on the Île-de-la-Cité unidentified bodies taken from the Seine were regularly put on public display. Most of the bodies had been caught in a net stretched across the river for that purpose downstream at Saint-Cloud. Some were murder victims, but the great majority were suicides. Stripped of their clothes, they lay stretched out on black marble tables, on the chance someone might claim them. Otherwise, after three days, they were sold to doctors for ten francs each. Crowds of people came to see. As Sanderson noted, "You can stop in on your way as you go to the flower market, which is just opposite."

Joining the throngs of promenading Parisians, the Americans walked the length of the Grand Avenue of the Champs-Élysées, nearly two miles, from the Place de la Concorde gently uphill to where Napoleon's colossal Arc de Triomphe, under construction since 1806, was at long last nearing completion. On a fine Sunday three or four thousand elegant carriages went rolling by on the avenue, in a show of fancy horses and the latest high fashions.

At a corner along the way, at the rue de Berri, stood the stone mansion where Jefferson had resided. Another few miles beyond the city was what had once been Benjamin Franklin's splendid estate on an elevated setting in the village of Passy. Less than a mile beyond that, at Auteuil, was the mansion where John and Abigail Adams had lived.

Such reminders of their own history were particularly refreshing for the Americans, engulfed as they were every day by a French past infinitely richer. A lightning rod Franklin installed at his estate at Passy was still to be seen. As the Americans were pleased to learn, it had been the first lightning rod in all of France.

In his *Notre-Dame de Paris*, describing the view from the top of the great cathedral, Victor Hugo had written that in all the eye could see there was "nothing that did not belong to the art of architecture." And from the countless miles they covered at ground level, and all they took in, the Americans, too, came to see and appreciate how much of the transcending appeal of Paris, the spell of Paris, derived from light, color, and architecture.

It was not just that they had never known a city of such size or variety, or with so much history, but they had never known one where the look and mood could be so strikingly different in different light. The Seine could be any of a dozen shades of mud-brown or chalky green, gleaming silver or a deep indigo, depending on the time of year, the time of day, or simply whether the sun was out. The change could be astonishing, theatrical. In the gloom of winter, sand-colored bridges and palaces could look as leaden as the skies overhead, just as in full sunshine—even in winter— the same bridges and palaces would glow with such golden warmth it was as if they were lit from within.

Naturally most Americans, unlike their countryman Cooper, greatly preferred Paris in sunshine. It was then—and there was no better time than late afternoon—when the gardens were at their loveliest, when strong, brilliant light and the sharpness of shadows presented great façades and belfries, gilded domes and chimney pots, at their best, vividly defining their character. Then especially it became manifest that whether the mode was the Gothic Hugo adored, or the Baroque or classical, architects built with light no less than with brick and stone.

Nathaniel Willis, having spent his first week walking the city in drizzling rain, said that when the sun burst forth at last it so changed all his previous impressions that he had to set off and see it all a second time. "And it seemed to me another city," he wrote. "I never realized so forcibly the beauty of sunshine. Architecture, particularly, is nothing without it."

II

The glories of the art of architecture, of the arts on all sides, in and out of doors, the conviction of the French that the arts were indispensable to the enjoyment and meaning of life, affected the Americans more than anything else about Paris, and led many to conclude their own country had a long way to go. Something had awakened within them. Most would never again look upon life in the same way, as they said themselves repeatedly in so many words.

Charles Sumner found himself feeling "cabined, cribbed, confined" by his own ignorance of art, but on a second visit to the Louvre during which he concentrated his attention on works by Raphael and Leonardo, he felt the thrill of a great awakening. "They touched my mind, untutored as it is, like a rich strain of music."

To his amazement, John Sanderson had begun to love art almost as much as he loved nature. "In our own country, we have nothing yet to show in the way of great works of art," he wrote. "It is a mighty advantage these old countries have over us."

To judge by their letters and journals, and the unabashed enthusiasm expressed, the performing arts surpassed anything the Americans had ever seen or imagined. They could hardly get enough of the opera and theater. Some, it would seem, went nearly every night.

"The evening need never hang heavy on the stranger's hands," wrote Ralph Waldo Emerson, having dispensed altogether with his initial misgivings about Paris. The very air now seemed charged with excitement. "More than twenty theaters are blazing with light and echoing with fine music . . . not to mention concerts . . . shows innumerable," he wrote. "The theater is the passion of the French and the taste and splendor of their dramatic exhibitions can hardly be exceeded."

There were two opera houses, both exuberantly ornate and spacious: the Théâtre Italien, on the Place des Italiens, where Italian opera was performed, and the Salle Le Peletier, home to the company now known as the Paris Opera, at that time sometimes called the Grand Opéra and known, too, for its corps de ballet.

Faultlessly attired and wearing a turban, Emma Willard went escorted by her son to the Italian Opera for a performance of *Otello*. She was pleased especially with the vantage point of their box seats, not so much for the view of the stage as the show of "genteel society," as she was frank to say. She later described the richly carved and gilded embellishments of the theater, the crimson curtain, the gorgeously lighted chandeliers. And the music, when it began, was much to her liking. But the audience interested her far more, and having had the foresight to bring "an excellent eyeglass," she studied every detail, every gesture.

> I never saw so many well dressed ladies together before; but
> it was not so much new forms of things which I saw as it was
> a greater perfection of material, of making and putting on. In
> manners also, one remarks a difference between these people
> and those we see at home under similar circumstances. All
> seem to live not for themselves, but for others. Nobody looks
> dreamy—but all are animated—gentlemen are on alert if a

French diligence (stagecoach).

The cathedral at Rouen.

GALIGNANI'S
NEW
PARIS GUIDE:

CONTAINING

A detailed and accurate Description of all the Public Edifices, Gardens, etc.; an Account of the Political, Scientific, Commercial, Religious, and Moral Institutions of the Capital; an Abstract of the Laws interesting to Foreigners; with an Historical Sketch of Paris, and all necessary and useful Directions to the Traveller previous to his setting out, upon his landing in France, and upon his arrival and during his residence at Paris; and an Account of the different Roads from the Coast to the Capital : to which is added an Historical and Picturesque

DESCRIPTION OF THE ENVIRONS,

INCLUDING A VERY AMPLE ACCOUNT OF THE PALACE, PARK, AND TOWN OF VERSAILLES;

ALSO CONTAINING

A PLAN FOR VIEWING PARIS IN A WEEK;

A COMPARATIVE SCALE OF WEIGHTS AND MEASURES, VALUE OF COINS, THE DUTIES ON GOODS ENTERING ENGLAND, A DIRECTORY OF PARISIAN BANKERS, TRADESMEN, ETC. WITH MANY INTERESTING PARTICULARS NOT TO BE FOUND IN ANY OTHER WORK OF THE KIND.

SEVENTEENTH EDITION,
WITH MAPS, TWELVE ENGRAVINGS, ETC.

PARIS:
PUBLISHED BY A. AND W. GALIGNANI,
AT THE ENGLISH, FRENCH, ITALIAN, GERMAN AND SPANISH LIBRARY, N° 18, RUE VIVIENNE.

JULY, 1830.

Title page of *Galignani's New Paris Guide,* indispensable companion for newly arrived Americans.

View of the Flower Market by Giuseppe Canella, with the Pont Neuf in the background.

The rue de Rivoli, with the Louvre on the left.

Writer Nathaniel Willis loved Paris from the start, but conceded, "It is a queer feeling to find oneself a *foreigner*."

A typical high-fashion French couple of the 1830s.

The Marquis de Lafayette by Samuel F. B. Morse, painted for the City of New York at the time of Lafayette's triumphal return to America in 1825–26.

Samuel F. B. Morse,
a self-portrait painted
at age twenty-seven.

James Fenimore Cooper
by John Wesley Jarvis,
painted when Cooper
was thirty-three.

On the following pages: Morse's *Gallery of the Louvre*, with Morse and student in the foreground, unidentified student to the right, Cooper with his wife and daughter in the left hand corner, Morse's friend Richard Habersham painting at far left, and (it is believed) sculptor Horatio Greenough in the open doorway to the Grand Gallery.

12

George P. A. Healy, self-portrait painted at age thirty-nine. Like nearly all American art students, Healy spent long hours at the Louvre making copies of works by the masters.

Schoolmistress Emma Willard, champion of higher education for American women, was delighted by the number of women at work on copies at the Louvre.

13

Four O'Clock: Closing Time at the Louvre by François-Auguste Biard. Americans were astonished by the spectacle of so many people of every kind taking an interest in art.

Art-Students and Copyists in the Louvre Gallery, wood engraving by Winslow Homer.

Oliver Wendell Holmes.

Henry Bowditch.

Jonathan Mason Warren.

Student ticket to the hospital.

Dr. Pierre-Charles-Alexandre Louis.

Dr. Guillaume Dupuytren.

The Amphithéâtre d'Anatomie (the dissecting room) on the rue d'Orléans.

The main entrance to the Hôtel Dieu, the oldest and largest hospital in Paris.

The church of the Sorbonne, the oldest part of the university.

Charles Sumner
by Eastman Johnson.

Sumner's Paris journal entry for Saturday, January 20, 1838, in which, after observing how "well-received" black students are at the Sorbonne, he writes, "It must be then, that the distance between free blacks and the whites among us [at home] is derived from education, and does not exist in the nature of things."

Thomas Gold Appleton by Robert Scott
Lauder. It was Appleton who said, "Good
Americans when they die go to Paris,"
the line made famous when quoted by his
friend Oliver Wendell Holmes. Of all the
Americans who came to Paris in his time,
few so enjoyed the city as did Appleton—
or returned so often.

Right: The Trois Frères
Provençaux, one of
the several elegant
restaurants at the
Palais Royal and a
great favorite of the
Americans.

The luxurious garden and arcades of the
Palais Royal. Oliver Wendell Holmes
liked to say that the Palais Royal was to
Paris what Paris was to Europe.

29

Marie Taglioni, considered the greatest dancer in the world and the sensation of Paris. "Have you seen Taglioni?" was often the first question a foreign visitor was asked.

glove or fan is dropped, and ladies never forget the appropriate nod, or smile of thanks.

Mrs. Willard approved entirely the French regard for fashion as an art unto itself. "We may make many valuable improvements from the instruction of French women in regard to dress, which after all is no unimportant affair to a woman."

> It is incredible what a nice eye a French woman has for dress and personal appearance. It is like a musician whose ear has become so acute that he discovers discords where to ordinary persons there seems perfect harmony.

Charles Sumner made a point of going to a performance of Mozart's *Don Giovanni*, notwithstanding that he could claim no more knowledge of music than of painting. The part of Don Ottavio was sung by Giovanni Battista Rubini, the leading Italian tenor of the day, but Sumner was surprised to find himself carried away by the "singular power" of all the performers. He had never heard anything like it, never known such feelings as swept over him.

While the Paris Opera was second to none in all of Europe in its elaborate scenery and costuming, and the glitter of the audience was no less than at the Italian Opera, it was the dazzling Marie Taglioni, considered the greatest dancer in the world, that "*tout Paris*" turned out for, filling all 1,300 seats of the Salle Le Peletier performance after performance. "Have you seen Taglioni?" was often the first question a foreign visitor was asked on arriving in Paris.

Her Italian father, Philippe Taglioni, a famous *maître de ballet*, had started her dancing as a child, and by age twenty-three she had made her debut at the Paris Opera. She had dark hair and large, luminous dark eyes. Her skin was uncommonly pale, her arms and legs uncommonly long and thin. By the time someone like Nathaniel Willis saw her perform, she was in her late twenties but looked younger. She had been one of the first to dance on the tips of her toes, and was known for her floating leaps and for her costume, with its tight bodice and short gauzy skirt, the prototype of the tutu. So lavish was the praise for her beauty and artistry that many went to see her for the first time wondering whether they might be disappointed.

"No language can describe her motion," wrote Nathaniel Willis after seeing her in the role of the dancing girl in *Le Dieu et la Bayadère*, the part that had made her famous. "She swims in your eye like a curl of smoke, or a flake of down. Her difficulty seems to be to keep to the floor."

> Her figure is small, but rounded to the very last degree of perfection; not a muscle swelled beyond the exquisite outline; not an angle, not a fault. . . . Her face is most strangely interesting, not quite beautiful, but of that half-appealing, half-retiring sweetness that you sometimes see blended with the secluded reserve and unconscious refinement of young girls just "out" in a circle of high fashion.

John Sanderson felt utter joy watching her. He had never seen anything to compare. "Mercy! How deficient we are in our country in these elegant accomplishments. In many things we are still in our infancy, in dancing we are not yet born."

Nathaniel Willis wondered to what degree the response of an audience enhanced the quality of a performance on stage. Taglioni's performance was a triumph of art, and she was applauded as an artist, but then the "overwhelming tumult of acclamation" she received for her most brilliant moments came from "the hearts of the audience, and as such must have been both a lesson and the highest compliment for Taglioni." Here, he thought, was the great contrast with the theater at home. "We shall never have a high-toned drama in America, while, as at present, applause is won only by physical exertion, and the nice touches of genius and nature pass undetected and unfelt."

What Willis appreciated most about the French theater was that the actors did not look like actors, or play their parts as if acting. He liked their naturalness, their "unstudied" facial expressions. "And when they come upon stage, it is singularly without affectation, and as the character they represent would appear."

Wendell Holmes and his fellow medical students, for all the pressures on them in their studies, took time to attend both the opera and the theater. Even James Jackson, Jr., the most intense of students, went along. By "indulging" himself this way, he was better able to study and maintain his health, he assured his father, knowing his father's own love of music.

> Indeed, while at the opera, I long for your company almost as much as while at the hospital, as I feel in both places how strongly you would sympathize with me—for I did not know what music was in America and I assure you I will not allow myself to neglect it altogether here. . . .

Like others, Holmes and Jackson wrote dutifully to their parents every week, sometimes comparing notes with one another in the process. "James Jackson has just come up to my room to write home a letter, and reminded me that I must have one ready for the next packet," Holmes began one letter. "Well, here we are, Jackson at my desk and I at my table, both of us in a little hurry, but not willing to let the day pass without our weekly tribute."

Of the many theaters in Paris, the famous old Théâtre Français, adjacent to the Palais Royal, was foremost and immensely popular largely because of Mademoiselle Mars, who was to French drama of the time what Taglioni was to dance. Here were performed the great classical French works—the plays of Corneille, Racine, and Molière—and in the finest style and according to strict rules. For the Americans intent on learning French, it was common practice to bring along a copy of the play to follow what was being said. Such theater was indispensable to the intelligent foreigner, Holmes explained to his parents, both as a guide to French manners and as "the best standard" of the language. In consideration of his parents' views on such matters, he added, "There is no need of cutting or tearing off this last page about theaters—where society is far advanced they must exist and are a blessing."

Mademoiselle Mars, whose real name was Anne Françoise Boutet, had been an unrivaled favorite on the French stage for nearly thirty years and had made Molière her *pièce de résistance.* Her pronunciation was considered the finest model of classic French.

"Molière could not have had a proper conception of his own genius, not having seen Mademoiselle Mars," wrote Sanderson, who had waited in line for more than two hours to buy a ticket. Charles Sumner saw her in Molière's *Les Femmes Savantes.* "Her voice is like a silver flute, her eye like a gem." He knew he would remember the evening as long as he lived.

———

And following the theater, there was more. "Thousands in merry moods throng the walks," wrote Thomas Appleton, who had no medical studies to cope with, and few if any worries about spending money. His wealthy father, a Boston merchant, banker, and textile manufacturer, had told him there was no reason to deny himself whatever was "comfortable."

Appleton adored the restaurants and cafés of Paris, especially after dark when the light from their windows was like "the blaze of day." He had made a point of dining at several of the finest, including the Rocher de Cancale, known for its oysters, and Tortoni's, on the boulevard des Italiens, where in summer after the opera the *haut ton* flocked to "take ices."

"*Cafés* abound in Paris, particularly in the principal streets and the boulevards," the newcomers read in their *Galignani's* guidebook.

> It is impossible to conceive either their number, variety, or elegance, without having seen them. In no other city is there anything to resemble them; and they are not only unique, but in every way adapted for convenience and amusement.

The most celebrated concentration was at the Palais Royal, where the modern restaurant had originated in the eighteenth century. The Café de Foy, the oldest and still one of the finest in Paris, Périgord, Café Corazza, and Véry were all in the Palais Royal. For the cost of a dinner at Véry, it was said, one could live comfortably in the provinces for a month. "Alas, my poor roasting and frying countrymen!" wrote Sanderson after dining at Véry and observing other Americans trying with equal difficulty to fathom the choices offered on the menu. "Your best way in this emergency," he advised, "is to call the garçon and leave all to him, and sit still like a good child and take what is given to you."

The gaslit Café des Mille Colonnes outdid them all in mirrors, and the elegant Trois Frères Provençaux was where Holmes, Jackson, Warren, and others of the medical students convened regularly on Sundays. As much as the food and the wine, they relished the talk that went with such evenings in such an atmosphere. Talk helped one shape one's thoughts, said Holmes, the greatest talker of the lot.

At Véfour, which many considered the most beautiful, rows of tables were covered with snow-white cloths, and the *garçons* [waiters] dressed to match. Each had one jacket pocket filled with silver spoons, another with silver forks, a corkscrew in a vest pocket and a snow-white napkin, or *serviette*, on the left arm. The menu was the size of a newspaper.

At the Café des Aveugles, below ground level, a small band of blind musicians played. The Café de la Paix was described in *Galignani's Guide* as richly decorated and much frequented by "ladies of easy virtue and Parisian dandies of the second order."

The Palais Royal, Holmes liked to say, was to Paris what Paris was to Europe. If enjoyment was the object of life, as some philosophers held, no one spot in the world offered such a variety of choices. The principal restaurants and the shops shimmering with jewelry and Sèvres china were on the garden level, as well as shoemakers, linen drapers, waistcoat makers, and tailors. On the level above were still more restaurants and a number of gambling houses. Some of the gambling houses were "*très élégantes*," and to the surprise of newly arrived Americans one saw "beautiful *women* engaged in various games of hazard." Other establishments catered to a rougher trade. As *Galignani's Guide* warned, in the Palais Royal were "haunts where the stranger, if he ventures to enter, should be upon his guard against the designs of the courtesan and the pickpocket."

(It was not that gambling went on at the Palais Royal only. It was everywhere and an unfamiliar spectacle for many Americans. In many states at home, gambling was a criminal offense. "Billiards, cards, faro, and other games of hazard, are to be found at every . . . street and alley of Paris," wrote John Sanderson. "The shuffling of cards or rattling of dice is a part of the music of every Parisian saloon. . . .")

Prostitutes of varying degrees of sophistication, allure, and price maintained a conspicuous presence throughout much of the city wherever crowds congregated. But the young Americans said little or nothing on the subject in their letters or even in the privacy of their diaries. Dire warnings by parents and teachers weighed heavily, as did the dread of syphilis, and few wished to acknowledge succumbing to the pleasures of the flesh or even suggest that when in Paris one might do as the Parisians did.

But then they were on their own as never before. "Young men are very fond of Paris no doubt," wrote Emerson, "because of the perfect freedom—freedom from observation as well as interference—in which each one walks. . . ." There were, it seemed, some advantages after all to being a "stranger."

While making no case for prostitution, John Sanderson could not bring himself to disapprove of, let alone scorn, the young working women of Paris who, because of pitifully meager wages as shop clerks and the like, chose to make "arrangements." These were the *grisettes*, so called because of the grey (*grises*) skirts and blouses they often wore.

"They are very pretty, and have the laudable little custom of falling deeply in love with one for five or six francs a piece," John Sanderson wrote. To many a student in the Latin Quarter, a *grisette* was "a branch of education."

> If a student is ill, his faithful *grisette* nurses him and cures him; if he is destitute, she works for him. . . . Thus a mutual dependence endears them to each other; he defends her with his life, and sure of his protection, she feels her consequence and struts in her new starched cap. . . . She is the most ingenious imitation of an innocent woman that is in the world.

If a young man's morals were "out of order" at home, Paris was not exactly the place to send him, Sanderson conceded. To keep a mistress was not only acceptable in Paris society, but was nearly always mentioned to one's credit.

If you can preserve him by religious and other influences from either, as well as from the dangers of an ascetic and solitary abstinence—for solitude has its vices as well as dissipation—so much the better. He will be a better husband, a better citizen, and a better man. But let me tell you that to educate a young man of fortune and leisure to live through a youth of honesty, has become excessively difficult even in any country; and to expect that with money and address he will live entirely honest in Paris, where women of good quality are thrown in his face—women of art, of beauty, and refined education—it is to attribute virtues to human nature she is no way entitled to.

Any problems or complaints the Americans had were comparatively few and seldom of great or lasting consequence. The long delay in mail from home remained a constant annoyance, and at times a worry. Family and friends were repeatedly urged to write, yet time after time when one went to pick up the mail, there was nothing. Months could pass with not a word from home. Emma Willard grew so distraught over this she was nearly ill, as she wrote to her sister. "My anxiety deprives me of sleep, and preys upon my health."

Many, like Charles Sumner, found winter's cold, unrelieved greyness—*la grisouille*, as it was called—more nearly than they could take. Emerson thought Paris unduly expensive. Nathaniel Willis thought one's time as well as one's money disappeared much too fast. Others besides Holmes did not care for the English men and women they met, and none of the Americans liked being taken for English.

Sumner hated seeing so many soldiers about the streets, the public gardens, and standing guard at every museum and palace. It seemed nearly impossible to be out of sight of soldiers. They were part of the picture, and this took getting used to.

Emma Willard was appalled to learn that more than a third of the children in Paris were born out of wedlock. During a visit to the Hospice des Enfants-Trouvés, the Hospital for Foundlings, seeing the numbers of babies ranged in rows of cribs, she was heartstricken, exactly as Abigail Adams had been on a similar tour long before. Like Abigail Adams, Mrs. Willard was touched by the devotion shown by the nuns to the care of the infants, but felt there had to be something dreadfully amiss about a society in which so many babies were abandoned.

But the long-awaited letters from home nearly always arrived. Charles Sumner found relief from the cold by moving to different lodgings. Those short of money seemed to find ways to get by. Those like Emma Willard and John Sanderson, who had left home in quest of better health, found their health greatly improved.

"*On prend l'essence de la vie dans la ville.*" "One captures the essence of life in the city," the French said. To be in Paris was to have the world at one's feet—"*le monde à ses pieds.*"

Wendell Holmes adjusted to the new life so quickly and easily it took him by surprise. Of all the young Americans none adapted to Paris so readily and enthusiastically. He felt entirely at home, as if he had always lived in Paris, which was remarkable, given he had known nothing the least like his new life. He had no trouble learning French, and from his friends among the French students he quickly picked up on the "little practical matters" that helped him make the most of the city, including "economy," he assured his parents:

> An American or Englishman when he first comes to Paris . . . is always extravagant and this for two reasons—first, because he is under an excitement to find himself in a strange place and indifferent to the base motive of economy, and next because he is totally ignorant of the thousand expedients for avoiding expense which have sprung from the philosophy of the Parisians. Thus he pays his *garçon* (servant) double what he ought to, he gives money to the little rascally beggars who never dare to ask a Frenchman. He takes a cabriolet when he should take an omnibus. He calls for twice as much at the restaurants as he wants—ignorant, poor creature, that while an Englishman values everything in proportion to its price, the Frenchman's eulogy is "*magnifique et pas cher!*"

Holmes liked the French. He adored the food and enjoyed especially congenial gathering places like the Café Procope, close to the École de Médecine, which everyone knew was once a favorite of Voltaire and Benjamin Franklin. It had been started in 1670 by a Sicilian named Francesco Procopio del Cotillo, who was said to have introduced coffee to Paris.

"I am getting more and more a Frenchman," Holmes told his parents. "I love to talk French, to eat French, to drink French every now and then. . . ." Paris was "paradise"—though, to be sure, a very different variety of paradise than envisioned in Boston. For years afterward Holmes would delight in quoting a remark of Appleton's, "Good Americans, when they die, go to Paris."

Appleton, who rarely ceased having a good time, chose after a month or so to move on and see more of Europe as he had always intended. But in 1836 he was back again when his father decided to bring five of the family to Europe in grand style, which included a suite of rooms at the famous Hôtel Meurice on the rue de Rivoli overlooking the Garden of the Tuileries. On the question of whether to be a painter or a writer, Appleton remained unresolved, and as it turned out, for all his considerable talent for both, he would be neither seriously. Nor would he ever settle for any fixed occupation. His father advised him not to be overly concerned about money and thanks to his father's fortune, he never had to be. He would continue as he had right along, writing and painting for his own pleasure, a convivial devotee of the arts, generous with his money, beloved for his wit, his gift for talk and for friendship. He was too devoted to Boston ever to choose the life of an expatriate, but he would travel to Europe and return to Paris time after time, never able to get enough of it.

For the rest there was work at hand and for all the limitless fascination and pleasures of Paris, the work mattered foremost and consumed much the greatest part of all their time and energy. Work was their reason for being there, and they never lost sight of that. Like the young Boston artist George Healy, they had a strong desire to make something of themselves, and with few exceptions they were working longer hours and with far greater concentration than ever in their lives. Even James Cooper, who had already made something of himself, not only completed *The Prairie*, the third of his "Leather-Stocking" novels, but six other books as well.

Some days, according to his wife, Susan, he worked such long hours and became so agitated he could hardly hold his pen.

Samuel Morse, who arrived in Paris on New Year's Day, 1830, had gone at once, predictably, to the Louvre and walked up and down the Grand Gallery for three hours, trying in his excitement to take it all in and decide which paintings to copy. Two weeks later he left for Italy, not returning until the following year and thus missing the July Revolution. But in September 1831, he returned, and that autumn at the Louvre conceived the idea for what was to be the most difficult, ambitious painting of his career.

George Healy had done little else but "study hard." How exactly he managed to get by—with scarcely any money and speaking no French at first—he never said. "But manage he did," a daughter would one day write. Somehow he talked his way into the studio, or *atelier*, of the then-celebrated painter Baron Antoine-Jean Gros. He was the sole American student, but having set up his easel, he became to all intents and purposes, in his daughter's words, a French painter, seeing things from a French point of view. "He lived like his comrades, whom he greatly liked. . . . It was often a hard life, but a singularly interesting and varied one also."

True to his assignment from the *New-York Mirror*, Nathaniel Willis kept turning out his letters, as did John Sanderson in his effort to be, as he said, "the Boswell of Paris." Sanderson went home to stay in 1836. His book *Sketches of Paris: In Familiar Letters to His Friends; by an American Gentleman in Paris*, as descriptive and delightful as anything on the subject by any American of the day, would be widely read on both sides of the Atlantic. It was published in Philadelphia in 1838, and in London that same year under the title *The American in Paris*. A French edition appeared in Paris in 1843.

Emma Willard never slackened in a busy social schedule that included Lafayette and Cooper and their families and grand soirées sufficient to feast her eyes on diamonds, rubies, emeralds, and ostrich feathers beyond anything she had ever imagined. She studied and approved highly the attention given to elevated conversation in such society. She spent more time at the Louvre. She undertook her own survey of French schools and arranged to stay longer than planned. "It seems as if a spell was laid upon me that I cannot go from this place," she explained. Before departing at last for home in the spring of 1831, her head filled with so much that she had seen and learned, she recruited a first teacher of French for her school, Madame Alphise de Courval. As would be said of Emma Willard, few people ever derived more benefit from a time abroad, and "the effect was speedily seen in the renewed *éclat* of the Troy Female Seminary."

Sumner, the ultimate industrious scholar, never let up attending lectures at the Sorbonne—on natural history, geology, geography, Egyptology, Greek history, the history of the English Parliament, the history of philosophy, Latin poetry, criminal law, the Byzantine emperor Justinian and the Justinian Code—and made time as well to sit in on lectures at the hospitals. He had been as determined in his efforts to master French as he was about nearly everything, and after a month, with the help of two tutors, he was able to follow the lectures with little difficulty. In six weeks he was taking part in conversations in French with students and faculty alike and on all manner of subjects.

CHAPTER THREE

MORSE AT THE LOUVRE

My country has the most prominent place in
my thoughts. How shall I raise her name?

—SAMUEL F. B. MORSE

I

Never during his time abroad had James Fenimore Cooper had so much to report about a friend and fellow countryman as he did now about Samuel Morse. Morse was "hard at work" at the Louvre, Cooper wrote in one letter. Morse "has created a sensation" at the Louvre, he said in another. "He is painting an exhibition picture that I feel certain must take." Beyond that, Morse was "just as good a fellow as there is going."

The "good fellows" of life mattered greatly to Cooper. "Friends are rare in any land," he had his frontiersman hero, Natty Bumppo, observe in *The Prairie*, and those he counted as friends knew his many kindnesses and genuine interest in their aspirations and concerns. He was a great organizer of clubs, a most faithful correspondent.

Cooper and Morse had met first at a reception at the White House seven years earlier, at the time of Lafayette's visit, and found how much they had in common. Back in New York they saw more of each other. But as often happens to sojourners far from home in foreign lands, their time together, first in Italy, now in France, had led to a fast friendship.

Growing up in Charlestown, Massachusetts, Samuel Finley Breese Morse had been known in the family as Finley. To Cooper he was Samuel, or Master Samuel, or plain Morse, and there was no mistaking Cooper's pride in him. "Crowds get round the picture, for Samuel has quite made a hit in the Louvre," Cooper wrote to William Dunlap, a painter and art critic in New York who would, Cooper knew, spread the word among their "set" at home.

It was the month of March in the year of 1832—a year that would prove to be one of the most calamitous in the history of Paris—and well before such other Americans as Wendell Holmes, George Healy, and Charles Sumner arrived on the scene. The weather, as Nathaniel Willis noted, was "deliciously spring-like."

———

At age forty-two, having spent half his life as an artist, Samuel Morse felt he had at last reached his stride, and that his time in Europe had already been of immeasurable value. During a year and more in Italy he had spent long days working in the Vatican galleries and other museums. He studied paintings, made copies on commission, including one of Raphael's *School of Athens,* for which he was to receive $100. He did landscapes, filled notebooks with sketches of and comments on churches, street scenes, and processions. At the Palazzo Colonna in Rome, a sixteenth-century portrait by Veronese had awakened him as no painting ever had to a new understanding of color.

Besides the time he had spent with Cooper and his family in Rome, including a moonlight tour of the Colosseum, Morse struck up a friendship in Florence with a young American sculptor, Horatio Greenough, a friend of Cooper's, whom Morse saw as a fellow spirit "wholly bent" on *"excellence in his art."* Greenough had paid Morse the compliment of doing a bust of him. To Greenough, who was still in his twenties, Morse seemed well on in years. He enjoyed teasing Morse for his straitlaced Puritan ways, calling him "wicked Morse," and kept telling him it was time he married again. A man "without a true love," insisted Greenough (who was happily single), "is a ship without ballast, a one-tined fork, half a pair of scissors."

When Morse returned to Paris in the fall of 1831, Cooper thought his work "amazingly improved." Morse had no sooner unpacked than Cooper commissioned him to paint a copy of a Rembrandt, *Tobit and the Angel*, that Cooper judged to be as difficult an assignment as any painting in the Louvre.

Cooper considered himself an artist as a writer, and reviewers of his novels often likened his eye for description to that of a painter. In France, Balzac wrote of Cooper that in his hands the art of the pen had never come closer to the art of the brush. Cooper took serious interest in painting and favored the company of artists. In the New York lunch club he had started—the Bread and Cheese—the artists outnumbered the literary men.

To Cooper, the art of portraiture, when it went beyond a skillful likeness to a delineation of character, had an especially strong appeal. Seeing a portrait of Jefferson by Thomas Sully, Cooper had experienced a complete change of mind. His staunch Federalist family background had given way, he said, and he saw "a dignity, a repose" in Jefferson he had never seen in other portraits. "I saw nothing but Jefferson standing before me, a gentleman . . . in all republican simplicity, with a grace and ease on the canvas. . . ."

From the time Morse took up his ambitious project at the Louvre, Cooper could not keep away. He came every day, climbing the long flight of marble stairs to the second floor to sit and watch.

It was to be a giant interior view of the Louvre. The canvas Morse had prepared measured six by nine feet, making it greater in size than his *House of Representatives* of a decade earlier. And it was to be an infinitely greater test of his skill. Instead of a crowd of congressmen's faces to contend with, he had set himself to render a generous sampling of the world's greatest works of art, altogether thirty-eight paintings—landscapes, religious subjects, and portraits, including Leonardo da Vinci's *Mona Lisa*—and convey in miniature the singular beauty and power of each.

Interior views displaying the treasures of great European art collectors had been an established convention since the seventeenth century. One stunning example of the genre was *The Picture Gallery of Cardinal Silvio Valenti Gonzaga*, painted in 1749 by Giovanni Paolo Panini, which presented the collection Morse had seen at the Palazzo Colonna in Rome, though in a setting only somewhat like that of the Palazzo. In 1831, just a year ahead of Morse, a British artist, John Scarlett Davis, had done one of the Louvre, a painting Morse probably knew about and may have been inspired by. But very few Americans had ever seen such paintings, and no American artist had yet undertaken the interior of the Louvre. Morse's view was to be nearly twice the size of the Davis canvas, which in conception, compared to what Morse had in mind, was prosaic, even banal.

American painters had been coming to Paris for a long time—notably Benjamin West, John Singleton Copley, and John Trumbull in the late eighteenth century—and they had registered great delight in the city. Trumbull had come as the guest of Jefferson, and in the library of Jefferson's home on the Champs-Élysées he and Jefferson had first discussed the idea of a painting to commemorate the signing of the Declaration of Independence. On a small piece of paper, Jefferson had drawn a rough floor plan of the room at Independence Hall as he remembered it, and Trumbull, on the same piece of paper, had made a quick thumbnail sketch of how he envisioned the scene that was to become the best-known work painted by an American.

Rembrandt Peale and John Vanderlyn were among the other American painters who came later to Paris, Vanderlyn spending seven years in all. Robert Fulton, artist and inventor, spent time there at intervals from 1797 to 1804, during which he both painted and worked on ideas for steamboats and submarines.

No American prior to Morse, however, had set himself to so great and difficult a Paris subject, a task that could require a year's work, as Morse appreciated.

He had decided, in effect, to rehang the walls of the elegant Salon Carré, or Square Room, the heart of the Louvre's picture galleries. He would select his own *chefs d'œuvre* from the museum's collection and arrange them on canvas to his liking. This in itself was an enormously ambitious undertaking, in that it meant walking the length and breadth of the Louvre for days, taking time to look seriously at some 1,250 paintings, then, as his own jury of one, decide which to include and how to arrange them.

As it was, the paintings hanging in the Salon Carré were contemporary French works, most in the Romantic style, including Théodore Géricault's highly dramatic *Raft of the Medusa*. Romantic art, with its emphasis on drama, color, and vigorous brushwork, was at its height. Just the year before, in 1831, at the French Academy's Salon, the annual exhibition of contemporary art held at the Louvre, Eugène Delacroix had presented his *Liberty Leading the People*, a huge heroic tribute to the Revolution of 1830, in which its commanding figure, the resolute Liberty, her breast bared, leads the charge to victory, the tricolor held high. The brilliant young Delacroix, who had become the commanding figure in the Romantic revolt against academic art, also included himself in the painting as a handsome, resolute citizen at Liberty's side, armed with a musket.

But Morse, whose work was fundamentally academic, failed to appreciate or take much interest in the Romantics and their revolt. He would choose instead those sixteenth- and seventeenth-century European masterworks—mainly from the Italian Renaissance—that he loved especially, and by the artists he most admired, but also, importantly, works he felt his fellow Americans ought to know and learn to appreciate. He was a man on a mission, a kind of cultural evangelical, as would be said. He would bring the good news of time-honored European art home to his own people, for their benefit and for the betterment of his country.

It was not a new idea. In the same spirit, Jefferson had purchased some sixty-three paintings while in Paris, mostly copies, in the belief that they, like the hundreds of books he selected from bookstalls by the Seine, could help increase American appreciation of the fine arts and the world of ideas.

The great virtue of Morse's project was that so many acknowledged masterworks could be seen all together. It would be his own *musée imaginaire*, which he would take on tour at home, though unlike the Louvre, he would charge admission. He had had the same idea with his *House of Representatives* and with no success. But this, he felt, was such a vastly different subject that the public would respond differently. He was intensely enthusiastic, but then he was by nature intensely enthusiastic.

Cooper loved what he saw emerging and the "sensation" it was causing. He had a regular routine—work at his desk in the morning, then proceed to the Louvre (a walk of a mile and a half or more from his home across the Seine) to spend the afternoon with Morse.

> I get up at eight, read the papers, breakfast at ten, sit down to the quill at ½ past ten, work till one, throw off my morning gown, draw on my boots and gloves, take a cane . . . go to the Louvre, where I find Morse stuck up on a high working stand. . . .

Morse worked from a tall, movable scaffold of his own contrivance, which he shifted about from point to point in the galleries to copy his chosen subjects, some of which were hung quite high.

His painting was of a wall full of pictures in the Salon Carré hung floor-to-ceiling and cheek-by-jowl—the standard mode for French exhibitions. Just left of center in the composition, through a large open doorway, could be seen the long, high-vaulted Grande Galerie with its skylights stretching away as if forever, like a glowing vista in a landscape. To the left and right of the main wall of paintings were portions of the sidewalls, these, too, solid with pictures though much foreshortened like the sidewalls of a stage set. In fact, the net effect of the whole arrangement was very like that of a stage set, and it was Morse's plan to place a half dozen or more figures on stage, as it were, for added interest and to give human scale to the room.

He worked all day "uninterruptedly," Sundays included, from nine o'clock until just before four, when the guards came through to call out that the museum was closing. Visitors flowed through the galleries the whole time, and other artists and students worked at their easels doing copies. But Morse up on his scaffold remained the undisputed center of curiosity and topic of conversation. Sitting astride a chair close at hand, Cooper enjoyed the show more than anyone, occasionally, for comic relief, offering his friend a little unsolicited advice: "Lay it on here, Samuel— more yellow—the nose is too short—the eye too small—damn it, if I had been a painter what a picture I should have painted."

Nathaniel Willis, who was fascinated by faces, tried to fathom why, in a crowd, he could always recognize an American. There was something distinctive about the American face, something he had never noticed until coming to Paris. The distinguishing feature, he decided, was "the independent, self-possessed bearing of a man unused to look up to anyone as his superior in rank, united to the inquisitive, sensitive, communicative expression which is the index to our national character."

To Willis, Cooper and Morse were the essence of the "national character," and on a gentle, sunny afternoon in the Garden of the Tuileries that March, seeing them approaching along one of the wide gravel walks, Willis took note. A fashion plate himself, he had been observing the passing parade of French dandies, their heads "fresh from the hairdresser" and sporting the whitest of white gloves. Then Cooper and Morse came into view, and what contrast there was between these two good American faces!

> Morse with his kind, open, gentle countenance, the very picture of goodness and sincerity; and Cooper, dark and corsair-looking, with his brows down over his eyes, and his strongly lined mouth fixed in an expression of moodiness and reserve.

The two faces were not equally just to their owners, Willis thought. Morse was all that his face bespoke, but Cooper was by no means as dark and moody as he appeared, as anyone who knew him could attest. Cooper himself called it his "chameleon face."

In a portrait painted at home ten years before by John Wesley Jarvis, it is an intensely serious James Fenimore Cooper who fixes his bright black eyes on the viewer. A ruddy face from the brow down, it is dominated by a nose burned red by the sun, while the unusually broad forehead is pale white, the mark of a man who spent much time out of doors, his hat pulled low over the eyes.

On a marble bust carved in Paris by a leading French sculptor, Pierre-Jean David, Cooper's face is leaner and handsomer, the brow, if anything, broader still, and there is a tenacious set to the jaw. Cooper's family thought it an excellent likeness, which was not the case of another bust by Horatio Greenough, where the "corsair-look" was too much in evidence.

Cooper and Morse were about the same height, and from Morse's passport we know he stood five feet nine. The rest of the passport description reads as follows:

> *Forehead: High*
> *Eyes: Black*
> *Nose: Straight*
> *Mouth: Large*
> *Chin: Regular*
> *Hair: Black & Grey*
> *Face: Long*

In several portraits Morse did of himself, starting in his college years, his countenance is quite as kind, open, and gentle as Nathaniel Willis said, and boyish verging on pretty. Greenough also rendered Morse and gave due emphasis to the high forehead, straight nose, and large mouth. The boyish look, however, is no longer in evidence. The face Greenough modeled is leaner, the hair tousled, and there are creases at the corners of the wide mouth. It might be the bust of a handsome actor or poet. It is a gentle, romantic, somewhat soulful face, yet with an unmistakable look of purpose about it.

II

Cooper's afternoons at the Louvre with Morse were a welcome diversion from much on his mind. They were part of that "little pleasure concealed in the bottom of the cup" he had hoped to find living abroad. In the eyes of many, Cooper, with his established reputation and attractive family, was the center of the small American circle in Paris. But for Cooper, Morse and Morse's work at the Louvre had become a redeeming center of interest and enjoyment.

Six months earlier, in September, Cooper's nephew William, who had become very like an adopted son, was taken ill. In October, William died of consumption at age twenty-two. With the onset of winter, Cooper's wife, Susan, came down with a fever of some lingering indeterminate variety that had the whole family worried. Paris was notoriously unhealthy in the chill gloom of winter, the season of colds and deadly fevers.

"*Ma femme est malade et . . . j'attends le médecin,*" Cooper notified a French friend. The family's Parisian doctor was doing too little for her, Cooper thought. He was too content to let nature take its course. "They [the French] are capital in all surgical or all anatomical applications, but when it comes to fevers and latent diseases, they are too timid by half."

His own health, though uneven, was better than it had been in New York, as he liked to tell others. He was less troubled by fevers and gastric attacks. At age forty-two, he was often told he looked thirty-five. "Of course, I believe them," he would respond. Susan, reporting in confidence to her sister, wrote that "Mr. Cooper" was quite well but for one problem. "When he goes into crowded rooms, then he is sure to suffer for the next twenty-four hours with an attack of nerves more or less violent." But of this nothing was to be said beyond the family.

For several months there had been warnings of a possible onset of the dreaded *cholera morbus*. Reports had appeared in the Paris and London newspapers starting in August, and concern kept growing. From Boston in November, Dr. James Jackson, Sr., wrote to his son in Paris asking, "What are you to do if the cholera reaches you?" His advice was to "fly"— to leave France as fast as possible.

Cooper dismissed the talk of cholera, suspecting "a good deal of exaggeration on the subject."

As usual, Cooper had a novel under way, his fourteenth. Beyond that he talked of doing a volume on his travels in Europe. He had been writing now for twelve years, and while the quality of his efforts was uneven, he took pride in the books and enjoyed the acclaim they brought. And he loved the money. It was for money that he had started writing in the first place, when the collapse of a family empire left him nearly destitute. According to the story told later by his daughter Sue, a story widely repeated, Cooper had been reading aloud to her mother from an English novel one evening when, after a chapter or two, he threw it aside saying he could write a better book. She had laughed at the idea, whereupon he set to work.

At no prior time had he shown the least interest in writing or entertained any thought of a literary life. At Yale, where he was the youngest student in the college, he had proven such a poor scholar and such a hellion that he was expelled at age sixteen. (Among other things, he had locked a donkey in a recitation room and exploded a homemade bomb under a dormitory door.) After a year under his father's supervision at home in Cooperstown, the village founded by his father beside Otsego Lake in upstate New York, it was arranged for him to go to sea on a merchant ship. Finding he liked the sailor's life, he had joined the U.S. Navy—it was then that he met his Paris walking companion, Captain Woolsey—and saw no reason not to make the navy a career, until he met Susan Augusta De Lancey, who thought it time he settled down.

Married in New York in 1811, they lived first with her parents at Mamaroneck, then moved to a farm by Otsego Lake. Cooper began building a stone manor house, and with a generous cash bequest from his father, who had died in 1809, he anticipated a serene future as an upstate country gentleman. Children were born. Debts accumulated. When his father's unsettled estate was found to be riven with debt, and the family land holdings worth little because of a poor economy, Cooper faced bankruptcy.

His first book, *Precaution*, was a romance set in England, somewhat in the manner of a Jane Austen novel. It was not very good and only moderately successful. In England it was taken to be an English novel. But Cooper had discovered he liked the work and liked the prospect of the influence he might attain as an author. Books mattered. Without delay he tried again.

"By persuasion of Mrs. Cooper I have commenced another tale," he wrote. (He called her his "tribunal of appeals," "an excellent judge in everything." He read all he wrote aloud to her and she went over every page of manuscript.) The result this time proved entirely different. *The Spy* was an all-out adventure tale set in America during the Revolutionary War. Its theme, as Cooper said, was patriotism, and it was an immediate hit.

From that point on, his success was phenomenal. The next tale, *The Pioneers*, sold 3,500 copies by noon of publication day. Less than a year later, a French translation appeared.

The Pioneers was published in 1823, the most difficult year of Cooper's life. The house he had built burned. His two-year-old son, Fenimore, died. He himself suffered from sunstroke as well as severe bilious attacks, as he called them, and a fever that may have been malaria.

In *The Pioneers* he had been writing about a world much like that of his boyhood, and largely to please himself. The setting was Cooperstown (called Templeton in the book), the year, 1793. It was in *The Pioneers*, too, that he introduced Natty Bumppo, a lean old frontiersman, known also as Leatherstocking for the long deerskin leggings he wore, a character very like Daniel Boone, who had died only a few years earlier.

Two more historical novels followed: *The Pilot*, a sea story, and *Lionel Lincoln*, set in Boston at the time of the Battle of Bunker Hill.

Natty Bumppo appeared again in *The Last of the Mohicans*, where again the setting was upstate New York, only this time it was the New York wilderness of sixty years earlier, during the French and Indian War, and Natty, a scout, was in the prime of life. Cooper had written *The Last of the Mohicans* at top speed in three or four months. It was intense, romantic, filled with violence and bloodshed, as Natty, now also known as Hawkeye, and a Mohican friend, Chingachgook, escorted two sisters, the daughters of a British general, in a flight through the forest. Long descriptive passages of the wild American scenery—of river and waterfall and "the vast canopy of woods"—stirred readers as nothing else had by an American writer, and the book was an immediate success on both sides of the Atlantic.

It appeared in 1826, the year Cooper sailed for France and was already at work on still another Natty Bumppo tale called *The Prairie*. "I think *Pioneers*, *Mohicans*, and this book will form a connected series," Cooper told a friend. "I confess *Prairie* is a favorite as far as it goes. . . ."

By the time he and the family were settled in Paris, he had become America's most famous author. Morse would write of seeing Cooper's books in the windows of every bookshop in the city. Not since the days of Benjamin Franklin had an American been so welcomed and liked— attention Cooper loved, not just for himself, but for his country.

He and Susan became frequent guests of honor at dinners given by Lafayette at his mansion on the rue d'Anjou, in the Faubourg Saint-Honoré, and were treated to overnight visits at La Grange, the general's towered, fifteenth-century château southeast of the city. They were made the center of attention at diplomatic dinners and lavish entertainments, after which Cooper filled pages of correspondence describing the "splendors"— the setting, the food, the eminence of those present. He was hailed as the American Walter Scott, a comparison intended as a high compliment, but which privately he disliked. Artists and sculptors asked him to sit for them.

As much as he enjoyed such attention and acclaim, Cooper was far from enamored with "the mere butterflies" of Paris society. Taken by Lafayette to be "presented," he found King Louis-Philippe perfectly courteous and was glad to hear him speak with pleasure of his time in America. But for others he encountered, Cooper had little use. "The fear of losing their butterfly distinctions and their tinsel gives great uneasiness to many of these simpletons," he wrote privately.

Yet Cooper loved Paris. There was no denying that. He liked living there and working there—finding himself subjected to fewer distractions than in New York—and took particular satisfaction in the education his children were receiving.

The contrast between the author's stately home and way of life, and the setting of the tale he was writing in *The Prairie*, could hardly have been more pronounced. This time, in *The Prairie*, Natty Bumppo was an old man who, to keep ahead of the advancing tide of settlement, had moved steadily westward, beyond the forests, beyond the Mississippi, just as Daniel Boone had in the last part of his life. No one had dramatized American history in such fashion. "It is a weary path, indeed," Cooper had Natty say, "and much I have seen, and something have I suffered in journeying over it." Even on the open prairie, Natty found it getting "crowdy."

That such a story in such a setting, an empty landscape with no visible history, could have been written in Paris would strike some readers as absurdly incongruous. To Cooper, wherever he found himself, it was "a point of honor to continue rigidly as an American author."

Meanwhile, he was being remunerated as no American author had been. The French edition of *The Last of the Mohicans* kept "gaining ground daily." He was making money and saving money as never before. By 1832 he reckoned his financial prospects for the year ahead were something on the order of $20,000, and $20,000 in Europe went a long way.

To other Americans in Paris, his presence, his success and fame, were a matter of much pride. He was "our countryman Cooper," and that he remained so distinctly American—and made no effort to conceal his prosperity—made them prouder still. A young medical student from North Carolina named Ashbel Smith, befriended by the Coopers, wrote that Cooper "more than anyone" was "the American par excellence," adding, "And what is of importance in Paris, he lives in fine style."

Indeed, Cooper and family—his wife, four girls, and a boy, plus three or four servants—occupied two well-appointed, spacious floors of a Louis XVI mansion, or a *hôtel particulier,* at 59 rue Saint-Dominique in the Faubourg Saint-Germain, in the Seventh Arrondissement, "a very *distingué* part of the town," as Susan explained in a letter to her sister. Cooper's was an altogether new kind of American success story. Such splendor for a writer!

> The salon is near thirty feet in length, and seventeen feet high [Cooper wrote]. It is paneled in wood, and above all the doors . . . are allegories painted on canvas, and enclosed in wrought gilded frames. Four large mirrors are fixtures, and the windows are vast and descend to the floor.

The salon, or parlor, with its long French windows, was on the second level, "adjoining Mr. Cooper's library," Susan reported. The dining room, on the floor below, opened onto a garden. "We are very comfortable, very quiet, and overlook a half dozen gardens besides our own, which besides being very agreeable, gives us good air."

The children were doing splendidly well with their music and art lessons. All five could by now "prattle like natives" in French, Italian, and German. Even the youngest, seven-year-old Paul, spoke the three languages and could read them with ease, as his father loved to boast.

But the glittering social whirl of their first years in Paris had become a thing of the past. "We [are] . . . very retired, don't go out much and see but little company," Susan wrote. Her health was the customary explanation, but neither of them cared for fashionable society, and Cooper's trouble with crowded rooms may have been no less a factor than her lingering ailments. "Instead of seeking society," he had written to a friend, "I am compelled to draw back from it, on account of my health and my pursuits." He had grown weary of the fuss the French made over him.

"The people seem to think it marvelous that an American can write." Most of them appeared ignorant that any book had ever been published in America, "except by Dr. Franklin and *M. Cooper Américain*, as they call me."

Though they rarely accepted an invitation, he and Susan regularly entertained such favorites among the "American circle" as Morse, Nathaniel Willis, Horatio Greenough (whenever he was in Paris), and Ashbel Smith, as well as those of any nationality sympathetic to Polish freedom, a cause Cooper fervently embraced. Willis would describe the uniquely generous hospitality of a Cooper breakfast for the Polish-American Committee, where, as probably nowhere else that side of the Atlantic, the guests were treated to hot buckwheat pancakes.

Every American welcomed into the enclave of the Coopers seems to have treasured the experience. "Some of the best hours are spent with Mr. Cooper and his family," Emma Willard had written. "I find in him what I do not in all who bear the name American, a genuine American spirit."

Morse became such an established presence it was as if he were part of the household. At the close of his day at the Louvre, he and Cooper would walk home to the Faubourg Saint-Germain, to join the family for dinner and conversation into the night. Morse began giving the Coopers' daughter Sue drawing lessons, which naturally inclined some to think he had more than a passing interest in her, gossip that soon reached New York and may have been true. Writing to her sister in January 1832, Susan Cooper seemed to go out of her way to stress that "our worthy friend, Mr. Morse" was drawn "more by the attraction of the father than the daughter." Cooper insisted that his friend Morse, though "an excellent man," was not "one to captivate a fine young woman of twenty."

Morse lived modestly in a few small rooms on a side street, the rue de Surène, on the Right Bank, which, to meet expenses, he shared with another American artist named Richard Habersham. Except for his evenings with the Coopers, he appears to have had no other life in Paris apart from his work at the Louvre—no theater, no opera, no convivial evenings at restaurants, no social life of any kind. Still, he and Cooper saw each other, as he recorded, "daily . . . almost hourly" in these "eventful years" of 1831, 1832.

———

They had much in common. Both were the sons of prominent fathers. Both had attended Yale and were of roughly the same age. Both were talented, ambitious, and bright. Each considered himself a historian in his way. Each was devout in his Protestant faith, Morse more so than Cooper, and fittingly for the son of a preacher, he would have preferred that Cooper were more religious. Morse gave time to prayer every day and saw the unfolding of his life, his burdens and struggles, the decisions he made, in religious terms. That Cooper said grace at meals and read family prayers every evening apparently did not suffice.

Both loved music—Cooper played the flute, Morse the piano—and both took with utmost seriousness their roles as gentlemen, "gentlemen in all republican simplicity," in Cooper's phrase. It was how they had been raised and educated. If asked, they would have said that, as Americans abroad, gentlemanly deportment was of even greater importance, since they were a reflection on their country.

(The question of what constituted a gentleman was given serious consideration by other Americans who came to Paris. Wendell Holmes decided, after looking at Titian's painting at the Louvre of the young man with a glove in his hand, that Titian "understood the look of a gentleman as well as anyone that ever lived.")

Cooper's father, William, remembered as a kind of "genius in land speculation," had served as the first judge of Otsego County and was twice elected to Congress. He had known George Washington. Gilbert Stuart had painted his portrait. His famous son would recall with affection "my noble-looking, warm-hearted father" who could "lighten the way with his anecdote and fun."

Morse's father, the Reverend Jedidiah Morse, was of an entirely different variety, a Congregational clergyman and scholar known across the country and abroad as "the father of American geography." He was the author of *Geography Made Easy* and *The American Geography*. His *Elements of Geography*, for children, was a standard in nearly every school. When young Samuel entered Yale as a freshman, he was at once, inevitably, nicknamed "Geography" Morse.

Cooper had been expelled from Yale by the time Morse arrived at age fourteen, and while Morse graduated with the class of 1810, he was only a fair student. His younger brothers, who followed him to Yale, were, as he acknowledged, "very steady and good scholars" and "much esteemed." He was always short of money, and continuously begging his parents for more, which, it happened, was exactly as it had been for his father when he was at Yale.

That Samuel had a lively mind was obvious. But with the exception of some courses in science, he had shown little serious interest in his studies. In one way only had he distinguished himself as an undergraduate, and that was in drawing and painting. Already he was doing miniature portraits for a dollar a piece.

But much differed between Cooper and Morse. Cooper was famous; Morse was not. Cooper had made himself fluent in French, Morse continued to struggle with the language. Morse had no family with him, nothing remotely like the financial security Cooper enjoyed. For Morse there had been no late awakening to what he wanted to make of his life. He had not just shown a knack for painting at Yale; he had known then that he must be an artist. "I was made for a painter," he told his parents at age nineteen, and pleaded for money enough to study under one of the most accomplished young artists of the time, Washington Allston of Boston.

For years his parents had worried that he was "unsteady." *Attend to one thing at a time*," the Reverend Morse preached repeatedly. The "steady and undissipated attention to one object" was the "sure mark of a superior genius." But when the boy declared he wanted to "attend" to painting as his "one object," his parents found that unacceptable. Best that he form no plans, his father wrote. "Your mama and I have been thinking and planning for you."

From the pulpit of the First Congregational Church of Charlestown,

Jedidiah Morse espoused an unyielding, orthodox Calvinism and sent his sons to his alma mater, in large part because Yale remained free from the corruptions of the new liberal Unitarianism espoused at Harvard. With his long, pale, Puritan face he seemed severe and humorless as the grave, as well as exceptionally learned. At home "Papa" preached hard work and frugality, dutiful obedience to parents and gratitude for the blessings of heaven. Samuel's mother, Elizabeth Morse, was of the same mind, but more plainspoken. The daughter of a New Jersey judge, granddaughter of the president of Princeton College, she had "no use of Segars or Brandy or Wine or anything of the kind," as she had reminded Samuel during his college years. "The main business of life is to prepare for death," she told him.

As he well knew, she had had more than her share of experience with death's reality. Of the eleven children she had given birth to, only three, Samuel and his two brothers, Sidney and Richard, had survived.

That Jedidiah and Elizabeth Morse were also attentive, warmhearted parents who cared deeply for their three sons and their welfare, the three sons would have been the first to confirm. And so it was that in a matter of months after Samuel's return home from Yale, having seen at first hand how intent was his desire to make the most of what God-given talent he had, they acquiesced. Not only could he study under Washington Allston, he could, as Allston strongly urged, go to London with him and his wife to study there.

To an acquaintance in London, the Reverend Morse wrote as follows, by way of an introduction for his son. The letter also said much about the father:

> His parents had designed him for a different profession, but his inclination for the one he has chosen was so strong, and his talents for it, in the opinion of some good judges, so promising, that we thought it not proper to attempt to control his choice.
>
> In this country, young in the arts, there are few means of improvement. These are to be found in their perfection only in older countries, and in none, perhaps, greater than yours.

In compliance, therefore, with his earnest wishes and those
of his friend and patron, Mr. Allston (with whom he goes to
London), we have consented to make the sacrifice of feeling
(not a small one), and a pecuniary exertion to the utmost of
our ability, for the purpose of placing him under the best advantage of becoming eminent in his profession, in the hope
that he will consecrate his acquisitions to the glory of God
and the best good of his fellow men.

In contrast to James Cooper, who had taken up the pen at age thirty
and burst virtually full-blown as a successful writer, having had no training or served any sort of apprenticeship, Morse spent four years in London, working as he never had, driven, as he said, by a desire to "shine."

His progress under Allston's tutelage was astonishing. Allston, who
was in his early thirties, was himself hard at it and painting better than he
ever had, and this Morse found thrilling to behold. As a teacher, Allston
was exceedingly demanding. His critiques could be "mortifying," Morse
wrote, "when I have been painting all day very hard and begin to be
pleased with what I have done . . . to hear him after a long silence say,
'*Very bad, sir. That is not flesh, it is mud, sir. It is painted with brick dust
and clay!*' " At such moments Morse felt like slashing the canvas with his
palette knife. He felt angry and hurt, but with reflection came to see that
Allston was no flatterer, but a friend, "and that really to improve I must
see my faults."

Allston could also take the palette and brushes from Morse and with a
few deft strokes show him just how it should be done. "Oh, he is an angel
on earth."

Allston introduced him to the legendary Benjamin West, under whom
Allston had studied. West, who had grown up near Philadelphia, was by
then in his seventies, yet youthful in spirit and revered as no other living historical painter. He had arrived in London in 1763, during what was
to have been temporary study abroad, and never left. In the half century
since, he had become the favorite of King George III and one of the greatest of all teachers. Among the many Americans who had studied under
West over the years were John Trumbull, Gilbert Stuart, Charles Will-

son Peale, and Thomas Sully. His interest in young artists was as great as ever.

Morse was amazed to learn West had painted more than six hundred pictures, and was then at work on nine or ten different pieces at once. West questioned him closely on the state of the arts in America, and "appeared very zealous that they should flourish there."

Morse met West just as the War of 1812 broke out between Britain and the United States, and thus found himself living among the enemy, which was exactly what had happened to West during the American War for Independence.

"Paint *large!*" West told him.

When Morse finished a historical canvas, *The Dying Hercules*, measuring six by eight feet, West came at once to see it and had only compliments. "Mr. West . . . told me that were I to live to his age, I should never make a better composition," Morse noted proudly. The painting was selected to hang in an exhibition at the Royal Academy, and for the first time Morse saw his work praised in print.

It was Allston, however, who had brought him to where he was in his work, Morse stressed. He could hardly say enough for Allston. Through him he met other painters, as well as an acclaimed young American actor, John Howard Payne, and the British poet Samuel Taylor Coleridge. Morse was reading Chaucer and Dante. ("These are necessary to a painter," he explained to his parents.) He took up the harpsichord and, contrary to the old home preachments, began smoking cigars and drinking wine. He attended the theater, saw the great tragic actress Sarah Siddons in one of her last performances, even tried his hand at writing a farce.

"You mention being acquainted with young Payne, the play actor," his mother wrote, plainly worried. "I would guard you against any acquaintance with that description of people, as it will, sooner or later, have a most corrupting effect on the morals."

Morse was busy, sociable, letting go of old enforced constrictions as much as he ever had or ever would, and he was as happy as he had ever been. According to a letter written years later, he even came close to falling in love, though with whom, he never said, adding only that after a time he had found love and painting to be "quarrelsome companions."

At Yale he had been constantly short of money. In London the problem became even more acute. He could afford "no nice dinners," he plaintively informed his parents. "I have had no new clothes for nearly a year; my best are threadbare, and my shoes are out at the toes."

He had to be more than a "mere portrait painter," he announced in another long letter dated May 2, 1814. He could not be happy unless pursuing the "intellectual branch" of art, namely history painting.

> I need not tell you what a difficult profession I have undertaken. It has difficulties in itself which are sufficient to deter any man who has not firmness enough to go through with it at all hazards, without meeting any obstacles aside from it. The more I study it, the more I am enchanted with it; and the greater my progress, the more I am struck with its beauties. . . .

He was thinking of his country. "My country has the most prominent place in my thoughts. How shall I raise her name?"

He longed to go to France to study, but again it was a matter of money. Paris, he reminded his parents, was a mere two-day journey. "I long to bury myself in the Louvre," Morse wrote fully seventeen years before finding himself perched atop his movable scaffold there.

His ambition, he had written in London at age twenty-three, was to be one of those who would revive the splendor of the Renaissance and rival the genius of a Raphael or Titian. Now in Paris in 1832, at age forty, painting large indeed, he was filling his enormous canvas with a virtual tour of the Renaissance that included Raphael and Titian and more.

The London years ended for Morse in the summer of 1815, when told by his parents it was time to come home and earn a living. Back in the United States, he concentrated almost exclusively on portraits, hoping to earn enough to go to France and continue his artistic education. He divided his time between New England; Charleston, South Carolina; Washington; and New York. That his work was as fine as that of any American portraitist of the day there was little doubt. He had been transformed by his years in London from a gifted student to a painter of the first rank.

In 1816 he met Lucretia Pickering Walker of Concord, New Hampshire. "She is very beautiful . . . and openhearted," he confided to his parents. "I ventured to tell her my whole heart. . . ."

"Is she acquainted with domestic affairs?" his ever-practical mother wished to know.

> Does she respect and love religion? How many brothers and sisters has she? How old are they? Is she healthy? How old are her parents? What will they be likely to do for her some years hence, say when she is twenty years old?
>
> In your next [letter] answer at least some of these questions. You see your mother has not lived twenty-seven years in New England without learning to ask questions.

His object now was to make money sufficient for a "domestic" future. At one point he painted five portraits in eight days for $15 each. With "industry," he calculated, he might average $2,000 to $3,000 a year.

But it was not enough. He tried to think of other ways and between portraits turned his mind to inventions. Working with his brother, he developed a flexible (leather) piston pump—for use on fire engines, or as a bilge pump on ships—for which they secured a patent. On his own, he built a machine for carving marble, as a faster way to make copies of statues.

Samuel Morse and Lucretia Walker were married at Concord in 1818. His fee for portraits had reached $60. In 1819 came his first major commission, to paint President James Monroe for the City of Charleston, South Carolina, for the almost unimaginable sum of $750.

It remained a largely itinerant life, not easy on him or Lucretia. With the addition of two children, making ends meet became an unrelieved worry. In the meantime his parents had moved to New Haven, close to the Yale campus, after the Reverend Morse was asked to leave the pulpit at Charlestown on the complaint that he was devoting too much time to geography. It was a severe blow, and particularly for a father who had so adamantly warned his son of the perils of not attending to one thing at a time.

Morse, too, then settled his small family in New Haven. But with an increase in commissions and income, he was able to establish a studio in New York at 96 Broadway, where he could report to Lucretia at last, in December 1824, that he was "fully employed" with portraits and providing instruction for several students as well. He had resolved, he told her, never to be rushed in his work, never to paint too fast. He had no desire to be "a nine days' wonder, all the rage for a moment and then forgotten forever."

"You will rejoice with me, I know, in my continued and increasing success," he wrote to her only days into the new year. He had been chosen out of all painters to do a life-size portrait of General Lafayette to hang in New York's City Hall. He was to receive as much as $1,000 and would be going to Washington just as soon as Lafayette could see him. His only regret was that it would mean more time away from her.

He returned to New Haven for a few days in late January when Lucretia gave birth to their third child, a son they named Finley.

He reached Washington on February 7, 1825, and met Lafayette the following day. "My feelings were almost too powerful for me," he wrote to Lucretia. The general had agreed to proceed with the portrait.

Morse had been advised that Lafayette's features were "not good," and in truth the general had an oddly shaped head with a slanting brow, ears that clung so close that from face-on they could hardly be seen. With advancing age (Lafayette was sixty-seven), the jowls seemed to have taken over. To Morse it was a "noble" countenance, a perfect example of "accordance between the face and the character," showing the "firmness and consistency" that so distinguished the man.

On the evening of February 9, Morse attended the president's levee, where he met Cooper for the first time. It had been a day of considerable excitement in Washington. In the recent presidential election, Andrew Jackson had won a popular majority, while John Quincy Adams had carried the electoral vote. That day, the House of Representatives had resolved the issue by electing Adams president.

"There was a great crowd [at the White House] and a great number of distinguished characters," Morse reported in a long letter to Lucretia.

> I paid my respects to Mr. Adams and congratulated him on his election. He seemed in some degree to shake off his habitual reserve. . . . General Jackson went up to him and, shaking him by the hand, congratulated him cordially on his election. The General bears defeat like a man. . . .

He was making good progress on the Lafayette portrait. "I have but little room in this letter to express my affection for my dearly beloved wife and children," he wrote at the bottom of the last page. "I long to hear from you. . . ."

She was never to read those words. Two days later, on February 11, in a letter from his father delivered to his hotel, Morse learned that Lucretia had died on February 7.

"My affectionately beloved son," the letter began. "The shock to the whole family is far beyond, in point of severity, that of any we have ever before felt. . . ." It had been a heart attack. She was twenty-five.

"My whole soul seemed wrapped up in her," Morse wrote a month later from New York. "I am ready almost to give up."

> To my friends here, I know, I seem to be cheerful and happy, but a cheerful countenance with me covers an aching heart, and often have I feigned a more than ordinary cheerfulness to hide a more than ordinary anguish.

He concentrated on work, of which he had more than ever, leaving the care of his children to his parents. Having completed the Lafayette portrait, he went on to paint one eminent figure after another, and of the kind with whom he liked most to associate, Americans known for their ideas and worthy accomplishments. They included William Cullen Bryant, poet, and editor of the *New York Evening Post;* Noah Webster, lexicographer and author of the *American Dictionary of the English Language;*

Governor DeWitt Clinton of New York, the great champion of the Erie Canal, which was completed that year, 1825; and Benjamin Silliman of Yale, who had been Morse's science professor and would later become the president of the college.

He took the lead in founding the National Academy of the Arts of Design in New York, as an alternative to the American Academy of Arts, then headed by John Trumbull, which Morse thought unnecessarily exclusive and stodgy. He became the first president of the National Academy and developed a series of lectures on art that he delivered at Columbia College, the first such talks ever given by an American artist.

At a gathering of the National Academy, while awarding prizes to young artists, he told them that if they expected a painter's life to be one of ease and pleasure, they were greatly mistaken. It was "a life of severe and perpetual toil." They must expect "continual obstacles and discouragements, and be prepared to encounter illiberality, neglect, obscurity, and poverty." Only an "intense and inextinguishable love of art" could sustain them to bear up, and if they did not feel this love, they should "turn while yet they might to other pursuits."

On June 9, 1826, the Reverend Jedidiah Morse died at New Haven, and, not long after, Samuel began explaining to his mother why he needed to go to Paris. In 1828 she, too, died. Thus, with his wife, father, and mother all taken from him, and feeling as he never had before that time was running out for him, Morse arranged for the children to stay with an aunt in New Hampshire and his brother Richard in New Haven. He lined up $2,800 in commissions to do copies in Europe, and sailed for France.

———

On the lovely, springlike March afternoon when Morse and Cooper were observed by Nathaniel Willis walking in the Garden of the Tuileries, the time appears to have been nearing five o'clock. Morse would have finished his day at the Louvre by then, and he and Cooper, as was their routine, would have been on their way to Cooper's house for the evening.

After they passed by, Willis remained in the garden, seated on a bench presumably, notebook in hand, savoring the scene a bit longer. The palace bell rang five o'clock.

The sun is just disappearing behind the dome of the Invalides, and the crowd begins to thin [he wrote]. Look at the atmosphere of the gardens. How deliciously the twilight softens everything. Statues, people, trees and the long perspectives down the alleys, all mellowed into the shadowy indistinctness of fairy-land. The throng is pressing out the gates . . . for the gardens are cleared at sundown.

It was a Friday, Willis said, but he gave no date. To judge by his description of the weather it must have been March 23.

III

Cholera morbus—Asiatic cholera or Indian cholera—had been a matter of some concern in European medical circles for more than fifty years, from the time outbreaks in Calcutta in the 1780s had taken the lives of many thousands. But the far-distant Indian origins of the scourge had made it seem an "exotic production," not the sort of thing that could strike a "civilized" European city.

In 1826 cholera had begun to spread toward Europe, following the old trade routes. By 1830 it reached Moscow, then Poland, then Vienna in the summer of 1831. At that point many in Paris had begun to worry.

The first word of cholera in Paris came on Wednesday, March 28, 1832, in reports in the afternoon and evening papers and in dispatches sent off to London and New York. Ten people had been taken to the old Hôtel Dieu, the main hospital on the Île-de-la-Cité, beside Notre-Dame. Seven of the ten had died. The autopsy of five bodies performed "in the presence of thirty-eight medical men and the Minister of Public Works" left no doubt.

The terror of the disease was that it struck with such ferocity. Its victims would be seized suddenly by savage cramps, followed by vomiting, convulsions, and violent diarrhea. Their faces turned purple and broke out in a cold sweat. The eyes bulged. Lips and fingernails turned blue. Nathaniel Willis, who managed to get inside the Hôtel Dieu by passing himself off as a doctor, described a young woman in her twenties convulsed with agony. "Her eyes were started from their sockets, her mouth foamed, and her face was of a frightful, livid purple. I never saw so horrible a sight."

The medical student James Jackson, Jr., had himself attended the death of another victim identified only as a *chiffonier,* a ragman. Drawing on his notes, he described for his father the autopsy that followed:

> Stomach contained a quart of reddish fluid. . . . Small intes-
> tines . . . contained a vast quantity of red fluid . . . the liquid
> flowing from these intestines had a somewhat sour smell to
> me like that of all undigested vegetable food which has been
> vomited. . . . Aorta contained a great quantity of black blood
> liquid. . . .

By April 2, there had been 735 reported cases and 100 deaths. "Vast numbers of people were leaving Paris," read a dispatch to the *New York Evening Post* that would not reach the United States for another month.

It was "a disease of the most frightful nature," wrote young Jackson, who, like almost every American physician, had had no experience with cholera. Walking one ward of the Hôtel Dieu, he had seen fifty or more patients in rows. "It is almost like walking through an autopsy room. In many nothing but the act of respiration shows the life still exists. It is truly awful." Jackson's fellow student Ashbel Smith wrote in his journal on April 3:

> The official bulletin of the morning gives 1,020 new cases from
> yesterday. . . . A young man came in the other day to inquire
> after his father and mother. They were found . . . side by side
> in the dead room, naked, and in a pile of bodies. The disease is
> rapidly spreading in every direction and the consternation is
> terrible. The Americans are almost all leaving the city.

Months before, when Jackson's father had told him that should the cholera reach Paris he must "fly," James had written to ask, "But if, as I think it highly possible, the disease is at some future time to prevail in our country, had I not better become acquainted with its physiognamy if I have an opportunity?" Jackson, who had never in his life gone against his father's wishes, wrote now to say he would stay, hoping his father would understand. Several other American medical students made the same decision, including Smith.

> We are bound as men and physicians to stay and see this disease [James continued]. As a physician you know it and feel it. As a father you dread it. For myself, I confess, I should be unwilling to return to America and not have at least made an effort to learn the nature and best treatment of this destroyer of life.

The common understanding was that miasmas—foul, noxious vapors from rotting garbage and human filth—were the carriers of the disease, just as malaria and yellow fever were supposedly spread. As sea air was beneficial to one's health, the bad air of city slums could be deadly. Thus cholera was understood to be a disease of the poor, while those living in the cleaner, more airy parts of the city were believed to be safe from the scourge.

In fact, no one knew the cause of cholera or what to do about it. "The physicians," Jackson conceded, "are in a state of the greatest incertitude, not knowing which way to turn."

The actual cause, which would not become known for years, was a microorganism, the *Vibrio cholerae*, carried mainly by contaminated water, and in some cases by infected food. It invaded the body by mouth and rapidly attacked the intestines, killing about half its victims by dehydration in a matter of days or even hours.

The death toll in Paris mounted. Wild rumors spread that the government was secretly poisoning the poor, and angry crowds streamed over the bridges to the Île-de-la-Cité to besiege the Hôtel Dieu, swearing revenge.

How could it be, many were asking, that something as hideous as a medieval plague could attack so great a center of civilized life and advanced learning?

When, on April 12, James Cooper judged the worst of the epidemic had passed, he could not have been more mistaken. The calamity surged on. Moreover, the agony and loss were spreading to every part of Paris, even Cooper's own supposedly safe Faubourg Saint-Germain. "We have had pestilence all around us, and we have had many deaths very near us," wrote Susan Cooper in alarm.

> I have seen two instances of it myself. One, the sister of our porter, who was taken with it while here on a visit, and the other, a poor woman who sold matches at the door of our hotel. Mr. Cooper had her brought into the courtyard and we took care of her, until she was carried to the hospital where I fear she died. . . .

While others fled the city in droves, the Coopers stayed, but only because they were too sick to move. He and Susan were both "in the doctor's hands," Cooper wrote, Susan confined to her bed with a severe "bilious attack," he suffering from the most excruciating headaches he had ever known.

Yet how were they to know whether they were better off remaining in Paris, where they had become in some measure acclimated, than expose themselves to the inconvenience of travel and the risk of going where "the horrors" might break out on their arrival? "It is spreading rapidly all over France," Susan wrote. "It has by no means spared the upper classes. . . ." Nearly all their countrymen had fled, she noted, except the heroic American medical students at the hospitals.

Morse, too, stayed. "Samuel was nervous even unto flight, nay so nervous he could not run," wrote Cooper, who speculated that a thousand people were already in their graves. Some estimates were ten times that. No one could say for certain.

"The churches are all hung in black," wrote Nathaniel Willis, reporting for his readers in New York. "There is a constant succession of funerals, and you cross the biers and hand-barrows of the sick, hurrying to the hospitals at every turn, in every quarter of the city."

A young French woman, Amandine-Aurore-Lucie Dupin, who had just published her first novel under the pen-name George Sand, lived directly across the Seine from the morgue on the Île-de-la-Cité and could see from her window the wagonloads of dead bodies being delivered. She and her friends had made a pact to meet at the Luxembourg Gardens every day at a certain time to be sure they were all still alive.

Strangely, though, much of life in Paris went on as usual. People strolled the parks and boulevards and dined at the cafés, as though they had not a worry. Willis attended a masquerade ball at the Théâtre des Variétés, where two thousand people carried on with their revels through the night, until seven in the morning. It was all unbearably macabre.

> There was a *cholera-waltz*, and a *cholera-galopade*, and one man, immensely tall, dressed as a personification of the cholera itself, with skeleton armor, bloodshot eyes, and other horrible appurtenances of a walking pestilence.

Week after week the weather remained incongruously delightful. Picture the most perfect day in June, but without the full heat of an American summer, wrote James Jackson, trying to fathom how this could be.

> I walk by the riverside and the waters are flowing mildly and calmly, undisturbed, while the glorious sun in its fullest splendor is glowing above and the sky is of the finest blue without a cloud and the air of the clearest and purest. All seems beauty.

Believing, like others, that the cholera was in decline, and exhausted from his efforts at the hospitals, Jackson decided after a month it was time he left for London. He had done all he could to help, he felt, and had seen more and learned more firsthand than he could ever have anticipated.

Meanwhile, at the Louvre, Samuel Morse toiled on. He was there each morning from the moment the great bronze doors opened. Friends knew always where to find him. There is no evidence that he missed a day, or that Cooper was not on hand to lend support. As would be said of Cooper's novels, his hero, his "model man," whether woodsman, sailor, or gentleman, was always "bent on bringing some especial thing to pass." Here now in the Louvre was his friend Morse, under pressures of a kind none could have foreseen, trying with all that was in him to bring some exceedingly special thing to pass.

Morse was terrified. In his youth he had taken the dying Hercules as a subject. Now, bending to this Herculean task, with death all about, he could only wonder if it was to mean his demise. Five weeks into the epidemic, on May 6, he wrote to his brothers, "My anxiety to finish my picture and return drives me, I fear, to too great application. . . ."

> All the usual securities of life seem to be gone. Apprehension and anxiety make the stoutest hearts quail. Any one feels, when he lays himself down at night, that he will in all probability be attacked before daybreak.

He had to be finished by August 10, the day the Louvre closed for the summer. By September, he prayed, he would be homeward bound.

———

Most days he could be found maneuvering his scaffold from one part of the museum to another, to work on copies of the different paintings in his composition. Possibly, in painting his copies, he made use of a camera obscura, a large dark box in which the image of an object may be projected through a small convex lens onto a facing surface. It was a device artists had employed for a long time, and the sort of thing Morse found fascinating.

The thirty-eight pictures in his painting-of-paintings included works by twenty-two masters. Five—Veronese, Poussin, Claude Lorrain, Rubens, and Guido Reni—were represented twice; two, Murillo and Van Dyck, three times. Titian appeared four times. The single work by Leonardo da Vinci was the *Mona Lisa*.

Each had to be so rendered as to catch the very character of the original. Each had to have the look of that particular painter. It was as if a single actor were required to play twenty-two different parts in a performance, and all so well that there could be no mistaking who was who.

That there be no question which paintings and painters he considered most important, Morse clustered several immediately beside and above the open door to the Grand Gallery, the focal point of his composition. He positioned Titian's portrait of Francis I, the king of France, at almost the exact center of the canvas, against the upper right-hand corner of the door, and painted it somewhat larger than it really was relative to the others. To Morse, Titian was a veritable god among painters, and Francis I was the French monarch who, in the sixteenth century, first began collecting paintings for the Louvre, including the *Mona Lisa*. Morse placed another Titian, *Supper at Emmaus*, directly over the door, and to the left he put Murillo's *Holy Family*.

By far the largest painting in the arrangement was the largest painting in the Louvre, the monumental work depicting Christ's first miracle, *The Marriage at Cana*, by the sixteenth-century Venetian Paolo Veronese. To have effectively created a foreshortened version of so complicated a painting was a tour de force in itself. Its position on the side wall at far left made it number one if the arrangement was "read" from left to right.

Significantly, a total of sixteen, or nearly half of the thirty-eight paintings chosen by the devout Morse, including the giant Veronese, were of religious subjects.

Some days, when copying a picture hung at the highest level—up at "the skyline," as artists said—he could be seen perched ten or twelve feet above the floor. There was, also, a certain irony to the fact that in this biggest undertaking of his career he had to spend the greatest part of his time painting small, not large, working with small brushes on his miniature renditions on the canvas.

So concerned was he about finishing in time, he decided to concentrate his efforts on the copies—work that could only be done at the Louvre—and paint the frames for each later, back in New York.

———

The bond of friendship between Cooper and Morse held fast through the long ordeal of the cholera epidemic. If anything, it grew stronger. Acutely sensitive to the extreme stress under which Morse worked, Cooper continued to praise and encourage him, even implying he might purchase the painting once it was completed. Or at least that was Morse's impression.

And as terrified for his own life as Morse may have been, he readily understood the weight of worry and responsibility for an entire family that Cooper had to bear.

But there was more. For some time Cooper had been subjected to criticism of a kind that cut deeply and that Morse thought unjust. The trouble had begun with the publication of a book of Cooper's titled *Notions of the Americans*, one of those he had written while in Paris. It was a novel in the form of a series of letters supposedly written by an Englishman traveling in America at the time of Lafayette's visit. Cooper had done it partly to please Lafayette, but mainly as a way to correct what he saw as egregious misconceptions about his country held by many in Britain and Europe. The book was not Cooper at his best. The writing was stiff, didactic, and so laudatory of his country and the "American Dream" that it raised outcries on both sides of the Atlantic at a time when real English authors were traveling the United States and offering a decidedly different view.

The most scathing and engaging of these had appeared that same calamitous spring of 1832 and became a huge success in England. *Domestic Manners of the Americans* was a rollicking satirical tour of the New World in which the author, Frances Trollope, had a grand time finding almost nothing to like about America and Americans. She made great sport of the way Americans ate, for example, describing the "total want of all the usual courtesies of the table, the voracious rapidity with which the viands were seized and devoured." She did not like Americans, she wrote in her concluding chapter. "I do not like their principles, I do not like their manners, I do not like their opinions." Her book, as well as the frequent anti-American snobbery to be found in publications like the *Edinburgh Review*, in addition to critical commentary of a like kind in print in his own country, riled Cooper as nothing ever had, and in defense he became still more boastful, even bombastic about being an American, and spoke more disparagingly of Europeans and their failings.

Nathaniel Willis had observed that Cooper's stern countenance ought not to be taken as representative of the man. So Morse felt Cooper and his opinions needed some explaining for those at home no less than in Europe. He knew the man, he knew the respect he commanded in Paris. "He has a bold, original, independent mind, thoroughly American," Morse wrote to his brothers in New York, who had established a religious newspaper, the *New York Observer.*

> He loves his country and her principles ardently. . . . I admire exceedingly his proud assertion of the rank of an American . . . for I know no reason why an American should not take rank, and assert it, too, above any artificial distinctions that Europe has made. We have no aristocratic grades . . . and crosses, and other gewgaws that please the great babies of Europe. . . .

Morse was exhausted and angry.

> There can be no *condescension* to an American. An American gentleman is equal to any title or rank in Europe, kings and emperors not excepted. . . .
>
> Cooper sees and feels the absurdity of these distinctions, and he asserts his American rank and maintains it too, I believe, from a pure patriotism. Such a man deserves the support and respect of his countrymen. . . .

Willis, who felt he had very much "arrived" by being included in Cooper's circle, said no American could live "without feeling every day what we owe to the patriotism as well as the genius of this gifted man." Reluctantly, Willis had decided the time had come for him to move on and continue his travels, to Italy next. "Paris is a home to me, and I leave it with a heavy heart," he wrote.

Morse kept working, the epidemic notwithstanding, and the crowds kept coming to see the American painter and his picture. Even Alexander von Humboldt, the world-famous naturalist and explorer, came to watch and to chat with Morse. In all Europe there was no more revered embodiment of the life of the mind.

He "took pains to find me out," Morse wrote, his spirits lifted.

———

By the start of summer, cholera had struck New York, and in Paris had abated somewhat. But by no means was the danger past, as some contended. Probably 12,000 people had already died in Paris. By summer's end at least 18,000 would be dead in six months' time, considerably more lives taken than during the entire Reign of Terror. According to surviving records, no Americans died in Paris of cholera. In New York the epidemic left 3,515 dead.

———

For several years now, it had become the custom among a number of Americans in Paris to celebrate the Fourth of July with a grand patriotic banquet, and to include General Lafayette as guest of honor. If, because of the cholera epidemic, there was any reluctance to hold the event that summer of 1832, or any thought of canceling it, no evidence is to be found. For Morse and Cooper, it was to be a particularly affecting occasion, their last Fourth of July in Paris and a last opportunity to honor Lafayette.

The dinner was held at Lointier on the rue de Richelieu, a favorite restaurant among Americans. Morse presided as President of the Day, with Cooper as Vice President. Eighty guests, including Lafayette and the American minister to France, William C. Rives, pulled up their chairs to the table and, before the evening was out, joined in toasts to George Washington and the new president of the United States, Andrew Jackson, King Louis-Philippe, and the City of Paris, some twenty toasts in all.

But Morse's toast to Lafayette brought the greatest response, with spirited applause following nearly every line. The imagery he chose for his windup, in tribute to the general's strength as a leader, suggests his own homeward voyage, and the ways of winds and storm-tossed seas, were also much on his mind. In any event, he brought the whole crowd cheering to its feet.

Some men were "like the buoys upon tide-water," Morse said. "They float up and down as the current sets this way or that."

> If you ask at an emergency where they are, we cannot tell you.
> We must first consult the almanac. We must know the quarter of the moon, the way of the wind, the time of the tide. . . .

But gentlemen, our guest . . . is a tower amid the waters. . . . He stands there now. The winds have swept by him, the waves dashed around him, the snows of winter have lighted upon him, but still he is there.

I ask you, therefore, gentlemen, to drink with me in honor of General Lafayette.

———

In the weeks remaining, before the Louvre closed for the summer, Morse pressed on. Concentrating on the immense canvas overall, he found himself well pleased, even to the point of bragging a bit to his brothers, calling it "a splendid and valuable" work. "I am sure it is the most *correct* one of *its kind* ever painted, for everyone says I have caught the style of each of the masters."

Whether he began work on the figures in the scene during these last days at the Louvre, or saved them for later, is not entirely clear, but most likely they were added in New York. Either way they were part of his plan and who they were—those he included and those he did not—was of no small importance.

In the completed painting which Morse titled *The Gallery of the Louvre*, there would be ten figures. And though he was to provide viewers a key to all the paintings in the scene, he would identify none of the people. Still, four were quite obvious to anyone who knew them.

Most conspicuous was Morse himself standing front and center, leaning over the right shoulder of an attractive young art student, giving her instructions. The subject she is sketching—and that Morse is helping her understand—is the colossal Veronese, *The Marriage at Cana*, on the left-hand wall. The identity of the student is not known. Nor is that of another young woman working on a miniature at a table to the right. The seated artist wearing a red turban on the left is believed to be Morse's American friend and roommate, Richard Habersham.

Upstage, by the doorway, a figure wearing the traditional peaked white cap of the women of Brittany, and the child she holds by the hand, are the only ones in the scene with their faces toward the glow and splendors of the Grand Gallery beyond. As an accent, her cap serves as an instructor's pointer calling attention to the painting above, *The Holy Family*, by Murillo. But she and the child serve, too, as reminders that the museum and its riches are there not for artists and connoisseurs only, but for people of all kinds and ages.

The well-dressed man entering the Salon Carré through the doorway, his high-crowned black hat in hand, has the appearance of Horatio Greenough, and fittingly, his eye is fixed on the single work of sculpture on display, *Diane Chasseresse—Diana of the Hunt*—at the far right.

But after the figure of Morse, it is the threesome in the left-hand corner who are of greatest interest, and they are, unmistakably, Cooper and his wife watching their daughter Sue at her easel working on a copy. Possibly, as later speculated, Morse included them because he expected Cooper to buy the painting. Morse himself never said. Most likely, he included the Coopers for the same reason he had added his father, the Reverend Morse, and his Yale professor Benjamin Silliman to the faces in the gallery in his *House of Representatives*, because it gave him great pleasure to do so.

With the presence of Cooper, his wife, and daughter, Greenough and young Habersham, the scene becomes something distinctly more than a tour de force showcase of Old World masterpieces. It may be taken as well as a kind of family portrait—Morse and his Paris family.

But seldom in family portraits does one member so upstage the others as Morse does here. By placing himself as he has, so conspicuously, so immodestly front and center and larger than anyone, he has rendered a self-portrait intended to present much that he wished to be known and remembered about himself, beyond the fact that the whole huge panorama is the result of his own efforts and ability. In the tableau with the student, most obviously, he is presenting himself not as an artist only, but as a teacher—a teacher in the spirit of Benjamin West and Washington Allston—and a founder and first president of the National Academy of Design. The Salon Carré becomes thereby a sumptuous, treasure-laden classroom for the master.

And if a man be known by the company he keeps, there in the corner is his friend Cooper, with his upraised finger pointing, like the white Brittany hat, to Murillo's *Holy Family*, as he, the cultivated gentleman, talks of what he sees and appreciates in a great work of art. Further, as a readily recognizable American somebody, Cooper provides a distinct note of national pride.

By rendering Sue Cooper as he did, with her head turned to listen to her father, Morse seems to suggest his interest in her may indeed have been romantic, and if not, here was visible reason why it could have been.

Of the ten figures in Morse's tableau, six, or more than half, are Americans—Americans in Paris making the most of their time. And six, counting the child, are females, which would appear Morse's way of encouraging women in their aspirations in art.

As may be said of nearly all paintings, nothing is included by chance. Every element is the result of conscious choice, and what an artist chooses to leave out is also of importance in understanding a finished work. That there is a complete absence in Morse's Salon Carré of French aristocrats, French soldiers and priests, could only have been intentional. Aristocrats, soldiers, priests, were ubiquitous, and as commonly present at the Louvre as they were in almost any public place or gathering in Paris.

Like Cooper, Morse had no use for the "mere butterflies" of Paris society, and no more liking for the sight of soldiers everywhere than would Charles Sumner. Such disdain for almost anything connected with the Catholic Church, for priests, and the dictates of the Vatican that had permeated Morse's Calvinist upbringing, had only hardened as a consequence of his experiences in Europe. In Rome he had written in his notebooks of priests "dissipating their time in gambling" and "disfiguring the landscape with their uncouth dress," of the "numberless bowings and genuflections and puffings of incense" at the Catholic services he attended. He had been willing to remove his hat when entering a Catholic church, but not in the street when religious processions passed. "If it were a mere civility I should not object," he wrote, "but it involves acquiescence in what I see to be idolatry and of course in the street I cannot do it. . . . No man has a right to interfere with my rights of conscience."

Once, on a street in Rome, when a religious procession passed and

Morse failed to remove his hat, a soldier, one of the cardinal's guards, had knocked it off with his gun, cursing him as *il diavolo*. Thinking about it later, Morse decided he could not blame the soldier, only a religion that would resort to such force.

In addition to aristocrats, soldiers, and priests, he chose not to include any representation of upper-middle-class Paris, the numerous bourgeois, or the many European tourists who comprised such a substantial part of the regular flow of visitors. As he had included only his pick of the more than a thousand paintings in the museum's collection, so, too, the clientele was limited to his personal preferences.

Nor did he provide the least sign or hint of the deadly scourge then raging outside the museum or the inner torment of the figure at center stage. Instead there is a feeling of great security and well-being. Far from cold or threatening, the painting glows with warmth, in the Salon's deep red walls, and promise, in the gleam of sunshine from the skylights down the vaulted Gallery.

Cooper had been on hand through the whole effort, keeping Morse company. "He is with me two or three hours at the gallery (the hours of his relaxation) every day as regularly as the day comes," Morse reported to his brothers in mid-July when more than 200 people a day were dying of cholera.

Shortly afterward Cooper and family departed for an extended sojourn in Germany and Switzerland, relieved to put Paris behind them at last. Ever the faithful correspondent, Cooper would write frequently to Morse, to describe the sights he and the family were seeing and the improvement in Susan Cooper's health. He hoped Morse would not leave Paris until the following spring, so they could all sail home together.

But Morse had made up his mind. By the time the Coopers returned to Paris in mid-October, Morse was gone. His work at the Louvre at an end, his affairs settled, and having paid an emotional farewell to Lafayette, he sailed from Le Havre on the American packet *Sully* on October 6. *The Gallery of the Louvre* was stowed securely belowdecks.

IV

But Morse was taking something of more importance home with him—
an idea inspired by a system used outside of Paris to send overland messages, a semaphore apparatus that used mechanically operated arms or
flaps from atop tall towers spaced six miles apart. Messages were read by
telescope. This served well enough in clear weather, but not in fog, rain,
or at night. For this French system the word "telegraph" had first come
into use.

Morse would later say his first mention of the possibility of an electric telegraph took place during the voyage home on the *Sully*. He would
recall "the manner, the place, and the moment when the thought of making an electric wire the means of communicating intelligence first came
into my mind and was uttered." But according to Cooper and his family,
Morse had talked frequently of the idea during their evenings together
through the spring of 1832, months before Morse ever left Paris. "I confess
I thought the notion evidently chimerical, and as such spoke of it in my
family," Cooper would later tell Morse. "I always set you down as a sober-
minded, common-sense sort of a fellow, and thought it a high flight for a
painter to make to go off on the wings of the lightning."

Richard Habersham, too, would remember passing the evening in the
rooms they shared listening to Morse go on about the French telegraph
being too slow, and that on the invitation of a French authority Morse had
gone to examine the French system at close hand.

> I recollect also [Habersham wrote] that in our frequent vis-
> its to Mr. J. Fenimore Cooper's in the rue Saint-Dominique,
> these subjects, so interesting to Americans, were often intro-
> duced, and that Morse seemed to harp on them. . . .

But whenever Morse began talking about an electric telegraph—and
the question would later become a matter of importance—there was no
doubt the germ of the idea had taken hold of him in France. Assuredly,

neither Habersham nor Cooper and his family would have said so had it not been true.

———

By the summer of 1833 in New York, Morse had completed the final touches on *The Gallery of the Louvre*. On August 9, he wrote to Cooper, "My picture, *c'est fini*." It went on public view in the second-floor gallery of the well-known bookstore Carvill & Company, at Broadway and Pine Street. The charge for admission was 25 cents.

The reviews were respectful, complimentary, even enthusiastic. "Every artist and connoisseur was charmed with it," wrote the critic William Dunlap. "Here shine in one grand constellation, the brilliant effusions of those great names destined to live as long as the art of painting exists," declared the *New-York Mirror*.

> We do not know which most to admire, in contemplating this magnificent design, the courage which could undertake such a Herculean task, or the perseverance and success with which it has been completed.
>
> We have never seen anything of the kind before in this country. Its effect on us is different from that made by any other painting. . . .
>
> We may truly congratulate the country that such a collection is in its possession. We can say with a friend of ours, a distinguished artist who has never been in Europe, that we never had an idea of the old masters until we saw Morse's picture of the Louvre.

The public, however, showed little interest. As a commercial venture, the painting was no more a success than Morse's *House of Representatives* had been.

Eventually it was bought by a man named George Hyde Clarke, who lived near Cooper's old home on Otsego Lake and whose portrait Morse had painted before leaving for France. The purchase price was $1,300. Morse had hoped to get $2,500.

That *The Gallery of the Louvre* would one day, in 1982, be purchased for a museum in Chicago for $3,250,000, the highest sum ever paid until then for a work by an American artist, would in Morse's time have been unimaginable.

Cooper and his family left Paris in the spring of 1833. They had been away from home longer than intended—for the younger children more than half a lifetime. But none ever regretted the time in Paris. Cooper had written eight novels since leaving home, and privately he talked now of calling a halt to his writing. But there would be much more to come, including *Gleanings in Europe*, devoted to his experiences and observations in France, and two more immensely popular Natty Bumppo tales, *The Pathfinder* and *The Deerslayer*, the latter of which many considered his masterpiece.

It had been seven years since Cooper and the family set sail for France from New York and the man on a passing ship had called out ominously, "You will never come back." Now he was on his way back, and he wanted to go. Unlike Morse, he was never to see Paris again.

CHAPTER FOUR

THE MEDICALS

It is no trifle to be a medical student in Paris.

—OLIVER WENDELL HOLMES

I

Like all great cities, Paris was a composite of many worlds within, each going about its particular, preoccupying ways quite independent, or seemingly independent, of the others. As notable as any of these worlds, and of far-reaching importance, was Paris Médicale, the Paris of numerous hospitals and illustrious physicians, of medical technicians, nurses, interns, and patients numbering in the many thousands; a celebrated medical school, the École de Médecine, and several thousand students from every part of France and much of the world.

This, too, was Paris—*their* Paris for those caught up in it— unmistakably different from fashionable Paris, or political Paris, intellectual Paris, financial Paris, or the visitor's Paris, not to say the Paris pictured in the minds of so many who had never been there, or the Paris of the desperately poor.

The population of medical Paris equaled that of a small city, and included every variety of humankind, virtually every known ailment and affliction, much suffering—suffering sometimes relieved, often not—and a constant presence of death. Much about the standard procedures in the hospitals and surgical amphitheaters was, to the uninitiated, revolting, and among some of the celebrated performers of such procedures, professional rivalries and jealousies flourished as much as within any opera company.

It was not a closed world. Visitors were welcome to nearly all of it, and more often than not what they saw, the dedication and kindness of the nurses, the orderliness and scale of the care given, seemed everything that could be desired. As a place to learn, it had no equal, and with all its components it was as proud an achievement as any Paris could claim.

Largest of the hospitals was the Hôtel Dieu, an immense five-story pile of a building that stood by Notre-Dame on the Île-de-la-Cité—on the square, or *parvis*, of Notre-Dame (to the right as one faced the cathedral), its back to the Seine. Founded in 1602, it was the oldest hospital in Paris and possibly in all Europe. Its only claim to architectural distinction was an entrance foyer with Doric columns approached by a broad three-sided stone stairway. An annex nearly as large as the main building stood directly behind, on the other side of the river, the two buildings connected by a covered bridge.

This one hospital, with 1,400 beds, served more than 15,000 patients a year, and as in all Paris hospitals, patients were treated free of charge.

Second in size of the general hospitals and more beautifully situated was the Hôpital de la Pitié, which faced the Jardin des Plantes, a short distance away on the other side of the Seine. It had 800 beds, and while the Hôtel Dieu was considered preeminent in surgery, La Pitié was known for its clinical medicine and particularly for the treatment of diseases of the chest such as tuberculosis.

The Hôpital de la Charité, also on the Left Bank, was half-again smaller and timeworn in appearance, but much on a par with the other two and distinguished by several acclaimed physicians especially popular among the medical students. La Charité stood on the narrow rue Jacob, almost directly across the street from one of the most important historic sites in American history, the Hôtel d'York, where in 1783, Benjamin Franklin, John Adams, and John Jay had signed the Treaty of Paris that officially ended the Revolutionary War. But few of the American medical students seemed aware of this.

The Hôpital des Enfants Malades, on the rue de Sèvres, was the first children's hospital in the world. The immense Hôpital de la Salpêtrière, founded originally for beggars in the seventeenth century and built on what had been a site for making saltpeter, was an asylum for indigent and deranged women. For indigent and deranged men, there was the larger Hôpital de Bicêtre on a hill well to the south. The Hôpital Saint-Louis, in the northeastern part of Paris, had been built by King Henry IV to combat the plague. A handsome complex of brick and stone pavilions with the look of a château, it served now as a hospital for diseases of the skin, the first of its kind anywhere.

In the single year of 1833, the year following the cholera epidemic, a total of twelve Paris hospitals provided treatment for 65,935 patients. In Boston, by comparison, the Massachusetts General Hospital and the McLean Hospital together cared for fewer than 800 patients.

The Hôtel Dieu, La Pitié, and La Charité, all within walking distance of each other, in combination with the nearby École de Médecine, formed the heart of medical Paris. Here, at these three hospitals primarily, as well as the medical school, the great luminaries of French medicine, many of international reputation, held forth in the lecture halls and allowed students to accompany them as they made their rounds of the patients in the wards.

Auguste-François Chomel was a leading clinical physician whose bedside comments during his morning rounds at the Hôtel Dieu attracted a large following. Guillaume Dupuytren held the supreme position of chief surgeon at the Hôtel Dieu. Alfred-Armand-Louise-Marie Velpeau, who lectured at La Charité and the École de Médecine, wrote the treatise on surgery used by most students and was considered a surpassing example of a man who by merit and hard work had risen from obscure beginnings to the forefront of his profession. Velpeau, as everyone knew, was the son of a blacksmith.

Philippe Ricord was a noted specialist in syphilis and one of the few medical professors who spoke English. Gabriel Andral lectured at the École on internal pathology and, in the view of many students, was the most eloquent professor of them all. Pierre-Charles-Alexandre Louis, though neither eloquent nor especially popular, was to have the greatest influence on the American students. Louis stood foremost in insisting on evidence—facts—as essential to diagnosis and was greatly admired as the best man in Paris with a stethoscope.

Compared to the hospitals, the magnificent École de Médecine on the rue de l'École de Médecine was brand-new. Its cornerstone had been laid in 1776, less than sixty years earlier. It was neoclassical in the grand manner, and enormous. Its central amphitheater for lectures seated nearly a thousand. There were exhibits, a library, everything open to all.

A public institution, the École was a showpiece of French education. In the time since the Revolution of 1789, opportunities for a medical education had been made available to a degree unimaginable earlier, the profession of medicine opened to all qualified young men irrespective of wealth or background. The social position of one's family no longer mattered, as the surgeon Velpeau's career testified.

In the spirit of opening wide the door, French, not Latin, had been made the language of instruction. A college education, or equivalent, was required for admission, as was not the case at American medical schools, but foreign students at the École did not have to meet this requirement. Further, for foreign students, including Americans, there was no tuition. For them, as at the Sorbonne, the lectures were free.

Nothing in the United States remotely compared to the École de Médecine. Medical education in America at the time was barely under way. There were still, in the 1830s, only twenty-one medical schools in the United States, or on average not even one per state, and these were small, with faculties of only five or six professors. Most aspiring physicians in America never attended medical school but learned by apprenticing themselves to "respectable" practitioners, most of whom had been poorly trained. In his novel *The Pioneers*, Cooper described the medical apprenticeship of a character named Elnathan Todd, said to have been based on a real-life doctor in Cooperstown. Though the setting of the story was earlier in the nineteenth century, and the portrayal a bit exaggerated, the education for "doctoring" had improved little in many parts of the country.

> [At about age eighteen] the lad was removed to the house of
> the village doctor, a gentleman whose early career had not

been unlike that of our hero, where he was often seen, sometimes watering the horse, at others watering medicines. . . .
This kind of life continued for a twelvemonth, when he suddenly appeared at meeting in a long coat . . . and a few months
later was called for the first time in his life, Doctor Todd. . . .

At the École de Médecine, a faculty of twenty-six delivered lectures on
Anatomy, Physiology, Physics, Medical Hygiene, Medical Natural History,
Accouchements (birth), Surgical Pathology, Pharmacology and Organic
Chemistry, Medical Pathology, Therapeutics, Pathological Anatomy, Op-
erative Surgery, Clinical Surgery, Clinical Medicine, Clinical Midwifery,
Diseases of Women and Children, and Legal Medicine.

Enrollment was as high as 5,000 students, or approximately twice the
number of students then in all medical schools in the United States. The
American students at the École in the 1830s and '40s were but a tiny part
of enrollment, numbering only 30 to 50 annually.

For those American students newly arrived in Paris, the prospect of
entering such a world was exciting and unnerving, quite apart from the
considerable problem of language. Some hesitated, putting it off as long as
possible, knowing, as one wrote, it would be a *"new* world from the circle
of which it will be difficult to escape when once I am in it."

———

But then once "in it," most of them wanted only to stay longer than they
originally intended. During his first days, Ashbel Smith had stressed in
letters home that his "attachment" to America could never be diminished,
and that he had every intention of returning soon to North Carolina.
Within a month, he was confiding to a cousin, "I dislike to fix the time of
my departure. I shall protract it as long as possible."

James Jackson, Jr., who had left Paris for the British Isles after serving
in the cholera wards, was, when he returned in the fall of 1832, jubilant to
be back. Nothing he had seen in the hospitals of London, Dublin, and Edinburgh had caused him to reconsider his high opinion of medical Paris.
The grandeur of the École, he felt, was the grandeur of great minds. A lecture he attended, soon after his return, was the most thrilling he had ever

heard. "The glory of the week has been Andral's introductory lecture on diseases of the brain," he wrote to his father. "What powers of mind and vastness of comprehension has this man!"

Jackson's Boston friend Mason Warren, one of the new arrivals, would describe himself later as having been "a perfect ignoramus" in the life of the world into which he was entering, and feeling "quite overwhelmed." With Jackson and another Bostonian, Henry Bowditch, Warren had found a place to live on the narrow, upward-sloping rue Monsieur-le-Prince. Shortly after, Wendell Holmes moved in on the same street near the top of the rise. Holmes described his room on the uppermost floor of a five-story house as having three windows and a view, a tile floor, and a "very nice" green carpet. The furniture included a bed, a marble-topped bureau, a mahogany table, two mirrors, two armchairs, and an ink stand, all of which cost him 40 francs a month, or about $8, which was average. A "little extra" went to the porter who woke him in the morning, made the bed, washed his clothes, and polished his boots. With the apartment only a few blocks from the École and his route on the rue Monsieur-le-Prince all downhill, Holmes found he could make it to his first lecture in under four minutes door-to-door.

At the request of his physician father back in Boston, Mason Warren described what constituted a typical day, once he was seriously embarked.

> I commonly rise a little after six. The servant comes in every morning to wake me and light my candle. From 6 until 8 I attend Chomel at Hôtel Dieu, a man at present very celebrated for his knowledge of diseases of the lungs. At 8 Dupuytren commences his visit which lasts an hour, that is till 9, and he afterwards lectures and has his consultations and operations, which occupies the time until 11. I then breakfast. . . .

Breakfast over, he attended a lecture on surgery, followed by another on surgical pathology until four o'clock. Dinner was at five, evenings occupied with "reading, etc.," and lessons in French from a private tutor.

Warren was an openly affable young man whose company everyone welcomed. It was said conversation never languished in his presence. He was always agreeable, remembered Henry Bowditch. "No one ever heard aught against him." Unlike Bowditch and most of the other Americans, Warren had come to Paris to concentrate on surgery, which, given his family background, was what everyone expected. As Holmes would write, he "never for a moment lost sight of his great objective—to qualify himself for that conspicuous place as a surgeon which was marked for him by the name he bore. . . ." That Warren had attended Harvard only three months before proceeding with his professional training, first at home under his eminent father, then at the Harvard Medical School, also distinguished him from others of "the medicals," as they were called.

Students at the École de Médecine chose "lines of study" in either general medicine or surgery, and while they all attended lectures in both as part of their training, and made the rounds of the hospitals with both physicians and surgeons, those training in surgery followed a different curriculum. Thus Warren's schedule had little resemblance to that of his friends Jackson, Bowditch, and Holmes, none of whom aspired to be surgeons. Indeed, he rarely saw them, other than for an occasional meal, even though they all lived next door to one another.

Warren was a slender, blue-eyed twenty-one-year-old. In a pencil drawing done by a fellow student named Robert Hooper, he is distinguished by a full head of hair, a thin cigar clenched in his teeth at a jaunty angle, and just a suggestion of the fancy attire for which he was known. Dressing to the nines was his nature, something inherited from his father. As a friend of the family would write, "He was, in truth, one who must have everything handsome about him, and . . . [he] was not slow to avail himself of the opportunities which Paris afforded for the adornment of his person. . . ." He liked especially bulky coats that made him look less slender, more manly, and whatever the season, his coats and trousers were "irreproachable," his shirts, "exquisite," each of his several waistcoats, "a separate triumph of varied color and design." The considerable running cost of such a wardrobe seems not to have distressed his father in the least.

Poor health, mainly digestive problems, had troubled Warren much of his life—it had been the reason for his leaving Harvard after only three months as an undergraduate—but since arriving in Paris, except for some troubles with his teeth, he had never felt better. Perhaps a regimen that allowed for only two meals a day had something to do with it. (His father had urged him to eat sparingly.) Or possibly, such miseries as he saw daily in the hospitals made any complaints of his own seem scarcely worth mentioning. Or it could have been that the combined excitement of his studies and just being in Paris on his own, far from his father, gave him a therapeutic lift.

As a student, Warren was not on a level with James Jackson—but then no one was—and he was slower than others taking hold of French. He could make himself understood well enough "in regard to the necessities of life," as he said, but in conversation felt "entirely lost." Still, he was uncommonly self-disciplined.

As the son and grandson of famous surgeons, Warren had long known how much was expected of him. Like James Jackson, he was obliged to report regularly to his father. It was not just that John Collins Warren cared greatly about the well-being and professional progress of his distant son, but that he insisted on being kept continuously apprised of all that was new and innovative in surgical practice abroad. "Observe operations. Get as near as possible," insisted his father, who had himself studied in Paris thirty years earlier. "Send me without delay every new book containing anything important. . . ." These were directions not to be taken lightly.

Like James Jackson, Warren provided his father with a detailed, running chronicle on how he was making use of his time, the procedures he was observing, his professors and what he thought of them, the books and professional journals he was reading. His letters, written in a strong, generally clear hand, customarily ran five to eight pages. In this way, as time passed, he would contribute the fullest, most descriptive of the many accounts by Americans of student life in the medical world of Paris.

II

Inside the ancient Hôtel Dieu, the long wards were each like the great hall of a castle, with rows of beds down both sides numbering nearly a hundred—a striking scene for anyone seeing it for the first time. The waxed oak floors were polished to a high gloss. All was quite orderly. Each of the beds was enclosed with its own white curtains, and high on the walls above each bed, a good-sized window provided ample light and ventilation. Even with as many as 1,200 patients in the hospital, it did not feel crowded.

Scores of Sœurs de la Charité, nuns of the order of Saint-Augustin wearing large white caps, went briskly about their tasks as nurses. Accounts by the Americans frequently express appreciation for "those excellent women," their skill and kindness. Seeing one he knew while walking with another student, James Jackson exclaimed, "There is a face I dearly love to look upon." Through the time of the cholera he had been witness to her unfailing devotion to the sick and the dying.

For students, the great advantage of study in a hospital of such size was in the number of sick and wounded of all descriptions, and thus in the number of different diseases and ailments to be observed firsthand. They might attend a physician's examination of half a dozen or more cases of tuberculosis, say, not just one or two, or any of a dozen other maladies as well. Over a period of a few months, a student might take part in the examination of as many as fifty cases of tuberculosis. In the United States, in all but a few medical schools, no experience of any kind in hospitals was required of students.

The first rounds of the wards began at six in the morning, before dawn. They were conducted by candlelight, and when led by one of the more eminent physicians, attended by as many as two-or-three hundred students, which for most made it nearly impossible to get near enough to the beds to see much. To the Americans the French students seemed inordinately eager to get as close as possible, and competition for a vantage point could be fierce. James Jackson described how on more than one occasion he had worked himself up to the bedside, determined to take part in the examination, only to find that when he went to put his ear to the patient's back, "a French head would slip between mine and that same back." And this, Jackson hastened to add, would be accomplished always with an ever-ready "*Pardon, Monsieur!*"

Wendell Holmes would remember students piling up on the back of the chief surgeon, Baron Guillaume Dupuytren, in an effort to see as he bent over a patient, to the point where he would "shake them off from his broad shoulders like so many rats and mice." (With his remarkable facility with language, Holmes had from the start little or no trouble understanding what was said in the lectures, and within a year was taking notes in French.)

Dupuytren, one of the medical giants of France, let no one doubt he was the reigning presence in the Hôtel Dieu. He was handsome, squarely built, and intimidating. A former battlefield surgeon, he had been made a baron by Napoleon. Clad in his long white apron, he marched heavily through the wards like "a lesser kind of deity," it seemed to the diminutive Holmes. He had the flushed face of a bon vivant and reputedly spent most nights at one of the better gambling houses at the Palais Royal. The state of his mood at the start of each morning, his students alleged, was the sign of whether he had won or lost the night before. Many mornings his temper was vile.

But to see Dupuytren at work with scalpel in hand was to witness a great performance. He talked the whole time he worked and loved to "make a show." To the French, it seemed, everything was theater—*un spectacle*—even surgery.

Mason Warren watched as Dupuytren, working by candlelight, removed cataracts from the eyes of several patients, and from another, a tumor of the tongue the size of a peach. He saw Dupuytren extract bladder stones from the bladder of a child, and perform the operation for an artificial anus for which he was also famous. "His operations are always brilliant and his diagnosis sometimes most wonderful," Warren wrote. "He is always endeavoring to convince us that he is a great man. . . ."

Warren attended as well the lectures and operations of surgeons Philibert-Joseph Roux at the Hôtel Dieu and Jacques Lisfranc at La Charité, both known for their skill at amputation. He thought Lisfranc's removal of toes and fingers "very neat and rapid." He saw Lisfranc remove a cancerous penis "with one stroke of a large amputating knife." Another day, he observed Roux amputate an arm from one patient, then a leg from another.

Surgeons were known for their steady, quick, dexterous hands. Theirs were the hands of an artist, it was said. To watch them was not simply a matter of seeing how it was done, but beholding an artist at work, and the work, one was told, must be done in the words of the ancient motto, *cito*, *tuto*, and *jucunde*—quickly, surely, and agreeably.

That the eminent Dupuytren and the other surgeons used no anesthetics or bothered ever to wash their hands before proceeding, or sterilized their instruments, was not recorded or remarked upon by Mason Warren and others for the reason that no one as yet knew anything about such precautions.

Nor did Warren write of the screams of the patients.

The attitude of several of the French surgeons toward their patients did, however, trouble Warren and others considerably. The show of professional sangfroid seemed overdone. Lisfranc's operations were performed in a "kind of off-hand way," it seemed to Warren, "depending entirely on the state of the disease for the extent to which he carries them. I have seen him work away on a cancer of the eye, chiseling the bones of the head, till I expected every instant to see part of the brain make its appearance."

Lisfranc was a phlebotomist, a great believer in drawing blood. On one occasion Wendell Holmes saw him order that ten or fifteen patients be bled. (The Hôtel Dieu maintained a ready supply of leeches for the purpose and a full-time keeper-of-leeches was part of the staff.) To Holmes, Lisfranc was little more than "a great drawer of blood and hewer of members."

Too often it seemed the surgeon's primary motivation was the desire to operate, with little or no consideration for the patient. Philibert Roux had insisted in carving open an old man for a tumor of the shoulder, and the patient died only an hour later. "Without it he would probably have lived five or six years longer," Warren wrote. How much of the surgery practiced, he wondered, was intended more "to perform an operation beautifully and quickly" than to save a life?

By Warren's estimate more than two-thirds of those upon whom amputations were performed died afterward. In fact, most patients who survived surgery of any kind at the hands of the most skilled surgeons later died and nearly always of infection. The work of the French chemist Louis Pasteur on the role of bacteria in the spread of disease and that of the English physician Joseph Lister in antiseptic surgery were still in the future.

Even the best of the surgeons seemed to have no feelings for the patient. They could be rough and ill-tempered. For outright physical brutality to a patient, "the great Guillaume Dupuytren" had no equal.

> If his orders are not immediately obeyed, he thinks nothing
> of striking his patient or abusing him most harshly [Warren
> wrote]. A very favorite practice of his during his consultation
> is to make a handle of the noses of his patients. Whenever a
> man enters with any disease of the head, he is immediately
> seized by the nose and pulled down onto his knees where
> he remains half in sorrow and half in anger at the treatment
> until he is allowed to rise and describe his disease.

The open, often vociferous enmity between some of the surgical prima donnas also came as a surprise to the Americans, and those like Jackson and Warren, who had been raised in the medical profession, found this disgraceful. It was said the tongues of the faculty were more cutting than their scalpels. Lisfranc in particular could hardly deliver a lecture without attacking the reputations of Dupuytren, Roux, or Velpeau.

At six feet, Lisfranc was taller than most men and had a voice like thunder. He wore a rusty black-and-red cap and baggy trousers that flapped in the wind as he rounded the front gate into La Charité. "In his lectures he speaks with that loud style and gesture used by our stump orators," Warren reported to his father. When angry, he would let fly with "a tremendous volley" of foul language. "When any other man's ideas come into collision with his own, he gives him no quarter, but lavishes upon his opponent every epithet of abuse that the language affords. . . ." His most savage invective he saved for Dupuytren, his former teacher and idol, whom he customarily referred to as *"le brigand,"* the highway robber, or worse.

Crude and unpleasant as all this could be, no student had cause to complain of dull lectures or that any of the faculty were below standards. The great Dupuytren was indisputably the greatest French surgeon of the time. His lectures were spellbinding. It was he who named the contraction of the palmar fascia of the hand, which is still known as "Dupuytren's contracture." Alfred Velpeau was to become increasingly popular with the American students, not just because of his celebrated rise from humble beginnings, but because he took an interest in them. In later years, Holmes, recalling Velpeau's origins and ability, said "a good sound head over a pair of wooden shoes is a good deal better than a wooden head belonging to an owner who cases his feet in calf-skin."

In addition to the quality of the hospitals, the number of patients, the ability and eminence of the faculty, and the variety of instruction provided, medical training in Paris offered two further important advantages over medical training in the United States. Both had almost entirely to do with the difference in how people saw things in the two countries.

The first was that students making the rounds of the wards in the hospitals of Paris had ample opportunity to examine female patients as well as men. This was not the case in America, where most women would have preferred to die than have a physician—a man—examine their bodies. It was a "delicacy" nearly impossible to surmount, and as a consequence a great many American women did die, and young men in medical training in America seldom had any chance to study the female anatomy, other than in books.

In France this was not so. "The French woman, on the contrary, knows nothing at all of this queasy sensibility. She has no hesitation, not only to describe, but to permit her physician to see every complaint," wrote a Philadelphia surgeon named Augustus Gardner, who came to observe medical practice and training in Paris. "In this respect therefore the Paris educated physician enjoys superior advantages to the homebred man."

The second great difference was in the supply of cadavers for dissection. In the United States, because of state laws and public attitude, dead bodies for medical study were hard to obtain and consequently expensive. Until 1831, trade in dead bodies in Massachusetts had been illegal, which led numbers of medical students of earlier years, including Mason Warren's father, to become grave robbers. The new Massachusetts law permitted only the use of corpses buried at public expense, which meant mainly the bodies of those who died in prison. New York, too, had such a law and other states—Connecticut, Maine, New Hampshire, Illinois, Tennessee—would follow. In the South it was the general attitude that, with the consent of the slave owner, the body of any slave could be dissected.

In Paris there was not the least prejudice against dissections. Even mortally ill patients in the hospitals, "aware of their fate," and knowing that two-thirds of the dead were carried off to the dissecting rooms, did not seem to mind. Beyond the hospitals, due in large part to the ravages of disease and poverty, cadavers were readily available and cheap—about 6 francs for an adult, or $2.50, and still less for a child.

John Sanderson, after taking a room in the Latin Quarter, where he was "living a kind of student's life" near the hospitals, described seeing carts "arrive and dump a dozen or so of naked men and women, as you do a cord of wood upon the pavement," these to be distributed to the dissecting rooms.

Delivery time for corpses at the Amphithéâtre d'Anatomie, on the rue d'Orléans near the Hôpital de la Pitié, was at noon. Wendell Holmes wrote of how he and a Swiss student split the cost of their "subject" and by evening had "cut him into inch pieces." Thus could all parts of the human body—nerves, muscles, organs, blood vessels, and bones—be studied, and this, Holmes stressed, could hardly be done anywhere in the world but in Paris.

The size of the stone-floored amphitheater was such that 600 students could practice operations at the same time. The stench in the thick air was horrific. The visiting Philadelphia surgeon Augustus Gardner left a vivid description of the scene.

> Here the assiduous student may be seen with his soiled blouse and his head bedecked with a fantastic cap. In one hand he holds a scalpel, in the other a treatise on anatomy. He carries in his mouth a cigar whose intoxicating fumes, so hurtful on most occasions, render him insensible to the smell of twenty bodies decomposing, putrefying around him. . . . Here, too, is the learned professor, who thus prepares himself for a difficult operation by refreshing his anatomy; and thus rehearses his part in the tragedy to be acted on the morrow. The blood and

pieces of flesh upon the floor he regards as the sculptor does
the fragments of marble lying round the unfinished statue.

Disposal of the discarded pieces was managed by feeding them to dogs
kept in cages outside. In summer, dissecting was suspended, because in
the heat the bodies decomposed too rapidly.

For all that was so morbidly unpleasant about work at the dissecting tables—the stench, the smoke—it was far better, every student came
to appreciate, that they practice on the dead than on the living. If the
work was laborious, they had chosen a laborious profession. For any of
the Americans to have given up and gone home would have been easy
enough, but there is no evidence any of them did.

The "medicals" found *their* Paris quite as inspirational as would the
Americans who came to write or paint or study or imbibe in ideas in other
fields. In Paris they felt the exhilaration of being at the center of things, as
Wendell Holmes tried to convey to his father:

> I never was so busy in my life. The hall where we hear our lec-
> tures contains nearly a thousand students and it is every day
> filled to overflowing. . . . The whole walls around the École de
> Médecine are covered with notices of lectures. . . . The les-
> sons are ringing aloud through all the great hospitals. The
> students from all lands are gathered. . . .

"Not a day passes," declared James Jackson, "that I do not gain something new in itself or something old with renewed force."

Of great importance, in addition to the hospitals and the lectures,
was the library at the École with its 30,000 volumes. (By comparison,
the library at the College of Physicians and Surgeons of New York City
had all of 1,200 volumes. The library at the Harvard Medical School had
fewer still.) There were, besides, the world-renowned exhibits and lectures
nearby at the Musée d'Histoire Naturelle at the Jardin des Plantes. One
enthusiastic medical student, Levin Joyce from Virginia, likened the museum at the Jardin to a great buffet banquet of knowledge. "What a feast
is here presented . . . !"

"By the blessing of God you shall never have reason to repent that you have sent me here," a grateful Henry Bowditch wrote to his parents. Like Warren, Holmes, and numbers of other medical students, Bowditch was making a point to attend lectures at the Sorbonne as well.

Bowditch had embarked on a medical career far from sure it was right for him. He entered Harvard Medical School with feelings of doubt mixed with repugnance at the thought of some of the elementary work necessary. The change had begun when an instructor in anatomy at Harvard showed him, during a dissection, the arrangement of muscles in a forearm.

Bowditch was another of those with an illustrious father. He was the son of Nathaniel Bowditch, the self-taught astronomer and mathematician who in 1802, after sailing much of the world, had published *The New American Practical Navigator*, which made his name known everywhere. A well-mannered, intelligent-looking young man with an active sense of humor, he worked hard and caught on quickly. Any squeamishness he may have felt about exercises in dissection had long since disappeared. Finding at the end of a day at the dissecting table that there was more he wished to examine, he put a lung under his hat and walked out, past the guard at the door, all going well as he proceeded through the streets until he felt blood trickling down his face.

James Jackson's friendship was a godsend to Bowditch. Jackson was the trailblazer, the guiding spirit, the one, they were all certain, destined to make a great mark in time to come. Jackson "devotes himself heart and soul to his profession," he wrote. "I love him much."

Jackson made sure Bowditch was headed in the right direction, stressing especially that he attach himself to Pierre Louis. Great as was Jackson's admiration for the eloquent Gabriel Andral, he had come to idolize Louis as the "Master of the Age" in diagnosis. Jackson saw that Bowditch was introduced to Louis first thing and included in Louis's rounds at La Pitié, which attracted a much smaller following than the rounds of more popular physicians. Where several hundred made the rounds with Dupuytren at the Hôtel Dieu, those with Louis at La Pitié might number fifteen at most, and Louis sensibly started later in the morning when the light was better.

When Holmes arrived in the spring of 1833, Jackson looked after him as well.

There was rarely a letup in the work, and never a shortage of additional opportunities to be pursued. "The days are so much occupied as to fly past almost like shadows," wrote Mason Warren, for whom a greatly increased facility with French had made a world of difference. With so many fields of study open, he tried to pursue all he could. He attended lectures on syphilis, observed operations at the Hôpital des Vénériens. He went several times to the Hôpital des Enfants Malades to hear talks on whooping cough, measles, and chicken pox. The diseases of children presented "an entire new field for examination," Warren wrote with enthusiasm. He sat in on lectures in chemistry at the Sorbonne. For a month he was engaged in "some very interesting experiments" on the intestines of dogs. He took up the study of skin diseases at the Hôpital Saint-Louis and followed with increasing interest the work of a German physician, Jules Sichel, in diseases of the eyes. "I was at a soirée at his house last night, at which there were four languages spoken," he wrote to his father.

And, importantly, he enrolled in a private course of lectures given by a *sage-femme*, a noted obstetrician, Madame Marie-Louise La Chapelle, in which students learned to examine with their fingers the wombs of pregnant women and came to understand a great deal more than they ever had about labor pains and the birth of a child. Madame LaChapelle was held in the highest regard by her students. Bowditch was to say he learned more of "midwifery" from Madame La Chapelle in her private course than he had in three years at the Harvard Medical School. To Wendell Holmes she was a shining case in point of why women should not be excluded from a medical education.

Between times, Warren was making himself known among the medical booksellers, surgical-instrument makers, and the preparers of anatomical specimens to be found in and about the crooked side streets of the Latin Quarter. He was shopping mainly for his father. "I send you by ship sailing direct to Boston," he wrote, "two boxes—a large one containing 50 to

60 specimens of morbid bones, some skulls . . . also the bones of the head separate." "Will you tell me to what extent I am to go on in my purchases?" he asked another day. "I have already laid out eighty dollars for bones."

On Sundays only, it appears, did Warren turn from work to the pleasures of Paris, when he, Jackson, Bowditch, Holmes, and others would cross the Seine to attend the opera or theater, and dine at their favorite Trois Frères Provençaux, where "full of warm blood, of mirth, of gossiping" (in Warren's words), they delighted in *soupe à la Ture* or *côtelettes à la provençale* or any number of other *spécialités* as well as a favorite Burgundy.

Warren even departed from the usual professional content of his letters home to report that Taglioni's performance in the ballet *La Sylphide* was wonderful beyond description. Another night, he attended a grand ball given by the most prominent American banker in Paris, Samuel Welles of Boston, in a mansion on the Place Saint-Georges, as brilliant an event as the young man had ever beheld. The host was the Welles of Welles & Company on the rue Taitbout, where Warren and the other Bostonians posted their mail.

One Sunday, Warren joined a great crowd gathered to watch a statue of Napoleon being placed atop the column in the Place Vendôme. Another day, at midweek, he sat in on a session of the Chambre des Députés, at which Lafayette was present looking very "sad on finding himself so entirely duped by the King."

> There is no doubt that if Lafayette had wished he could have been chosen president and established a republic [Warren informed his father]. Although at present he does everything in his power to show his devotion to the Republican party, he is looked upon by many of them with an evil eye.

Though the world of French politics impinged little on the day-to-day lives of the American medical students, some, like Warren and Holmes, made an effort to keep abreast of what was in the newspapers and the increasing "grumbles" over Louis-Philippe, and in part because they knew how great was the interest in all this at home. "There is a notion that the old gentleman, who is said to be a cunning fellow, has slackened a little in his zeal for the liberal principles," wrote Holmes of Louis-Philippe. "The papers talk without the slightest ceremony about his defection from the principles of the Revolution of July.

> The King is caricatured without mercy. If you have ever seen his portrait, you know that he has a narrow forehead and large fat cheeks. This has been ingeniously imitated by the outline of a pear—so that on half the walls of Paris you will see a fig- ure like this [outline of a pear] done in chalk or charcoal. . . .

It was very likely, Holmes thought, that in the course of time the French would have a "sober revolution" and a republic.

To ease his mind from work and take a little exercise, Holmes liked to roam about "using my eyes to see everything life had to show." He loved the broad paths and open sky of the nearby Luxembourg Gardens, and to walk by the Seine, where he felt closest to the essence of Paris. Just to stand on the Pont Neuf and gaze at the river, its passing boats and barges, was, he said, all the occupation one could ask for in an idle hour.

Bowditch preferred the Jardin des Plantes, where in good weather he walked mornings and evenings, often reading Virgil. Bowditch was the only one of the Bostonians known to have had a serious love affair in Paris, but then Bowditch was said to have been of an "impulsive, ardent, and romantic disposition." His heart had been won by Olivia Yardley from England, who was finishing her education in Paris and lived nearby in the Latin Quarter.

The one hint that Holmes paid the least attention to the numerous young women of the Latin Quarter is a wistful little poem titled "La Gri- sette." Whether he wrote it at the time or later is not clear.

> *Ah, Clemence! When I saw thee last*
> *Trip down the rue de Seine,*
> *And turning, when thy form had past,*
> *I said, "We meet again,"*

I dreamed not in that idle glance
Thy latest image came
And only left to memory's trance
A shadow and a name.

Another medical student, Louis Frazee from Kentucky, would later write in a book he published about his time in Paris that it was perfectly acceptable for a student to live on the most intimate terms "with his *grisette* in many of the hotels, without giving offense to the landlord or landlady." A *grisette* could visit a young man's room whenever she pleased, and stay as long as she pleased.

But of the many surviving firsthand accounts by American medical students, only one diary chronicles in brief but candid detail some off-hours carousing of a kind in which more than a few undoubtedly indulged but never mentioned in what they wrote. In the 1840s young Philip Claiborne Gooch of Richmond, a graduate of the University of Virginia, wrote in his diary in not very good French of countless hours at the billiard tables, of nights playing cards, and getting drunk on champagne and cognac. (In one such session, Gooch duly noted, he and a friend consumed a bottle of cognac each.) He wrote of visiting brothels and of vicious hangovers, but also of working diligently at the hospitals and his studies all the while.

Gooch took up with a *grisette* named Clementine, while a friend named Theodore favored another, Emeline, both of whom, it seems, were dancers. "I worked all day," Gooch recorded in one diary entry, the rest of which he devoted to dinner and events following that evening.

> I uncork the bottle of champagne. Theodore begins to eat. We drink. I take Emeline, who has the shivers, in my arms and put her on her knees. We kiss. We start to cry. They kiss. We kiss also. She says *tu toi*. I say *tu* . . . The familiar form. We are friends. The three bottles of champagne are empty. We are warm. The cognac flows. Emeline is drunk. We put her to bed. The three of us drink some more. Everyone goes to bed and—and—what follows . . .

The next morning he wrote, "We got up at 10. An enormous breakfast, and then each goes his way, the girls to the rehearsal at the Opera, me to the dissections, where I stayed until 4."

Every morning the work resumed. "At 6 A.M. I go to the hospital and from that time to 6 P.M. I am, at least 8 hours, there in the wards . . . observing, writing . . . sometimes fifteen pages a day," wrote James Jackson, who, by the spring of 1833, was spending nearly all his time working with Pierre Louis. But by then they were all under the spell of Louis, including Mason Warren, who said the effect on his friends had been enough in itself for him to make "great sacrifices" to spend six months under Louis's instructions.

That summer of 1833, Warren's father wrote to ask if he had "fixed the time" for his return home, but the young man felt he was hardly getting started.

III

Of the celebrated teachers and practitioners of the medical arts who held sway in Paris in the middle of the nineteenth century, none was so esteemed by the American students, or had such influence on them, as Pierre-Charles-Alexandre Louis. For twenty years and more he was to inspire American medical students as did no other French physician.

Louis did nothing for show. He was neither spellbinding nor flamboyant. He could never have filled the amphitheater at the École as did Gabriel Andral. He spoke quietly. Some thought him "dry." Henry Bowditch would remember him as ill at ease as a teacher and awkward when lecturing. Yet he had a power. What set him off from the others was his clearheaded approach to the treatment of disease, his insistence on the need for analysis based on evidence, on "*facts*." As Holmes said, he taught "the love of truth."

Louis was in his forties. After completing his training in Paris, he had gone to Russia, where he practiced medicine for seven years. Since his return, he had given up general practice to devote himself to the study of disease. That he was married to the sister of Victor Hugo gave him, in the eyes of many of his students, an added importance.

He was known—and at times ridiculed—for his extended questioning of patients, his slow, careful examinations and endless note-taking. Seeing Holmes taking notes one morning during the rounds at La Pitié, Louis exclaimed, *"Vous travaillez, monsieur. C'est bien ça!"* ("You are working, sir. It is well, that!")

He insisted on "exact observation," by which he meant listening to what the patient had to say and listening carefully, methodically with the stethoscope, the instrument for the examination of the chest first introduced by the French physician René Laënnec in 1819. As Holmes would write, the stethoscope was "almost a novelty in those days. The microscope was never mentioned by any clinical instructor I listened to while a medical student."

"The mind of this gentleman is not a brilliant one," Henry Bowditch wrote of Louis.

> It is an observing and calculating spirit, which examines with the utmost exactness the symptoms of disease at the bedside, weighs the different values of them under different circumstances. [Louis] is, in fact, what he wished to be considered, a careful observer of facts, and deduced from these facts laws which regulate disease.

Eagerly embracing the Louis approach, Holmes would spend upward of five hours a day sitting at the bedsides of patients, asking questions and filling his notebook.

Diseases of the chest were Louis's main interest, and he had made tuberculosis, a leading killer of the time, his forte. At times Louis's interest in the disease seemed greater than his interest in curing the patient, as even James Jackson conceded.

Tall and soft-spoken, Louis wore small spectacles on a long nose, and when not at the bedside of a patient, he moved swiftly through the wards. Holmes described him as a man of "serene and grave aspect, but with a pleasant smile and kindly voice." Mason Warren would remember especially that when, after a long run of perfect health, he took ill for several days, Louis came to see him.

Like the surgeon Velpeau, Louis was partial to American students, and like Velpeau, he saw the promise of this particular group of Americans—Jackson, Warren, Bowditch, and Holmes. Jackson was the master's favorite, and working with Louis during the cholera epidemic had left Jackson in even greater awe of him. He had come to think of Louis as a second father. And Louis, as he would later tell James Jackson, Sr., thought of James as a son.

Jackson had decided he must stay longer in Paris than originally planned. He wished, as Louis strongly encouraged him, to devote more time to science. He had found his mission in life. "In very truth I look forward with fear and trembling to the day when I must employ my time to earn money, instead of to learning truth," he wrote in a long thoughtful letter to his father.

> I once laughed when I was told the student's is the happiest life. Persuaded as I am that there is very much in the exercise of our profession, that develops and satisfies the affections—that delights the moral man—yet I must acknowledge that had circumstances favored it, I should have been pleased to pass at least eight or ten years in the study of the sciences of pathology and therapeutics, in the hopes of establishing some important truths. . . .
>
> We live indeed in darkness, and it costs more time to discover the falsity of pretended truth than it would perhaps to reach something truly valuable. . . . I believe that we admit many things in America as axioms, which are very far from being proved. We have too long believed that because demonstration on many points was impossible in medicine, it was not worthwhile to study it like an exact science. It is a very false position.

Louis wrote to Jackson's father urging that James stay on in Paris several more years to concentrate on pathological research. But James

Jackson, Sr., though wholly sympathetic to his son's desire, wanted him home. James was needed, he would explain in a letter to Louis. "We are a business-doing people. We are new.... Among us, where the hands are few in proportion to the work to be done, every young man engages as soon as he can in the business of life."

It was settled. On July 13, 1833, James wrote to his father, "In two hours I am to be out of Paris. I will not attempt to describe to you the agony it gives me to quit Louis."

———

Inspired by Louis and his approach, Bowditch decided to concentrate on diseases of the chest. "Thrice happy am I that I have trod French soil, and breathed a French atmosphere; have known Louis," he wrote.

Enthralled with Louis's scientific approach, Holmes felt as intellectually exhilarated as he had ever been and even more adamant about the value of all he had come to understand that he never would have had he remained at home. Here was the future of medicine. Were he asked why he would prefer the intelligent young man who had been studying in Paris to a venerable practitioner of the old school, Holmes's answer would be this:

> ... because the young man has experience. He has seen more cases perhaps of any given disease. He has seen them grouped so as to throw light upon each other. He has been taught to bestow upon them far more painful investigation. He has been instructed daily by men whom the world allows to be its most competent teachers—by men who know no masters and teach no doctrine but nature and her laws, pointed out at bedside for those to own who see them, and for the meanest student to doubt, to dispute if they cannot be seen. He has examined the dead body oftener and more thoroughly in the course of a year than the vast majority of our practitioners have in any ten years ... merely to have breathed a concentrated scientific atmosphere like that of Paris must have an effect on anyone who has lived where stupidity is tolerated, where mediocrity is applauded. ...

In another letter, Holmes wrote, "I am more and more attached every day to the study of my profession and more and more determined to do what I can to give [to] my country." To mark the end of his first year in Paris, he wrote still again in an effort to define what he felt he had accomplished thus far:

> My aim has been to qualify myself so far as my faculties would allow me, not for a new scholar, [or] for a follower of other men's opinions, [or] for a dependent on their authority, but for the character of a man who has seen and therefore knows, who has thought and therefore arrived at his own conclusions. I have lived among a great and glorious people. I have thrown my thoughts into a new language. I have received the shock of new minds and new habit. I have drawn closer the ties of social relations with the best formed minds I have been able to find from my own country. . . . I hope you do not think your money wasted.

His expenses, he told them, were $1,200 a year, for books, instruments, private instructions, everything. "I tell you that it is not throwing away money, because nine tenths of it goes straight into my head in the shape of knowledge."

In the second week of April 1834, violence broke out in Paris in protest of the government. Barricades went up in the streets of the poorest quarters of the city, and in the "pacification" that ensued, scores of citizens were killed and wounded. In response to gunfire from a building on rue Transnonain, government troops broke down the door and massacred all within—12 men, women, and children—a scene of horror later depicted in a powerful lithograph by the caricaturist Honoré Daumier.

For days wheelbarrow loads of the wounded kept arriving at the hospitals, and the students had their first sight of gunshot and bayonet wounds. Mason Warren wrote of "one poor fellow" who had been hit by ten musket balls and a woman who had had part of her leg shot away.

"Many of the dead were disposed in the morgue, some of them horribly slashed up."

Then, only weeks later in May, came heartbreaking news that hit Holmes, Warren, and Bowditch as nothing had. For all they and others had been dealing with daily at the hospitals, all the diseases they had been exposed to, not one of them had been seriously ill during his time in Paris. Now came word that James Jackson, Jr., had died in Boston of typhoid fever.

Earlier that winter the news that Jackson was ill had caused much concern among his friends in Paris. "No one could excite a greater interest in our minds on all accounts," Holmes had written to his parents. But the warning had in no way lessened the blow, nor was it felt by the Bostonians only. "I have seldom seen such a general feeling expressed on all sides," wrote Mason Warren. Pierre Louis was "altogether overcome, quite unable to contain himself."

As James Jackson, Sr., was to explain, his son had become actively involved with work at the Massachusetts General Hospital from the time he arrived home.

> Our autumnal fever was prevalent much more than usual, and with uncommon severity. The opportunity to study this and to compare it with the fever of Paris, on which Louis had written so admirably, was one which he could not forego. And when he found that this disease exhibited in the living and in the dead the same characteristics, which his master had so accurately delineated, his ardor was increased more and more and he put all his powers to their greatest trial. It is not surprising, in the retrospect, that he became affected with the prevailing disease.

After weeks of severe illness and a slow convalescence, James appeared to recover, when suddenly he took a turn for the worse, his mind "gave way," and he died.

"What shall I say of his ambition?" his father asked.

I think his young friends and associates will agree that he was not anxious for honorary distinctions. He had not such a spirit of emulation as leads one to study hard so that he may get the highest rank among his fellows. . . . But he had the strongest ambition to be worthy of the esteem and love of the wise and good. He rejoiced openly when he made an acquisition in knowledge.

That same month of May 1834 marked the death of Marie-Joseph-Paul-Yves-Roch-Gilbert du Motier, the Marquis de Lafayette. The legendary hero breathed his last on May 20, at age seventy-six, at his house on the rue d'Anjou, in the Faubourg Saint-Honoré. The day of the funeral, crowds of 200,000 or more lined the route of a long military procession to the Picpus Cemetery, where the interment in the family vault was private, as he had requested. In Washington, President Andrew Jackson declared a time of national mourning, and former president John Quincy Adams, now a member of the House of Representatives, read a lengthy tribute to the heroic friend of liberty.

For those Americans in Paris for whom Lafayette had been such a looming symbolic presence, it was an especially heavy loss. To many like Nathaniel Willis, who happened to be back in Paris briefly, the military funeral was a sham and a disgrace. "They buried the old patriot like a criminal. Fixed bayonets before and behind his hearse, his own National Guard disarmed, and troops enough to beleaguer a city, were the honors paid by the 'citizen king' to the man who made him!"

"They have buried liberty and Lafayette together," another American told Willis gloomily. "Our last hope in Europe is quite dead with him!"

———

In the fall of 1834, Mason Warren noted the rising number of "fine young men" from New York, Philadelphia, and other parts of the United States who had lately arrived in Paris to take up their studies in medicine, adding proudly that among all the students, "the Americans stand as high as those of any nation who come here, and they are surpassed by none. . . ."

Early in 1835, Warren was pleased to report that Dr. Louis was delivering his lectures with increased facility and now had a "great crowd" of students following him. Louis had been discovered, and in large part because of the American students, and recognition of his "value" was to last for years to come. Acolytes like Warren, Bowditch, and Holmes would carry the word home to Boston and beyond—Bowditch was already translating into English one of Louis's principal works on typhoid fever.

Bowditch departed for Boston in 1834, sooner than intended. He had sent a letter to his family announcing that he and his English love, Olivia Yardley, were engaged to be married. His father responded by telling him he must return home with no delay and alone.

Mason Warren departed in 1835. By then, except for a few side trips elsewhere in Europe, Warren had been in Paris nearly three years.

Holmes, who had been in Paris for more than two years, kept urging his parents to let him stay longer. The issue was money. He knew it would mean "hard squeezing" at home, but his cause was noble, he insisted. His pleading was to no avail. Reluctantly he sailed in the fall of 1835.

Meanwhile, more American students kept arriving, including another Bostonian destined for a distinguished medical career. George Shattuck began his studies under Louis (who thought so highly of Shattuck that he entrusted him with the translation of his text on yellow fever), and it was Shattuck in 1838 who encouraged Charles Sumner to join the "medicals" in their morning rounds at the hospitals as a part of Sumner's self-directed, eclectic education.

Sumner, whose line of study at the Sorbonne included everything from the history of Greece to civil law to geology, welcomed the chance. At six feet two he loomed over everyone making the rounds and had no trouble observing.

Following Alfred Velpeau at the Hôpital de la Charité, Sumner saw "every kind of hurt, swelling, and loathsome complaint," all observed with "an undisturbed countenance" by students and teachers. "Blessed be science," he wrote, "which has armed man with knowledge and resolution to meet these forms of human distress!" What struck Sumner especially about Pierre Louis was the spirit with which he expressed his love of science.

The strong impression made by the hospitals and the French approach to medicine was to figure importantly in Sumner's life to come. But of far greater future consequence was the impression made by something he observed at the Sorbonne.

On Saturday, January 20, 1838, as he recorded in his journal, Sumner attended a lecture at the Sorbonne on the philosophical theory of Heraclites delivered by Adolphe-Marie du Caurroy, a distinguished grey-haired scholar who spoke extremely slowly. Sumner began looking about the hall.

"He had quite a large audience," Sumner wrote, "among whom I noticed two or three blacks, or rather mulattos—two-thirds black perhaps—dressed quite *à la mode* and having the easy, jaunty air of young men of fashion. . . ." He watched closely. The black students were "well received" by the other students, he noted.

> They were standing in the midst of a knot of young men, and
> their color seemed to be no objection to them. I was glad to
> see this, though with American impressions, it seemed very
> strange. It must be then that the distance between free blacks
> and whites among us is derived from education, and does not
> exist in the nature of things.

It was for Sumner a stunning revelation. Until this point he is not known to have shown any particular interest in the lives of black people, neither free blacks nor slaves. On his trip to Washington a few years earlier, traveling by rail through Maryland, he had seen slaves for the first time. They were working in the fields, and as he made clear in his journal, he felt only disdain for them. "They appear to be nothing more than moving masses of flesh, unendowed with anything of intelligence above the brutes." He was to think that way no longer.

It would be a while before Sumner's revelation—that attitudes about race in America were taught, not part of "the nature of things"—would take effect in his career, but when it did, the consequences would be profound. Indeed, of all that Americans were to "bring home" from their time in Paris in the form of newly acquired professional skills, new ideas, and new ways of seeing things, this insight was to be as important as any.

Like so many, Sumner, too, wished he could stay longer in Paris. In the spring of 1838, with only a few days remaining, he wrote of his regret over "a thousand things undone, unlearned, and unstudied which I wished to do, to learn and to study." But in another letter he added, "I have never felt myself so much an American, have never loved my country so ardently. . . ."

———

The flow of Americans to the "medical mecca" of Paris continued through the 1840s, and the same illustrious French physicians—Lisfranc, Velpeau, Roux, Louis—continued to make their rounds and deliver their lectures. The only one missing from the professional galaxy was Guillaume Dupuytren. On the day of his funeral, on the way to Père Lachaise Cemetery, students had unharnessed the horses from the hearse and dragged it themselves to the tomb.

Between 1830 and 1860 nearly seven hundred Americans came to Paris to study medicine, and nearly all returned home to practice their profession greatly benefited by what they had learned. And much of this they would pass on to others.

Considerable attention and respect were given to nearly every young Paris-trained physician on his return. What was said of Mason Warren could have been said for most of them. "Apart from all other considerations, the mere fact of his long absence in Europe caused a degree of importance to be attached to him, as in those days few of our countrymen traveled abroad. . . ." Inevitably some returned from Paris a bit too pleased with themselves, while others in the profession who had never left home belittled the whole idea of study abroad or were openly critical of French medicine.

Decades later, in the 1890s, William Osler, one of the founders of the Johns Hopkins Medical School and as respected a figure as any in American medicine, would write that "modern scientific medicine" had had "its rise in France in the early days of this century." More than any others, it was the pupils of Pierre Louis who gave "impetus" to the scientific study of medicine in the United States.

Approximately seventy of those who had trained in Paris in the 1830s, or one out of three, later taught in American medical schools, and several ranked among the leading physicians in the nation. The Philadelphian William Gibson became chief of surgery at the University of Pennsylvania. A student from Salem, Massachusetts, Henry Williams, having discovered an interest in diseases of the eyes during his time in Paris, was made the first professor of ophthalmology at Harvard. George Shattuck became dean of Harvard Medical School. Furthermore, all contributed in other ways as well. Williams, as an example, wrote three books on diseases of the eyes that were considered the best of their time.

Henry Bowditch became a professor of clinical medicine at Harvard, where diseases of the chest remained his first interest, tuberculosis his specialty. In 1846, Bowditch published *The Young Stethoscopist*, a work used by medical students for half a century. His "greatest service," however, was in the field of public health, in which he was to have more influence nationally than anyone of his day.

Mason Warren "gave himself at once" to a large and popular practice as a surgeon in Boston. On October 16, 1846, in the operating theater at the Massachusetts General Hospital, he was present for the historic moment when his father, John Collins Warren, at age seventy, performed the first operation ever in which ether, administered by a Boston dentist named W. T. G. Morton, was used as an anesthetic. Morton had been experimenting successfully with the use of sulfuric ether fumes as a way to make tooth extractions painless. When word of this novelty reached John Collins Warren, he decided to proceed with a public surgical demonstration. The removal of a tumor from the neck of a young man took five minutes. The patient felt no pain.

A month later, on November 12, 1846, Mason Warren himself performed the first successful operation under ether done in private practice, and the month following he employed ether for the first time during surgery on a child.

Wendell Holmes was the illustrious, beloved professor of anatomy at the Harvard Medical School for thirty-six years, and for part of that time, he served as dean of the school. His lectures on anatomy began promptly at one in the afternoon five days a week. "He was never tired, always fresh, always eager in learning and teaching it," remembered one of his students.

Holmes's writings on medical subjects drew professional attention nationally, but it was in his spare hours that he continued his literary pursuits, publishing poetry and essays, for which he was even more widely known. In 1857 he began a series of witty essays in the new magazine he had helped found, the *Atlantic Monthly.* The first of these, "The Autocrat of the Breakfast Table," and a number that followed, published as a book, were to become an American classic, in which, among other things, Holmes defined Boston as "the hub" of the solar system and was the first to call Boston aristocrats Brahmins—a category he himself qualified for in every way except wealth.

Each of the three eminent Bostonians married and had children. Bowditch, after waiting patiently for several years, at last married his Paris true love, Olivia Yardley. Warren married Anna Crowninshield of Boston, and Holmes wed Amelia Jackson, a first cousin of James Jackson, Jr. The oldest of the three Holmes children, the eminent Oliver Wendell Holmes, Jr., was born on March 8, 1841.

Except for his two years in Paris as a student, Holmes lived all his life in or near Boston, but the immense importance of his Paris years may be judged by the fact that half a century later, in 1886, on the eve of his retirement from Harvard Medical School, having reviewed in his mind so much that he had seen and learned in his long career, he chose to talk about the remarkable French physicians under whom he had once studied in Paris. And Pierre Louis figured foremost.

"He had that quality which is the special gift of the man born for a teacher—the power in exciting an interest in that which he taught."

> You young men [Holmes continued] . . . hardly know how much you are indebted to Louis . . . I say, as I look back on the long hours of the many days I spent in the wards and in the autopsy room of La Pitié. . . .

Once, when Emerson referred to Pierre Louis in public as an example of French theatricality, Holmes wrote to him to say that while Louis had "assimilated to himself" many of the best and most industrious American students, there had been "nothing to keep them around him except his truthfulness, diligence and *modesty in the presence of nature.*" The "master key" to all Louis's success, Holmes said, was "honesty."

Yet, with the passage of years, Holmes wondered whether he and the other American students had "addicted" themselves too closely to the teachings of the master. He felt, Holmes said, "that I gave myself up too exclusively to his methods of thought and study." As essential, as invaluable as was the study of specific diseases through close, scientific investigation, there had to be more to the physician's comprehension and approach. There had to be concern for and some understanding of the patient. Medicine was a science to be sure, but also an art, "the noblest of arts."

He had been thinking about this duality for a long time. In an introductory lecture at the medical school some years earlier, recalling the strengths of his first great teacher, James Jackson, Sr., Holmes had talked of Jackson's kindness as one of his greatest professional strengths. He had always applied "the best of all that he knew for the good of his patient. . . . I never saw the man so altogether admirable at the bedside of the sick as Dr. James Jackson."

Much that Holmes had come to value about his time in Paris had to do with what he had learned beyond Paris Médicale, by just being in Paris, living in Paris—so much of art, music, poetry, and of good conversation.

The same could have been said of Warren and Bowditch. For as long as they lived, they would remember the feeling of walking into the Louvre and of beholding its treasures for the first time, the thrill of the Paris Opera, of seeing Molière performed onstage, seeing Taglioni. This, too, they knew, had made them better prepared to understand the human condition and thereby better able to serve in their profession.

Bowditch's son, Vincent, would write of his father, "He never allowed his interests in his patient's case to hide the fact that he was dealing with a fellow human being." When Vincent was himself about to leave for medical training abroad, Henry Bowditch told him:

While medicine is your chief aim, remember that I want you
to see all you can of art and music. I often think I have done
more good to some poor, weary patients by sitting down and
telling them of a delightful European experience than by all
the drugs I have ever poured down their throats.

———

Bowditch, Warren, and Holmes remained friends as well as colleagues
for the rest of their lives, none ever forgetting they had Paris in common.
After attending an address by Warren before the Massachusetts Medical
Society, Holmes told him in a note that regrettably he had not been able
to hear very well. "I suspect that my ear-drums may not be quite as tightly
corded up as in the days when we saw our young faces in the Burgundy of
the Trois Frères."

Each of them would return to Paris as time passed, and in some cases
more than once. Sometimes it was for their health—in the hope that just
being there would provide the needed lift of outlook—and sometimes that
worked. Mason Warren, who struggled with poor health all of his life,
with the exception of his student years in Paris, returned three times. Suffering from depression, he made his first trip in 1844 and came home sufficiently "refreshed" to work steadily another ten years. He had revisited
all the old haunts, as would both Bowditch and Holmes.

During his return in 1867, Bowditch discovered the same porter still
on the job at his old lodgings in the Latin Quarter. "Found my old garçon,
John, who remembered me well," he wrote in amazement. He revisited the
spot where he had first met Olivia Yardley and, as a highlight, dined with
Pierre Louis, who was then eighty years old. Louis, Bowditch wrote, was
"as beautiful in his old age as you can imagine a man to be." Louis died
five years later.

Holmes returned just once, in 1886, for what he called a Rip Van Winkle experiment. Like the others, he walked the rue Monsieur-le-Prince,
his head filled with memories.

For all of them, to judge by so much that they wrote in later years,
the life they had known as "medicals" in Paris had been what James Jackson, Jr., had said then—the happiest life.

PART II

CHAPTER FIVE

AMERICAN SENSATIONS

*We were met on the steps by half a dozen huge and splendid
looking porters, in flaming scarlet livery and powdered wigs,
who conducted us in, and being met by one of the King's* aides-
de-camp, *we were conducted by him into His Majesty's presence. . . .*

—GEORGE CATLIN

I

"Plus ça change, plus c'est la même chose"—"The more things change, the
more they remain the same"—was the oft-quoted observation of a French
writer, Alphonse Karr. But while much about life would assuredly go on as
usual, very much was to be profoundly, irretrievably different.

Change was coming—dramatic, unprecedented change: scheduled
Atlantic crossings by steamship in half the time; communication between far-distant points at the speed of lightning; a surprise discovery
by a Parisian artist named Louis Daguerre that Samuel Morse, seeing it
for the first time, called "the most beautiful" of the age; centuries-old European monarchies brought down by tumultuous political upheaval that
began in Paris; and Paris itself transformed on a scale no one could have
imagined—and all within less than twenty years.

The year 1838 marked the beginning, when in April the paddle steamer

Sirius crossed from Cork to New York, followed closely by another steamship from Bristol, the *Great Western*. Although both ships had a full complement of sails, both had the "unceasing aid" of steam engines the entire way.

Under steam a ship could now cut a straight furrow at sea, from point to point, with no more, or very little, tacking this way and that at the will of the winds. As never before, there could now be scheduled departures, no more waiting for wind when there was none, causing delays that could drag on for days.

On Tuesday, May 1, the *Sirius* departed New York on her return voyage. It was the first time a steamship ever set off from America for Europe, and thousands of people crowded the wharf to witness the historic event. Among those on board was James Gordon Bennett, publisher of the *New York Herald*, who on reaching England would declare, "We are positively in the beginning of a new age."

It had been a rough crossing, with gale winds and heavy seas, still it had taken only seventeen days. Samuel Morse, who left New York by sailing ship shortly after, did not reach London until mid-June, a full month later.

As they were to discover, Morse and Bennett were both on their way to Paris.

Of those Americans who had braved the Atlantic to come to Paris earlier in the 1830s, only two would return for reasons other than a pleasurable or nostalgic visit, and Samuel Morse was one. The other, Charles Sumner, would not arrive until 1856, and as it was with Morse, Sumner's purpose this time was entirely different from what it had been at first.

There was, however, one of the original adventurers who had never gone home, nor diverged in the slightest from his original objective. George Peter Alexander Healy, "Little Healy" from Boston, was still happily, industriously pursuing what he had come to Paris for in the first place, to make himself a master in the art of portraiture.

Arriving in Paris at age twenty-one, knowing no one and speaking no French, he had gone to the Louvre for his first look at the works of the old masters, and, to his surprise, found himself thinking they were overrated. "Perhaps many a young and audacious ignoramus has thought and even said as much before and since," he would later write. It was the experience of trying his hand at a copy of a Correggio that opened his eyes to the genius of the masters and to an appreciation of the long way he had still to go with his work.

Yet the fact that he was accepted as a student at the atelier of Baron Antoine-Jean Gros, to begin his first serious training, suggests his efforts at the Louvre were hardly lacking.

He "went to work with a will," trying all the while to catch up enough in French to make his way. The only American among the students, he was well received from the start, which was unusual. In the world of the Paris atelier, rigorous hazing was an established tradition for any newcomer, let alone an *étranger*.

Proficiency in drawing came first and foremost. Drawing was the foundation of everything, it was preached, and most of every day was devoted to drawing a live model, the students packed at their easels elbow-to-elbow. Once, during an early session, while the model was taking a break and Healy concentrated on looking over his efforts, another student, short, rough-mannered, and older than the rest, suddenly stepped in and shoved him aside, saying *"Donne-moi ta place, Petit."*

> He coolly turned over my sheet of grey paper [Healy would remember] and sketched the model, who resting, had fallen into a far better attitude than that which we had copied. The outline drawing was so strong, so full of life, so easily done, that I never had a better lesson.

The rough-mannered student, Thomas Couture, was to become one of the celebrated French painters of the day, and as a teacher have great influence on many more Americans to follow. He and Healy became fast friends. "There was in Couture's talent such vigor, such frankness, and so much of life and truth that my admiration for the artist equaled my liking for the man."

Genial by nature, always well-disposed to others, Healy made friends easily, a quality that was to serve him to great advantage in his career. He loved good conversation, and the more his French improved, the more he caught on with the others in the studio, one of whom, a particularly affable young man named Savinien Edme Dubourjal, who painted miniature portraits, became another favorite.

Healy openly revered the master, Antoine Gros, who had studied under the great Jacques-Louis David and won acclaim for paintings glorifying Napoleon. Gros was still widely respected, but he had become, in his sixties, "a saddened and almost despairing man," brooding constantly over the fact that he was no longer in fashion. In some quarters he was often the subject of outright dismissal. *"Gros est un homme mort!"* one critic had exclaimed. "He had outlived his popularity, and his heart was broken," wrote Healy.

On June 25, 1835, Antoine Gros drowned himself in the Seine. Shaken by the loss, his studies in the atelier at an end, Healy refused to despair.

> My life at this time was a life of extreme sobriety and very hard work. I was full of respect for the dollars I had brought with me, and my noonday meal often consisted of a small loaf with fruit, or cheese when there was no fruit. But I had good health, high spirits, and immense pleasure in the progress I felt I was making day by day.

His physical appearance was also in his favor. He stood about five feet eight and had by this time, in the Paris mode, succeeded in growing a small mustache. He parted his full head of dark brown hair down the middle and the beginnings of a frown, a vertical crease between the eyebrows of the kind that comes from much close concentration with the eyes, gave what might have been simply a handsome face an appealing degree of intensity. All this he captured quite well in his early self-portraits. In time he would wear eyeglasses and add a small goatee. In self-portraits done some years afterward, he looks very much like Eugène Delacroix.

His energy was phenomenal. He was seldom still. In 1837 he accepted an invitation to London to do portraits there. A year later, with two young

French artists, he set off from Paris on a painting tour of France and Switzerland on foot, often covering twenty or thirty miles a day. Then he was back again in London filling more canvases with the faces of English gentry.

Word of his talent spread. In Paris in 1838, the American minister to France, General Lewis Cass, asked Healy to paint his portrait, then another of Mrs. Cass, for which Healy would later win his first medal at the Paris Salon. The general was exceedingly proud of his gifted young countryman and spread the word further still.

In June of 1838, Healy was back in London in time to witness the coronation of Queen Victoria, and later decided to introduce himself to John James Audubon, much as he had once gone to see the beautiful Mrs. Otis on Beacon Hill, knowing that Audubon, too, in his youth had made ends meet painting portraits. Audubon was in London to supervise production of the fourth and final volume of his monumental work *The Birds of America* and was living with his wife on Wimpole Street. After protesting he was too busy to take time to sit for a portrait, Audubon said yes. Lewis Cass had been Healy's first chance to paint an American notable. Audubon was the second, but also a hero to Healy and considerably more picturesque than the buff, well-fed general. He painted Audubon in the garb of a backwoodsman with his bird gun in hand.

Life for Healy was advancing rapidly, for by now he had met a shy young English woman, Louisa Phipps, one glimpse of whom, he said, was "enough to fix my destinies." Fond of talking as he worked, Healy told Audubon he was in love. Audubon, who had been married for thirty years, immediately became more animated, assuring the young man the only real happiness in life was a good marriage.

In the spring of 1839, Healy received word from General Cass of an important commission awaiting him in Paris. He at once proposed to Miss Phipps. They were married in a quiet ceremony at St. Pancras Parish Church in London. Louisa wore her traveling dress, and as soon as the ceremony was over, they started for Paris. Healy had a hundred dollars; Louisa, "not a penny." Nor could she speak a word of French.

General Cass, who was on excellent terms with King Louis-Philippe, had told His Majesty he wanted very much to have a portrait of the king for his Paris residence and that he wished to commission young Healy to do it. Cass, who had fought bravely in the War of 1812, and afterward served as the territorial governor of Michigan and as secretary of war under President Andrew Jackson, was a man of considerable charm, as well as ample means, and lived on the avenue Matignon in as grand a manner as any American in Paris. After being shown the large, assured portrait Healy had done of Cass, the king agreed to sit.

The first session at the Tuileries Palace commenced with a moment of unanticipated drama.

> Before beginning the portrait [Healy wrote], I advanced toward the King, so as to take the measure of his face, using a compass for that purpose. One of the courtiers, seeing the gleam of steel in my hand, rushed upon me and pushed me aside. With a smile, Louis-Philippe said, "Mr. Healy is a republican, it is true, but he is an American. I am quite safe with him."

Like other Americans, Healy found Louis-Philippe easy to talk to and particularly happy to recall his own years in the United States. As the painting progressed, and the king grew increasingly interested in it, he recounted for Healy how once he had watched Gilbert Stuart at work on a full-length portrait of George Washington.

Healy had never been happier. He was delighted with his work, blissful in his new married life. He and Louisa had moved into tiny quarters on the Left Bank, on the rue d'Assas near the Luxembourg Gardens. The larger of two rooms served as a studio, the other as their bedroom.

> The concierge kept the place clean, and we went out for our meals. It was not a complicated way of living, but it never struck us that we were not the happiest mortals under the sun.

They began entertaining. To compensate for a complete lack of silverware, their friend Dubourjal, the miniaturist, would arrive at the door with his coat pocket full of knives and forks, and bearing several bottles of wine, which he loved to uncork and pour with due ceremony. Thomas Couture came also, though his loud voice and idea of humor did not sit well with shy Louisa. Where Dubourjal offered silverware from his pocket, Couture would pull out a live lizard and delighted in provoking disgust by showing raw oysters still alive at the moment they were swallowed.

King Louis-Philippe had chosen not to present himself in the portrait as the bourgeois gentleman frequently seen in the Garden of the Tuileries with his black suit and green umbrella. Instead he posed with his head held high by a stiff, gold-embroidered military collar, and wearing a chest full of decorations, heavy gold epaulettes, and a bright red sash over his right shoulder. Healy included the jowls, but the lift of the chin helped to compensate, and there was no suggestion that the head of black hair was a wig. In the completed work the overall look was of a vigorous man of military bearing clearly fit for his royal role. It was a long way from the pear-shaped Louis-Philippe of the political cartoons, yet a strong likeness nonetheless, and with life in it. All were pleased.

———

Healy rose early every morning and worked all day. On the rare occasions when he took time off, it was usually to go to the Louvre to stand for an hour or more studying a Rembrandt or Titian.

A larger, more commanding full-length portrait of Foreign Minister François Guizot followed that of Louis-Philippe. Guizot was the king's chief advisor, and if not the real ruler of France, as many contended, he was possibly the greatest parliamentary manager of the age. A brilliant intellectual and former professor of history, he, like the king, spoke English fluently and preferred to converse in English while Healy worked. As a young man, he told Healy, he had translated Gibbon's *Decline and Fall of the Roman Empire*, and more recently had published a biography of George Washington. The conversation between painter and sitter never flagged, Healy would remember. He found Guizot courteous and "perfectly charming," but beneath it all, "cold."

On a canvas measuring nearly 8 by 4½ feet, Guizot was shown standing at a table covered with official documents, his right hand clasping one of them. He was in a black coat, straight of spine, and he stared straight at the viewer with the unmistakable look of a man of keen mind and substance, with no time for fools or views contrary to his own. "Inflexible" was another word Healy used to describe Guizot. It was one of Healy's finest portraits yet, not just a deft likeness, but delineating character as well.

Thomas Appleton, who had known Healy and admired his work since Healy painted his sister Fanny in Boston, was in Paris again in the summer of 1841 and saw Healy at about the time the Guizot portrait was finished. "Healy is an excellent fellow," Appleton wrote, adding prophetically, "and, if he perseveres [he] will come back to us someday with the best reputation for portraits of any American of his time."

To what extent Healy's fees may have been increasing all the while is not known, but he and Louisa moved from their two rooms on the Left Bank to "a rather better place" on the other side of the river, on the rue Saint-Lazare, with a studio "more fitted to receive distinguished sitters," and more space for their expanding family. Louisa by now had given birth to two children, a boy and a girl, Arthur and Agnes.

In 1842, at the request of the king, Healy departed for America for the first time in eight years to make a copy of the Gilbert Stuart full-length portrait of Washington, which was hanging in the White House. Before the year was out, he was back in Paris with the Washington copy, as well as portraits he had done of President John Tyler and Senator Daniel Webster. When the king and others at the palace gathered for a first look, it is said, the portrait of Webster, "a magnificent-looking man," attracted the most attention.

In the spring of 1845, Louis-Philippe asked Healy to go again to the United States and as soon as possible. Word had reached Paris that former president Andrew Jackson was seriously ill and the king wanted a portrait done from life while there was yet time. Further, he wished Healy to paint for him a whole series of portraits of living American statesmen to hang in his private gallery at Versailles. It was a commission such as no American artist had ever received until then, not Stuart or Copley, not Charles Willson Peale or Trumbull or Sully.

It was late May by the time Healy reached the Hermitage, Jackson's home near Nashville, Tennessee, and the gaunt old president, propped up with pillows in a big armchair (as Healy would remember), told him he was too late.

"Can't sit, sir—can't sit!" Jackson said.

"But, General, the King of France . . ." Healy began.

"Can't sit, sir, not for all the kings in Christendom!"

Nashville was a world apart from Paris, as Healy knew from the time and effort it had taken him to get there. Yet he was pleased to find the plantation home of the supposedly rough-hewn Jackson decorated with fine French wallpaper and French mirrors. The dining room table was heavy with French china, the cellar stocked with French wine. The visitor from Paris was made to feel immediately at home and with the urging of young Mrs. Jackson, the general's adored daughter-in-law, the old president changed his mind and agreed to sit. As it turned out, Healy painted two portraits, one for the king, the other, at Jackson's request, for the daughter-in-law. When Jackson died on June 8, Healy was among those at the bedside.

From Tennessee, Healy traveled on to Kentucky to paint Henry Clay, then to Massachusetts, where he did the aged John Quincy Adams, who was still serving as a member of Congress. In their conversation over several days, Healy found him as fascinating as anyone he had ever met, and particularly when Adams began reminiscing about his boyhood years in France with his father.

> It seemed odd [Healy would recall] to talk to one who had been in France before the [French] Revolution, whose father had spoken to him familiarly of Voltaire, of Buffon, of the Encyclopédistes, of the French court; who had been at school near Paris with Franklin's grandson . . . the sensation was a strange one.

Adams openly enjoyed sitting for his portrait, and this, Healy said, was not always the way with celebrated people. Webster, as he told Adams, likened artists to horseflies on a hot day. "Brush them off on one side, they settle on another," Webster exclaimed.

Adams disagreed and talked of sitting for Gilbert Stuart and of the time he had spent at the Louvre looking at paintings. He talked of Lafayette and Lafayette's beautiful wife. "I was but a small boy then, but I still remember what a deep impression the lovely Marquise made on my youthful imagination." Talking about books and his favorite classical authors, Adams went on with such fervor that he visibly trembled with emotion. As Healy would observe years later, "In those far-away days cold indifference was not yet in fashion."

II

"Having been delayed seven weeks in England, endeavoring to obtain a patent," Samuel Morse wrote to his daughter Susan from Le Havre on July 26, 1838, "[we] are now on our way to Paris, to try what we can do with the French government."

> I confess I am not sanguine as to any favorable pecuniary re-
> sult in Europe, but we shall try, and at any rate we have seen
> enough to know that the matter is viewed with great interest
> here. . . . I am in excellent health and spirits. . . .

Morse was traveling with James Gordon Bennett. The weather was ideal, the sky blue, and the Seine just as blue the whole way to Paris. "The beauty of the Seine is exquisite," Bennett reported for his readers in the *New York Herald.* "The natural scenery along its placid winding banks, reminded me of the Mohawk above Albany. . . ."

Morse thought their hotel on the rue de Rivoli and the view from his window of the Garden of the Tuileries as delightful as any in Paris. It was a grand time to be back. Summer crowds filled the boulevards. The colossal Arc de Triomphe, the largest triumphal arch ever built, now completed at long last, offered from its summit yet another breathtaking panorama of the city.

In the six years since Morse left Paris, he had known seemingly endless struggles and disappointments, and then, just that February, a vivid triumph. He was now forty-seven, his hair turning grey. He remained a widower and still felt the loss of his wife, Lucretia. "You cannot know the depth of the wound that was inflicted, when I was deprived of your dear mother," he wrote to Susan, "nor in how many ways that wound has kept open." He welcomed the prospect of marrying again, but a few halfhearted attempts at courtship had come to nothing. Moreover, to his extreme embarrassment, he was living on the edge of poverty. His time in Europe thus far had already cost him most of what little money he had.

A new position as professor of art at New York University provided some financial help, as well as studio space in the tower of the university's new building on Washington Square, where Morse worked, slept, and ate his meals, carrying in his groceries after dark so no one would suspect the straits he was in. His two boys, meanwhile, were being cared for by his brother Sidney. Susan, the oldest child, was in school in New England.

For a long time Morse had hoped to be chosen to paint a historic scene for the Rotunda of the Capitol in Washington. It would be the fulfillment of all his aspirations as a history painter, and would bring him a fee of $10,000. He openly applied for the honor in letters to members of Congress, including Daniel Webster and John Quincy Adams. Four large panels had been set aside in the Rotunda for such works, but as yet no decisions had been made. In 1834, in remarks on the floor of the House he later regretted, Adams had questioned whether American artists were equal to the task. James Fenimore Cooper, responding in a letter to the *New York Evening Post*, insisted the new Capitol was destined to be an "historical edifice" and must therefore be a showplace for American art. With the question left unresolved, Morse could only wait and hope.

That same year, 1834, to the dismay of many, Morse had joined in the Nativist movement, the anti-immigrant, anti-Catholic outcry sharply on the rise in New York and in much of the country. Like others, he saw the American way of life threatened with ruination by the hordes of immigrant poor from Ireland, Germany, and Italy flooding into the country, bringing with them their ignorance and their "Romish" religion. In Morse's own birthplace, Charlestown, Massachusetts, an angry mob had sacked and burned an Ursuline convent.

Writing under a pen name, "Brutus," Morse began a series of articles for his brothers' newspaper, the *New York Observer*. "The serpent has already commenced to coil about our limbs, and the lethargy of his poison is creeping over us," he warned darkly. The articles, published as a book, carried the title *Foreign Conspiracy Against the Liberties of the United States*. Monarchy and Catholicism were inseparable and unacceptable, if democracy was to survive, Morse argued. All the old fears and dire warnings he had been raised on, plus the memory of the soldier in Rome knocking off his hat, came rushing back. Asked to run as the Nativist candidate for mayor of New York in 1836, Morse accepted. To friends and admirers he seemed to have departed his senses. An editorial in the *New York Commercial Advertiser* expressed what many felt:

> Mr. Morse is a scholar and a gentleman—an able man—an accomplished artist—and we should like on ninety-nine accounts to support him. But the hundredth forbids it. Somehow or other he has got warped in his politics. . . .

On election day, he went down to a crushing defeat, finishing last in a field of four.

He kept on with his teaching at the university and his involvement with the National Academy of Design. And he kept painting. A portrait of the Reverend Thomas Harvey Skinner was as deft as any he had ever painted, and a large, especially beautiful portrait of his daughter Susan received abundant praise.

But when word reached Morse from Washington that he had not been chosen to paint one of the historic panels at the Capitol, his world collapsed. Friends and fellow artists wrote to express their disappointment and sympathy, and if possible to lift his spirits. "Dismiss it then from your mind, and determine to paint all the better for it," wrote his former teacher, Washington Allston.

Morse felt sure that John Quincy Adams had done him in. But there is no evidence of this. More likely, Morse himself had inflicted the damage with the unvarnished intolerance of his anti-Catholic newspaper essays and ill-advised dabble in politics.

He "staggered under the blow," in his words. It was the ultimate defeat of his life as an artist. Sick at heart, he took to bed. Morse was "quite ill," reported James Cooper, greatly concerned. Nathaniel Willis would recall later that Morse told him he was so tired of his life that had he "divine authorization," he would end it.

Morse gave up painting entirely. He abandoned for good all his dreams of accomplishment and recognition as an artist, the whole career he had set his heart on since college days. No one could dissuade him.

"Painting has been a smiling mistress to many, but she has been cruel to me," he would write bitterly to Cooper. "I did not abandon her, she abandoned me."

He must attend to one thing at a time, his father had preached. The "one thing" henceforth would be his telegraph, the crude apparatus for which was also to be found in his New York University studio apartment. Later it would be surmised that had he not stopped painting when he did, no successful electromagnetic telegraph would have happened when it did, or at least not a Morse electromagnetic telegraph.

Essential to his idea, as he had set forth earlier in notes written in 1832, were that signals would be sent by the opening and closing of an electrical circuit, that the receiving apparatus would, by electromagnet, record signals as dots and dashes on paper, and that there would be a code whereby the dots and dashes would be translated into numbers and letters.

The apparatus he had devised was a strange, almost ludicrous-looking assembly of wooden clock wheels, wooden drums, levers, cranks, paper rolled on cylinders, a triangular-shaped wooden pendulum, an electromagnet, a battery, a variety of copper wires, and a wooden frame of the kind used to stretch canvas for paintings (and for which he had no more use)—all "so rude," so like some child's wild invention, he was reluctant to have it seen.

His chief problem was that the magnet had insufficient voltage to send a message more than about forty feet. But with help from a colleague, a professor of geology at New York University, Leonard Gale, the problem was overcome. By increasing the power of the battery and magnet, they were able to send messages a third of a mile on electrical wire strung back and forth in Gale's lecture hall. Morse then devised a system of electromagnetic relays, and this was the key element, in that it put no limit to the distance a message could be sent.

A physician from Boston, Charles Jackson, charged Morse with stealing his idea. Jackson—who was no relation to James Jackson, Jr.—had been a fellow passenger on Morse's return voyage from France in 1832. He now claimed they had worked together on the ship, and that the telegraph, as he said in a letter to Morse, was their "mutual discovery." Morse was outraged, and answering Jackson, setting him straight, as well as responding to other charges that would come out of Jackson's claim, were to consume hours upon hours of Morse's time and play havoc with his nervous system. "I cannot conceive of such infatuation as has possessed this man," he wrote privately. And for this reason Cooper and Richard Habersham spoke out unequivocally in Morse's defense, attesting to the fact that he had talked frequently with them of his telegraph in Paris well before ever sailing for home.

Morse sent a preliminary request for a patent to Henry L. Ellsworth, the nation's first commissioner of patents, who had been a classmate at Yale, and in 1837, with the country in one of the worst financial depressions to date, Morse took on another partner, young Alfred Vail, who was in a position to invest some of his father's money. Additional financial help came from Morse's brothers. Most important, Morse worked out his own system for transmitting the alphabet in dots and dashes, in what was to be known as the Morse code.

In a larger space in which to string their wires, a vacant factory in New Jersey, he and Vail were soon sending messages over a distance of ten miles. Demonstrations were staged successfully elsewhere in New Jersey and Philadelphia.

There were continuing reports of others at work on a similar invention both in the United States and abroad, but by mid-February 1838, Morse and Vail were at the Capitol in Washington ready to demonstrate the machine that could "write at a distance." They set up their apparatus and strung ten miles of wire on big spools around a room reserved for the House Committee on Commerce. For several days members of the House and Senate crowded into the room to watch "the Professor" put on his show. On February 21, President Martin Van Buren and his cabinet came to see.

The wonder of Morse's invention was thus established almost overnight in Washington. The Committee on Commerce moved quickly to recommend an appropriation for a fifty-mile test of the telegraph.

Yet Morse felt he must have government support in Europe as well, and thus was soon on his way over the Atlantic, only to confront in official London the antithesis of the response at Washington. His request for a British patent was subjected to one aggravating delay after another. When finally, after seven weeks, he was granted a hearing, the request was denied.

"The ground of objection," he reported to Susan, "was not that my invention was not original, and better than others, but that it had been published in England from the American journals, and therefore belonged to the public."

Paris was to treat him better, up to a point. The response of scientists, scholars, engineers, indeed the whole of academic Paris as well as the press, was to be expansive and highly flattering. Recognition of the kind he had so long craved for his painting came now in Paris in resounding fashion and in the most appropriate setting possible. The French knew how such occasions should be orchestrated.

For the sake of economy Morse had moved from the rue de Rivoli to modest quarters on the rue Neuve des Mathurins, which he shared with a new acquaintance, an American clergyman of equally limited means named Edward Kirk. Morse's French had never been anything but barely passable, nothing close to what he knew was needed to present his invention before any serious gathering. But the Reverend Kirk, who was proficient in French, volunteered to serve as his spokesman and, in addition, tried to rally Morse's frequently sagging spirits by reminding him of the "great inventors who are generally permitted to starve when living, and are canonized after death."

They arranged Morse's wires and apparatus in their cramped quarters and made every Tuesday "levee day" for anyone who wished to climb the stairs to witness a demonstration. Kirk, who knew little of science or inventions, caught on quickly enough to serve as "the grand exhibitor." Distinguished visitors and complete strangers alike came in increasing numbers to see the show.

> I explained the principles and operation of the telegraph [Kirk would recall]. The visitors would agree upon a word themselves, which I was not to hear. Then the Professor would receive it at the writing end of the wires, while it devolved upon me to interpret the characters which recorded it at the other end. As I explained hieroglyphics, the announcement of the word, which they saw could have come to me only through the wire, would often create a deep sensation of delighted wonder.

Kirk would regret in later years that he had failed to keep notes on what was said. "Yet I never heard a remark which indicated that the result obtained by Mr. Morse was not NEW, wonderful, and promising immense practical results."

Between times Morse went off on long walks through the city, and at least once, perhaps more often, he took the old route across the river to the rue Saint-Dominique where Cooper had lived.

One wonders, too, if during this time in Paris, or later, Morse ever crossed paths with George Healy. He had to have known about Healy's success—Healy was to be made an honorary member of the National Academy of Design. And one wonders what Morse, who had given up painting, may have felt about such success achieved at so young an age.

Back when Morse was resettling in New York, after his work at the Louvre, Healy had been just setting off on his first venture to Paris. On reaching New York, and finding the departure of his ship delayed, he had gone to call on Morse.

"So you want to be an artist?" Morse had said. "You won't make your salt!" Healy's grandmother had earlier told him the same thing in almost the same words.

"Then, sir," Healy replied, "I must take my food without salt."

In the first week of September, one of the luminaries of French science, the astronomer and physicist Dominique-François-Jean Arago, arrived at the house on the rue Neuve des Mathurins for a private showing of the "wonderful discovery." "He gave it a thorough examination, questioned the inventor with great minuteness," wrote Edward Kirk, "and declared himself satisfied with the results and its capacity to do all that was claimed for it."

Arago offered at once to introduce Morse and his invention to the Académie des Sciences at their next meeting to be held in just six days on September 10. To prepare himself, Morse began jotting down notes on what should be said: "My present instrument is very imperfect in its mechanism, and only designed to illustrate the principle of my invention. . . ."

The savants of the Académie convened in the great hall of the Institut de France, the magnificent seventeenth-century landmark on the Left Bank facing the Seine and the Pont des Arts. Just over the river stood the Louvre, where, six years earlier, Morse the painter had nearly worked himself to death. Now he stood "in the midst of the most celebrated scientific men of the world," as he wrote to his brother Sidney. There was not a familiar face to be seen, except for Professor Arago and one other, Alexander von Humboldt, who in those other days at the Louvre had come to watch him at his labors.

At Morse's request Arago explained to the audience how the invention worked, and what made it different and superior to other such devices, while Morse stood by to operate the instrument. Everything worked to perfection.

It was, as would be said, the proudest triumph of Morse's career thus far. "A buzz of admiration and approbation filled the whole hall," he wrote to Alfred Vail, "and the exclamations, *'Extraordinaire!' 'Très bien!' 'Très admirable!'* I heard on all sides."

The event was acclaimed in the Paris and London papers and in the Academy's own weekly bulletin, the *Comptes Rendus*. In a long, prescient letter written two days later, the American patent commissioner, Morse's friend Henry Ellsworth, who happened to be in Paris at the time, said the occasion had shown Morse's telegraph "transcends all yet made known," and that clearly "another revolution is at hand."

> I do not doubt that within the next ten years, you will see electric power adopted between all commercial points of magnitude on both sides of the Atlantic, for purposes of correspondence, and men enabled to send their orders or news of events from one point to another with the speed of lightning itself. . . . The extremities of nations will be literally *wired* together. . . . In the United States, for instance, you may expect to find at no very distant day the Executive messages, and the daily votes of each House of Congress made known at Philadelphia, New York, Boston, and Portland—at New Orleans, Cincinnati, etc.—as soon as they can be known in Baltimore or even the opposite extremity of Pennsylvania Avenue! . . . Abstract imagination is no longer a match for reality in the race that science has instituted on both sides of the Atlantic.

That he was in Paris made him feel greater pride than ever, Ellsworth conceded. "In being abroad, among strangers and foreigners, one's nationality of feeling may be somewhat more excusable than at home."

Acclaim from the savants and the press was one thing, progress with the French government was another. Minister Lewis Cass provided Morse with a "most flattering" letter of introduction to carry on his rounds, but to no effect. After his eighth or ninth call at the office of the Ministre de l'Intérieur, Morse was still able to speak to no one above the level of a secretary, who asked only that he leave his card.

"Everything moves at a snail's pace here," he lamented a full two months after his day of glory at the Academy. "Dilatoriness" was to be expected, Lewis Cass told him, and little could be done about it.

Morse, who had intended at midsummer to stay no more than a month in Paris, was still there at the start of the new year, 1839, and with Edward Kirk's help, still holding his Tuesday levees upstairs on the rue Neuve des Mathurins. That there was no decline in interest in his invention made the "dilatoriness" even more maddening.

It would be at home in America that his invention would have much the best chance, Morse decided. "There is more of the 'go-ahead' character with us. . . . Here there are old systems long established to interfere, and at least to make them cautious before adapting a new project, however promising. Their railroad operations are a proof in point." (Railroad-building in France had been later starting than in the United States and was moving ahead at a much slower pace.)

By March, fed up with the French bureaucracy, embarrassed by the months wasted in waiting and by his worsening financial straits, Morse decided it was time to go home. But before leaving, he paid a visit to Monsieur Louis Daguerre, a theatrical scenery painter. "I am told every hour," wrote Morse with a bit of hyperbole, "that the two great wonders of Paris just now, about which everyone is conversing, are Daguerre's wonderful results in fixing permanently the image of the camera obscura and Morse's electro-magnetic telegraph." And so, for a second time, Samuel Morse would bring home to America an idea from France of consequences far beyond what he or anyone could then have foreseen.

Morse and Daguerre were of about the same age, but where Morse could be somewhat circumspect, Daguerre was bursting with *joie de vivre*. Neither spoke the other's language with any proficiency, but they got on at once—two painters who had turned their hands to invention.

Skilled in theatrical lighting and scenic effects from years in the theater, Daguerre had devised his own secret technique for painting scenes on huge, transparent theater drops, or scrims, as large as seventy-one by forty-five feet—a view of a Swiss valley or the interior of an English cathedral—which when lit from behind and set off by a few well-placed props, had a reality beyond anything seen before. He had built his own large theater, the Diorama, in which to put on his show, and from its opening day, in 1822, Parisians had come "flocking."

Daguerre had proven himself a master illusionist with light. The audience sat on a revolving platform, so it was as if the scenes were passing before them, and they found it almost impossible to believe what they were seeing was not real. The Diorama, proclaimed a reviewer in the *Journal de Paris*, marked an "epoch in the history of painting." "We cannot sufficiently urge Parisians who like pleasure without fatigue to make the journey to Switzerland and to England without leaving the capital."

Seeing the results of Daguerre's latest invention, Morse was struck with amazement. Years before he had tried to see if it were possible to fix the image produced with a camera obscura, by using paper dipped in a solution of nitrate of silver, but had given it up as hopeless.

Daguerre had been experimenting with the idea of reproducing visual images for a long time, working with an older colleague named Joseph-Nicéphore Niépce, who had since died. What Daguerre finally accomplished with his little daguerreotypes was clearly, Morse saw—and reported without delay in a letter to his brothers—"one of the most beautiful discoveries of the age."

> They are produced on a metallic silver-coated [copper] surface, the principal pieces about 7 inches by 5 [inches], and they resemble aquatint engravings, for they are in simple chiaroscuro, and not in colors. But the exquisite minuteness of the delineation cannot be conceived. No painting or engraving ever approached it. For example: In a view up the street, a distant sign would be perceived, and the eye could just discern that there were lines of letters upon it, but so minute as not to be read with the naked eye. By the assistance of a powerful lens, which magnified fifty times, applied to the delineation, every letter was clearly and distinctly legible, and so also were the minutest breaks and lines in the walls of the buildings and the pavements of the streets. The effect of the lens upon the picture was in a great degree like that of a telescope in nature.

The daguerreotype marked the birth of photography, but other artists seeing Daguerre's accomplishment were not so enthusiastic as Morse. To Delacroix it marked the death of art.

Morse stayed more than an hour and came away overjoyed. But a return visit by Daguerre to Morse's rooms on the rue Neuve des Mathurins, to see Morse's telegraph, was cut short when word came that the Diorama had caught fire and burned to the ground, those in the audience barely escaping with their lives.

Morse's account of his visit with Daguerre, published by his brothers in the *New York Observer* on April 20, 1839, was the first news of the daguerreotype to appear in the United States and was quickly picked up by newspapers all over the country. Once Morse arrived back in New York, having crossed by steamship for the first time, aboard the *Great Western*, he wrote immediately to Daguerre to assure him that "throughout the United States your name alone will be associated with the brilliant discovery which justly bears your name." He also saw to it that Daguerre was made an honorary member of the National Academy, the first honor Daguerre received outside of France.

With help from a professor of chemistry at New York University, John William Draper, Morse experimented with making daguerreotype portraits, something Daguerre himself had not bothered with, deciding it was impractical, since the subject would have to remain motionless for as long as fifteen or twenty minutes. By 1840, Morse and Draper were sufficiently satisfied with their results to open a daguerreotype portrait studio on the top floor of the university building. Thus, Samuel Morse, the painter of portraits, had proudly become a portrait photographer.

Still he kept plugging away with work on the telegraph, his old longing "to shine" by no means dormant.

———

Four years later, in July of 1844, news reached Paris and the rest of Europe that Professor Morse had opened a telegraph line, built with Congressional appropriation, between Washington and Baltimore, and that the telegraph was in full operation between the two cities, a distance of thirty-four miles. From a committee room at the Capitol, Morse had tapped out a message from the Bible to his partner Alfred Vail in Baltimore: "What hath God wrought!" Afterward others were given a chance to send their own greetings.

A few days later, interest in Morse's device became greater by far at both ends when the Democratic National Convention being held at Baltimore became deadlocked and hundreds gathered about the telegraph in Washington for instantaneous news from the floor of the convention itself. Martin Van Buren was tied for the nomination with the former minister to France, Lewis Cass. Ultimately, on the eighth ballot, the convention chose a compromise candidate, James K. Polk of Tennessee.

In Paris, *Galignani's Messenger* reported that newspapers in Baltimore were now able to provide their readers with the latest information from Washington up to the very hour of going to press. "This is indeed the annihilation of space."

III

The spring of 1845, just a year following Morse's triumph at Washington, marked the appearance in Paris of a decidedly different variety of American, the first wave of American curiosities or exotics—"*les sensations américaines*"—who were the cause of great popular commotion.

It began with P. T. Barnum—Phineas Taylor Barnum—the flamboyant New York showman, and his tiny protégé Tom Thumb, and not even Barnum, for all his extravagant claims, foresaw the sensation they caused.

Almost immediately afterward came the American painter of Plains Indians, George Catlin, bringing an entire gallery of his pictures, more than five hundred in total, as well as a party of painted and feathered real-life "Ioways." It was the most memorable visit of an American painter to Paris of all time.

Coinciding with all this excitement, a virtuoso American pianist, Louis Moreau Gottschalk from New Orleans, gave his first concert in Paris at the Salle Pleyel on the rue de Rochechouart, which appears to have been the first solo performance ever by an American on a Paris stage. What made it particularly notable was that Gottschalk was fifteen years old.

With a genius for publicity and humbug, P. T. Barnum had made himself famous a few years earlier when he opened his American Museum on

Broadway. In no time it became the most popular attraction in New York. "The people like to be humbugged," he would explain. By chance, Barnum had also discovered a child from Bridgeport, Connecticut, named Charles Stratton, a midget who stood not quite two feet high and weighed sixteen pounds. The boy was five. Barnum renamed him Tom Thumb, or General Tom Thumb, fitted him out in a miniature uniform something like that of Napoleon, and said his age was eleven.

> He was a perfectly formed, bright-eyed little fellow with light hair and ruddy cheeks [Barnum later wrote] and . . . I took the greatest pains to educate and train [him] . . . devoting many hours to the task by day and by night, and I was very success-ful, for he was an apt pupil. . . .

Barnum had opened his museum, he was frank to say, "for the op-portunity it afforded for rapidly making money." In the tiny "General" he had found a gold mine. He paid the boy's parents $3 a week and put him on display in the museum, where he became such an instant favorite that Barnum raised the weekly salary to $20. Then "to test the curiosity of men and women on the other side of the Atlantic," Barnum took Tom, his par-ents, a tutor, and three or four others on a trip to Europe, first to London, then Paris. Under a new agreement, Tom was to receive a weekly $50.

In London the Lilliputian Wonder was a "decided hit" on stage in Pic-cadilly and, later, resplendent in his uniform, at a command performance before Her Majesty Queen Victoria at Buckingham Palace. But London was not Paris. "The French are exceedingly impressionable," wrote Bar-num, "and what in London is only excitement, in Paris becomes a furor."

He settled Tom and his entourage in the Hôtel Bedford on the rue de Rivoli and swung into action. He hired a brand-new auditorium with a seating capacity of 3,000, the Salle de Concert on the rue Vivienne, hired an orchestra, and made the rounds of the Paris newspapers to drum up publicity.

The winter in Paris had been unusually severe and signs of spring were late in coming. The branches of a well-known chestnut tree in the Garden of the Tuileries, normally mint-green by early March, were still as bare as in the middle of winter. Then, suddenly, on the first official day of spring, March 21, the sun shone brilliantly and the boulevards were at once fully "animated" in the spirit of the season. Crowds thronged the Champs-Élysées. *Tout Paris* paraded by in their elegant equipages, providing a first glimpse of the new spring fashions.

Yet Tom Thumb stole the show, sporting a top hat, riding in a no-less-fancy miniature carriage with four grey ponies and four tiny liveried coachmen. The crowd along the avenue broke into cheers for "General Tom Pouce."

Because of the reception given "the General" at Buckingham Palace, Barnum had no trouble arranging for a comparable appearance before King Louis-Philippe and his royal court at the Tuileries Palace on the evening of March 23. Tom came attired this time as the perfect upper-bourgeois gentleman in a well-fitting black coat, white vest, and a glittering diamond shirt pin, and was at once the center of attention and delight. Barnum had coached his "apt pupil" well.

When a lady (who undoubtedly had also been coached) asked Tom in English if he planned to marry, he replied, "Certainly."

"And how many have you engaged to marry?"

"Eight, all told."

"But they tell me you are fickle and faithless."

"It is true."

"In England the ladies ran after you a great deal, and you let them kiss you."

"That was to avoid hurting their feelings."

"How many times have you been kissed?"

"A million."

The king asked the General if he spoke French.

"A little," he replied.

"What can you say in French?" asked the king.

"*Vive le Roi!*"

Tom performed an original dance, posed in imitation of such well-known statues as *David and Goliath, Samson,* and *Hercules.* Resuming his role as perfect gentleman, he consulted a tiny pocket watch and offered a pinch of snuff from a tiny box sparkling with faux jewels. For his last act he danced a Highland fling in Scottish bonnet and kilts.

Reportedly the wardrobe he brought to Paris could be packed in a hat box, and while on tour he slept in a bureau drawer.

The following day the Paris papers announced drolly the public levees, "FOR A SHORT TIME ONLY," for "The American Man in Miniature" at the Salle de Concert:

> He is smaller than any infant that ever walked! He is lively, intelligent, and symmetrical in his proportions. He will relate his history, sing a variety of songs, DANCE . . .

Admission for the best seats in the hall was 3 francs; second-best, 2 francs.

As reported three days after the opening, the levees were "crowded to excess."

> The grace, readiness, and address of this wonderful little fellow are, in truth, scarcely less extraordinary than his miniature size, and have already rendered him the reigning favorite of the fashionable world, particularly among the ladies.

Shop windows were by now displaying miniature statues of Tom Pouce in plaster and chocolate. There were songs about him. One café even changed its name to Tom Pouce.

So great was the attendance at his two daily performances at the Salle de Concert as the weeks went on that Barnum had to hire a cab each night to haul his bag of silver back to the hotel.

The pale, slender young American who walked on stage at the Salle Pleyel and seated himself at the piano on the evening of Wednesday, April 2, 1845, knew how much was expected of him. Moreau, as he was called, had been studying music in Paris for four years, and in musical circles there was much talk about him. In the audience waited his mother and five younger brothers and sisters, as well as his teacher, Camille Stamaty, who had studied under Mendelssohn. There, too, waiting attentively, were two of the most adored pianists of the time, Sigmund Thalberg and Frédéric Chopin, who had had his own first performance in Paris at the Salle Pleyel. Paris devotees of music had turned out in force, every seat was full, in response to a printed invitation to hear the debut of "Young Moreau Gottschalk of New Orleans."

The boy had been born in 1829. His mother, Aimee Brusle Gottschalk, was a Roman Catholic Creole whose first language was French. Moreau was raised as a Catholic, but educated in English. His father, Edward Gottschalk, Jewish by birth, made his living trading in land and slaves. Moreau was said to have shown his first interest in the piano at age three and at age twelve, with strong encouragement from one of his piano teachers in New Orleans, he had been sent off on a sailing ship to France under the care of the captain.

With all its historic and old family ties with France, its French-speaking population, its French food, and French ways, New Orleans had a natural affinity with Paris. Many in New Orleans felt a far closer kinship to Paris than to any city other than their own. Well-to-do Creole families frequently sent their children to be educated there. Or they themselves took an extended turn at *la vie parisienne*. One immensely wealthy young woman from New Orleans, Micaela Almonaster y Rojas, had moved to Paris following her marriage to her cousin Celestin de Pontalba, and wound up at the center of a sensational incident that would be gossiped about in Paris and New Orleans for generations. In 1834 in Paris, her father-in-law had tried to kill her—apparently in the hope of inheriting her money—by shooting her point-blank with dueling pistols. Two balls lodged in her breast; another destroyed part of her left hand. When she managed to escape to another room, he turned and killed himself. Miraculously she survived, and not long afterward, to let there be no doubt about her financial position, or her intention to stay in Paris, she built one of the city's most glorious mansions, on the rue du Faubourg Saint-Honoré, which would one day, in another era, become the official residence of American ambassadors to France.

Young Moreau was enrolled in a private boarding school run by a couple named Dussert in their apartment. Already fluent in French and eager to learn, the boy did well in all the usual studies, but so excelled at the piano as to draw attention almost at once. The Dusserts arranged for him to meet Sigmund Thalberg, who, after hearing Moreau play, took him by the hand saying, "This child is surprising." Meanwhile, Moreau's father, who had endless troubles staying solvent, assured him he could meet all the expenses of Paris, which were not inconsiderable, given that the boy liked fine clothes and had already, at age thirteen, arranged to have his portrait painted. The work, by an artist named J. Berville, showed a long-haired youth with wide-set, wistful dark eyes, holding a quill pen and a sheet of music and looking lost in thought.

Moreau had been in Paris three years when, in the fall of 1844, his mother and her five younger children arrived for an extended stay. Aimee Gottschalk was all of thirty-one, fond of society and elegant comforts, and ready to make the most of Paris. In a way, the evening of April 2 was to be her debut as well.

For a piano prodigy especially, Paris just then was the ideal place and time to be heard. It had supplanted Vienna as the musical capital of Europe, and never had the piano, or any musical instrument, been so popular. According to one study there were as many as 60,000 pianos in the city and some 100,000 people who could play them. If this was so, then approximately a third of the youth in Paris were playing, or attempting to play, the piano. Virtuoso pianists and composers like Thalberg, Chopin, Franz Liszt, and Hector Berlioz were at the height of their popularity, as brilliant as any stars in the Paris firmament. Chopin in particular, with his music and his celebrated love affair with George Sand, had become the very embodiment of artistic genius and the romantic spirit. To young Moreau, Chopin outshone them all.

Musical prodigies were not uncommon in Paris—they were even something of a tradition—but Moreau was an *American* prodigy, and that was new.

His debut at the Salle Pleyel was with full orchestra and he opened the program with Chopin's Concerto in E Minor. Then followed compositions by both Thalberg and Liszt, and the burst of applause at the end left no doubt that he had more than lived up to expectations.

Chopin himself came backstage afterward. Greeting Moreau, according to one account, he exclaimed in French, "Good, my child, good, very good. Let me shake your hand once more." But Moreau's sister Clara would later say Chopin had placed his hands on the boy's head, as though conferring a benediction, and said, "I predict that you will become the king of pianists."

La Revue Musicale praised the young American for "the neatness and elegance of his playing," and predicted that in time to come his fame would equal that of any pianist. Back home the *New Orleans Courier* reported on the front page that 1,200 people belonging "chiefly to the upper ranks of society" had been in attendance and that a "glorious future" was in store for "this young and interesting child of Louisiana." A brilliant career had been launched in memorable fashion.

Midway into April, three weeks or so after the premiere appearance of General Tom Thumb at the Salle de Concert, and two weeks following the Gottschalk debut, George Catlin and his party of Iowa Indians took up residence at the Victoria Hotel on the rue Chauveau-Lagarde, just behind the Church of the Madeleine. Besides the more than five hundred paintings of his Indian Gallery, Catlin had brought with him an enormous collection of Indian artifacts—tomahawks, scalping knives, rattles, drums, skulls, cooking utensils, and four complete wigwams—making altogether eight tons of paintings and artifacts packed in giant crates.

Catlin's story was like that of no other American artist. A sturdy, clean-shaven, rather stern-looking man of medium height and with a granite set to his jaw, he was part painter, part scholar, part explorer, dreamer, entrepreneur, and showman. He had been born in Pennsylvania, started out to be a lawyer, then quit to paint, specializing at first in miniature portraits. Still, like Samuel Morse, he had longed to be a history painter. When in Philadelphia he saw a visiting delegation of western Indians in full regalia, it was, as he said, enough to inspire "a whole lifetime of enthusiasm."

In 1832, as cholera raged in Paris and Morse was laboring on his *Gallery of the Louvre*, James Fenimore Cooper faithfully keeping him company, George Catlin, at age thirty-six, had been on his way up the

Missouri River. His courageous mission, to record "a vast country of green fields, where men are all red," had been influenced almost certainly by Cooper's Leatherstocking Tales, and *The Prairie* especially. Over a stretch of nearly eight years, traveling by steamboat, canoe, and horseback, and often alone, Catlin studied and lived with and painted forty-five of the tribes of the Great Plains. He had gone up the Missouri as far north as Fort Union and down the Mississippi all the way to New Orleans. No artist had attempted the subject on such a scale or kept at it so long or with such intense commitment. He painted portraits, landscapes, scenes of buffalo hunts, violent Indian games, and religious ceremonies— "the proud and heroic elegance of savage society, in a state of pure and original nature, beyond the reach of civilization," as he put it. He knew there was little time left before a whole way of life would vanish, corrupted or altogether destroyed, and which he was determined to "rescue from oblivion" with his brush and pen. He also hoped to make himself famous and earn a living sufficient to support his wife, Clara, and their children.

At no point had Catlin benefited from government or private support for his mission. In 1839 he offered his entire collection for purchase by the United States government, but to no avail. So he sailed for England, taking the collection with him, hoping for better luck. Clara and the children would follow later.

The paintings went on display at London's Egyptian Hall in Piccadilly. Catlin gave lectures, and for added effect often dressed as an Indian. He took the paintings on tour to other cities, all the while going deeper in debt. When two or three delegations of Ojibwas and Iowas showed up in London of their own accord, intending to exhibit themselves, Catlin invited them to join him and strongly resented—then and later—those who denounced him for exploiting the Indians.

The "real" Indians added greatly to the show. Their translator, Jeffrey Doraway, also became part of the company, and Catlin enlarged the gallery by doing portraits and drawings of each of the Iowas. When the Ojibwas announced they had had enough of London and sailed for home, Catlin, who had been in England for years, decided it was time to move the whole enterprise to Paris. His family, meanwhile, had also become part of the entourage. What kind of reception he expected to receive in Paris is not known.

It was well after dark when they reached their hotel. Not until the next morning did the Iowas, leaning from their windows as far as they dared, get a first real look at the city, and the spectacle of so many red painted and crested heads on high, greeting the start of the day, quickly drew an excited crowd in the street below.

> The servants in the house were at first alarmed [Catlin wrote], and the good landlady smiled at their unexpected appearance, and she roared with laughter when she was informed that the beds were removed from their rooms, that they spread their own robes and, in preference, slept upon the floor. All in the house, however, got attached to them in a few days.

Climbing aboard an omnibus, they toured the city, rolled by the Tuileries Palace, the Louvre, crossed over the Seine and back on the Pont Neuf, and wound up at the Hôtel de Ville—City Hall—where several thousand people were waiting for a glimpse. "There was a great outcry when they landed and entered the hall, and the crowd was sure not to diminish whilst they were within," wrote Catlin, thrilled by the reception. Inside, champagne was uncorked and the *préfet de police* presented the chief of the Iowa delegation, Mew-hew-she-kaw—White Cloud—with a silver medal.

"My father," responded White Cloud in a brief speech, "we were astonished at what we saw in London, where we have been, but we think your village is much the most beautiful."

Others in the delegation included Ruton-ye-we-ma—Strutting Pigeon—the wife of White Cloud; Se-non-ty-yah—Little Wolf—a warrior; his wife, O-kee-wee-me—Female Bear that Walks on the Back of Another—and their infant daughter, wrapped in a papoose. In all there were seven men and a boy, four women and two infant girls. Their daily itinerary, their names and appearance, were news everywhere.

The Iowas, reported *Galignani's Messenger*, were "of fine stature, pleasing features, and mild manners," inferring that no one need be afraid.

Phrenologically they have all the indications of superior faculties. They are a deep copper color inclining to red, but with
features many Europeans might envy. Their costumes are picturesque and even elegant. They appear devotedly attached
to their chief, and are in their own way exceedingly religious,
never partaking of food without praying for the blessings of
the great spirit, and returning thanks for the benefits they receive.

While the Indians continued their sightseeing, drawing crowds at
every stop, Catlin moved his exhibition into the cavernous Salle Valentino on the rue du Faubourg Saint-Honoré. The paintings were put up side
by side, filling every foot of wall space. One of the strongest, most vivid of
the portraits was that of Little Wolf, his face painted bright red, his eyes,
nose, and mouth encircled by a band of orange and green, his shoulders all
but concealed under a heavy necklace of giant grizzly bear claws, beside
which the presidential gold medal he wore looked all but lost. In another
portrait a Mandan chief, Four Bears, stood proudly in full regalia, a magnificent headdress of eagle feathers reaching to the ground, his long deerskin shirt decorated with accounts of his bravery in war. Describing Four
Bears arriving the day of his first sitting for the painting, Catlin had said,
"No tragedian ever trod the stage, nor gladiator ever entered the Roman
Forum, with more grace and manly dignity. . . ."

There was a portrait of a handsome Cheyenne woman, She Who
Bathes Her Knees, wearing a dress of mountain sheepskins embroidered
with beautiful blue quillwork, but also scenes of gruesome self-torture
ceremonies, war dances, scalp dances, a dying buffalo in its agony, bright
red blood spurting from its wounds, and a tallgrass prairie ablaze, the
swirling black sky above brushed on by Catlin with fitting fury.

At the center of the gallery, to help set the scene, he had placed a huge
Crow wigwam. When he said later that Paris had never seen an exhibition
remotely like it, he was by no means exaggerating.

Of the many notables of the day—members of the king's inner circle,
eminent scientists, writers, painters, newspaper publishers—who were
captivated by Catlin's paintings and the contingent of Iowas, none re-

sponded with such spontaneous interest or obvious pleasure as the king himself. Louis-Philippe, Queen Marie-Amélie, and the royal family received the Americans at the Tuileries Palace on the afternoon of April 22, 1845, the Iowas, as Catlin noted proudly, "in a full blaze of color . . .

> all with their wampum and medals on, with their necklaces of grizzly bear claws, their shields and bows and quivers, their lances and war clubs, and tomahawks and scalping knives . . . their painted buffalo robes wrapped around them. . . .

Louis-Philippe, "in the most free and familiar manner," launched at once into conversation in English—with Jeffrey Doraway translating—about his own experiences in America, only this time with even greater enthusiasm than usual and to the delight of his guests from the Great Plains.

"Tell these good fellows I am glad to see them," he said by way of greeting, "that I have been in many of the wigwams of Indians of America when I was a young man, and they treated me everywhere kindly, and I love them for it."

He talked of his adventures in the American wilderness half a century before as though it had been only the other day. "Tell them I was amongst the Senecas near Buffalo . . . in the wigwams of the chiefs—that I was amongst the Shawnees and Delawares on the Ohio."

In the winter of 1797–98, Louis-Philippe and his two younger brothers, on their own, starting from Pittsburgh, had descended the length of the Ohio River to the Mississippi in a small boat, then continued down the Mississippi all the way to New Orleans, just as Catlin had. He, too, had been the guest of Cherokees, Chickasaws, and Choctaws, smoked a friendly pipe, and learned some of their language.

"This," wrote Catlin, "made the Indians stare, and the women, by a custom of their country, placed their hands over their mouths, as they issued groans of surprise."

"Tell them also, Jeffrey, that I am pleased to see their wives and children they have with them here, and glad also to show them my family, who are now nearly all around me," said Louis-Philippe, who then introduced, one by one, his wife, sister, two sons and their wives, and two grandsons.

With ceremony befitting a head of state, the king then presented a gold medal to Chief White Cloud, and silver medals to each of the warriors. Then everyone moved to the grand ballroom, where the Indians, seating themselves in the center of the floor, began singing and beating drums, then broke into an eagle dance, flailing their weapons.

The dance ended with resounding applause, and the Iowas resumed their sitting positions. Then the drums beat again, and louder now and with increased tempo. Little Wolf, throwing aside his buffalo robe, sprang from the floor with his tomahawk and shield, "and sounding the frightful war-whoop, which called his warriors around him," as Catlin wrote.

> Nothing could have been more thrilling or picturesque than the scene at the moment presented of this huge and terrible-looking warrior, frowning death and destruction on his brow, as he brandished the very weapons he had used in deadly combat, and in his jumps and sudden starts, seemed threatening with instant use again! The floors and ceilings of the Palace shook with the weight of their steps, and its long halls echoed and vibrated the shrill-sounding notes of the war-whoop.

Suddenly Little Wolf stopped, and shaking the tomahawk overhead, ordered the others to stop. He advanced toward the king.

> My Great Father [he said], I present to you my tomahawk with which I killed one of my enemies . . . and you see the blood remaining on its blade. . . . My Father, since we came among the white people, we have been convinced that peace is better than war, and I place the tomahawk in your hands—I fight no more.

As he watched from the side, Catlin kept thinking of how this king in his life, in his journey down the Ohio and Mississippi, had seen more of the great western regions of America, and the ways of its people, than all but one in a thousand Americans ever had or would. (Alexis de Tocqueville, as recently as 1835, in the first volume of his *Democracy in America*, had described the Mississippi as "the most magnificent place God ever prepared for men to dwell in," but reminded his readers it was still "a vast wilderness.")

Catlin admired, even revered, the king, in a way few other Americans could have, knowing as he did what such adventures demanded in "energy of character and skill." And here he was, the king of the French, "taking the poor Indians of the forest by the hand in his palace, and expressing to them the gratitude he had never lost sight of. . . ."

Such thoughts were rapid, Catlin wrote, but often recurring during his solitary walks in Paris.

> In the midst of such reflections I often strolled along in a contemplative mood through the wilderness throngs of boulevards, the central avenue and crossing-place—the aorta of all the circulating world—to gaze upon the endless throng of human beings sweeping by me, bent upon their peculiar avocations of business or pleasure, of virtue or of vice, contrasting the glittering views about me with the quiet and humble scenes I had witnessed in various parts of my roaming life.
>
> In the midst of this sweeping throng, knowing none and unknown, I found I could almost imagine myself in the desert wilderness, with as little to disturb the current of contemplative thoughts as if I were floating down the gliding current of the Missouri in my bark canoe. . . .

Long descriptive accounts of the Iowas at the Tuileries Palace appeared in the Paris papers, but when Catlin opened his Indian Gallery, or Museum, at the Salle Valentino a few days later, the exhibition was not as well attended as hoped, nothing like the continuing clamor over Tom Thumb, who by this time was appearing nightly at the Théâtre du Vaudeville. Soon, though, as noted in *Galignani's Messenger*, the exhibition was attracting "crowds of savants and others," and by late May the paintings and the dances of the Iowas were "drawing full and fashionable audiences," both in the afternoons and evenings.

It was not only the subject matter of Catlin's paintings that appealed, but the direct strength of his work, the raw color and a simplicity of form verging on naïve. The paintings had much the same fascination for the French as the Indian tales by James Fenimore Cooper. This was the America they imagined, "wild America," and that they found almost irresistible. The Iowas themselves, said the *Journal des Débats*, seemed to have come to Paris "for the very purpose of serving as living commentary to the well-known novels of the famous Cooper."

The old yearning among the French intelligentsia for the primitive and exotic, the Romantic idolization of the unspoiled "natural man" that began with Rousseau, had much to do with the response, particularly among writers and artists. In the early 1830s, at the time Catlin was out on the Great Plains, Eugène Delacroix had been in Morocco sketching and painting Arab chieftains and lion hunts, and Delacroix was among those who now spoke in praise of Catlin, *le peintre américain*. George Sand described how the whole combination of the paintings, the artifacts, and then the dances had gripped her as nothing in her experience.

> At first, I felt the most violent and unpleasant emotion that any show has ever given me. I had just seen all the frightening objects of the Catlin Museum, primitive tomahawks . . . flattened and deformed skulls spread on a table, of which several showed the mark of a scalp, bloody spoils of war, repulsive masks, paintings showing hideous scenes of the initiation to mysteries, extreme corporal punishments, tortures, great hunts, murderous fights. . . . When the noise of sleigh bells which seemed to be announcing the coming of a herd of cattle told me to run for my seat, I was ready to be frightened, and when I saw appear in the flesh these painted faces, some blood red as if they were seen through a flame . . . these half nude bodies, magnificent models of statuary, but also painted

in many colors . . . these bear claw necklaces which seem to tear the torso of those wearing them . . . I admit that I started being afraid and my imagination took me to the most lugubrious scenes of *The Last of the Mohicans*. It was even worse when the savage music gave the signal for the war dance.

With the roar and commotion, the "delirious rage" of the dance under way, she became utterly terrified. "I was in a cold sweat, I thought I was going to witness a real scalping of some vanquished enemy or a scene of torture which would be even more horrible."

The carefree Parisian audience, who has fun being surprised, laughed around me, and this laughter seemed to me that of the spirit of darkness. I came to my senses only when the dance stopped and the Indians were again, as if by miracle, showing this expression of simple good-heartedness and cordiality which makes them look like better men than us.

So moved was she by the whole show, she went back the next day, bringing several others. She was sure Catlin's paintings were far more important than the public realized, and Victor Hugo and Charles Baudelaire were of like mind.

Baudelaire, as important as any French critic, loved especially Catlin's portrait of Little Wolf and another of a Blackfoot chief, Buffalo Bull's Back Fat, for the way Catlin had captured "the proud, free character and noble expression of these splendid fellows." As for Catlin's color, something of the mysterious about it delighted him. Red, "the color of blood, the color of life," abounded and the green of wooded mountains and immense grass plains. "I find them again singing their melodic antiphon of the very faces of these two heroes."

The Catlin Indian Gallery, said a review in the *Constitutionnel*, was "one of the most curious collections that has ever been seen in Paris, as much because of the naïve character of the painting style as because of the originality of what it represents." Still, the American painter's lack of skill and finesse, the review continued, made it especially arresting.

Mr. Catlin paints quietly from the start, by placing one color which is right and pure next to the other, and it doesn't seem he goes back over his work either through glazing or impasting. But his feeling is so deep and in some ways so sincere, his execution so naïve and so spontaneous, that the effect, rightly seen, is rightly expressed.

Seeing the collection, said another journal, the *Observateur*, one found it hard to believe it was all the work of just one man. Catlin was compared to Herodotus in his journeys to chronicle remote peoples, praised for his "remarkable power" as a lecturer. Knowing little French, he spoke in English only and his manner was described as "coldly polite, his face severe and thoughtful, like the face of a man who has seen many things."

The approval was far more glowing and emphatic than what Catlin received in London, and further, the time in Britain had been cast in shadow toward the end by a death among the Iowas. The infant daughter of Little Wolf and Female Bear that Walks on the Back of Another had died during a visit by the whole company to Scotland. And so the responses of Paris meant that much more.

But just as all seemed to be going so right in Paris, Little Wolf's wife herself suddenly and unexpectedly died of tuberculosis. She was buried in the cemetery of Montmartre and Little Wolf, shattered, "heartbroken," went every day to sit by her grave. The story was in all the papers and talked about everywhere. Chopin mentioned her in a letter to his family that summer.

Having had enough, the Iowas were soon packed and on their way home.

Catlin and his family had only just moved to new quarters on the avenue Lord Byron when Clara Catlin took ill with what at first seemed no more than the usual sore throat. But rapidly "her feeble form wasted away," as Catlin wrote, and on July 28, 1845, Clara died of pneumonia.

In the midst of his grief Catlin arranged for her remains to be shipped home for burial and did all he could to console the children. He and Clara had talked of leaving Paris, and Catlin was inclined now to go as soon as his lease on the Salle Valentino expired. His expenses were high, his debts increasing. But when a party of Canadian Ojibwas turned up, having heard of the Paris success of the Iowas, and were ready to take their place, Catlin decided to stay.

Still more acclaim followed. Louis-Philippe conferred what to some was the ultimate recognition by having Catlin's entire collection temporarily installed in a gallery at the Louvre, so that he and his family might enjoy it privately. This would have been a rare honor for any artist, let alone one from America. Moreover, Louis-Philippe asked Catlin to copy fifteen of the works for his gallery at Versailles.

Neither P. T. Barnum nor Tom Thumb, nor Moreau Gottschalk, nor George Catlin, was in any hurry to leave Paris and return home that fall of 1845. Ever the showman, Barnum felt he had been born to play the part of a Paris bon vivant. He relished French cuisine, the theater, the opera, and strolling the boulevards. Barnum would speak later of his extended stay in Paris as the happiest time in his life.

Moreau Gottschalk, who grew increasingly handsome and was always the perfect young gentleman, continued to be embraced by the *monde musical*. He became something of a fashion plate and began performing his own compositions, based on Creole melodies he had heard in childhood. Two in particular, "Bamboula" and "La Savane," first performed in Paris a few years later, were to make him famous and beloved on both sides of the Atlantic. In one three-year period he would give 1,100 concerts in the United States and Canada. He toured California and Central America. Then, on tour in Brazil in 1869, he suddenly took ill and died at age forty.

George Catlin, still in mourning over the loss of his wife, "retired" to his Paris apartment to concentrate on his work and look after his children, three girls and a boy ranging in age from three to ten. "I thus painted on," he wrote, "dividing my time between my easel and my little children . . . resolving and re-resolving to devote the remainder of my life to my art. . . ."

Catlin's Indian exhibition, which had been moved from the Louvre to the Galerie des Beaux-Arts on the boulevard Bonne-Nouvelle, closed at last at the end of June. Catlin kept at his easel, turning out one Indian portrait or scene after another. Before leaving Paris he would produce more than fifty such pictures, largely out of economic necessity. If ever he considered other subjects for a change, a Paris view perhaps, or considered doing a copy at the Louvre, there is no sign of it.

In the summer of 1846, tragedy struck again. All four of Catlin's children were stricken by typhoid fever. "My occupation was changed to their bedsides, where they were all together writhing in the agonies of the disease." The three little girls survived, but the youngest, his son, George, did not. Still, Catlin stayed on in Paris nearly a year longer and with no letup in his work.

The ever-persistent Samuel Morse, now known as "the Lightning Man," was also in Paris once more, having arrived in the fall of 1845, still in quest of a patent from the French. Yet again he faced disappointment. His friend and still ardent supporter Dominique Arago presented him to the Chamber of Deputies, where, after demonstrating his telegraph, Morse was generously acclaimed. But as would be said, he came away loaded with honor and nothing more.

George Healy did not return to Paris until the following year, 1846, and in less than six months he was on his way back to the United States. Expecting to stay longer this time, he took his wife, Louisa, with him. The children, who now included another daughter, Mary, were left in the care of Louisa's mother. His mission was to gather material for a major painting he was determined to undertake portraying Daniel Webster at the summit of his oratorical powers, delivering his famous reply to Robert Y. Hayne in the Senate in 1830. By the time Healy returned to Paris, his generous client, the king of France, would be gone and prospects quite uncertain.

CHAPTER SIX

CHANGE AT HAND

How then can strangers hope to look
into the veiled future of France?

—RICHARD RUSH

I

The new American minister had no sooner landed at Le Havre than he began hearing how unpopular the king and his government were. It was not what he had expected, and at Paris expressions of discontent and accusations "increased a hundred fold," as he reported. The papers poured "daily fire" on nearly every public measure, their hostility coupled always with distrust of Louis-Philippe. He was accused of being selfish, crafty, senile, of breaking promises, of neglecting his duties to the nation. And all this seemed completely at odds with what the previous American minister, Lewis Cass, had had to say, and, for that matter, the impression one received from nearly every American who had spent any time with Louis-Philippe.

The post of minister to France was one Richard Rush had neither expected nor sought, but for which he was eminently qualified. In a long career in public service he had distinguished himself as attorney general of Pennsylvania (at age thirty-one), attorney general of the United States (at thirty-three), secretary of state, and then minister to the Court of St. James's, where, facing a variety of critical disputes, he proved firm and candid while creating no ill will. In four years as secretary of the treasury under President John Quincy Adams, he had never missed a day on the job. When, as Adams's running mate in the election of 1828, they went down to defeat against Andrew Jackson, he quietly retired to private life. Yet even then he continued to serve, settling boundary disputes and securing the bequest from the Englishman James Smithson that made possible the establishment of the Smithsonian Institution.

Minister Rush had as well the advantage of a distinguished name. His father, Dr. Benjamin Rush, a Philadelphia physician, had been a signer of the Declaration of Independence. Like his father, he was a man of wide intellectual interests, and at sixty-seven he was still impressively handsome, with penetrating blue eyes and a high, broad forehead. In all, he was as well suited to his new assignment as any American envoy since Jefferson. His one obvious deficiency was that he did not speak French.

Rush reached Paris in mid-July 1847, accompanied by two of his ten children, daughters Anna Marie and Sarah Catherine, who were both in their twenties. Their mother, suffering from poor health, had remained behind in Philadelphia. Rooms had been arranged at the Hôtel Windsor on the rue de Rivoli until a suitable residence could be found at a rent he could afford. Unlike his predecessor Cass, Rush was not a wealthy man.

On the afternoon of July 31 he made his first official call on the king, to present a "Letter of Credence" from President James K. Polk and deliver a brief statement about the honor of representing his country to France. The king responded in kind and in perfect English. The ceremony over, the king asked him to return for an informal dinner that evening.

By September, Rush had found a "sufficiently grand" house on the rue de Lille in the Faubourg Saint-Germain. He felt obliged to hire a carriage and a few servants as well, but only, he wrote, because they were essential to the role he must play.

> I am representing a great nation at a great court. I cannot live
> like a curmudgeon or mechanic, but must live like a gentle-
> man and foreign minister. . . . Still, I hope to meet it all if pos-

sible with the seven thousand dollars . . . the struggle will be severe. . . .

In a short time he was on cordial terms with both Louis-Philippe and the formidable foreign minister, François Guizot, careful always to take no sides in discussions concerning French politics. He saw the king often and conversed on a range of topics. He called frequently on Guizot and attended the requisite diplomatic receptions and dinners, where he kept seeing Baron von Humboldt, who, at nearly eighty and gregarious as always, happily recalled dining at the Rush home in Philadelphia when Richard was a boy. All in all, to judge by his diary, Rush was having a grand time, his deficiency in French and financial concerns notwithstanding.

> Last night we were at Mr. Walsh's [Robert Walsh, the American consul in Paris]. The party was large. Among those present were the venerable Humboldt . . . M. de Tocqueville . . . some of the DeKalb family whose French ancestors rendered gallant services in our Revolution, and others of note in French society. Many of our own country, including ladies, were there. . . . There was much intellectual conversation, and much that was sprightly, with music at intervals.

Yet he was troubled, as so many were, by the growing political unrest. Reform banquets, as they were called, had become the unofficial gathering places for those most vociferously critical of the king. At one such event held at the Château Rouge outside the city, more than a thousand people turned out, including members of the Chamber of Deputies. The old "Marseillaise" was sung and nearly every act of government since 1830 vigorously denounced.

Were the grievances real, Rush wondered. To judge by "the appearance of things," France was full of prosperity and contentment, he wrote to Secretary of State James Buchanan on September 24, 1847. "Production is everywhere increasing. Tranquility everywhere prevails." Were Napoleon to come back again, "he would hardly know the Paris he left, so much has it advanced in size, commerce, beauty, and above all, cleanliness."

Taxes were high, to be sure, but no higher proportionately than any other European power. For a king, Louis-Philippe lived quite modestly. To be both a king and a republican on the same throne was difficult, Rush acknowledged. The only explanation he had for such simmering hostility and unrest was the French themselves. They were always excitable. "They will find fault with their rulers when there is cause and when there is not."

These were "loose thoughts" only, Rush cautioned. "They are thrown out with the distrust which my short residence and limited opportunities of authentic information and observation up to this date ought to inspire."

As for Louis-Philippe, he seemed as active and involved as ever, but looked tired and was often irritable. The death of a beloved sister, Adélaïde, had hit him hard. Further, and as Rush did not mention, predictions of the king's downfall had been voiced for years and from many quarters. James Fenimore Cooper had long thought the king would be forced to "decamp." Writing from Cooperstown only that fall, Cooper told a friend that all Europe was on the verge of "serious troubles," and Louis-Philippe could well be on the way out.

In response to such forewarnings as he heard, the king himself observed that the people of Paris were not given to revolutions in winter.

With the new year under way, the Paris papers were calling the discontentment in the country "profound and universal." Still, Rush sensed nothing to be alarmed about. "Notwithstanding all the reform banquets, I see no present prospect of a change," he reported to Washington on January 22, 1848.

A week later, Alexis de Tocqueville warned his fellow members of the Chamber of Deputies, "We are sleeping on a volcano."

On February 20, in fear of a revolt, the deputies and the government canceled a reform banquet scheduled for two days later. At once a great public clamor erupted. The whole issue had become "formidable," Rush wrote privately to his family.

What followed happened with a speed no one foresaw.

On February 22, crowds marched and barricades went up in the streets to stall the advance of troops. The day after, still larger crowds turned angry, looting shops and throwing up more barricades. That night, full-scale riots broke out. When confronted by a line of troops stationed outside the residence of Foreign Secretary Guizot, the mob kept coming. A sergeant fired a shot. Then the rest of the soldiers opened fire, killing or wounding 50 people.

An American student named Richard Morris Hunt, who had been swept along with the crowd near Guizot's house, wrote afterward of how people kept pressing the soldiers from all sides.

> We were too near to be pleasant, we saw the flash and we heard the noise of guns. For a moment we thought it was fireworks. We were pushed on by the crowd . . . and on and on, stopped from time to time by soldiers who will not let us advance. We cannot believe that they have drawn on the people.

Hundreds of the National Guard joined the insurgents and through the night church bells tolled across the city. At the Palace of the Tuileries an exhausted Louis-Philippe kept saying over and over, "I have seen enough blood."

The following morning, Thursday, February 24, shaken by all that had happened and refusing to order further bloodshed, Louis-Philippe abdicated.

He and his wife fled out a side door and through the Garden of the Tuileries to a waiting carriage. After a breakneck ride out of Paris to Le Havre, and a day or two in hiding, Louis-Philippe and Marie-Amélie— "Mr. and Mrs. William Smith"—crossed the Channel to refuge in England.

Thus ended the eighteen-year reign of the last king of the French.

Shortly after his arrival in England, Queen Victoria wrote in a letter to old Lord Melbourne:

> The poor King and his government made many mistakes within the last two years, and were obstinate and totally blind at the last till flight was inevitable. But for *sixteen years* he did

a great deal to maintain peace and made France prosperous,
which should *not* be forgotten. . . .

Louis-Philippe would die in exile at Claremont, Surrey, two years later
in 1850, at age seventy-seven.

———

On the fateful morning of Thursday the twenty-fourth, at his desk on the
rue de Lille, Richard Rush had dashed off a letter to Secretary Buchanan
reporting all he then knew of the riots and the lives lost the day before,
and to say "general confusion [and] uncertainty" still prevailed. "Even
now . . . cavalry are hastily passing through streets within my hearing,
and my servants bring in rumors that the King has abdicated. . . ."

What he did not yet know was that the mobs, delirious with success,
had marched on the Palace of the Tuileries, broken in, and gutted it. Furniture and clothing were thrown down from the windows and burned in
the garden. The king's throne was carried off to be paraded through the
streets as the ultimate symbol of triumph before it, too, was burned.

A week later Rush had more to report. On the evening the king made
his escape, a new government had sprung into being as suddenly as the
old monarchy had fallen, the provisional government of a republic char-
acterized so far by "moderation and magnanimity." But "foremost of all"
in what he had to report was that he, as the American minister, "acting
under a sense of independent duty in the emergency," had taken it upon
himself to recognize the new government without delay.

It was a momentous step. "I shall remain inexpressibly anxious until I
know it will be officially received at home," he wrote. "The responsibilities
of my public station were upon me. What would my country expect from
me? And what did I owe to my country under this emergency?"

He had never viewed Louis-Philippe and his government as did the
French opposition, and he prided himself in having remained aloof from
political conflicts. To have done otherwise would have been improper.
"But the French people were themselves the arbiters of the conduct of
their government, and the sole judges of what form of government they
would have."

Paris had quickly returned to life as usual. It was hard to believe. Shops and theaters reopened. People were out and about their business, as though nothing had happened. The new government seemed to be exercising its power appropriately, and no one was moving against it. Two months might pass before news of the abdication reached Washington and Rush received his instructions in response. What was he to do? "Was it for me to be backward when France appeared to be looking to us?"

At two o'clock in the afternoon on Monday, February 28, in formal diplomatic attire, he appeared at the Hôtel de Ville, headquarters of the new government. A great crowd was gathered outside. Once inside, having been formally presented, he delivered his address, saying:

> As representative of the United States, and charged with the interests and rights of my country, and my fellow citizens residing in France, and too far off to wait for instructions, I seize on the first opportunity to offer you my felicitations, persuaded that my government will sanction the course I thus adopt. Nor can I either fail to state to you that the remembrance of the alliance and ancient friendship which have joined together France and the United States is still living and in full force among us.

Cries of *"Vive la République des États-Unis"* went up among those gathered inside and out.

None of the European diplomatic corps had made such a move. The United States was first and alone in recognizing the new republic. The rest were awaiting instructions.

In Washington, Rush's decisive role was roundly approved. President Polk assured Congress that the American minister to France had his "full and unqualified approbation."

Paris continued "wonderfully, miraculously tranquil." Elections to the National Assembly went ahead in perfect order. Visitors were returning to the city. The weather in late April and early May was as lovely as ever at that time of year. Back for another visit, Ralph Waldo Emerson wrote of the timeless beauty of scenes along the Seine, the "very civil and good tempered, polite and joyous" people of Paris.

Americans had long since read in *Galignani's Guide* that the volatile populace of the city was easily led into "criminal excesses," but also quick to recover, ever eager in the pursuit of pleasure. "Living entirely for the present, the Parisian soon forgets his afflictions, consoles himself with the amusements of the day, and is too gay to think of the future." The one disturbing note to Emerson was the great number of trees that had been cut down during the February uprising to build barricades.

But, appearances and guidebooks to the contrary, all was not well. A government program of national workshops to provide bread and work for the unemployed had problems from the start. As Rush explained in a long report:

> They did not and could not employ everybody. . . . The work was ill-done into the bargain, whilst the accumulating over-surplus of workmen who could not be employed at all were thrown as a charity upon the government. . . . This made up a heavy aggregate of expense to the government without satis-fying the workmen. The consequence was discontent among the whole of them.

Unemployment grew steadily worse. Tens of thousands had no jobs and were suffering dreadfully, many starving. Children were starving. In the meantime, revolutionary fervor and violence were spreading rapidly across Europe, in Germany, Italy, and Poland.

Emerson departed on June 3. On June 23, riots in Paris flared into a full-scale, raging insurrection.

By decree the National Assembly conferred supreme authority—unlimited power—on the minister of war, General Louis-Eugène Cavai-gnac. Paris was declared in a state of siege and an additional 30,000 troops were rushed in from outside the city. The fighting turned savage, and General Cavaignac responded with brutal force, ordering the use of can-non and bayonet, and refusing to give the least quarter to the insurgents.

The archbishop of Paris, Denis Affre, asked permission to go himself to the scene of the worst of the fighting, to try to mediate. "On his way he passed my door in his full clerical robes," wrote Rush. When the archbishop climbed a barricade in clear view, the firing stopped for an instant on both sides, and then he was shot. He died the next day.

The "June Days of 1848," as they were to be known, numbered four. "So vast and horrible a desolation wrought in the heart of a city by the hands of her own citizens the world has not witnessed," reported the New York and London papers. Possibly as many as 5,000 were killed, including some 1,200 soldiers. Another 11,000 were arrested and thousands of these would be shipped off to Algeria. It made what happened in February seem only a minor disturbance.

(A young German writer and professed communist, Karl Marx, who had been living in Paris until ordered to leave a few years before, wrote that the February revolution was the "*beautiful* revolution," the one in June, the "*ugly* revolution, the repulsive revolution.")

With the fighting ended, Rush, like thousands of others, set off to view the "battlefield," to find that, the battlefield being Paris, the dead and wounded had been taken away as they fell. Only the barricades and houses shattered by cannonballs or riddled by musket fire stood as evidence of the havoc and slaughter. The great boulevards looked like abandoned encampments. "Scattered wisps of hay and the litter of cavalry, horses tied to iron palisades, detachments of infantry, their arms stacked, the men lying down on straw, looking jaded, some asleep . . . such is the picture of these streets now," wrote Rush.

What would come of it all was impossible for him to predict, knowing how much he had failed to foresee since his arrival.

> None can understand a country or have full claim to speak of its future, but those who belong to it, or live in it long enough to catch its whole genius and characteristics. . . . How then can strangers hope to look into the veiled future of France?

Though the official state of siege would not be lifted until October, and thousands of troops remained a conspicuous presence, daily life resumed again and at a quickening pace. The National Assembly opened, and Rush found himself back playing his part at diplomatic receptions or dining in splendor with the president of the assembly and members of the cabinet.

In November the first snow fell, whitening all of Paris. On December 10, the election for the first president of the Republic took place, and the winner by an enormous margin was Prince Louis Napoleon, who was hardly more than a name to most of the country, but the name was quite enough. He was opposed by General Cavaignac and the poet and politician Alphonse de Lamartine. Of the more than seven million votes cast, Louis Napoleon won over 5 million.

On New Year's Day, 1849, the new president moved into the Palais de l'Élysée on the rue du Faubourg Saint-Honoré. Though more modest than the Palace of the Tuileries, and a bit shabby, the Élysée, as everyone knew, had been a favorite residence of the Emperor Napoleon. At a first grand ball at the Élysée in February, it was taken as no small matter that the servants were wearing the green and gold livery of the emperor.

II

The flow of Americans into Paris continued all the while, their numbers including the usual range in age, vocation, interests, social standing, purpose, and wherewithal—students, journalists, writers, social reformers, salesmen, merchants, tourists, the young, the old, the ambitious, the indisposed, the idle rich. But there was a notable change to be seen in the increasing number of American women. One of these, a New York literary critic and ardent feminist named Margaret Fuller, decided all who came to Paris from her country could be classified in three distinct "species."

The first she called the "servile" American, whom she considered "utterly shallow," all but worthless.

> He comes abroad to spend his money and indulge his tastes.
> His object in Europe is to have fashionable clothes, good foreign cookery, to know some titled persons, and furnish himself with coffee house gossip. . . .

Then there was the conceited American, "instinctively bustling and proud of he knows not what" and "profoundly ignorant." Still, she thought this a creature not without hope.

And third was the artist, the "thinking American," the one she approved of and with whom she felt a common bond.

> [He] recognized the immense advantage of being born to a new world . . . yet does not wish the seed from the past to be lost. He is anxious to gather and carry back with him every plant that will bear a new climate and a new culture. . . .

But plainly there were new arrivals distinctively different from any who preceded them and who would make way for others like them to follow. And Margaret Fuller was herself of this different variety, in that she was the first American woman of great talent as a professional writer to visit and describe Paris. A Bostonian by birth and upbringing, she had begun her career working with Ralph Waldo Emerson, editing the Transcendentalist publication the *Dial*, before joining the staff of the *New-York Tribune*. At age thirty-six, she was at last seeing Europe, a desire of long standing, and filing "letters" to the *Tribune*, a number of which were carried on the front page. Much, though not all, about Paris charmed her. She wrote of "passably pretty ladies with excessively pretty bonnets, announcing in their hues of light green, peach blossom and primrose the approach of spring." But the men "sauntering arm-in-arm" were another matter.

> The air, half military, half dandy, of self-esteem and *savoir-faire*, is not particularly interesting, nor are the glassy stare and fumes of bad cigars, exactly what one most desires to encounter when the heart is opened by the breath of spring. . . .

Hearing Chopin perform at the piano was to hear his music for the first time, she wrote. In the Library of the Chamber of Deputies, she feasted her eyes on the original manuscripts of Rousseau.

I saw them and touched them—those manuscripts, just as
he has celebrated them, written on the fine white paper, tied
with ribbon—yellow and faded age has made them, yet at their
touch I seemed to feel the fire of youth, immortally glowing,
more and more expansive with which his soul has pervaded
this century.

She met and conversed with George Sand, whom she greatly admired.
She "takes rank in society like a man, for the weight of her thoughts," and
had "every reason to leave her husband—a stupid, brutal man." The "brilliant shows" of Paris days and nights were entrancing, but of the French
overall, she was not so sure. "French people I find slippery," she confided
in a letter to Emerson, though she knew that with her limited command
of the language it was difficult to "meet them in their way."

"It is too plain that you should conquer their speech first, which is to
unlock such jeweled cabinets for you," Emerson responded.

When a French tutor told her she spoke and acted like an Italian, it
suited her fine, since she was on her way to Italy and thus might find herself more at home there.

Margaret Fuller would meet and marry a penniless Italian aristocrat,
Angelo Ossoli. On a voyage to New York in 1850, she, her husband, and
their small son would die when the ship went down in a storm off Long
Island, within sight of land.

Another American who amply qualified for Margaret Fuller's third category was Richard Morris Hunt, the student who had found himself carried along with the mob on the day of the February bloodshed. Hunt was
the first American to be admitted to the school of architecture at the
École des Beaux-Arts—the finest school of architecture in the world—and
the subsequent importance of his influence on the architecture of his own
country can hardly be overstated.

He was, in addition, one of the earliest of the American children
brought to Paris by wealthy parents to improve their education, specifically in the arts. Richard, who grew up in Brattleboro, Vermont, had ar-

rived in Paris first in 1843, at sixteen, with his four brothers and sister and widowed mother. The family fortune had come from land speculation in New England. His father, a member of Congress, had died of cholera in Washington during the epidemic of 1832.

Ambitious to become an architect, Richard had prepared for the famously difficult entrance examination at the École des Beaux-Arts under the guidance of a noted French architect, Hector-Martin Lefuel. When he failed the exam, he resolved to try harder. The second time, he passed.

Meanwhile, his brother, William Morris Hunt, who had thought he wanted to be a sculptor, switched to painting after seeing a picture in the window of an art store. It was a portrait called *The Falconer* by George Healy's friend Thomas Couture. "If that is a painting, I am a painter," William is said to have exclaimed. He became Couture's first American student, and his favorite.

The two Hunt brothers were both slim, dark-haired, good-looking, and socially at ease. William, the older by three years, was the more witty and theatrical, but also short-tempered. Each was genuinely fond of the other. They enjoyed each other's company and for some years shared a bright, fifth-floor apartment at 1 rue Jacob, a short walk from the École des Beaux-Arts.

Richard began his studies at the École and William started painting under Couture in 1846, and for brief periods, Richard, too, enrolled in Couture's atelier to study painting and drawing. William was also among the first Americans attracted to the work of those French artists—and particularly the influential painter of peasants, Jean-François Millet—who had settled in the picturesque hamlet of Barbizon thirty miles southeast of Paris.

From the training and inspiration each of the brothers was to experience in the next several years in France would come great strides for each in his work. "Mr. William Hunt is our most promising artist here," reported Thomas Appleton to his father.

———

In the spring of 1849, Elizabeth Blackwell, "with a very slender purse and few introductions of any value," found herself in the "unknown world" of

Paris. What made her situation different from that of other American visitors was her profession. She was a doctor—the first American woman to have become a doctor. Like her male counterparts from the United States, she had come to Paris to further her training in medicine and surgery. (Given that medicine was still understood to be an art, she, too, belonged in the third of Margaret Fuller's categories.)

English by birth, she had moved to America as a child, settling eventually with her family in Cincinnati. As a young woman, she taught school, before declaring her ambition to become a doctor, and preferably a surgeon, at a time when any woman who entertained such ideas was commonly considered "either mad or bad." A physician writing in the *Boston Medical and Surgical Journal* categorically declared that women were "not constituted" for the profession, they being of such *"nervous or excitable"* temperament. "Let woman not assume the prerogatives of *man* by entering the arena and noisy business of life, for which she has not the faculties in common with *man.*"

The idea of winning a doctor's degree, Elizabeth would write, gradually assumed "the aspect of a great moral struggle, and the moral fight possessed immense attraction for me." When she mentioned what was on her mind to a well-known Cincinnati doctor, he was horrified by the very thought. However, Harriet Beecher Stowe, who was then living in Cincinnati and a neighbor, told her the idea, though impractical, if carried out might prove highly useful.

Refused by medical schools in Philadelphia and New York, Elizabeth finally gained admission to the Geneva Medical School in upstate New York. In 1849, after little more than a year of study, she was granted a medical degree.

Yet she felt still the need to know more, and as she later wrote, her teachers and friends urged her to go to Paris. She was twenty-eight, a tiny woman only five feet one, according to her passport application, with a round face, light grey eyes, and sandy hair.

One after another the Paris physicians she saw showed no interest in her or any inclination to help, until she met Pierre Louis, who advised her to enter La Maternité, the world's leading maternity hospital.

On the last day of June, Elizabeth Blackwell stepped through a small door in a high grey wall on the rue Saint-Jacques, into the cloistered life of La Maternité, where young women trained to become midwives under the famous *"sage-femme*-in-chief," Madame Madeleine-Edmée-Clémentine Charrier. "So send a welcome greeting to the Voluntary Prisoner," Elizabeth wrote the next day to her family.

> Imagine a large square of old buildings, formerly a convent, set down in the center of a great court with a wood and garden behind, and many little separate buildings all around, the whole enclosed by very high walls, over the tops of which, shining out beautifully against the clear sky, may be seen the dome of the Panthéon [or] the Hôtel des Invalides. . . . The inner court is surrounded by *les cloîtres*, a most convenient arched passage which gives covered communication to the whole building, and which I suppose was formerly traversed by shaven monks on their way to the church. . . .

She lived in a long dormitory, or *dortoir*, with twenty girls, all French, most of whom were ten years younger than she, and "all pretty and pleasant, of no education except their studies in the institution." Each was provided a narrow bed with an iron bedstead, one chair, and a small lamp. The brick floors were so highly polished she had difficulty walking on them. She should be pictured trying to get about in a great white apron, she wrote to her mother. "And how French girls do chatter!"

From the time the morning began at five-thirty, their whole day was occupied with lectures and work in the wards and clinics. There was scarcely a pause. No distractions were permitted, no newspapers, no books unless medical works. A bell at noon announced the first meal of the day, which consisted of a loaf of bread, a small bottle of wine, soup, boiled meat and vegetables, all "eaten in haste."

Madame Charrier, by Elizabeth's description, was "a little deformed woman, elderly, but with a fresh color still and kind blue eyes," and generally loved by her students. In consideration of Elizabeth's foreignness, Madame insisted she sit beside her during lectures, so she would thoroughly understand.

Several days out of the week were *"en service,"* when each student spent the day (or night) serving in the wards. Every morning three students went before Madame Charrier for a one-hour oral examination of what they had learned, and in her volatile Gallic responses to the answers, Madame Charrier seemed to mimic the extremes of mood of Paris itself. "If they answer promptly and well . . . her face grows beautiful, and her *'Bien! très bien!'* really does me good, it is so hearty," Elizabeth wrote. But if the student hesitated, or answered in too low a voice, or seemed not to know what she should, then followed a terrific scolding.

> Alternately satirical and furious, she becomes perfectly on fire, rises upon her chair, claps her hands, looks up to heaven, and the next moment if a good answer has redeemed the fault, all is forgotten, her satisfaction is as great as her anger. . . . At first I was a little shocked at this stormy instruction, but really it seems almost necessary now, and produces wonderful results.

It was a routine and life, a world within the medical world of Paris, entirely separate from and very unlike that of the male "medicals," but as one of the French physicians stressed to Elizabeth, it offered the opportunity of "seeing all that was remarkable" in the deliveries of more babies in a shorter space of time—four months—than anywhere else in the world, indeed, as many as in the entire practice of some doctors.

With her time at La Maternité nearing its end, Elizabeth contracted a serious eye infection that confined her to bed for weeks and ultimately cost her her sight in one eye, thus ending whatever aspirations she may still have had for a career in surgery.

"How kind everybody was!" she wrote of the care she received.

The training at La Maternité had been a trying time, she conceded, with no privacy, poor air, poor food, hard work, and little sleep. "Yet the medical experience was invaluable at that period of pioneer effort. It enabled me later to enter upon practice with a confidence in one important branch of medicine that no other period of study afforded."

Within a few years, she would found the New York Infirmary and College for Women, a hospital run entirely by women.

The same summer of 1849, while Elizabeth Blackwell was confined to her study of obstetrics, yet another American pioneer was making his presence felt in a different way and in the altogether different setting of an international peace conference presided over by Victor Hugo at the Salle Sainte-Cécile on the rue Saint-Lazare. William Wells Brown, one of the eight hundred delegates, was a lecturer and writer, an ardent abolitionist, and a fugitive slave.

Born in Kentucky, he had told his story in *Narrative of William W. Brown, a Fugitive Slave*, a book published in 1847. His mother was a slave, his father a slave master. At age ten he had heard the cries of his mother as she was being flogged by an overseer. Several times he tried to escape to freedom before succeeding at last, at age eighteen, by getting away to Ohio, where he found shelter with a Quaker named Wells Brown, whose name he took for his own. In the years since, he had worked on steamships on Lake Erie, acquired an education, and made a name for himself as a speaker for abolitionist societies in Pennsylvania, New York, and Massachusetts. He was handsome and articulate, and audiences invariably found his story extremely compelling.

When Brown first applied for a passport earlier that summer, in a letter to Secretary of State John M. Clayton, saying "I am a native of the state of Kentucky and I am a colored man," he never received a direct answer but was later informed that passports were not granted to "persons of color." Only through the government of Massachusetts was he able to obtain a certificate permitting him to get as far as England. Once there, he succeeded in arranging for a passport through the American embassy in London.

Nor had he been given financial help by any antislavery society or by friends to cover the cost of his trip. He went, as he said, entirely at his own expense.

On the final day of the Paris conference, August 24, at the request of Victor Hugo, Brown spoke for peace and against slavery in a speech quoted at length in the Paris papers. With the abolition of war, he proclaimed, "we shall break . . . in pieces every yoke of bondage and let all the oppressed go free," to which the audience broke into sustained cheers. He had been a slave for nearly twenty years. He knew whereof he spoke. Here in Paris he could utter his sentiments "freely." To do so in the United States, he reminded them, would be to risk his life.

He was tremendously pleased by the response of the audience, and even more by the welcome he received later at a lavish reception given by the French foreign minister, Alexis de Tocqueville. At home he could have been present at such a reception only as a servant. Curious to know more about him, Madame de Tocqueville asked him to sit beside her on the sofa. The only disapproving look he saw among the many watching was from the American consul, Robert Walsh.

Before his stay in Paris ended, Brown covered much of the city on foot, setting off from the Hôtel Bedford at first light before the sessions of the conference began. He saw most of the major sights on both sides of the Seine, and though unable to speak French, he enjoyed it all. Never once, under any circumstance, was he made to feel anything but welcome.

William Wells Brown was to become a prolific author, historian, and the first black American novelist and playwright, with his novel titled *Clotel; or, The President's Daughter* (1853) and a play, *The Escape; or, A Leap for Freedom* (1863). Having come to Paris while in his early thirties, he would continue writing for another thirty years.

That summer of 1849 also marked the return to Paris of George Healy and his family from their time in the United States, and the start of preparations for the departure for home by Richard Rush and his daughters.

There had been a change in the administration in Washington and, to his regret, Rush was recalled. He felt he had done his job well, never abandoning his duties for a single day since he arrived. Alexis de Tocqueville sent a note that touched him deeply. "It is with great concern that I see you leaving the position you have occupied here and have filled with so much usefulness to the interests of your country and our own." Rush and his daughters would sail in October.

Healy established himself in an enormous studio on the rue de l'Arcade and set to work on the largest, most ambitious painting of his career, his *Webster's Reply to Hayne*, which measured a colossal fifteen by twenty-seven feet. (Samuel Morse's *Gallery of the Louvre*, at six by nine feet, was small by comparison.)

The scene was the United States Senate on January 26, 1830, the culminating moment of the historic debate over whether the states that had created the Constitution had the right to withdraw support from the policies of the federal government. An ardent "nationalist," Webster championed the position that all of the states had created the Constitution and the federal government, and that no state or states could nullify that government. "Liberty *and* Union, now and forever, one and inseparable," was the ringing declaration of the speech so long remembered and quoted.

Healy positioned Webster in the foreground, standing foursquare in the classic orator's manner—back arched, left hand on the corner of a desk—addressing the packed chamber. Webster wears a white cravat, a buff-colored vest, and a blue dress coat with brass buttons. A play of light on him, like a sunbeam, adds to his dramatic presence.

In addition to Webster, Healy rendered no fewer than 120 other identifiable faces, including those of Senators Joseph Y. Hayne, James K. Polk, John C. Calhoun, and General Lewis Cass. John Quincy Adams, who can be seen looking on from the visitors' gallery, was not actually present for Webster's great moment. Nor were several others whom Healy chose to make part of the scene, such as Henry Wadsworth Longfellow. Healy even included two of his favorite Frenchmen, Alexis de Tocqueville and Thomas Couture, seating them near Adams.

According to a pamphlet testifying to the authenticity of the painting, 111 likenesses were "carefully executed" from life. But it also appears Healy relied in part on daguerreotype portraits. Such details of the Senate chamber as the great carved eagle over the Senate president's chair and the spindled storage space of the desks crammed with papers were presented quite as they were.

Healy labored at what he called "my big picture" for two years, and with no guarantee of compensation. Further, in 1850, he and his wife, Louisa, suffered the tragic loss of two children, when their youngest son,

George, Jr., succumbed to scarlet fever and the eldest, Arthur, at age ten, fell down some stone steps during play hour at school and died soon afterward.

Healy put the final touches to *Webster's Reply to Hayne* in his Paris studio in the summer of 1851 and in a matter of weeks was on his way with the painting to Boston, where in September it was shown for the first time at the Boston Athenaeum on Beacon Hill. People came by the hundreds to pay a 25-cent admission fee. One Saturday, escorted by Healy, Webster himself came, and as reported, "It was a proud moment that, for our young American artist. . . ."

"Receive my sincerest compliments on your great picture," wrote Henry Longfellow. "You have done wonders with a subject of extreme difficulty, and I am rejoiced to see your labors crowned with such complete success."

The painting later went on display in New York at the National Academy of Design, and as in Boston, the public response was enthusiastic, while mixed among the critics. Much the fullest praise was for Healy's portrayal of Webster, the strongest part of the painting.

> The countenance—an admirable likeness of the statesman— is kindled with the inspiration of eloquence [said the *New York Times*]. The person . . . is drawn up with a majestic self-reliance, expressive of strong inner consciousness of adequacy for the remarkable occasion which prompted the effort. The eyes are glowing with animation, the shaggy brows, rather raised, show the exultant, triumphant gaze of the orator. . . .

Does the painting have artistic greatness? asked the *New York Evening Post*. "We must answer decidedly that it does not." A man making a speech, said the reviewer, was no fit subject for the realm of Art, whatever the painter's skill.

As a commercial enterprise, at 25 cents a ticket, the painting proved a disappointment as it continued on tour. Before long it was back in Boston, on display at no charge in Faneuil Hall, one of the nation's most historic sites. Eventually, following Webster's death in 1852, it was purchased by the city of Boston for $2,500, less than half what Healy had hoped to receive, to hang permanently in the Hall.

Healy would never regret the time he had devoted to the painting. "However onerous to an artist such undertakings usually are, and this one proved particularly so to me," he said it had been an honor to paint so many of his illustrious countrymen and Webster most especially.

———

On September 14, 1851, James Fenimore Cooper died at his home in Cooperstown, one day from his sixty-second birthday. His death was the first of an American writer of international reputation.

Old friends who had seen him in New York not long before had thought he looked in fine health, "a very castle of a man," as Washington Irving said, but in fact he had been suffering from diseases of the intestines and kidneys for some time.

Irving was one of those notables who spoke at a memorial tribute in New York, and a published *Memorial* included letters from Emerson, Longfellow, Charles Sumner, Samuel Morse, and Richard Rush. Morse chose to keep his remarks short, recalling simply the "eventful time" he and Cooper had spent in Paris together twenty years past. "I never met with a more sincere, warm-hearted, constant friend."

They were words that would have touched Cooper more than any, unless it was the tribute from Richard Rush, who said—and perhaps with Morse in mind as well—that the nation's enduring fame would rest above all on the great American names in literature and science.

CHAPTER SEVEN

A City Transformed

At last I have come into a dreamland.

—HARRIET BEECHER STOWE

I

Louis Napoleon Bonaparte, the improbable president of the Second Republic—or prince-president, as some preferred to call him—was not an easy man to fathom. His face in repose was nearly impossible to read: pale, grave in expression, and dominated by a large nose, an outsized mustache, its tips waxed, and a pointed goatee. The small pale blue eyes showed scarcely a sign of life. The eyelids drooped, causing him to look half asleep. George Sand likened him to a "sleepwalker." Yet he had a surprisingly bright smile, and though of less than average height and a bit bowlegged, he sat a horse well and looked perfectly cast parading on horseback.

Some of the political elite of Paris took him for a *"crétin,"* certain he would be easy to manipulate. Victor Hugo, on the other hand, was favorably impressed. The British ambassador was "charmed." Richard Rush found the president "courteously attentive," and Rush's replacement as American minister, William C. Rives of Virginia, would report being received in a manner "most cordial and flattering."

As time passed, Louis Napoleon was seen more and more as a study in contrasts, a mixture of opposites, at once naïve and calculating, sincere and full of schemes. "He was very much better than what his previous life and crazy enterprises led one to expect," wrote Alexis de Tocqueville, who in a brief turn as foreign minister had the opportunity to observe the president at close hand.

> As a private person he possessed some attractive qualities—a kindly disposition, humanity, gentleness and even tenderness, a perfect simplicity. . . . His power of concealing his thoughts, resulting from his conspiratorial past, was aided by the immobility of his countenance . . . for his eyes were as dull as opaque glass.

The president was, in addition, a notorious womanizer, a *"grand coureur de femmes,"* which was considered highly admirable by some, regrettable by others, and either way a common explanation for the half-asleep look. "His vulgar pleasures weakened his energies," was all de Tocqueville had to contribute on the subject.

The one American who enjoyed anything like a friendship with the president was Dr. Thomas W. Evans, a sociable Philadelphian who had become the foremost dentist in Paris, due both to his professional skill—he was reputedly the first in Paris to specialize in gold fillings—and the fact that Louis Napoleon was his patient. To Evans, the president was a "charmer" whose "extraordinary self-control" and "seeming impassiveness" were greatly to his advantage. Rather than cold and calculating, Evans found him generous and affectionate. Those who spoke ill of him, according to Evans, were either his political enemies or people who did not know the man.

"My power is in an immortal name," he himself was fond of saying, and indeed, except for the name, he would seem to have come out of nowhere and with almost nothing to qualify him for high position or to account for his popularity. Except in childhood, he had never lived in Paris. As a consequence of schooling in Switzerland and Germany, he spoke French with a slight German accent, and after years of exile in London, enjoyed a cup of tea quite as much as any Englishman.

Born in 1808, the son of the first Napoleon's brother Louis Bonaparte, he had lived abroad with his mother during most of his youth, and in 1836, having tried and failed at a ludicrously inept attempt to overthrow King Louis-Philippe, he had been exiled to the United States, where he stayed but a short time, eventually settling in London. (Like Louis-Philippe, he spoke English with ease and, as Thomas Evans had discovered, preferred conversing in English when he did not care to have others nearby understand what was said.)

In 1840, still trusting to his star, he had launched a second clumsy attempt at insurrection, but this time was sentenced to life imprisonment northeast of Paris in the medieval Castle of Ham, replete with moat and drawbridge. There, provided with a young companion, a laundress who bore him two sons, he spent five and a half years reading history, political theory, and military treatises. To those surprised by the range of his knowledge, he liked to say, "Do you forget my years of study at the university of Ham?"

Then in 1846 he shaved off his mustache and beard, disguised himself in the clothes of a workman, put a plank over his shoulder, walked out of the prison, and escaped to London to pursue his "destiny" still again.

His popular strength, as shown by his overwhelming victory in the presidential election of 1848, was mainly in rural France. Yet even in Paris, what opposition there was remained relatively quiet. In the time since the election, he had become more popular still. His name, he liked to say, was a complete program in itself. "It stands for order, authority, religion, the welfare of the people, national dignity. . . ." And this, after so much unrest and appalling bloodshed, was what people longed for—order above all.

As a leader, Louis Napoleon also had a marked gift for grand-style theatrics and display of a kind long missing in the life of the nation. Presidential balls at the Élysée Palace were now large and exuberantly lavish, with guests announced by title even though titles had been done away with by the constitution. Paris dearly loved a show, as he understood. At public appearances, he was commonly greeted with cries of "*Vive l'empire! Vive l'empereur!*"

The autumn of 1851 was particularly beautiful—like Indian summer at home, wrote a correspondent for the *New York Times*. The air was "soft and hazy, the sunlight rich and mellow." The misery of so many was "crouching out of sight" no less than ever, off in the narrow, crooked streets, and being out of sight, was "as usual out of mind." The well-dressed, well-fed populace filled the boulevards. The fashionable avenue of the Champs-Élysées was as crowded as on the finest days of spring.

There was talk, of course, of political unrest, of hidden plots and coups d'état, and it seemed to matter not at all to the Parisians.

> They eat, drink, and make merry, and make the most of the passing day. Future probabilities or possibilities are not allowed to interfere with the pleasures of present possession. This way of taking life is wise enough—for, remember, it is French life.

On the first day of December 1851, Louis Napoleon sent for his American dentist friend, Thomas Evans, who on arriving at the Élysée Palace found the president more than ordinarily affectionate toward him. There were, however, Evans later wrote, moments when it seemed the president had something he wished to talk about, yet did not.

At a formal reception at the palace that evening, he stood greeting his guests in his usual calm, attentive way, showing no sign that anything out of the ordinary might be on his mind. About ten he excused himself and went behind closed doors to join a small coterie of trusted fellow conspirators. As they gathered about his desk, he opened a bundle of secret papers bearing a single code word, "Rubicon."

Soon after midnight, in the first hours of December 2, 1851, the surprise coup was under way.

Before daybreak more than seventy political figures, generals, and journalists had been roused from their beds and arrested. By dawn troops lined the boulevards and occupied the National Assembly, the railroad depots, and other strategic points. Proclamations put up on the walls of buildings proclaimed the National Assembly dissolved. The constitution

Louis Napoleon had taken an oath to uphold had been done away with and a new constitution called for.

Everything had been considered. Soldiers posted at newspaper offices kept them from opening. Even the ropes of church bells had been cut so they could not be used to summon protest.

In a matter of hours, Louis Napoleon had made himself dictator. Later that morning he rode through Paris on horseback without incident. Not for another two days did protest flare, and it was quickly, decisively crushed, leaving hundreds dead.

Two weeks later, in a national referendum, the country voted overwhelming approval of Louis Napoleon's coup d'état.

Many were outraged. The American minister, William Rives, felt so incensed he refused to attend the president's diplomatic receptions until gently reproved from Washington by Secretary of State Daniel Webster. Victor Hugo, who had thought well of the president at the beginning, fled to Belgium that he might speak his mind freely about "Napoleon the Little." "On 2 December, an odious, repulsive, infamous, unprecedented crime was committed," he wrote.

> The author of this crime is a malefactor of the most cynical and degraded kind. His servants are the comrades of a pirate. . . . When France awakes she will start back with a terrible shudder.

Hugo would remove himself further to the English Isle of Guernsey, where he would live in exile for fifteen years.

The usual bustle of Paris resumed yet again, crowds in the streets taking up the familiar pace of business and pleasure. Many of those arrested were released. Newspapers resumed publication, though by a new decree anyone found propagating false news would be immediately arrested, which in effect meant no real freedom of the press.

Political discord and violence had been put to rest at last, it seemed, and for the greater part of the population, even in Paris, that was sufficient for now. When the words *Liberté, Égalité, Fraternité* were removed from the façades of public buildings, there was hardly a word of protest.

The following October, Louis Napoleon, age forty-four, was proclaimed Emperor Napoleon III, and the close of the year 1852 marked the official beginning of the Second Empire. To a large part of the nation, however, it was not until a bright morning in January 1853, when, at the Cathedral of Notre-Dame, he married the beautiful Spanish countess Eugénie-Marie de Montijo—and France once again had both an emperor and an empress—that the Second Empire was truly under way.

II

As for what he intended to do with his power, the new emperor was emphatically clear on one thing above all. He would make Paris more than ever the most beautiful city in the world and solve a number of intolerable problems in the process.

The great appeal of the city had long been what man built there. There was nothing stunning about its natural setting—no mountain ranges on the horizon, no dramatic coastline. The river Seine, as Emma Willard and other Americans had noted, was hardly to be compared to the Hudson, not to say the Ohio or the Mississippi. The "genius of the place" was in the arrangements of space and architecture, the perspectives of Paris. Now far more—almost unimaginably more—was to be built, and the perspectives to become infinitely longer.

No time was taken up with extended discussion. The emperor disliked discussion. He put a new prefect of the Seine in charge, a career civil servant and master organizer named Georges-Eugène Haussmann, and the choice proved decisive. On the day Haussmann was sworn in, the emperor showed him a map on which he had drawn in blue, red, yellow, and green pencils what he wanted built, and "according to their degree of urgency."

The work would go on for nearly twenty years. Haussmann liked to call himself a "demolition artist," and from the way great, broad swaths were cut through whole sections of the city, and entire neighborhoods leveled with little apparent regard for their history or concern for their inhabitants, it seemed to many that headlong destruction was truly his main purpose. On the Île-de-la-Cité, the historic center of Paris, the ancient slums clustered close to Notre-Dame would be leveled. Streets that Victor Hugo knew and wrote about in *Notre-Dame de Paris* totally disappeared. The Hôtel Dieu would be demolished without the least hesitation. "I could never forget the sinister air of that bit of river wedged between two hospital complexes with a covered walkway between them, polluted with evacuations of every kind from a mass of patients eight hundred strong or more," Haussmann wrote. A resident population of some 15,000 people on the Île-de-la-Cité would be reduced to 5,000.

Broad avenues were to radiate from the Arc de Triomphe like the spokes of a colossal wheel. North from la Cité would run the new boulevard de Sébastopol, and south, the boulevard Saint-Michel. In a long east-west arc on the Left Bank, back from the river, a broad thoroughfare, the new boulevard Saint-Germain, would cut through the heart of the old Latin Quarter.

Haussmann was vigorous and opinionated, a broad-shouldered man, six feet two, who could be ruthless with anything or anyone standing in his way—as often said, just the sort who might succeed in such an ambitious and difficult task.

With its population now more than a million people and still growing, the city had urgent need of modern improvements. Its problems were many and serious. The old tangle of medieval Paris, the crowding, the filth, squalor, foul air and water could be ignored no longer if only for the physical health of the people. It was not that no notable progress had been accomplished in recent years. Much had been done for the betterment of city life under Louis-Philippe. But far more was needed.

The plan was to improve public health and reduce crime, improve the flow of traffic and commerce, provide better sanitation with a vast new sewer system, improve the city's water supply, and provide more open space and clean air, as well as years of employment for tens of thousands of workers. It was true that straight, wide streets would be less suitable for building barricades and better for the rapid deployment of troops, or for directing artillery fire, as critics often said. But a free flow of traffic and a sense of grandeur were far more important to the planners. The making of a more splendid city was always the paramount objective. The longest of the boulevards planned, the rue Lafayette, was to run three miles in a perfectly straight line. Eventually seventy-one miles of new roads would be built.

Along the great boulevards new apartments would rise—whole apartment blocks of white limestone—none more than six stories high and in a uniform Beaux-Arts architectural style, with high French windows and cast-iron balconies. Sidewalks were to be widened. Streets and boulevards would be lined with trees and glow at night with 32,000 new gas lamps. Gaslight everywhere would turn night into day, making Paris truly *la ville lumière.*

And with the boulevards came such novelties as newspaper kiosks, public urinals, and cafés with their tables and chairs set outside on the sidewalks.

The emperor directed that the Bois de Boulogne, the vast woodland west of the city, must become a public park surpassing that of any city, and include a magnificent approach, the avenue de l'Impératrice—the avenue of the Empress. Miles of new walking paths, flower beds, lakes, and a waterfall were part of the plan. And other, smaller parks were to be developed, such as the beautiful Parc Monceau.

"At every step is visible the march of improvement," Haussmann wrote proudly in his diary. But the gulf between the rich and the poor grew greater, and as Haussmann himself acknowledged, over half the population of Paris lived still "in poverty bordering on destitution."

The Louvre would be completed at last. New libraries were built. A new Palais de Justice would rise on the Île-de-la-Cité, and in time an all new Hôtel Dieu. For all that was lost to demolition on the Île-de-la-Cité, an essential part of the plan was to keep it the heart of the city, and much of historic importance was spared. With most of the dense slums removed, the glorious façade of Notre-Dame would stand in a wash of open light and in full view as it never had.

Les Halles, a great new central market, with cast-iron girders and a skylight roof, would go up, and as a kind of architectural crescendo, the grandest, most exuberant expression of the Second Empire opulence, a new Théâtre de l'Opéra at the head of a new avenue de l'Opéra, was to be the surpassing centerpiece of the new Paris.

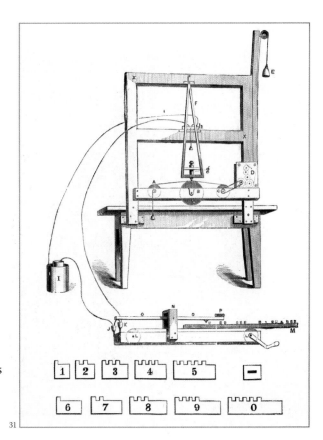

Samuel F. B. Morse's
first telegraph.

Early daguerreotype of Paris, with the Pont des Arts in the foreground,
the Pont Neuf and the towers of Notre-Dame in the distance.

Andrew Jackson by George P. A. Healy. Painted in Tennessee only days before Jackson's death in 1845. Jackson was one of several prominent Americans painted by Healy at the request of King Louis-Philippe of France.

33

Webster's Reply to Hayne by Healy.

34

William Wells Brown, fugitive slave, writer, and ardent abolitionist.

Elizabeth Blackwell, the first female doctor in America.

37

P. T. Barnum and Tom Thumb.

38

Pianist Louis Moreau Gottschalk.

No American artist ever caused such a stir in Paris as Catlin, painter of the Plains Indians, who arrived with an enormous exhibition of his work and a troupe of Iowas, who performed their dances at the Tuileries Palace before King Louis-Philippe and his family, as portrayed in a painting by Karl Girardet.

39

George Catlin by William Fisk.

Little Wolf by George Catlin.

Napoleon III and Georges-Eugène Haussmann at the start
of the remaking of Paris. Painting by Adolphe Yvon.

Empress Eugénie.

43

Dr. Thomas Evans, the popular American dentist who, at the fall of the Second Empire, arranged the daring escape of the empress to England.

44

45

Author Harriet Beecher Stowe, in Paris in 1853 to escape the fanfare over her novel *Uncle Tom's Cabin,* felt at once the "dreamland" charm of the city, its people, its architecture and art. At the Louvre, Géricault's vast, dramatic *The Raft of the Medusa* (upper right) seemed to "seize and control" her whole being.

46

The Raft of the Medusa by Théodore Géricault, showing the victims of an 1816 disaster at sea.

47

The laying of the Atlantic Cable in 1858 changed transatlantic communication forever.

Second Empire opulence on display at the Grand Hôtel.

48

49

50

As the German army marched on Paris, Augustus Saint-Gaudens, an American student of sculpture, decided he must leave.

Mary Putnam chose to stay, determined to pursue her medical studies no matter what.

51

With Paris under siege, Léon Gambetta makes his dramatic escape by balloon. As few people knew, the second balloon (right) carried two Americans, Charles May and William Reynolds.

52

A Soup Kitchen During the Siege of Paris by Henri Pille.

Rat Seller During the Siege of Paris by Narcisse Chaillou.

American minister to France Elihu B. Washburne.

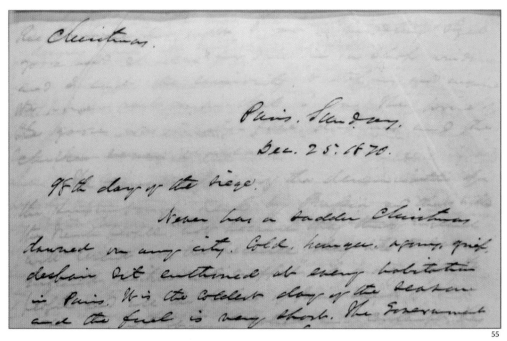

A December 25, 1870, excerpt from the diary Washburne
kept every day through the entire siege.

56

57

Communard corpses.

Paris aflame the night
of May 23–24, 1871.

58

Georges Darboy, Archbishop of Paris by Jean-Louis-Victor
Viger du Vigneau. Archbishop Darboy was arrested,
imprisoned, and secretly executed on orders from the
Communard Chief of Police Raoul Rigault.

Raoul Rigault
dead in the gutter.

59

The Ruins of the Tuileries Palace by Jean Louis Ernest Meissonier.

Clouds of dust and mountains of rubble became part of the scene. Traffic would be brought to a halt on the rue de Rivoli by the accidental shattering of a water main. The removal of paving stones on the Place du Panthéon revealed an ancient underground cavity very like the catacombs. With the demolition of an old convent, the skeletons of eleven nuns were exhumed, some still retaining parts of their woolen habits. Workers were badly injured or killed in accidents.

To be sure, not all were pleased with the transformation. When a character in an English novel of the time, *The Parisians* by Edward Bulwer-Lytton, asked, "Is there not something drearily monotonous in these interminable perspectives?" more than a few readers nodded in agreement.

"How frightfully the way lengthens before one's eyes!" the same character, a French *vicomte*, continued.

> In the twists and curves of the old Paris one was relieved from the pain of seeing how far one had to go from one spot to another; each tortuous street had a separate idiosyncrasy; what picturesque diversities, what interesting recollections—all swept away! *Mon Dieu!* And what for?

The cost of it all, exceeding even the most extravagant expenditures of times past, was to be met with some government funds and a great deal of borrowed money. By 1869 some 2.5 billion francs would be spent, forty times the cost of Louis-Philippe's improvements. Such an investment, it was promised, would be more than compensated for by increasing prosperity. "When building flourishes, everything flourishes in Paris," went an old saying. And with order and prosperity the people might continue to forget the loss of their essential liberties.

Contrary to what many assumed, neither the emperor nor Haussmann profited personally from the project, though certainly others close to the emperor did, and handsomely, including the American dentist Thomas Evans. Acting on "inside" information, Evans purchased land that would rise thirty times above what he paid for it. He would, as well, build his own grand mansion on the broad new boulevard leading from the Place de l'Étoile, where the Arc de Triomphe stood, to the entrance of the Bois de Boulogne.

That the final splendor achieved would make Paris more appealing than ever, few had any doubt.

————

The number of visitors was already increasing noticeably in the early 1850s. Railroad service to and from the rest of Europe and French ports on the Channel was by now well established, clean, and efficient. At sea, larger and ever-finer steamships were crossing from America on regular schedules year-round, and offering comforts on board unimaginable only a few years earlier. The change was dazzling.

American steamers like the *Atlantic, Pacific,* and *Arctic* of the Collins Line were appropriately called "floating palaces." The *Arctic,* as an example, offered accommodations for 200 first-class passengers, a grand dining salon, a gentlemen's smoking room, a gentlemen's barber shop. Interiors were richly embellished with satinwood and gilded ceilings, plush armchairs, oversized mirrors, marble-topped tables. On the *Pacific,* where the décor was equally resplendent, five especially large staterooms were designated bridal suites, and the wine cellar carried more than 3,000 bottles.

Such ships were steam-heated for winter travel and featured indoor plumbing. Ice rooms carried as much as forty tons of ice. Fresh fish, fruits, and vegetables were staples. The cooking was comparable to that of the best restaurants. There were no steerage passengers aboard such vessels, and first-class passage was predictably high-priced, about $150 one way. (For an additional $24 one could bring a dog.) "God grant the time will come when all mankind shall be as luxuriantly cared for at home as they are when they go abroad," wrote a New York correspondent describing life aboard the *Arctic.*

The great majority of those crossing the Atlantic in both directions still traveled by sailing ships, and by far the greatest number of those passengers were headed in the opposite direction from Americans bound for France. They were sailing for America in steerage, fleeing famine in Ireland and revolution in Europe—over 200,000 Irish in the peak year of 1851, and even more, 350,000, from Germany in 1853 and 1854.

Still, the number of Americans who could afford to travel by luxury steamships and enjoy comparable accommodations once abroad, was steadily on the rise, and even more were now giving the idea serious consideration. In 1851, largely because of interest in the Great Exposition at London's Crystal Palace, the *Pacific* put out from New York carrying 238 passengers, a new steamliner record for a single crossing.

Many who were headed for London went on to Paris, and increasingly the more affluent of them brought their families. No longer was it uncommon, as in the time of James Fenimore Cooper, to see a husband and wife come aboard with three or four young children, as well as a servant or two.

Among the earliest of such couples were Robert and Katherine Cassatt of Pennsylvania, who in the summer of 1851 embarked on an extended sojourn abroad, stopping first in London before moving on to Paris with their three young children, Alexander, Lydia, and Mary. In Paris they settled in for an extended stay at the Hôtel Continental, and seven-year-old Mary was to remember the day of Louis Napoleon's coup d'état the rest of her life. It would also be said that her interest in painting began then, which would appear to make her the youngest American thus far to have come under the spell of the arts in Paris.

———

Two years later, in the spring of 1853, another notable but very different American family began its time abroad.

The year before, in 1852, a new novel titled *Uncle Tom's Cabin* by an unknown author had caused the greatest stir of anything published in America since Thomas Paine's *Common Sense*. The book had since become a sensation in Britain as well, and its author, Harriet Beecher Stowe, unknown no longer, was on her way to England in the "hope of doing good" for the cause against slavery, as she had told her friend Senator Charles Sumner of Massachusetts.

In Britain, *Uncle Tom's Cabin* had been acclaimed for having accomplished greater good for humanity than any other book of fiction. Over half a million British women had signed a petition against slavery. In Paris, where the Stowes were also headed, publishers were still scrambling to finish translations, but George Sand, writing in *La Presse*, had already called Mrs. Stowe "a saint. Yes—a saint!"

Traveling with her were her husband, the preacher-scholar Calvin Stowe, her younger brother, Charles Beecher, also a preacher, and three of her in-laws, but none of her children. They crossed on the steamship *Canada*, and for Hatty, as she was known in the family, it was, at age forty-one, her first time at sea.

The author's British tour was long and exhausting. Having taken no part in the antislavery movement prior to writing her book, she suddenly found herself the most influential voice speaking on behalf of the enslaved people of America. From the day her ship docked at Liverpool, crowds awaited her at every stop of the tour through England and Scotland. Husband Calvin was so undone by it all that he gave up and went home.

By the time Hatty reached Paris, in the first week of June, she craved only some peace and privacy, and wanted her presence in the city kept as quiet as possible. Rather than staying at one of the fashionable hotels, she moved into a private mansion on the narrow rue de Verneuil in the Faubourg Saint-Germain, as the guest of an American friend, Maria Chapman, known as "the soul" of the Boston Female Anti-Slavery Society.

"At last I have come into a dreamland," Hatty wrote. "I am released from care. I am unknown, unknowing. . . ."

With her time all her own, she used it to see everything possible, starting the next day, a Sunday, with church service at the Madeleine, her first "Romish" service ever. She usually went accompanied by her brother Charles, whose energetic, good-humored companionship she relished. For nearly three weeks she moved about Paris unnoticed, a small, fragile-looking woman of no apparent importance—"a little bit of a woman," as she said, "about as thin and dry as a pinch of snuff, never very much to look at in my best days."

She was tireless and saw everything that so many Americans had seen before her, but took time to look hard and to think about what she saw. Hatty was a natural "observer," wrote Charles, "always looking around on everything." And for all that others had had to say on the same subjects, there was a freshness, an originality in what she wrote.

She loved Paris at once. She needed no coaching, no interlude in which to acclimate herself. She felt immediately at home, as Oliver Wendell Holmes had, and better just for being among the people. "My spirits always rise when I get among the French."

The days were unseasonably warm, the temperature eighty degrees in the shade, as she recorded in her journal, describing the pleasure of sitting beneath the trees in the Garden of the Tuileries, observing the human show.

> Whole families come, locking up their door, bringing the baby, work, dinner, or lunch, take a certain number of chairs and spend the day. As far as the eye can reach you see a multitude seated, as if in church, with other multitudes moving to and fro, while boys and girls without number are frolicking, racing, playing ball, driving hoop, etc., but contriving to do it without making a hideous racket.

How French children were taught to play and enjoy themselves without disturbing everyone else was a mystery to her.

> There were grayheaded old men and women, and invalids. And there were beautiful demoiselles working worsted, embroidery, sewing; men reading papers, and, in fact, people doing everything they would do in their own parlors. All were graceful, kind, and obliging; not a word nor an act of impoliteness or indecency.

No wonder the French adore Paris, she thought.

Pausing for an ice at a garden café at the Palais Royal after a long day, she was delighted to find so many others doing the same. No one recognized the plain little American or paid her any attention—just as she wished.

Another day, after climbing with Charles up the spiral staircase to the top of the Arc de Triomphe, she made no mention of the nearly three hundred steps, only the thrill of the view. But, whatever the vantage point, she refused to let slip from her mind how much might lay out of sight. "All is vivacity, gracefulness, and sparkle to the eye, but, ah, what fires are smoldering below."

Seeing the emperor and empress ride by in their carriage on the boulevard des Italiens, she thought he looked stiff and homely, she beautiful but sad.

Until the evening her host Marie Chapman held one of her salons on the rue de Verneuil, setting out cake and tea for a gathering of Parisian friends, neither Hatty nor Charles had ventured to say much in French. Charles decided to throw caution to the winds and "talked away, right and left, and right and wrong, too," as he wrote, "a perfect steeple chase, jumping over ditches and hedges, genders and cases . . . nouns, adjectives, and terminations of all sorts." The guests were amazed and delighted, as was his sister. "Poor Hatty!" he wrote. "She could not talk French, except to say, '*Oui, madame. Non, monsieur.*' "

The attention paid to her at this and other small gatherings by those who knew who she was, was "very touching," Charles thought. "She is made to feel perfectly free. . . . And the regard felt for her is manifested in a way . . . so considerate that she is rather *strengthened* by it than exhausted."

———

What was the mysterious allure of Paris, she wondered. What was its hold on the heart and imagination? Surely the "life artery" was the ever-flowing Seine, she mused one day when crossing the Pont d'Austerlitz. Her years in Cincinnati, living in the presence of the Ohio and writing about it in her book, had given her a strong inner sense of the river as a divider, an open highway, a measure of the turning of the seasons, of life. But the Seine, embellished with such bridges and show of monumental architecture, was like no river she had ever known. "And there is no scene like this, as I gaze upward and downward, comprehending in a glance the immense panorama of art and architecture—life, motion, enterprise, pleasure, pomp, and power."

> As the instinct of the true Parisienne teaches her the mystery
> of setting off the graces of her person by the fascinations of
> dress, so the instinct of the nation to set off the city by the
> fascinations of architecture and embellishment.

Much in the way Emma Willard and others of New England Puritan background were transported by the Cathedral of Rouen, Hatty Stowe, gazing upward within Notre-Dame, felt a "sublimity" she found impossible to analyze or express. It was a long way from the kitchen table in Brunswick, Maine, where she had written *Uncle Tom's Cabin*, a baby in a clothes basket at her feet.

She had become increasingly interested in art. So the Louvre occupied the greater part of her time. She knew nothing of the "rules of painting," as she said, but confident in what she knew of the art of literature, she compared the painters who most strongly appealed to her to one or another of her favorite writers. Rembrandt struck her as very like Hawthorne, for example.

> He chooses simple and everyday objects, and so arranges light
> and shadow as to give them a somber richness and a mys-
> terious gloom. *The House of Seven Gables* is a succession of
> Rembrandt pictures done in words instead of oils. Now this
> pleases us because our life really is a haunted one. The sim-
> plest thing in it *is* a mystery, the invisible world always lies
> round us like a shadow. . . .

There were no paintings in the museum to which she returned as often as those by Rembrandt.

Rubens—"the great, joyous, full-souled, all powerful Rubens!"—whom she loved no less, was like Shakespeare, she decided. Yet Rubens bothered her. He was full of "triumphant, abounding life, disgusting and pleasing, making me laugh and making me angry, defying me to dislike him."

> Like Shakespeare, he forces you to accept and forgive a thou-
> sand excesses, and uses his own faults as musicians use

discords only to enhance the perfection of harmony. There certainly is some use even in defects. A faultless style sends you to sleep. Defects rouse and excite sensibility to seek and appreciate excellences.

Walking back and forth the length of the Grande Galerie, pausing to look at pictures from a distance and up close, she found few "glorious enough to seize and control my whole being." Too many artists "painted with dry eyes and cool hearts," she thought, "thinking only of mixing their colors and the jugglery of their art, thinking little of heroes, faith, love, or immortality."

For the large works of Jacques-Louis David hanging with other French paintings in the Salon Carré, she had little use. The problem with David was that he had neither heart nor soul. His paintings were but the "driest imitation" of the classics.

She saw French painting as representative of the "great difficulty and danger" of French life in general:

> that passion for the outward and visible, which all their edu-
> cation, all arrangements of their social life, everything in their
> art and literature, tends continually to cultivate and increase.
> Hence they have become the leaders of the world in what I
> should call the minor artistics—all those particulars which
> render life beautiful. Hence there are more pretty pictures
> and popular lithographs from France than from any other
> country in the world, but it produces very little of the deepest
> and highest style of art.

But there was one stunning exception, she was quick to concede, *The Raft of the Medusa*, the tremendous (16 by 23½ feet) dark canvas by Théodore Géricault showing the tragic victims of an 1816 disaster, when the ship *Medusa* went aground off the coast of Senegal. There are no heroes on the crude raft in Géricault's wild, dark, unforgiving sea. At least two of the figures in the foreground are already dead. Those still alive cling to one another, and the whole thrust of the pyramid of their bodies is to the upper right-hand corner, where the strongest of the living, a black man, waves a shirt or rag toward one dim semblance of hope, the mere speck of a ship on the far horizon.

If any great work in the Louvre had the power to "seize and control" her whole being, she wrote, it was this. She spent a full hour in front of it.

> I gazed until all surrounding objects disappeared, and I was alone in the wide Atlantic. Those transparent emerald waves are no fiction. They leap madly, hungering for their prey. That distended sail is filled with the lurid air. The dead man's foot hangs off in the seething brine a stark reality. What a fixed gaze of despair in that father's stony eye! What a group of deathly living ones around that frail mast, while one with intense eagerness flutters a signal to some far-described bark! Coleridge's *Ancient Mariner* has no colors more fearfully faithful to his theme. . . . And there is no voice that can summon the distant flying sail!

Here was the work of a man "who had not seen human life and suffering merely on the outside, but had felt in the very depths of his soul the surging and earthquake of those mysteries of passion and suffering which underlie our whole existence in this world." She was sure no more powerful piece had ever been painted. It was as though this one picture had been worth the whole trip to France.

After not quite three weeks she and her party were on their way to the Swiss Alps and Germany, but soon were back in Paris for a longer stay.

She had been thinking about the human need for beauty and how in childhood she had been starved for that side of life. She felt she had been senselessly, cruelly cheated. "With all New England's earnestness and practical efficiency, there is a long withering of the soul's more ethereal part—a crushing out of the beautiful—which is horrible."

> Children are born there with a sense of beauty equally delicate with any in the world in whom it dies a lingering death of smothered desire and pining, weary starvation. I know because I have felt it.

It was a severe indictment of her own upbringing, indeed of American life, and not until she came to Paris had it struck her so emphatically.

More important was the realization that the beauty of Paris was not just one of the pleasures of the city, but it possessed a magically curative power to bring one's own sense of beauty back to life. "One in whom this sense had long been repressed, in coming into Paris, feels a rustling and a waking within him, as if the soul were crying to unfold her wings." Instead of scorning the lighthearted, beauty-loving French, she decided, Americans ought to recognize how much was to be learned from them.

Of the outstanding New Englanders whose brilliance distinguished American letters in the 1850s, Oliver Wendell Holmes, Henry Wadsworth Longfellow, Ralph Waldo Emerson, and now Harriet Beecher Stowe had all made pilgrimages to Paris. In 1858 followed yet another, Nathaniel Hawthorne. Herman Melville had passed through in 1849, but his stay had been so brief and uneventful it seems to have mattered little to him. The only one of the New England "immortals" who did not come was Henry Thoreau, but then he seldom went anywhere.

Hawthorne, his wife, and three children arrived for a week's visit in the bitter cold of January. They had come over from England, where Hawthorne was serving as the American consul at Liverpool, and they stopped at the newly opened Hôtel du Louvre, just across the rue de Rivoli from the museum.

"The splendor of Paris, so far as I have seen, takes me altogether by surprise," Hawthorne recorded at the end of his first day. London was nothing by comparison. The emperor deserved great credit for the changes brought about in so little time, he thought. Every visitor looking at Paris ought, selfishly, to wish him a long reign. As for the masterpieces in the Louvre, Hawthorne found them "wearisome," much preferring to watch the crowd of Sunday visitors. If he took any interest in the paintings by Rembrandt, or saw any similarity to his own work, as Mrs. Stowe had, he made no mention of it.

Great as were the improvements in transatlantic travel, the perils of the sea had by no means become a thing of the past. In 1854 came news of a terrible tragedy, when the largest of the American "floating palaces," the *Arctic*, on a return voyage to New York, collided with another ship in the fog off the Grand Banks of Newfoundland. The death toll numbered between 350 and 372 passengers and crew. Two years later, a Cunard steamer, *Pacific*, set out on a winter crossing from Liverpool to New York, with 186 passengers and crew, and was never heard from again.

Still, the ocean travelers from America kept coming, and with the approach of the 1855 Paris Exposition, their numbers grew even larger. "Perhaps never before have there been so many Americans in Europe as at the present time," reported the *New York Times*. Among them were the James family of New York, beneficiaries of an inherited fortune—father, mother, four sons, and a daughter. His intention, said the elder James, was "to educate the babies in strange lingoes." The oldest of the children, William and Henry, were fourteen and twelve respectively. Set loose on their own in Paris, the two boys would often head down the Champs-Élysées and through the Tuileries to the Louvre. Henry would remember how he "looked and looked again" at the pictures, and how he wondered at the "still-present past" of Paris, the "mysteries of fifty sorts," as he tried to fathom what he might make of his life.

The exposition, staged largely on the Champs-Élysées, was an enormous success. There were more than 5,000 exhibits, and in the course of the year more than 5 million visitors descended on Paris. When Queen Victoria and Prince Albert arrived, 800,000 people lined the streets to see them ride by. (With France and Britain then joined as allies of the Turks against the Russians in the Crimean War, the presence of the British monarchs had more than conventional symbolism.)

Flags flew everywhere. Hotels posted COMPLET (FULL) signs. Prices soared. For the emperor and his prefect of the Seine, Haussmann, it was a clear confirmation of their claim that the sums being spent on the city would be returned in full with the money spent by ever-more visitors.

Although the vast demolition and construction continued, it was astonishing how much had already been accomplished. "Paris is singly transformed," wrote an amazed and approving Prince Albert.

French intellectuals complained that in planning the exposition too much attention was devoted to the Palais de l'Industrie, too much fuss made over the material products of industry and technology. American visitors, however, were delighted to see such attention and the gold medals conferred on Singer sewing machines, Colt revolvers, McCormick reapers, and Professor Morse's telegraph.

Of the 796 French artists represented at the Gallery of Fine Arts, there were forty paintings by Ingres, the official favorite of the French government, and thirty-five by Delacroix. American painters, by contrast, were so few—a scant twelve in all—as to be barely noticeable. Among them were William Morris Hunt and George Healy, who had thirteen of his portraits accepted, as well as his latest work—Benjamin Franklin pleading the cause of American independence before Louis XVI—for which Healy received a gold medal.

If the emperor and others in power drew one clear conclusion from the Exposition, it was that the next one must be bigger and more dazzling still.

———

In his years painting portraits, George Healy had had the pleasure of conversing while he worked with many outstanding talkers, but he had never met the equal of William B. Ogden from Chicago, who that summer of the exposition came to Healy's studio for several sittings. Ogden, a real estate developer and railroad man, had been Chicago's first mayor when it had numbered all of 4,000 people, and he loved to go on about the city's "marvelous future." The more Ogden talked, the more interested Healy grew. Now forty-two, he had been wondering if it might be time for a change.

> I had often thought of returning to the United States and set-
> tling there; but the difficulties of moving with a large family,
> the uncertainty as to where I should go, the fear of being con-
> sidered by my country-people, according to a frank saying of
> the time, as a "blasted foreigner," had made me hesitate.

Ogden offered the hospitality of his Chicago home until Healy could get settled, and promised "a rich harvest" of commissions among those he knew. So in the fall of 1855, Healy joined the hundreds of other Americans homeward bound from the Exposition. Because Louisa was soon to give birth to another child, she, the baby (a son), and five little girls would follow later. It had been twenty-one years since Healy arrived in Paris as a student. Whether it crossed his mind that he might return again is not known.

With the departure of Healy, one generation in American art made its exit from the stage of Paris while another, as if on cue, made its entrance, and fittingly, in a decidedly different form.

James McNeill Whistler was only just twenty-one. He was small (five feet four inches) and a dandy—slim, with long curly black hair and a black mustache. So high-spirited and noisy was he, so overflowing with wit and self-confidence, many failed to take him seriously.

Much of his boyhood had been spent in St. Petersburg, Russia—his father, Major George Whistler, a civil engineer and West Point graduate, had helped build the first railroad connecting St. Petersburg to Moscow for Czar Nicholas I—and there the boy had first shown his gift for drawing. At sixteen, like his father, he entered West Point, which he instantly loathed. The only course in which he excelled was drawing. In his third year he was discharged for failure in chemistry. "Had silicon been a gas," he loved to say, "I would have been a major general."

Like the young George Healy, Whistler had come to Paris for proper training in an atelier, but with the difference that he already spoke excellent French and had all but memorized a recent French novel about the carefree life of artists in the Latin Quarter, *Scènes de la Vie de Bohémienne* (Scenes of Bohemian Life) by Henri Murger, which was later adapted for the libretto of Giacomo Puccini's *La Bohème*.

American students who knew "Jimmie" Whistler in Paris at that time described him as full of "go," "eccentric," "always smoking cigarettes, which he made himself," and "no end of fun." Nor would his "peculiar" hat be forgotten—a big yellow straw hat with a broad brim and low crown wrapped in a broad black ribbon with its long ends hanging down. It was the signature touch of his *Vie de Bohémienne* look.

Elated with the new life, he seemed in no hurry to decide on an atelier or settle down to work. He did, however, take up with a young dressmaker named Héloïse, and together they moved into a small studio-bedroom on the rue Jacob. When eventually he entered the popular atelier of Charles Gleyre, he seems to have spent limited time there. Yet what he took away from the experience was of lasting value—that line mattered more than color, and that of all colors, black was of greatest importance, black "the universal harmonizer."

He and Héloïse moved from the rue Jacob to cheaper quarters, then moved again. "I don't think he stayed long in any rooms," another student remembered. He never had enough money, yet kept on enjoying himself expansively at restaurants like Lalouette's, famous for its burgundy at one franc a bottle and for allowing art students unlimited credit.

"His genius, however, found its way in spite of an excess of the natural indolence and love of pleasure," said another of his student circle. In fact, Whistler was concentrating on work more than it appeared. In a sense, he was never not working. As would be said, "Everything he enjoyed as a student he turned to his profit as an artist. The women he danced with at night were his models by day." He was drawing, doing etchings of exceptional vitality, and spending long days at the Louvre working on copies.

He made many friends among the French students, including one Henri Fantin-Latour, who would prove as valued as any of his lifetime. He also began going back and forth to London, and in 1859, having parted company with Héloïse, he moved there, his student days at an end. But by no means was Whistler finished with Paris, or Paris with him.

He left owing Monsieur Lalouette, the restaurant owner, 3,000 francs, all of which, in time, he paid back.

III

In the nearly twenty years since his student days at the Sorbonne, Charles Sumner had become one of the most eloquent and disputatious figures in American politics. With his imposing height, his rare command of the English language, and his deep, powerful voice, he could rouse and inspire audiences as could few others, and when unleashing his passion for causes, he seldom failed to provoke storms of criticism, even outrage. He had argued for world peace, spoken out fearlessly against the Mexican War and slavery, and with little or no apparent concern over whom he offended. His friends worried for his safety. "For heaven's sake don't let him do himself harm while trying to help other people," Thomas Appleton wrote to his father from England.

It was Sumner's continuing part in the "question" of slavery, above all, that had propelled him to national prominence. He was one of the founders of the Free Soil Party and, in 1851, at age forty, was elected to the United States Senate. Having once concluded—while observing how black students were treated at the Sorbonne—that the attitude toward and treatment of African-Americans at home was contrary to the "natural order of things," Sumner had made plain his hatred of slavery and never gave up on it. "I think slavery a sin, individual and national," he wrote, "and I think it the duty of each individual to cease committing it."

The first news of the savage physical attack on Sumner in the United States Senate reached Paris on June 9, 1856. Within days all Europe knew the sensational story.

The assault had taken place on May 22, after Sumner, earlier in the week, delivered his longest, most strident and contentious speech yet, "The Crime against Kansas," as he called it. Like Webster's reply to Hayne, it was one of the most important orations in the history of the Senate and was delivered to a packed chamber over the course of two days. And again it was a Massachusetts senator who stood at center stage.

But such was Sumner's wrath that, unlike Webster, he launched into personal attacks of a kind traditionally not tolerated in the Senate, with the result that the speech and the ensuing attack on Sumner were to have consequences far beyond those resulting from what Webster had declaimed.

He would expose "the whole crime" of slavery "without sparing language," Sumner told a friend in advance, and he did. In printed form the speech ran more than a hundred pages, and he had memorized every word. He denounced not only "the reptile monster," slavery, and the "swindle" of the Kansas-Nebraska Act, which was the center of the debate, but he singled out for acid scorn several members of the Senate who had perpetuated "human wrongs," one of whom, Senator Andrew P. Butler of South Carolina, was not present to reply. Sumner likened Butler to a silly old Don Quixote in love with the "harlot slavery." "He cannot open his mouth but out there flies a blunder."

To no one's surprise the speech was immediately denounced in the South and acclaimed in the North. The abolitionists, and especially in Massachusetts, were overjoyed. "Your speech," wrote Sumner's close friend Henry Longfellow, "is the greatest voice on the greatest subject that has yet been uttered."

An incensed congressman named Preston S. Brooks of South Carolina, who was a slaveholder and kinsman of Senator Butler, brooded for more than a day over what he ought to do to defend the honor of South Carolina in the face of such insults. The main question on his mind was whether to go after Sumner with a horsewhip or his heavy, gutta-percha cane. He chose the cane, having decided, he later explained, that Sumner with his size and strength might readily "wrest" a whip from his hand and turn on him with it, and then where would he be?

It was early afternoon when Brooks slipped into the back of the Senate Chamber and stood waiting. Only a few others were still present. Sumner was alone at his desk busily signing papers.

Brooks approached and addressed him. "Mr. Sumner," he said, "I have read your speech over carefully. It is a libel on South Carolina and Mr. Butler, who is a relative of mine. . . ." When Sumner looked up, Brooks struck the first backhanded blow to the head.

Sumner's desk, like other desks in the Senate, was screwed to the floor, and with his long legs, he could sit only with his knees wedged tightly underneath. Desperate to defend himself, he rose up with such explosive force that he ripped the desk loose from the floor.

Brooks kept striking, left and right—"thirty first-rate stripes," he later boasted—until the supposedly unbreakable cane shattered. "I wore my cane out completely, but saved the head which is gold."

Sumner lay on the floor unconscious and covered with blood. Brooks slipped quietly out of the chamber. After several minutes, Sumner regained consciousness and was taken to his lodgings and put to bed.

In Kansas, abolitionist John Brown and his men, hearing the news of the attack on Sumner, "went crazy," as one of them would recall, and rushed off to slaughter five innocent men in the infamous Pottawatomie Massacre.

Congressman Brooks received only a fine of $300 for what he had done. Instead, he was a hero in the South, greeted with cheers wherever he went and presented with gifts of gold-headed canes.

Sumner never fully recovered from the attack. After a long convalescence, he tried to return to his work in the Senate but found it impossible. He could walk only with difficulty. Getting out of a chair was painful. His condition was described as "an oppressive sense of weight or stricture on the brain," and this was greatly increased by any mental effort, even by conversation.

With the arrival of the New Year, when he tried again to resume his duties in the Senate, he found even one day too much for him. His doctors advised a trip abroad—for the beneficial effects of days at sea and for "a complete separation from the cares and responsibilities that must beset him at home."

———

The voyage was a far cry from what it had been on the packet *Albany* in 1837. Sumner departed New York this time in the comforts of the steamship *Fulton*, with flags flying and a booming thirty-one-gun salute in his honor.

He had come on board looking extremely feeble, walking with the support of a cane. At forty-six, he might have been taken for a man in his late sixties. For the first seven days he was confined to his stateroom, suffering from seasickness. But the morning he emerged, it was obvious the voyage, seasickness included, had done worlds of good. A newspaper correspondent on board described how the senator could rise from a chair without difficulty and could be seen walking the deck with no cane.

> To look at Mr. Sumner now and converse with him as he stands firmly on the unsteady deck . . . I can understand why a ruffian, a chivalric ruffian, would choose knocking such a man when he was down rather than attempt to knock him down.

He became openly sociable, taking time to talk with nearly everyone among the passengers and crew. It was said he could have been elected by a landslide to any office he wished on board.

"The sea air, or seasickness, or absolute separation from politics at home, or all combined, have given me much of my old strength," he wrote after landing at Le Havre. For the first time since his student days in France, he was keeping a journal again.

On the overland ride to Paris—by rail rather than diligence—he stopped at Rouen as before and again took time to visit the cathedral. From Rouen to Paris, the day was fine. "Civilization seemed to abound," he wrote of the passing scenery. He was looking forward with greatest anticipation to so much he remembered of Paris—the opera, the theater, a few favorite restaurants, and time with old friends, like the peripatetic Thomas Appleton, who, he knew, was already there.

Once in Paris, he "sallied forth" without delay, "astonished at the magnificence which I saw, beyond all my expectations." He was off to the opera the first night, for two hours of *Guillaume Tell.* The next morning he and Appleton took a drive through the city. "The improvements are prodigious," he wrote, his spirits soaring. He attended performances at the French opera, the Italian opera, and the Opéra Comique seven or eight nights running, and the theater as well. He did it all, it seems—strolled the Garden of the Tuileries, went to the Louvre, "played the flâneur" at the Palais Royal, dined at Trois Frères Provençaux, Véry's, the Café Anglais. Sumner dined with Appleton at least a dozen times. He crossed the Seine and "revived" old recollections at the Sorbonne. From his "beautiful apartment" at the Hôtel de la Paix, on the rue de la Paix, he could watch "all the movement of Paris."

Not only had Paris been transformed; he had, too. Such vitality as he had shown walking the deck of the *Fulton* was even greater now, as he kept a schedule that might have exhausted someone half his age.

Alexis de Tocqueville came to call and converse candidly about the political picture in France. ("He did not disguise his opposition to the government . . . said that it was a *'gouvernement de bâtards.'* ") Another day Sumner joined de Tocqueville for breakfast with several French political figures, among whom was François Guizot, who assured Sumner that he, too, opposed slavery. When someone at the table asked which of the foreign accents in French was the least agreeable to a Frenchman, Guizot, with no hesitation, said German, and recalled that Louis-Philippe judged a man's ability by the languages he spoke. In a matter of days, Sumner had arranged for a French tutor who spoke no English to come to his hotel every morning to read and speak French to him.

He met and conversed at length with the poet-politician Alphonse de Lamartine, who told him nobody could anticipate the future of France: "With a people so changeable, nothing is certain but change."

At a dinner party he met the American dentist Thomas Evans. "He speaks of the emperor in warmest terms of admiration," Sumner recorded, "and describes him as laborious and happy, beginning the day with a cold bath, and meeting his wife with a kiss."

Sumner had never married. His interest in women was considerable, and the face of a particularly beautiful woman could move him deeply. But he was often uncomfortable with women. His work and his friends were his life, and he had many close friends to whom he was devoted, like Longfellow, Appleton, and Samuel Gridley Howe, ardent antislavery leader and pioneer in education for the blind.

On April 23, from Paris, Sumner wrote a long letter to Howe. His time, he said, was indeed "intensely occupied," but he did tire. His legs dragged after a walk that once would have been nothing. By then he was also fighting a cold—"they call it *la grippe* here." But *la grippe* or not, he was in Paris, and Paris, he could report, was "very gay and beautiful, and abounding in interesting people."

He began feeling a little of the old urge to get back to Washington. "I tremble for Kansas. . . . How disgusting it seems the conduct of those miserable men who thus trifle with the welfare of this region! My blood boils at this outrage, and I long to denounce it again from my place."

Young Henry James, who through his father met Sumner at this time, was surprised to find the martyr looking so well, his wounds all "rather disappointingly healed."

The pace of sightseeing and social occasions with "interesting people" hardly slackened. At one evening affair he chatted with the Russian novelist Ivan Turgenev, who predicted that serfdom would be abolished in Russia within ten years. At two other gatherings he had the chance to catch up with Harriet Beecher Stowe, who was back in Paris and making her own effort to learn French.

He visited the Imperial Library, watched in amazement a military review on the Champ de Mars, where 60,000 troops paraded, more soldiers than he had ever seen or expected ever to see again. He made a return visit to the École de Médecine, even "plunged into the dissecting rooms, strong with the stench of human flesh."

Appleton accompanied him on a shopping expedition for gifts to take home, including a dessert service for Appleton's sister, Fanny, who had become Mrs. Henry Longfellow. Dining together night after night, they talked on for hours as only they could.

They were two thorough Bostonians close to the same age—Sumner the older by a year. They had known each other for more than twenty years, ever since they had met at Harvard. Appleton had chosen a life devoted mainly to his own enjoyment, nothing like Sumner's. (As Appleton had written to his father earlier from Paris, "I dine out very often, eat and drink as much as I wish, sleep well after it, paint in pastels, talk a good deal in a very superior way. . . .") Still, it would have been hard to find two Americans of the day who had anything approaching their range of common interests, their knowledge and love of opera, theater, art, books, travel, and ideas. Or who could expand on any or all with such compelling vitality.

Possibly there was a homosexual side to their friendship, but there is no evidence of this. Appleton may have been ambiguous sexually, but beyond that nothing is known, and while Sumner's political enemies would have leapt at the chance to destroy him with charges of scandal of any kind, none was ever made.

Sometimes when dining in Paris they were joined by another guest. One evening it was an American naval officer, William Lynch, the author of a recent, popular book about his explorations of the River Jordan and the Dead Sea. More often it was the two friends to themselves. Regrettably neither recorded anything of these occasions. Still, it is easy to picture them in a setting such as Trois Frères Provençaux, enjoying perhaps a salt cod with garlic, a *spécialité de la maison*, and a bottle or more of Château Carbonnieux from Bordeaux, the evening sailing along on all manner of observations on Mozart or Verdi or Donizetti's *Maria Stuarda*, one of the operas they had recently attended and enjoyed, or going on about Keats or Dumas or the cathedral at Rouen or Paris itself. And while Sumner would have contributed little in the way of humor, Appleton would have more than compensated.

For Sumner it was the best medicine possible, talk of the kind he thrived on, and hardly to be found among the politicians in Washington. If Preston Brooks with his attack had brought him near death, was it not his old friend Appleton who had observed, "When good Americans die they go to Paris"?

On May 24, after a stay of two months, Sumner left for a tour of the provinces. Then followed another two months of headlong sightseeing in London, Germany, the Netherlands, Brussels, and Scotland, until it became too much. Feeling unwell again, he consulted a London specialist in phrenology, who told Sumner that his brain, "although apparently functionally sound," would ultimately give way under the pressure of public life in America.

By early December 1857 he had returned to Washington, in time for the new session of Congress, only to find himself exhausted by just sitting and listening. He could neither work nor abide the whole "vileness and

vulgarity" of the capital. When in late December he left again, he felt better almost at once. Still, he tried returning to Washington several times,
but to no avail.

Through all his prolonged disability and absence from the Senate, the
people of Massachusetts remained loyal to Sumner. There were no serious
calls for his resignation, little or no talk of someone taking his place, and
in this, as he knew, he was extremely fortunate.

When several doctors advised a return to Europe, he sailed again for
Le Havre, leaving on May 22, 1858, two years to the day since the attack in
the Senate.

———

The excruciating ordeal Sumner was subjected to in the summer of 1858
need never have happened. Some American acquaintances in Paris had
recommended that he see a French-American physician named Charles
Edward Brown-Séquard, reputedly "a bold experimenter on animals and
human beings, adventurous in practice as in theory."

Brown-Séquard came to see Sumner at his hotel and after a three-
hour examination determined to his satisfaction that the blows inflicted
by Congressman Brooks had, because of Sumner's seated position, se-
verely damaged certain key points in his spinal cord. The cure the doctor
recommended was "fire." He would burn the naked skin on Sumner's back
at the key points using cotton soaked in some combustible substance. The
treatment, warned Brown-Séquard, could be painful. Sumner asked him
to begin at once and, at his choice, without anesthetic, lest it reduce the
effect of the procedure.

Through the agony of the ordeal—conducted there in the hotel room—
Sumner gripped the back of a chair with such force that he broke it in two.

Over the next two weeks he was subjected to an additional five such
"treatments," again without anesthetic. "The doctor is clear," he explained
in a letter to Longfellow, "that without this cruel treatment I should have
been a permanent invalid, always subject to sudden and serious relapse.
Surely this life is held sometimes on hard conditions."

Apparently he had no second thoughts about the procedure or about

Brown-Séquard. But a number of friends and physicians at home were convinced he had been the victim of a quack experimenting with a "baseless theory" at his expense.

There seems little doubt that Brown-Séquard thought he was doing the right thing, and the fact that such a treatment was prescribed by a physician of reputation in Paris, the world's center of advanced medicine, gave it great credence, and particularly to a patient desperate for relief.

From what is known from surviving records, the attack by Brooks had neither fractured Sumner's skull nor caused a concussion, and this, with other evidence, strongly indicates that much of what he suffered after the attack was from what would later be called psychic wounds. His suffering was entirely real, but the indications are it derived far more from the psychological trauma of the attack than from a neurological cause.

That Sumner could barely endure being back in the Senate—back at the scene of the attack—and that his condition so noticeably improved the farther from Washington he was, strongly suggests this, as indeed it did to several physicians at the time. Almost any change of scene would have helped him. Had there been no "cruel treatment" as administered by Brown-Séquard, Paris by itself would almost certainly have proven quite as therapeutic again that summer of 1858 as it had the year before.

When in August, six weeks after the last of the treatments, Sumner received an invitation to a grand banquet to be given by a number of other Americans in Paris in honor of Samuel Morse, he was, as he told Morse in a note, still too weak and beset by pain to attend.

Morse had at last, at age sixty-seven, attained the success and recognition he had longed for. His telegraph was an established part of American life. A few years earlier in a letter to Dominique Arago, the first of the French savants to have acclaimed the importance of the invention, Morse had written proudly, "At this moment my system of telegraphing comprises about *fifteen thousand* English miles of conductors on this continent." How many thousands of miles it reached in Europe he did not know.

Financially he was secure as he had never been, even wealthy to the point where he had been able to establish his first real home and in the grand manner, an Italianate mansion called Locust Grove, which he built on the eastern bank of the Hudson River just below Poughkeepsie. He had married Sarah Griswold, and had had four more children. He was still bothered with rival claims to his invention and lawsuits, but all that seemed of far less consequence now, as the most enormous telegraph project yet was nearing completion, the laying of an Atlantic cable connecting America and Britain. An announcement of its success was expected any day, which made the prospect of the banquet all the more cause for excitement.

Morse arrived in Paris with nearly all his large family—his wife, three young boys, his mother-in-law, a party of fifteen in total—and checked into the Hôtel du Louvre.

On August 17, with perfect timing, on the eve of the banquet, came the news of the completion of the Atlantic cable. Messages of greeting had been exchanged across the sea by telegraph between Queen Victoria and the president of the United States, James Buchanan. As later reported in a *New York Times* account of the dinner in Paris, "the utmost enthusiasm prevailed."

Of the eighty gentlemen gathered in formal attire at the Trois Frères Provençaux, at least one in four appear to have had something to say in tribute to Morse. "Every figure of rhetoric was exhausted in his praise," continued the *Times* coverage of the "Great Telegraphic Festival." Morse himself, when it came his turn, spoke modestly of his accomplishments and why all Americans should feel proud, and he was roundly and repeatedly applauded.

Greatest of all was the standing acclaim when the new American minister to France, John Y. Mason, announced that the governments of Europe, with France in their lead, had agreed to honor Professor Morse as a "benefactor of mankind." He was to be awarded the sum of 400,000 francs (approximately $80,000), with France contributing the largest part of it.

It was a night of nights for Morse and of the kind Charles Sumner, with his oratorical flair, would have thrived on. As it was, in his note to Morse declining the invitation, he had said in a single paragraph what so many had tried to say with such formality and at such length:

> I seize the moment to express in this informal manner my humble gratitude for the great discovery with which your name will always be associated. Through you civilization has made one of her surest and grandest triumphs beyond any ever won on a field of battle. Nor do I go beyond the line of most cautious truth when I add, that if mankind had yet arrived at a just appreciation of its benefactors, it would welcome such a conqueror with more than a marshal's baton.

Morse wrote immediately to express his gratitude.

When in early September, it became known that messages over the Atlantic cable had suddenly stopped, that something had gone wrong, no one took it as anything more than a temporary inconvenience. As said in *Galignani's Messenger*, there was "no great cause for despondency in the present interruption. It rather sets forth the necessity for more cables. . . ."

———

Feeling strong enough to get about again, Sumner departed on an excursion to Brittany, then the French Alps, to Aix-les-Bains, to try the mineral springs known for their curative value since Roman times. Noticeably improved, he moved on to Italy, then to Vienna, Prague, and Dresden, and afterward to Munich and down the Rhine to Cologne, and then back to Paris. Through the whole journey, he kept up correspondence with old friends at home and took time to be with other friends encountered en route. He was determined, by staying on the move and keeping his mind fully occupied, to "turn the corner" on his health. When, in Paris, Dr. Brown-Séquard warned that he was not yet ready to return to the United States, he promptly went off to Montpellier in the south of France and by the spring of 1859 was in Italy again, then back to France for still more sightseeing in Brittany and Normandy, stopping at Mont-Saint-Michel, Saint-Malo, and Rennes. "If anybody cares to know how I am doing, you can say better and better," he reported to his brother.

By the autumn of 1859, once more in Paris, he was preparing at last to leave for good, ready to go home and get back to his work in the Senate. In the last few days he treated himself to a shopping binge, in true American tourist fashion, buying china, bronzes, old manuscripts, engravings, and rare books, for which he had a passion, all to take back with him, and made an excursion to La Grange, to pay final homage to the memory of Lafayette.

A friend from Boston, the controversial Unitarian minister Theodore Parker, who had come to Europe in hope of relief from health problems of his own, was amazed by the miraculous change in "dear old Sumner."

> He walks on those great long legs of his at the rate of four or five miles an hour. His countenance is as good as ever. He walked upright and sits upright. All the trouble has vanished from his brain. . . . He is full of information—knowledge of facts, men, and ideas. . . . I never found him more cheerful or more hopeful. It is a continual feast to see him.

By the fall of 1860, George Healy and his family were well established in Illinois. Another child had been born, a sixth daughter, which made a total of seven children, and Healy had commissions aplenty, just as his Chicago friend, William Ogden, had promised. One of those who sat for his portrait was Bishop John Bernard Fitzpatrick, who conversed with Healy in French and persuaded him to return to the Catholic faith, from which he had long since strayed.

In the second week of November 1860, following the presidential elections, Healy was asked to paint the president-elect, Abraham Lincoln. On November 15, Healy took the train to Springfield for the first of several sittings in the Illinois State House. A visiting politician who happened by described how Lincoln "sat to the artist with his right foot on top of the left and both feet turned inward—pigeon fashion," and how, telling stories the whole while, he "laughed at his own wit . . . and made a couple of hours pass merrily."

During one session Lincoln sat glancing through letters and began laughing aloud over one from an unknown correspondent. "She complains of my ugliness," he told Healy. She suggested he grow a beard, "to hide my horrible lantern jaws." Would Healy like to paint him with a beard, Lincoln asked. He would not, Healy said, and Lincoln laughed again "with perfect delight."

The portrait was one of Healy's strongest and most sensitive, and of great importance because it recorded Lincoln in color and without the beard. The head is in profile. His face is not yet marked by the burdens and strain of the years to come. It is a younger, still-untested Abraham Lincoln and as surely rendered as any portrait ever done of him.

Less than five months later, in April 1861, Healy was in Charleston, South Carolina, finishing a portrait of General Pierre Gustave Toutant Beauregard, just before Beauregard, having joined the Confederates, ordered the fateful bombardment of Fort Sumter in the harbor on April 12. Charleston went wild with excitement. Healy, who had never mixed in politics, was nonetheless, as he said, "a Northern man with Northern feelings and anti-slavery principles." A Charleston newspaper declared that if the Yankee painter had "not left the city before the sun went down, he should be tarred and feathered." When Healy laughed on hearing about it, his host assured him it was no laughing matter and said a carriage would be at the door in an hour and he most certainly must leave.

Back in Washington, on receiving word of the firing on Fort Sumter, Senator Charles Sumner went directly to the White House to assure President Lincoln of his full support, "heart and soul," and told him that "under the war power the right had come to him to emancipate the slaves."

In Paris the April weather was all it was supposed to be. One fine, sunny day followed another, the temperature in the seventies. Some days not a cloud was visible. Along the Champs-Élysées the fashionable paraded themselves as customary, pleased with the weather and the crowds, delighted to be seen in their new spring finery and to be part of the glittering show.

Wagner's *Tannhäuser* had its premiere (the consensus was that it needed work), and among the new translations available in the bookshops was Longfellow's *Hiawatha*. In the Garden of the Tuileries and the Luxembourg Gardens, strollers slowed or paused to enjoy the long beds of flowers in bloom.

With great military pageantry and solemnity, the mortal remains of Napoleon were transferred from the Chapel of Saint-Jérome in the Invalides, where they had rested for twenty years, to lie at last beneath the church's great dome. Emperor Napoleon III in full uniform and the Empress Eugénie in "deep mourning" descended into the crypt to sprinkle holy water on the coffin.

The emperor's vision of a great imperial city moved steadily forward, with no little racket and raising of dust, and still mountains of rubble were everywhere. Demolition for the "prolongation" of the broad boulevards continued—the boulevard Malesherbes was on schedule for completion that summer—and it was announced that the French architect Charles Garnier had won the design competition for the Théâtre de l'Opéra, the monumental structure intended to epitomize more than any other the splendor of the Second Empire. Like Harriet Beecher Stowe, Nathaniel Hawthorne, and Charles Sumner, most Americans liked what they saw of the new Paris.

News of Fort Sumter broke by trans-Atlantic "telegraphic dispatches" on Saturday, April 27. "THE CIVIL WAR IN THE STATES," ran the headline in *Galignani's Messenger* the next day. The city of Washington was described as "in a frantic state of excitement."

As the news grew steadily more alarming, more and more Americans in Paris were hurriedly making ready to leave. A correspondent for the *New York World* wrote of the crowds of Americans gathered day after day at Galignani's and other centers for dispatches, and how, though there was some excitement and "a little angry discussion," the general feeling was one of gloom and sadness.

> We who are residing in a foreign country, away from the immediate scene of action, perhaps can feel more deeply than those at home the evil effects of the present distracted condition of our country. Here men from every section of it . . . heretofore felt a pride and a pleasure in grasping the hand of an American, from whatever portion of the Union he may have come from. But this has given place to the feeling of bitterness, and the men from the North and South are now, in

Europe, looking upon each other as enemies. The effect of the last news will be to send to America most of those who are now here, as the feeling on both sides appears to be that in the present crisis every man should be where his services may be obtained if needed.

For Americans the good time in Paris was put on hold, and no one could say for how long.

CHAPTER EIGHT

BOUND TO SUCCEED

I was chiefly impressed by Gus's possessing so strongly the qualities of a man who was bound to succeed.

—ALFRED GARNIER

I

Augustus Saint-Gaudens came to Paris the first time in 1867, the year it seemed the whole world came to Paris for the Exposition Universelle, the grand, gilded apogee of Second Empire exuberance.

He arrived on an evening in February, by train after dark and apparently alone. He was nineteen years old, a redheaded New York City boy, a shoemaker's son, who had been working since the age of thirteen. He was not one of the first ambitious young Americans to come to Paris following the Civil War. He was younger than most, however, and in background and the future he had in store, he was like no one else. Until now he had never been away from home.

> I walked with my heavy carpet bag from the Gare du Havre
> down to the Place de la Concorde where I stood bewildered
> with the lights of that square and of the avenue des Champs-
> Élysées bursting upon me. Between the glory of it all and the

terrible weight of the bag . . . I made my way up the interminable avenue des Champs-Élysées to the Arc de Triomphe. . . .

His French father, the proprietor of a shoe shop on Fourth Avenue, had
asked if he would like to attend the great exposition and offered to pay
his passage. He crossed on the steamer *City of Boston* in steerage and was
"sicker than a regiment of dogs" the whole way.

The young man had more in mind than the exposition. He planned to
enroll at the École des Beaux-Arts and remain in Paris as long as need be.
Like young George Healy more than thirty years before—and Wendell
Holmes, Charles Sumner, Elizabeth Blackwell, and others—he had something he was determined to accomplish, and thus become accomplished
himself. He was, as he said, bound to be a sculptor. That no American had
ever been accepted as a student in sculpture at the École did not deter
him. But first he needed a job. In his pocket he had $100 saved by his fa-
ther for him from his own small wages.

Gus, as he was known, had been born in Dublin, Ireland, on March 1,
1848. His father, Bernard Paul Ernest Saint-Gaudens, who came from the
village of Aspet, in the foothills of the Pyrénées in southern France, had
found work in a Dublin shoe factory. There he met Mary McGuiness of
Ballymahon, in a shoe store where she did the binding for slippers. It was
because of the famine in Ireland that the couple emigrated to America
when Gus was six months old.

In New York, after a struggle, Bernard Saint-Gaudens managed to establish his own small store on Lispenard Street. The sign read FRENCH
LADIES' BOOTS AND SHOES, and with virtually everything French much in
fashion, he did well enough to get by, the clientele of his "small establishment" including some Astors and Belmonts.

Two more children were born, sons Andrew and Louis. At home the
father addressed the children in French, and in the accent of southern
France, and they customarily spoke French to him. Their mother spoke
always in English in her "sweet Irish brogue," as Gus said. He would describe his father as short and stocky, with dark red hair, red mustache, and
a "picturesque personality." His mother had wavy black hair and a "typical
long, generous, loving Irish face."

They lived for a time on Duane Street, then Forsyth Street, then the Bowery, then in an apartment over a grocery store on 21st Street. The boy survived countless street fights with neighborhood gangs, "heroic charges and counter charges" amid showers of stones. There was Sunday school at St. Patrick's Cathedral on Mulberry Street, and the inevitable recital of a prayer ending with the words "through my fault, through my fault, through my grievous fault," which always left him wondering what in the world his fault might be. School was "one long imprisonment." But there were also "the delights" of *Robinson Crusoe*, the first book he read, and a friend of his father's, an ophthalmologist named Cornelius Agnew, who had studied in Paris and who, after seeing some drawings Gus had done of shoemakers at work, encouraged him to keep drawing.

When, on the boy's thirteenth birthday, his father announced it time he went to work and asked what he would like to do, Gus said he hoped it could be something that would help him become an artist. His father apprenticed him to a cameo cutter named Louis Avet, a fellow Frenchman.

Cameos for men were much in style as scarf pins, with the heads of dogs, horses, and lions—lion heads were especially in demand—cut from amethyst and other stones. Louis Avet was highly accomplished in the art and, as Gus quickly learned, an exceedingly hard taskmaster who flew into rages and made the boy's time "a miserable slavery." But the training was superb, and Saint-Gaudens later attributed his habit of work to Avet— and of singing at his work, as Avet had. "When he was not scolding me, he sang continuously."

The boy worked ten-hour days and spent the first part of his apprenticeship polishing the backgrounds of stone cameos done by his master, but was soon allowed to do more, including custom-colored cameo portraits on conch shells.

The art of cutting cameos, as said, was a species of sculpture rather than engraving. The artisan worked at a small bench with a multitude of steel engraving tools, or burins, with different-shaped points, these powered by a foot pedal that the cutter pumped as one did a sewing machine. The piece of stone or shell was fixed with cement to a stick, to hold it fast while the cutter worked. As said in an article in *Scientific American* magazine, "Sculptured heads are the best model for the learner to study and the figures of statuary the best guide." For portraits most cutters worked from photographs.

To work with painstaking care was of the essence. There could be no rushing the process. The success of a cameo was in its design, and thus Gus learned the infinite importance of design to any work to be taken seriously. In little time he was producing remarkably accomplished, even exquisite, work.

The apprenticeship with Avet lasted three years, until the day when, in one of his rages, Avet fired him for dropping crumbs on the floor during lunch. Quite possibly the temper outbursts came from jealousy—that someone so young had such talent and had advanced so far so rapidly. In any event, recognizing the mistake he had made, Avet went to Bernard Saint-Gaudens and offered to hire Gus back at a higher wage. The boy refused. He later spoke of it as one of his most heroic acts ever and would treasure all his life the memory of the look of pride on his father's face.

He went to work for another French cutter, Jules Le Brethon, who specialized in larger shell cameos and who, in temperament and understanding, was the antithesis of Avet, except that he, too, sang the whole day long.

Large shell cameos with carved portraits had become highly fashionable as part of the well-dressed woman's attire, and it was working with and learning from his new employer for another three years that decided Gus on a career as a sculptor. Not only did he like giving physical dimension to a subject; he had come to appreciate the importance of faces. Generously, Le Brethon allowed him an hour a day in which to model in clay on his own.

Encouraged by his father, Gus began taking evening drawing classes at the Cooper Institute. Later he attended evening classes at the National Academy of Design. "I became a terrific worker," he would remember, "toiling every night until eleven o'clock after class was over, in the conviction that in me another heaven-born genius had been given the world."

> Indeed, I became so exhausted with the confining work of cameo-cutting by day and drawing at night that in the morning mother literally dragged me out of bed, pushed me over

to the washstand, where I gave myself a cat's lick somehow
or other, drove me to the seat at the table, administered my
breakfast, which consisted of tea and large quantities of long
French loaves of bread with butter, and tumbled me down-
stairs out into the street, where I awoke.

The apprenticeship years under the two cameo cutters were also the
years of the Civil War, and the day-to-day presence, the excitement and
tragedy, of the war were seldom out of mind. Bernard Saint-Gaudens became an outspoken abolitionist. Soldiers thronged the streets. Once, from
an open window while at Louis Avet's workshop, the boy had watched
a whole contingent of New England volunteers march down Broadway
on their way to war singing "John Brown's Body." Another day he saw
"Grant himself" with his slouch hat parade by on horseback. Greatest of
all was the thrill of seeing President Lincoln, who with his height seemed
"entirely out of proportion" with the carriage in which he rode.

The boy would remember the crowds outside the newspaper offices,
and the sight of legless and armless men back from the battlefields would
never be forgotten. One day during the Draft Riots, Monsieur Le Brethon
sent him home for his safety.

Of the many American art students and artists who came to Paris after
the Civil War, scarcely any had been unaffected by the war. Some had
served in it; others had been witnesses to camp life and the horrors of a
war that had left more than 600,000 men dead. Henry Bacon, a landscape
painter, had enlisted in the Thirteenth Massachusetts Regiment and was
badly wounded at the Second Battle of Bull Run. Winslow Homer had
covered the war as an artist correspondent for *Harper's Weekly*. By the
end of 1866, when he came to Paris, Homer had done more than twenty
paintings with the war as his subject, including *The Veteran in a New
Field*, a powerful image of a lone figure swinging a scythe, like the reaper
of death, in a golden wheat field, evoking memories of slaughter in the
wheat field at Gettysburg.

In the weeks that followed the Battle of Gettysburg, the wounded had
arrived by the trainload in Philadelphia, the home of Thomas Eakins, then
a student of painting. Like many parents, Eakins's father, a man of limited

244 · D A V I D   M c C U L L O U G H ·

means, paid the required $25 so Thomas could avoid being drafted, a difficult decision for both father and son.

It would be hard for future generations to imagine—or would simply be forgotten—that in a city like Philadelphia more than half the male population between ages eighteen and forty-five served in the Union Army.

Most heart-wrenching for young Saint-Gaudens was seeing Abraham Lincoln lying in state at New York's City Hall. He had waited hours in an "interminable" line, and after seeing Lincoln's face, he went back to the end of the line to go through a second time.

In France, as he and other newly arrived Americans soon learned, the Civil War was viewed with indifference or, more often, overt sympathy for the defeated Confederates. Thus it had been since the start of the war and seemed strangely at odds with French opposition to slavery, not to say the traditional goodwill between the governments of France and the United States from the time of the American Revolution. In 1863, matters had been further complicated. With America preoccupied with the war, Napoleon III chose to install his own puppet emperor in Mexico, the young Austrian Ferdinand Joseph Maximilian. That so many Americans had taken this as a clear breach of the Monroe Doctrine only added to French sympathy for the South.

Congressman Elihu B. Washburne of Illinois, who was soon to become the American minister to France, affirmed later that Louis Napoleon had been in "full sympathy with the Rebellion" and "desirous of giving it aid and comfort as far as he dared.

> That was well known to everybody in Paris, which was filled with Confederates, who were flattered and feted not only at the Tuileries, but by the people generally of the city. The loyal men of our country were everywhere in the background.

A Confederate mission had been established in Paris at 25 avenue d'Antin, and a Confederate Woman's Aid Society, organized by Southern women, collected medical supplies and clothing for the Confederate army and staged fundraising concerts and bazaars.

The one time when the "excitement" of the Civil War had come to

France's doorstep was on June 19, 1864, the day the Confederate raider *Alabama* and the steamer USS *Kearsarge* fought to the finish off Cherbourg, within view of several thousand spectators crowded on hilltops along the shoreline. The *Alabama*, which had been wreaking havoc with Union shipping, had put in to Cherbourg for repairs. When the *Kearsarge* arrived on the scene, the *Alabama* went out to meet her. The battle raged for an hour and a half before the burning *Alabama* went to the bottom. Engravings of the drama filled the illustrated French newspapers and magazines. The painter Édouard Manet produced a dramatic portrayal of the scene. The Paris papers were filled with editorial sympathy for the *Alabama* and her brave crew. According to one journal, the *Constitutionnel*, the loss of the *Alabama* had caused "profound regret from one end of France to the other."

For Augustus Saint-Gaudens, nothing about his growing up had been easy or shielded from the hard realities of existence. The combination of New York street life, work, and the war had made him mature beyond his years. Physically full grown by the time he arrived in Paris, he stood five feet eight. He had his father's full head of wiry dark red hair, a long pale face like his mother, rather small, deep-set, intent pale grey-blue eyes, and a long nose his friends made fun of and that he himself made fun of in cartoons and caricatures.

People liked him for his sense of humor and exuberance, his "Celtic spirit." "In his spare but strong-knit figure, his firm but supple hands, his manner of carrying himself, his every gesture," a friend would write, "one felt the abounding vitality, the almost furious energy of the man." He seemed happy by nature. He loved to sing at work or with friends, most any time, and was blessed with a rich tenor voice. One friend, Thomas Moore, would remember how, on Saturday nights after class hours at Cooper Institute, he, Gus, and two others named Herzog and Grotemeyer, "took long walks arm-in-arm to Central Park shouting airs from 'Martha,' the 'Marseillaise,' and the like, in which Gus was always the leader with his voice and magnetic presence."

Known for looking always on the bright side, he would later in life suffer acute spells of melancholy and insist there had been "always the *triste* undertone in my soul that comes from my sweet Irish mother."

He had demonstrated uncommon talent in his extraordinary cameo carvings and freehand drawings. Before leaving for Paris he had modeled a remarkably strong, confident bust of his father. He considered a pencil portrait he drew of his mother to be his most prized possession. Yet he knew the question of how far his talent could take him, and how it would measure up against serious competition, had still to be resolved, and as for so many others, this was among the main reasons for his being in Paris.

He moved in at first with his Uncle François, his father's brother, on the avenue de la Grande-Armée, and "at once" found a part-time job working for an Italian cameo cutter on Montmartre. Told his application to the École des Beaux-Arts could take months to process, he enrolled in both morning and evening classes in modeling at one of the so-called "*petites écoles*" held at the École de Médecine. From Montmartre to the École de Médecine in the Latin Quarter was a two-mile walk. On the days he was working he made the round trip.

Uncle François, who made his living as a demolition specialist, had been doing well as long as Georges Haussmann kept tearing Paris apart. But with the emperor's plan for the city nearly completed, and the demolition about over, Uncle François was in "bad straits." Forced to find somewhere else to live, Gus began moving from "cheaper to cheaper lodgings." He was soon barely surviving, "miserably poor," as he wrote years later, but he said nothing about it at the time, such was his refusal to "dwell on the ugly side of things."

Classes at the *petite école* were a joy to him. Not even the conditions under which they were conducted could dampen his spirits.

> We worked in a stuffy, overcrowded, absolutely unventilated theater, with two rows of students, perhaps twenty-five in each row, seated in a semicircle before the model who stood against the wall. Behind those who drew were about fifteen sculptors and I look back with admiration upon the powers of youth to live, work, and be joyful in an atmosphere that must have been almost asphyxiating.

II

As promised, the glittering Exposition Universelle of 1867 was bigger and more spectacular than anything the world had yet seen. One giant, oval-shaped, glass-and-cast-iron exhibition "palace" and more than one hundred smaller buildings filled most of the vast Champ de Mars on the Left Bank. More than 50,000 exhibitors took part. The theme was "objects for the improvement of the physical and moral condition of the masses." By the time the fair closed, on the last day of October, 11 million people—more than twice the number who attended the Exposition of 1855—had poured across the Pont d'Iéna to the banner-festooned main entrance on the Quai d'Orsay.

They came from virtually every country. Emperor Napoleon III played host in lavish fashion to the czar of Russia, the kings of Prussia, Bavaria, and Portugal, the pasha of Egypt, and the sultan of Turkey in a red fez. There were soirées and dinners night after night, and grand balls at the luxuriously renovated Palais des Tuileries. Count Otto von Bismarck, chief minister to the king of Prussia, could be seen resplendent in his white uniform and invariably enjoying himself as much as anyone. At a ball at the Austrian Embassy, amid "mountains" of lights and flowers, grottoes, and cascades of real water, guests waltzed to music by Johann Strauss's orchestra from Vienna. Strauss himself conducted the first performance of *The Blue Danube* in Paris, and the dancing went on until nearly daybreak.

To add to the pleasures of the city for visitors of all kinds, a new line of steam-powered sightseeing boats called Bateaux Mouches now plied the Seine.

Because of bad weather in March, the exposition had been embarrassingly slow getting under way. At the time of the official opening on April 2, nearly half of the exhibits were still unpacked. (People were calling it "The Universal Exhibition of International Boxes.") But by May all was in full swing and Paris more dazzling than ever. No one had ever seen so many flags flying, so many lights blazing, so many people of all kinds.

"At the Grand Hôtel they were making up beds in the dining room," reported the *New York Times*. With the start of summer the throngs grew greater still. "Even the Americans are coming at last. The registers are filling with their names from Boston to New Orleans, and so on to San Francisco." Among the crowds of Americans was the author Mark Twain, who, taking time out from a tour of Europe and the Holy Land, checked into the Hôtel du Louvre.

"Paris is now the great center of the world," wrote Samuel F. B. Morse, who, at age seventy-eight, had returned with his wife and four children. (So indispensable had the telegraph become to daily life at home in the United States by this time that 50,000 miles of Western Union wire carried more than 2 million news dispatches a year, including, in 1867, the latest from the exposition in Paris.)

The displays of novel manufactured items included an almost overwhelming array of things large and small, things almost unimaginable— magnificent locomotives, steam engines, a feather-weight metal called aluminum, a giant siege gun by the German cannon maker Krupp, and a new kind of brass horn, *le saxophone*, devised by Napoleon III's official instrument maker, Adolphe Sax. The favorite American import, to judge by the crowds it drew, was a soda fountain. The Philadelphia art student Thomas Eakins wrote to his family of waiting in a line a block long for a drink from it.

Mark Twain and a few traveling companions spent only a few days in Paris before continuing on the tour he would describe in often hilarious fashion in *Innocents Abroad*, which was to remain his best-selling book throughout his lifetime. Neither he nor any of his group had been abroad before. Travel was a "wild novelty" to them, and Paris "flashed upon us a splendid meteor," he wrote, but he thought considerably less of the Parisians, and what humor he evoked was chiefly at their expense. He was, as would be said, not so much an American Francophobe, but a Parisphobe. The Paris barbershops were hopeless. He detested Paris guides. They "deceive and defraud every American who goes to Paris for the first time or sees the sights alone or in the company with others as little experienced as himself."

With few exceptions the women of Paris struck him as downright homely. The *grisettes* were the biggest disappointment of all. "I knew by their looks that they ate garlic and onions . . . and I sorrow for the vagabond student of the Latin Quarter now, even more than I formerly envied him." Seeing the "renowned" can-can danced for the first time, he covered his face with his hands, he claimed, but "looked through my fingers."

> The idea of it is to dance as wildly, as noisily, as furiously as you can; expose yourself as much as possible if you are a woman; and kick as high as you can. . . . Heavens!

Of the especially conspicuous presence of prostitutes in the city because of the exposition, he chose to say nothing. Yet when his brief stay was over, as he acknowledged, he gave "the beautiful city a regretful farewell."

The number and importance of contemporary paintings and sculptures on exhibit surpassed anything seen before in one place. Though the American section of the Fine Arts Department was quite modest compared to that of the French, it was larger than it had been at the Exposition of 1855 and contained a number of works that, in time, would rank as American masterpieces. The most admiring crowds gathered about two enormous, dramatic landscapes—both befitting subjects for America, it was felt—Albert Bierstadt's *The Rocky Mountains* and Frederic Church's *Niagara Falls*, the only American painting to be honored with a silver medal. Among several works evoking the Civil War from a Northern point of view were John Ferguson Weir's *The Gun Foundry*, showing the munitions works near West Point, and Winslow Homer's *Prisoners from the Front*, in which three Confederate prisoners under guard stand before a Northern general.

James McNeill Whistler's *White Girl*, a near-life-size, full-length portrait of his beautiful red-haired Irish model and mistress, Joanna Hiffernan, dressed in white against a white background, had been rejected from an earlier exhibition at the Royal Academy in London and was considered, even in Paris, too suggestive by far, in that the young woman's hair was undone and she stood on a wolf's skin.

Many visitors found the exhibitions of American art disappointing. "Infantile arrogance," "childish ignorance," were two of the harsher comments from French critics, though one thought "M. Homer ought not, in good justice, be passed over unnoticed" and another saw promise of better things to come.

> Count on the fact that the Americans, once they begin the business of the fine arts, will go quickly, and will go looking toward the future. Go ahead! Forward!

Homer, who had arrived in Paris in December, stayed nearly all of 1867. "I am working hard and improving much," he wrote a friend in August. But his correspondence was infrequent and provides little in the way of details. He shared a studio in Montmartre, studied for a while with a French artist, Frederick Rondel, and spent time painting landscapes in the artists' colony at Cernay-la-Ville.

A painting by Homer called *The Studio* that appears to have been done in Paris had, in any event, as Henry James said, "a great deal of Paris in it." Two painters sit playing chamber music on cello and violin, the score propped on their easels. They have the requisite beards and mustaches, and in a photograph taken in Paris that year, Homer has the tips of his large mustache waxed to sharp points in the Louis Napoleon mode. Presumably, like other American artists and students, he spent time at the exposition, but how much is unknown.

Nor, regrettably, is there any account of how much of the exposition Augustus Saint-Gaudens saw. Probably he had not money enough to attend more than once or twice. But with his zest for getting "his money's worth," he doubtless covered a lot of ground, and he did see something of lifelong importance to him. It was a small bronze, a standing figure by the French sculptor Paul Dubois, of *St. John the Baptist as a Child.* It "seemed extraordinary to me," he would write years afterward, and Dubois's work and Dubois himself were to have "profound" influence.

Americans filled Paris in such numbers as to please themselves and annoy some of those from other countries, and the British in particular. Hotel managers, shopkeepers, clerks, and floor managers at the sumptuous new department stores—*les grands magasins* such as Le Printemps and La Samaritaine—welcomed Americans as no others. "They spend money profusely, are not much given to bargaining, and put on no airs," wrote the *New York Times* correspondent.

In addition to the huge influx of American tourists, the size of the American colony in Paris had been growing steadily to the point where there were now more than 4,000 Americans living in the city. This was far fewer than the number of resident English or Germans, but still four times what it had been a generation earlier.

The bad feelings that had developed among many of the French toward Americans on the side of the North during the Civil War had subsided rapidly. Further, on July 2, word reached Paris that Emperor Maximilian of Mexico had been executed by a firing squad on orders from the rebel leader, Benito Juárez. Napoleon III first learned of the calamity as he was preparing to present awards before a crowd of 20,000 at the exposition.

Clearly his misadventures in Mexico were finished, and this, too, had a notable effect on how Parisians felt about the throngs of American visitors that summer.

> The great majority of thinking minds are . . . heartily glad that an end has been put to the Emperor's projects in that direction [the *Times* correspondent wrote], and they seem desirous to make up by their present cordiality to Northerners for the dislike and hostility which was evinced toward them during the rebellion. For the prompt revival of the old feeling of friendship, we have no doubt in a great measure to thank the Exhibition.

Europeans marveled at the industrial might that had been marshaled by the North during the Civil War and America's surging productivity since. In the words of the soon-to-be American minister to France, Elihu Washburne, a former congressman from Illinois, "The United States, having astonished all Europe by triumphantly crushing out the most stupendous rebellion the world had ever known, and after one of the most gigantic wars in history, had bounded forward to a position of first rank among the nations of the earth."

Such an enormous increase in productivity also meant unprecedented prosperity for a great many Americans, and with money at hand as never before in their lives, what better place to spend it than Paris? Well-to-do American women were now making annual trips to Paris to enhance their wardrobes at Worth's. The famous couturier Charles Frederick Worth, an English expatriate, had made his establishment at 7 rue de la Paix a Paris destination, his name the very emblem of good taste in New York and San Francisco, no less than Paris or London. And if Worth's proved insufficient, there were other high-priced dressmakers like Bobergh or Felix.

Bringing one lady to Paris cost as much as two men, wrote a young American civil engineer, Washington Roebling, who, with his wife, Emily, was in Europe gathering technical information in preparation for what was to be America's greatest bridge, connecting Brooklyn to New York. Their money had vanished so rapidly in Paris that they had to leave earlier than they wished.

Another American of note, Henry Adams of Boston, wanted only to get out of Paris as soon as possible, but to his annoyance he and his wife, Clover, were held over for days, "waiting for ladies' dresses and the milliner's bills." Paris was "horribly" expensive and crowded, the fastidious Adams reported. He had never imagined the city could be so overrun with "hordes of low Germans, English, Italians, Spaniards, and Americans, who stare and gawk and smell, and crowd every shop and street. I did not detect a single refined-looking being among them. . . ."

Every month, on average, one hundred Americans sojourning in Paris applied to the United States minister for the chance to be presented at court, and nearly all felt obliged to turn out in the finest, latest thing. Dr. Thomas Evans regularly supplied the emperor with the names of "présentable" Americans to be invited to reviews or grand balls at the Palace of the Tuileries or gala days at the palace at Saint-Cloud, Fontainebleau, or Compiègne.

One resident American in Paris who, like Evans, figured frequently on the royal guest list was Lillie Greenough Moulton, the wife of an independently wealthy American named Charles Moulton. Still in her twenties, and known for her exquisite singing voice, as well as her beauty, she had become a favorite of the emperor and empress. In her diary, along with descriptions of the flowers and diamond tiaras, the dazzling uniforms and other extravagances of the court, she included this account of what was involved in just preparing for a week in the country at *la Maison de l'Empereur* at Compiègne.

> I was obliged to have about twenty dresses, eight day cos-
> tumes (counting my traveling suit), the green cloth dress for
> the hunt, which I was told was absolutely necessary, seven ball
> dresses, five gowns for tea. . . .
> A professional packer came to pack our trunks, of which I
> had seven and C[harles] had two; the maid and the valet each
> had one, making, altogether, quite a formidable pile of luggage.

Transportation was provided by a special train marked IMPÉRIAL.

There was increasing talk in Paris financial circles of the great railroad under construction across the North American continent and what it could mean to world trade, especially in combination with the new sea-level ship canal being dug at Suez with French financing and under the leadership of the French diplomat Ferdinand de Lesseps. The future had never looked so large with possibilities.

"The American flag is freely displayed all over Paris, as if our countrymen were welcome," wrote a Philadelphia physician, Dr. FitzWilliam Sargent, who for some years had been coming to Paris to study French medical practices, but was now, with his wife and children, living full-time in Europe.

"Lincoln's portrait is often seen in shop windows with other notabilities. In short the United States are 'looking up.' . . ." Dr. Sargent's twelve-year-old son, "Johnnie," was also a source of much pride to him. "He sketches quite nicely and has a remarkably quick and correct eye."

III

When a formal notification arrived at last, informing Augustus Saint-Gaudens he had been admitted to the École des Beaux-Arts after a wait of nine months, he enrolled immediately in the atelier of François Jouffroy. As students in painting at the École, like Thomas Eakins, aspired to study under Jean-Léon Gérôme, master of the classical mode, who put great stress on drawing the human figure, so for those who would be sculptors, Jouffroy's atelier was, as Saint-Gaudens said, "the triumphant one."

Jouffroy was sixty-two, the son of a baker, tall, dark, and spare, "with little, intelligent black eyes," as Saint-Gaudens remembered. When making his critique of a student's work, he spoke in a low, nasal voice and while customarily gazing off the whole time in some other direction from the model and the student's efforts.

As he acknowledged, Saint-Gaudens had not yet shown himself to be a brilliant student. But Jouffroy's compliments consoled him. He was not the least discouraged, nor did he suffer any doubts about himself, such was his youthful vanity, as he also acknowledged years afterward. The doubts came later.

At a student party soon after he joined the class, the others asked him to sing the "Marseillaise," which, under the Second Empire, was forbidden in public places. He sang it in English, as he had with his friends at home in New York, and his performance brought a roar of approval. They urged him to sing it again. They praised his voice, told him how beautiful it was, and he believed them. In the days to follow he sang the song many times over, only to realize they were making fun of him.

"I was finally admitted to full membership and teased no more, becoming in my turn one of the most boisterous of the students."

He made friends—friends for life, in several cases—and mostly with those from southern France, who spoke with a southern accent just as he did, because of his father.

Reminiscing later, he recalled nothing in the way of "amorous adventure." When a girl he liked in New York wrote to ask whether he still meant to "keep company" with her, he never replied. How truly chaste he remained is impossible to know, so extremely circumspect was he always about what he considered private matters. Friends and working associates, however, would talk a good deal later of his fondness for women.

His afternoons cutting cameos provided only the barest living. Long afterward, walking with friends in the narrow back streets of the Latin Quarter, he would point out the miserable little cafés where he had been forced to eat dreadful food as a student in order to survive. But so "soaring" was his ambition, as he later said, and so "tremendously austere" was he, he felt a kind of "Spartan-like superiority."

A close friend, Alfred Garnier, would describe him as "possessing so strongly the qualities of a man who was bound to succeed," yet he remained as well "the most joyous creature." For exercise he, Garnier, and others went regularly to a gymnasium. (Gus was "crazy about wrestling.") On holiday hiking expeditions, they would sometimes cover thirty miles, with Gus setting the pace. On one such venture they set off for Saint-Valéry-en-Caux on the coast of Normandy. "Five minutes after we reached the seashore," Garnier remembered, "we were in the water in spite of the heavy waves, for as soon as he saw the water Gus had to enter. . . ." On another trek, in Switzerland, when they climbed a cathedral spire, none exclaimed over the view with such enthusiasm as Gus. "Nobody got his money's worth so well as he. Everything seemed enchanting, everything beautiful!"

For more than a year he remained the only American among Jouffroy's students, until 1869 when Olin Warner joined the class. Older than Gus by four years, Warner came from Vermont and was a former telegraph operator. In a stream of letters to his "Dear Ones at Home," he expressed with appealing clarity the feelings of many American students of every kind:

> Paris is the most splendid city I ever saw. . . .
> Wine is cheaper than milk. . . .
> I could not have gone to a better part of the world to study. . . .
> I am entirely out of money. . . .
> The further I go the harder it looks to me and the more
>   difficulties I encounter, but I am determined to succeed. . . .

In Jouffroy's atelier Gus led all in determination, and in making noise, "singing and whistling to split the ears." He would happily recall how he loved to "bawl" the andante of Beethoven's Seventh Symphony, or the serenade from Mozart's *Don Giovanni*. Yet for all the *joie de vivre*, the carryings-on with friends, he remained oddly shy with people he did not know. He cared nothing about what he wore, or what was in or out of fashion, and greatly disliked any and all affectations, as he would through life.

Concentrated effort at modeling and drawing day after day for three years produced clear progress. Jouffroy, while not a sculptor of the highest rank, was an exceptional teacher, and his atelier a center for what was the new movement in sculpture in France, which took its inspiration from the Italian Renaissance. In this regard, Saint-Gaudens had come to his studies in Paris at a highly advantageous time.

It was then, too, in his student years in Paris that he reached certain conclusions about work that were to stand as his guiding principles, and that he was one day, in turn, to stress again and again to students of his own.

> Conceive an idea. Then stick to it. Those who hang on are the only ones who amount to anything.
>
> You can do anything you please. It's the way it's done that makes the difference.
>
> A good thing is no better for being done quickly.

In November 1869, with all appropriate pageantry, the Suez Canal was opened, joining the Mediterranean with the Red Sea. The Empress Eugénie, present for the ceremony, stood on the deck of the imperial yacht wearing a big straw hat and waving a white handkerchief. "There was a real Egyptian sky," she would remember, "a light of enchantment, a dreamlike resplendence. . . ." The canal was a triumph. It brought France *la gloire*. Its builder, Ferdinand de Lesseps, was Europe's reigning hero. The timing seemed perfect. In America, earlier that summer, the transcontinental railroad had been completed. As the popular French novelist Jules Verne would postulate, it was now theoretically possible to go around the world in just eighty days. Those in France who had invested in the de Lesseps project—and there were thousands—would profit handsomely.

All the while "the resplendence" and pageantry of the Second Empire and its capital city continued. The exposition had come and gone, but the show of Paris never closed. The lights burned bright. Such arrays of the newest, most fashionable merchandise displayed in countless shops and grand department stores tantalized no less than ever. The music of Gounod and Offenbach, the can-can, the opening of the new Folies Trévise music hall, restaurants that stayed open through the night, the daytime spectacle of top-hatted and bonneted gentry at their leisure in the dappled sunshine of public gardens all continued, as did the steady incoming flow of affluent Americans.

Of the prominent, well-to-do American families in Paris in 1869, two from New York are particularly of note, and chiefly because of their children: the Theodore Roosevelts, the frail, asthmatic oldest son of whom, young Theodore, or "Teedie," was eleven; and the George Frederick Joneses (whose way of life was said to have inspired the expression "keeping up with the Joneses"), and whose studious, red-haired daughter Edith, the future Edith Wharton, had her first portrait painted in Paris at age eleven, during what turned out to be a family stay of two years.

But all this was worlds apart from the life of the impoverished young New Yorker trying to become a sculptor. So desperately poor was Saint-Gaudens still that out of pride as much as necessity he had assumed an attitude of "deepest scorn" for all "ordinary amusements." His one indulgence was the opera. He had come to adore the music of the opera, and with orders for cameos increasing somewhat, was inclined to treat himself now and then.

As it happened, Saint-Gaudens and several friends were at the opera the night of July 15, 1870, the night no one in Paris would ever forget, when news came that France had declared war on Prussia.

It was near the end of a performance of Daniel-François Auber's *La Muette de Portici.* One of the leads, Madame Marie Sasse, came onstage carrying a tricolor flag and asked the audience to join in singing the "Marseillaise." "Then," remembered Alfred Garnier, "everyone went crazy."

The audience poured out onto the boulevard des Italiens, where crowds were shouting *"À Berlin"*—"On to Berlin!" To Gus and Garnier, it seemed utter madness. They found themselves hammering with fists and canes at some of those shouting the loudest.

To Gus the empire was nothing but "nonsense" and "rottenness." He and his friends were ardent republicans and saw the war as the emperor's doing. None of it made sense, any more than singing the "Marseillaise," the hymn of the French Revolution, had any connection with any of the Napoleons—yet now it was the emperor's war song!

The madness grew worse by the day. Paris rang with the "Marseillaise." More crowds marched shouting for war. The government-controlled press unanimously called for war.

"No language can measure the probable consequences and results," wrote the American minister Elihu Washburne in a dispatch to President Ulysses S. Grant. "Everything is brought to a standstill and ordinary people stand aghast with amazement. But the great crowd[s] are mad with excitement and things are rushed as in a giddy whirl." The French minister of war assured the people that any conflict with Prussia would be "a mere stroll, walking stick in hand."

The emperor, who was ill and suddenly aged, privately opposed the war. He knew France to be unprepared, the same conclusion Otto von Bismarck had reached during his visit to Paris in 1867. The fact was, the Germans had more than 400,000 well-trained, well-equipped troops, whereas the French soldiers numbered only 250,000 and were poorly equipped. The issue supposedly at stake, the succession of the Spanish throne, was hardly cause for war. But that seemed of little interest, and the emperor let himself be swayed by those close around him whose hubris greatly exceeded their judgment.

On July 28, pale and tired and dressed in the full uniform of a general, he departed for the front from Saint-Cloud by private train, looking anything but confident, the pain of a bladder stone too great for him to have appeared on horseback. He was entering the campaign in command of the army poorly prepared for war. On reaching the front, at Metz, he reported to the Empress Eugénie that nothing was prepared. "I regard us as already lost."

In the first weeks of August one humiliating French defeat followed another in rapid succession, at Wissembourg, Forbach, and Wörth. An American observer with the German army, General Philip Sheridan, called the German infantry "as fine as I ever saw." The Krupp guns had twice the range of the French pieces.

The news, when it reached Paris, was devastating. Many refused to believe it. "No person not in Paris at the time could have any adequate idea of the state of feeling which the extraordinary news from the battlefield had created," wrote the American minister, Washburne.

(Telegraph dispatches from American newspaper correspondents in France had also stirred great popular interest in the war in the United States. Papers in New York or Boston or Cincinnati now carried on-the-scene descriptions of battles only days after they happened. To enable a correspondent for the *Cincinnati Commercial* to follow the French army, Washburne had devised a special passport and "covered it all over with big seals.")

On September 2 came the ultimate, overwhelming French defeat at the small border fortress of Sedan, where Napoleon III insisted, despite the pain he was in, on riding into battle, as if preferring to be killed rather than face the disgrace to come.

Sedan was the most sudden, catastrophic defeat in French history. More than 104,000 of the emperor's troops surrendered and the emperor was taken prisoner.

Paris learned what had happened late the afternoon of September 3 and the Second Empire instantly collapsed. It had been all of seven weeks since the night in July when war was declared and jubilant crowds swarmed through Paris shouting "*À Berlin!*"

On September 4, a beautiful sunny Sunday, in the midst of disaster and with the certain prospect of the Germans marching on Paris, the new minister of the interior, the flamboyant Léon Gambetta, climbed onto the sill of an enormous open window at the Hôtel de Ville to proclaim to the crowd below the birth of the Third Republic.

"Louis Napoleon Bonaparte and his dynasty have forever ceased to reign in France," he shouted. Suddenly it had become a day for rejoicing. And for Elihu Washburne no less than any other "*étranger*" in Paris. "I am rejoiced beyond expression at the downfall of this miserable dynasty and the establishment of the Republic," he wrote privately.

"So perishes a harlequin, and all his paraphernalia of Empire collapses as suddenly as a windbag pricked with a pin," wrote an American medical student named Mary Putnam, equally overjoyed.

> France, or at least Paris, gives itself up not to panic, but to a perfect outburst of joy, to the jubilation of a fête day. It crowns the statue of Strasbourg with flowers, it promenades on the Place de la Concorde, the rue de Rivoli, before the Hôtel de Ville, as if to salute the return of a triumphant army. It forgets Prussia, it forgets even the Emperor, it is wild with delight crying, "Vive la République, à toi citoyen! Nous avons la République!"

Augustus Saint-Gaudens knew nothing of what had happened, however. Early that same Sunday he had left Paris by train for Limoges, to visit his brother Andrew, who had found work in a porcelain factory there. He had felt a need to get away and think about what he ought to do.

On the fateful afternoon the Republic was proclaimed, with the clamor growing louder and more threatening outside the Palace of the Tuileries, the Empress Eugénie decided it was time to attempt an escape. She never believed this could happen to her, that she would exit in disgrace like King Louis-Philippe and Queen Marie-Amélie. For days, looking pale and worn, she had stayed on courageously. Others urged her to leave while she could. Now servants were departing, throwing aside their livery on the way out the doors.

"I yield to force," she said calmly at last. Leaving everything behind— money, jewelry—she went by way of rooms that connected the palace to the Louvre. She was accompanied only by the ambassadors of Austria and

Italy and a few loyal attendants. There was no prearranged plan. No attempt was made at disguise. She left wearing the same simple black cashmere dress she had been wearing for days, plus a dark shawl and a black derby hat with a veil.

She hurried down the long Grande Galerie of the Louvre and through the Salon Carré into the Salle des Sept-Cheminées, where, for an instant, Géricault's *Raft of the Medusa* caught her eye. How strange, she later said, that this painting of ill omen should be the last she ever saw of the Louvre.

Once outside, on the rue de Rivoli, she and a lady-in-waiting, Madame Adélaïde-Charlotte Lebreton, went off by a common, one-horse cab as fast as possible up the Champs-Élysées to the avenue de l'Impératrice, on an impulse that Dr. Evans might help her.

They arrived at about five o'clock to find Evans not at home. When he returned an hour or so later, accompanied by a long-time American colleague, Dr. Edward Crane, he was told two unidentified ladies "very anxious" to see him were waiting in the library.

Thomas Evans had been well established in Paris professionally and socially for nearly twenty years. He had come to France knowing no one, speaking no French, and with little in savings. He now resided on the avenue de l'Impératrice, where, as said in the *Paris Guide* of 1867, one saw "smiles everywhere, people dressed to the nines . . . elegance, too, and what splendors!" The house he and his wife, Agnes, called Bella Rosa had, in addition to a fine library, a white and gold ballroom, stained-glass windows, and a grand staircase of Pyrénées marble designed by Charles Garnier, the architect for the new Opéra. There were extensive grounds, a fountain, a stable with stalls for twenty horses. Evans knew all the prominent and well-to-do Americans in Paris, as well as Minister Washburne, who lived farther down the avenue. He and Agnes entertained in lavish style and customarily spent holidays at the most fashionable seaside resorts. Agnes was at the moment on holiday at Deauville on the Normandy coast.

He was charming and handsome, if a bit too well fed, and had every reason to be pleased with himself, having received the highest professional honors, including the French Legion of Honor. Such heights were unimaginable for a dentist at home in the United States or in France. In

Paris, when he first arrived, he had found those who specialized in treating diseases of the teeth ranked with barbers. Physicians looked down on dentistry, considering it hardly comparable to their own profession. Dentists sent for by well-to-do patients were expected to enter the house by the back door, like ordinary tradesmen.

For all that he had adapted to life in Paris, Evans never lost his strong allegiance to his own country. Most obvious had been his open support of the North throughout the Civil War, lobbying the emperor on the subject at every chance, despite the Southern sympathies of much of his clientele, not to say the emperor himself.

Further, from the time France went to war that summer, Evans had taken a lead in preparing for the medical emergency to be faced. He wasted no time establishing what he called the American International Sanitary Committee, paid for by him and a circle of American friends in Paris.

On a flat stretch of open land across the avenue from Bella Rosa, tents went up for a field hospital, or "field ambulance," over which he flew an American flag. Supplies of canned beef, biscuits, candles, ether, bedding, and clothing were stocked—all under the direction of Evans and his colleague Crane. The sick and wounded to be cared for would be more than the Paris hospitals could handle, and a well-supplied, well-staffed facility in the open air would be far preferable to crowding them into airless churches and public buildings, as was the usual way. No one with any realistic sense of the gravity of the crisis to come failed to appreciate the value of how much Dr. Evans had already accomplished.

As soon as he stepped into the library and saw who was waiting, Evans knew what was expected of him. Without hesitation, he offered the empress his help, despite all he stood to lose if things went wrong, as they both knew without saying. "We were thoroughly impressed with the idea that we were about to engage in an undertaking attended with many risks," he would write, "and that it would require great discretion on our parts if it was to be successfully executed."

They agreed to wait until morning before leaving the house. The empress had had little or no sleep for days. Evans made up a bed for her himself, in his wife's bedroom, because he dared not trust the servants.

At five o'clock he knocked at her door and they were on their way before daybreak, both dressed as they had been the night before. They were a party of four—Evans and Crane, the empress and her lady-in-waiting—traveling in Evans's own enclosed landau, a trusted coachman driving. They headed straight for Deauville, anxious and fearful, with Evans doing the talking at every checkpoint. No one recognized the empress, not even at Deauville.

Evans appealed to an English yachtsman, Sir John Burgoyne, and his wife to take the empress across the Channel to asylum in England. Lady Burgoyne responded, "Well, why not?"

After an extremely rough crossing, the empress and Evans were landed safely on the other side.

In Paris, meantime, no one knew anything about this. There were only rumors, the most common of which was that the empress had managed to get away to Belgium. Later the same day as her escape from the city with Evans, September 5, Victor Hugo, after years in exile, returned to Paris to wild acclaim.

Augustus Saint-Gaudens learned the news of a new republic only after arriving at Limoges. "I am heart and soul in the French cause," he declared, and departed for Paris again on the next available train.

But on the train with him on all sides were women weeping for husbands and sons at the front. At Paris he saw volunteers from Brittany marching into the city with no uniforms other than simple white blouses. Crowded with them, "in utter confusion and dust," as he wrote, were droves of sheep and cattle being led to the Jardin des Plantes in preparation for the coming siege. "They seemed to me like so many innocent men condemned to death marching to their doom," he wrote to an American in Connecticut named Elmira Whittlesey, who, during a stay in Paris, had commissioned some of his cameos. To judge by the length and candor of the letter, she was someone in whom he placed considerable trust. "I could not restrain my feelings and I kissed some of the poor fellows as they marched along. I feel sure now that most of them are already dead, a sacrifice to the ambition of a couple of scoundrels."

He had received an eight-page letter from his mother "in terrible grief," begging him to stay out of French political affairs and come home, whatever the cost. He had never felt so low, so seized by the *"triste* undertone" of his nature. He may have been heart and soul in the French cause, but he was not French. He was an American.

Earlier that summer there had been an estimated 13,000 Americans in Paris, mostly tourists. Since the declaration of war in July, they had been leaving by the thousands. The American colony in Paris that numbered over 4,500 would all but disappear. Other American artists and art students had already gone. Thomas Eakins had left in July. Mary Cassatt, another Philadelphian, had departed. Gus's French relations in Paris all urged him to go. Even his brother Andrew intended to leave. By September it seemed anyone with an American passport was getting out while it was still possible. The crush of the crowds at the railroad stations was "awful," recorded one American who had seen his family off. Trains for Le Havre, or the south of France, as Gus knew, were jammed to capacity.

His French friends, however, were going off to fight. Alfred Garnier had not hesitated to enlist. Olin Warner, though an American, had signed up to serve with a corps of friends of France, organized as a supplement to the regular forces.

Back in Limoges again, Gus wrote plaintively to Garnier, *"Je suis persuadé, et je ne t'en blâme pas, que tu dois te dire: Voilà un lâche!"*—"I feel persuaded you think me a coward, and I don't blame you!"

If only his parents were there in France, it would make such a difference. He would not hesitate to enlist. "But they are getting old, and love me. They have worked hard all their lives, are poor, and are still working. What would happen if they should lose me now?"

He made up his mind. He would stick to the pursuit he had come for. He would keep going in his mission to become a sculptor. He had not yet reached the point in his work where he was ready to go home. If unable to continue his studies in Paris, then he would go to the next-best place. For the time being, he would go to Rome.

PART III

CHAPTER NINE

UNDER SIEGE

I shall deem it my duty therefore to remain at my post. . . .

—ELIHU WASHBURNE

I

From the window of the *grand salon* of his residence on the avenue de l'Impératrice, by the entrance to the Bois de Boulogne, the American minister Elihu Washburne looked out on two large, imposing cannon newly positioned close to his front door. Beyond in the fading light, soldiers were cooking their suppers. It was a lovely, clear September evening and, as he wrote in his diary, all was perfectly still except for the occasional distant sound of cannon fire.

> There are no carriages passing on the grand avenue, that great artery through which has passed for so many years all the royalty, the wealth, the fashion, the frivolity, the vice of Paris . . . and there is the silence of death.

"Has the world ever witnessed such change in so short a time," he wondered. "It to me seems like a dream."

Paris had become an armed camp. There were soldiers everywhere— encamped all about the Arc de Triomphe and down the Champs-Élysées—

more than 300,000, he had been told, regular army troops in red *képis* and red trousers, reservists of the Garde Mobile and the Garde Nationale, "the People's Army," in blue uniforms and armed with whatever was available. Streets and avenues were filled with tents, baggage wagons, horses, and forage. The Tuileries Garden had become an artillery park, the Bois de Boulogne, a vast stockyard for 100,000 sheep and 80,000 head of cattle.

The day before, Sunday, the Germans had cut all roads into the city. At one o'clock Monday afternoon, September 19, 1870, the last train left Paris. The Germans were at the gates and nearly 2 million people, civilians and soldiers, were now trapped.

"And it seems odd to be in this world, and still not in it," Washburne wrote.

He had become accustomed to constant, almost instantaneous communication with Washington. At the time the new Republic was proclaimed two weeks before, he had sent off one telegram after another reporting the situation as it developed, and Washington had responded at once with telegraphed instructions to recognize the new government without delay—a very different situation from what Richard Rush had experienced in 1848. Now all telegraph lines had been cut.

How another nation could willfully do harm to Paris, the capital city of "light and civilization," was more than most Parisians could fathom. "It is in Paris that the beating of Europe's heart is felt. Paris is the city of cities," Victor Hugo had written in a widely circulated appeal to the Germans. "There has been an Athens, there has been a Rome, and there is a Paris. . . ." And Paris would not yield to force, Hugo declared: "Paris, pushed to extremities; Paris supported by all France aroused, can conquer, and will conquer; and you will have tried in vain this course of action which already revolts the world."

Until war broke out that summer, the Paris life for the Washburne family had been entirely to their liking. A French governess for the children had been found and a cordon bleu cook—a Madame Francis and her husband, who served as her assistant—a chambermaid, and a nurse. A French tutor worked with the children every morning but Sunday, and with the children about the house day and night, it seemed more like a home than an official residence.

So relatively small was the "American Colony" in Paris that Washburne had soon become acquainted with many. They came to the house for consultation and advice, and to attend receptions. A few even came to the house to be married, with the American minister often performing the service. Daughter Marie would remember her father's first secretary, Colonel Wickham Hoffman, saying that if the bride was pretty, the minister kissed her, otherwise it fell to his lot.

Compared to Washburne's life in Washington and the strain of the Civil War years on the congressman, the assignment to Paris had been "most agreeable." His wife, Adele, fluent in French, was a great help. He spoke French well enough, but compared to her he "hobbled" in the language, as he said. "Her tact, her grace, her cordial unaffected manner have won her many friends," he had written proudly to a friend in Illinois.

At the start of summer he had had sufficient free time even to sit for George Healy, who was back in Paris briefly and doing a portrait of Washburne's brother Cadwallader. There was enough similarity, Healy told him, that his cooperation would be of great help, and Washburne had been glad to oblige. Such tranquil days now seemed a world apart.

He had sent Adele and the three youngest children, Susie, Marie, and two-year-old Elihu, Jr., to Brussels for their safety. Of their three older children, Hempstead was in school in the United States, William in school in London. Only the oldest son, twenty-one-year-old Gratiot, had remained with his father.

Troops were now quartered in the house next door. Other houses up the avenue had been left in the care of servants. Washburne's friend Dr. Evans, having managed the escape of the empress, was still in England, and the other neighbors had "picked up their hats in a hurry," in Washburne's expression.

Of all the ambassadors of major powers in Paris, he alone had chosen to remain, along with the representatives of Belgium, Denmark, the Netherlands, Sweden, and Switzerland. All the rest "ran away," as Washburne put it privately in his diary. (In explanation for his departure, the British diplomat Lord Richard Bickerton Pennell Lyons would write, "I thought it would be, on all accounts, inexpedient for me to allow myself to be shut up in Paris. . . .")

Washburne had felt duty-bound to stay and do everything he could for those of his countrymen still there, come what may. Nearly all had wanted to get out but, with business to attend to or other preoccupations, had missed their chance. Charles May and another American named William Reynolds, salesmen for the Remington Arms Company, had simply waited too long. A few, like the medical student Mary Putnam, chose to stay of their own free will. Another was Nathan Sheppard, a lecturer on modern English literature at Chicago University and an acquaintance of Washburne's, who was trying his hand as a war correspondent for the *Cincinnati Gazette.* For some Americans, like the elderly Moultons of the banking family, Paris had been home for so long they simply could not bring themselves to leave.

Now choice in the matter was no longer anyone's privilege to make, and Washburne least of all. "However anxious I might be myself to get away, I would deem it a species of cowardice to avail myself of my diplomatic privilege to depart and leave my *nationaux* behind me to care for themselves."

He had, besides, just succeeded with the most overwhelming task of his life, and while it had left him totally exhausted, he had learned a great deal and gained immeasurable respect in many quarters at home and in Europe.

Through the panic and confusion of the past several weeks, before the start of the siege, Washburne had not only had the responsibility on his hands for the safe, efficient departure of thousands of Americans, but of some 30,000 Germans who had been ordered to leave the country. Numbers of Germans were being arrested as spies and in some cases convicted and shot.

Some of the German population of Paris had long established businesses and owned property, but the great majority were men and women employed in the most menial kind of labor, as laundresses, street cleaners, and garbage collectors. They were poor and uneducated and with numerous children. As the one remaining representative of a neutral power, Washburne found himself called upon by both the French and Prussian governments to see to the safe exodus of the Germans in the midst of the most tense of days.

"Employers discharged their [German] workmen. Those who would gladly have kept them dared not," wrote Colonel Hoffman, the first secretary.

> The suffering, both moral and physical, was very great. It must be borne in mind that many of these people had been settled for years in Paris. They had married there. Their children had been born there. . . . We have heard much . . . of the expulsion of the Moors from Spain, and of the Huguenots from France, and our sympathies are deeply stirred. . . . I do not see why the expulsion of the Germans does not rank with these. . . .

Washburne and his staff at the legation issued safe-conduct passes and arranged for special trains that left from the Gare du Nord every night. Washburne worked twelve to eighteen hours a day, so hard that the rest of the staff felt duty-bound to keep up. As an assistant secretary named Frank Moore wrote, there was "no holding him back" when he decided to do something.

The American Legation occupied a shabby apartment up two flights of winding stairs in a seven-story building at 95 rue de Chaillot, just off the Champs-Élysées. It was a walk of nearly two miles from Washburne's house, up the avenue de l'Impératrice to the Arc de Triomphe, then down the Champs-Élysées, which, door to door, took about half an hour.

His office was anything but impressive, of medium size only and furnished with a single desk, a few chairs, and a black marble mantelpiece on which stood a clock made of the same gloomy material. To add to the overall depressing mood, there was a dark green rug worn nearly black with age.

So great were the crowds waiting at the front door of the legation each morning, and packed inside on the winding stairs, that six *gendarmes* were needed to keep order. Day after day 500 to 1,000 people stood waiting. Many were old and obviously in no condition to travel. Some had no money. There were women in various stages of pregnancy. One day a child was born on a bench outside near the door.

"I am depressed and sad at the scenes of misery, suffering, and anguish," Washburne wrote to his wife Adele on September 2.

> Yesterday forenoon a poor woman came into the Legation with three children, a babe in arms, one about three and the oldest about five. When about to leave the depot the night before her husband was seized as a . . . spy—and carried off to prison. There she was left in the depot without a cent of money . . . and there she remained all night and yesterday made her way to the Legation bringing the children with her. She wept as if her heart would break and the two little children joined in—the baby alone unconscious of the situation. I at once gave her money to go out and get something to eat and sent off a man to look after her husband. . . .
>
> The crowd to go off last night was so great that I went to the depot myself. There were at least two thousand persons to whom we had given . . . cards entitling them to tickets, and such was the mob . . . pulling . . . squeezing, yelling, and swearing [such as] you never heard. It was impossible for the railroad to send them off and about 500 were left. They broke down the railing and one of my men was nearly squeezed to death. I did not get away from there until midnight.

Not all the Germans had gotten out by the time the city was cut off, but most, more than 20,000, had departed in safety, thanks to numerous French officials and those who ran the railroad, but mainly because of the unstinting efforts of the American minister. As Wickham Hoffman would write, "Everything that energy and kindness of heart could do to facilitate the departure of those poor people, and to mitigate its severity, was done by our minister.

"And here let me remark that no one could have been better fitted for the difficult task. . . .

> Had he been brought up in diplomacy, he would have hesitated and read up on precedents which did not exist, and so

let the propitious moment pass. . . . It is quite as well that the head of an embassy should be a new man. He will attach much less importance to trifles, and act more fearlessly in emergencies.

Elihu Benjamin Washburne, who turned fifty-four that September, was a remarkable man who had served energetically and effectively in Congress for sixteen years but whose appointment as minister to France by President Ulysses S. Grant was regarded in some quarters as woefully inappropriate and he himself quite unsuited for a diplomatic role of almost any kind, let alone one of such prestige and importance as Paris.

Raised on a farm in Maine, he had gotten his start in the law and politics in the rough mining town of Galena, Illinois, and by appearance and manner, he could far more readily have passed for an ordinary countryman than a diplomat. Five feet ten-and-a-half inches tall, he dressed plainly in dark blue or black broadcloth. In a day when nearly every man adorned his face with some variety of beard or mustache, he remained unfashionably clean-shaven. His iron-grey hair, cut long in back, overhung his shirt collar. He had a high forehead and bushy eyebrows. His large, intense eyes, his most striking feature, were grey-blue. An enthusiastic talker, he spoke in a deep, full voice and seldom left any doubt about what he meant.

He had had no prior diplomatic experience. For all his influence in Congress, he had served on no committee concerned with foreign affairs. Nor had he shown any interest in such matters. That he had none of the easy savoir faire considered requisite for his new role was taken as a further serious drawback. A judgment expressed by *The Nation* at the time of his appointment was the accepted view of many: "He goes as minister to France, a post for which he may have some qualifications, but what they are it would be difficult to say."

The *New York World* had called him "a man of narrow mind" who had "never originated an important measure, never acted a distinguished or influential part on any occasion." A still more biting dismissal was that of the habitually spiteful Gideon Welles, President Lincoln's secretary of the navy, who considered Washburne "coarse, uncultivated," and devoid of "enlarged views." "He may represent correctly the man who appoints him [Grant], but is no credit to his country."

———

"Our family was very, very poor," Washburne was later to write in his reminiscences. He was the third of the eleven children—seven boys, four girls (one of whom, a boy, died in infancy)—of Israel and Martha Benjamin Washburn. He had been born on September 23, 1816, in the crossroads village of Livermore in Androscoggin County, Maine, on a windy hill far inland from the sea. His father had come north from Massachusetts and bought a sixty-acre farm and the small general store that stood nearby. The front door of the gambrel-roofed house faced toward the western mountains bordering New Hampshire. On clear days one could see Mount Washington more than fifty miles in the distance.

From behind his store counter Israel Washburn talked politics and extended credit in such generous fashion that people came inordinate distances to trade there. When the business failed in 1829, the sheriff arrived with several yoke of oxen and hauled the store away.

The family struggled to survive on the farm, growing potatoes, corn, apples, wheat, and oats. It was exceedingly hard living, with long bittercold winters, and unending hard work for everyone. Maine was known as "a devilish place for oats" and just about everything else, so "unwilling" was the rocky soil. It would be said of the Washburn children that they never knew hardship because they never knew anything like luxury. It would also be said of their capacity for hard work that they had never known work that was not hard. In fact, none of them ever forgot the hardships or the example of their parents, and their mother especially, her courage in the face of adversity and her high ambitions for her family. To judge by the subsequent careers of several of her children, she must have been a force.

She had been born in Livermore. Her father, of whom she was notably proud, had served through the entire Revolutionary War, from Lexington to Yorktown. She had had little education and worried that her plain, country ways could be an embarrassment to her children, but, as Elihu wrote, her mind was "quick." She was an ardent reader of the newspapers that arrived weekly by post rider and, like her husband, took great interest in public affairs. Her pride in their children and how far they could go in life had no limits. "The foundation that is layed in youth lasts throu[gh] life," she wrote to Elihu after he had headed west. He must remember that "if a man's word is not good he is good for nothing."

> When I think of her labors [remembered Elihu], her anxieties, her watchfulness, her good and wise counsels and her attention to all our wants, my heart swells with emotions of gratitude toward her which no language can express.

Four of her sons would serve in the United States Congress, elected— and reelected—from four different states, Maine, Illinois, Wisconsin, and Minnesota. At one point there were three brothers—Israel, Elihu, and Cadwallader—in the House of Representatives at the same time, something that had never happened in the history of the country. Israel, the oldest, later became the governor of Maine. Cadwallader, who came after Elihu in age and was the first of the family to go west, made a fortune in banking, railroads, and especially flour-milling. (As one of the founders of General Mills, he made Gold Medal flour known everywhere.) Later he became a Union general in the Civil War. William, the youngest, who settled in Minnesota, also succeeded handsomely in railroads and milling, and helped found the *Minneapolis Tribune*, before serving in the United States Senate.

Because there was not food enough for all the mouths to feed on the farm, Elihu was "hired out" as a farmhand by the time he was twelve. "I dug up stumps, drove the oxen to plow and harrow, planted and hoed potatoes," and he longed the whole while for something "more congenial." At age fourteen, forced to fend for himself, he left home in a suit made for him by his mother and went to work as an apprentice printer on a newspaper thirty miles away in the town of Gardiner, a job he loved that provided room, board, and the promise of $24 a year. It was then, too, that he decided to add an *e* to his name, spelling it Washburne, as it had been originally in England.

When the Gardiner newspaper failed, Uncle Reuel Washburn took Elihu into his Livermore law office and taught him Latin.

At eighteen Elihu tried teaching, which he liked even less than farm-work, then started again as a "printer's devil" at another paper, the *Kennebec Journal* in Augusta, where he was as happy as he had ever been. "There is no humbug about the trade of a printer," he would later explain. "A man may be a bogus lawyer, doctor or clergyman, but he cannot set type unless he has learned the art and mastery of printing."

Between times he got what education he could at public schools and, for a while, at a private seminary in nearby Readfield, having earned enough from haying to pay his board. Reading all he could at public librar-ies, he acquired a lifelong love of Shakespeare, Dickens, and English po-etry. In 1839, after another two years working in a law office in Hallowell, he was admitted to Harvard Law School.

Meanwhile, brother Cadwallader had headed west, and in 1840, at age twenty-three, after little more than a year in law school, Elihu followed. Asked later why her sons left Maine, their mother said no state was big enough to hold any one of her family.

Cadwallader, who had settled for the time in Rock Island, Illinois, per-suaded Elihu to try nearby Galena on the Galena River, a tributary of the Mississippi.

He arrived by stern-wheeler on April Fool's Day, knowing no one, found lodgings in a decrepit log building by a cattle yard, and quickly took hold. The population numbered perhaps 4,000, and the mud in the streets was "knee deep." But because of the lead mines close by at places with names like Bunkham, Hardscrabble, and Roaring Camp, Galena had be-come a boomtown, and the people, as Elihu said, were "a litigious set." In less than a month he was sending money home from his legal fees.

In a rough, wide-open town where other lawyers included drunks and gamblers, he vowed never to smoke or drink hard liquor or gamble, a vow he kept. He joined a church. At home the Washburns were Universal-ists, but with only a few churches to choose from in Galena, he joined the Episcopalians.

He liked the life in what he later called the "Golden Years" in Galena, and his success and stature in the community were to be seen in the handsome Greek Revival house he had built on Third Street. In 1845, at twenty-nine, he married Adele Gratiot, who was ten years younger, small, slender, dark-eyed, well educated, and of French descent. Like Elihu's mother, she had been born on the frontier, there in Galena. Indeed, she could proudly claim to have been the first white child born in the settlement. Sent to a seminary school in St. Louis, she studied under French nuns and learned French. Thus, Elihu resolved to learn the language, too, and in time French would be spoken within their growing family.

According to an old Washburn family history, "He was not under the influence of anyone except his wife who had much to do with the directing of his career," and again like his mother, "she never had a doubt that he could do anything which he set out to do."

Defeated in his first run for Congress in 1848, he tried again in 1852 and won. In little time he became chairman of the House Committee on Commerce. He was praised as "independent," "intrepid," "scrupulously honest," "brimful of things to say and do." But he could also be abrupt and impatient to the point of rudeness. An Ohio newspaperman watching from the gallery described how Representative Washburne could hardly bear listening to others speak, not even his own brothers, for more than a few minutes before plunging into paperwork at his desk or darting off to talk with someone in the gallery. Or he would tilt back in his seat, hands clasped behind his head, and "blow off like a steam engine." As chairman of the Committee on Appropriations he was famous for saying no as if it were spelled with two o's.

He and his brothers took up the antislavery cause and became early enthusiasts for the new Republican Party. (It was Israel Washburn, in a speech in Maine, who reportedly first used the name "Republican" for the party.) As debate over slavery grew more heated in Congress, the brothers played an increasingly prominent part and were in the thick of a long-remembered scene on the floor of the House.

It happened at about two in the morning on February 6, 1858. The House had been in session for hours, arguing over slavery, when two representatives—one from the North and one from the South—suddenly began throwing punches. Others rushed to join the fray, and, as reported, "Mr. Washburne of Illinois was conspicuous among the Republicans dealing heavy blows." Seeing Representative William Barksdale of Mississippi take a swing at Elihu, brother Cadwallader jumped in and grabbed Barksdale by the hair of his head, which proved to be a wig that came off in Cadwallader's hand. The astonishment was enough to stop the fight and set everyone laughing. When Cadwallader returned the wig and Barksdale put it on backward, the merriment grew still greater. Among their constituents back in the Midwest, esteem for both brothers rose appreciably.

At home in Illinois, Elihu had become involved with the political prospects of a former congressman, Abraham Lincoln, whose company he greatly enjoyed. They had first met in 1843. In 1860, when Lincoln ran for president, Washburne wrote a campaign biography for him. On the day Lincoln stepped off the train in Washington, in advance of his inauguration, wearing a makeshift disguise because of a rumored attempt on his life, Washburne alone was at the station to greet him and drive him to his hotel.

Through the grim, painful years of the Civil War, Washburne remained as staunch a supporter of the president as anyone in Congress and, more than any, championed the advancement of Ulysses S. Grant. He had "discovered" Grant earlier, when Grant, having retired from the army and failed successively as a farmer and a real estate agent, came to Galena to work as a clerk in his father's leather store. As Lincoln himself said, Washburne "always claimed Grant as his right of discovery."

In long letters to Adele through the war years, Washburne provided a vivid account of people and events in Washington, as well as the realities of the desperate struggle in the field, where, too, he was often on the scene. Of his confidence in Grant there was never a doubt. "Without doing any injustice to anyone, I can say I fully believe this army would have been defeated before this, and in its retreat, had it not been for him," he wrote to her from Grant's camp near Spotsylvania, in May of 1864, after some of the fiercest fighting of the war. He was with Grant at Appomattox, saw the final surrender on April 9, 1865, and it was in the library of the Washburne home in Galena in November 1868 that Grant received word that he had been elected president.

The confidence Washburne placed in Grant, Grant returned in kind, appointing Washburne secretary of state, a position from which Washburne withdrew after only a few days. He had been stricken suddenly by what at the time was called a "congestive chill" and remained desperately ill for days. "His life was despaired of," wrote his daughter Marie, "and I can remember prayers being said for him at our house." Once recovered, he felt too shaken and exhausted to take on so great a responsibility as secretary of state. He had had his fill of Washington, he decided. When Grant offered the alternative of going to Paris—and with Adele's full concurrence—he accepted, expecting to enjoy at last a little "quiet and repose."

Whatever the editorial skepticism about the appointment, or scorn of the kind expressed by Gideon Welles, those who knew Elihu Washburne, including Grant, had every confidence he would prove a great credit to his country.

II

In its long history Paris had been under siege fifteen times before. In the first ordeal, in 53 B.C., the native Parisii on the Île-de-la-Cité had been set upon by the Romans. In the most recent, in 1814, when the combined forces of northern Europe, some 200,000 troops, converged on the city, it held out for just over six months. But Paris had been half the size then, its defenses few compared to those now in place, and most Parisians seemed to feel quite secure, their spirits remaining remarkably high given the circumstances.

The ideal weather continued day after day. Even with soldiers drilling in the streets, Paris seemed much as ever. "The weather is charming and Paris seems wonderfully cheerful," Washburne wrote to Adele on September 28, the tenth day of the siege. In the interest of keeping communications open with the American minister, Prussian Prime Minister Otto von Bismarck was permitting his correspondence to come through the lines by diplomatic pouch.

The formal exchange of dispatches took place every Tuesday morning at a point two miles southwest of Paris at Sèvres, the village on the Seine famous for its china factory. At the sound of trumpets and the raising of a white flag at exactly ten o'clock, a German officer in full dress would march forward to a broken arch on the Sèvres Bridge, give a military salute, and address a French officer who came to meet him, saying, "Gentlemen, I have the honor to present you my salute."

"Sir, we have the honor to salute you," came the reply.

"Gentlemen, I have the honor to inform you my mission is to place in your hands Mr. Washburne's dispatches."

"Sir, we are going to have the honor to send them."

Each officer, having again saluted, returned to his end of the bridge and stepped down to the riverbank. The French would then send a boat across the river to receive other dispatches and mail from the hands of the German officer. Again salutes were exchanged. Each officer immediately returned to his respective trenches, and the instant the white flag came down, both sides opened fire again.

Others in Paris had begun trusting their correspondence to "balloon mail." On September 21, a daring balloonist had taken off from the city and successfully proven that balloons could carry word of what was happening to the outside world. From that point on, the balloons kept flying and became the topic of headline stories and great public interest in the United States. Eventually some sixty-five balloons took flight from Paris carrying more than 2 million pieces of mail. To send dispatches into the city, carrier pigeons were used.

"I have never before so much realized the want of your society and the presence of the darling children," Washburne wrote to Adele. "But I find enough to do every day to take up my time and so I am not idle." This, she knew, was a large understatement.

To his brother Israel in Maine, Washburne stressed that the French had 500,000 troops in the city, counting the National Guard, and that their spirits were high, the defenses strong. All approaches to Paris were defended by a wall thirty feet high, a moat, and sixteen fortresses that made up a sixty-mile circle around the city. But there also seemed little likelihood that the French could ever succeed in breaking out through the formidable German lines.

On the morning of September 30, after unusually heavy cannonading, French troops made an all-out sortie against two German positions with what Washburne described as "great courage and spirit," but against immense odds. Their losses were heavy—500 killed, 1,500 wounded—and nothing was gained.

The morning crowds at the door of the legation had diminished considerably, but the desire of Americans to get out of the city by almost any means was greater than ever and thus far there seemed little Washburne could do to help. In early October the American arms salesman Charles May, thinking he had come up with the perfect solution, asked Washburne to arrange a German passport for him. Washburne said he could not. But when, on the morning of October 7, Léon Gambetta, the French minister of the interior, made a sensational escape from Paris by balloon, the enterprising May and his business associate Reynolds went, too, as Gambetta's guests in an accompanying balloon.

They took off from the summit of Montmartre, to the cheers of a huge crowd. Gambetta, wrapped in a fur cape and looking extremely pale and apprehensive, waved from the wicker basket swinging beneath a great yellow balloon. The balloon bearing the two Americans was snow-white.

Other Americans in Paris over the years had had a considerable variety of adventures, but until now none had ever escaped by balloon.

It was another perfect day and "a beautiful sight it was to see our friends there, waving hats and handkerchiefs as we gradually ascended," Charles May would write.

> The air was clear and the sky cloudless. A fair even temperature, quite mild, with just enough wind to float us on.
>
> Gambetta's balloon was just over us a little to the northwest, and soon we were passing the suburbs of Paris near St.-Denis, when I heard the horses galloping below, saw German artillery exercising, and crack, bang went the guns and we realized their eyes were on us, and they meant to bring us down if possible. The firing became more and more frequent, the balls whistled around us, still we kept rising.

One of Gambetta's crew cupped his hands at his mouth and shouted, *"Dépêchez-vous! Dépêchez-vous!"* ("Hurry! Hurry!")

So we opened the sand bag [May continued], which quick-
ened our rising and away we floated, and after twenty minutes
the firing ceased and we had the heavens for our way without
anything to molest or make us afraid.

"There was no sense of motion, no noise, no friction, no jarring—the
perfection of traveling," May recounted. He had thought to bring a basket
of crackers, chocolate, canned oysters, and wine. "So we had a very agreeable time."

The two balloons were filled with coal gas. It would have taken only
a few stray shots to have turned them into balls of flame. As it was,
Gambetta eventually landed safely beyond the German lines near Tours,
150 miles to the south. May and Reynolds came down at Roye, 70 miles
north of Paris.

The following day it rained for the first time in a month, a "blue dull"
rain, as Washburne recorded. It was the twenty-fourth day of the siege,
and the problem of food could no longer be ignored. "The days go and the
provisions go," he wrote. The government began rationing meat and set
the price. Ration cards were issued. Soldiers stood posted at the *bouche-
ries*, the butcher shops, to check the cards. Washburne, as he reported to
his family, had earlier "laid by" his own sufficient stock of food.

His reputation for energetic, levelheaded attention to problems spread
rapidly in Europe and at home. "Were it not for Mr. Washburne, who was
brought up in the rough-and-ready life of the Far West, instead of serving an apprenticeship in courts and government offices, those who are
still here would be perfectly helpless," wrote a correspondent for London's
Daily News, Henry Labouchère. "He is worth more than all his colleagues
put together." During an afternoon at the American Legation, Labouchère
was amazed to see Washburne walking about "cheerily shaking everyone
by the hand, and telling them to make themselves at home."

How different American diplomats are to the prim old women
who represent us abroad, with a staff of a half dozen dandies
helping each other to do nothing, who have been taught to
regard all who are not of their craft as their natural enemies.

"The world cannot fail to admire the firm purpose which keeps him at his post in the midst of danger," wrote the *Chicago Journal*.

In mid-October, Washburne was struck ill by what he called his "old Galena ague," great dizziness and violent vomiting. Two days later, on October 15, he was still "suffering . . . so sore I can hardly move . . . cold feet and ague pains in my limbs . . ." But he refused to give in. On October 17 he was back at his office "quite early" and "busy all day."

> Many people called. At noon went to the prison [of Saint-Lazare] to see the poor German women. I found seventy-four of them imprisoned for no offense except being Germans. . . . I have made arrangements to have them all released tomorrow and shall have them cared for till the siege is over.

Pressure on him to get people out of Paris grew greater. Under the new government of Paris, the Government of National Defense, General Louis Trochu was at its head, and Jules Favre served as minister of foreign affairs. Trochu refused to permit anyone to leave the city for any reason for fear of a demoralizing effect on the army.

"But Washburne," wrote Wickham Hoffman, "was not a man to sit down quietly under a refusal in a matter like this." He went directly to Trochu's headquarters at the Louvre and after an "interminable gabble" of three hours, in which Jules Favre also took part, Trochu relented. So on October 27 a caravan of nineteen carriages piled high with baggage departed from the city under military escort carrying forty-eight Americans—men, women, and children—and twenty-one others with passes provided by Minister Washburne.

He had wanted to ride with them as far as the German lines and see them safely delivered, but was suffering "the ague" still and, he had to confess, "a little depression of spirits" from so long a separation from his family. Instead, he sent Hoffman and his son Gratiot.

"We drove to the French outposts, and thence sent forward the flag with an officer of Trochu's staff," wrote Hoffman.

> While we waited, a German picket of six men advanced toward us, dodging behind the trees, muskets cocked, and fin-

gers on trigger. I confess I was not much impressed with this specimen of German scouting. It looked too much like playing at North American Indian. . . . The necessary arrangements having been made, we proceeded to the German outposts. Here the Prussian officers verified the list, calling the roll name by name, and taking every precaution to identify the individuals. I heard afterward, however, that a Frenchman of some prominence had escaped disguised as a coachman.

The Americans now remaining in Paris numbered no more than 150.

On October 31, Trochu's army launched another attack on the Germans, this time at the village of Le Bourget, in an attempt to enlarge the perimeter of Paris. The attack seemed to have succeeded at first and in Paris was immediately proclaimed a resounding victory. But then it turned out to be a horrendous failure.

That same day, to compound the shock of disappointment, came official word that at the French stronghold of Metz, east of Paris, which had been holding out until now, a French army of over 170,000 men had surrendered. To make matters inconceivably worse, rumors spread that at the Hôtel de Ville that morning Trochu and his Government of National Defense were secretly discussing the surrender of Paris.

It was Halloween, and as Washburne wrote in his diary, events "marched with gigantic strides."

A shouting crowd of workers and citizen soldiers marched on the Hôtel de Ville—angry over any talk of an armistice and determined to save Paris. Washburne was busy all day at the legation, but his friend Nathan Sheppard joined the throngs who converged to see what was happening. "People, and people, and people hurrying to the Hôtel de Ville," Sheppard wrote, ". . . ten thousand, fifteen thousand . . . packing all the vast open space before the palace, and all the streets emptying into it."

Women with big feet and ankles of prodigious circumference; maidservants in their clean white caps; boys as frolicsome as only boys can be, playing hide-and-seek among the forest of legs, followed by small dogs in full bark; old men, who totter as they hasten. . . . Mobiles and Nationals in half uniform and full uniform, full-armed and half-armed—in they pour and here they gather, and shout, and squeeze, and sway. . . .

Placards and banners proclaimed NO ARMISTICE! RESISTANCE TO DEATH! VIVE LA RÉPUBLIQUE, VIVE LA COMMUNE.

A tall well-bred-looking gentleman, in officer's undress uniform, ventures to deplore such factious behavior, and looks down haughtily on the ruffians who hustle up around him with menacing faces and fingers. But he folds his arms and continues to look formidable to his tormentors, who gradually skulk before his cool disdainful eye. . . .

Delegations wedge their way through to the iron gates [of the Hôtel]. . . . The clock over the entrance chimes the quarter-hour. The pleasant melody is sadly out of keeping with the angry and vindictive shouts. . . . The gates come open. The crowd pours in. . . . There is a parley with the sentinels, who give way. Shots are fired, by whom, at whom, no one knows. . . . Ten thousand people run hither and thither crying, "To arms! To arms! They are attacking the Government. They are firing on the people." Now a spectacle of panic, stampede, and lunacy such as only Paris can furnish.

Inside the Hôtel de Ville, the insurgent "Red Paris" seized control of the government. On hearing what was happening, Washburne left the legation and reached the Hôtel de Ville at about six o'clock. Forcing his way through the crowd, he succeeded in getting inside the Hôtel only to find mostly National Guard soldiers wandering about carrying their muskets upside down, the sign of peace. "They all seemed to regard the revolution as an accomplished fact, which was only to be ratified by a vote of the people of Paris." So Washburne departed, thinking "a genuine Red

Republic" was a *fait accompli*. "God only knows what is yet in store for this unhappy country," he wrote that night in his diary.

But the uprising melted away as rapidly as it began. By the next day Trochu and the Government of National Defense were back in place. "What a city!" concluded Washburne. "One moment revolution, and the next the most profound calm!"

To add to his troubles, more and more British citizens were descending on him, "perfectly raving" to have learned that through his efforts so many Americans had slipped out of Paris while they were left behind. But by this time Bismarck had informed Washburne there would be no further passports granted to anyone. The exit door was closed.

III

The rumble of distant cannon remained an everyday presence. Wounded soldiers kept arriving at the city's hospitals and the American Ambulance, a field hospital. There was much talk of holding out at all costs and "dying to the last man"; still, overall the adjustment of the populace remained surprisingly, admirably smooth.

The great majority of the people believed the defenses of the city were impregnable, and in Washburne's opinion, they had reason to feel secure. He had made several tours of miles of the outer defenses, and was amazed. He had seen many forts and immense earthworks during the Civil War, but these were "a prodigy of strength and wonder," he recorded. "Indeed, the defenses all round the city present a spectacle without parallel in the whole world." The entire defense circle was manned by troops of the regular army, and by French sailors who were in charge of the cannon. Washburne could conceive of nothing "so complete." "I do not see for the life of me, how the city can be taken by assault."

Though all private building construction had been halted in the city in order to concentrate on defenses, there was no shortage of work. Small shops were busier than ever making war materials. Department stores, theaters, hotels, and public buildings had been turned into hospitals. Flags of the Red Cross flew from the rooftops of the Grand Hôtel, the

Comédie Française, the Palais Royal, and the Palais de Justice. Architect Charles Garnier's still-uncompleted Opera House served as a military supply depot. The Orléans railroad station had been converted into a balloon factory.

At the Louvre, where Trochu established his headquarters, windows were covered with sandbags. Paintings and statuary had been boxed up and carried away for safekeeping. In the great galleries, instead of painters quietly at work at their easels making copies, one saw and heard gunsmiths at workbenches noisily converting old muskets into breechloaders.

In a city cut off from all news from the outside, there were more newspapers being published than ever—thirty-six or more—and representing every shade of political opinion. Hungry for news of almost any kind, Parisians now read newspapers as they walked down the streets. Yet at the same time there seemed even less faith that much of anything published could be trusted for accuracy.

At first all theaters were closed, but when the Comédie Française reopened, with productions using no sets or costumes, a few others followed. Restaurants and cafés remained open, but only until ten at night. Supplies of bread were still plentiful and cheap, but not meat. Reportedly 50,000 horses or more were to be slaughtered before long. Horse-drawn cabs and carriages were growing noticeably fewer in number. But dining on cats and dogs was as yet spoken of only in jest.

Paris continued taking things in stride. Little if any outspoken complaining was to be heard. The crime rate dropped significantly.

For the American population, though they were but a tiny fraction of the total, the hard truth of their lot was little different from the rest. "The situation here is dreadful," wrote Washburne, summing things up on November 12. "The Prussians can't get into Paris and the French can't get out." Nor did it help that the weather had turned damp and raw. "Nothing of interest today," he recorded on November 22. "Raining outside—cold, cheerless, dreary . . ." When he took time off to sit for a portrait, the photographer told him his expression was "too sober."

"Oh, for an opportunity to escape!" wrote Nathan Sheppard, who to fill the time walked the city at all hours. "One felt an intense desire to have one's capacity for hearing, seeing, and comprehending increased a hundredfold, to be enabled to be everywhere at once, and to miss not one phase of the situation." He was annoyed only by the "furtive glances" he encountered, the suspicion of any and all "*étrangers*" as spies. On the Champs-Élysées one evening, he and two other Americans were arrested on the charge of talking in a foreign tongue.

Worst of all, he wrote, was the mental strain, the *ennui*:

> It is the intolerable tension of expectation and the baffling un-
> certainty that besets every hour and minute of the day which
> tries us. One really knows nothing of what is going on, and
> there is an all-pervading sense of something that is going to
> happen, and which may come at any moment. This gives a
> sense of unreality to one's whole life.

Anything more dreary than the boulevards in the evening would be difficult to imagine, wrote London's *Daily News* correspondent Labouchère. Only one streetlamp in three was lighted, and the cafés were on half-allowances of gas.

For many not the least of troubles was severe insomnia. An American physician from Pennsylvania named Robert Sibbet, who had come to Paris expecting to attend lectures at the École de Médecine just as the École closed its doors in the emergency, found himself "overtaken" with insomnia and reported many others suffering in the same way. The worst of it was the cannonading. "The cannonading produces a decided effect upon nervous constitutions." Many nights he could not sleep at all, not even for an hour.

The American medical student Mary Putnam had the advantage, she said, of something to do of overriding importance to her. She concentrated on her academic work, and on tending the sick and wounded at the Hôpital de la Pitié. The steadily diminishing supply of food, the inconveniences, bothered her comparatively little. Nor had she any desire to leave.

She was staying with a French family whose congenial, cultivated company and outlook she greatly enjoyed. Her only pain she seems to have kept to herself. She had fallen in love with another medical student, a young Frenchman, and they had become engaged. But he had gone to the front to serve. She refused to brood or complain. She had set herself to completing her thesis by the end of the year. Her chosen topic was *"De la Graisse Neutre et des Acides Gras"* ("Natural Fat and Fatty Acids"). It was the last hurdle to her becoming the first American woman to be graduated from the École de Médecine.

"It is not at all probable that the war will last until December," she had written to her mother on the eve of the siege, "and if school opens then I have all I need." She had offered her services to the doctors at the American Ambulance, but was told they had more volunteers than they had places for.

With the passage of days the toll of disease—and especially of smallpox—mounted steadily. In the first week of the siege 158 people died of smallpox. By the fourth week the number exceeded 200. By the eighth week, 419 would die of the disease.

After nearly two months of siege, the gas that made Paris the City of Light finally gave out, along with food and firewood. An order appeared that instead of only one in three streetlamps lighted at night, it would now be one in six.

As darkness fell earlier and more heavily, Washburne found himself thinking increasingly of life at home in Galena and such examples of fortitude as he had grown up with in the Maine of his boyhood. On November 18 he noted in his diary that it was his father's eighty-sixth birthday, and that it would not be long before his father and the last of the settlers of Livermore were all gone.

> And what a class of men they were [he wrote], distinguished for intelligence, nobility, honor, thrift, illustrating their lives by all these virtues which belong to the best type of the New England character. . . . And here in this far off, besieged city, in these long and dismal days, I think of them all. . . .

To Parisians it came as no surprise that they would still, in the face of everything and in large numbers, turn out for a Sunday stroll on the boulevards, quite as though they had not a care, and especially if the sun were shining, as it was on Sunday, November 20. "The sun was just warm enough for comfort," Nathan Sheppard noted. "The atmosphere was kindly." He saw nothing dejected in the look of the crowd. "On the contrary, nothing could be more indicative of the satisfaction and contentment than the faces of the people under the genial November sun. They were each and every one the picture of self-congratulation." Shoes were polished, children "sportive." At one of the public concerts, a young lady who had performed beamed when she received, instead of a bouquet of flowers, a generous portion of cheese.

In the meantime, the cattle and sheep that had filled the Bois de Boulogne were to be seen no more. Horsemeat had become the mainstay of Paris. And all knew there was worse to come. "They are arriving down to what we call in the Galena mines the *hard pan*," Washburne wrote, referring to the part all but impossible to drill.

Because the German command continued to grant him the privilege of receiving by diplomatic pouch news from the outside world, he was in a position like that of no one else. No newspapers from elsewhere got into Paris except those that came to the American Legation. But he could also send out written correspondence and so felt he must report what he knew as responsibly and accurately as possible. When time allowed, he tried to get out and see all he could of what was happening, hoping in this way that he might be better able to forecast what was to come. But could anyone predict how Paris would respond under such circumstances? There seemed no telling with the French. So much that they did seemed such a contradiction. "With an improvised city government, without police, without organization," he recorded in the last week of November, "Paris has never been so tranquil and never has there been so little crime. . . ."

The radical political clubs had begun to "agitate" again. "Hunger and cold will do their work," he wrote. But whatever the given situation, he reported to Washington, no one could tell how soon it might all change.

The American Ambulance, the large, well-equipped field hospital established by Thomas Evans and others at the start of the war, had proven a tremendous success and a source of pride for every American who knew anything about it. At its head were two American physicians, Dr. John

Swinburne, the chief surgeon, and Dr. W. E. Johnston, the physician-in-chief, assisted by several additional American doctors and nearly forty American volunteers, including Gratiot Washburne.

Of the many hospitals and ambulances throughout the city, it was the only tent encampment, intended specifically to provide as much fresh air as possible. "Here were order, system, and discipline," wrote Wickham Hoffman. The work went on without stop in all weather.

To warm the large tents in cold weather a trench had been dug the length of each on the inside and a pipe laid to carry heat from a coal stove set in a hole at one end of the tent on the outside. Thus the ground was dried and warmed, and this warmed the whole tent. It was a solution devised during the Civil War and it worked perfectly. No patient in the American Ambulance was to suffer from the cold. "I have known the thermometer outside to be 20 degrees Fahrenheit, while in the tents it stood at 55 degrees," wrote Hoffman.

Swinburne, a battlefield surgeon in the Civil War, had been traveling in France when the Franco-Prussian War broke out and had stayed in Paris to serve. He spoke perfect French, seemed never to sleep, and was admired by everybody. He and Dr. Johnston both served without remuneration.

"Is it necessary that we should dwell upon the scrupulous cleanliness of this ambulance, or the assiduous care [with] which our wounded are treated?" asked an editorial in the *Électeur Libre*, adding that it was "truly touching" to see these foreigners "giving themselves up without reserve to this humane work." The surgeon general of the French Army told Elihu Washburne he thought the American hospital superior to anything the French had.

On December 1, following yet another futile French assault launched on the German lines, Washburne stood in the cold of the afternoon watching as the wounded, numbering more than a hundred, were hauled to the tents of the ambulance by the carriage load. Gratiot had been with the volunteers who went to the battlefield to help. One soldier had died in Gratiot's arms.

The cold of winter had arrived, and Washburne continued to chronicle in his diary the steady worsening of conditions and decline of hope. Numbering the days of the siege, he filled page after page, writing in a clear, straightforward hand, leaving little margin on either side and rarely ever crossing out or changing a word.

December 2. 76th day of the siege. Cold . . . ice made last night half an inch thick.

December 3. 77th day of the siege. . . . There has been no fighting at all anywhere today. There was a very light snow last night and this evening it rains a little. The suffering of the troops on both sides must have been fearful these last days. The French are without blankets and with but little to eat, half-frozen, half-starved, and raw troops at that. . . . I have just come from the American Ambulance where I saw a poor captain of the regular army breathing his last and his last moments were being soothed by some of our American ladies who are devoting themselves to the sick and dying.

December 4. 78th day of the siege. A snapping cold morning. . . . Have remained in my room nearly all day hugging my fire closely. This evening went to Mr. Moulton's with Gratiot as usual . . . on Sunday evening. Nothing talked of or thought of but the . . . siege and the absent ones and our "bright and happy homes so far away. . . ."

December 6. 80th day of the siege. . . . Another sortie threatened which only means more butchery. The more we hear of the battles of last week, the more bloody they seem to have been. The French have lost most frightfully and particularly in officers. They have shown a courage bordering on desperation.

December 8. 82nd day of the siege. . . . A more doleful day than this has not yet been invented. . . .

> December 11. 85th day of the siege. My cold worse than ever and I am unable to go out. . . . People come in and say the day is horrible outside. For the first time there is [talk] about the supply of bread getting short. . . .

> December 15. 89th day of the siege. . . . Went to the Legation this P.M. at two o'clock. The ante room was filled with poor German women asking aid. I am now giving succor to more than six hundred women and children. . . .

As he explained in a letter to one of his brothers at home, money for support of the refugees on his hands came from the German government, but the time was fast approaching when money would buy neither food nor firewood.

In ten days there had not been ten minutes of sunshine. It had become one of the coldest winters anyone could remember. The Prussian command began threatening Paris with bombardment, but the people showed no sign of panic. There was still no discernible lessening of spirit.

In the United States, sympathy and admiration for the people of Paris could be heard everywhere. "Too much cannot be said in praise of the conduct of the population of Paris in these days of suffering and privation," wrote a correspondent for the *New York Times*.

> Never did any population under similar circumstances exhibit greater patience, resignation and heroism. The Prussians imagine that when they begin their threatened bombardment, those qualities will fail them. They are mistaken. The people of the capital know well what is before them, and are prepared for everything.

In Washington, Secretary of State Hamilton Fish did what he could to boost Washburne's spirits, assuring him his efforts were not going unappreciated. "There is universal approbation for your course from Americans," he wrote. "Nothing has been omitted [by you] that ought to have been done and what has been done, has been done well. I think you have earned the title 'Protector General.' "

All over the city, long lines, mostly of women, stood in the bitter cold outside butcher shops and bakeries, lines of a thousand people in some cases. Lines formed as early as four in the morning and the waiting could last five or six hours, only to buy nothing more appetizing than horses' hooves and horrible dirt-colored bread. On the rue de Clichy a jeweler now displayed eggs wrapped in cotton in the part of his window usually reserved for fine silver.

As firewood began running out, bands of thousands of people roved the streets at night to cut down trees and rip apart wooden fences for fuel. Many poor families were burning their furniture to keep warm.

Christmas Day was the coldest day yet, "the climax of the forlorn," Nathan Sheppard called it. "Thermometer at zero, snow dribbling, scowling heavens, slippery pavements, ominous silence all round . . . thousands of people lying abed to save food and fuel."

"Never has a sadder Christmas dawned on any city," wrote Washburne. "The sufferings . . . exceed by far anything we have seen." Of so much that was horrible, the continuing slaughter of horses seems to have distressed him particularly.

> The government is seizing every horse it can lay its hands on for food. It carries out its work with remorseless impartiality. The omnibus horse, the cab horse, the work horse, the fancy horse, all go alike in mournful procession to the butcher's block. . . .

For his part, determined not to let Christmas go by unrecognized, he sacrificed two laying hens for a Christmas dinner at home for Wickham Hoffman, Dr. Johnston, Nathan Sheppard, and a few other American friends, in addition to Gratiot. The bill-of-fare included oyster soup, followed by sardines, roast chicken, corned beef and potatoes, tomatoes, cranberries, green corn, and green peas—all but the chicken from Washburne's supply of canned goods.

As Hoffman was to explain, the French were accustomed to shopping for fresh food day-to-day, not only because of their love of fresh food, but because so many lived in apartments with little if any room for stores. Americans liked being well stocked with canned goods, and consequently many Paris grocers had obligingly imported large quantities for the *colonie américaine*. With the greater part of the *colonie* having departed by the time the siege began, a quantity of canned fruits, vegetables, oysters, even lobsters, had remained on the market. "The French knew nothing of these eatables till late in the siege, when they discovered their merits," Hoffman wrote. "In the meantime the Americans bought up nearly all there was at hand."

For dessert Washburne offered a selection of canned fruits, in addition to chocolates, of which there was still no shortage in Paris. Indeed, supplies of French chocolate, mustard, and wine appeared to be inexhaustible.

———

The day after Christmas, he recorded a stark winter scene he had never thought imaginable—a "wood riot" virtually at his front door.

> The large square across the street diagonally from our house was filled with wood from the Bois de Boulogne, which has been saved up to burn into charcoal. At about one o'clock this P.M. a crowd of two or three thousand women and children gathered . . . right in our neighborhood and "went for" this wood. . . . Nearly all the wood was carried off.

It was probably only the beginning, he speculated. "These people cannot freeze to death or starve to death."

Two days later, on December 28, he hit a new low, despairing over everything, including himself. "The situation becomes more and more critical . . . I am becoming utterly demoralized."

I am unfitted for anything. This siege life is becoming unen-
durable. I have no disposition to read anything. . . . I am too
lazy to do any work and it is an immense effort to write a dispatch once a week. . . .

By New Year's Day, Paris was both freezing and starving to death. People were eating anything to be had—mule meat, dogs, cats, crows, sparrows, rats, and bread that was nearly black and as heavy, Washburne said,
as the lead from a Galena mine. To Nathan Sheppard it tasted of "sawdust,
mud, and potato skins."

Sheppard sampled just about everything, and out of necessity, it
seems, as much as curiosity. He found dogmeat preferable to horsemeat,
but could not honestly say he liked it. Cats he considered "downright good
eating," as apparently did many people. The price of a cat on the market
was four times that of dog. For the poor, nothing was a bargain. By the
second half of December a single egg was 3 francs, twice the daily pay
of a soldier in the National Guard. A single sparrow cost 1 franc. For weeks
along the Champs-Élysées and in the Tuileries and Luxembourg Gardens,
and on the quays by the Seine, people had been busy shooting sparrows, to
the point that some felt it dangerous to be out walking there.

A rat cost only a little less than a sparrow. A rat, Sheppard was surprised to find, tasted a lot like a bird. It had been estimated that at the
start of the siege the number of rats in Paris exceeded 20,000. It was also
generally agreed that the flavor of a brewery rat surpassed that of the
sewer rat, due to its diet. Rat pâté was considered a delicacy, but Sheppard
knew of only one shop that carried it.

Food had become the principal topic of conversation. "The worst of it
is," he wrote, "the more one talks about eating, the more one wants to eat."
Many Parisians, with their abiding affection for dogs, were keeping them
hidden. One elderly woman assured him she would sooner starve to death
than eat her cat.

With little or nothing to feed the animals in the zoo, the government
began butchering them as well, until nearly all had gone to feed the starving city—bear, kangaroo, reindeer, camel, yak, even porcupine, and two
long-popular elephants named Castor and Pollux.

But as bad as things became, there was no time when money—preferably gold—would not buy good food (a point vividly made by Honoré Daumier in a caricature of a fat, well-heeled epicure, a great bib at his neck, happily gorging himself). Nor did anyone in Paris doubt that across the lines the enemy's army had all it wanted in the way of bread and German sausage.

Everyone dreamed of white bread, café au lait, and green vegetables, wrote Mary Putnam. "But bah!!! Such things are not worth speaking about."

"The incessant and exceptional cold weather continues, and the suffering in the city is steadily increasing," Washburne stressed in a dispatch to the secretary of state in the first week of January, doubtless wondering whether anyone enjoying the comforts of Washington had the least idea of the agony of Paris, and of the army as well as the people. Several hundred French soldiers had been disabled by the extreme cold or had frozen to death.

So severe was the suffering of the indigent Germans who still came to him in desperation, pleading for his help, that Washburne had converted the whole first floor of the legation building into a dormitory where he housed, fed, and kept warm more than a hundred men, women, and children.

The poor suffered the most. The death toll in the city, not counting those dying in the military hospitals, had reached more than 4,000 a week, five times the usual average, and the heaviest toll was among infants and the elderly poor. "Great discontent is now prevailing among the poorer classes, yet there seems to be a disposition to hold out until the last extremity," wrote Washburne.

IV

With the ground frozen as hard as marble to a depth of a foot and a half, the Prussians were able to bring up the biggest of their Krupp cannon, and on January 5, 1871, the 109th day of the siege, they commenced bombardment of Paris itself. Many had predicted it would never happen, that

Bismarck would not allow it. In fact, Bismarck had wanted to begin bombarding the city as early as October, convinced that "two or three shells" would be enough to scare the Parisians into surrendering.

"At 2 P.M. I walked down the Champs-Élysées," wrote Washburne, "and to say that the firing was then terrific would give no idea of it. I supposed, however, it was only a bombardment of the forts and I had not thought that the shells were coming into the city."

The initial barrage struck on the Left Bank, the first shell on the rue Lalande. Olin Warner, who had not gone off to fight with the French army as he originally intended, but stayed on living on the Left Bank, wrote of German shells hitting "on all sides" all night in his neighborhood. "Sometimes they would strike and burst so near I could smell the powder from the explosion and once I heard a woman scream. . . ."

The thundering assault on the Left Bank continued day and night. An old woman had her head blown off. Near the Luxembourg Gardens a little girl was cut in two on her way to school. An American student from Louisville, Kentucky, named Charles Swager had part of one foot torn to pieces when a shell struck his room on the Left Bank. Taken to the American Ambulance, he had to have his leg amputated. The operation was performed by doctors Swinburne and Johnston, as Washburne duly noted, but a month later the young man would die.

The poor were especially to be pitied, wrote the American doctor Robert Sibbet.

> They carry with them, through the deep snow which has fallen, their children and their bedding. They are crowding into the basement stories of the theaters, the churches and other buildings, where they are safe from the cold and the shells.

With shells bursting all around the house where she lived on the Left Bank, Mary Putnam had to move out. One night, with four or five hundred others, she slept in the vast crypt beneath the Panthéon, where the heroes of French liberty were buried. "It was singularly dramatic," she wrote, "the tombs of Voltaire and Rousseau sheltering the victims of the Prussian barbarians. . . ."

The bombardment continued with great fury. The shells rained down at a rate of three or four hundred a day, all striking the Left Bank. (The domes of the Panthéon and the Invalides remained favorite German targets.) But the number of people killed was surprisingly low, given the size of the city's population. "Nearly twelve days of furious bombardment has accomplished but little," Washburne wrote on January 16. "The killing and wounding of a few men, women, and children and the knocking to pieces of a few hundred houses in a city of two millions is no great progress. . . ." "The bombardment so far," he reported to Secretary of State Fish that same day, "has not had the effect of hastening the surrender of the city. On the other hand it has apparently made the people more firm and determined."

The total number of those killed by the bombardment would be estimated to have been 97 over three weeks, or less than a third of the number dying of smallpox in the hospitals each week, week after week.

In the privacy of his diary, on January 18, Washburne wrote, "I am more and more convinced that we can only be taken by starvation." The weight of despair had never been worse. "Four months of siege today and where has all this gone to? It seems to me as if I had been buried alive. I have accomplished nothing and, separated from my family and friends, cut off from communication to a great extent from the outside world, those dreary weeks might as well be struck off my existence."

A great movement of some 100,000 troops was under way. The Paris National Guard, with little or no experience in fighting, was to launch a last, desperate sortie to the west of the city. "The ambulances have all been notified, and I shudder for the forthcoming horrors." Some of the units had had only a few days of training.

The French novelist Edmond de Goncourt wrote of the "grandiose, soul-stirring sight" of the citizen army "marching towards the guns booming in the distance—

> an army with, in its midst, grey-bearded civilians who were fathers, beardless youngsters who were sons, and in its open ranks women carrying their husband's or their lover's rifle slung across their backs.

The following day, as the battle raged near Saint-Cloud, Washburne and Wickham Hoffman went as far as Passy, to the historic old Château de la Muette, to observe with Jules Favre and other French officials as much as could be seen by telescope from an uppermost cupola.

> One hundred thousand men are struggling to break through that circle of iron and of fire which has held them for four long, long months [Washburne wrote]. The lay of the country is such that we cannot see the theater of the conflict. . . . The low muttering of the distant cannon, and the rising of the smoke indicate, however, the field of carnage. The crowd of Frenchmen in the cupola were sad indeed, and we could not help feel for their anxiety.

From the château, Washburne returned to the American Ambulance, where carriages from the battlefield were arriving one after another with "loads of mutilated victims."

> They had brought in sixty-five of the wounded. . . . The assistants were removing their clothes all wet and clotted with blood, and surgeons were binding up their ghastly wounds.

Dr. Johnston and Gratiot told him the slaughter of French troops had been horrible, that the "whole country was literally covered with dead and wounded."

"All Paris is on the *qui-vive* and the wildest reports are circulating," he wrote by day's end. "The streets are full of people, men, women, and children. Who will undertake to measure the agonies of this dreadful hour!"

The weather turned thick and foggy. Rumors spread of "trouble in the city" and of Trochu being "crazy as a bed bug." On the morning of Sunday, January 22, the pounding of the bombardment seemed heavier than ever.

That afternoon some of the National Guard and an angry mob marched on the Hôtel de Ville once again but were confronted by troops of the Mobile Guard, who fired on them, killing five and wounding a dozen more. "And then such a scatteration," wrote Washburne, "these wretches flying in every direction . . . and in twenty minutes it was all ended." But for the first time French troops had fired on their fellow Frenchmen.

Again he and Hoffman had made their way down the Champs-Élysées in an effort to see what was happening, but to no avail, so dense were the crowds and the numbers of troops drawn up.

" 'Mischief afoot,' " Washburne surmised in his diary that night, evoking a line from Shakespeare's *Julius Caesar*. "The first blood has been shed and no person can tell what [a] half starved . . . Parisian population will do."

Four days of continuing fog, rumors, and bombardment followed. He had never seen such gloom everywhere, he wrote on January 24. Hardly anyone was to be seen except those cutting down the great trees along the avenues. "The city is on its last legs. . . ."

And then it happened. The surrender of Paris—and the end of the war—was announced on the morning of Friday, January 27, 1871, the 131st day of the siege.

" 'Hail mighty day!' " wrote Washburne. "Not a gun is heard today, the most profound quiet reigns. . . ."

CHAPTER TEN

MADNESS

*In the madness which prevails here, I will not un-
dertake any prediction of what will happen. . . .*

—ELIHU WASHBURNE

I

The terms of the surrender became public on the twenty-ninth day of the
new year, 1871. All troops in Paris were immediately to give up their arms.
Cannon on the ramparts were to be thrown in the moats. The Germans
would not enter the city for several days, and agreed to remain a brief time
only. There was to be no occupation of Paris.

For France it had been the most ill-advised, disastrous war in history,
with total defeat coming in little more than five months. The cost to France
in young men killed and wounded in battle was 150,000. For the German
Empire it was 117,000. The death toll in Paris was reported to have been
65,591, of whom 10,000 died in the hospitals. Three thousand had been
killed in the battle for Paris. The infants who died in the city also numbered somewhere between 3,000 and 4,000.

By the terms of the surrender, France was subjected to a staggering
war indemnity of 5 billion francs and forced to cede to Germany the provinces of Alsace and Lorraine, a point of extreme humiliation to the French
that was only to fester.

Emotions in Paris ranged from stoic acquiescence to abject gloom and bewilderment to burning fury, and this especially among the poor and those of the political left who had wanted to fight on and felt they had been betrayed by their own government.

"The enemy is the first to render homage to the moral strength and courage of the entire Paris population," read the government's own proclamation. "France is dead! Long live France!" declared the conservative paper *Le Soir*. But the liberal *Le Rappel* expressed the mood of tens of thousands that "Paris is trembling with anger."

Olin Warner spoke for nearly every American who had been through the siege when he wrote of the utter relief he felt just to have it over. If ever again he found himself in similar circumstances, he assured his parents, he would remain no longer "than packing up of my clothes requires."

Yet to Mary Putnam, who refused to abandon her faith in the ideal of a republic, the surrender had been unwanted and unnecessary. Paris could have held out another three months, she insisted, as did so many Parisians. "We are all furious," she told her father in a letter written from the legation, where she had gone partly to get warm but also because she knew the letter would have a better chance of getting out.

The very gloom of the streets, shrouded day after day by a persistent, thick fog, seemed entirely in keeping.

Shipments of food, including barrels of flour from America, began arriving in increasing quantities. In a matter of weeks food of all kinds had become widely plentiful and cheaper than before the siege. Trains ran once more, people were free to come and go. News and mail from elsewhere began circulating. And the weather at last cleared. By late February, with a spell of "pleasant days," Elihu Washburne could report that Paris was again "quite Parisian," its "bright-hearted population" back filling the streets.

He eagerly anticipated the return of his family and, in the meantime, was being warmly commended for all he had done through the crises to help so many in distress, everyone assuming, as did he, that the worst was over. When his friends the Moultons asked what those shut up in Paris would have done without him, he answered, "Oh, I was only a post-office." And praise was plentiful at home:

61

Henry James.

62

Mary Cassatt, self-portrait.

63

John Singer Sargent.

Augustus Saint-Gaudens by Kenyon Cox.

Augusta Saint-Gaudens
by Thomas Wilmer Dewing.

Living room interior of the
apartment at 3 rue Herschel by
Augusta Saint-Gaudens.

Farragut Monument, Madison Square Park, New York City, unveiled in 1881.
In the distance, Saint-Gaudens's *Diana* stands atop the tower of Madison
Square Garden, built later.

Reading Le Figaro by Mary Cassatt, the portrait of her mother, Mrs. Robert (Katherine Johnson) Cassatt, that marked her arrival as an Impressionist.

69

Lydia at a Tapestry Frame by Mary Cassatt (above). Lydia Cassatt, who suffered from Bright's disease, posed repeatedly for her sister, Mary, as in *The Cup of Tea* (below).

70

71

Carolus-Duran by John Singer Sargent, the portrait of the celebrated
French master that launched Sargent's career at age twenty-three.

Vernon Lee by Sargent.

72

Sketches of Sargent
reading Shakespeare
(top) and painting by
his fellow student and
roommate James
Carroll Beckwith.

73

74

75

El Jaleo (left top) and
*The Daughters of Edward
Darley Boit* (left bottom)
by John Singer Sargent.
*El Jaleo, The Daughters
of Edward Darley Boit,*
and Sargent's *Madame X*
(Madame Pierre Gautreau)
were all painted in Paris
within just two years, 1882
to 1884, when Sargent
was still in his twenties.
Below, the painter in his
studio with the portrait
that caused a sensation
like no other.

The Statue of Liberty rises over Paris in a painting by Victor Dargaud.

The grounds of the 1889 Exposition Universelle with the newly completed Eiffel Tower, the world's tallest structure.

Thomas Alva Edison by Abraham Archibald Anderson. So great was popular interest in Edison that he spent much of his time in Paris hiding out with his American friend Anderson, who took the opportunity to paint Edison's portrait.

Students at the Académie Julian in a painting by Jefferson David Chalfant (detail).

Robert Henri.

Henry O. Tanner by Hermann Dudley Murphy.

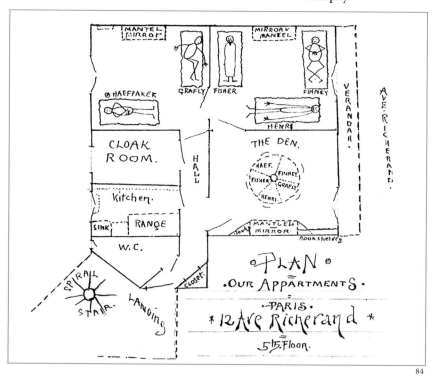

Henri's plan of the apartment he shared with four other American art students and their sleeping arrangement on "little iron beds."

Henry Adams.

Cover of a 1900 Exposition
Universelle guide book.

The continuing thrill of the fair—Paris seen from the Eiffel Tower.

Augustus Saint-Gaudens in his Paris studio, with a variation of his *Amor Caritas*.

Gus and Gussie aboard ship
on a trip to Spain, 1905.

90

91

Sherman Monument (with *Victory*) at 59th Street and Fifth
Avenue in New York City at the entrance to Central Park.

The conduct of Mr. Washburne during the war, and especially during the siege of Paris [wrote the *New York Tribune*] was marked by such discretion, such courage and energy that it gained the respect and esteem of the French and the German people. . . . We do not recall an instance in our diplomacy of a more brilliant and successful performance of duty in circumstances of such gravity and delicacy.

From Secretary of State Fish came a personal expression of gratitude. "No Minister . . . ever discharged a difficult and trying duty with more tact and ability and skill than you have. . . ."

Washburne longed only for peace and rest. He hoped he had done his duty, he told a friend, but feared too much praise. "It is always perilous to be too popular. . . ."

As soon as he saw his way clear, he was off to Brussels for a few days with Adele and the children.

The German army marched into Paris and down the Champs-Élysées on Wednesday, March 1. The city looked as if closed for a funeral. By general "understanding," shops and restaurants along the path were shut tight. No omnibuses or carriages were to be seen. No newspapers were published, no placards posted.

The first of the conquerors appeared at nine in the morning, three blue-uniformed German cavalrymen advancing slowly down the avenue, their horses at a walk, their carbines cocked, their fingers on the triggers. More of the advance guard followed, both cavalry and infantry.

The day had started out cloudy and grey, but after noon the sun appeared bright and warm. By half past one, the Royal Guards of Prussia, with glittering bayonets, surrounded the Arc de Triomphe. Then came the main body of the army marching by for two hours.

Washburne, who watched much of it from the balcony of a friend's apartment on the Champs-Élysées, wrote that a good many people were on the sidewalks on both sides of the avenue.

At first the troops were met with hisses, cat-calls and all sorts
of insulting cries, but as they poured in thicker and thicker . . .
the crowd seemed to be awed into silence, and no other sound
was heard but the tramp of the soldiery and the occasional
word of command.

That evening no crowds appeared on the boulevards. Not a restaurant
opened its doors, except for two on the Champs-Élysées that the Germans
had ordered to stay open. "Paris seemed literally to have died out," Washburne wrote.

The gas was not yet lighted, and the streets presented a sinister and somber aspect. . . . It is just to say that the people of
Paris bore themselves during all that cruel experience with a
great degree of dignity and forbearance which did them infinite credit.

Trying to see as much as possible, he had been, he reported to Adele,
"about on foot all day and at night was used up, feet blistered, etc."

On the morning of March 3, after an occupation of little more than
forty-eight hours, the conquerors marched away. Stores, restaurants, and
hotels threw open their doors. The Champs-Élysées was scrubbed clean.
Fountains in the Place de la Concorde began to spout again. "At 3 o'clock
in the afternoon (the day was splendid) . . . people looked happier than I
had seen them for many long months."

Gaslights burned once more. A sum of 200,000 francs was received
from the city of New Orleans in aid of the French wounded. Work began
to repair the damages done to the Tuileries Garden and the Bois de
Boulogne. Some of the galleries at the Louvre reopened. People who had
fled the city were pouring back by the thousands.

But any thought that things might go smoothly into spring was soon
dashed. On March 17, Washburne mentioned in a dispatch to Washington
that units of the National Guard had seized more than a hundred cannon and fortified themselves on the heights of Montmartre. As he later

said, he had no premonition of what followed early the next day, Saturday, March 18, 1871.

In a surprise move the government sent a force of army regulars to recover the cannon, and almost instantaneously the National Guard soldiers on Montmartre were joined by a huge angry crowd in which many were armed. At the moment of confrontation a regiment of regulars suddenly held their rifle butts in the air and joined in shouting down the government.

A general in command of the regulars, Claude Lecomte, was pulled from his horse, and with another general, Jacques Clément-Thomas, who had been taken captive irrespective of the fact that he was in civilian clothes, marched away to a nearby house on the rue des Rosiers with the mob following after and shouting for their death. General Thomas, an elderly man known for his Republican sympathies, had been doing no more than watching from the sidelines, but he had been long despised for his part in crushing the Revolution of 1848.

In an improvised mock trial, by a show of hands, the two captives were found guilty, then taken into the garden, tied together against a wall and shot, after which, reportedly, a number of the women from the crowd urinated on the bodies.

The violence on Montmartre marked the start of the insurrection that became known as the Paris Commune.

II

The Commune, as often mistakenly assumed later, had nothing to do with communism. The word *commune*, meaning something communal or shared, was used for a town or city government as a mark of regional autonomy. Thus the Paris Commune was now in charge of Paris and, ideally, devoted to politics more representative of the will of the people of Paris.

Washburne, who had gone to the country that Saturday with his friends the Moultons, did not learn of what happened on Montmartre until the following day, and by then, Sunday, March 19, the Central Committee of the National Guard had taken over at the Hôtel de Ville and the government, led by Adolphe Thiers, had fled to Versailles. Placards posted everywhere proclaimed a *comité* now in charge. As no one needed to be told, the National Guard in the city numbered 50,000 troops, all still armed. No less than 20,000 were now encamped outside the Hôtel de Ville with forty to fifty cannon drawn up.

It seemed the "culmination of every horror" to Washburne, whose family arrived from Brussels late that same day.

On March 21, several thousand citizens calling themselves the "Friends of Order" staged a protest, parading down the rue de la Paix to the Hôtel de Ville unarmed and without incident. But when, the day after, thousands more of Les Amis de l'Ordre marched down the same route to the cheers of spectators, a contingent of the National Guard stood ready at the Place Vendôme to stop them. Someone opened fire. From which side was never determined. Instantly the street was filled with gunfire and screaming, and a dozen of the Amis and at least one guardsman lay dead.

Through the week that followed, Washburne sent off one letter or dispatch to Washington after another in an effort to describe what was happening. With the official government now at Versailles, and little chance of its return to Paris anytime soon, he was obliged to travel back and forth by carriage almost daily to Versailles, twenty miles round-trip. He was gravely worried, concerned about the safety of his family, exhausted, and feeling ill much of the time.

The situation, he wrote, was already worse by far than during the siege. In a city of 2 million people there was "no law, no protection, no authority except that of an unorganized mob." In the first days of the Communards, he had spoken in their defense among friends, saying they were acting in good faith, but by now he was "utterly disgusted" by them.

True to form, he had no more intention of leaving Paris than he had had on the eve of the siege. And again he was the only chief of mission of a major country who chose to stay. The rest had moved to Versailles, where he set up a temporary office with Wickham Hoffman in charge, but where he refused to reside himself so long as other Americans remained in Paris.

On March 28, with great to-do, the Commune officially installed itself at the Hôtel de Ville. Military bands played. Officers of the Guard and members of the Comité Central wore red scarves. Red flags flew everywhere and the crowd, Washburne reported to Secretary of State Fish, exceeded 100,000 people. In response to every speech by members of the Comité, great cheers went up, and shouts of "*Vive la Commune!*"

At the same time, as Washburne also reported, the Paris journal *Nouvelle République*, a semiofficial organ of the Commune, announced that the deliberations of all representative bodies would no longer be public, and there would be no further reports of the sessions. Only decrees would be issued.

Newly printed placards posted in the streets of Montmartre announced the appointment of certain citizens who would henceforth receive any "denunciations" of anyone suspected of being in "complicity" with the government at Versailles.

Elsewhere, in several other parts of the city, houses were being searched and arrests made—more than four hundred arrests in a matter of days—on the orders of the new chief of police, Raoul Rigault, a former journalist in his twenties.

Such a system of "denunciation," Washburne assured Secretary Fish, would very soon fill the prisons of Paris. His private secretary, a young man named James McKean, had been to the Prefecture of Police and found an enormous crowd gathered, all looking for friends who had been arrested and "spirited away."

Washburne was not only disgusted with the Communards, but had come to think of pronouncements from the government at Versailles as mostly "rubbish." "Imbecility and indecision rule . . . at Versailles," he wrote privately. Adolphe Thiers, whom he admired, told him it would take at least two weeks for Marshal Patrice de MacMahon, the government's commander, to gather a sufficient force to attack the insurgents in Paris. Jules Favre, on the other hand, thought that once such a force was in place the insurgents would immediately cave in. "He is mistaken," Washburne wrote in his diary.

"The Commune is looming up and means business. Everything has a more sinister look," he recorded on March 31. "There never was such a hell upon this earth as this very Paris."

He kept trying every way he knew to find out what was happening. But to get to "the truth of matters" in such wild excitement seemed impossible. He was not frightened for himself, as frightening as things were, but he worried about his staff, worried constantly about his family and getting them safely away before it was too late.

———

The morning of that same day, March 31, Lillie Moulton, the beautiful daughter-in-law of his friends known for her exquisite singing voice, went to the office of the new chief of police, Rigault, to obtain a passport to leave Paris. The Prefecture of Police, a prison on the Île-de-la-Cité by the Palais de Justice, was enough to strike fear in anyone. Washburne described it as "a horrid place," even in the best of times. "What mysteries within these walls, what stories of suffering, torture and crime . . ."

Raoul Rigault, as he himself made plain, was the epitome of the impassioned Left Bank radical, half journalist, half student, bent on destroying all established privilege and authority, and at the moment he held more power than any other man in Paris. He despised nearly every social convention, the upper class, the middle class, and the church and its clergy most of all. "I want sexual promiscuity. Concubinage is a social dogma," he had earlier proclaimed.

Lillie Moulton described him later as "short, thick-set, with . . . a bushy black beard, a sensuous mouth, and a cynical smile." Extremely nearsighted, he wore heavy tortoiseshell glasses, but even these, she said, "could not hide the wicked expression of his cunning eyes." Washburne, with reason, was to call Rigault one of the most "hideous" figures in history, "strange and sinister . . . [with] the heart of a tiger."

Lillie was admitted to Rigault's office only after being kept waiting a considerable time. When finally she stood before the desk where he sat writing, he neither looked up nor acknowledged her presence. Again she waited, feeling, she said, "like a culprit." Two uniformed policemen stood immediately behind his chair. Another man, whom she did not recognize, leaned against a small mantelpiece at the other end of the room. He was Pascal Grousset, the Commune's delegate for external affairs and someone Washburne had had dealings with and liked. Possibly, Washburne had something to do with Grousset's presence in the room. Otherwise, one wonders why he would ever have allowed Lillie to face Rigault alone.

Breaking the silence, she told him she had come for a passport and handed him Washburne's card.

Did she wish to leave Paris? he asked. Yes, she said, and as she later wrote, "He replied, with what he thought was a seductive smile, 'I should think Paris would be a very attractive place for a pretty woman like yourself!' "

Was she an American? Yes, and glad to be so, she answered.

"Does the American minister know you personally?"

"Yes, very well."

Opening a desk drawer, he took out a blank passport form and began filling it in while asking the standard questions, but in a slow, insinuating way that she found "hateful." She thought she might faint. It was only when Pascal Grousset stepped forward to intervene and speed things along that the ordeal ended and she was safely out the door.

"No Elsa ever welcomed her Lohengrin coming out of the clouds as I did my Lohengrin coming from the mantelpiece," she later wrote.

———

For several days and nights the roar of cannon fire was heard again, exactly as during the siege, except this time it was the French firing on the French.

On April 4, the Commune formally impeached all members of the government at Versailles and confiscated their Paris properties. After dark that night, moving swiftly and with great secrecy, Chief of Police Rigault had the archbishop of Paris, Monseigneur Georges Darboy, arrested and jailed, along with twenty other priests. The archbishop had committed no offense, nor was any reason given for the arrest. Like Washburne, he had refused to leave the city, feeling it his duty to face every danger and stay with his people in their time of trial.

News of the arrest spread great alarm and outrage among many. Newspapers reported that the archbishop was taken before Raoul Rigault, who proceeded with "icy coolness" to interrogate the prisoner.

At first M. Darboy attempted his usual clerical attitudes, turning his eyes up and called the persons present, *"Mes enfants!"* Citizen Rigault, however, immediately interrupted him with the remark that he was not speaking to children, but to judges.

As the cannonading grew heavier, the exodus from Paris became a stampede of hundreds of thousands of people, everyone carrying as much money as could be safely concealed. All the gold and silver found in churches had been confiscated by the Commune. Placards on buildings denounced priests as thieves.

By the second week of April, all able-bodied men were forbidden to leave the city. Railroads suspended service. When cannon fire began hitting close to the American minister's home on the avenue de l'Impératrice—one shell striking within fifty feet—Washburne moved his family to a safer part of town.

"Big firing this morning and shells coming in fast," he wrote in his diary on April 10.

> I started downtown to the Legation. The shells were hissing through the air and exploding in the neighborhood of the Porte Maillot and the Arc de Triomphe. I got within about two hundred yards of the Arc when pop went the weasel—a shell struck [and] burst against the Arc. A piece of shell fell in the street, which a National Guard picked up, all warm and smoking, and sold to me for two francs.
>
> April 17. . . . The firing is going on all the time . . . so near it seems almost under the windows. . . . Every day makes things worse. . . . The house adjoining ours was entered and sacked the night before last. . . . I hardly know what to do.
>
> April 19. . . . All is one great shipwreck in Paris. Fortune, business, public and private credit, industry, labor are all in "the deep bosom of the ocean buried" [from Shakespeare's *Richard III*]. The physiognomy of the city becomes every day

more sad. All the upper part of the Champs-Élysées is completely deserted in fear of the shells. Immense barricades are going up at the Place de la Concorde. The great manufacturies and workshops are closed. . . . Where I write, at 75 [avenue de l'Impératrice], always the roar of cannon, the whizzing of shells and rattling of musketry. When I came home at 6½ this evening the noise was terrific. . . . Gratiot went to Fontainebleau today to find a place for the family, but was unsuccessful.

When the pope's nuncio, Monseigneur Chigni, made a strong appeal to the American minister, as the only senior diplomat still in Paris, to intervene on behalf of the imprisoned archbishop, stressing how perilous the situation had become, Washburne agreed to do what he could.

On the morning of Sunday, April 23, accompanied by young McKean, he made an official call on General Gustave-Paul Cluseret, the secretary of war under the Commune, who had the unusual distinction for a French officer of having served in the Union Army during the Civil War. With help from Senator Charles Sumner he had become a Union colonel and commanded troops in the Shenandoah Valley. Washburne had known him at the time, and Cluseret received him now most cordially and expressed his sympathy for the archbishop. But unfortunately, given "the state of feeling in Paris," he said, "no man would be safe for a moment who proposed his release."

Like an attorney in court, Washburne "remonstrated" against the "inhumanity and barbarism" of seizing such a man accused of no crime, dragging him to prison, then allowing no one to speak to him. If it was not within Cluseret's power to release the archbishop, then he, Washburne, must be permitted to visit him in prison.

Cluseret thought it a reasonable request and agreed to go at once with Washburne to see Chief of Police Rigault.

"So we all started off (Mr. McKean was with me) and made our way to the Prefecture," Washburne recorded. Arriving at about eleven o'clock, they were told Rigault was still in bed. Cluseret went alone to see him and soon returned with a pass. Washburne and McKean then proceeded directly to the infamous Mazas Prison on the boulevard Mazas, opposite the Gare de Lyon, where the archbishop was being held.

To their surprise they were admitted without delay and ushered to a visitors' cell. Minutes later the prisoner was led in.

Monseigneur Georges Darboy was fifty-eight years old. Born in Fayl-Billot, in the Haute Marne, he had come to Paris thirty years earlier to serve as inspector of religious instruction at the colleges of the diocese of the city. He became the archbishop in 1863. Washburne, who had never met him, was stunned by his appearance.

> With his slender person, his form somewhat bent, his long beard, for he has not been shaved apparently since his confinement, his face haggard with ill health, all could not have failed to have moved the most indifferent.

He was extremely pleased to see them, the archbishop said, for until then he had been permitted to see no one from the outside. Nor had he been allowed even to see a newspaper.

> He seemed to appreciate his critical situation, and to be prepared for the worst. He had no word of bitterness or reproach for his persecutors, but on the other hand remarked that the world judged them to be worse than they really were. He was patiently awaiting the logic of events and praying that Providence might find a solution to these terrible troubles without the further shedding of human blood.

He was confined, he told his visitors, to a cell ten by six feet with one small window, a single wooden chair, a small table, and a prison bed. In the same prison forty other priests were now being held. When Washburne offered him any assistance he might want, he said he had no need for anything.

Washburne, a Protestant and *un étranger*, left determined to do everything possible to have the archbishop released. He would be an agent of freedom still again, as he had been for so many during the siege and in battles at home in Congress against slavery. Two days later he was back at the prison bringing a stack of newspapers for the archbishop and a bottle of old Madeira.

On April 25, Adele and the family, with McKean as their escort, left the city to stay in Vieille-Église, thirty miles from Paris, beyond Versailles. "It is a little French village four hundred years old," Washburne wrote to a friend in Galena during an overnight visit. "We occupy a cottage near an old château, splendid yard, garden, etc. It is very pleasant and healthy and Mrs. W. and the children are very well, happy, and contented."

He himself was not so well, however. "I have been so run down and so overwhelmed with care and responsibility. . . ." What he did not say was that he had lost so much weight his suits hung on him. "The children are growing," he added, "and they chatter French like birds. . . ."

Back in Paris an incident involving the elderly Charles Moulton provided a momentary lift of spirits for Washburne, as it did for every American in Paris who heard the story.

For years Moulton had been known for his inability to say almost anything in French as it should be pronounced. After more than twenty years in Paris, he remained the ultimate Yankee mangler of the language, and much to the embarrassment of the rest of his family. He had no trouble reading French, and, seated in his favorite parlor chair, he often insisted on reading aloud to the others from the Paris papers, which, as he keenly appreciated, was enough to send them scurrying from the room.

On the morning of May 9, a mob of Communards descended on the Moulton estate on the rue de Courcelles. As the family well knew, anyone of obvious wealth was by this time in grave risk. "We thought our last day had come," said Lillie Moulton.

When no one in the house, neither servant nor family member, expressed sufficient courage to step out and face the mob, Moulton decided to go himself—"like the true American he is," wrote Lillie, who volunteered to go with him.

Small, slight, and bespectacled, he was hardly an imposing figure, and, against the backdrop of the enormous house, he seemed smaller still.

A rough-looking leader of the crowd pushed forward holding a sheet of paper with the official seal of the Comité de Transport and demanded in the name of the Commune every animal on the premises.

> Mr. Moulton took the paper [Lillie wrote], deliberately adjusted his spectacles, and . . . read it very leisurely (I wondered how those fiery creatures had the forbearance to stay quiet, but they did. I think they were hypnotized by my father-in-law's coolness). . . .

No sooner did Moulton open his mouth to reply than the crowd began to giggle, his pronunciation working its spell. When, raising his voice to an unusually high pitch, he declared they could have the horse, "*le cheval*," but not "*le vache*," using the masculine pronoun *le* for cow, it was more than they could bear.

"The men before us were convulsed with laughter," wrote Lillie.

Moulton's French saved the day, she later acknowledged, adding that, rough and threatening as the men in the crowd were, they "could not but admire the plucky old gentleman who stood there looking so calmly at them over his glasses."

A beloved family horse was led away, but "*le vache*" was permitted to stay. No damage whatever was done to the house or to anyone in it.

––––––––

The Commune issued a decree ordering the demolition of the famous Vendôme Column in the Place Vendôme honoring the victories of French armies under Napoleon. Other decrees followed, one to burn the Louvre, because it contained works of art celebrating gods, kings, and priests, and another to demolish Notre-Dame, the ultimate symbol of superstition.

Hundreds of laborers were already at work in the Place Vendôme, preparing to topple the 155-foot column. At the point where it was calculated to hit the ground, horse manure was being piled high to cushion the fall.

In another part of the city, on the Place Saint-Georges, Communards were busy demolishing the home of Adolphe Thiers and carrying off his possessions, including one of the finest private libraries in Paris.

For days crowds converged at the Place Vendôme, expecting to see the column come crashing down at almost any moment. Bands played as if at a festival. Thousands stood watching—as many as 20,000, Washburne judged from what he saw at midafternoon on May 16.

The engineers had cut through the bronze veneer and into the thick stone core of the column at its base, as a giant tree would be felled. Cables were attached to the top, just below the statue of Napoleon, and winches and pulleys set in position to pull.

At five-thirty, down it came, shattering in pieces even before it hit the manure pile. ("I did not see it fall and I did not want to," Washburne later wrote.)

To most of the throng who cheered the spectacle of such destruction, it symbolized an end to imperialism and the start of the new era under the Commune. A red flag was at once mounted on the now-vacant pedestal, and for days afterward the giant statue lay on its back, the head separated from the body, the right arm broken loose.

Writing in his diary the next day, Edmond de Goncourt noted the increasing number of people he saw walking about in the streets talking to themselves "aloud like crazy people."

A large placard in bold letters issued by the Commune went up on walls throughout the city:

> Citizens,
>
> Enough of militarism, no more general staffs loaded with stripes and gilded on every seam! Make way for the people, for fighters with bare arms! The hour for revolutionary war has struck. . . .
>
> If you want the loyal blood that has flowed like water for the last six weeks not to be in vain; if you want to live free in a France that is free and equal to all; if you want to spare your children from both your sorrows and your miseries, you will rise up as one man. . . .
>
> Citizens, your leaders will fight, and, if necessary, die with

you; but in the name of glorious France, mother of all popular revolutions, fountainhead of the ideas of justice and solidarity which must be and shall be the laws of the world, march to meet the enemy. Let your revolutionary energy show him that they may sell Paris but cannot deliver her; nor can they conquer her.

The Commune is counting on you, count on the Commune.

Every day seemed worse than the one before, Washburne wrote on May 19. "Today they threaten to destroy Paris and bury everybody in its ruins before they will surrender." In his official capacity he said nothing derogatory about the Communards. But in his diary they were "brigands," "assassins," and "scoundrels." "I have no time now to express my detestation. . . ."

Demands on his time by people desperate to get away grew proportionately. Already he had issued 4,450 *laissez-passers*. Yet at eight o'clock that morning two hundred people stood waiting outside the legation below his window.

The precarious fate of the archbishop weighed heavily and efforts in his behalf occupied many hours. The Communards wanted an exchange of the archbishop for one of their heroes, Auguste Blanqui, an idealistic radical conspirator who had been held prisoner for so long and by so many political regimes that he was known as "the imprisoned one." Washburne understood why the Versailles government might oppose such a trade. Yet whatever the difficulties, it seemed to him, the government stood to lose nothing by agreeing and thus saving the archbishop's life. He went to Versailles to make the case in person. It was, as he later said, "a very delicate piece of business," but he had become intensely interested in that "venerable and excellent man." Thiers and the government stubbornly refused to exchange Blanqui.

On another visit to the Mazas Prison, Washburne found the archbishop very "feeble" and confined to his bed.

Back again at the prison on the afternoon of Sunday, May 21, he discovered "everything in a vastly different state." There were new men in charge, most of them drunk and highly annoyed by his presence. Instead of allowing him to go to the prisoner's cell, as he had before, they brought the weakened archbishop out into a passageway and stood by watching and listening. He had greatly changed, Washburne later wrote. "He had lost his cheerfulness, and seemed sad and depressed. The change in the guardings prevailing there foreboded evil."

III

Like most of Paris, Washburne went to bed and slept through that night, May 21–22, unaware of what was happening, and like most of Paris he was stunned when he awakened to the news. The Tricolor flew atop the Arc de Triomphe, he was told by an excited servant at first light. The Versailles army had entered Paris.

He and Gratiot both dressed at once and raced out to see with their own eyes. It was true. Others already on the avenue were happily congratulating one another on delivery of Paris at last.

The regulars had marched in at Porte de Saint-Cloud in force at three o'clock the previous afternoon, and against little opposition advanced steadily along the Right Bank of the Seine on the avenue that connected Versailles and Paris, heading for the Commune stronghold at the heart of the city, at the Place de la Concorde.

Nothing had foretold the attack. The Commune command was taken completely by surprise. As night came on and the Versailles troops moved forward in the dark, National Guard units manning the barricades at Porte Maillot and on the avenue de la Grande-Armée, beyond the Arc de Triomphe, hastily abandoned their positions, and so another corps of regular troops poured into that quarter of the city. An enormous barricade by the Arc nearly thirty feet high that had taken great labor to build "served no earthly purpose," as Washburne observed.

He and Gratiot followed the regular troops down toward the Place de la Concorde, fully expecting to see the National Guard defense there quickly overrun. But it did not happen. Orders had gone out from the Central Committee at the Hôtel de Ville to throw together more barricades, barricades "in all haste," barricades in every direction. As reported later in *Galignani's Messenger,* "Everyone passing was forced to bring forward a paving stone or an earth bag, and any refusal would have been dangerous. Women and children worked just as actively as the National Guards themselves."

At about nine o'clock the Communard batteries on Montmartre opened fire on the city and the shells came in "thick and fast."

Tired of waiting and doing nothing, Washburne mounted a horse and rode off to see more, entirely without concern for his own safety, it would seem. "5:45 P.M. Have just taken a long ride," he wrote. "The havoc has been dreadful—houses are all torn to pieces, cannon dismantled, dead rebels, etc., etc. One can hardly believe such destruction."

"To arms!" read an urgent appeal posted by the National Guard. "To the barricades! The enemy is within our walls! Let there be no hesitation! Forward the Republic, the Commune and Liberty."

By late in the day more than 80,000 Versailles troops had arrived and the western third of the city was in their hands. Still, at the Place de la Concorde and elsewhere, the fighting raged on, gunfire and the screams of the wounded filling the night.

So began "La Semaine Sanglante," the Bloody Week.

On May 23 a city of 2 million people became a deafening full-scale battlefield. For twelve hours there was no letup in the roar of cannon. Montmartre, the symbolic stronghold of the Commune, fell to the regular army, the Communards leaving behind the dreadful spectacle of twelve regular soldiers taken prisoner who, because they refused to join the Commune, had had their hands cut off. Vicious street fighting took heavy tolls on both sides, but of the Communards especially. Some 4,000 Communards were taken prisoner. Any suspected of being deserters from the regular army were shot at once.

The Communard positions at the Place Vendôme, the Place de la Concorde, the Tuileries Palace, and Hôtel de Ville continued to hold.

Everyone in Paris tried to keep out of harm's way, indoors. Washburne, for his part, decided to make still another effort to save the archbishop. He went by carriage to the Versailles army headquarters at Passy to urge Marshal MacMahon to take possession of the Mazas Prison as quickly as possible to save the archbishop and the other prisoners. "He [MacMahon] hopes they will be there in a day or two," was all Washburne could claim for his efforts in his diary that night.

At one o'clock (Wednesday, May 24) he was again awakened in bed, this time to be told the Palace of the Tuileries was in flames. He left as quickly as possible, and from a window at the Legation, six flights up on the top floor, much of the city was spread before him.

It was a terrible, unimaginable spectacle. The blazing palace lighted the sky. The Legion of Honor and the Ministry of Finance, too, were on fire. For a while it appeared the Invalides was burning, but this proved not to be so. "Tremendous [cannon] firing in another part of the city and the windows of the Legation shake."

Like so many days that had followed one after another, the morning that dawned, May 24, was perfectly beautiful, except, as Washburne wrote, that over the city thick smoke obscured the sun. He went "down town" at about eleven o'clock. The insurgents had been driven from both the Place Vendôme and the Place de la Concorde. The fires, it was said, were the insidious work of women carrying petroleum or kerosene who numbered in the thousands—*pétroleuses*, they were called. "Every woman carrying a bottle was suspected of being a *pétroleuse*," wrote Wickham Hoffman, who found it hard to believe the story.

"I can give no adequate description of what I saw," Washburne wrote.

> All the fighting in all the revolutions which have ever taken place in Paris has been mere child's play compared to what has taken place since Sunday and what is going on now. . . . You can scarcely imagine the appearance of the streets. . . . Went as far as the burning Tuileries, the front of all falling in and flames bursting out in another part of the building. . . . Fires in all directions raging—many of them under the guns of the insurgents so they cannot be put out.

With the Palace ablaze, the Louvre was in imminent danger, but as Washburne could report in a long dispatch to Secretary Fish sent that night, the museum had been saved.

Two days earlier Police Chief Rigault and a coterie of extreme Communards had met in secrecy and ordered the execution of Archbishop Darboy and five other priests. The hostages were then moved from Mazas to
La Roquette Prison in the Belleville quarter, which was still under Communard control.

At approximately six o'clock on the evening of May 24, as Paris was
burning, the archbishop and the others were ordered out into the courtyard of the prison. They then descended a stairway, stopping at the ground
floor, where they embraced one another and exchanged a few last words.
When a cluster of National Guard soldiers at the door made insulting
remarks, an officer demanded silence, saying, "That which comes to these
persons today, who knows but what the same will come to us tomorrow?"
Darkness had come on, and the six prisoners had to be led into the courtyard and up to the wall by the light of lanterns. The archbishop was placed
at the head of the line. At a signal the firing squad shot all six at once.

Late that night the bodies were tumbled into a cart, hauled to nearby
Père Lachaise Cemetery, and thrown into an open ditch.

At the Mazas Prison another fifty-three priests were murdered in cold
blood.

Nothing of these atrocities was reported until late the next day. Nor
was it yet generally known that on the afternoon of May 24, before the
execution of the archbishop, Versailles soldiers had found Raoul Rigault
hiding in a hotel on rue Gay-Lussac and, upon discovering who he was,
took him into the street and shot him in the head. The body lay in the gutter for two days.

Flames raged through the night. The Hôtel de Ville had been set afire,
along with the Palais de Justice and the Prefecture of Police. The Palais
Royal and houses along the rue de Rivoli were burning. After nearly a
month with no rain everything was dry as tinder.

Punishment for anyone caught, or suspected of, setting fires was immediate and merciless. Correspondents for the foreign press wrote of the

"savage feeling" among the Versailles troops. Such hatred as was let loose in Paris had become terrifying beyond description, Washburne stressed in another hurried dispatch. The victims were strewn everywhere in the streets. That afternoon on the avenue d'Antin, an employee of the legation had counted the bodies of eight children, none more than fourteen years of age, who had been caught distributing incendiary boxes and shot on the spot.

The insurgents fought on "like fiends," and the killing continued through Thursday and Friday as the first rain fell—heavy rain. Many hundreds of insurgents taken prisoner were summarily executed in the streets, in prisons, in the Luxembourg Gardens, and outside the Louvre. Thousands more were herded off through the rain, along streets where enraged crowds screamed for their death.

"They are as they were when caught, most without hats or caps, their hair plastered on the foreheads and faces," wrote Edmond de Goncourt, as he watched several hundred prisoners pass on their way toward Versailles.

> There are men of the common people who have made a covering for their heads with blue-checked handkerchiefs. Others, thoroughly soaked by the rain, draw thin overcoats around their chests under which a piece of bread makes a hump. It is a crowd of every social level, workmen with hard faces, artisans in loose-fitting jackets, bourgeois with socialist hats, National Guards . . . two infantrymen, pale as corpses. . . . You see middle-class women, working women, street-walkers, one of whom wears a National Guard uniform. . . . There is anger and irony on their faces. Many of them have the eyes of mad women.

The nearer the end came, the more the atrocities accelerated on both sides. On Friday, 50 prisoners of the Communards were taken from La Roquette Prison and shot. That night another 38 were led to the Père Lachaise Cemetery and executed, followed by another 4 the next day, making 92 victims in all.

On Sunday, May 28, when the last of the Communards still fighting were finally overrun, Marshal MacMahon declared Paris "delivered." But the atrocities continued, growing still more horrific. One of the most infamous took place again at Père Lachaise when 147 Communards were lined up and shot against a wall to be henceforth known as the Wall of the Communards.

"There has been nothing but general butchery," Washburne wrote in his diary.

> The rage of the soldiers and the people knows no bounds. No punishment is too great, or too speedy, for the guilty, but there is no discrimination. Let a person utter a word of sympathy, or even let a man be pointed out to a crowd as a sympathizer and his life is gone. . . . A well-dressed respectable looking man was torn into a hundred pieces . . . for expressing a word of sympathy for a man who was a prisoner and being beaten almost to death.

"The vandalism of the dark ages pales into insignificance before the monstrous crimes perpetrated in this great center of civilization in the last half of the nineteenth century," he wrote in an impassioned dispatch to Secretary Fish.

> The incredible enormities of the Commune, their massacre of the Archbishop of Paris and the other hostages, their countless murders of other persons who refused to join them in their fiendish work, their horrid and well organized plans of incendiary intended to destroy almost the entire city . . . are crimes which will never die. I regret to say that to these unparalleled atrocities of the Commune are to be joined the awful vengeances inflicted by the Versailles troops. . . . The killing, tearing to pieces, stabbing, beating, and burning of men, women, and children, innocent and guilty alike, by the government troops will stain to the last ages the history of France, and the execrations of mankind will be heaped upon

the names who shall be found responsible for acts which disgrace human nature. . . .

Although estimates of the total carnage inflicted by the regular troops vary, there seems little doubt that they slaughtered 20,000 to 25,000 people. No one would ever know for sure what the total numbered, but nothing ever in the history of Paris—not the Terror of the French Revolution or the cholera epidemic of 1832—had exacted such an appalling toll. At one point the Seine literally ran red with blood.

The value of the architectural landmarks and other treasures destroyed was inestimable.

Olin Warner, like Washburne an eyewitness to events, was later to write a lengthy defense of the Communards, in which he compared their initial idealism to that of the American rebels of 1776. At the time, however, in a letter to his "Dear Ones at Home" he said he had seen more than enough. "I hope it will never be my lot to see a drop of blood shed again. I never want to hear another cannon roar as long as I live. . . . I am disgusted with everything pertaining to war."

On June 1, three days after the fighting had ended, Elihu Washburne went to La Roquette Prison to see the cell in which the archbishop had been held, and to pay homage at the spot in the prison yard where the archbishop and the five priests had been executed. The marks of the bullets on the wall could be plainly seen.

The body of the archbishop, having been rescued from the ditch at Père Lachaise before decomposition had taken place, lay in state at the palace of the archbishop at 127 rue de Grenelle. For several days thousands came to pay their respects, Washburne among them. On June 7, still greater numbers lined the streets to see the funeral procession pass on the way to Notre-Dame, where services were held with all appropriate majesty. To Washburne it was one of "the most emotional and imposing" services he had ever attended.

IV

Charred beams, dead animals, shattered doors and window frames, the remains of broken lampposts, wagons, mountains of wreckage, and all the barricades were hauled away. With people working day and night, life steadily resumed. Omnibuses began running, restaurants opened. It was not that the horrors of what had happened were put out of mind, any more than the horrendous damage done vanished entirely from sight. The blackened ruins of the Palace of the Tuileries were to be left standing for more than ten years as a mute reminder.

On June 3, *Galignani's Messenger* carried an item from the *Times* of London declaring, "Paris, the Paris of civilization, is no more. . . . Dust and ashes . . . smolder and stench are all that remain. . . ." Cook's Tours of London was already selling special trips to see the ruins of the fire. But there seemed a united, pervasive zeal to put Paris in order again as quickly as possible. By July the Tuileries Garden had reopened and some 60,000 stonemasons were at work repairing, rebuilding, building anew, a force of stonemasons equivalent to the entire population at the time of Portland, Maine, or Savannah, Georgia.

The Hôtel de Ville would be rebuilt, the Column of the Place Vendôme put together again and restored to its old pedestal.

The Venus de Milo was recovered from a secret hiding place and returned to the Louvre. The incomparable Greek statue, dating from before the birth of Christ, had been buried during the siege in, of all places, the cellar of the Prefecture of Police. Packed into a giant oak crate filled with padding, it was taken in the dead of night to the end of one of the many secret passages in the Prefecture, where, as only a few knew, a wall was built to conceal it. Stacks of documents of obvious importance were piled against the wall, then a second wall built to make it appear the hiding place was for the documents. When the Prefecture caught fire the night so much of Paris went up in flames, the anxiety of those in the know about the Venus was extreme. It seems a broken water pipe "miraculously" saved the statue. Once the smoking ruins were removed, the oak crate was found intact and brought back to the Louvre to be opened.

Everyone leaned forward eagerly to look [read the account in *Galignani's Messenger* at the end of August]. Lying in her soft bed . . . she seemed to look gratefully on her preservers. . . . All her features and limbs were complete, no injury has been done. . . .

To many her return from the ashes seemed a resurrection of the Paris of art and culture, a Paris that would not die.

Those Parisians who had fled the city for their safety returned like an incoming tide. With them were foreign students, business people, diplomats, and the families of diplomats, including Adele Washburne and her children. The Americans who had never left tried to pick up their lives where they had left off.

Lillie Moulton ordered several fine dresses from Worth, in preparation for a September concert tour in America. ("And if my public don't like me," she wrote, "they can console themselves with the thought that a look at my clothes is worth a ticket.")

Mary Putnam, like many of her French friends, had seen her initial fervor for the Republic vanish, not because of the excesses of the Commune so much as the brutal vengeance of the Versailles government. Her engagement, too, had ended when the return of her fiancé brought "a sense of estrangement." Part of the problem was that as a woman she would face inevitable difficulties practicing medicine in France and he was unwilling to leave France. She did, however, complete her dissertation, for which she was awarded the highest honors, just as she received the highest possible marks in each of her five examinations. "I have passed my last examination [and] . . . passed my thesis, and am now *docteur en médecine de la Faculté de Paris*," she wrote to her mother on July 29. She was the first American woman ever to attain such a professional standing.

Her achievement received notice in the New York and Paris papers, and in the *Archives de Médecine*, which mattered most to her. That a woman had acquired the legal right to practice medicine, said the learned professional journal, was "not without importance at large."

By then also, the American minister to France, Elihu B. Washburne, after several restorative weeks "taking the waters" at Carlsbad, the famous health spa in Bohemia, decided that, if needed, he would happily stay on in Paris.

―――――

Tributes were to be published celebrating the part Washburne had played. At home he would be talked of as a possible candidate for president. There were dinners in his honor in Paris, and much said in diplomatic circles about the courage and perseverance he had shown.

"Speaking of diplomacy, hasn't our Minister in Paris done splendidly," wrote Frank Moore, the assistant secretary at the legation who had served with Washburne through the siege and the horrors of the Commune and was still on the job.

> By the use of sound common sense, a kindly, generous dispo-
> sition and a true appreciation of the right, he has during the
> past year brought more credit to our government and people
> at home than they can ever reward him for. His name is on
> every tongue and I am sure that he will not escape the fate
> of other honest men for whom thousands of boy babies have
> been and will affectionately and admiringly be named. . . .
> That it will ever be a pleasant chapter for Americans to read
> in future history which must say that the U.S. Legation alone
> remained in Paris throughout the siege and the fearful scenes
> of the Commune of 1870 and 1871.

What no one could yet appreciate, other perhaps than Washburne himself, was the additional, immeasurable value of the diary he had kept day after day through the entire ordeal, recording so much that he witnessed and had taken part in, writing often at great length late at the end of an exhausting, horrible day, aware constantly of the self-imposed duty he felt to keep such an account. He could very well have done nothing of the sort. Or the daily entries might have been abbreviated notes only, telegraphic in style, something to be "worked up later" as a memoir. But Washburne was not so constituted. He had to set it down there and then, and the wonder is that what he wrote was not only substantial in quantity, but that he wrote so extremely well, with clarity, insight, and such great empathy for the human drama at hand.

Numbers of his famous American predecessors in diplomatic roles in Paris had written perceptively, often eloquently of their experiences and observations while there, beginning with Benjamin Franklin, John Adams, and Thomas Jefferson. Still greater numbers of American authors of high reputation—Cooper, Longfellow, Emerson, Hawthorne, Mark Twain, Harriet Beecher Stowe—had written of their Paris days before Washburne ever arrived, and many more would take their turns in years to come. But no one ever, before or after, wrote anything like Washburne's Paris diary, and if his decision to stay and face whatever was to come had resulted only in the diary, he would have made an enormous, singular contribution.

CHAPTER ELEVEN

PARIS AGAIN

I began to live.

—MARY CASSATT

I

"I have never seen Paris so charming as on this last Christmas day," wrote Henry James, Jr., in the fourth of his "letters" to the *New York Tribune.* "The sky was radiant and the air was soft and pure. . . . It was a day to spend in the streets and all the world did so."

He had first seen Paris as a boy of twelve while touring Europe with his family. He had returned now, twenty years later, to work on a novel. To help meet expenses, he was doing two letters a month for the *Tribune,* for which he received the sizable sum of ten gold dollars a week.

In the first of his letters, dated November 22, 1875, he stressed that any American who had been to Paris before found on return that his "sense of Parisian things becomes supremely acute." He wrote of Charles Garnier's new opera house, finished at last and "the most obvious architectural phenomenon in Paris," and a new play by the son of Alexandre Dumas in rehearsal at the Théâtre Français.

In the fourth letter he extolled the "amazing elasticity" of France:

> Beaten and humiliated on a scale without precedent, de-
> spoiled, dishonored, bled to death financially—all this but
> yesterday—Paris is today in outward aspect as radiant, as
> prosperous, as instinct with her own peculiar genius as if her
> sky had never known a cloud.

Highly knowledgeable about art, no less than music and theater, James
wrote admiringly of several paintings hanging in the Théâtre Français,
and particularly a portrait of a lady pulling off her glove by Carolus-Duran,
who, of all the modern emulators of the seventeenth-century Spanish
master Diego Velázquez, James declared "decidedly the most successful."

At age twelve, James had spent hours in the Louvre with his older
brother, William, where they "looked and looked again" at paintings, all
the time wondering what he would make of his life. But now, at thirty-two,
his career was well established. He had published dozens of reviews, travel
sketches, and more than twenty-four short stories. A first novel, *Roderick
Hudson*, was about to be published. The second was his reason for being
back in Paris. Called *The American*, it began in the Louvre, with its pro-
tagonist, Christopher Newman, reclined on a "commodious" divan in the
Salon Carré, contemplating Murillo's *Immaculate Conception.*

That James was in Europe to stay seems not yet to have entered his
mind. After an uneventful crossing of the Atlantic and a brief stopover
in London to freshen his wardrobe, he had had little trouble finding a
suitable apartment—two bedrooms, parlor, and kitchen—on the rue de
Luxembourg (now the rue Cambon), a block from the Place Vendôme. The
street was relatively quiet and his windows, facing south, caught the full
sunlight. "If you were to see me, I think you would pronounce me well off,"
he wrote to his father, in Cambridge, Massachusetts, who had inherited
his wealth and took great interest in how the family money was spent.
"Considering how nice it is, it isn't dear," Henry assured him.

He wrote faithfully week after week—to father, mother, sister Alice,
brother William—in an effort to portray the new life he had embarked
upon and especially his excitement over the French writers he had already
met, including Edmond de Goncourt, Émile Zola, Gustave Flaubert, and
the Russian Ivan Turgenev, whom he liked best. He had also, he reported

to his mother, knowing how it would please her, "taken a desperate plunge" into the American circle by attending two balls and a dinner party. But he had no relish for such company.

He missed his family dreadfully. "I am waiting anxiously for the letter from William who was to write to me on the Sunday after yours," he wrote to his father. "But make mother write too. I have heard from her but once since I left home. It seems an age." "Love to all in superabundance," he would end a long letter to his mother.

He was in Paris to work, and Paris was "an excellent place to work," he assured his editor at the *Atlantic*, William Dean Howells, who would be publishing the new novel in installments.

Quite unlike James himself, the novel's main character, Newman, who was new to Paris, had come solely to be amused: "I want the biggest kind of entertainment a man can get. People, places, art, nature, everything." James portrayed him as tall, lean, and muscular, a veteran of the Civil War, a success in business with money aplenty and ready to spend, awkward still in French but decidedly interested in the company of attractive women—none of which applied to the author himself. A graduate of Harvard Law School, James had been exempted from military service because of a physical infirmity. He had never worked in business, not even a day, and was neither tall nor muscular, nor, it seemed, much interested in women beyond spirited conversation, at which he excelled. But as it was with his main character, the longer he stayed in the great French capital, the greater its appeal.

"What shall I tell you?" he began a letter to Howells one April morning. "My windows are open, the spring is becoming serious, and the soft hum of good old Paris comes into my sunny rooms. . . ."

"The spring is now quite settled and very lovely," he told brother William a few weeks later. "It makes me feel extremely fond of Paris and confirms my feeling of being at home here. . . . I scribble along with a good deal of regularity. . . ." And that, as he knew William understood, was the point.

———

Since the brutal catastrophes of 1870–71, the numbers of Americans coming to Paris had been growing steadily. In a single week in September 1872, the Grand Hôtel, always popular with Americans (including James's fictional Christopher Newman), had to refuse accommodations to two hundred people. Many, like James, were back for a second or third time. Among them was Senator Charles Sumner, who, at sixty-two, had returned once more in need, his physicians said, of rest and relaxation. And as before in Paris, he was "the recipient of much attention from all quarters."

In a city focused on swift revival, Americans were welcome as never before. The economic effect of their presence was phenomenal, as confirmed by *Galignani's Messenger:*

> It is generally acknowledged that the trade of Paris is now mainly sustained by American visitors who spend more money among the shopkeepers than all the rest put together. . . . we only wish there were more of them, for this is about the best and most effective way in which Uncle Sam can aid the new French Republic.

But an appreciable number of the French looked to America for more than monetary sustenance only. For those whose faith in the ideal of a republican form of government held firm, America remained the shining example. Indeed, one group of the faithful had conceived the idea of creating an unprecedented gift from France to the United States, to coincide with the approaching centennial of American independence in 1876.

It was to be a colossal monument called *Liberty Lighting the World.* A French sculptor chosen for the design, Frédéric-Auguste Bartholdi, had already been to America to see something of the country and meet with numerous Americans who shared an appreciation for the bonds between their country and France. He had returned with a plan to build an immense statue at the entrance to New York Harbor. The new Franco-American Union, established in Paris to promote the project, included several prominent Americans among its honorary members, one of whom was Minister Elihu Washburne.

As in times past, the great majority of the talented and aspiring Americans coming to the city to study were young and altogether unfamiliar with France, its language and ways. Many would one day rank among the eminent American artists and architects of their time. James Carroll Beckwith, J. Alden Weir, Theodore Robinson, Thomas Dewing, George de Forest Brush, Abbot Thayer, Will Low, and architect Louis Sullivan were among those who arrived in Paris in the 1870s and, like so many before, their excitement was such as they would never forget. Will Low, an art student, expressed perfectly how it felt "to wake up in Paris" for the first time. "I was not yet twenty. I was quite alone. I did not speak a word of French . . . but I was in Paris and the world was before me."

Those not new to the city felt much the same. Like Henry James, they had returned because for them Paris was the best of all places to get on with their work. Of particular note were painters George P. A. Healy, returning again at age fifty-nine, nearly forty years after his first arrival, Mary Cassatt of Philadelphia, and John Singer Sargent, who was young enough to have been Healy's grandson and an American prodigy such as had not been seen in Paris since the days of Louis Moreau Gottschalk, who, as it happened, was one of the young man's favorite composers.

Unlike all but a few of their American counterparts, each of these four spoke fluent French, and, with the exception of James, they were there in Paris with their families.

George Healy, with his wife, Louisa, several daughters and a son, took up residence in 1872 in an ample eighteenth-century "hôtel" on the heights near Montmartre, in what was known as the painters' quarter, at 64 rue de la Rochefoucauld, which had an enormous studio next door. Healy was an American success story of a kind the French greatly respected, and both the house and the workspace befitted a figure of renown. There were numerous spacious rooms with numerous French windows, tall mirrors, white-and-gold woodwork, as well as a small conservatory and lovely walled garden with a rococo grotto. "We can give garden parties here!" exclaimed the youngest daughter, Kathleen, who was fourteen.

The Healys had been among the thousands dealt a devastating blow by the catastrophic Chicago Fire of 1871. None of the family was injured—all were away at the time—but their home on Wabash Avenue had been completely destroyed and everything in it, including much of Healy's work, correspondence, journals, account books, and other papers of record.

Healy had thought at first of relocating in Italy. They must think carefully and choose "exactly the right place," he told the family, "for this is really and truly our last move." The choice was Paris, "the only logical conclusion."

Commissions came steadily. "Healy is strong in portraits," reported Thomas Gold Appleton to Henry Longfellow, Appleton having by then resumed his annual visits to Paris. As once Healy had painted the protagonists of the Civil War—Lincoln, Beauregard, Sherman, Grant—so now, in relatively little time, he would paint those of the Franco-Prussian War—Adolphe Thiers, Léon Gambetta, Otto von Bismarck, all three at the request of Elihu Washburne.

As a kind of postscript to his Civil War portraits, he produced a posthumous Robert E. Lee, for which Lee's son Custis, the president of Washington and Lee College, posed in the studio on the rue de la Rochefoucauld.

Working as industriously as ever, Healy painted a full-length portrait of Emma Thursby, an American concert singer acclaimed on both sides of the Atlantic, standing with a musical score in hand and wearing a magnificent blue silk and lace gown. In 1879, Nathan Appleton, half-brother of Thomas Gold Appleton and one of the American backers of a French plan to build a Panama canal, brought the celebrated leader of the project, Ferdinand de Lesseps, "The Hero of Suez," to Healy's studio for a portrait. "This will be an historical picture," Healy wrote in his diary the day he completed a first sketch showing de Lesseps pointing to the place on the map where the canal was to go.

Between commissions he painted his own portrait and one of Louisa, then another of Louisa and daughter Edith sitting in the garden, Edith knitting while Louisa read aloud to her. Healy, too, loved to listen to Louisa read from Dickens, Balzac, or George Sand while he worked. If she were away or for some other reason unable to read, he would turn gloomy. "I go every morning and read . . . to Papa, but . . . that is not what Mama's reading is, so he looks rather glum," Edith wrote in her diary.

Healy could not have felt better about his work and the whole change in the life of the family. One daughter, Mary, would marry a French writer and professor, Charles Bigot. Another, Emily, chose to become a nun and took her vows in the great house at Conflans-Sainte-Honorine. Son George decided to study architecture in Paris rather than return to college in the United States. For the genial Healy himself much of the pleasure of Paris came from providing generous hospitality to young American artists who had come to "study hard," as once he had, and to give them encouragement.

———

Mary Cassatt, too, had been hard hit by the Chicago Fire, and her loss, though nothing like what happened to the Healy family, had also led to her return to Paris.

Like Henry James, she had spent a good part of her childhood in Paris in the company of a well-traveled, well-to-do family and was said to have shown her earliest interest in art there at age seven. In 1866, at twenty-one, traveling with another young Philadelphia painter, Eliza Haldeman, she had returned to Europe to study and paint, much of the time in Paris, where she entered the studio of a distinguished portrait painter, Charles Chaplin, one of the few French masters who held classes especially for women. She made copies of masterworks at the Louvre, painted in the nearby countryside, worked hard and steadily.

> I think she has a great deal of talent and industry [Eliza Haldeman wrote in a letter to her mother]. One requires that latter living in France, the people study so hard and the results are wonderful. . . . The difference between Americans and French is that the former work for money and the latter for fame, and then the public appreciate things so much here.

In an atelier at Villiers-le-Bel, Mary studied with George Healy's old friend Thomas Couture. Later, in 1868, she was in Paris when one of her paintings, *A Mandolin Player*, which showed clearly the influence of Couture's spirited, unacademic style, was accepted and hung in the Salon. She exhibited the work under her middle name, Mary Stevenson. "It is much pleasanter," Eliza Haldeman explained, "when one is a girl as it avoids publicity."

For Mary her time in France had determined she would be a professional, not merely "a woman who paints," as was the expression. Commenting in a letter on just such an acquaintance, she was scathing: "She is only an amateur and you must know we professionals despise amateurs. . . ."

With the outbreak of the Prussian war during the summer of 1870, she had headed home to Philadelphia, where she kept painting but felt so deprived of the presence of great art at hand, so downhearted, that she was nearly ready to give up. Thinking Chicago might be a better market for her work, she went west to investigate, traveling with two of her cousins. And thus she was there when the city burned. Neither she nor any of her party suffered any injury, but two of her paintings on display at a jewelry store were destroyed.

Returning to Philadelphia, she resolved to change her life. "Oh how wild I am to get to work, my fingers fairly itch and my eyes water to see fine paintings again," she wrote to another Philadelphia friend and fellow painter, Emily Sartain. By December the two were on their way to Europe.

They found Paris bitterly cold and smothered in fog. It had been less than a year since the final agonies of the siege, only six months since the Bloody Week. "The Hôtel de Ville seems like a Roman ruin. . . . the fog was so thick everything was lost at fifty feet off," wrote Emily. "I could scarcely see the pictures in the Louvre, it was so dark."

She and Mary soon moved on, this time to Parma, in Italy, to work with a teacher, Carlo Raimondi, who told Mary, "Don't be disheartened—remember you can do anything you want to."

The following spring Emily left Mary at Parma to join her family in Paris. On one excursion out of the city, they passed the site where one of the great battles had been fought between the French and the Germans and where the dead, they were told, were buried in eight enormous pits. A putrid smell still hung in the air.

At Parma, Mary worked on, concentrating especially on paintings by Correggio, and making such progress that she began to draw attention. In Paris in the spring of 1872, *Galignani's Messenger* carried an article from the *Gazzetta di Parma* in which a distinguished Italian art critic,

Parmetto Bettoli, wrote of seeing a copy of the Correggio masterpiece *L'Incoronata*, done by a young American:

> I must candidly confess that when I am called to criticize feminine essays in the Fine Arts or *Belles-Lettres*, my eulogisms are generally qualified by the restriction embraced in the phrase, "It is not bad for a woman." But as regards this picture I find myself in a very different position. The copy of this great work, executed by Miss Cassatt, betrays such a surprising knowledge of art that a male artist, no matter how great his experience, might feel honored at having the authorship of this work attributed to him.

Later, from Madrid, Mary wrote to tell Emily that she had discovered Velázquez. "Velázquez oh! my but you knew how to paint!"

She worked without letup, in Madrid and Seville, then Antwerp for a summer, then Rome for seven months, with intermittent stops in Paris, which, she claimed, she had come to dislike.

In 1873, after a series of rejections of her work by the Paris Salon, she learned that one of her Spanish paintings, a large canvas of a bullfighter and his lady, had been accepted.

The pull of Paris proved too strong. Back in the city in 1874, after years of roving over half of Europe, she said she had come to stay. "She astonished me by telling me she is looking for an atelier here," wrote Emily Sartain. "She has always detested Paris so much that I could scarcely believe it possible . . . but she says it is necessary to be here. . . ."

Mary Cassatt had been born in 1844 in western Pennsylvania, in what was then known as Allegheny City on the opposite side of the Allegheny River from Pittsburgh. Her mother, to whom she was devoted, was Katherine Kelso Johnston, the daughter of a Pittsburgh banker of Scotch-Irish descent. Her father, Robert Simpson Cassatt, whose forebears were French (the name was originally Cossart), became the first mayor of Allegheny

City and succeeded so rapidly in finance and mercantile enterprises that by the time he reached his early forties he felt ready for retirement, whereupon he moved the family east, settling first in Lancaster County.

Mary was the fourth of five children. The oldest, Lydia, was followed by two brothers, Alexander and Robert. The youngest, Joseph, arrived when Mary was five. Childhood was set in perfect comfort, amid books and fine furniture, and in as handsome a country home as could be found in Lancaster County. But the mother and father had desired city life and so moved to Philadelphia. Then followed four years in Europe—two in Paris, two in Germany—at the end of which the family returned to Pennsylvania, first to West Chester, outside Philadelphia, then Philadelphia again.

They were not people of immense wealth, rather, as they would have said, they were respectably "comfortable." Refined in their tastes, they frowned on ostentation. The children attended the best private schools. Good grammar and proper manners were insisted upon. Everyone dressed well, and father Robert Cassatt continued to see no necessity for a return to gainful employment.

At sixteen Mary, "Mame," as she was called in the family, enrolled at the Pennsylvania Academy of the Fine Arts on Chestnut Street. When, at twenty, she announced her wish to continue her studies abroad, her father exploded, declaring he would almost rather see her dead than become an artist. But Mary persisted. She always persisted. He gave his consent and was not known to have ever regretted it.

The summer of 1874 she spent back at Villiers-le-Bel working with Thomas Couture. That fall she rented a studio in Paris and, with sister Lydia, moved into a small nearby apartment on the rue de Laval (now Victor Massé) at the foot of Montmartre.

The course of her life was set. If becoming a *professional* artist—never a "woman who paints"—meant giving up marriage and a family of her own, so be it. She was adamant, at times even abrasive, on the matter.

Her appearance remained consistently, entirely ladylike. She stood not quite five feet six, considered tall for a woman. Her hair was light brown, her chin a bit sharp for her to have been considered pretty. Hers was a strong, intelligent face. The grey eyes were large and alert. And she had the slender figure and perfect carriage for her well-tailored ensembles.

"Miss Cassatt's tall figure, which she inherited from her father, had distinction and elegance, and there was no trace of artistic *négligé*, or carelessness, which some painters affect," wrote Louisine Elder of New York, who was struck even more by how much Miss Cassatt knew and how animated she became.

> Once having seen her, you could never forget her—from her remarkable small foot to the plumed hat with its inevitable tip upon her head and the Brussels lace veil without which she was never seen. She spoke with energy, and you would as soon forget her remarks when she conversed as to forget the motion of her hands.

Louisine Elder and Mary Cassatt met in Paris in 1874, at a time when Mary's work was going well, her name becoming known in art circles in both Paris and New York. (She listed herself now as Mary Cassatt.) A portrait of hers, *Madame Cortier*, had been hung in the Salon.

In Paris with her mother and two sisters, nineteen-year-old Louisine was eager to see and learn as much as possible. She was enthralled by all that the vibrant Miss Cassatt had seen and accomplished, the places she had been, and wondered how she had ever summoned the courage to go off to Italy and Spain.

Mary took her to the opera and theater, talked long and fast about Correggio and Velázquez. "I felt that Miss Cassatt was the most intelligent woman I had ever met and I cherished every word she uttered. . . ." It was the threshold of a fifty-year-long friendship of far-reaching consequences.

At the same time, another friendship went on the rocks. For Emily Sartain, Mary's strong-willed, occasionally dictatorial ways became too much. There was a dispute over some unknown matter and bitter feelings resulted. "Miss C. is a tremendous talker and very touchy and selfish, so if you hear her talking of me at home, as she has done lately in Paris, you will know the origin of it all," Emily confided to her father. "I shall never become intimate with her again. . . ." Emily went home to Philadelphia to teach at the School of Design for Women, where she would have a long, distinguished career.

Not long afterward, in 1875, Mary discovered the work of a new group of artists who called themselves La Société Anonyme des Artistes—the Impressionists, as they were to be known, among whom were Claude Monet, Pierre-Auguste Renoir, Édouard Manet, Camille Pissarro, and Edgar Degas. In much the way the American painter William Morris Hunt had the direction of his career changed by seeing a portrait by Thomas Couture in a Paris art store window, so Mary Cassatt reacted to seeing for the first time pastels by Degas in a window on the boulevard Haussmann.

"I would go there and flatten my nose against that window and absorb all I could of his art," she would remember. When she said later, "It changed my life," she was by no means exaggerating. It changed her life because it changed her work. An entirely new way of seeing and painting, for which she was to become famous, began then.

She took Louisine to see a Degas pastel titled *Répétition de Ballet* (Ballet Rehearsal) and urged her to buy it. "It was so new and strange to me!" Louisine wrote. "I scarcely knew how to appreciate it, or whether I liked it or not . . . [but] she left me no doubt as to the desirability of the purchase and I bought it upon her advice."

The price was 500 francs, or about $100. By contrast, the American dry goods impresario A. T. Stewart had recently paid $60,000 for a painting by the French master Ernest Meissonier.

The purchase by Louisine Elder was the first of many to follow. She was to become, with her future husband, Henry O. Havemeyer—and with the continued guidance of Mary Cassatt—one of the great art collectors of the era and the first to bring works of the Impressionists home to America.

Mary Cassatt's first major work in the Impressionist manner was to be a portrait of her mother.

II

Charles-Émile-Auguste Durand—Carolus-Duran, as he preferred—was still in his thirties, young to be the master of an atelier. Primarily a portraitist, he was flamboyant in appearance and manner, and exuberantly unorthodox in his teaching. His atelier on the boulevard Montparnasse was the most avant-garde in Paris.

Wild black hair, a sweeping, upturned black mustache, goatee, and a swarthy complexion, made him an arresting sight quite apart from his usual showy attire. A black velvet suit might be accented by a yellow shirt, a green tie, frilled cuffs, and a good deal of gold jewelry. He looked like a magician, which to his students he was.

He had spent two years in Spain and the influence of Velázquez had been powerful. His most arresting and important work thus far, *The Woman with the Glove*, a full-length portrait of his wife measuring five by seven feet, had all the drama and strong use of black of the Spanish master himself.

As a teacher, Carolus-Duran put far less emphasis on drawing than did such long-respected masters as Meissonier or Jean-Léon Gérôme. He stressed form and color. He wanted his students to paint directly—to take up the brush and draw and paint at the same time. To learn to paint, one had to paint, he preached. Painting was no mere "imitative" art.

Unlike the masters of other ateliers, Carolus-Duran kept his classes small—ten or fifteen students—and most of them were "happy American youths" who looked upon their master "as an elder brother," as one wrote. Work commenced at seven-thirty in the morning. Twice weekly the master gave critiques, these sometimes accompanied by his virtuoso demonstrations, most often portraits of one or two of the students done with miraculously few strokes in what seemed mere minutes. The fee for students was $4 a month, or a dollar a week.

Those young Americans at work with Carolus-Duran in the spring of 1874 included several of marked ability and substantial prior training. Before coming to Paris, Will Low had been supporting himself as an illustrator in New York. J. Alden Weir had grown up drawing and painting under the guidance of his father, a noted artist who taught drawing at West Point. James Carroll Beckwith had studied for three years at Chicago's Academy of Design and a year at the National Academy in New York.

But none among them showed anything like the ability of John Singer Sargent, as was evident from the morning he first entered the atelier that

May. Years later, recalling the "advent" of Sargent, Beckwith said it was either a Tuesday or a Friday, the days when Carolus came to criticize the work.

> I had a place near the door, and when I heard a knock I turned to open it. There stood a grey-haired gentleman, accompanied by a tall, rather lank youth who carried a portfolio under his arm, and I guessed he must be a coming nouveau. This gentleman addressed me politely in French, and I replied in the same language, but with less fluency. . . . He evidently saw that I was a fellow countryman, for he then spoke in English and we held a short conversation in subdued tones. . . . Carolus soon finished his criticism, and I presented my compatriots. Sargent's father explained that he had brought his son to the studio that he might become a pupil. The portfolio was laid on the floor, and the drawings were spread out. We all crowded about to look, and . . . [we] were astonished. . . .

There were paintings of nudes, portrait studies, copies in oil and watercolor of Tintoretto and Titian, sketches in watercolor of scenes and figures in Venice, Florence, and Rome. Long afterward Will Low could still feel the "sensation" of the moment.

> The master studied these many examples of adolescent work with keenest scrutiny, then said quietly, "You desire to enter the atelier as a pupil of mine? I shall be very glad to have you do so." And within a few days he joined the class.
>
> Having a foundation in drawing which none among his new comrades could equal, this genius—surely the correct word—quickly acquired the methods then prevalent in the studio, and then proceeded to act as a stimulating force which far exceeded the benefits of instruction given by Carolus himself.

At age eighteen Sargent looked even younger. He was just over six feet tall, extremely well-mannered, multilingual, and considered himself an

American though he had never been to the United States and spoke with an English accent. He had spent his whole life in Europe. His expatriate mother and father had been wandering about Europe, moving from one city or spa to another for twenty years, according to the seasons of the year, always in search of a more amenable climate or more economical accommodations, seldom settling anywhere for long. They never found reason to be anywhere for long. John, who was born in Rome, had lived in Florence, London, Paris, various cities in Spain, Pau, Biarritz, Salzburg, Nice, St. Moritz, Venice, Lake Maggiore, Dresden, then Florence again before his return to Paris in 1874.

His father, Dr. FitzWilliam Sargent, who gave up a Philadelphia medical practice at age thirty-two, had long since grown weary of such self-imposed exile. "I am tired of this nomadic sort of life," he had written from Florence to his mother in the fall of 1870.

> The spring comes and we strike our tents and migrate for the summer. The autumn returns and we must again pick up our duds and be off to some milder region. . . . I wish there were some prospect of our going home and settling down among our own people and taking permanent root.

It was not the romantic expatriate life commonly imagined, free from the constraints of provincial America. In many ways it was a captive life and his a sad case. His wife, Mary Singer Sargent, had no desire to go home. She adored Europe—its art and music were the stuff of life for her. She sketched and painted quite well in watercolor. She loved to entertain, loved to shine in cultivated circles. She also suffered spells of bad health, as did John's two younger sisters, Emily and Violet, and so they needed Europe for their health, she insisted, and flatly refused to go home.

Further, there was the matter of money. If one managed one's resources prudently in Europe, one could not only get by but keep up appearances at far less expense than at home, and there was great appeal in that alone. Were one to return to the United States, one's financial deficiencies would soon become all too apparent, and appearances mattered exceedingly to Mary Sargent. Since it was her money they were living on, not her husband's, her wishes prevailed.

As FitzWilliam wrote privately, "Mary's income is only such as enables us to live on with constant effort to spend as little as possible. . . ." That income was approximately seven hundred dollars a year.

Mary was short, round, ruddy-faced, and brimful of *joie de vivre* when feeling well. He was lean, grey, austere, and melancholy. John's only known portrait of his father, done a few years later, might have been titled *A Study in Sadness*. Everything about the long, thin face is downcast—the eyes and mouth, the drooping walrus mustache.

The joy of the parents in their children was expansive nonetheless, and in "Johnny" increasingly as his exceptional talent became ever more evident.

As a small boy, he had filled his schoolbooks with so many drawings his teachers despaired of his ever learning what was printed in them. He seemed not ever to have been unaware of beauty, a cousin, Mary Hale, later wrote. His first memory, he told her, was of a deep red cobblestone in the gutter of the Via Tornabuoni in Florence of a color so beautiful that he thought of it constantly and begged his nurse to take him to see it on their daily walks.

Seeing how advanced he was for his age, his mother insisted he draw and paint nearly every day. "Drawing seems to be his favorite occupation and I think he has the elements of a good artist," FitzWilliam wrote proudly to his own father, adding in a summary appraisal what numbers of others were to say as time passed. "He is a good boy withal, and everyone seems to like him."

He did well in school, in Latin and Greek, geography, history, and European languages. He loved music, learned to play the piano and mandolin. He also studied art in school and with tutors during the summer months. "I see myself that he studies well and with pleasure," FitzWilliam reported, "and that he is very much pleased with his teachers—which is almost as essential to progress as that his teachers should be pleased with him."

His mother went sketching with him, insisting always that no matter how many drawings or watercolors he began each day, one at least must be finished.

By thirteen the boy knew he wanted an artist's life more than any other and both mother and father strongly encouraged him. In Florence in the winter of 1870 he was enrolled in classes at the Accademia di Belle Arti and on spring days went sketching with his mother in the Boboli Gardens.

Then in the spring of 1874 the whole family moved to Paris. "We hear that the French artists, undoubtedly the best now-a-days, are willing to take pupils in their studies," John himself explained to a cousin. On May 19, FitzWilliam informed his father from Paris, "We came on here especially to see if we could not find greater advantages for John in the matter of his artistic studies. . . ." But to locate somewhere "comfortably and cheaply" proved difficult, "everything in the way of lodgings being very dear."

A "smallish" apartment was found on the rue Abbatrice, close to the Champs-Élysées, and seemed near to heaven except for a nurse (to look after the young Violet), a "hard customer" who came with the apartment and soon had to be fired. She loved telling them in detail how she witnessed the whole rise and reign of the Commune and how much she had enjoyed it. She described the burning of the Hôtel de Ville and the Palace of the Tuileries and said she would love to see it all again. "So," explained FitzWilliam, "we were afraid to trust the child to her, lest she would sell or otherwise dispose of our flesh and blood."

As for Paris, he was exceedingly happy to be back. He genuinely liked and admired the French.

> Paris is judged unfairly, I am convinced. Behind the gaiety, vice and debauchery which floats on the surface and which the transient comer only sees . . . there is a solid substratum of honesty and probity and economy and virtue, of intelligent, honest hard-work, and of indefatigable search for truth in morals and happiness and domestic virtues equal to what can be found anywhere in the world. . . .

Foremost was the importance of Paris to young John, who "works with great patience and industry and bids fair to succeed."

With the arrival of summer, when Carolus-Duran moved his classes to Fontainebleau, John followed. That autumn he was accepted at the École des Beaux-Arts, where J. Alden Weir, also enrolled there, described him as "one of the most talented fellows I have ever come across. . . . Such men wake one up." Hardworking Carroll Beckwith from Chicago said much the same, noting in his diary that Sargent's work "makes me shake myself."

Weir, Beckwith, Will Low, and others of the Americans, all still struggling to learn French, were hardly less astonished by the way Sargent could rattle on in perfect French—or Italian or German, whichever suited—quite as well as in English.

Work with Carolus-Duran continued, John's power of concentration no less a wonder to the others than was his ability. One must look for the middle-tone, Carolus preached, and begin there. "*Cherchez la demi-teinte,*" he would say again and again. And they must study Velázquez without respite. "*Velázquez, Velázquez, Velázquez, étudiez sans relâche Velázquez!*"

Years later, in the course of a conversation with Henry James's brother, William, Sargent would remark of painting, "If you begin with the middle-tone and work up from it towards the darks—so that you deal last with your highest lights and darks—you avoid false accents. That's what Carolus taught me."

Living with his family, concentrating on his work, young John knew virtually nothing of after-hours student life on the Left Bank, until one night when, as he wrote to a friend,

> we cleared the studio of easels and canvases, illuminated it with Venetian or colored paper lanterns, hired a piano and had what is called "the devil of a spree." Dancing, toasts and songs lasted till 4, in short they say it was a very good example of a *Quartier Latin* ball.

Then he added, "I enjoyed our spree enormously, I hope not too much, probably because it was such a new thing for me."

Of his fellow students, he got on with Beckwith especially well. In 1875, encouraged by his parents, he left the family and with Beckwith moved into a fifth-floor studio on the rue Notre-Dame-des-Champs on the Left Bank. In off-hours, in a series of quick sketches, Beckwith recorded the remarkable Sargent (now sporting the beginnings of a beard) at the piano, Sargent at his easel painting, Sargent stretched in an armchair reading Shakespeare. It was as if Beckwith and the others were mesmerized by him. "Of course, we are dealing with a phenomenal nature," Will Low explained.

"There were no difficulties for him," remembered another American, Walter Gay. Yet John worked harder than anyone, which seemed surprising in someone so gifted. Those for whom things came easily usually made less of an effort than others, not more. Further, he had lived his whole life in a family in which no one worked, not his father, not his mother, not anyone.

It was rare, too, for any American student in Paris to have a family of such interesting and hospitable people residing close at hand, and the pleasure of being one of John's guests at Sargent gatherings, his friends found, was great indeed. Beckwith, Alden Weir, Will Low, and others were invited frequently to join the Sargents for Sunday dinner, and always to their delight. Weir described those gathered as "the most highly educated and agreeable people I have ever met." Among them were several young ladies—John's sister Emily and three cousins of the Sargents, the Austin sisters—all "very sensible and beautiful," as Weir said.

"The society of the Sargents and the Austins . . . has given me many charming Sunday evenings . . . and the habit of ease in ladies' society, which I feared I had lost, I have again recovered," Beckwith recorded happily in his diary.

From two portraits done by John at about this time, of his sister Emily and cousin Mary Austin, it is easy to see why the young men responded as they did.

———

In the spring of 1876, with the Centennial Exposition in Philadelphia a subject of much talk in Paris, Mary Sargent decided to take the two oldest, Emily and John, on a first visit to America. They were gone four months, during which they visited relatives in Philadelphia and toured the exposition. Presumably, John saw the elegant portrait by Carolus-Duran prominently placed in the French art show, and the works of such American painters as Thomas Eakins and Winslow Homer, who, too, had once studied in Paris. Nor could he or any of the hundreds of thousands attending the exposition have missed the giant hand and torch standing outdoors, the only part of sculptor Bartholdi's Statue of Liberty far enough along to display.

It was also the summer when, with much fanfare, the first wire for the cables of the new Brooklyn Bridge was strung across the East River in New York, and the summer of General Custer's downfall at the battle of the Little Bighorn. Yet curiously nothing is known of what John or his mother and sister thought of any of this, or anything else other than that Mary found unbearable Philadelphia's record heat of 97 degrees in the shade.

His Philadelphia cousin, Mary Hale, would remember John entertaining everyone with a performance at the piano, playing and singing his own version of a passionate Italian love song, the words composed entirely of the names of patent medicines.

The three touring Sargents went on to New York, Newport, and Niagara Falls, and for all John recorded of the trip, he might never have left France. He apparently wrote no letters. Some drawings and paintings that he did were his closest thing to keeping a diary, but they were few. The scenes he put the most time and feeling into were done at sea, in watercolor and oil, and one in particular of a raging storm during the return voyage.

III

In spring, John's friend Will Low liked to say, Paris "atoned" for all her "climatic misdeeds of the winter." It was the season of renewal, *renouveau*, as the old French calendars said. On such days one felt a "joyousness," the feeling that one could "undertake anything" or, better still, go off on a good walk across the city, over its bridges, through its gardens.

In the spring of 1877, Paris was "overflowing with people glad to enjoy the sunshine," reported a new English-language Paris paper, the *American Register*.

> The lilac bushes at the Bois are in full bloom and the air is heavy with their fragrance. In all the public gardens and squares flowers have been planted, and are thriving. . . . The streets are thronged with ladies in beautiful *toilettes*. There are crowds of persons sitting in front of the cafés and restaurants, the boulevards are filled with vehicles of every description, yet there is no unpleasant hurry, no pushing.

Pedestrian traffic on the Pont Neuf, which had been freshly scraped and cleaned, and looked brand-new, was said to be 63,000 people a day.

Henry James, who only the year before delighted in saying he was thoroughly "Parisianized," had decided in 1876, with the first sign of the return of a Paris winter, to pack up and leave. His work on *The American* finished, he was ready to move on. So by that spring he was settled in London. But, like James McNeill Whistler, who had abandoned Paris for London, James was to return often.

George Healy, after several weeks in Berlin, had come home to the rue de la Rochefoucauld, bringing his portrait of Otto von Bismarck, which he put on display in his studio. The *American Register* hailed it as a noble work of art. "Among our American portrait painters there is no one whose success has been more thorough or gratifying to our national pride than has that of Mr. Healy."

Another of Healy's subjects was Dr. Thomas Evans, who had returned to Paris, reestablished his dental practice, and was living handsomely as ever.

Mary Cassatt, too, was working almost exclusively on portraits, but with a much higher-keyed palette. Her range of color, now that of the Impressionists, included almost no black any longer. ("One morning one of us, having no black, used blue instead, and Impressionism was born," Renoir once explained.) Velázquez and Correggio were all but forgotten.

She had turned a corner, inspired by a new hero, Degas, whom she had at last met. Having seen some of her work, he had asked a friend to arrange an introduction. They came to her studio, and after an hour's conversation, Degas asked her to join the Impressionists, making her the first and only American among the group. She would also be one of only two women. The other was the beautiful, ladylike, and immensely gifted French painter Berthe Morisot, whom Mary very much liked.

"I accepted with joy," she wrote.

She who was so entirely, properly conventional in dress, manner, and background felt fully free now from the constrictions of conventional art. "Finally I could work with absolute independence without concern for the eventual opinion of the jury. . . . I detested conventional art and I began to live."

Wellborn like Mary and ten years older than she, Degas was dark-eyed and dark-haired, with a grey beard. He dressed always in the dark suit and black top hat of a gentleman. Further, unlike all but a very few French painters, he had been to the United States and loved it. His mother was an American, and in 1872 he had made a trip to New Orleans to visit a brother. One of his finest paintings, *The Interior of a Cotton Broker's Office at New Orleans*, had resulted.

Degas called frequently at Mary's studio to talk and comment on her work. With her excellent French, she could converse readily and comfortably. It became an open friendship, but apparently no more than that. By nature contentious, he was not an easy man to get along with, and there would be long spells when she would have little to do with him. The American art student Walter Gay, who greatly admired Degas's work and received "much good advice" from him, later said he was extremely hard to know. "He was very difficult, very witty, but his wit left a sting."

Years later, when Louisine Elder Havemeyer asked Mary what Degas was like, she replied, "Oh, my dear, he is dreadful! He dissolves your willpower."

How then could she get along with him?

"Oh," Mary answered, "I am independent . . . and I love to work. Sometimes it made him furious that he could not find a chink in my armor, and there would be months when we just could not see each other. . . ."

Great as Degas's influence was, she never became a disciple. He painted ballet dancers and laundresses, scenes in Paris cafés and at the racetrack. Only rarely did she choose subjects anywhere beyond her own private, domestic circle.

In the fall of 1877 she found her métier of choice, when her mother, father, and sister all returned to Paris to move into a new apartment with her. It was another momentous change for her. The Cassatts had given up the family home in Philadelphia and come to Paris to stay, and largely for the same reason the Sargents had chosen their self-imposed exile. Faced with diminishing means, they could expect their money to go further in Paris. Contrary to what was often assumed, then and later, Mary never had limitless family resources to draw on.

A further reason for the move to Paris was sister Lydia's health, which had become a cause for concern for all of them.

Father, mother, Lydia, and Mary moved into a sixth-floor apartment at 13 avenue Trudaine, on the heights just below Montmartre, not far from the Healy residence. "You know we live up very high," Katherine Cassatt wrote to a grandchild, ". . . but we have a balcony all along the front of the house from which we can see over houses opposite, so we have a magnificent view!" Paris was "a wonder to behold," wrote Robert Cassatt, whose primary pleasure was to go off alone on long walks.

Mary had always been close to her mother, whose company she thoroughly enjoyed. Extremely well read and a lively talker, her mother was, as Louisine Elder Havemeyer wrote, "interested in everything, and spoke with more conviction and possibly more charm than Miss Cassatt." To give her mother something to do—and the opportunity for them to get caught up with each other after so long a separation—Mary asked if she would sit for a painting. Thus with the onset of winter, 1877, Mary began work on the portrait that was to mark her debut as an Impressionist.

The setting for the painting was entirely private, her mother plainly at ease comfortably seated in an upholstered chair reading *Le Figaro* through dark shell pince-nez glasses. She wore a casual white morning housedress. The chair was chintz-covered with a floral pattern. Behind, on the left, was a large gilt-framed mirror, a favorite visual device among the Impressionists and one Mary was to employ repeatedly.

It was the antithesis of a formal academic portrait. The subject was not set off by a conventional dark background. Nor did the subject look directly at the viewer. She was busy at something else, her mind elsewhere. She could have been anyone and she seemed altogether unaware of anyone else's presence.

The title did not provide the subject's name. The painting was called simply *Reading Le Figaro* and would be greatly admired for portraying its subject so honestly, so entirely without pretense. "It is pleasant to see how well an ordinary person dressed in an ordinary way can be made to look, and we think nobody . . . could have failed to like this well-drawn, well-lighted, well-anatomized, and well-composed painting," an admiring American art critic wrote. For her part Katherine Cassatt was extremely pleased. She thought it made her look ten years younger.

With her work and her family about her, Mary had little time for much else. She also had subjects to paint right at hand as she never had, as well as her own approving audience. Shipping the portrait of Katherine off to their son Alexander in Philadelphia, Mary's father said in a note, "Here there is but one opinion as to its excellence."

Sister Lydia agreed to pose next, and Mary undertook the first of a series of portraits—Lydia reading the paper, Lydia at tea, Lydia crocheting in the garden, Lydia working at a tapestry frame—the settings always private, domestic, refined, safe, quiet, and secure, with never a hint of the world beyond.

Since the move to Paris, Lydia's health had continued to decline, and in 1878 a Paris physician warned that her trouble could be Bright's disease, a degenerative disease of the kidneys. But the diagnosis was not conclusive. "The doctor frightened us out of our wits," her mother wrote. "It seems it isn't as hard to cure a person as it is to find out what is the matter. . . ." Much of the time Lydia felt too miserable and weak to go out. On days when she felt better, sitting for Mary gave her a sense of playing a constructive part, and like her mother, she was good company.

Mary also undertook a portrait of a little girl in a white party dress sprawled in a big blue chintz-covered armchair and looking totally uninterested in anything around, not even the small dog lying in another chair beside her. She was the daughter of a friend of Degas's, who continued to take a close interest in everything Mary was doing. In this case Degas advised her on how to do the background, *"even worked on the background,"* as she herself later acknowledged, never at all reluctant to give credit where it was due.

The family kept almost entirely to themselves. Paris or not, their life together was little changed. They could as well have been in Philadelphia. They had no interest in Paris society or any society—Mary had no patience for it—and they rarely entertained. They lived "as usual," Katherine said in a letter to her son Alexander. "We . . . make no acquaintances among the Americans who form the colony, for as a rule they are people one wouldn't want to know at home. . . ." Of Mary's French Impressionist friends, only Degas and Berthe Morisot, given their social class, were considered acceptable.

Just as in the Sargent family, where no one did much of anything but John, so the Cassatts did little else besides sit and read, or sit for Mary, or go off for a walk, while she worked away, intent, as she later said, "on fame and money."

IV

After eight and a half years of unstinting service as the American minister to France, Elihu Washburne had concluded the time had come to step aside. He had served longer in the role than anyone else. A new president, Rutherford B. Hayes, had taken office. Adele's health had become a concern, and the lease on the residence on the avenue de l'Impératrice was about to expire.

He submitted his resignation and on September 10 he and the family said goodbye to Paris. But not before he had George Healy paint his and Adele's portraits, and commissioned Healy to do still another of Ulysses S. Grant. The former president, having embarked on a world tour, was expected in Paris two months later.

"After a reasonably good passage to New York," Washburne would write simply in his *Recollections*, "we reached what was thereafter to be our home at Chicago. . . ."

As expected, the arrival of General Grant and his family caused considerable stir, though it hardly compared to the fuss once made over General Tom Thumb or George Catlin and his Indians. The former president, his wife, Julia, and their son Jesse, stayed at the Hôtel Bristol on the Place Vendôme. They were feted by President MacMahon at the Élysée Palace and at a dinner given by the new American minister, Edward Noyes. They attended the opera, shopped at the Palais Royal and Worth's, strolled the boulevards and gardens. At the invitation of the Committee of the Franco-American Union, they went to the workshops of Gaget, Gauthier & Compagnie on the rue de Chazelles, to view the progress being made on Monsieur Bartholdi's statue.

Grant agreed that Paris was beautiful, he wrote to friends at home, but could not imagine wanting to live there. "It has been a mystery to me how so many Americans can content themselves here, year after year, with nothing to do."

The sitting for Healy went well. Grant had posed for the painter ten years before and enjoyed his company. As always, Healy talked the whole time he worked. When Grant learned that Healy had recently completed a portrait of Léon Gambetta and expressed an interest in meeting him, Healy arranged a family dinner at his home. "The contrast between the two was a very striking one," he later wrote:

> Grant with his characteristic square American head, full of will and determination, his reddish beard sprinkled with grey, his spare gestures, and taciturnity; and this Frenchman, with his southern exuberant manner, his gestures, his quick replies, the mobility of expression on his massive face. . . . They seemed typical representatives of the two nations.

Grant spoke no French, Gambetta no English, but they traded flattering comments sufficient to keep one of Healy's daughters busy translating.

The Grants' stay in Paris lasted five weeks. In early December they were on their way once more, moving from one national capital to another for another year and a half.

On Christmas Day in Paris the first snow of the winter fell.

CHAPTER TWELVE

THE FARRAGUT

His whole soul is in his art.

—AUGUSTA HOMER SAINT-GAUDENS

I

Augusta Homer, an art student from Roxbury, Massachusetts, had been living in Rome, devoting her time principally to copying masterpieces in the Palazzo Barberini, when she met Augustus Saint-Gaudens and fell in love.

Four years later in Paris, in the summer of 1877, the newlywed couple moved into a tiny first apartment on the boulevard Pereire and set up housekeeping. "We have bought a Persian rug for which we gave 110 francs, $22.00," she wrote to her mother. "We think our little parlor looks prettily now. We had it papered last Saturday and now we must have the floors waxed. . . ."

Her husband had his heart set on living in Paris. The "art current" was stronger there than anywhere, she explained to her mother, and his "whole soul" was in his art.

Once settled, she began going with him to his new studio to paint or to help him with his work. Other days she went to the Louvre, as she had to the Palazzo Barberini, to do copies.

Tall, slender, still in her twenties, she was known as "Gussie" and could be fairly described as attractive rather than pretty. She had large, clear blue eyes and, when smiling, her face turned radiant. Her mother and father had sent her abroad with one of her brothers, to Italy to pursue her ambitions in art. (A love of painting seemed to run in the family. Winslow Homer was her first cousin.) But she went, too, in the hope of improving her health. She suffered spells of fatigue and low spirits, and more seriously from increasing deafness, which also ran in the family. Her father, Thomas Homer, had written earlier of how "painful" it was to observe Gussie's deafness steadily increasing and know of no way to help. Since meeting her "Mr. Saint-Gaudens," she wrote, her hearing was no better, but her outlook and health had much improved.

The more she knew him, the more she liked him, she had confided in the early stages of their romance. Those at home had no idea what a sculptor's studio was like or how the work was done, or what a "perfect marvel" it was to see it done.

And perhaps they should know what he looked like:

> Medium sized, neither short nor tall, blue eyes, straight nose. . . . Neither handsome nor homely and when you first meet him does not impress you as particularly talented. But the more you know him the better you like him and a more upright man I never met.

"Mr. St.-G. is very much in love with me," she announced to her mother in a letter from Rome dated February 8, 1874, and marked "PRIVATE."

"Now I must tell you who he is," she said, and proceeded to explain that his father was a French shoemaker in New York and poor, but that there was nothing "Frenchy" about her "Mr. St.-G." except his name and the fact that he spoke French extremely well. She stressed how much he had accomplished in his career through his own determination, and told how he had gone to work cutting cameos at age thirteen and succeeded later in being accepted at the École des Beaux-Arts. She described his years in Rome, where again he had supported himself cutting cameos, and the statue he had done of Hiawatha, and the praise it was receiving.

Some of the most influential men in New York had taken an interest in his career, she wrote, and there seemed little doubt he would be successful ultimately. She thought he was twenty-six, or perhaps twenty-seven.

> His education in everything regarding art is complete, but he occasionally makes mistakes in speaking. But he is every inch a gentleman and there is an innate refinement about him. His treatment of me has been just what a noble man ought to do and I have told him I think a great deal of him. He does not ask or wish me to make any promises for the future as it must be at least two years before he can think of it and of course I would do nothing without your and father's sanction.

"I am not *dead* in love as they say, but perhaps would be if I thought I ought," she added in conclusion.

"I am very sure that the only possible objection to him is that his father is French and his mother Irish," she wrote in another "PRIVATE" letter. "But, mother, he is neither: an American to the backbone."

To her New England Protestant parents, a French father and an Irish mother could only mean that the young man was a Roman Catholic. But Gussie said nothing on the subject, nor, to ease their worries, did she mention that Gus was a lapsed Catholic. That he was both a gentleman and an American, she felt, was more than sufficient qualification.

Whatever letters he may have written to her during this period have not survived. Probably they were destroyed with much else in a studio fire long afterward. Years later, however, in an uncharacteristic burst of candor about his private life, he would mention in his *Reminiscences* having had love affairs with five women before meeting Gussie, and that the fifth was a very "beautiful" model named Angelina with whom he had wanted to elope to Paris, but that she had been "wise enough to refuse."

He hated writing letters, but in several addressed to Gussie's parents, he made clear his honorable intentions and the seriousness of his feelings for their daughter. In a straightforward summary of his life thus far in which he expressed his reasons for feeling optimistic about his work, he concluded, saying, "What I have is a splendid future and a fine start."

If successful, and with your consent, I shall claim Miss
Homer's hand immediately. If not I shall then have to delay
until . . . I am guaranteed our future welfare. . . . I ask your
consent to my attentions to your daughter, nevertheless leaving her completely free and binding her to nothing.

He cut her a cameo engagement ring and bought himself a new high
silk hat, his first ever, and "so great was his enthusiasm," he put it on and
"promptly walked across the Piazza di Spagna in the rain, and without an
umbrella," to visit her.

"You'll have to get used to a Gus and Gussie in the family," she told
her mother. "How does it sound to you? . . ." But permission for Gussie to
marry him, her parents made plain, was not to be granted until he had a
commission for a major work, something he had not as yet achieved.

They were naturally concerned about her happiness, but also about her
future financial security. Once prosperous, they were living at a much-
reduced standard, due to "reverses" in Thomas Homer's mercantile business. They stood ready to help, of course, but the amount would have to be
limited, all of which Gussie understood perfectly.

In 1875, Saint-Gaudens left Rome and returned to New York, crossing again, as he had the first time, in steerage. By telegraph en route
he learned that his mother had died. It was his first great sorrow, one
of the most painful moments of his life, a trial, he said, "like a great
fire."

He rented a shabby studio in the German Savings Bank Building at
14th Street and Fourth Avenue, where he also slept, his father's house
being too overcrowded as it was.

Hearing from Gussie that there was a competition for a statue of
Charles Sumner to be placed in the Boston Public Garden, he decided to
try for it. But his entry was rejected. (The sculptor chosen was Thomas
Ball, who had done the great equestrian statue of George Washington that
stood at the entrance to the garden.)

Soon after, Saint-Gaudens learned of plans to create a memorial in
New York to Admiral David Glasgow Farragut—"Damn the Torpedoes"
Farragut, the Civil War hero of the battle of Mobile Bay and the surrender

of New Orleans two years before. A committee had been formed to pick a sculptor. A sum of $9,000 was said to be available from the City of New York. Saint-Gaudens applied at once and contacted everyone he knew who might put in a word for him.

To do a man like Farragut justice in bronze would be no easy undertaking. The admiral had had as long and distinguished a career as any officer since the founding of the U.S. Navy. The son of a naval officer, he had gone to sea with the navy at age ten, even briefly commanded a captured ship at the age of twelve. Serving on ships of the line, he had seen much of the world before he was twenty.

He was resourceful and intelligent—without benefit of formal schooling, he learned to speak French, Italian, Spanish, and Arabic—and above all, courageous. By the outbreak of the Civil War he had served in the navy nearly fifty years. When assigned to capture New Orleans, he commanded the largest fleet to have sailed under the American flag, and at the war's end he became the first man ever to hold the rank of full admiral in the U.S. Navy.

"I have made two models, a large drawing and a bust," Saint-Gaudens wrote to Gussie's mother. "As far as I can see I am in a fair way to have the commission."

His career and his marriage were riding on it. And he got it.

Of the $9,000, he was to receive $2,000 on signing the agreement, $3,000 on completion of the statue in clay, $2,000 when the statue was cast in bronze, and a final check for $2,000 on delivery of the finished work to New York.

In an account book later he would record, "On hand June 1, 1877 when I was married, [$]2,821.00."

He and Gussie were married at her family home on Winthrop Street in Roxbury. Two days later they were at sea on the steamer *Abyssinia*—and no steerage this time—on their way to a honeymoon in Paris and the start of work on "the Farragut."

Paris was essential to the work, Gus felt, not only because the "art current" ran stronger there, but because sculpture as an art form was taken more seriously than at home, and experienced craftsmen—plaster molders, foundrymen, and the like—were plentiful. The project at hand was greater and more challenging by far than anything he had ever undertaken, and he would need the best help he could get.

II

As an American bride in Paris, she was something of a rarity, even with the great numbers of young Americans in the city, and she was doing her best to adapt to her new role. He knew French; she did not. He knew Paris; she did not, and at this point she knew almost no one else in the city.

Her health improved. Gus said it was the wine. She thought freedom from worry was the reason. He worked most of the time in his studio near the Arc de Triomphe. She tried to keep busy. She painted at the Louvre, went shopping for gloves at Le Bon Marché. On a night when they attended the opera, she marveled at the grand stairway and tried to imagine the glittering Paris social life she had heard so much about. "I wish someone would invite us to a big party or reception," she wrote to her mother. "I should like to wear my wedding dress. . . ."

> Only think there are twenty-four families in this house who use the same entrance we do and twelve who use the same staircase [she wrote in another letter], and although we have been here more than three months we do not know by sight anyone but the family whose door is directly opposite ours. Doesn't it seem kind of strange?

"Aug keeps wracking his brain all the time to think of something good and original," she reported.

He also took time to report to her parents on her health, to kid about the weight she had put on, and to express his gratitude for their financial help. "While Gussie is wrestling with the preparations for dinner, I'll try and wrestle with a letter," he began one evening in the fall of 1877. "She eats more, sleeps more, walks more, talks as much . . . [as] I have seen her in three years."

You write splendid letters to her and the best part . . . is when you tell her, "Don't work too hard." She is inclined that way. . . . She manages to be occupied all the time and I wish we could fix it so she might be able to paint more. She can give you some lessons in cooking, if you wish any. First rate soups, first rate mackerel, first rate everything in fact . . . she takes care of the inner man splendidly. . . .

I am much obliged to you, Mr. Homer—"much obliged" expresses very mildly how much I thank you for all you are doing and have done in regard to my finances. . . .

The following spring, they moved to a larger, more beautiful, partially furnished apartment in a choice location, No. 3 rue Herschel on the Left Bank, just off the boulevard Saint-Michel and less than a block from the Luxembourg Gardens. It was all they could wish for: on the fourth floor with a fair-sized parlor and tall French windows, two bedrooms, a dining room, kitchen, a servant's room upstairs, and a balcony off the parlor with nothing blocking the view of the gardens and the towers of the Church of Saint-Sulpice. In her letter to her parents reporting the news, she drew a plan on a separate sheet of paper. She and Gus could hardly believe their good fortune.

They found additional furniture at bargain prices—two brass-studded Louis XVI chairs, a handsome carved chest said to be three hundred years old—and bought "a beautiful Japanese matting" to cover one wall in the parlor from floor to ceiling.

Gussie set up her easel and painted two interior studies of the apartment and took time to write long descriptive letters to her family, her love of Paris and her happiness overflowing.

You have no idea how beautiful the view is from my windows this morning [July 25, 1878]. The air is clear and everything is very lovely. I watch my plants on the balcony just as father does his pear trees. My geranium has two buds. The calla is putting out a new leaf. . . .

Oddly, when invitations came for evening events hosted by other Americans, "Aug," as she called him, would go while she remained at home like "Cinderella." Late hours left her feeling "not very bright" the next day, she explained. But it may also have been that she was self-conscious about her hearing and the fact that she spoke so little French.

Gussie's younger sister, Eugenie ("Genie") Homer, arrived in the autumn for a stay in Paris. Then Gus's younger brother Louis became one of the household.

Gus was devoted to Louis and had done all he could for him since boyhood in New York when he had been Louis's protector from bullies. He had long encouraged Louis in his own ambitions to become a sculptor, first by teaching him how to cut cameos. Later, Louis had joined Gus in Rome, where he proved himself both a hard worker and talented. But in June 1876, Louis had disappeared. For two years no one knew his whereabouts, until suddenly in 1878 Gus heard he was in London and in desperate straits. Gus made a quick trip from Paris to rescue him.

Louis said only that he had been married to an American girl and that she had died in childbirth. He was also in financial trouble and appeared to have a drinking problem.

Gussie agreed to take him in—as her sister Genie wrote, Louis "tucked himself" into the servant's room upstairs. Gus put Louis to work in the studio, glad to have his help and his company on the job. Everyone was happy with the arrangement, it seems, including Gussie, who wrote of Louis, "He is certainly the easiest person to have in the house and it's very pleasant all around."

One of the few surviving letters by Bernard Saint-Gaudens, the father, reached Paris later that fall. It was addressed to his "Dear Children." "Let Louis judge now of my anxiety during all of the time he left us without sending us news," he began.

> However, I forgive you so long as you continue in the way you say you have marked for yourself in the future. For I say to you my dear son you will never find any peace for your soul and mind excepting in work. That is the only true source of our welfare. Through work the soul aspires to God who be-

stows upon it a power of will and wisdom which nothing can overthrow. . . .

Working as never before and needing more space, Gus had leased a huge barnlike studio on the Left Bank at 49 rue Notre-Dame-des-Champs, at the center of a growing community of American artists. By cutting through the Luxembourg Gardens, he found, he could get from the apartment to the studio in twenty minutes or less.

A painter, unless working on a huge mural, rarely needed the help of others and comparatively little in the way of equipment and material beyond paint, brushes, palette, and canvases. But a sculptor, and especially one undertaking a monumental project, needed great space for others on the job and all manner of clay, sacks of plaster, ladders, scaffolding, and tools. A sculptor's studio was a workshop.

The new studio had once been a public dance hall, and with fourteen windows overhead, each ten feet square, there was plenty of light. But Gus decided everything had to be whitewashed—ceiling, walls, woodwork—to make the light better still. With room to spare, he told some of his favorite painter friends to set their easels "high up" on the balcony formerly used for the orchestra. One of them, Maitland Armstrong, remembered being amused "by the alternate waves of exaltation and despair that swept over Saint-Gaudens as he worked," and how, when somebody would break out in a song, the rest would join in and Gus especially.

For additional help on the Farragut, besides brother Louis, he hired Will Low, who also became a consistent guest at dinner. As Gussie explained to Genie, "He hasn't a cent."

She kept the accounts, paid for everything, kept close records of what Gus gave Louis or loaned to some of the old friends who came around, like Alfred Garnier.

"Gus lent Garnier $5.00," reads one entry. "Gus gave Louis [$]5.00. Odds and ends for studio [$]2.00."

She also paid the monthly rents—$350 for the apartment, $465 for the studio—and recorded when Garnier and others paid back what they owed.

In addition to the Farragut in its various stages, which Gus positioned at the center of the studio, he was busy with a number of low reliefs in clay, and had still another project of importance under way.

Before leaving New York for Paris, he had been asked to help with the new Trinity Church in Boston. Henry Hobson Richardson, the architect chosen to design the church, had assigned the decoration of the interior to a gifted artist, John La Farge, who in turn had recruited Saint-Gaudens to assist him. Like Saint-Gaudens, Richardson was a product of the École des Beaux-Arts, and was emerging as one of America's most brilliant architects. La Farge, too, had studied in Paris, though briefly, and Saint-Gaudens jumped at the chance to work with both of them. (He would later call LaFarge "a spur to higher endeavor equal if not greater than any other I have received.") On the eve of Saint-Gaudens's departure for Paris, La Farge had asked him to do an altar screen, a sculptured panel of angels in high relief, for St. Thomas Church in New York. Now this, too, occupied long hours in the Paris studio.

Two others of importance who had worked on Trinity Church and thus became friends of Saint-Gaudens were architects Charles McKim and Stanford White. Still in their twenties, they had since left Richardson's employ—McKim to start his own firm, White to see something of the world. Saint-Gaudens liked them both, but particularly White, whose high spirits and humor, uninhibited love of art and architecture and music, seemed as limitless as his energy.

White had grown up in New York in an atmosphere of art and music and books. His father was a recognized authority on Shakespeare, a composer and cellist. As a boy, Stanford had shown exceptional talent for drawing and painting, but La Farge, a friend of the family who was constantly short of money, had warned that as an artist he would have trouble supporting himself, and told him to take up architecture. So at age nineteen he went to work as an apprentice to Richardson.

He and Saint-Gaudens had met first in New York. White was climbing the cast-iron stairway in the German Savings Bank Building one day when he heard a strong tenor voice at full volume singing the Andante of Beethoven's Seventh Symphony. Deciding to investigate, he found Gus at work in his studio.

The friendship with Charles McKim came a little later, and according to Saint-Gaudens, it was their "devouring love of ice cream" that brought them together.

Early in 1878, hearing that White was planning a trip to Europe, Saint-Gaudens wrote to say he was "pegging away" at the Farragut, but that the limited interest of his subject's clothing made the job "a hard tug." From the point of view of sculpture, Saint-Gaudens disliked modern clothing. Here he had only a cap, sword, field glasses, belt, and buttons to work with—not much, he lamented, adding, "When you come over I want to talk with you about the pedestal. Perhaps something might be done with that."

White's response came at once, "I hope you will let me help you with the Farragut pedestal. . . . Then I should go down to Fame, even if it is bad, reviled for making a poor base for a good statue." In June, White reported he was on his way to Paris and that McKim was coming, too.

They arrived in midsummer, 1878, and after extended discussions with the sculptor in his crowded "ball-room studio," and much conviviality with Gus, his wife, and friends—dining at Foyot's, a favorite restaurant of students beside the Luxembourg Gardens, seeing Sarah Bernhardt in Racine's *Phèdre*—they succeeded in convincing Gus it was time he took a break and head off with them to the south of France.

Gus was itching to go. As he wrote long afterward, there had been, before White's arrival, "little of the adventurous swing of life" he had once known in his student days.

Gussie encouraged him to go, apparently. It seems the only thing she ever flatly said no to was his wish that they get a dog.

The stated purpose of the expedition was to look at Gothic and Roman architecture along the Rhône. "It's really a business trip," she assured her mother. They were to be gone less than two weeks and traveling third-class.

So, as Saint-Gaudens wrote, the "three red-heads" started on their way. (White, in addition to a thick, reddish-brown mustache, had close-cropped red hair that stood straight up as stiff as a brush. And though McKim had little hair left on top of his head, it, too, was red.) Their route was from Paris by train to Dijon, Beaune, and Lyon, then by boat from Lyon down the Rhône to Avignon, Arles, Saint-Gilles, and Nîmes; then back northward over the mountains by diligence to Langogne, Le Puy, and to Bourges, Tours, and Blois, then back to Paris by way of Orléans.

In letters to his mother White described Dijon as clean and cheerful. Beaune, besides the beauty of the town itself, could be said to have "good wine and pretty women." Most enjoyable was moving with the swift current of the Rhône. The boat was a side-wheel steamer with a single, tall stack and built on the lines of a canal boat. "[It] is 275 ft. long and not over 20 ft. wide, *comme ça*," White wrote, and drew a sketch. "She holds about two hundred passengers. . . ."

Avignon, with the remains of the ancient Pont d'Avignon and the enormous Palace of the Popes, both dating from feudal times, was much the most impressive spectacle on the river. Years later Saint-Gaudens would remember arriving at Avignon after nightfall, and as he walked the narrow streets, hearing "the sound of a Beethoven sonata floating from an open window into the warm summer night. . . ."

Stanford White thought the portal of the twelfth-century Church of Saint-Gilles "the best piece of architecture in France." It was later to be the inspiration for a porch he designed for St. Bartholomew's Church in New York.

At Nîmes they visited the great Roman amphitheater with its seating capacity of 20,000. "We sat on the top row and imagined ourselves ancient Romans," White wrote. While Saint-Gaudens and McKim stayed seated where they were, White went down and rushed out into the arena, "struck an attitude and commenced declaiming" for their benefit. Warming to the role, he began stabbing imaginary gladiators until a guard appeared and chased him off.

After Nîmes, they set off by diligence over the mountains to Le Puy, the highest town in France, at 4,000 feet, then on into Burgundy and the Loire Valley. By August 13, they were back in Paris. Gus felt they had learned even more by traveling third-class than from the architecture they had seen.

To commemorate the fellowship of the expedition, he made a mockheroic Roman medallion six inches in diameter featuring in relief caricatures of each of the three. Mock-Latin tributes decorated the circumference. At the center was a large architect's T-square at the base of which were inscribed the letters "KMA," believed to have been an abbreviation for "Kiss My Ass." Saint-Gaudens presented bronze reproductions to each of his two friends, and kept the third for himself.

Gus had "a most successful trip," Gussie reported to her mother. "He feels he has learned a great deal from his architect friends."

―――――

When Saint-Gaudens returned to work on the Farragut monument, White went with him to the studio to help with plans for the pedestal. For a while White stayed overnight at the apartment, until he found a place of his own. McKim lingered only a little while before returning to New York. Then White headed off again to see more of France, and returned bringing superb sketches he had done of landscapes, houses, street scenes, and cathedrals inside and out. Then it was back to work with Saint-Gaudens, their efforts marking the start of collaborations to come on some twenty projects.

Gussie appears to have welcomed White's presence. "He is one of the nicest fellows I have ever met and Aug says he is tremendously talented," she told her mother. White, however, was of another mind about her.

He loved being back in Paris, he wrote to his mother, "I hug S[ain]t-Gaudens like a bear every time I see him, and would his wife if she was pretty—but she ain't—so I don't.

> She is very kind, however, and asks me to dinner, mends my clothes, and does all manner of things. She is an animated clothes rack, slightly deaf—a double barreled Yankee, and [I] mean to that extent that no comparison will suffice. Why fate should have ordained that such a man should be harnessed to such a woman, Heaven only knows. Nevertheless, she has been very kind to me, and I ought to be ashamed of myself for saying anything about her.

He thought Gussie's sister Genie far prettier.

Gussie also showed uncommon patience about Gus heading off with White on social whirls. One night, with another gregarious American,

William Bunce, they went to a masked ball at the Opera and, as she reported to her parents, did not come home until half-past six the next morning.

"I have just taken this paper from Gussie as she has a headache, and I don't think she should write any more," Gus scrawled in his own hand. "I close this epistle and fill the page so that Gussie can't put anything else in it."

"I am writing in the studio," she began another letter. Aug was washing his hands in a pail of water and talking to a friend. White was tasting some bread for his lunch and she was seated at a table writing.

> The model has just come in the second day and has retired behind a curtain to get himself up in Farragut's coat and fixings and presently will mount on the stand where Aug will go to work. He and Mr. White are still working on the pedestal. . . . There is to be a high circular stone seat so fashioned.

Then she made a small diagram of the pedestal. "Please don't say anything about this as yet, [as] it is by no means fully decided upon."

"Do you want to know how I pass my day?" White wrote to his mother. He was awakened at his lodgings by a servant at nine-thirty, then chose to stay in bed for another half-hour, until he headed out for breakfast at 3 rue Herschel—"and ring the doorbell five times, which is my private ring."

> Coffee, eggs, and oatmeal being swallowed, we forthwith make our way to the studio, and both set to work at our respective businesses. Then comes lunch hour. This is a very simple matter for Saint-Gaudens, who partakes of an unappetizing lunch packed up by his *femme*. With me it is quite an event. I go and buy all my provisions and lunch like a Seigneur [a lord] on 20 cents. Something in this way: *Pâté de foie gras;* boned chicken, or sardines, 4 cts.; two *petits pains*, well toasted, 2 cts.; rhum pudding, 3 cts.; *un petit fromage suisse*, 5 cts. and about 5 cts. worth of wine. . . .

Then we go to work again, and darkness—which comes
here now at five o'clock—gives us a rest.

———

Great as the demands of the work had become, Gus and Gussie were taking more time for some pleasure together, and with others. They dined
out, attended an occasional social event, and went again to the opera.

Gus loved the opera no less than ever. But he loved the theater still
more. The drama of the stage, the techniques of stagecraft—costume,
lighting, scenery—all appealed tremendously. He loved watching actors at
work and imagining himself in their place. If he could be anything other
than what he was, he liked to say, he would be an actor. "I am convinced,"
he later wrote, "that if I would overcome the sense of [self-] consciousness,
I should be a wonderful actor." And if not an actor, then a playwright,
which might be better still, he thought. "How wonderful," he would say,
"to create characters to portray every phase of emotion, present all points
of view, and with these characters work out their destinies."

> I think anything and everything. This seeing a subject so
> that I can take either side with sympathy and conviction I
> sometimes think is a weakness. Then again I'm thinking it's a
> strength. I could put it to good use as a dramatist.

With her trouble hearing and her inadequate French, Gussie found
the Paris theater extremely difficult to follow, and so seldom went with
him. But she seems to have had a particularly good time at one evening
affair put on by George and Louisa Healy. "We went to a dancing party at
Mr. Healy's and really enjoyed it very much," she reported to her mother.

How often Gus and Healy saw each other, or what they may have
talked about, is regrettably unrecorded. Certainly they had much in common. But whether they ever compared notes on their modest beginnings
in Boston and New York, or their early student years in Paris, or the Civil
War and its heroes, is impossible to know.

On her growing enjoyment of Paris, Gussie was explicit: "Every time I
go out I like it better and better."

In addition to the Healys, they were meeting other noted Americans, among them Phillips Brooks, the minister of Trinity Church in Boston, and Mark Twain, who had returned to Paris with his wife. Twain would be remembered at one after-dinner gathering at 3 rue Herschel consuming one black cigar after another until he finally asked, "What is Art?" which was the signal for all to go home. Gus never liked to "talk art" and hated art theory.

Art students like Carroll Beckwith and John Sargent were regularly in and out of the apartment and the studio. The studio the two young painters shared was on the same street as Gus's, at 73 rue Notre-Dame-des-Champs. A few old friends from Gus's own student days, like Alfred Garnier and Paul Bion, also made appearances.

Gus took great interest in students and was unusually generous with his encouragement of those he thought promising. But beyond that, as Will Low would write, he had a manner of expressing himself, "of making one 'see things,' " that they long remembered.

> He, in all simplicity, believed himself to be virtually inarticulate [Low wrote]; and for any personal exercise of the spoken or written word he quite honestly professed much the same aversion as he, the skilled artist, would feel for the bungling attempt of the ignorant amateur.
>
> But it was precisely because he was so intensely an artist that his mental vision was clear, and that which he saw he in turn made visible—there is no other word—to others.

Sargent particularly impressed Saint-Gaudens. Further, he liked the young man. They exchanged work—Sargent gave Saint-Gaudens one of his watercolors; Saint-Gaudens fashioned a small medallion, a sketch in relief of Sargent in profile, which he gave to him. It was the start of a long stretch of mutual admiration.

Still, the struggle to "break away" with the Farragut and achieve something beyond the ordinary continued, and grew increasingly difficult as Saint-Gaudens became ever more demanding of himself. His Civil War memories from boyhood were strong within him—of watching from the cameo cutter's window as the New England volunteers came marching down Broadway singing "John Brown's Body," of seeing Lincoln and Grant in person, and the wounded back from the battlefields. "I have such respect and admiration for the heroes of the Civil War," he had written earlier, "that I consider it my duty to help in any way to commemorate them in a noble and dignified fashion worthy of their great service."

New York was still, and always, home to Saint-Gaudens, and the Farragut, he knew, was to be New York's first monument to the Civil War.

In late March he was suddenly stricken with violent intestinal pains and a high fever. "It was all Mr. White, Louis, and I could do to take care of him night and day," Gussie wrote. Days passed before he felt strong enough to walk slowly beside her in the Luxembourg Gardens, and weeks went by before he was able to resume work. Feelings of depression—the "*triste* undertone" of his soul, as he called it—set in. Worst was the awful sense of time a-wasting. "You have no idea how hard it is for him to remain inactive when there is so much waiting for him to do," Gussie told her father.

It was the largest piece Saint-Gaudens had yet attempted, and the wonder is someone who had begun as a cameo cutter and mastered that tiny, exacting craft to such perfection could now, not so long afterward, undertake a project of such colossal scale. But the lessons of cameo cutting, of working "in the small," were not to be dismissed, even when working so large.

His inspiration had been the taller-than-life marble St. George by the Italian Renaissance sculptor Donatello, which he had seen in Florence and never forgotten. Donatello was his hero, second only to Michelangelo, and the effect of the St. George, of a man standing in repose yet clearly ready to take on the world, was just what he hoped to attain with his Farragut.

In how he faced a difficult task, Saint-Gaudens was at heart much akin to his subject. "Conceive an idea. Then stick to it. Those who hang on are the only ones who amount to anything," he often said. In a tribute published following Farragut's death in 1870, the *Army and Navy Journal* had written, "Once satisfied that a course must be pursued, it was utterly impossible to hold Farragut back from it."

Saint-Gaudens's Farragut had begun with a clay study of a nude figure two feet high. "Don't leave any serious study to struggle with in the big," was another of his working rules. It was in the small-scale model that the most serious attentions must be focused, "the whole ensemble together in the small," he liked to say.

The procedure was then to enlarge the two-foot figure to life-size and again in clay, but supported now by an armature of iron braces. Once work on the life-size statue was complete, it would serve as the model for still another statue of more than eight feet in height, this again done in clay and with an even heavier armature.

The giant clay figure would require still more work before a plaster mold could be made, in sections, from which a giant plaster statue would then be cast, and it in turn would need considerable final going over before taken to the foundry to be cast in bronze.

At every stage it was a complex process involving many others besides the sculptor, and it took much time and close attention.

The subject of all these efforts, David Glasgow Farragut, was a man Saint-Gaudens had never known, never laid eyes on. He had only pictures to go by—photographs and engravings—plus descriptions provided by the admiral's widow and son. As he would also admit privately, "I don't fully understand about the sea."

In real life the hero had stood about five feet six. To transpose the life-size clay model into its final heroic scale required that hundreds of measurements be made with calipers, and so a large scaffold had to be built beside the statue from which the workers could reach the uppermost portions of the figure.

But the mathematics of the system and even the most skilled use of calipers were never sufficient in and of themselves. The artist's eye and the desire to breathe life into the clay had to be the deciding factors at almost every stage.

Saint-Gaudens would write of the "toughness" of the sculptor's challenge, all the problems to be dealt with, the different helpers, the equipment and rubbish, and "all the while trying to soar into the blue."

He excused the delays that came with the work on the ground that a sculptor's efforts endured so long that it was nearly a crime to fail to do everything possible to achieve a worthy result. He had a terrible dread of making a bad sculpture. "A poor picture goes into the garret," he would write, "books are forgotten, but the bronze remains, to amuse or shame the populace and perpetuate one of our various idiocies."

The finished work had to convey the reality and importance of a singular personality. It had to be more than "a good likeness." It had to express the character of the man.

"Farragut's legs seem to be pretty troublesome," Gussie reported. Farragut must stand braced on proper sea legs, Gus insisted. But how to achieve that?

A friend from New York, the editor of *Scribner's Monthly*, Richard Watson Gilder, who was visiting Paris and was short like Farragut, agreed to pose for the legs. Still Gus fretted. "He has been very much bothered by one of Farragut's legs, and has been working on it for weeks. He is not satisfied yet," Gussie wrote later, just before he took ill.

The admiral's buttons and braid, his cap, sword, all had to be true to fact and a natural part of him, like his stance. Greater still was the importance of the face, and the face, the head, unlike a portrait on canvas, had to look right from every angle. The whole work must look right from every angle.

Even with Saint-Gaudens back on the job following his illness, the work fell steadily further behind schedule. Expenses kept mounting, and to her parents, who were still faithfully providing financial help, Gussie felt obliged to explain what the work now involved and why even more help was needed. "Am sorry to bother you so much but we must have some money or else collapse," she wrote bluntly at one point. Just the wheels of the dolly on which the clay model turned cost $40, she emphasized.

Her unshaken belief in her husband was plain. She wanted those at home to know how hard he was working and how much he had to put up with on the job. Almost no one seemed to understand how much he needed time to work and to think without interruptions. "He is very much bothered by visitors [to the studio] at all hours. He can't turn them out. He isn't made so. . . ."

"Gus is working on Farragut's left leg today," she wrote on May 8, 1879. A week later she could report, "Augustus . . . seems to be conquering the legs which have been his *bête noire*." On May 30 she could at last announce, "Farragut has two legs to stand on," but had to say also that Farragut still "bothers Gus a great deal. He finds it hard work to satisfy himself."

By June he had moved on to the flap on the admiral's coat, intending that it appear to be blowing in the wind. To Gussie it was a marvel how he made the silk lining and the cloth of the coat look as if made of silk and cloth.

She felt increasingly happy—with what he was creating and with their life together. One Sunday they spent an entire afternoon in the Bois de Boulogne, just the two of them, picking wildflowers and sitting talking under the trees. She had never loved Paris more. "It is strange how fascinating the life here becomes after living a couple of years. There is always so much to see and do." She painted a portrait of a friend, the wife of an expatriate American doctor named Farlow. The doctor was so pleased with the result he asked her to do him as well.

Work on the pedestal with Stanford White continued, but when, with the return of summer, White chose to go off to Italy, Gus decided to go, too. His doctors told him he needed rest and a change of scene. Gussie traveled with her sister Genie to Château d'Oex in Switzerland, to wait for Gus to join them there. He arrived on August 6, bringing her a beautiful lamp to hang in their parlor in Paris, and together with White they stayed on in Switzerland for another few days.

The time away had done Gus great good. "[He] feels like a lion," she said. Decisions on the pedestal had been resolved, and White returned to New York. All was fine, it seemed.

But something had gone wrong between Gus and White. What happened is not altogether clear. The nearest thing to an explanation was provided later by sister Genie. Gus's "friendship, or perhaps I should say affection, was limited," Genie wrote, due to certain sides to White's personality and way of life.

> In early days, mingled with White's enthusiasm, extraordinary activity and capacity for work, kindly instinct and friendliness, which made him personally attractive, were his aggressive, violent prejudice and a certain snobbishness that annoyed [Gus]. . . .

Gus cared nothing about food or clothes, no more now than in his student days in Paris. He would wear shirts until they were filled with holes, as Gussie lamented, and, according to Genie, he came to view with contempt White's adoration of food. Food was the way White "showed his self-indulgence in those days," Genie said, and recalled how, when crossing a mountain pass in Switzerland, White insisted on delaying everything for several hours in order that he could taste some famous dish at a local inn, which infuriated Gus.

Undoubtedly there was more to it than that, and whatever the issue, it appears to have begun in Italy. In a letter to White later, Gus said he was "feeling sorry for things [he had done] in Italy," but in response White urged no more apologizing: "If ever a man acted well [in Italy], you did, and I ought to have been kicked for many reasons."

Whatever the cause of the disagreement, the friendship was not broken; it only cooled somewhat. Their work together continued.

Much of great importance had still to be resolved, not the least of which were the final height and location of the monument.

Correspondence between Gus and White continued. There were questions about the kind of stone to be used for the pedestal and the design of two relief angels representing Courage and Loyalty that Gus was to do. Union Square, at Broadway and 14th Street, remained the favorite choice for the location among members of the Farragut Commission, and Saint-Gaudens was inclined to agree, though he had some concern about the height of the statue of Lafayette by Bartholdi in the square.

In New York, White went to look over the site and reported that the Lafayette stood not more than eight feet, four inches. "If you stick to eight feet, six inches, I do not think you will go much wrong," he told Saint-Gaudens.

White thought Madison Square Park, farther uptown between 23rd and 26th streets, on Fifth Avenue, and in particular at the corner of 26th and Fifth, was a far preferable spot—"a quiet and distinguished place . . . where the aristocratic part of the avenue begins . . . and the stream of people walking down Fifth Avenue would see it at once." He also reminded Gus that Delmonico's, the most fashionable dining place in town, was directly across the street, and Gus understood what that alone meant to White.

"*Go for Madison Square,*" Gus responded.

He and White both knew how important the monument could be to New York, as well as their own careers. He was calling on everything in his power, Gus wrote to former minister to France John Dix, a member of the commission, "to break away from the regular conventional statues."

October 14, 1879: . . . Aug is just as busy and bothered as he can be. He has three men at work in the studio besides Louis, and the molder much of the time and so much going on distracts him very much. They are getting ready to enlarge the statue and yesterday they made some mistakes and it took the whole lot of them all today to undo and [re]do what they did yesterday. A sculptor friend of Aug told him he would be made nearly wild with it and that for a long time apparently nothing would seem to be accomplished. I tell you all this to give you an idea of what is going on. Aug is going to enlarge the head in wax and will do it here [in the apartment] in the evenings. He is fussing over the Farragut and working on angles [for the pedestal] now. I wish I could help him but there seems to be nothing I can do but keep the house going and his clothes in order. Louis works as hard as he can and is never satisfied unless he is doing something. As daylight is so precious we are going to try going to bed at nine and getting up at half past six or thereabouts. I don't know how it will work, but we will try anyway. . . .

November 14: The Farragut statue looks much finer to us in the big than it did in the life-size one. If necessary it could be cast now, but Aug will probably work over it off and on for two months before having it cast.

The "fussing" went on, and on. He seemed never quite satisfied with what he had done. He hated to let his work go.

Gussie had been assigned to making the braid on the sleeve of "our Farragut." It was a "purely mechanical thing . . . but it takes ever so much time. . . ."

But life was not all work. Gus had acquired a flute and she a piano on which to accompany him. Rental for both, she assured her parents, was only three dollars a month.

Sometimes he would scratch in a few good-spirited lines of his own at the end of her letters, or add a cartoon or caricature of himself, his head with the beard drawn the shape of a wedge, his long nose a straight line down from the forehead, his eyes two tiny dots.

———

Through the whole slow, drawn-out process, the great volume of clay had to be kept constantly moist on the surface. If it were allowed to dry out, the statue would crack. In December came the coldest winter since the year of the siege, with snows in Paris over a foot deep. The Seine froze over, and the worry inside the studio was that the wet clay might freeze and the statue crack. Two large coal stoves had to be kept burning, the temperature in the room and the surface of the clay carefully monitored day and night. "Poor Aug is driven, he does not know which way to turn and the days are so short and dark he can seem to accomplish very little in them," wrote Gussie. "Louis sleeps there, and keeps the fires up all the time," she reported a week later.

Writing to Richard Gilder on December 29, 1879, Gus said, "All my brain can conceive now is arms with braid, legs, coats, eagles, caps, legs, arms, hands, caps, eagles, eagles, caps, and so on; nothing, nothing but that statue."

In a letter to La Farge written the same day, he confided, "I haven't the faintest idea of the merit of what I've produced. At times I think it good, then indifferent, then bad."

By the last week of January 1880, the work in clay was nearly done to the satisfaction of the sculptor—all but for one troublesome leg. "One of Farragut's legs has always bothered him and I am afraid he has used a great many swear words about it," Gussie said, "but yesterday for the first time he got the leg and trousers to suit him and when I went up to the studio he was singing, so I knew that he was very happy about something. . . ."

The admiral stood eight feet, three inches tall, his legs apart, the left leg (the one giving the most trouble) slightly back from the right, the toes of the great fourteen-inch-long shoes pointed nearly straight ahead. The sword hanging from his left side and the fieldglasses grasped in the large left hand were also of heroic proportions.

He stood as if on deck at sea braced for whatever was to come, chin up, eyes straight ahead. The flap of his long double-breasted coat seemed truly to blow open with the wind, and the back of the coat, too, billowed out. And while due attention was paid to the braid on the sleeves, the buttons, belt, and straps that held the sword, there was an overall, prevailing simplicity that conveyed great inner strength, no less than the presence of an actual mortal being, for all the figure's immense size. The admiral had missed buttoning the third button on his coat, for example.

The intent, weather-beaten face said the most. The look on the face, like the latent power in the stance, leaving no doubt that this was a man in command.

Casting the statue in plaster was scheduled to begin on Monday, February 9. "There are nineteen great bags of plaster here," Gussie reported from the studio, "and any quantity of bars of iron and they will all go into the statue. They will be four days making the mold and then . . . the plaster statue will be cast."

Once that cast was finished, Gus went to work again, and when done, "thought better of it," as he reported to Stanford White.

A few writers for newspapers were permitted to come in and take a look, with the understanding that nothing was to be said in print until the statue was finished.

"I have seen nothing finer of its kind, even in France," the correspondent for the *New York World* wrote at once. "The statue is admirably naturalistic in the best sense. It does not seem like a man of clay, but like a man of flesh and blood." It was a first rave review, but Gus was furious that anything at all had been published at this stage.

Only days later, with all ready for the next step, there was an accident. In the process of getting the statue free from the scaffolding, it slipped and landed hard, cracking one of the troublesome legs. Twenty men had been helping with ropes and rollers. No one seemed at fault. "It was immensely heavy," Gussie explained in a letter. Saint-Gaudens and others at once went to work, and the damage was repaired.

To the delight of everyone, the weather was suddenly like summer, Gussie wrote. "Clear and cloudless and everything growing green. . . . Every window . . . open wide all day long. . . . There is nothing like Paris in spring." Aug was "very well and very happy over his statue. . . ."

———

In April, Gussie discovered she was pregnant and wrote to tell her mother that her sickness each morning passed quickly and that immediately afterward her appetite returned better than ever.

Gus decided to submit a plaster Farragut, along with five of his bas-reliefs, to the Paris Salon. For a brief time, before being placed on exhibition inside, the statue stood out in the open air, as Gus had never seen it until then. "He felt very much pleased," Gussie wrote, "and says he knows now that he has done a good thing. . . ."

His entries were awarded an Honorable Mention, and the Farragut received especially strong praise from French critics. Saint-Gaudens had captured "that initiative and boldness which Americans possess and which Farragut exemplified," wrote Émile Michel in *Revue des Deux*

Mondes. The statue, said Paul Leroi in *L'Art*, was "the incarnation of the sailor, better cannot be done."

By the middle of May the plaster statue was ready to be moved to the long-established Gruet Foundry, there to be cast in bronze. It was not only essential that such a foundry be experienced, Saint-Gaudens insisted, but that he be on hand to supervise the entire process. The cost was substantial, $1,200, as Gussie wrote to her parents. She was going with him to the foundry to watch. "You know it is quite an exciting thing. . . ."

Taking part in the whole process day after day at the foundry, Saint-Gaudens became a nervous wreck. Two weeks later, when the lower half of the statue was cast, again something went wrong and it had to be done all over, and again at considerable expense.

When at last the whole cast was done, the statue complete in bronze, its entire outer surface had to be expertly finished, and, as Saint-Gaudens wanted, with the admiral's buttons and insignia given a slightly brighter gloss.

Finally the completed work—eight feet, three inches in length and weighing nine hundred pounds—had to be carefully packed up, shipped by rail to Le Havre and sent on its way aboard ship to New York. It was the largest work of sculpture in bronze by an American ever shipped from France until then.

Not until midsummer was everything sufficiently in order for Gus and Gussie themselves to leave for home.

III

The baby, a boy, was born in Roxbury on September 29, and christened Homer after his maternal grandfather. Through the months that followed, while Gussie and the infant remained with her family, Saint-Gaudens was busy finding a studio in New York and concentrating on work on the Farragut pedestal.

As finally resolved with White, and after much wrangling with the commission over the costs involved, the pedestal would place the statue fully nine feet above ground level and include tall, slightly curved stone façades reaching out to either side, these to provide a comfortable place to sit—an exedra, as it was known—as well as space for the two large allegorical figures in relief representing Loyalty and Courage, combined with a motif of fish and waves at sea. This entire composition was being done in Hudson River blue stone, with the thought that its color would add further to the nautical theme. A lettered tribute to the admiral was also to be included, this composed by White's father.

The relief figures of Loyalty and Courage were a major work unto themselves, and here again Louis Saint-Gaudens took part. They were to be seated figures and as large in scale as Farragut, their arms reaching out three feet. They were beautiful and unadorned, with the look of twin sisters, though the expression on the face of Courage was a touch more resolute and she wore breast armor, while Loyalty was partly bare-breasted. It was to be a pedestal unlike any ever seen in New York or anywhere else in the United States.

"Yesterday I had a good long day's work, also today—I expect that in about two weeks to have both Loyalty and Courage finished," Saint-Gaudens wrote in high spirits to Gussie, "Darling ole smuche," in an undated letter from New York. "They have commenced cutting the fishes and they look very fine. The piece of blue stone that goes directly under the Farragut is the largest piece of blue stone ever quarried."

"Did I ever tell you what a lot of handsome females there are here," he kidded her, "a great many more than in France and all of them have a rare thing, fine breasts." Who posed for Loyalty and Courage is not known.

How was the "Babby," he asked at the end. "Is he President yet?"

The grand unveiling took place at Madison Square on the afternoon of May 25, 1881.

A Marine band played; sailors marched. The celebrated New York attorney and orator Joseph H. Choate delivered an extended tribute to the admiral, and 10,000 people stood in the hot sun through the length of it.

Seated on the speakers' platform, along with some forty-five "notables"—including Mrs. Farragut, the mayor, the governor, church pastors, admirals, generals, and commissioners—could be seen the sculptor Augustus Saint-Gaudens and his wife. It was his first experience with public acclaim, and happening in his own hometown.

The monument was a stunning success. The critics were exuberant, the whole art world electrified. The *New York Times* hailed the Farragut with the headlines: A BEAUTIFUL AND REMARKABLE WORK OF ART, and MR. SAINT-GAUDENS'S TRIUMPH.

> It is Farragut just as he looked, quiet, unpretending, stern, re-
> solved to do his duty. The heroic is not obtruded. . . . For the
> great point of this statue is the absence of "fuss and feathers"
> in the attitude as well as the dress. It would be commonplace,
> if it were not so simple and true.

The two bas-relief figures of Loyalty and Courage ought to be ranked among the finest achievements of sculpture in America, the *Times* continued. "The faces are naturally . . . and most carefully worked. Here a weak man would fail."

The character of the indomitable admiral "shines from the sculptured face," said the critic for the *New York Evening Post.* The sculptor's work impressed one not as a statue but as a living man. "The spectator does not feel the bronze, he does not feel the sculptor; he feels the presence of the Admiral himself."

"In modeling severe, broad yet minute in finish . . . full of dignity and reserved force," wrote Richard Gilder in *Scribner's*, making no mention of the legs he had posed for. Saint-Gaudens's Farragut, he continued, might be called the work of a "new Donatello," which must have pleased Saint-Gaudens as much as anything said in print.

Praise came from all sides. Most touching for Saint-Gaudens were the reactions of his fellow artists and friends. The statue took his breath away, wrote Maitland Armstrong, who had also returned from Paris. "The sight of such a thing renews one's youth, and makes one think that life is worth living after all."

A few days after the unveiling, at about midnight, Saint-Gaudens and Gussie and a friend were walking up Fifth Avenue, on their way home from a party. As they approached Madison Square, they saw an elderly man standing alone in the moonlight looking at the statue. Recognizing his father, Saint-Gaudens went to him and asked what he was doing there at such an hour.

"Oh, you go about your business!" his father answered. "Haven't I got a right to be here?"

———

It had been fourteen years since Augustus Saint-Gaudens had sailed for Paris in steerage at the age of nineteen with little more than high ambition and the $100 in boyhood earnings his father had put aside for him.

Now he had a wife and a son of his own. The last three years in Paris had been for him and Gussie as difficult, productive, and as happy as any they had known. With his brilliant debut as an artist he had indeed "soared into the blue" and achieved recognition such as he had dreamed of. There seemed little likelihood he would ever again have to struggle to find work, or depend on the support of others. He and Stanford White were already started on another project.

Further, he had established himself as an artist brilliantly capable of doing justice to the memory of the Civil War. In time he would sculpt six of the most remarkable public monuments to the war ever created. And another of these, like the Farragut, would be made in Paris.

CHAPTER THIRTEEN

GENIUS IN ABUNDANCE

Paris! We are here! . . .
We feel our speechlessness keenly . . .

—ROBERT HENRI

I

When Mary Cassatt made her debut as an Impressionist at the opening of the Fourth Impressionist Exhibition in Paris in 1879, she was thirty-four years old. John Sargent, then at the start of his career, was her junior by eleven years. Cassatt's family was still with her in Paris and to a large degree her life remained centered around them. Sargent's family, on the other hand, had resumed their nomadic ways, departing Paris late in 1878 for Savoy, then Nice, leaving John to fend for himself.

The Impressionist Exhibition opened on April 10 at a gallery on the avenue de l'Opéra. Cassatt had eleven paintings and pastels on display, including her portrait of her sister Lydia, *Woman Reading*. A few weeks later Sargent's first major portrait, of his teacher Carolus-Duran, could be seen at the Paris Salon.

The work of both Americans received warm acclaim. "The *Woman Reading* . . . is a miracle of simplicity and elegance," said one review. Mademoiselle Cassatt and Monsieur Degas were "perhaps the only artists who distinguished themselves in this group," said another critic who in general looked askance on Impressionists.

Sargent's *Carolus-Duran* received an honorable mention at the Salon, and much approval from the public and critics. "There was always a little crowd around it, and I overheard constantly remarks of its excellence," wrote his father, who had made a return visit to Paris for the occasion.

"No American had ever painted with such quiet mastery . . . equaling the French on their own ground," declared an American review. "There is no feebleness, no strain, no shortcoming in the art . . . it is alive."

May Alcott of Boston, who was studying art in Paris and had made a conscientious effort to see nearly everything by Americans shown at the galleries and the Salon, concluded that, were one to leave out the work of Sargent, women clearly ranked first among American painters, with Mary Cassatt at the forefront. Miss Alcott, who was the sister of Louisa May Alcott, would write:

> If Mr. John Sargent be excepted, whose portrait of Carolus-
> Duran alone undoubtedly places him in the first rank of paint-
> ers, there is no other male student from the United States in
> Paris today exhibiting in his pictures the splendid coloring
> always found in the work of Miss Cassatt of Philadelphia. . . .

With their upper-class demeanor, fluency in French, general sophistication, and extraordinary talent, Cassatt and Sargent had a great deal in common, despite the differences in gender and age. They lived and worked in the same city—of their own choice and for many of the same reasons—and Sargent, with some of his fellow students, had met Cassatt sometime in the 1870s. But they had no more than a passing acquaintance and their lives remained worlds apart.

Where Cassatt's days were confined almost entirely to her studio and the fifth-floor family residence on the avenue Trudaine, life for young Sargent was as free as it had ever been. He had a number of companionable friends and was frequently off and about, at times traveling more even than his parents, with the difference that he kept working wherever he was.

Most of the summer of 1877 he spent at the small Breton port of Cancale. The next summer he traveled to Naples, then sailed to Capri before returning to Nice to be with his family. In the summer of 1879 he went overland to Madrid to copy masterworks at the Prado Museum, as urged by Carolus-Duran. From Madrid he moved on to Granada, then Morocco and Tunis.

The steady production of work resulting from these expeditions was phenomenal. He found interest in everything. At Cancale he sketched and painted studies of oyster gatherers on the beach—women with large baskets and the children who accompanied them—and produced three major canvases on the subject. He did ships and boats, boatmen and wharf scenes in both oil and watercolor. He painted portraits and studies of women in Capri, children bathing on the shore, olive groves, and more than a few of an especially beautiful model named Rosina in silhouette dancing on the white rooftops.

At the Prado he devoted weeks to painting a copy of the Velázquez masterpiece *Las Meninas*. He did pencil, ink, and oil sketches of Spanish dancers and musicians in Madrid, and at Granada, luminous watercolors of the architectural details of the Alhambra. In Morocco he painted street scenes, mosques, and Berber women wearing their haiks.

No subject seemed to daunt him. Once back in Paris, he undertook scenes out in the city itself, something very few American painters had yet attempted. Two brilliant black and white oil paintings of the Pasdeloup Orchestra in rehearsal at the Cirque d'Hiver amphitheater on the rue Amelot left no doubt of his amazing virtuosity. A scene of a couple strolling in the Luxembourg Gardens at twilight, which he painted twice, evoked the romantic spell of Paris as few works ever had. And he was only getting started.

He and Carroll Beckwith continued to share the studio apartment at 73 rue Notre-Dame-des-Champs, and counted French as well as American painters among their "circle," including Paul Helleu from Brittany, who introduced Sargent to Claude Monet.

Unlike Mary Cassatt, Sargent had no impulse to embrace the Impressionist mode, nor would he allow himself to be so classified, as much as he admired the work of Monet, Manet, and others. It was to portraits above all that he devoted the most time and effort and that were rapidly bringing him attention and increasing income.

He painted his American student friends Ralph Curtis, Francis Chadwick, and Gordon Greenough. Paul Helleu—lean, dark, and a lifelong friend—seemed never to tire of posing for him. FitzWilliam Sargent sat for his melancholy portrait, and the French playwright Édouard Pailleron became the first full-fledged patron, commissioning not only a portrait of himself but two more of his wife and children.

But it was the portrait of Carolus-Duran that launched Sargent's career, just as he hoped it would, and intrinsic to its appeal was an unmistakable feeling for the theatrical that was to characterize his strongest, most arresting works to follow.

So relaxed, confident, almost flippant was the pose struck by Carolus-Duran, he might well have been seated downstage at the footlights about to deliver an entertaining soliloquy, or produce a rabbit out of a hat. He looks at the viewer straight on, as though his dark eyes never blinked. An actor assigned to play the part would have only to look at the painting to know what to do.

It was seeing the portrait of Carolus-Duran that led playwright Pailleron to ask Sargent to paint him in a comparable pose. Sargent's brushwork and use of a dark background to accentuate his subjects in both portraits were unmistakably in the manner taught by Carolus-Duran, yet still more an expression of Sargent's own genius for catching the essence of the subject with only a few, seemingly effortless brush strokes.

A small, candid portrait done in London the next year, 1881, of an American novelist and essayist, Vernon Lee, was another virtuoso performance. It was a brilliant likeness that appeared to have been captured in a flash, without a moment's hesitation.

Vernon Lee was the pen name of Violet Paget. She had been one of Sargent's childhood playmates in Nice, where her parents, too, were living the expatriate life. Describing for her mother the day she sat for Sargent, she wrote, "I enjoyed it very much; John talking all the whole time and strumming the piano between times." She thought the painting "extraordinarily clever," if "mere dabs and blurs." "He says I sit very well; the goodness of my sitting seems to consist in never staying quiet a single moment."

She was as much a whirlwind talker as he, and the "dabs and blurs" caught the animation of her chattering face, the glints of light from her eyeglasses and uneven teeth. It was, she conceded, "more like me than I expected anything could [be]—rather fierce and cantankerous."

Greatly as they enjoyed each other's company, Sargent and Vernon Lee rarely talked about art. As a writer and critic, she had become interested in the "application to art of psychological research." But like Augustus Saint-Gaudens, Sargent wished only to be spared such talk. "In his eyes," she later wrote, "all this was preposterous, and I suspect, vaguely sacrilegious." And she went further:

> Now, as I declined to yield to my dear old playfellow's dictation on this subject, and failed to make him recognize that art could afford to other folk problems quite apart from those dealt with by the artist and the art critic; as, moreover, Sargent did not like opposition nor I dogmatism, a tacit understanding henceforth kept us off anything which might lead to either. So our conversation turned more and more to books, music and people, about all of which John Sargent was a delightful talker and an often delighted listener.

Word spread that he made sitting for a portrait highly pleasurable, and affluent women in increasing numbers wished to do so. Among them were Eleanor Jay Chapman and her sister Beatrix, the daughters of a New York stockbroker, and Madame Ramón Subercaseaux, the wife of the Chilean consul in Paris, who later described going with her husband to Sargent's studio and finding it, to their surprise, "very poor and bohemian while the artist himself seemed a very attractive gentleman," though "very young." Her sittings took place at the Subercaseaux apartment on the avenue du Bois-de-Boulogne. He had her pose at her piano, her right hand on the keyboard as if about to perform.

> He concentrated on each detail and took great care of the effect of each object and color. He was a man of great skill who felt secure and at ease while working. He was very fond of

music and had me play for him. He brought me several pieces
from Louis Moreau Gottschalk . . . whom he admired very
much, specially his interpretations of Spanish and South
American dances.

Sargent's love of music and the flamboyant were intrinsic to his work,
and sometimes in small inventive ways. In a sparkling portrait of beautiful Madame Paul Escudier, in which she is dressed to go out, her coat and
the background—virtually three-quarters of the canvas—are black, but
the face radiates life and the white ribbon of her hat, in combination with
her red hair, is a showpiece unto itself.

Little is known of Sargent's interest in any of the women who sat for
him, beyond the work at hand, with two exceptions and even then there
was only hearsay. Fanny Watts, the subject of the first picture he sent to
the Salon, was, like Vernon Lee, a friend from childhood in Italy. Their
families moved in the same social circles and he was clearly fond of her.
There was talk of a romance, even an engagement, but supposedly his
mother put an end to it, saying marriage at such an early age would interfere with his career.

Later came even more talk of a romance with Louise Burkhardt, the
subject of a full-length portrait by Sargent, *Lady with the Rose*, much admired by critics. He and Louise were together frequently in Paris and,
with Carroll Beckwith and others, went off on summer excursions to
Fontainebleau and Rouen. Her mother strongly encouraged the supposed
romance, and again there was talk of an engagement that never happened.

How strongly attracted Sargent was to the opposite sex, or to his own,
was and would remain difficult to determine. It would be said that no man
indifferent to the physical appeal of stunning women could possibly have
painted them as he did. But it would also be said that some of his drawings and paintings of his male friends argued the opposite, and that his
rendering of women was his way of concealing his homosexuality. But no
one ever knew or said so if they did. He kept that side of his life entirely
private.

Vernon Lee, who knew him as well as anybody, later wrote, "More and
more it has seemed to me that Sargent's life was absorbed in his painting,

and that the summing up of a would-be biographer must, I think, be: *he painted."*

That the same could have been said of Mary Cassatt remained as evident as ever. Except for occasional spells of poor health and the interruptions required to attend to her family's needs, her devotion to her work was no less ardent than ever. Her life, too, was her art.

Her father complained of dyspepsia and lumbago. Her mother suffered from a hacking cough and insomnia. Sister Lydia, her health steadily declining, remained a constant worry. Her sufferings from intermittent headaches and stomach pains had become more severe, at times alarming, though she seldom complained—"she has wonderful spirits considering all things," her mother reported to her son Alexander—and with Lydia still willing to sit for Mary when the pains subsided, Mary kept painting her.

In 1880, primarily for Lydia's benefit, the family began spending summers in the country at Marly-le-Roi. Alexander, his wife, Lois, and their four children made a long-promised visit to France to join them at Marly, and the atmosphere seemed to agree with everyone. Mary painted several of her finest pictures—*Lydia Crocheting in the Garden at Marly, Lydia Seated in the Garden with a Dog in Her Lap, Katherine Cassatt Reading to Her Grandchildren.*

Again it was the safely sequestered, quiet, unstrained, unthreatened feminine world of family and privilege that she portrayed and that, by all evidence, she had no desire to venture away from. Nor do any of her subjects ever look directly at the viewer. They are all quietly seated, preoccupied with some private, genteel interest of the moment. Even Alexander, who at home in the United States played an active part in the often rough-and-tumble world of giant railroads, is seen in an oil sketch with a book in hand, quietly gazing off as if lost in some philosophical thought.

Unlike Sargent's subjects, Cassatt's were never in the least flamboyant or theatrical. There is no drama to her settings, no suggestion of noise or merriment or mystery, only peace and quiet, and nearly always with an edge of sadness. Not only is there no dancing, no one is even seen standing. Apparently she, too, like her subjects, sat at her easel to work at eye level.

The nearest she came to portraying the Paris world of music and drama were paintings of women at the opera and theater, but there as well her ladylike subjects sit safely sequestered in a loge or box seat.

She received abundant praise—she was a "veritable phenomenon"— and her paintings were selling. "Mame's success is certainly more marked this year than at any time previous," her father was glad to report to Alexander in the spring of 1881.

> The thing that pleases her most in this success is not the newspaper publicity, for that she despises as a rule—but the fact that artists of talent and reputation and other persons prominent in art matters asked to be introduced to her and complimented her on her work. She has sold all her pictures or can sell them if she chooses—

Alexander, who had spent his whole career with the Pennsylvania Railroad and had recently been made a vice president of the company, had now, under Mary's guidance, begun his own collection of Impressionist works. But early in 1882, when the Impressionists began quarreling among themselves, Mary withdrew from the group. Worse still, that summer at Marly, Lydia became "very ill" and Mary became extremely sad and unproductive. "Mary being the worst kind of alarmist does not help when things look gloomy . . . and is not doing much in the way of art," her father wrote. After a private meeting with Lydia's doctor, who said there was no hope for a cure, Mary went home so depressed she had to take to her bed.

"Poor dear!" her father wrote of Lydia in mid-September. "This is the first time she has spoken plainly and directly of her death. . . ." Mary, Lydia had told him, had developed into a "most excellent nurse."

Lydia Cassatt died in Paris of Bright's disease at age forty-five on a dismal, rain-soaked November 7, 1882.

Mary had never known the death of someone close to her. When Alexander, Lois, and the children arrived in Paris three weeks later, Mary told

Lois how desperately lonely she felt. Perhaps she would have been better off to have married, she said, than face being "left alone in the world."

II

In 1882, the year of Lydia Cassatt's death, John Sargent's genius took hold as never before. In that one year, at age twenty-six, he painted not only his *Lady with the Rose* and the stunning small portrait of Madame Escudier, but a second portrait of her standing in her sumptuous parlor, as well as eight other portraits and two of the largest, most arresting works of his career, *El Jaleo* and *The Daughters of Edward Darley Boit*, in neither of which was there any holding back on his sense of theater and love of dramatic light and shadow.

The French critic Henry Houssaye called *El Jaleo* "the most striking picture of the year." Eight feet high and nearly twelve feet long—so huge no one could fail to take notice—it was Sargent's passionate, bravura tribute to Spanish dance and music. In a scene lit by footlights, a dark-haired flamenco dancer in a flowing silver-white skirt flings herself into her performance, as behind her, against a wall, a line of musicians and singers, all in black, play and sing, and other seated dancers clap hands.

Painted far from Madrid on the rue Notre-Dame-des-Champs, with a French model posed as the dancer, it was the exuberant culmination of innumerable pencil, ink, and oil sketches from Sargent's time in Spain three years earlier and in Paris as part of his preparation. The Spanish word *jaleo* denotes the burst of clapping and shouts of *olé* that are part of flamenco dancing. Once Sargent had the immense canvas under way, such was the vigor and clarity of the brushwork in the highlights of the dancer's skirt that it was as if he, too, were shouting *"olé!"* to the loud stamp of her high heels. The darkly shadowed back wall, the dramatic lighting, the singer who throws back his head in a kind of ecstasy, are all pure, unabashed theater.

Nor was there much less theater in the second masterpiece, painted only months later, with the difference this time that the curtain had opened on an altogether silent tableau in which four very proper figures stand perfectly still, all but one looking directly at the audience—a scene made especially arresting in that they are children.

Edward Darley Boit and Mary Louisa Cushing Boit were the rich American expatriates and friends of Sargent's who commissioned him to paint their four daughters. Boit had given up being a Boston lawyer to paint, specializing in watercolor, at which he was highly proficient. His wife, whose inherited wealth exceeded even his, was described by Henry James as "brilliantly friendly."

Apparently they had no specific requests or requirements of Sargent, leaving the setting, individual poses—everything about the picture—to him. And what resulted, the whole arrangement and mood of the painting, could hardly have been more unorthodox. That the canvas was a huge square, seven by seven feet, was in itself a departure, and the composition, the placement of the subjects, was a clear echo of *Las Meninas*, the Velázquez masterpiece of children in the Spanish court that Sargent had copied at the Prado.

The two oldest Boit daughters, Florence, who was fourteen, and Jane, twelve, stand together at the side of a high, wide doorway. Jane is positioned at the exact center of the canvas, Florence with her face in profile is so shadowed she is barely recognizable.

Further forward on the left, seven-year-old Mary Louisa stands alone, hands behind her back, her face fully lit, while "the baby," three-year-old Julia, also fully lighted, sits on a Persian rug in the right foreground.

A pair of giant Japanese vases several heads taller than the two tallest girls also stand on either side of the doorway. With the Persian rug, they constitute the only props suggesting the luxurious Boit way of life. (Such was family pride in the vases that they were shipped back and forth between Boston and Paris every time the Boits crossed the Atlantic, year after year.)

The three older sisters wear the starched white pinafores considered proper play attire, and the three-year-old holds her doll. But the play attire notwithstanding, none is at play, and each seems oddly alone.

Other artists of the day painted children at play in the sunlight of public gardens in Paris, often accompanied by stylish, chattering mothers or white-capped nursemaids. Sargent placed these four young Americans not only indoors, but in a sunless interior with a dark void of a background made to seem darker still by a gleam of light reflected in a mirror to the rear. To add further drama and mystery, part of a red screen makes a bright, dagger-shaped slash down the right side of the doorway.

The children surely have a story to tell, and one waits for them, like actors onstage, to begin speaking, perhaps in turns, to unfold the story.

Contrasting with the rigid geometric composition of the tableau and the motionless pose of its protagonists is Sargent's characteristic vitality in the brushwork—in his rendering of the white pinafores, most conspicuously, and the decorative pattern of the Japanese vases. He is like a virtuoso pianist who, playing rapidly, strikes every key perfectly. Moreover, along with the air of mystery there is great warmth in the wall and the parquet floor, but especially in the pretty faces of the two younger girls in the foreground.

Vernon Lee would later write, "I am persuaded that the individual temperament of every artist expresses itself with unconscious imperative far more in *how* he paints than in what he chooses to be painting. . . ." It was, she felt, in such "perfectly pure and contrasted colors" and "the unerring speed of his hand and eye" in such paintings as *El Jaleo* and the portrait of the Boit daughters that the true temperament of John Sargent was to be found.

Finished in late 1882, the picture of the Boit daughters was intended for the Paris Salon the next spring. But Sargent could not wait, and so put it on exhibit under the title *Portraits d'Enfants* at Georges Petit's gallery on the rue de Sèze in December.

Reaction to it then and later when shown at the Salon was uneven. Some viewers were troubled by its mood. One French critic described the children as *"en pénitence,"* being punished. Henry James, writing in *Harper's Weekly*, would declare without hesitation that Sargent had never painted anything "more felicitous and interesting." The picture was "astonishing," James said, and praised "the complete effect, the light, the free security of execution, the sense it gives of assimilated secrets and instinct and knowledge. . . ."

In London, a critic for the *Art Journal* reported that Sargent now found himself "the most talked-about painter in France, with every opportunity to have his head turned by the admiration he had received." Another English reviewer wrote that *El Jaleo* not only put Sargent at the head of the American school in Paris, but "on equal ground with the most prominent French painters."

A visiting Boston merchant named T. Jefferson Coolidge had wasted no time buying *El Jaleo*, paying 1,500 francs, or about $300, for it. And while some expatriate Americans chattered about the feeling of loneliness and mystery in the *Portraits d'Enfants*, speculating over what it might be saying about Sargent's own childhood, people at Georges Petit's gallery and later at the Salon kept coming back for a second or third look.

Sargent paid little or no attention to all this. He was too excited about a new project, a portrait of a famous Paris beauty, Madame Gautreau.

Sargent was by nature, as Vernon Lee wrote, always "especially attracted by the *bizarre* and outlandish," the very essence of Virginie Amélie Avegno Gautreau, who, contrary to the impression most people had, was an American.

Born in New Orleans, she had been brought to Paris as a child of eight by her widowed, socially ambitious mother. Her father, a major in the Confederate army, had been killed at the battle of Shiloh. She was, by 1883, twenty-four years old, two years younger than Sargent.

To her mother's great approval, she had married a wealthy French banker, Pierre Gautreau, and became what was called a "professional beauty," the perfect "*parisienne*," someone known for her remarkable looks and social stage presence, and who, in her appearances in society, was expected to fill that role with all due attention to wardrobe and the artful use of cosmetics, no less than a great actress. In her particular case a heavy use of a chalky lavender powder on face and body gave her a pallor distinctive enough in itself to draw attention. To her critics she was all too plainly an arriviste.

Her beauty was distinctly different, almost eccentric, her nose too long by accepted standards, her forehead too high. Yet the total effect, and particularly given her hourglass figure and her way of moving, was striking in the extreme, her appeal unmistakably seductive, as she well knew.

An American art student named Edward Simmons wrote of being "thrilled by every movement of her body."

> She walked as Virgil speaks of a goddess—sliding—and seemed to take no steps. Her head and neck undulated like that of a young doe, and something about her gave you the impression of infinite proportion, infinite grace, and infinite balance. Every artist wanted to make her in marble or paint.

After meeting her socially, Sargent, some said, had become obsessed by her. He let it be known that he wanted to do "homage to her beauty" in a portrait to be shown at the Salon, the implication being it could bring each of them notoriety in the way Manet's sensational *Olympia* had, albeit she need not pose in the nude.

> Do you object to people who are *fardées* [made up] to the extent of being uniform lavender or blotting paper color all over [he wrote to Vernon Lee]. If so you would not care for my sitter. But she has the most beautiful lines and if the lavender or chlorate-of-potash lozenge color be pretty in itself I shall be more than pleased.

He did one line drawing after another of her head in profile, made studies in pencil and watercolor of her relaxing on a settee in a low-cut evening dress, painted her in oil drinking a toast, and here again in profile. In the summer of 1883, from the Gautreaus' country estate in Brittany, he wrote to tell Vernon Lee he was "still struggling with the unpaintable beauty and hopeless laziness" of his subject.

That he and Amélie Gautreau were both Americans was by no means immaterial to their ambitions. The same year they met, a society journal noted that "Yankees" in Paris were gaining ever-greater prominence. "They have painters who carry off our medals, like Mr. Sargent, beautiful women who eclipse ours, Mme. Gautreau. . . ." If they were to be known always as Americans, then all the more reason to be at the forefront.

Finished with his preliminary studies, Sargent left Brittany for Nice to pay his annual visit to his parents, before moving on for an autumn stay in Florence.

"His life is a pleasant life," FitzWilliam Sargent wrote to a brother in Philadelphia.

> He seems to be respected, even admired and beloved (according to all accounts) for his talent and success as an artist, for his conduct and character as a man. His work is a pleasurable occupation to him and brings him a very handsome income. He travels about in countries which provide him with materials for his pictures as well as with bread and butter and elements of health and enjoyment. He is well received everywhere for his manners are good and agreeable. He is good looking, plays the piano well and dances well, converses well, etc., etc. In short, he has given us, his parents great satisfaction so far. . . .

In the winter of 1883–84, Sargent moved from the Left Bank to a new studio across the Seine at 41 boulevard Berthier, in the then fashionable neighborhood near the Parc Monceau. It was there in a workplace elegantly furnished with comfortably upholstered chairs, Persian rugs, and drapery befitting his new professional standing, and an upright piano against one wall, that he painted his full-length portrait of Madame Gautreau, the whole time suffering what he called "a horrid state of anxiety."

She was dressed in a long black satin skirt and low-cut black velvet bodice, her shoulders bare except for two slim jeweled straps. She held both shoulders back and her head cocked sharply to the left, giving full cameo emphasis to the remarkable profile.

Her left arm on her hip, she held her skirt with the left hand, while the right arm was oddly turned back on itself, her right hand gripping the top of the side table. She wore her hair up, with a tiny diamond tiara on top.

It was a flagrantly stagy pose, which could only have been difficult to hold for any length of time, even for one who was a poser by nature.

Against the deep black of the dress, the deathly blue-white of her pow-dered skin was even more strange and striking. When, during one sitting, her right shoulder strap dropped suggestively over her arm, Sargent re-quested she leave it that way.

In contrast to his usual approach, he worked and reworked the canvas, simplifying and redefining edges.

> One day I was dissatisfied with it and dashed a tone of light rose over the former gloomy background [he reported to a friend]. I turned the picture upside down, retired to another end of the studio and looked at it under my arm. Vast im-provement. The *élancée* figure of the model shows to much greater advantage.

No doubt Madame Gautreau saw how the portrait was emerging under his brush from one sitting to another. Possibly her mother, too, may have been present occasionally. If they found anything about it disturbing at the time, there is no evidence that a word was said.

When Carolus-Duran came by for a look, he told Sargent he could submit the painting to the Salon with perfect confidence. Sargent was not so sure.

Another who dropped in was Henry James. In Paris briefly, James had met and quite liked the young artist, calling him "the only Franco-American product of importance" in France. But, as James confided to a friend, he only "half-liked" the portrait of Madame Gautreau.

The 1884 Paris Salon, an exhibition filling thirty-one of the *grandes salles* in the Palais de l'Industrie, opened on a beautiful May morning with much excitement among the customary well-dressed crowds in attendance. So great had the number of American painters in Paris become, and so im-portant to their careers was representation at the Salon, that they were now second only to the number of French artists included. For Sargent it marked the sixth consecutive year he had exhibited at the Salon, and each time with increasing acclaim.

Paintings filled every wall. The portrait of Amélie Gautreau, ideally placed at eye level, was hung in Salle 31, and the doors had been open scarcely an hour when it became the talk of the exhibition.

For all that would be written and said, no eyewitness account of the event and of its effect on Sargent compared to what his friend Ralph Curtis wrote to his parents the next day. Whether the opening marked Sargent's birthday as an artist or his funeral, Curtis could not say.

> Walked up the Champs-Élysées, chestnuts in full flower and a dense mob of *"tout Paris"* in pretty clothes, gesticulating and laughing, slowly going into the Ark of Art. In 15 minutes I saw no end of acquaintances and strangers and heard everybody say, *"Où est le portrait Gautreau?" "Oh, allez voir ça."*

Curtis had seen Sargent the night before. "He was very nervous about what he feared," he wrote, "but his fears were far exceeded by the facts of yesterday. There was a *grand tapage* [great fuss] before it [the portrait] all day."

> In a few minutes I found him dodging behind doors to avoid friends who looked grave. By the corridors he took me to see it. I was disappointed by the color. She looks decomposed. All the men jeer. *"Ah voilà 'la belle!' " "Oh, quelle horreur!"* Etc. Then a painter exclaims, *"superbe de style, magnifique d'audace!"* [Magnificent audacity!] *"Quel dessin!"* [What drawing!]

In an exhibition wherein paintings of nudes were commonplace, that of Madame Gautreau in her black evening dress was considered scandalously erotic.

But what was unacceptable to *"tout Paris"* was the blatant, self-centered impropriety of it all—the heavy powder, the odd, arrogant pose, the décolletage. Such vulgar flaunting was simply not done by women of social standing.

"All the A.M. it was one series of *bons mots, mauvaises plaisanteries* and fierce discussions," Curtis continued in his letter. "John, poor boy, was *navré* [full of sorrow]. The tumult of talk lasted through the day, but by evening the tone of opinion about the picture had changed. It was discovered to be the knowing thing to say '*étrangement épatant.*' [Shocking, amazing!]

"I went home with him," Curtis continued, "and remained there while he went to see the Boits." Madame Gautreau and her mother came to the studio "bathed in tears." Curtis "stayed them off," but Madame Avegno came back again, after Sargent had returned, and made "a fearful scene." "All Paris mocks my daughter," she said. If the painting were to stay on exhibit, she would "die of chagrin."

Sargent, obviously put out, told her there was nothing he could do, that it was against the rules of the Salon to retire a picture and that he had painted Amélie exactly as she was dressed.

"Defending his cause made Sargent feel much better," wrote Curtis. "Still we talked it over until 1 o'clock here last night and I fear he has never had such a blow."

The reviews were essentially of three kinds, those that objected to Madame Gautreau's décolletage, those repulsed by the color of her skin, and those that, seeing "modernity" in the approach, applauded Sargent's courage.

The *New York Times* dismissed the painting out of hand as a "caricature," far below Sargent's usual standard. "The pose of the figure is absurd, and the bluish coloring atrocious." The *Times* of London conceded only that the portrait was "most interesting." But the French critic Louis de Fourcaud, writing in the *Gazette des Beaux-Arts*, called it a masterpiece of characterization. It should be kept in mind, he wrote, that "in a person of this type everything relates to the cult of self and the increasing concern to captivate those around her.

> Her sole purpose in life is to demonstrate by her skills in contriving incredible outfits which shape her and exhibit her and which she can carry off with bravado. . . .

Sargent had been living and working in Paris for a full decade and in that time had received only expressions of admiration and praise. He had never known an adverse review or even mild criticism, let alone public mockery. His portrait of Madame Gautreau was in fact a masterpiece and in time would be so recognized. He hung on to it, renaming it *Madame X*. He also repainted the fallen shoulder strap, restoring it to its proper place. Years later, when he sold the painting to the Metropolitan Museum in New York for $1,000, he would remark that it was perhaps the best thing he had done.

He and Amélie Gautreau seem to have had no further contact, though she, too, eventually changed her opinion about the painting and expressed pride in it.

Yet hard hit as he was and angry over what had happened, Sargent appears to have had no doubts about his ability or his ambition to keep painting. Feeling an immediate need for a change of scene, he followed up on an earlier plan to go to London. He left Paris in late May 1884, not to return until December.

III

All the while that Sargent was painting his Spanish dancer, the Boit daughters, and *Madame X*, work had been proceeding in Paris on another very different rendition of the female form on a scale never before seen.

Lady Liberty, France's colossal gift to America, had been rising steadily within her scaffolding upward from the courtyard of the Gaget, Gauthier & Cie. workshop on the rue de Chazelles, until she loomed high over the rooftops. Sculptor Auguste Bartholdi's unprecedented creation was now on display for all to see.

The first rivet of her skin of copper sheets had been driven in 1881. And with the support of an inner skeleton—pylon and ingenious trusswork—designed by France's master-builder in iron, Gustave Eiffel, the gigantic goddess had been growing steadily higher until the spring of 1884, when she was complete all the way to the tip of her upheld torch, 151 feet above street level.

She was a startling spectacle even to Parisians accustomed to spectacles, and her presence was to be brief, as everyone knew. The whole gigantic structure would soon be taken down piece-by-piece to be shipped to New York.

Photographers set up tripods and cameras to record the phenomenon of her towering over her Paris neighborhood. A French artist, Victor Dargaud, painted a scene of people in the street below craning their necks to see the uppermost reaches of the arm and torch, where men still at work looked like mere specks against the sky.

The disassembly began in December. Every piece was labeled, packed in more than two hundred wooden chests, and shipped off by rail to Rouen to be put aboard a French war vessel, the *Isère*, which sailed on May 21, 1885.

The pedestal on which Liberty was to stand on little Bedloe's Island had been designed by Richard Morris Hunt, the first American architect to have been trained at the École des Beaux-Arts. Hunt's pedestal stood eighty-nine feet tall, and thus Liberty and her torch would reach more than 240 feet above New York Harbor.

———

Even before the statue was on its way over the Atlantic, word began circulating in Paris that the civil engineer Eiffel had a still more audacious project in mind, a wrought-iron tower nearly 1,000 feet tall to be completed in time for the 1889 Exposition Universelle. Nothing like it had ever been attempted. The towers of Notre-Dame were by comparison a mere 226 feet high. The Washington Monument, the world's tallest stone structure, was, at 555 feet, little more than half the height of Eiffel's proposed centerpiece for the exposition.

It was to stand on the Champ de Mars, the old military parade ground where every exposition had been held since 1867. Eiffel's estimated cost for the project was 5 million francs, approximately $1 million.

Though the great majority of Parisians seemed taken with the idea, protests erupted at once. The tower was denounced as much too large, too dangerous, unacceptably ugly—"a project," it was said, "more in character with America (where taste is not very developed)."

In the past twenty years, since the end of the Civil War, feats of American engineering and construction had been attracting the attention of the world. The Mississippi River had been spanned for the first time, at St. Louis, with an unprecedented steel-and-masonry railroad bridge designed by James Buchanan Eads. The newly completed Brooklyn Bridge, the largest suspension bridge in the world, demonstrated dramatically the first use of steel cables.

Further, American inventions were the talk everywhere and rapidly becoming part of European life, as Samuel Morse's telegraph had. Paris was particularly affected. Alexander Graham Bell's telephone, invented in 1876, and Thomas Edison's electric light bulb, introduced in 1879, as well as his system to generate electricity, took hold rapidly. In 1880 there were nearly 500 telephone "subscribers" in Paris. By 1883 there were more than 2,000. The Paris Opera and the Saint-Lazare railway station had converted from gas to electric lights.

That France, too, was well advanced in science and technology, pioneering with numerous inventions like the use of caissons for underwater construction, a system adopted by the builders of the Brooklyn Bridge, seemed wholly beside the point to those opposed to Monsieur Eiffel and his tower. So greatly did they fear the takeover of art by industry and technology that the very thought of such a monstrous intrusion on the beauty of Paris was completely abhorrent.

The general understanding was that the tower would not be permanent, but would be taken down at some point in the future. In the fall of 1886 a government committee voted to proceed. When, at the start of 1887, the first stages of construction got under way on the Champ de Mars and it could be seen, by the placement of their foundations, that the four great angled legs upon which the tower would stand encompassed an area of fully two and a half acres, those against it became even more incensed. They saw the whole centuries-long preeminence of art and architecture, the entire human scale of the Paris they loved, direly threatened. The glorious evidence of their country's past and culture would be hideously overshadowed by an iron monstrosity. And what possible use would it serve, they asked.

Le Temps carried a petition signed by fifty highly prominent, highly irate figures in French arts and letters, including Charles Garnier, architect of the Opera, painter Ernest Meissonier, composer Charles Gounod, writers Alexandre Dumas and Guy de Maupassant.

> We, writers, painters, sculptors, architects, and devoted lovers of the beauty of Paris, to date intact, do protest with all our strength and with all our indignation, in the name of unappreciated French taste, in the name of French art and French history, now under attack, against the erection, in the very heart of our capital, of the useless and monstrous Eiffel Tower, which public spitefulness, often characterized by common sense and the spirit of justice, has already baptized, "the Tower of Babel."

Not even "the commercial nation of America" would want such a structure, the petition insisted.

In his response Eiffel asked whether it was because of their artistic value that the pyramids had so captured the imagination of the world. "The tower will be the highest edifice which men have ever built. So why should what is admirable in Egypt become hideous and ridiculous in Paris?" Addressing the question of artistic value, he said the tower would have its own beauty.

He also correctly sensed that the majority of the people of France favored the project as a stunning symbol of the amazing rejuvenation of their country since the "*Débâcle*" of 1870. In less than twenty years, under the Third Republic, the national income had nearly doubled, industrial production tripled. The whole idea of the forthcoming 1889 exposition was to celebrate such modern progress, as well as the centennial of the French Revolution.

The steady advance of French accomplishment would have seemed without limit were it not for recent unsettling reports from Panama that Ferdinand de Lesseps's attempt to dig a canal there at sea level like his prior triumph at Suez, was proving far more difficult and costly than promised.

But if anyone of the day embodied the French genius for success, it was Gustave Eiffel. Indeed, faith in the Panama canal had revived almost from the moment it was announced that Eiffel—who had warned against attempting a sea-level canal at Panama—would now be designing locks for the project. No other civil engineer in France inspired such confidence. To a large degree the decision to go ahead with the tower rested on his reputation.

Born and raised in Dijon, and trained in Paris at the École Centrale des Arts et Manufactures, Eiffel had, by 1887, become France's master builder. Without question, he was one of the engineering geniuses of the Industrial Age, known especially for such unprecedented iron structures as the Garabit Viaduct, with its arches four hundred feet above the Truyère River. For nearly thirty years he had built railroads, train stations, and bridges all over France, Europe, even in Russia and China. Nothing he had built had ever failed.

The chief problem to contend with in constructing the tower, he knew, was wind, and it was in answer to that reality that the design emerged. As the great French architect and earlier builder in iron, Henri Labrouste, had preached, "in architecture form must always be appropriate to the function for which it is intended." (Or as the Paris-trained American architect Louis Sullivan would later say more succinctly and famously, "Form follows function.")

The tower would rise in three stages. Once under way, it proceeded upward in amazingly rapid time. Its critics were even more taken aback by the spectacle. It was called "a metal spiderweb," "a work of disconcerting ugliness" and utter "coarseness." A professor of mathematics predicted from his calculations that at a height of 748 feet the tower would collapse. Others stressed that in any event it would never be finished in time for the exposition.

By April it had reached its first platform level, where a visitor's promenade and four restaurants were to be located at an elevation of 189 feet. By September, it was up to the second platform at 379 feet. From there the ironwork of the enormous spire began its long tapering ascent to the top, the men on the job working in all weather.

By March 1889, the tower was finished, not only ahead of schedule but ahead of every other building under construction for the exposition. On

Sunday, March 31, Eiffel and a delegation of ten willing to brave a climb of 1,170 steps unfurled a huge Tricolor from on top.

"You will remember always," Eiffel told them against a stiff March wind, "the great effort we have made in common to show all that, thanks to her engineers and her workers, France still holds an important place in the world. . . ."

From such a height, wrote a reporter from *Le Figaro* who had made the climb, Paris appeared like a tiny stage set.

———

In the years since his exit from Paris, John Singer Sargent had returned several times, traveled to Nice to see his parents, engaged a London studio on Tite Street that had once belonged to James McNeill Whistler, gave up his Paris studio, and continued working no less than ever and with outstanding results.

In his naturally affable fashion he had also acquired a number of new friends, such as Henry James, Robert Louis Stevenson, and the American painter Edwin Austin Abbey, all of whom were to mean much to him for as long as they lived.

"We both lost our hearts to him," wrote Stevenson, speaking for his wife as well, after Sargent came to their home in Bournemouth to do their portrait. At first, Stevenson continued, Sargent seemed to have "a kind of exhibition manner," but on closer examination proved "a charming, simple, clever, honest young man." As for the portrait, Stevenson thought it "poetical but very chicken-boned."

To Sargent, Stevenson was "the most intense creature" he had ever met, and, wishing to paint him again, he asked if he might return. This time it was a scene with long, lean Stevenson striding across a room, in a black velvet jacket, twisting his long mustache, as if caught in the midst of a thought, his American wife, Fanny, slouched on a sofa off in the background to the far right, wrapped in a glittering shawl from India. She looked like a ghost, Stevenson thought. She adored the picture. "Anybody may have a 'portrait of a gentleman,' but nobody had one like this," she wrote. "It is like a box of jewels."

"Walking about and talking is his main motion," Stevenson wrote, describing Sargent's manner at work. Palette in one hand, brush in the other, Sargent would look at his subject then advance on the canvas, as if in a duel, make a few swift strokes, back off, look again, then advance again and again, and all the while talking.

With such constant back-and-forthing in his studio, Sargent himself once calculated, he covered four miles a day. Work, work every day, work, was his way. "John thinks of nothing else," his friend Edwin Abbey wrote, "and is always trying and trying . . . he is absolutely sincere and earnest."

He painted indoors, outdoors, portraits, landscapes. On a return trip to France, during a visit to Giverny, he did a scene of Monet painting by the edge of a woods. And again he chose to do children in one of his most ambitious canvases, which he called *Carnation, Lily, Lily, Rose,* after a popular song of the day, which he happened to be humming as he worked. Two little English girls in summer dresses, the daughters of an artist friend, Fred Barnard, are seen lighting paper lanterns in a garden at twilight. It had been inspired by a scene Sargent witnessed one evening on the Thames, and it took a considerable time to complete, since he insisted on working on it only at dusk when the light was right and then only for twenty minutes or so. Many considered it his finest picture to date.

Portrait commissions were plentiful as his reputation continued to spread. And he was traveling no less than ever, always packing books in his luggage. It was said no one traveled with more books than Sargent, who usually chose several on a particular period if, say, history was his interest at the moment, or if it were fiction, a number by the same author. He loved French literature especially—Voltaire, Balzac, Flaubert, Stendhal—and read with remarkable speed.

In September of 1887 he boarded a steamer for Boston to paint portraits there. He had his first-ever one-man show at Boston's St. Botolph Club, and included his *El Jaleo* and *The Daughters of Edward Darley Boit.* In New York, Stanford White hosted dinners at which Augustus Saint-Gaudens and others of "the Paris old boys" raised toasts in his honor. By the start of 1889, he had six paintings ready for exhibit at the Exposition Universelle.

The number of American artists working and studying in Paris in the 1880s had never been greater, and nearly every new arrival was young. Frank Benson, Dennis Bunker, Willard Metcalf, Edmund Tarbell, John Twachtman, Childe Hassam, and Robert Henri were all in their twenties, and all enrolled in the Académie Julian, now the most popular of the Paris ateliers, with nearly 600 students. Among the American women were Mary Fairchild, Ellen Day Hale, Anna Klumpke, Elizabeth Nourse, Cecilia Beaux, and Clara Belle Owen.

A group of aspiring young Mormon painters who called themselves "art missionaries" arrived from Utah, many to enroll at the Académie Julian. Their expenses were being provided by the Church of Jesus Christ of Latter-day Saints in return for work they would later contribute, painting murals in the Temple at Salt Lake City. As one of their leaders, an especially gifted painter named John Hafen, said, their motivation was the belief that "the highest possible development of talent is the duty we owe to our Creator."

Though no exact count was made of the American art students in Paris at the time, they undoubtedly numbered more than a thousand. And nearly all, judging by what they wrote then and later, were thrilled at the chance to be in Paris and found themselves working harder than they ever had.

Anna Klumpke, a tiny young woman who walked with a cane as a result of a childhood injury, was one of those in the women's classes at the atelier of Rodolphe Julian. As a child in San Francisco, she had a doll named Rosa Bonheur and even then knew of Bonheur's acclaimed painting *The Horse Fair*. Bonheur was her hero. Now in the atelier she heard Julian say, "Prepare yourselves to compete favorably with my men students." There was no reason, he said, why one should not succeed "even as Rosa Bonheur." In 1898 Bonheur would sit for a portrait by Klumpke.

Cecilia Beaux from Philadelphia, another enrolled in the Académie Julian, decided that for all one learned from such instruction, it was of secondary importance. "The immense value to the student in Paris," she wrote, "lies in the place itself."

A number of them were, like Mary Cassatt, greatly influenced by the Impressionists. Willard Metcalf, John Twachtman, and Childe Hassam were to become foremost American Impressionists. Hassam, like John Sargent, got out into Paris to paint the city itself. "I am painting sunlight," he wrote when doing his *Grand Prix Day*, a scene set near the Arc de Triomphe. He painted Notre-Dame, winter along the Seine, and *April Showers* on the Champs-Élysées. Asked long afterward what his greatest pleasure had been in those years, he said, "To go about Paris."

Like generations of ambitious students before them, many devoted hours to making copies at the Louvre, an experience they found unsettling at first. Robert Henri was not alone in thinking, as he set up his easel in front of a Rembrandt, that everyone was staring at him. He had never seen a Rembrandt before, let alone tried to copy one.

Clara Belle Owen actually found encouragement in the work going on around her. "The people I saw copying at the Louvre were not doing so wonderfully well," she reported to her mother at home in Chicago. "I can do better than they do, I know. . . ."

Rather than enroll in an atelier, she spent every available hour painting at the Louvre or the gallery of the Luxembourg Gardens. "The day was so short, and the weeks go by so rapidly," she wrote again to her mother one December evening. "I do not have time to do half what I want to. Perhaps it is because I want to do so much."

She liked especially working at the Luxembourg Museum and appreciated "the privilege we have of working there more and more. . . .

> Just think how they keep the place warmed, furnish people with easels and stools, take care of your pictures, and charge nothing for it, except what one has a mind to give.

She had thought she might get homesick, but no. "I am too busy for that."

When it came time, in 1885, for John Twachtman to leave Paris and sail for home, he wrote, "I hardly know what will take the place of my weekly visit to the Louvre . . . perhaps patriotism."

"Paris! We are here!" Robert Henri had written boldly in the "Log" he kept. "We feel our speechlessness keenly. . . ."

A lanky New Yorker, Henri was twenty-one years old and highly talented. He and four other American students had rented an apartment on the Right Bank, on the rue Richerand, five floors up a spiral stairway.

"Dust and dirt are everywhere," he wrote on September 26, 1888, after moving in:

> But with soap and muscle we did great work. The red tiles in the kitchen fairly shone and everything was in good shape for the reception of the little iron beds, the straw seated chairs and other bits of furniture which we soon got in order. . . .
>
> When we turned in, it was with feelings of pleasure, we were in our house at last! Our own little iron beds!

Not even the population of fleas or his "bungling attempts" at French seemed to bother him. "The other fellows admit the same [inability with French] and we all laugh at the ridiculous situations we get ourselves into."

So crowded was the studio at the Académie Julian every morning that it meant a scramble for a place close enough to see the model, "a pretty woman." Emphasis at the academy was on mastering drawing in advance of painting.

"Made start—poor one—hard lines and poor expression," he recorded of one morning's effort. But then the day brightened:

> Julian treats the school—all hands to [the] café. Usual noise and circus, wine, fully 200 fellows. Leaving the café the crowd formed in line—hands on shoulders and went running up [the rue] St.-Denis, stopping wagons, creating excitement. . . . All out of breath, return to studio. The model was along with us, undresses and work is resumed. . . .

In a letter to his parents Christmas Day, 1888, Henri wrote that the praise he received and seeing his work displayed on the studio wall were certainly encouraging, but they must not expect too much. He had a good way to go.

Since I have been here my eyes have opened and the immense mountain I am to climb, to win my success, appears before me with all its formidable aspect. . . . I am nevertheless more determined to make the attempt and I shall stick to the struggle as long as I live.

Another day he wrote, "Who would not be an art student in Paris?"

On the night of May 5, 1889, like just about everyone else, Henri and his friends were swept up in the spectacle of brilliant illuminations across the city, music and dancing in the streets. It was the eve of the grand opening of the exposition.

Flags everywhere [he wrote the next day]. Great crowds along the river, bridges . . . boats all wonderfully illuminated. Trees full of . . . Chinese lanterns . . .

IV

Despite all the criticism of the Eiffel Tower, despite the late opening of many exhibits, despite the dreadful shock earlier in the year from the financial collapse of the Ferdinand de Lesseps Panama Canal Company—the bursting of the giant "Panama Bubble" that affected hundreds of thousands of French investors—and despite innumerable tiresome forecasts that the exposition could never possibly come up to those of other years, the great Exposition Universelle of 1889 was the biggest, best, most profitable, and enjoyable world's fair ever until then.

From its opening on May 6 to closing day six months later on November 6, the crowds far exceeded expectations and the attendance at all previous fairs. The first day, half a million people poured through the twenty-two entrances. The total number by November was 32 million. Some 150,000 Americans came to the fair, and in the words of the *American Register*, they, with thousands more foreigners and millions of French, "shed over Paris a shower of gold" like nothing before.

Never had the city looked so scrubbed and appealing. The ruins of the

Palace of the Tuileries were gone at last. Thousands of electric bulbs lit up the Eiffel Tower. Every night featured a show of fountains illuminated by electricity.

So much that had been created was so unimaginably colossal, quite apart from the tower. The Palais des Machines, built of iron and glass, was the largest space ever constructed under a single roof. It measured more in length than the tower in height, and the weight of its iron was greater even than that of the tower.

American machinery and products on display included giant steam engines and steam pumps, most of them in motion, lawnmowers and typewriters, which were still a novelty to Parisians. A New York confectioner provided a full-size replica of the Venus de Milo in chocolate.

The Thomas Edison display alone filled a third of the American exhibit space in the Palais des Machines, the inventory of Edison's inventions and devices totaling no less than 493, and of all those creative Americans whose work was shown, none had such celebrity as Edison. "What Eiffel is to the externals of this exposition," said the *New York Times*, "Edison is to the interior. He towers head and shoulders in individual importance over any other man. . . ." So great was the crush of admirers around him whenever he appeared anywhere that he felt forced to hide for days at a time, out of sight in the studio of an American artist friend, Abraham Anderson, who used the opportunity to paint his portrait.

One of the many new productions on display at the Palais des Machines was a small four-wheeled motor car powered by a new kind of petroleum engine—a two-cylinder internal-combustion engine—developed by a German engineer and inventor, Gottlieb Daimler. Most people thought it a toy only. As a writer in *Le Petit Journal* observed a short while later, "Off in this hidden corner . . . was germinating the seed of a technological revolution."

The works of art on display at the Palais des Beaux-Arts totaled more than 6,000, making it the largest art exhibit ever assembled in one place except at the Louvre. American works numbered 572, second only to the volume of French paintings and sculpture.

Pictures by Thomas Eakins, Cecilia Beaux, Walter Gay, Edwin Abbey, Will Low, Theodore Robinson, Anna Klumpke, James Carroll Beckwith, and Alden Weir were to be seen. William Merritt Chase showed eight pictures, the most of any American, and Kenyon Cox entered a portrait of Augustus Saint-Gaudens at work completing a clay relief of William Merritt Chase.

A portrait of Lord Lytton by George P. A. Healy was hung on the same wall with Sargent's *The Daughters of Edward Darley Boit.*

Everybody had an opinion. "A remarkable portrait picture of little girls by John Sargent . . . takes the cake," wrote Robert Henri in his diary.

One young American, John Douglas Patrick from Kansas, a student at the Académie Julian, caused a sensation with an enormous dark canvas called *Brutality*, portraying a Paris wagon driver savagely beating his horse with a club. It was a scene of a kind he and other Americans had witnessed and found appalling. Indeed, a U.S. government commission report on the exposition had only praise for nearly everything about Paris, except for "the unchecked brutality" of cab and wagon drivers and the sufferings of their horses.

Buffalo Bill Cody arrived with his Wild West Show, his troupe of cowboys, Indians, and horses, and star performer "Little Sure-Shot," Annie Oakley, creating a sensation of a kind not felt in Paris since the days of Tom Thumb and George Catlin and his Indians. Performances were staged on show grounds in the Parc Neuilly, just beyond the Arc de Triomphe, and drew steady, enthusiastic crowds. Buffalo Bill even posed for a large portrait by Rosa Bonheur seated astride his favorite white horse.

Added to all this was the fascination of the constant human parade, at the fair and up and down the avenues, a show many visitors enjoyed as much as anything.

Still, nothing about the exposition so symbolized its glamour, its theme of modern achievement and progress, or attracted such throngs through the entire event as the Eiffel Tower. As colorful as anything at the highly colorful fair, it had been painted five shades of red, from a dark, bronze-like color at the base to a golden yellow at the top. Few would have disagreed with the Boston correspondent who wrote that it deserved to be ranked with "the wonders of the world."

People stood for hours in long lines waiting their turns to go up. By the close of the fair, 1,968,287 tickets had been sold—at the equivalent of

40 cents to go to the first platform, 60 cents to the second—bringing in more than a million dollars, a sum equal to the entire cost of building the tower. Nor did this include profits from the popular restaurants on the first platform.

To the Americans who made the ascent it was a matter of no small import that the ride up to the first platform was made possible by the Otis Elevator Company of New York, by a device more like a steep mountain railway than an elevator.

While disdain for the tower did not disappear, it was greatly exceeded by resounding public approval, and nothing confirmed that quite so much as the blessing conferred by Edison. He had been up the tower several times before August 16 when he went still again to join a group of friends. During lunch at one of the restaurants, somebody at the table dismissed the tower as nothing more than the work of a builder. Edison at once objected. The tower was a "great idea," he said. "The glory of Eiffel is in the magnitude of the conception and the nerve in execution." He liked the French, he added. "They have big conceptions."

———

Among the wealthy, prominent New Yorkers in Paris that summer were Henry O. Havemeyer and his wife, the former Louisine Elder, and their three children. They had come for the fair but also on a serious mission to buy art. Henry—Harry, as his friends called him—was considered one of the brilliant entrepreneurs of the day, having newly organized the first American sugar trust and thereby rapidly increased an already large family fortune. He had now set about collecting paintings. He and Louisine both took a serious interest in art and in their new mansion under construction on Fifth Avenue, there would be ample walls to fill.

For Louisine a great part of the excitement of being back in Paris was the prospect of seeing Mary Cassatt again and introducing her husband.

The meeting was "indelibly graven" on her mind, Louisine would later write. She and Harry called at 10 rue de Marignan, where Mary, with her parents, had been living for two years, and found Mary confined to bed with a broken leg. "Her horse had slipped upon the pavement of the

Champs-Élysées and she sustained a fracture," Louisine wrote. Still, Mary was "very dear and cordial."

> It is difficult to express all that our companionship meant. It was at once friendly, intellectual, and artistic, and from the time we first met Miss Cassatt was our counselor and our guide.

Louisine announced that in the few days since arriving in Paris, she and Harry had already bought a landscape by Gustave Courbet. "What a man Courbet was!" Mary exclaimed in approval.

With Mary on the "lookout" for them, the Havemeyers were to buy the works of Renoir, Monet, Cézanne, Pissarro, and Degas, in addition to several by Cassatt herself.

Since the death of her sister Lydia in 1882, Mary's work had fallen off, her life become even more secluded. The move to a smaller apartment had been made because of her father's increasing lameness and her mother's sufferings from rheumatism and other ailments, and though Mary had kept her former studio, she often found herself in no mood to work.

There were financial worries besides. In an effort to help, Mary's brother Alexander sent occasional checks. Still, sales of her work became of increasing importance. "Mame has got to work again in her studio, but is not in good spirits at all. One of her gloomy spells," her father wrote at one point. "All artists, I believe, are subject to them."

He found her "lamentably deficient in good sense" about many things, and "unfortunately the more deficient she is the more her mother backs her up," he complained to Alexander. "It is the nature of women to make common cause against the males and to be especially stubborn in maintaining their opinions. . . . They try my patience to the last point of endurance sometimes. . . ."

Mary insisted they make a trip to London, to which he objected on the grounds that she was subject to dreadful seasickness. Besides, he had no wish to go anywhere. As he reported to Alexander afterward, Mary was so sick from crossing the Channel she had to be carried off the boat. "She is dreadfully headstrong. . . ."

For her part Mary told Alexander she was so worried about her mother and her headaches that she had no time for painting or anything, "and the constant anxiety takes the heart out of me." A long stay at Biarritz was tried for her mother's benefit, but to little effect.

The paintings Mary produced were, as before, almost exclusively of genteel women—*Lady at the Tea Table, Girl Arranging Her Hair.* An exception was a portrait of Alexander and his son Robert, painted in 1885 while they were visiting in France.

In 1886, when the French art dealer Paul Durand-Ruel arranged a first-ever Impressionist show in New York, some of her paintings were included with those by Degas, Manet, Monet, Pissarro, Morisot, and Renoir.

Nothing of hers was to be seen at the exposition, however, and with all that was being written and said about art at the time, her name rarely received mention.

But it was then, in 1889, the year of the exposition and her reunion with the Havemeyers, that Mary Cassatt took up the theme of mother-and-child, *maternité*, the subject that would occupy her for years and result in many of her finest, most-celebrated works.

Berthe Morisot had been painting mothers with children for ten years or more, since the birth of her own daughter. But Cassatt, who never had a child, embraced the theme heart-and-soul as few painters ever had. Much as when she first discovered Impressionism, she began to live again.

Of the six paintings John Sargent exhibited at the exposition, all portraits, that of the Boit daughters attracted by far the most attention. Groups of people continually clustered about it, and often returned to look again, drawn by its air of mystery, but also by its warmth and vitality.

Sargent was "easily the most distinguished and original of American artists abroad," wrote a critic for the *New York Times* reporting on the fair. "He does not know how to be commonplace or conventional."

For his works on display, Sargent, at age thirty-three, received one of the exhibition's gold medals and was made chevalier of the Légion d'Honneur. The fuss over *Madame X* seemed, like the uproar over the Eiffel Tower, to have largely disappeared.

For Sargent such tributes just then meant more than was generally understood. Earlier in the year, at Bournemouth, England, his father had died. As Vernon Lee wrote, FitzWilliam Sargent "had become a silent and broken old one, and the end had come slowly." John, who was seldom ever ill and not known to have much patience with those who were, stayed faithfully with him, looked after him the whole while. "I can never forget," she wrote, "the loving tenderness with which, the day's work over, John would lead his father from the dinner table and sit alone with him till it was time to be put to bed."

Meanwhile, happily, the work he was engaged in, another ambitious portrait, offered a perfect chance to paint as freely and as much from the heart as he ever had.

He had been to see the opening night of *Macbeth* in London, with the great English actors Henry Irving and Ellen Terry in the leading roles. At the moment when Ellen Terry first appeared on stage, Sargent was heard to exclaim quietly, "I say!"

She wore a long flowing robe of dazzling green, blue, and gold and it was thus that Sargent painted her, at her crowning moment in the tragedy, literally lifting a gold diadem over her head. He felt deeply the infinite power of music, books, and great theater, and at his best, in his most serious work, he strove to express his own deepest emotions about life.

He chose a large canvas—interestingly it was almost exactly the same dimensions as his *Madame X*—and he rendered Ellen Terry's powdered face in shades nearly as deathly pale. But here there was no labored reworking of the paint. He put it on with his natural flair, in swift, sure strokes and dashes, and with greatest pleasure obviously in her sense of show. There was no holding back. She had been on the stage since age nine and was at the height of her career, as the gold crown suggested. And he and she both wanted that to be apparent.

The painting, his only literally theatrical work, left no doubt of Sargent's love of her artistry in that powerful moment in the play—her moment—in addition to his own power.

The brilliance of the work was recognized at once. It went on exhibit in London in May of 1889, at the New Gallery. The critic for the London *Times* said that to stand before it was "to enter a new world altogether."

The painter has deliberately chosen a costume which taxes his power to the uttermost . . . and a moment when the intensity of the emotions displayed might well daunt the boldest attempt in art to realize them. . . . The face is pallid as death and on it the artist has striven to express the meeting point and clash of two supreme emotions of ambition and of the sense of crime accomplished and moral law thrown down.

It was, said *The Times*, certain to be the most discussed painting of the year, and "without exception the most ambitious picture of our time."

CHAPTER FOURTEEN

AU REVOIR, PARIS!

But coming here has been a wonderful experience, surprising in many respects, one of them being to find how much of an American I am.

—AUGUSTUS SAINT-GAUDENS

I

No particular notice was taken of the small elderly gentleman strolling with the younger woman on the rue de la Paix and in the garden of the Palais Royal. No heads turned, no one responded to his characteristic smile with a sign of recognition.

At home in Boston everybody knew who he was. In London in recent weeks, he had been a center of attention at grand dinners, warmly greeted by the prime minister, dukes and earls and literary notables like Robert Browning and Oscar Wilde. He had been given a party by the Royal College of Surgeons and received honorary degrees from all three of Britain's greatest centers of learning: Oxford, Cambridge, and Edinburgh.

But in the Paris he so loved, he knew "not a soul" and no one knew him. As he would write, "Our most intimate relations were with the people of the hotel," and given his amiable outlook, this was perfectly acceptable.

At the peak of summer 1886, seventy-seven-year-old Oliver Wendell Holmes, Sr., had returned to Europe accompanied by his widowed daughter, Amelia, on what he called a "Rip Van Winkle experiment," a trip he had long promised himself. Fifty years earlier, he had left the France of Louis-Philippe and François Guizot. Now nearly all his Boston comrades from those earlier Paris days, his fellow "medicals," fellow poets and authors, were gone. Mason Warren, Charles Sumner, Ralph Waldo Emerson, even Thomas Appleton and Henry Longfellow, were all dead. Of those close companions who had sat with him through lectures by Dupuytren or followed the legendary Dr. Louis on his hospital rounds, only Henry Bowditch remained.

The only familiar faces to be seen now in Paris were in paintings at the Louvre, though at first nothing was to be found where he looked for it, so extensively had things been rearranged. "But when I found them, they greeted me, so I fancied, like old acquaintances. The meek-looking 'Belle Jardinière' was as lamb-like as ever. . . . Titian's young man with the glove was the calm, self-contained gentleman I used to admire."

He and Amelia were in Paris for a week only. While she did some shopping, he walked the old neighborhood of the École de Médecine, pleased to find the house where he lived on the rue Monsieur-le-Prince unchanged except for a shop on the street level. Tempted to go inside and make inquiries, he decided against it. "What would the shopkeeper know about M. Bertrand, my landlord of half a century ago; or his first wife, to whose funeral I went; or his second, to whose bridal I was bidden?"

From the rue Monsieur-le-Prince, Holmes made the short walk to the Panthéon, not, he explained, to pay homage to it as a "sacred edifice" or the final resting place of great men, but to see León Foucault's famous pendulum. "I was thinking much more of Foucault's grand experiment, one of the most sublime visible demonstrations of a great physical fact in the records of science." And there it was, a heavy weight swinging slowly back and forth from a wire reaching nearly three hundred feet to the dome overhead, proving, as its direction appeared to change, the rotation of the earth.

Only one man did Dr. Holmes hope to meet while in Paris, and this he resolved by going on his own initiative to the office of Louis Pasteur at 14 rue Vauquelin to pay an unannounced call.

"I sent my card in . . . and presently he came out and greeted me. I told him I was an American physician who wished to look in his face and take his hand—nothing more."

Reflecting later on the great changes he had seen as a result of French strides in science since he was a student in Paris, Holmes wrote that the stethoscope was almost a novelty in those days, the microscope never even mentioned by any clinical instructor he had had.

It was not just that the world of his student days was long past, or that he and his American contemporaries had all but disappeared, but that American medical students in Paris now numbered relatively few. Due in good part to what he and others had brought back from Paris, medical education in the United States had so greatly advanced that study in Paris was not necessarily an advantage any longer. Those who were ambitious to excel in clinical medicine or surgery could get superb training at home.

It being summer, much of Paris was characteristically quiet, and at night Holmes found himself too tired to go to the theater or the opera.

But there was joy still in seeing the beautiful bridges on the Seine. "Nothing looked more nearly the same as of old than the bridges," he wrote. The Pont Neuf looked not the least different to him and evoked all the good feelings of old.

Stopping at the Café Procope, once his favorite for breakfast, he thought it much improved in appearance. He sat contentedly over a cup of coffee, daydreaming of Voltaire and the other luminaries of the far past who had gathered there.

"But what to me were these shadowy figures by the side of the group of my early friends and companions that came up before me in all the freshness of their young manhood?" He need never chase off to Florida in search of Ponce de León's fountain of youth, Holmes decided. It was here. In Paris.

———

Three years after Holmes's visit—at the time of the 1889 exposition— Augustus Saint-Gaudens, too, returned to Paris, and his stay was also short. Apparently he came alone, and he wrote nothing of a wish to see the fair or anyone in particular, only that he was "desirous of returning in what measure I could to my student life and environment."

He appears to have kept largely to himself, staying not at a hotel, but in "a little box of a room" on the Left Bank, in the studio apartment of a friend and former assistant, sculptor Frederick MacMonnies. Of his impressions of Paris, he mentioned no more than its "monumental largeness." As for his opinions on the fair, he said only that they were "too complex and result in so much vanity that I'll modestly refrain. . . ."

What seems to have made the most lasting impression was a scene he observed the first morning in the small garden below his window in the "box." From the door of a studio opening onto the garden came a man of about his own age, "an old chap," in dressing gown and slippers and smoking a pipe.

> He trudged along in among the paths over to one particular flowerbed which was evidently his little property, and with great care watered the flowers with a diminutive watering pot. Soon after another codger appeared in another door, in trousers and slippers. He also fussed and shuffled in his little plot.

Such "codgers" could well be the very comrades of his youth at the Beaux-Arts, he thought, and here they were in the midst of crowded, bustling Paris so contentedly cultivating their flower gardens, "the blue smoke from their pipes of peace rising philosophically among the greenery, in harmony with it all." He envied that harmony and their contentment.

It would be said in the family that Saint-Gaudens had made the trip in 1889 out of a "deeply felt need" to see what was being done in Paris, "thereby widening his artistic horizon." This may have been true. But there was more to the explanation. He had his own private reasons, as would come to light later.

———

Great numbers of aspiring American artists, sculptors, and architects kept arriving in the city all the while, and among them several who, in the future, were to figure prominently in the arts at home.

Maurice Prendergast, the son of a Boston grocer, had crossed the Atlantic in a cattle boat to enroll in the Académie Julian in 1891. John White Alexander was in his thirties when he and his wife settled in Paris the same year. In very little time his large, strikingly composed paintings of beautiful young women in elegant settings were to have wide recognition.

James Earle Fraser had spent most of his boyhood on a ranch in South Dakota. His father was a railroad engineer. The talented young man had come to study sculpture at the École des Beaux-Arts, where he would later be "discovered" by Saint-Gaudens.

Henry O. Tanner was tall, cultivated, and the only African-American at the Académie Julian. The son of a minister in the African Method-ist Episcopal Church, he had been born in Pittsburgh. At the Pennsyl-vania Academy of the Fine Arts in Philadelphia, where he studied under Thomas Eakins, he had been the lone black student. He, too, sailed from America in 1891, but intended only to stop briefly in Paris before going on to study in Rome. As he wrote, "Strange that after having been in Paris a week, I should find conditions so to my liking that I completely forgot . . . my plans to study in Rome. . . ."

In a café on the Left Bank, on one of his first mornings in Paris, Tanner met Robert Henri for the first time. They found they had the Pennsylvania Academy in common and a friendship began. "He's modest . . . not in the opinion that he is a big man, so he will get on," wrote Henri, who helped give Tanner "a start" at the Académie Julian.

Tanner's expenses were being covered by patrons at home, a white American minister and his wife named Hartzwell, and by a $75 commis-sion he had received before setting sail. His total expenses the first year in Paris would come to $365, as he carefully recorded. In addition to having little money, he spoke no French.

Never had he seen or heard such bedlam as at the Académie, Tanner was to write in a lively chronicle of his student experiences. Nor had he ever tried to see or breathe in such a smoke-shrouded room.

> Never were windows opened. They were nailed fast at the be-
> ginning of the cold season. Fifty or sixty men smoking in such
> a room for two or three hours would make it so that those in
> the back rows could hardly see the model.

At no time was he made to feel unwanted or inferior because of his color, which had not always been so in Philadelphia. Only in some restaurants did he know he was unwelcome, but that, he knew, was because he did not drink wine. "In the cheap restaurants to which I went, they did not care to serve one unless one took wine—they made little or no profit on the food. . . . I was thus an undesirable customer and several times forced to change my restaurant."

The occasional appearance of students' parents in Paris was not uncommon. The chance to see the new life their offspring were leading, and enjoy a bit of Paris themselves, was all but irresistible if one could afford it, and the effect of the experience could be profound.

William Dean Howells, the novelist and former editor of the *Atlantic Monthly*, whose son John was studying architecture at the École des Beaux-Arts, had been enjoying himself thoroughly, buoyed by the spirit of Paris and the chance to catch up with old friends like James McNeill Whistler, whose part-time residence on the rue du Bac had become something of a rendezvous for visiting Americans of like mind and interests. But then at a gathering in Whistler's garden, Howells was seen standing alone, uncharacteristically downcast. He had just received word that he must return home. His father was dying.

Sensing something was wrong, a younger American came over to speak with him. Suddenly, Howells turned and put his hand on the young man's shoulder and said, "Oh, you are young, you are young—be glad of it and *live*."

> Live all you can. It's a mistake not to. It doesn't matter what
> you do—but live. This place makes it all come over me. I see
> it now. I haven't done so—and now I'm old. It's too late. It has
> gone past me—I've lost it. You have time. You are young. Live!

Some years later the young man, Jonathan Sturges, told the story to Henry James, stressing the intensity with which Howells had spoken. It became the germ of another James novel set in Paris, *The Ambassadors*, in which the main character, in an outburst, delivers the same message in almost exactly the same words.

In the spacious comforts of the home that he and Louisa had established on the rue de la Rochefoucauld twenty years before, George Healy had begun slowing down. He still went out to his studio part of every day, still walked down to the Church of the Holy Trinity to hear daily mass, though on the uphill walk home he moved considerably more slowly than he once had.

His large family was Healy's delight. A note in his diary at Christmastime, 1891, reads:

> My grandson, Georges De Mare, came to the studio to say they are waiting for me. The Christmas tree was all lighted up; about fifty children crowded around it, joy reflected in their faces; the parlors filled with people. Indeed, it was the loveliest picture one could see.

Healy was the last one left in Paris of those aspiring young Americans who had sailed to France filled with such high hopes in the 1830s. It had been nearly fifty-seven years since he set off from Boston with scarcely any money, knowing no French and knowing no one in Paris.

His love for the city was greater than ever. But for all the years he had lived there, he never thought of himself as anything other than an American. "His love of France and the French never changed him from an out-and-out American," a granddaughter, Marie De Mare, would write.

In 1892, Healy decided it was time to go. In March he and Louisa sailed for home, to spend their remaining years in Chicago.

II

The Augustus Saint-Gaudens who arrived in Paris again in October of 1897 for an indefinite stay was by almost any measure a stunning example not only of success, but of persistent hard work and great talent justly recognized and rewarded. At age fifty-one, he was America's preeminent sculptor, honored, revered by colleagues, repeatedly in demand for projects of national importance. Consequently, too, he had become wealthy. His finest work, it seemed certain, would stand down the years as some of the highest achievements of American art.

Since the unveiling of his Farragut in New York in 1880, he had never been without work. For a public park in Springfield, Massachusetts, he had done *The Puritan*, a striding, heroic figure in bronze that seemed to embody all the courage and purpose of seventeenth-century New England Protestant fervor.

A pensive, standing Lincoln unveiled in 1887 in Chicago's Lincoln Park captured as no work of sculpture yet had the depth of mind of the Great Emancipator.

In Rock Creek Cemetery in Washington sat the hooded figure of the Adams Memorial, Saint-Gaudens's most enigmatic, mysterious creation, and the subject of never-ending speculation about its meaning.

In contrast were the *Amor Caritas*, a magnificent winged angel for a funerary monument raising a tablet over her head, and his beautiful *Diana*, the archer, the only nude he ever rendered, which stood thirteen feet high atop the tower of New York's new thirty-two-story Madison Square Garden, designed by Stanford White.

Greatest of all, many felt, was another Civil War monument, this at Boston, which for the first time portrayed African-Americans as heroes. The Shaw Memorial, a giant bronze frieze, set at the edge of the Boston Common opposite the Massachusetts State House, commemorated the bravery and sacrifice of the Fifty-Fourth Massachusetts Regiment, the first black unit in the Union Army, most of whose members, including Colonel Robert Gould Shaw, were killed in a frontal attack on Fort Wagner in Charleston Harbor in 1863.

The positioning of Shaw on horseback moving forward with his marching men, the unflinching look in their faces and distinct individuality of each face, had a total effect beyond that of any memorial in the nation.

Saint-Gaudens had never taken such infinite pains with a work. It preoccupied him over a span of fourteen years before he was satisfied. Commissioned in 1884, it was not unveiled until May 31, 1897.

Presenting him with an honorary degree that spring, the president of Harvard, Charles Eliot, had said: "Augustus Saint-Gaudens—a sculptor whose art follows and ennobles nature, enforces fame and lasting remembrance, and does not count the mortal years it takes to mold immortal fame."

Between times, he had produced numerous relief portraits of Robert Louis Stevenson, Cornelius Vanderbilt, the artists William Merritt Chase and Kenyon Cox, his son Homer Saint-Gaudens, and John Singer Sargent's sister Violet, one of the loveliest of all his reliefs, in which she sits strumming a guitar and for which Sargent, in return, painted a portrait of young Homer with his mother.

For a while, Saint-Gaudens taught at the Art Students League in New York. He served as an advisor on sculpture for the Columbian Exposition at Chicago in 1893, and along with Sargent and Edwin Abbey, he agreed to help with the sculpture and murals for a magnificent new Boston Public Library to be located opposite Trinity Church on Copley Plaza. Charles McKim was the architect. His inspiration for the building had been the Bibliothèque Sainte-Geneviève in Paris.

More recently, as a kind of capstone to Saint-Gaudens's major contributions to the memory of the Civil War, New York City had commissioned an equestrian statue of General William Tecumseh Sherman to stand at Fifth Avenue and 59th Street by the entrance to Central Park, and work on it was under way.

By the late 1890s Saint-Gaudens was operating four studios in New York. He and Gussie were living in considerable style at a new address on West 45th Street and had purchased a country home in Cornish, New Hampshire.

So it came as a shock when suddenly, with so much going on, he announced they were moving to Paris, and that work on the Sherman would continue there.

"I suppose through overwork I had become nervous and completely disaffected with America," he would later offer in explanation. Nothing would "right things" but "getting away from the infernal noise, dirt, and confusion" of New York. Worst on his nerves was the unending din outside his main studio at 36th and Broadway:

> . . . with the elevated road discharging oil on the persons be-
> neath, the maddening electric cars adding their music, the
> ambulance wagons tearing by, jangling their diabolic gongs
> in order that the moribund inside may die in the spirit of
> the surroundings, and the occasional frantic fire engine rac-
> ing through it all with bells clanging, fire, smoke, hell, and
> cinders.

More besides his own troubles beset him. Gussie had suffered a miscarriage in 1885. His father had died after a prolonged struggle. And so
had his friend Robert Louis Stevenson, of tuberculosis, at age forty-four.

The Scottish writer had come to matter greatly to Saint-Gaudens.
Stevenson's books, beginning with *New Arabian Nights*, had set him
"aflame," and during five sittings for a relief portrait, as the ailing Stevenson lay propped in bed in a hotel room in New York, writing and smoking
a cigarette, they had talked steadily on all manner of subjects. Saint-
Gaudens brought young Homer to meet the famous author, and would
eventually do numerous reliefs and medallions of him.

Brother Louis Saint-Gaudens, still a mainstay for Gus, suffered a nervous breakdown as a result, Louis said, of "the high pressure tension" at
the studio. "So Augustus went [on] to more and greater glories, and Louis
went to a sanitarium," Louis would write. But then Augustus, too, said
Louis, began to "show the strain of his heroic labors. . . ."

That he had, indeed, become seriously depressed, Saint-Gaudens acknowledged. "But I was sick," in a "deplorable mental condition," "miserably blue," he would write. And Gussie had been suffering in the same way.

The medical term in fashion was "neurasthenia," its symptoms described as "mental irritability" and "morbid fear" often experienced by
"gentlemen of middle life," insomnia, "dyspepsia"—all brought on by nervous exhaustion.

> *A Feeling of Profound Exhaustion* [reads a contemporary med-
> ical text] . . . Attacks of a sensation of absolute exhaustion, as
> though the body had not strength to hold together. . . . This
> feeling of exhaustion, though not exactly pain in the usual

sense of the word, is yet, in many cases, far worse than pain.
These attacks may come on suddenly without warning. . . .
The *going-to-die* feeling is quite common in these cases. . . .

The definition given a century later would be "a syndrome marked by ready fatigability of body and mind usually by worrying and depression. . . ."

In photographs taken about the time he returned to Paris, Saint-Gaudens appears truly exhausted. He looks almost haunted, and older than his age. Always thin, he had become gaunt. There was more gray in his thick head of hair and the short beard had turned nearly white. William Dean Howells was to describe him as having the face of "a weary lion."

His son Homer would later say that New York had taken its toll, that his father had been "crippled for the remainder of his life by the ardor of his work." But, Homer insisted, his father's sickness was not what had taken him back to Paris.

> Quite on the contrary, it was his knowledge that his art had
> reached its strength . . . [and] in Paris alone he could measure
> himself with his contemporaries, place his work before the
> world's most critical audience, and learn, once for all, wherein
> it was good and wherein bad.

Doubtless all this was valid, and from much he said later, there is no question that Saint-Gaudens agreed. But it would appear, too, that the burden of the very success he had achieved, and the added complications and responsibilities such success brought with it, had become too much for him.

At some point early in the 1880s—it may have been after the triumph of the Farragut monument—Saint-Gaudens began having an affair with the stunning young Swedish model who had posed for the nude *Diana* and probably for the *Amor Caritas* as well. She was Albertina Hulgren but went by the name Davida Clark.

Relatively little is known about her, but in the summer of 1889, she had a baby, a boy, whom she named Louis, and this, it would seem, had something to do with Saint-Gaudens heading off to Paris that same summer. After his return, he established a separate ménage for her and the child in Noroton, Connecticut, and it is believed he provided support for the child thereafter.

It has been speculated that Gussie found out soon afterward, but no one knows. The only supposed details of the affair came nearly fifty years after Saint-Gaudens's death, from a woman in New Hampshire named Frances Grimes, who was then ninety-two. She had been an assistant to and reputed confidante of the sculptor late in his life and told a local newspaperman that Saint-Gaudens had had "many affairs," but that in the case of Davida he was "madly in love." How much of what she said was valid, how much the imaginings of a very old woman, is impossible to know. It is clear, however, that her claim that Gus and Gussie no longer lived together after Gussie learned of the affair is wholly mistaken.

With age Gussie's deafness and the sense of isolation it brought became an increasing handicap. Her battles with poor health and depression were equal, if not greater, than his own. She suffered back pains and, with her deafness, an almost constant ringing in her ears. Some people found her difficult to like, as Stanford White had in Paris years before, and attributed her ailments to hypochondria. But Saint-Gaudens is not known ever to have written or said a critical word about her.

She began spending much of her time away from home, traveling to health spas in places like Nova Scotia and Bermuda, whether for her health only or for relief from the strains of their marriage is again not clear. Probably it was both.

Long adamant about keeping personal matters private, Saint-Gaudens became even more so. His infidelity was not a subject about which he was proud. That some of his circle, like Frederick MacMonnies and Stanford White, both of whom were married, were known as "ladies' men" and seemed to enjoy talk of their philandering, Saint-Gaudens found repellent.

His and Gussie's marriage was badly shaken. Assuredly she felt a dreadful sense of betrayal and loss. And he suffered as well, from regret and self-reproach over his failings and the hurt he had inflicted on her. He loved her still, as he told her in an undated, heartfelt note. It is the only surviving, authentic evidence of what they were going through.

> Sweetness and kindness in women is what appeals mostly to men and a blessed charity for human failings makes one well loved. The quiet dignity of Mrs. MacMonnies and Mrs. White for the gross action of their husbands is far finer and commands a deeper respect than any other attitude they could possibly have taken, and way down their husbands respect them all the more. Although my action is a mere peccadillo in comparison to others, it has caused me a misery of mind you do not dream of.
>
> You are a noble woman, Gussie, and I love, admire, and respect you more than you have any conception of. We are both sick and for our mutual peace of mind on this earth I beg you not to come down from the high place you hold in my heart.
>
> Gus

Love and courage were "the great things" in life, he felt. That he saw both in her there is no doubt.

In October of 1897, a memorial fund in Chicago agreed to pay Saint-Gaudens $100,000 for another Lincoln statue and provided a substantial advance. That same month he, Gussie, and Homer left for Paris.

They found a suitable apartment off the Champs-Élysées. Homer was enrolled in a Paris *lycée*, to prepare for Harvard, and, after a "maddening" search up and down the Left Bank, Gus found the studio he wanted at 3 rue de Bagneux near the Luxembourg Gardens and his old studio on the rue Notre-Dame-des-Champs. He called it one of those "out-of-the-way corners of Paris the mere existence of which makes life worth living."

Any thought he may have entertained of finding peace of mind in Paris, or in such tranquil pleasures as watering flowers—as once he imagined while watching the old "codgers" in their gardens—was not to be. It was not in him. He had much work to do on his Sherman, assistants to hire, equipment to assemble.

It was to be a colossal statue representing Sherman on horseback at the head of his army and led by a winged goddess of Victory, holding a palm branch. Sherman would be bareheaded and wearing a cloak. Horse, rider, and goddess would all be gilded and stand thirteen feet tall.

On Sherman's march "from Atlanta to the sea," in late 1864, more than 60,000 Union troops crossed Georgia destroying towns, plantations, railroads, factories, virtually everything in their path for three hundred miles. Twenty-four years later, Sherman, who by then was living in New York and with only a few years left, agreed to more than a dozen sittings as Saint-Gaudens sculpted a bust to serve as a study for the larger work.

Seen up close, the finished head was not easy to look at. Grim, whiskered, and pockmarked, it seemed the very image of the horrors of war. It could have been the face of a madman.

Saint-Gaudens hated war, despised what it did to people. Sherman agreed. "I am tired and sick of war. Its glory is all moonshine. . . . War is hell," Sherman had said in a widely publicized speech.

Several busts and studies of Victory had also been done in New York prior to Saint-Gaudens's departure for Paris. The young woman who posed for him was a twenty-four-year-old model named Hettie Anderson from South Carolina, whom he described as "the handsomest model I have ever seen. . . ." Few were to know that she was an African-American, but for Saint-Gaudens and the others who did, it must have seemed especially fitting that she be the one to lead the triumphant Union commander on his way.

Her youth and beauty, as Saint-Gaudens sculpted her, are unmistakable, and particularly in contrast to the face of Sherman. But there is no joy, no gleam of triumph or glory in her expression. Her eyes are wide, her mouth open, as if she were under a spell.

For the horse Saint-Gaudens had chosen as his model a famous, powerful, high-jumper of the day named Ontario. To give power to the work, he knew, he must embody the power of the horse.

In Paris he began the full-size group, and for sufficient space for a work of such scale, he had taken over not one but three adjoining ateliers at

3 rue de Bagneux, knocked out the walls between two of them for the main studio, leaving the third for himself. Eventually he would have a crew of fifteen on the job.

Good fortune came with the addition of a highly gifted Beaux-Arts student in sculpture, James Earle Fraser, the young man who had grown up on a South Dakota ranch. He had come to Paris with a small statue of his own called *End of the Trail* of a "spent Indian brave" slumped on his pony. Seeing it, Saint-Gaudens told him, "You haven't done a man. You've done a race," and immediately offered him a job.

Homer Saint-Gaudens would later write that the "state of turmoil" at the studio became "only too like" what it had been in New York, and "constant."

In addition to the Sherman, Saint-Gaudens was working on another version of the *Amor Caritas*, which stood against one wall. He had no aversion to doing the same subject many times over, striving always for something stronger. "I make seventeen models for each statue I create," he once said.

Friends kept coming by for visits, and just as in New York and in former days in Paris, he would feel obliged to stop what he was doing. The new assistant, Fraser, would remember tiny James Whistler appearing at the door in top hat and long coat, and how "being a dominating little character," he made it impossible for Saint-Gaudens to work just when work was most needed.

John Singer Sargent stopped to talk about the murals for the Boston Public Library that he was painting in London. "He is a big fellow," Saint-Gaudens wrote of Sargent, "and what is, I'm inclined to think, a great deal more, a *good* fellow."

Gussie seems to have come and gone often, as she had at home, traveling to health spas at St. Moritz, Aix-les-Bains, and elsewhere. From the relatively few surviving letters between them, it is difficult to know where she was or how extended were her absences. But write they did, continuously, and nearly always assuring one another of their affection. (As Homer Saint-Gaudens would explain, "the entire collection of the most vital letters" between his mother and father was lost in a studio fire in New Hampshire in 1904.)

Gus continued to suffer spells of severe gloom, his "blue fits," and especially in winter. But they would pass. "I am feeling very well now," and the Sherman was progressing "very well," he reported to her early in 1898. "Lovingly, Gus," he closed the letter, "for I love you more than you think or than I ever express."

With the arrival of spring he felt better than ever, and the work went better. Paris was having exactly the effect he had hoped for.

"This Paris experience, as far as my art goes, has been a great thing for me," he wrote to a favorite niece, Rose Nichols, the daughter of Gussie's sister Eugenie. "All blindness seems to have washed away. I see my place clearly now." Great was his longing to "achieve high things."

As progress on the full-size statue went forward in the large studio, Saint-Gaudens concentrated on small studies and other details in his own adjoining space. He could hear through the wall the clamor of the crew at work, and they, on his good days, could hear him singing as in his student years. He still had a "magnificent voice," James Fraser would remember. "I believe he could have gone on to the Metropolitan in the baritone or bass parts of Faust and given a very good account of himself."

Late that summer, in a long letter addressed to "Dear old Fellow," Saint-Gaudens told Will Low that coming back to Paris had been a "wonderful experience," and surprising in many respects, one of which was "to find how much of an American I am."

"I belong in America," he continued, "that is my home. . . ." So much that he had found unbearable about New York was exactly what he longed for now. He was unabashedly homesick.

> . . . the elevated road dropping oil and ashes on the idiot below, the cable cars, the telegraph poles, the skyline, and all that have become dear to me, to say nothing of attractive friends, the scenery, the smell of the earth, the peculiar smell of America. . . .

"Up to my visit here I felt as if I was working in a fog. I knew not 'where I was at.' This is dispelled, and I see now my ground clearly."

I have acquired a strange feeling of confidence that I never
have felt before (and which, oh, irony, may mean that I am
losing ground), and together with a respect for what we are
doing at home. In fact, I shall return a burning hot-headed
patriot.

But then he added, "What a place this is over here, though, seductive
as a beautiful woman with her smile. I suppose when I get back, I shall
want to return again!"

The letter was dated September 2, 1898. Just ten days later he was writing again to Rose Nichols, but this time about "a feeling of weariness at
this life of work," and again on September 23, after working "late in the
gloom," he said it was "too sad in this big studio with the lamp flinging
great shadows on the walls."

Life went on to the full, he reported to Gussie at the start of the
new year, although he had had, he admitted, "another of those fearful
depressions . . . so much that I felt I would cry at any moment." Another
day he claimed to be feeling "like a fighting cock."

Next he became convinced he was seriously ill, until a physician assured him he had had only a light attack of neurasthenia, and that there
was nothing the matter with his heart. His gloom faded still more with
the passing of winter and the coming of spring.

"I had come to appreciate Paris in a way I never dreamed of in the
heyday of my youth," he would remember. "Paris in the spring is wonderful. There are two or three weeks when the pride and joy of life is at
its full there as it is nowhere else. The people appreciate life more than
we do."

The pressure of the work increased steadily. A plaster cast of the horse and
rider was to be exhibited at the Salon, and the turmoil inside the studio on
the rue de Bagneux was no less than in former days in New York.

Seeing the giant horse and its rider emerge in full size gave the sculptor cause for reconsidering one thing after another. Nothing satisfied. He

needed to change first this, then that. Months earlier Sherman's cloak had been the issue. "Your father . . . is beginning the Sherman cloak all over again and I have been making lots of little cloaks," Gussie had written to Homer. The cloak was still troubling him, and the fact that others said it was perfectly fine as it was mattered not at all.

Once Farragut's leg had been his bête noire. Now the left hind leg on the plaster horse was broken by accident. Saint-Gaudens sent a man to New York to make a duplicate from the clay original and bring it back as quickly as possible. The man returned with the wrong leg.

In a letter to Homer, he later described the "insane asylum" atmosphere at 3 rue de Bagneux in the days leading up to the Salon. "Eleven moulders, some of them working all night with the boss lunatic, your illustrious father, at their head. Whew!!! Sometimes I'd cry, then I'd laugh, then I'd do both together, then I'd rush out into the street and howl and so on."

By late April the statue was ready and in position at the Salon on the Champ de Mars. Its placement was more than Saint-Gaudens could have hoped for, at the very center of the garden. "The Sherman is in the place of honor," he told Gussie. "I am so tickled that I am ready to dance a jig at any time of the day or night."

Feeling a need to get away, he and Gussie went off on a trip to Spain.

———

Among those expressing approval of the Sherman and Victory was the renowned American historian Henry Adams, who was so taken by it that he stopped nearly every day for another look. But then Adams's feelings about the sculptor were like those of no one else, because of what Saint-Gaudens had achieved with the Adams Memorial.

It had been their mutual friend John La Farge who had urged Adams to commission Saint-Gaudens to make the statue in memory of Adams's wife, Clover, following her suicide in Washington in 1885. Suffering from depression, she had swallowed potassium cyanide, the chemical she used for retouching photographs.

At a meeting with Saint-Gaudens in New York, Adams had given the sculptor a general idea of what he had in mind for the monument, where-upon Saint-Gaudens is said to have seated a young assistant on a stand and thrown an Indian rug over his head.

Adams requested that the figure be neither conspicuously male or fe-male. He wanted it to convey complete repose and he wanted no name or anything inscribed on it. Lastly, he had no wish to see it until it was finished. He then left on extended tours of Japan and the Pacific Islands, taking La Farge with him as a companion.

Upon seeing the monument for the first time, after its installation at Rock Creek Cemetery, Adams was entirely satisfied. "The whole meaning and feeling of the figure is in its universality and anonymity," he wrote. His name for it was *The Peace of God.*

Adams had been coming to Paris much of his life and professed to dislike it. Yet one way and another he managed to return often. This time, staying at the Hotel Brighton on the rue de Rivoli, he found Paris surpris-ingly to his liking. Several American friends were in town, and most days were taken up with buying books, reading, and making notes for a new project on medieval cathedrals. Not even the heat of summer appeared to bother him.

"Paris delights me," he wrote to his friend John Hay, the American ambassador to the Court of St. James's, "but not for its supposed delights. It is the calm of its seclusion that charms . . . the cloister-like peace that it brings on in the closing years of life. I reflect on the goodness of all things. . . ."

Pleased to learn Saint-Gaudens was in Paris, Adams invited him to dine, even "risked" going to Saint-Gaudens's studio "to draw him out for a stroll" in the Bois de Boulogne.

Adams was ten years older than Saint-Gaudens and, at five feet four, a good six inches shorter. Where Saint-Gaudens's thick head of hair re-mained a distinguishing feature, Adams was, as he said, "very—very bald." They made a distinctive pair when seen together, quite apart from the fact that one was the descendant of American presidents and diplomats, the other the son of an immigrant shoemaker.

That the sculptor was, for all his great talent, "most inarticulate" when discussing his work utterly fascinated Adams, and especially when he considered the other artists with whom Saint-Gaudens consorted.

> All the others—the Hunts, Richardson, John La Farge, Stanford White—were exuberant [Adams wrote]; only Saint-Gaudens could never discuss or debate on an emotion, or suggest artistic arguments for giving to his work the forms that he felt.

Such simplicity of thought was "excessive," Adams decided, though he did recognize that the sculptor's health was poor, his spirits low that summer, and that he, Adams, who suffered his own spells of *ennui*, may not have been the ideal companion for him.

That Saint-Gaudens sensed what Adams found wanting in him is suggested in a letter he wrote to Gussie, who had gone home to Boston to be with her dying mother.

He had been tearing up his old letters, he told her, so "inane" did they seem. The only "readable" parts he found were in her handwriting. "Evidently I must content myself with expression in bronze. That makes me mad for we always wish for what is around the corner out of reach."

But in a letter to Will Low he showed no hesitation about expressing his feelings, going on at length about his love of France, but also said he intended to remain in Paris only until the 1900 exposition.

He confided, too, that he had been "very sick" and knew now the meaning of nervous prostration. "It is fearful, and I pity from the bottom of my heart many whom I had looked upon before as possessing a *maladie imaginaire.*"

From a surviving note in his hand to his brother Louis, it is also known that his mistress, Davida Clark, had come to Paris with their son, Louis, and that she did not like France and wanted to go home. But how long she had been there, whether she had come of her own accord or at his request, where she was staying, or when she and the boy left, there is no telling.

Gussie arrived back in Paris on November 12.

> Your father is about the same, perhaps less nervous than when I went away, and he is still poking about on the Victory [she wrote to Homer], so that even the studio is very little changed. . . . I have been here four days and have been three times to the bronze founders at Mont Rouge, so you can see I have little time for anything else. . . .

"Your father has been made a member of the Institut de France," she reported again to Homer two weeks later. "It is a very great honor, higher than the Legion of Honor . . . a *much* greater honor.

"Your father sends a great [deal] of love and hopes you are getting [on] well in every way. He only *signs* his letters now. I write even to White, McKim . . . and the like. . . ."

The main concentration at 3 rue de Bagneux was on the fine points of the "big" Sherman. Inevitably, there was further trouble with the horse's upraised left hind leg, which kept sagging, even as Saint-Gaudens's assistants kept plugging the cracks. When he said it looked as if it might be out of proportion, they assured him everything was as it should be. He insisted he was right. A measurement was taken and the leg was found to be three inches too long. So more work was required.

Between times he had begun studies for a group of figures for the entrance to the Boston Public Library, a project for which his brother Louis had also been recruited.

Louis was to create two large marble lions to stand guard on a grand marble stairway inside the main entrance. He had been working off and on for Gus in Paris, still battling depression and alcoholism. But his talents were great, as no one appreciated more than Gus, who counted on him and continued to stand by him.

His own principal preoccupation at the studio had become the finishing touches on the figure of Victory, upon which, he felt, the effect of the entire work depended. And at long last, as he wrote to Gussie, he was "on the homestretch with Victory."

Late in October, feeling the need again for a break, Saint-Gaudens invited two French friends to go with him on a visit to the famous cathedral at Amiens, north of Paris on the Somme River. He wanted especially to see the statues on the doorways of the west front, which were considered among the greatest of all Gothic sculpture.

Knowing Henry Adams's interest in the subject, he invited him to join them. He had come to quite like Adams for all his prickly manner and obvious disdain for a large portion of humanity. Adams openly disliked much about his own country, just at the time when Saint-Gaudens was feeling more of a patriot than ever. Adams loathed bankers, robber barons, and the crass, boorish politicians he observed all about him in Washington. He was anti-Semitic, though he would get over that with time. But those who knew him knew how much heart and kindness were beneath the surface, and the brilliance of mind. Later, in a caricature relief, Saint-Gaudens would portray Adams as a porcupine—"Porcupine Poeticus"—to illustrate the "outward gruffness and inner gentleness" of the man.

More than a hundred years earlier, alone at a desk in Paris, Adams's great-grandfather, John Adams, had written for those at home a statement of his purpose in life that had come down in the family as a kind of summons:

> I must study politics and war that my sons may have the liberty to study mathematics and philosophy. My sons ought to study mathematics and philosophy, geography, natural history, naval architecture, navigation, commerce, and agriculture in order to give their children a right to study paintings, poetry, music, architecture, statuary, tapestry, and porcelain.

For his part Henry Adams had produced a monumental, multivolume *History of the United States*, covering the administrations of Jefferson and Madison, that many then and later considered the finest American history ever written. Now he had ventured into the Middle Ages.

French cathedrals had had the same powerful effect on Adams as on Charles Sumner and others years before, when seeing the cathedral at Rouen for the first time. His travels and studies for his book had already made him an authority on the subject, while to Saint-Gaudens it was all still new.

Adams had chosen to concentrate on Mont Saint-Michel and Chartres, and had come to see architecture as an expression of the energy of a given age. The energy of the Middle Ages, he surmised, was the power of the image of the Virgin Mary, while at the center of his own time was the power of the electric dynamo.

As between the twelfth century and the approaching twentieth century, he had no difficulty recognizing which he preferred. "Every day opens new horizons and the rate we are going gets faster and faster till my twelfth century head spins, and I hang on to the straps and shut my eyes," he would write to his friend Elizabeth Cameron.

(The automobile, considered a curiosity or toy only ten years earlier, could now be seen and heard all through Paris. A bicycle maker, Armand Peugeot, had introduced a French-built car in 1891. By 1895 there were more than two hundred Peugeot automobiles on the road, as well as others made by Louis Renault. On a single day in Paris in the spring of 1900, fifty "automobilists" were arrested for speeding.)

For Adams his day at Amiens with Saint-Gaudens would serve as part of what he would later call his "education," but not because of the cathedral. As he was to write in his autobiographical *The Education of Henry Adams:*

> Not until they found themselves actually studying the sculpture of the western portal, did it dawn on Adams's mind that, for his purposes, Saint-Gaudens on the spot had more interest to him than the cathedral itself.

As for Saint-Gaudens's two French friends, they were far too bourgeois for Adams, "conventional as death" and of no matter whatever.

Saint-Gaudens, Adams concluded, was a man of the Renaissance, the natural child of Benvenuto Cellini, the Italian sculptor who had worked under Michelangelo, in contrast to Adams himself, "a quintessence of Boston," who through curiosity, not heredity, had come to think like Cellini.

Standing before the Virgin at Amiens, Adams felt her become for him "more than ever a channel of force," while for Saint-Gaudens she remained only "a channel of taste." The sculptor, Adams wrote, did not feel her as a power, "only as reflected emotion, human expression, beauty, purity. . . ."

Adams would later conclude that for a symbol of power, Saint-Gaudens "instinctively preferred the horse," as was "plain" in the horse of his Sherman monument. "Doubtless Sherman also felt it so." But at the time, in a letter to Elizabeth Cameron, Adams said that the cathedral at Amiens was "a new life" for Saint-Gaudens, that it "overpowered him."

III

As expected, the Exposition Universelle of 1900 offered just about everything for everyone. The largest world's fair yet, it covered nearly 250 acres on two sides of the Seine and included an American rolling sidewalk, a *trottoir roulant*, on which to get about, something never seen before. A glorious new Pont Alexandre III, as beautiful as any bridge in Paris, now spanned the river with a single arch to link the two sides of the fairgrounds. The first part of a new Paris metro system had been opened, and there was a Big Wheel to ride, a copy of the one built by George Ferris that had caused a sensation at the Columbian Exposition at Chicago in 1893. And there was still, of course, the ever-popular Eiffel Tower, which had not been taken down for the very reason of its popularity.

Tickets for general admission to the fair were cheap, the equivalent of eleven cents. Attendance far exceeded even the record numbers set in 1889. Fifty million people would crowd through the gates this time.

The public response was overwhelmingly favorable. Newspapers and magazines on both sides of the Atlantic were filled with praise. American papers described the "number of smart, well-dressed persons" in attendance and Paris aglow with electric illumination. *Scientific American* magazine called the new Pont Alexandre III one of the most beautiful ever built.

Some people were disappointed; others disapproved. "It is too big, and there are too many things to do," some visitors said. Among a certain number of intellectuals the whole affair was dismissed as an "odious bazaar," no more than a vulgar display of nationalism. And inevitably some who had traveled a long way to be there felt let down. Two representatives of the American Midwest were overheard expressing their views as follows:

> FIRST CHICAGOAN: "It don't compare with the World's Fair of
> Chicago."
> SECOND CHICAGOAN: "Of course not. I knew that before I left
> Chicago."

Henry Adams's great objection was the number of Americans everywhere. "All Americans are in Paris," he wrote. "I pass my time hiding from them."

More than forty countries participated, again a record. American products and inventions drew much attention, and grand prizes and gold medals went to American machinery, farm equipment, cameras, even a California wine—a higher total in awards than any other country except France.

Adams, who could not stay away, toured the Galerie des Machines one day with a friend from Washington whom he greatly admired, Samuel Pierpont Langley, the head of the Smithsonian Institution. For more than ten years Langley had been experimenting with flights of his own heavier-than-air machines, a field much ridiculed at the time, and using lightweight steam engines he had had great success. His experimental "air-ships" looked like gigantic, four-winged dragonflies. In 1896, one flew under its own power 3,000 feet over the Potomac River, another more than 4,000 feet—the first free flights of heavier-than-air machines in history.

Langley was to be yet another part of Adams's "education" in France. Ignoring most of the industrial exhibits, he led Adams straight to see the "forces" of power. "His chief interest was the new motors to make his airship feasible, and he taught Adams the astonishing complexities of the new Daimler motor and of the automobile," which to Adams had become a "a nightmare."

From the internal combustion engine they moved on to the great hall, where Adams "began to feel the forty-foot dynamo as a moral force, much as the early Christians felt the cross."

The exhibition of American art (which Adams and Langley took no time for) brought many of those young Americans who had been studying in Paris their first international recognition. Paintings by Cecilia Beaux, Robert Henri, Henry O. Tanner, and others of their generation were to be seen alongside those of such established American masters as Winslow Homer, Thomas Eakins, and James Whistler. Mary Cassatt had entered one of her mother-and-child paintings. John Singer Sargent had several of his recent portraits.

One American whose work was not to be seen this time was George P. A. Healy, who had died in Chicago in 1894. Healy had shown his work at every Paris exposition since 1855, when he had fourteen of his paintings hanging.

Among the French and other European artists on display, along with Carolus-Duran and Edgar Degas, was a nineteen-year-old Spaniard, Pablo Picasso.

The paintings and sculpture were all to be seen in the exposition's Grand Palais, built especially for the fair, an enormous wedding cake of a building entirely in the spirit of the Belle Époque, which stood between the new Pont Alexandre III and the Champs-Élysées. And for all who entered, the first spectacle—indeed, one of the most memorable spectacles of the fair—was a vast ground-floor space flooded with light from a giant glass-and-iron dome overhead and crowded from end to end with sculptures of all shapes and sizes.

For Saint-Gaudens it was the setting for a public display of his work such as he had never experienced. Though it annoyed him that so many pieces had been placed together "pell-mell," he knew such a collection had never been seen all in one place, nor was such an exhibit likely to occur again. And while patience was required getting about the maze of "arms, legs, faces and torsos in every conceivable posture," there were many "very remarkable" works to be seen.

Four of his own major works were on display—plaster casts of General Sherman and Victory, the Shaw Memorial, *The Puritan*, and *Amor*

Caritas—and Sherman and his horse rode highest among them. In addition, fourteen reproductions of his relief portraits were on exhibit, including those of William Dean Howells and Robert Louis Stevenson.

For his work overall Saint-Gaudens received the Grand Prize and the *Amor Caritas* would be purchased by the French government for the Luxembourg Museum.

But it was an incident witnessed by only a few apparently that had to have meant worlds to him. Auguste Rodin was seen to stop before the Shaw Memorial and take off his hat and stand silently bareheaded in respect.

Saint-Gaudens had mixed feelings about Rodin. He liked much of his early work, but Homer Saint-Gaudens would remember standing with his father in front of Rodin's famous *Balzac* and hearing his father say the statue gave him "too much the effect of a guttering candle."

Still, Rodin was France's greatest living sculptor, and here he was paying public tribute to an American. For Saint-Gaudens it was one of life's choice moments.

———

Just as Saint-Gaudens was riding so high, everything turned black as night. Gussie had left for the United States to make arrangements for their return home. In late June of 1900, struck by severe stomach pains, Gus went to three leading Paris physicians, all of whom told him he had a tumor of the lower intestine and that an operation must be performed without delay.

Almost at once he was overcome by a terrifying suicidal depression. If the end were near, let it be at his own time and choosing. Life was no longer bearable.

Of those still with him in Paris, none was closer on a day-to-day basis, or more devoted to him or aware of his changing moods than James Fraser, who knew nothing of Saint-Gaudens's cancer but worried increasingly about his worsening state of mind.

Years later Fraser put down on paper, as best he could remember, what happened and what Saint-Gaudens had said.

Fraser had come to work at 3 rue de Bagneux early one morning that

June and was in the large studio alone when suddenly Saint-Gaudens burst through the door and went straight into his own studio. Then Fraser heard the outer door of Saint-Gaudens's studio open and slam shut, after which all was silent.

An hour or so later, Saint-Gaudens returned and asked Fraser to come into his office. He had something he must tell him.

"I went in," Fraser wrote, "and I noticed that his look was unusual and very excited. . . ."

> "I have just had the most extraordinary experience [Saint-Gaudens began] . . . it now appears that I am seriously ill and must go home for an operation. I am greatly worried and have been sleepless for many nights.
>
> "Suddenly, this morning, I decided that I would end it all, and when I came here this morning I had definitely made up my mind to jump in the Seine. As I left here I practically ran down the rue de Rennes toward the Seine, and when I looked up at the buildings they all seemed to have written across the top a huge word in black letters—'Death—Death—Death.' This on all the buildings . . .
>
> "I ran—I was in so much of a hurry! I reached the river and went up on the bridge and as I looked over the water, I saw the Louvre in the bright sunlight and suddenly everything was beautiful to me, the Louvre was wonderful—more remarkable than I had ever seen it before.
>
> "Whether the running and the hurrying had changed my mental attitude, I can't say—possibly it might have been the beauty of the Louvre's architecture or the sparkling water of the Seine—whatever it was, suddenly the weight and blackness lifted from my mind and I was happy and found myself whistling."

"And he still seemed excited and happy and I felt he had passed a dreadful crisis and was safe for the time," Fraser wrote. Saint-Gaudens had said it was Paris—the morning light of Paris, the sparkle of the Seine from the Pont des Arts, the architecture of Paris—that had saved him.

———

Saint-Gaudens left in mid-July 1900, but not before stopping at 3 rue de Bagneux to give a few final instructions on Sherman and Victory, which he insisted be cast in bronze in Paris.

At the very time many thousands of Americans were arriving by ship for the exposition, Saint-Gaudens sailed for home so ill he had to be accompanied by a physician. Gussie met the ship at New York, and they went directly to Boston, where he was admitted to Massachusetts General Hospital for the first of two operations. The second followed that November.

Afterward, having settled to stay at their home in Cornish, New Hampshire, Gussie did everything possible to see to his care and well-being. He established another studio and kept on working, though at an easier pace.

———

The arrival of the new year, 1901, marked the start of the twentieth century, and by spring—with both the exposition and winter behind—Paris was Paris once again, all its particular magic in abundant evidence.

As reported in the press, the Champs-Élysées and the Bois de Boulogne were "in the most charming phase of delicate spring foliage." With skies clear above, the temperature ideal, the white blossoms of the horse chestnut trees at their peak, "the whole world" was out strolling the avenues and public gardens, or just sitting in the outdoor cafés contentedly "indulging in that refined kind of loafing at which the nation excels."

And daylight stayed longer, making evening promenades all the more pleasurable.

At the Opera, Gounod's *Faust* and Wagner's *Tannhäuser* were being warmly received. At the École des Beaux-Arts, a first-ever retrospective show of the drawings and paintings of Honoré Daumier had become one of the most successful attractions of the season, and was "daily thronged" by American art students only just discovering Daumier.

Notice appeared also of a young American "making her mark" with a performance of Greek and Florentine dances at a studio on the avenue de Villiers. Isadora Duncan was twenty-three. She had arrived in Europe with her mother, brother, and sister the year before. So great was their excitement at being in Paris that she and her brother, an artist, would get up at five in the morning and begin the day by dancing in the Luxembourg Gardens.

"We had no money . . . but we wanted nothing," she would remember.

What the new century might hold for them and their generation, there was no telling. For now it was enough just being in Paris.

EPILOGUE

The Sherman Monument was not unveiled in New York until 1903, Augustus Saint-Gaudens having decided after his recovery from surgery that both Sherman and Victory needed further attention. Thus, with the help of his brother Louis, James Fraser, and ten or so additional assistants, "final touches" continued at Cornish, New Hampshire.

The home he and Gussie had established, called Aspet after his father's birthplace in France, was set on an open hillside above the Connecticut River, with an uninterrupted view of Mount Ascutney to the west, across the river in Vermont. It was as beautiful a setting as any in New England, with Hanover and Dartmouth College just up the river.

Gus put Fraser in charge of building a barn-size studio, and he and Gussie continued efforts begun earlier to turn what had been an old inn into a comfortable home. Inevitably, Gus made a number of architectural changes to the exterior. Inside, the parlor was furnished with the same chairs, lamps, and wall hangings they had bought in Paris when first married. On the parlor walls were hung two of Gussie's interior paintings of the apartment at 3 rue Herschel.

To his surprise, Gus discovered he loved living in the country, and greatly enjoyed time spent out-of-doors, even in winter.

Still, as ever, work came first.

Work on the Sherman involved mostly details such as the reins on the horse's bridle. The plaster cast that had been in New York was shipped to New Hampshire. Then casts of the changes were dispatched to Paris, where the finished bronze was still in progress. Mainly it was a process of switching parts, but all this took another year.

When the finished bronze arrived from France, it was set up on the lawn outside the studio and the gilding applied there by hand.

On the morning of the unveiling in New York—Memorial Day, May 30, 1903—Gus and Gussie chose to be seated where there seemed the least chance of being noticed.

Thousands of people had gathered on the Grand Army Plaza at Fifth Avenue and 59th Street. There were flags and banners flying, a marching band, dignitaries, speeches, and well above the crowd, on an eleven-foot pedestal designed by Charles McKim, rode the gleaming, golden Sherman on his horse heading southward, his cloak flying and with the golden Victory, her palm branch held high, leading the way.

"The sculptor took no part in the exercise," wrote the *New York Times*, "but was the recipient of many congratulations when he had been discovered with Mrs. Saint-Gaudens in an inconspicuous place. . . ."

In 1904, a fire destroyed the studio at Cornish. In 1906, Gus's old friend and collaborator Stanford White was murdered, shot to death at Madison Square Garden by the crazed husband of a former mistress, Evelyn Nesbit. All this was extremely hard on Gus, while his health and strength kept deteriorating.

Yet, with a new studio under roof, the work moved forward.

"We are not dead yet, By Jingo! are we!" he wrote one fine spring day to Edwin Abbey. "If you were to see the establishment I have here, you would think I was, although I am stretched out on a couch at this moment in the flickering sunlight. I will stick at it until I am finally straightened out. That's the only thing, after all. Work, I mean. . . ."

He did more relief portraits, more busts and statues. At the request of President Theodore Roosevelt he created designs for the United States gold coinage.

Gussie conscientiously looked after him, saw to his comforts and needs, and more even than in previous years kept the accounts, handled sales of duplicate castings, and managed the property.

The last and one of the most spirited of his relief portraits was of her standing in profile with his beloved sheepdog. (Whatever objections she had had in Paris to his having a dog had long since vanished.) He gave the dog a face very like what he drew of himself in his cartoons and, as a close look revealed, he put a heart on Gussie's sleeve.

By early summer 1907 it was plain that he was dying.

In late July, an assistant, Henry Hering, described how Saint-Gaudens had become so weak and in such pain from his illness that he had to be carried to the studio each day, and how, once he was seated before his work, the look of pain and worry would vanish from his face.

Hering wrote also of "Mrs. St-G," describing her devotion to her husband through it all as "very true and beautiful."

In the evenings Hering often joined the Saint-Gaudenses, Homer, and a nurse at the dinner table, where Saint-Gaudens wished the others to talk and let him listen. "Now and then," Hering wrote, "he would ask that we talk louder so that Mrs. might hear, though it was harder than usual with her, for, poor lady, she said almost nothing—sitting there with the love of her youth."

Augustus Saint-Gaudens died at home in Cornish, of cancer, on the evening of August 3, 1907, at age fifty-nine. Only the doctor was at the bedside. Gussie was waiting outside the door. It is said that when the doctor told her, she fainted on the floor.

Of the later lives of Davida Clark and son Louis, little is known.

Gussie lived until 1926, devoting most of her time to seeing to the memory of her husband and appreciation of his work. In 1919, at her wish, their home at Cornish and its furnishings, his studio, and much of his work, became the Saint-Gaudens Memorial, incorporated by the State of New Hampshire. Later, it would become, and remains, a property of the National Park Service.

Homer Saint-Gaudens, after a career as a writer and in the theater as a Broadway director, served for twenty-eight years as the director of arts at the Carnegie Institute in Pittsburgh.

———

John Singer Sargent, while maintaining his studio and residence in London, spent more and more time in the United States, as if making up for what he had missed in his youth. He traveled back and forth repeatedly, working on the murals for the Boston Public Library and doing portraits, including a full-length portrait of Theodore Roosevelt, but devoting increasing time to landscapes in oil and watercolor. He painted in Maine, Florida, and the Rocky Mountains.

Informed that he was to be knighted in England, he declined the honor, saying it would be impossible since he was an American.

Sargent never married and never stopped painting until his death at age sixty-nine, from heart failure while he slept, the night of April 14, 1925, at his home in London. His glasses had been pushed up on his forehead. Beside him lay an open volume of *Dictionnaire Philosophique* by Voltaire.

Mary Cassatt died a year after Sargent, on June 14, 1926, at her château at Beaufresne, north of Paris. She was eighty-one.

She had stayed on in France with no wish to live anywhere else, even through the First World War, and she kept painting until she began to lose her eyesight from cataracts. Looked after by a devoted maid-companion, Mathilde Valet, she found her greatest pleasure in her gardens, where she had more than two hundred varieties of chrysanthemums, and in being taken for daily drives in her 1906 Renault Landau.

A much younger American painter named George Biddle, who had been greatly influenced by her work, was invited to join her for lunch at Beaufresne a few months before her death. On arrival he was told by Mathilde Valet that Miss Cassatt was unable to join him for lunch, but she would see him in her room afterward.

He found her propped up in bed, "quite blind" and "terribly emaciated," he wrote, but when she began to talk, the whole room became charged with her "electric vitality."

She regretted missing lunch with him, she said, but hoped he found the Château Margaux to his liking. It was the last bottle of a case of wine given to her by her brother fifteen years before.

"Miss Cassatt as usual did the talking. Her mind galloped along. . . . What abysses and reinforcements of courage and life and enthusiasm still lay hidden inside that frail body. . . ."

ACKNOWLEDGMENTS

For the steadfast, resourceful part he played in the research for this book, and for his unfailing good cheer, I wish to express my gratitude first of all to Mike Hill. As with three of my previous books, his efforts have been vital, and it was he who unraveled, as no one had, the full extent of the Elihu Washburne diary at the Library of Congress. (See the Notes for Chapter 9.)

My daughter Dorie Lawson has been of immense editorial help with the source notes and proofreading, and for that and all her other efforts I am extremely thankful. And my great appreciation to Melissa Marchetti, who has typed and retyped the entire manuscript in its many drafts, handled correspondence, and assisted with the source notes and illustrations.

I am most grateful also to my son-in-law Tim Lawson, a highly gifted artist who went with me to look at particular paintings and sculpture in Boston, New York, Chicago, and at the Saint-Gaudens National Historic Site in New Hampshire, and who, from his professional experience and knowledge, offered many valuable insights.

Betsey Buddy has provided research help in Paris, and for this and much that she and her husband, Mike Buddy, have had to say about Paris, and much that is second nature to her from teaching French for thirty years, I am most grateful.

In the course of writing the book I have been fortunate to draw on the resources of some thirty-two institutions as well as the knowledge and advice of many people who gave generously of their time. Any inaccuracies there may be in what I have written are my doing, not theirs.

I thank especially Jeffrey Flannery, the always helpful head of the

Manuscript Reading Room at the Library of Congress, and Gerard Gawalt, Grant Harris, Carol Armbruster, Jerome Brooks, Norman Chase, Elizabeth Faison, and Elvin Felix also of the Library of Congress; Henry J. Duffy, curator of the Saint-Gaudens National Historic Site, who knows more about Augustus Saint-Gaudens than anyone; Elizabeth Kennedy of the Terra Foundation for American Art, who provided a private viewing of Samuel Morse's *Gallery of the Louvre* at a time when it was in storage in Chicago and who was good enough to read and comment on a first draft of my account of the painting and its story; Erica E. Hirshler, senior curator at the Museum of Fine Arts in Boston, who graciously led me on a tour of the museum's collection of the works of Mary Cassatt and John Singer Sargent, as well as providing a backstage look at the Paris water-colors by Edward D. Boit; Jock Reynolds and Helen Cooper of the Yale University Art Gallery for their guidance and insights; Peter Drummey of the Massachusetts Historical Society, from whom I always learn something of value; Stephen Z. Nonack of the Boston Athenaeum, who put me on to the remarkable account by Charles May of his escape from Paris by balloon; Sarah Cash and Beth Shook of the Corcoran Gallery of Art; Beth Prindle of the Boston Public Library; Jack Eckert of the Countway Library of the Harvard Medical School; Jennifer M. Deprizio of the Isabella Stewart Gardner Museum; Nancy Iannucci of the Emma Willard School; Jay Satterfield, head of special collections at the Rauner Library, Dartmouth College; Howard J. Kittell, president of the Hermitage, the home of President Andrew Jackson, and Judge George Paine and Ophelia Paine, who generously arranged for the tour there; Lynn Turner, collections manager at the U.S. State Department; Marisa Bourgoin, Margaret Zoller, Wendy Hurlock Baker, and Liza Kirwin at the Smithsonian Institution's Archives of American Art; Jim Shea and Anita Israel at the Longfellow House, George Washington's Headquarters in Cambridge, Massachusetts; Pat Heller at the University of Pennsylvania Dental School Library; Elder Marlin Jensen at the Library of the Church of Jesus Christ of Latter-day Saints, Salt Lake City; Nancy Anderson at the National Gallery of Art; Nancey Drinkwine and Jen Colby-Morse at the Washburn-Norlands Living History Center, Livermore, Maine; Diana Skvarla, Scott Strong, and Melinda Smith at the Office of the Senate Curator; William Truettner at the Smithsonian American Art Museum; Stephanie Malmros, University of Texas Center for American History; Adam Lovell, Detroit Historical Society; and old friends Richard A. Baker, former historian of the U.S. Senate, and Charles Bryan, former head of the Virginia Historical Society.

For their assistance and many courtesies I wish to thank also the staffs of the Beinecke Library of Yale; the New-York Historical Society; the Houghton Library at Harvard; the Boston Art Commission; Faneuil Hall in Boston; the Simpson Library at the University of Mary Washington, Fredericksburg, Virginia; the Alderman Library at the University of Virginia; and in Paris, the Bibliothèque Nationale and the Bibliothèque Sainte-Geneviève.

Others to whom I am greatly indebted are Ed Wise, for introducing me to the music and story of Louis Moreau Gottschalk; sculptor Lawrence Nowlan, for taking the time to explain in his studio the processes and challenges of large-scale sculpture; Dr. Robert P. Laurence, Ryan O'Donnell, Arthur and Kim Grinnell, Anne Simonnet, Zoe Geer, Kerck Kelsey, James A. Percoco, Denny daRosa, Karen Ogden, David Acton, Tom Ford, James Symington, Dr. William Maguire; and in Paris, Alice Jouve, Fred and Marie-Cécile Street, Odile Hellier, proprietor of the Village Voice Bookshop, Agnes and Laurent Perpère, the staff of the historic Hôtel du Louvre, and especially concierge Carmelo Helguera, and former U.S. ambassador to France Craig R. Stapleton and Dorothy W. Stapleton for their hospitality in Paris and their stories about the ambassador's residence at 41 rue du Faubourg Saint-Honoré.

I thank again each of the following who read and offered valuable suggestions on part or all of the manuscript: John Zentay, Steven Barclay, Dr. Edward Kaplan, Dr. William B. McCullough, Philip W. Pillsbury, Jr., Dr. Fred Pittman, Robert Doran, and the late George Cochran.

To my longtime editor Michael Korda of Simon & Schuster, and to Carolyn Reidy, Jonathan Karp, Bob Bender, David Rosenthal, Julia Prosser, Jackie Seow, and Gypsy da Silva of Simon & Schuster, to Amy Hill, who designed the book, and Wendell Minor, who designed the jacket, I can only emphasize what joy it has been to work with them and how fortunate I feel to have their support and their friendship.

Again I must express my particular thanks to Fred Wiemer, copy editor extraordinaire, for his superb, sharp-eyed editing, and this time in both English and French. Proofreaders Jim Stoller, John Morgenstern, Bill Molesky, and Ted Landry, and indexer Chris Carruth were all part of the team.

To my exceptional literary agent, Morton L. Janklow, I am greatly indebted, and especially for his enthusiasm for the idea for this book right from our first conversation about it.

My family has once again played an important part as first readers and as listeners to my continuing talk about the project as it moved forward year by year. Daughter Melissa McDonald and son Geoffrey have read every chapter in successive drafts. Son David has given astute editorial comment throughout, and son Bill accompanied me on the rounds of historic sites in Paris.

My wife, Rosalee Barnes McCullough, has been as always the first of my first readers and the best, wisest provider by far of advice and encouragement. To her I am indebted above all.

—David McCullough
January 24, 2011

SOURCE NOTES

1. The Way Over

A great part of the source material for this book is, in addition to being of historic value, a pure joy to read because so many of the protagonists were superb writers. This is vividly clear from the very start, in what they wrote of their time outward bound for France. Such descriptions to be found in the letters and journals of even those who did not regard themselves as professional writers—like Emma Willard, Charles Sumner, or Thomas Appleton—amply qualify as American literature of the sea. Anyone wishing a sample of the professional virtuosity of a writer like Nathaniel Willis need only read his hilarious account of dining on board the brig *Pacific* in rough weather.

PAGE

3 The thought of going abroad: Pierce, *Memoir and Letters of Charles Sumner*, Vol. I, 190.

4 *"a little pleasure concealed"*: Cooper, *Letters and Journals of James Fenimore Cooper*, Vol. I, 126.

4 *"when standing in a pair of substantial boots"*: Ibid., 56.

4 *By contrast, his friend Charles Sumner*: Pierce, *Memoir and Letters of Charles Sumner*, Vol. I, 92.

4 *Emma Willard, founder*: Lutz, *Emma Willard: Pioneer Educator of American Women*, vii.

4 *"My dear mother was rather alarmed"*: Cooper, *Correspondence of James Fenimore Cooper*, Vol. I, 52.

5 *"got entirely out of trim"*: Franklin, *James Fenimore Cooper: The Early Years*, 395.

5 *"How long do you mean to be absent?"*: Cooper, *Gleanings in Europe: France*, Vol. I, 5.

5 *"classic features"*: Lutz, *Emma Willard: Pioneer Educator of American Women*, 87.

5 *"She was a splendid looking woman"*: Ibid., 45.

6 *"Old Ironsides"*: Morse, *Life and Letters of Oliver Wendell Holmes*, Vol. I, 81.

6 *"tasted the intoxicating pleasure"*: Ibid., 80.

6 *tried law school for a year*: Ibid., 78.

6 *"anything better than a rural dispenser"*: Ibid., 82.

6 *"sameness"*: Ibid., 74.

6 *"We learned nominally"*: Ibid., 38.

7 *Mathematics utterly bewildered him:* Pierce, *Memoir and Letters of Charles Sumner,* Vol. I, 47.

7 *"an indefatigable and omnivorous student":* Ibid., 106.

7 *"The thought of going abroad":* Ibid., 190.

7 *In 1822 he had undertaken:* Morse's *House of Representatives* hangs in the Corcoran Gallery of Art in Washington. His *Marquis de Lafayette* still hangs in New York's City Hall.

8 *Word came of the death of his wife:* Morse, *Samuel F. B. Morse: His Letters and Journals,* Vol. I, 265.

8 *"My education as a painter":* Ibid., 289.

8 *"historical painter":* Morse passport, Samuel F. B. Morse Papers, Library of Congress, Washington, D.C.

8 *"right hand man":* Healy, *Reminiscences of a Portrait Painter,* 18.

8 *"quite prettily":* Ibid., 17.

8 *"terribly timid":* Ibid., 18.

8 *When the friendly proprietor:* Ibid., 22.

9 *"Little Healy":* Ibid., 25.

9 *"I told her that I was an artist":* Ibid., 31.

9 *One small, especially lovely:* The portrait of Fanny Appleton is on display at the Longfellow House—Washington's headquarters in Cambridge, Massachusetts.

9 *I knew no one in France:* Healy, *Reminiscences of a Portrait Painter,* 35.

10 *"anticipation of Oscar Wilde":* Holmes, *A Mortal Antipathy,* 4.

10 *"dress them up one day":* Sanderson, *The American in Paris,* Vol. I, preface.

11 *When news of the July Revolution:* New York Evening Post, September 8, 1830.

11 *He had worked for a while:* Proud part of the Union Oyster House history, Boston, Mass.

11 *Steamboats by this time:* Allington and Greenhill, *The First Atlantic Liners,* 7.

12 *a London packet fittingly named* Crisis: Cooper, *Gleanings in Europe: France,* Vol. I, 9.

12 *But a wide sea voyage:* Washington Irving, *The Sketchbook of Geoffrey Crayon, Gent* (NY: Heritage Press, 1939), 8.

13 *Fare to Le Havre:* Sanderson, *The American in Paris,* Vol. I, 14.

13 *Acquaintances who had made the trip:* Susan Cooper to her sister, May 30, 1826, James Fenimore Cooper Papers, Beinecke Library, Yale University.

13 *"I am very glad, my dear":* Pierce, *Memoir and Letters of Charles Sumner,* Vol. I, 210.

13 *"Follow, my dear boy":* Ibid., 212.

14 *The written "Instructions":* Warren, *The Parisian Education of an American Surgeon,* 8.

14 *"fond of theaters and dissipation":* Arnold, *Memoir of Jonathan Mason Warren, M.D.,* 48.

14 *"And a sad time":* Pierce, *Memoir and Letters of Charles Sumner,* Vol. I, 213.

14 *"great depression":* Silverman, *Lightning Man,* 94.

14 *"We have left the wharf":* Pierce, *Memoir and Letters of Charles Sumner,* 211.

14 *And as she came down the river:* Willis, *Pencillings by the Way,* 12.

15 *"the fairest wind":* Morse, *Samuel F. B. Morse: His Letters and Journals,* Vol. I, 300.

15 *"inquire into everything":* Brogan, *Alexis de Tocqueville,* 145.

15 *"In rough weather":* Willis, *Pencillings by the Way,* 19–20.

16 *"It is a day":* Ibid., 13.

16 *in contrast to Wendell Holmes:* Morse, *Life and Letters of Oliver Wendell Holmes,* Vol. I, 83.

16 *"The accommodations":* New York Evening Post, February 28, 1833.
17 *I felt nothing of that do-little:* Appleton, *Life and Letters of Thomas Gold Apple-ton,* 86.
17 *"voice in the steerage":* Ibid., 87–88.
17 *"the still-life of the day previous":* Ibid., 88.
17 *"chattering in terror":* Ibid.
17 *"deeply, darkly, beautifully blue":* Ibid., 89.
17 *"A most delightful evening":* Ibid., 90.
17 *What an odd, good-for-nothing:* Ibid., 91–92.
18 *"vast islands of ice":* Ibid., 92.
18 *"Some of the older passengers":* Willard, *Journal and Letters, from France and Great Britain,* 11.
18 *"Then the waters rise up":* Ibid., 10–11.
18 *Thus with the raging element:* Ibid.
18 *"the rocking and rolling":* Ibid., 2.
19 *"If any lady of your village":* Sanderson, *The American in Paris,* Vol. I, 14.
19 *"Literally 'cabined' ":* Donald, *Charles Sumner and the Coming of the Civil War,* 45.
19 *"Bay of Fundy tide":* Pierce, *Memoir and Letters of Charles Sumner,* Vol. I, 215.
19 *In going abroad at my present age:* Ibid., 214.
20 *"cataract of French postulation":* Willis, *Pencillings by the Way,* 27.
20 *"vexatious ceremony":* Sanderson, *The American in Paris,* Vol. I, 25.
20 *In conversation with an English-speaking:* Ibid.
20 *"to pay the Virgin Mary":* Ibid., 15.
21 *"Everything was old":* Pierce, *Memoir and Letters of Charles Sumner,* Vol. I, 218.
21 *"beyond the reach":* Ibid.
21 *"none of the prestige":* Ibid.
21 *"If you feel very aristocratic":* Sanderson, *The American in Paris,* Vol. I, 26.
22 *I looked at the constantly occurring ruins:* Willis, *Pencillings by the Way,* 32.
23 *"inexpressible magic":* Willard, *Journal and Letters, from France and Great Brit-ain,* 27.
23 *I had heard of fifty:* Ibid., 26–27.
23 *"the great lion of the north":* Pierce, *Memoir and Letters of Charles Sumner,* Vol. I, 221.
24 *And here was I:* Ibid., 222.
24 *In an account of his own first stop:* Cooper, *Gleanings in Europe: France,* Vol. I, 76.

2. *Voilà Paris!*

Of the contemporary books about Paris drawn on for this chapter, *Pencillings by the Way* by Nathaniel Willis, John Sanderson's two-volume *The American in Paris,* and James Fenimore Cooper's *Gleanings in Europe: France* are outstanding. Sanderson's first volume in particular is a jewel, one of the best books about Paris by an American ever written. Of the letters and journal entries, those by Charles Sumner and Oliver Wendell Holmes are invariably descriptive and revealing.

PAGE
25 The origin of Paris: *Galignani's New Paris Guide,* 1827, 1.
26 "Voilà Paris!": Sanderson, *The American in Paris,* Vol. I, 31.
26 *"And with my mind full":* Willis, *Pencillings by the Way,* 36.
26 *"The streets run zig-zag":* Sanderson, *The American in Paris,* Vol. I, 33.

26 *"dirt and gilding":* Cooper, *Letters and Journals of James Fenimore Cooper,* Vol. I, 145.

26 *"We were amidst":* Willard, *Journal and Letters, from France and Great Britain,* 30.

27 *"quite pretty" rooms:* Willis, *Pencillings by the Way,* 37.

27 *There are few things:* Ibid., 37.

28 *indispensable was* Galignani's New Paris Guide*:* See, for example, *Galignani's New Paris Guide,* 1827, 182.

28 *"the bread is fine":* Willard, *Journal and Letters, from France and Great Britain,* 32.

28 *"Miss D":* Ibid., 33.

28 *We took the rounds:* Ibid., 34.

29 *a few "wearable things":* Ibid.

29 *"When I went in":* Morse, *Samuel F. B. Morse: His Letters and Journals,* Vol. I, 316.

29 *In her turn:* Willard, *Journal and Letters, from France and Great Britain,* 39.

29 *"His heart seemed to expand":* Ibid., 40.

29 *"If he keeps near the wall":* Oliver Wendell Holmes to his parents, May 31, 1833, Holmes Papers, Houghton Library, Harvard University.

30 *Holmes, like his fellow Bostonians:* Morse, *Life and Letters of Oliver Wendell Holmes,* Vol. I, 85; Dowling, *Oliver Wendell Holmes in Paris,* 184.

30 *The cold continues intolerable:* Pierce, *Memoir and Letters of Charles Sumner,* Vol. I, 241.

30 *"I freeze behind":* Ibid.

31 *"My voyage has already been compensated":* Ibid., 234.

31 *flâner:* Morse, *Life and Letters of Oliver Wendell Holmes,* Vol. I, 88.

31 *"Ah! To wander":* Balzac, *Works of Honoré de Balzac,* Vol. II, 133.

31 *Interestingly, "Home, Sweet Home":* Overmyer, *America's First Hamlet,* 202.

31 *"If you get into melancholy":* Sanderson, *The American in Paris,* Vol. I, 128.

32 *"uniform politeness":* Galignani's New Paris Guide, 1827, 27.

32 *"Indeed," wrote Holmes:* Morse, *Life and Letters of Oliver Wendell Holmes,* Vol. I, 101.

32 *"the originality of American civilization":* Tocqueville, *Democracy in America,* 46.

33 *"You ask a man the way":* Appleton, *Life and Letters of Thomas Gold Appleton,* 135.

33 *"Don't you hate to see":* Sanderson, *The American in Paris,* Vol. I, 57.

33 *how he had "decorated" himself:* Longfellow, *Letters of Henry Wadsworth Longfellow,* Vol. I, 173.

33 *"the glory of a little French hat":* Ibid.

34 *"You should remember that you are an American":* Calhoun, *Longfellow: A Rediscovered Life,* 44.

34 *No matter what is the article of trade:* Willis, *Pencillings by the Way,* 38.

34 *"caressing and caressing":* Sanderson, *The American in Paris,* Vol. I, 67.

35 *"The French dine to gratify":* Ibid., 87.

35 *"in blending flavors":* Cooper, *Gleanings in Europe: France,* Vol. I, 124.

35 *A dinner here:* Ibid., 125.

35 *"loud modern New York":* Emerson, *The Journals and Notebooks of Ralph Waldo Emerson,* ed. Ferguson, Vol. IV, 197.

35 *"the most hospitable of cities":* Ibid.

36 *Then a person who cut profiles:* Ibid., 198.

36 *Nathaniel Willis kept seeing:* Willis, *Pencillings by the Way*, 84.

36 *"impatient of all levity":* Arnold, *Memoir of Jonathan Mason Warren, M.D.*, 51.

37 *Happy the nation:* Sterne, *A Sentimental Journey Through France and Italy*, 125.

37 *John Sanderson hired a cabriolet:* Sanderson, *The American in Paris*, Vol. I, 47.

37 *"It is a queer feeling":* Willis, *Pencillings by the Way*, 43.

37 *No sooner had Cooper settled in Paris:* Cooper, *Gleanings in Europe: France*, Vol. I, 277.

37 *"He calls the Tuileries":* Ibid., 281.

38 *The captain commenced:* Ibid., 278.

38 *best "look-out":* Ibid., 88.

38 *We were fortunate:* Ibid., 89.

38 *The domes sprung up:* Ibid., 90.

39 *"peculiarities":* Ibid.

39 *"confused glittering":* Ibid.

39 *Charles Sumner, for his part:* Pierce, *Memoir and Letters of Charles Sumner*, Vol. I, 276.

39 *"streets without houses":* Ibid., 133.

39 *"It only grows under":* Ibid.

39 *"great design":* Ibid.

40 *"We must, if it be possible":* Hugo, *Notre-Dame of Paris*, 28.

40 *"That, its author":* Ibid.

40 *"The atmosphere brightened":* Sanderson, *The American in Paris*, Vol. I, 166.

41 *"that most chivalrous":* Willard, *Journal and Letters, from France and Great Britain*, 77.

41 *The bridge immediately:* Ibid., 55, 77.

41 *"very heart of Paris":* Ibid., 53.

42 *"with a throb":* Pierce, *Memoir and Letters of Charles Sumner*, Vol. I, 88.

42 *"Holmes and I actually were at the Louvre":* Appleton, *Life and Letters of Thomas Gold Appleton*, 130.

42 *Another day Appleton returned on his own:* Ibid., 132–33, 137–38.

42 *"much esteemed and bear a high price":* Willard, *Journal and Letters, from France and Great Britain*, 247.

42 *"little or no drapery":* Cooper, *Gleanings in Europe: France*, Vol. I, 302.

42 *No, my dear girls:* Willard, *Journal and Letters, from France and Great Britain*, 62.

43 *"running and hiding their faces":* Cooper, *Gleanings in Europe: France*, Vol. I, 302.

43 *"Who would live in this rank old Paris":* Sanderson, *The American in Paris*, Vol. I, 98.

43 *Garden of the Tuileries:* See, generally, *Galignani's New Paris Guide*, 1827, 147–52.

44 *"the most fashionable promenade":* Ibid., 152.

44 *"I have been there repeatedly":* Willis, *Pencillings by the Way*, 78–79.

44 *"I never venture":* Sanderson, *The American in Paris*, Vol. I, 102.

44 *"every inch of it":* Ibid., 104.

45 *Let us have gardens:* Ibid., 106.

45 *"a library on the street":* Ibid., 60.

46 *"You can stop in on your way":* Ibid., 164.

46 *"nothing that did not belong":* Hugo, *Notre-Dame of Paris*, 136.

47 *"And it seemed to me":* Willis, *Pencillings by the Way*, 74.

47 *"In our own country":* Sanderson, *The American in Paris*, Vol. I, 88.

48 *"The evening need never hang"*: Emerson, *The Journals and Notebooks of Ralph Waldo Emerson*, ed. Ferguson, Vol. IV, 202.

48 *Faultlessly attired*: Willard, *Journal and Letters, from France and Great Britain*, 37.

48 *"genteel society"*: Ibid.

48 *I never saw so many*: Ibid.

49 *"We may make many valuable improvements"*: Ibid., 164.

49 *Charles Sumner made a point*: Pierce, *Memoir and Letters of Charles Sumner*, Vol. I, 236.

49 *dazzling Marie Taglioni*: Willis, *Pencillings by the Way*, 48.

50 *"No language can describe"*: Ibid., 50.

50 *Her figure is small*: Ibid., 49–50.

50 *"Mercy! How deficient"*: Sanderson, *The American in Paris*, Vol. I, 46.

50 *"overwhelming tumult"*: Willis, *Pencillings by the Way*, 51.

50 *"We shall never have"*: Ibid.

50 *"And when they come upon stage"*: Ibid.

51 *Indeed, while at the opera*: James Jackson, Jr., to his father, March 20, 1832, Jackson Family Papers, Countway Library, Harvard Medical School.

51 *"James Jackson has just come up"*: Morse, *Life and Letters of Oliver Wendell Holmes*, Vol. I, 98.

51 *"There is no need of cutting"*: Ibid., 120.

52 *"Molière could not have"*: Sanderson, *The American in Paris*, Vol. II, 129.

52 *"Her voice is like a silver flute"*: Pierce, *Memoir and Letters of Charles Sumner*, Vol. I, 234.

52 *"Thousands in merry moods"*: Appleton, *Life and Letters of Thomas Gold Appleton*, 129.

52 *"the blaze of day"*: Ibid.

52 "Cafés *abound in Paris"*: *Galignani's New Paris Guide*, 1827, li.

52 *It is impossible to conceive*: Ibid.

52 *"Alas, my poor roasting"*: Sanderson, *The American in Paris*, Vol. I, 84.

52 *"Your best way"*: Ibid., 85.

53 *the elegant Trois Frères Provençaux*: Les Trois Frères Provençaux no longer exists. Le Grand Véfour, in the Palais Royal, is the oldest restaurant in Paris still operating at its original site and one of the finest in the city.

53 *As much as the food and the wine*: Holmes, *The Autocrat at the Breakfast Table*, 24.

53 *"ladies of easy virtue"*: *Galignani's New Paris Guide*, 1827, 176.

53 *The Palais Royal, Holmes liked to say*: Morse, *Life and Letters of Oliver Wendell Holmes*, Vol. I, 99.

53 *"haunts where the stranger"*: *Galignani's New Paris Guide*, 1827, iii.

53 *"Billiards, cards, faro"*: Sanderson, *The American in Paris*, Vol. I, 94.

54 *"Young men are very fond of Paris"*: Emerson, *The Journals and Notebooks of Ralph Waldo Emerson*, ed. Ferguson, Vol. IV, 201.

54 *"arrangements"*: Sanderson, *The American in Paris*, Vol. I, 88.

54 *"They are very pretty"*: Ibid., 199.

54 *If a student is ill*: Ibid.

54 *"out of order"*: Ibid., 203.

55 *If you can preserve him*: Ibid., 204.

55 *"My anxiety deprives me"*: Willard, *Journal and Letters, from France and Great Britain*, 209.

55 *Sumner hated seeing so many soldiers:* Pierce, *Memoir and Letters of Charles Sumner,* Vol. I, 238.

55 *Emma Willard was appalled to learn:* Willard, *Journal and Letters, from France and Great Britain,* 235, 236.

56 *An American or Englishman when he first:* Oliver Wendell Holmes to his parents, September 28, 1833, Holmes Papers, Houghton Library, Harvard University.

57 *gathering places like the Café Procope:* The Café Procope continues in business, though much enhanced from what it was in Holmes's day.

57 *It had been started in 1670 by a Sicilian:* Barclay, *A Place in the World Called Paris,* 51.

57 *"I am getting more and more a Frenchman":* Morse, *Life and Letters of Oliver Wendell Holmes,* Vol. I, 109.

57 *"Good Americans, when they die":* Holmes, *The Autocrat at the Breakfast Table,* 121.

58 *Some days, according to his wife, Susan:* Susan Cooper to her children, May 15, 1828, Cooper Family Papers, Beinecke Library, Yale University.

58 *"But manage he did":* Bigot, *Life of George P. A. Healy,* 9.

58 *"He lived like his comrades":* Ibid., 13.

58 *"the Boswell of Paris":* Sanderson, *The American in Paris,* Vol. I, 43.

58 *"It seems as if a spell":* Willard, *Journal and Letters, from France and Great Britain,* 241.

59 *recruited a first teacher of French:* See copy of Madame Alphise de Courval's contract dated March 19, 1831. Courtesy of Nancy Ianucci, Emma Willard School Archives.

59 *"the effect was speedily":* Lord, *The Life of Emma Willard,* 134.

3. Morse at the Louvre

The six volumes of *Letters and Journals of James Fenimore Cooper* are a treasure trove, not only for so much that Cooper writes, but for the thorough notes provided by editor James Franklin Beard. Cooper was a far more interesting man and the popularity of his work abroad far greater than generally appreciated in our time. Of considerable interest, too, are the letters of Susan Cooper, in the collection of the Beinecke Library at Yale. The main sources for Morse and his travails have been *Samuel F. B. Morse, His Letters and Journals,* in two volumes; *The Life of Samuel F. B. Morse* by Samuel I. Prime; *The American Leonardo* by Carleton Mabee; and the more recent *Lightning Man: The Accursed Life of Samuel F. B. Morse* by Kenneth Silverman.

PAGE

61 My country has the most: Morse, *Samuel F. B. Morse: His Letters and Journals,* Vol. I, 33.

61 *"hard at work":* Cooper, *Letters and Journals of James Fenimore Cooper,* 235.

61 *"has created a sensation":* Ibid., 172.

61 *"He is painting":* Ibid., 239.

61 *"just as good a fellow":* Ibid.

61 *"friends are rare":* Cooper, *The Prairie* (Penguin), 29.

61 *Cooper and Morse had met first:* Morse, *Samuel F. B. Morse: His Letters and Journals,* Vol. I, 263.

62 *"Crowds get round the picture":* Cooper, *Letters and Journals of James Fenimore Cooper,* Vol. II, 239.

62 *"deliciously spring-like":* Willis, *Pencillings by the Way,* 107.

62 *"wholly bent":* Silverman, *Lightning Man,* 109.

62 *"wicked Morse":* Ibid.

62 *"without a true love":* Ibid.

63 *"amazingly improved":* Cooper, *Letters and Journals of James Fenimore Cooper,* Vol. II, 163.

63 *Morse had no sooner unpacked:* Ibid., 167, 172.

63 *Bread and Cheese:* Silverman, *Lightning Man,* 89.

63 *"I saw nothing but Jefferson":* Cooper, *Letters and Journals of James Fenimore Cooper,* Vol. I, 96.

63 *One stunning example of the genre:* Tatham, "Samuel F. B. Morse's Gallery of the Louvre: The Figures in the Foreground," *American Art Journal,* Vol. XIII, No. 4 (Autumn 1981), 41.

64 *On a small piece of paper, Jefferson had drawn:* The piece of paper with Jefferson's floor plan and Trumbull's sketch is one of the treasures of the Trumbull Collection at the Yale Art Gallery.

65 *Cooper loved what he saw emerging:* Cooper, *Letters and Journals of James Fenimore Cooper,* Vol. II, 239.

66 *I get up at eight:* Ibid.

66 *"Lay it on here, Samuel":* Ibid.

67 *"the independent, self-possessed":* Willis, *Pencillings by the Way,* 43–44.

67 *Morse with his kind:* Ibid., 110.

67 *"chameleon face":* Morse, *Samuel F. B. Morse: His Letters and Journals,* Vol. I, 415.

68 *Morse's passport:* Papers of Samuel F. B. Morse, Library of Congress, Washington, D.C.

68 *"little pleasure concealed":* Cooper, *Letters and Journals of James Fenimore Cooper,* Vol. I, 126.

68 *Cooper's nephew William:* Ibid., Vol. II, 144.

68 *Cooper's wife, Susan:* Ibid., 168.

69 *"They [the French]":* Ibid., 175.

69 *"Of course, I believe them":* Ibid., 109.

69 *"When he goes into crowded rooms":* Susan Cooper to her sisters, November 29, 1830, James Fenimore Cooper Papers, Beinecke Library, Yale University.

69 *"What are you to do":* James Jackson, Sr., to James Jackson, Jr., November 25, 1831, Jackson Family Papers, Countway Library, Harvard Medical School.

69 *"a good deal of exaggeration":* Cooper, *Letters and Journals of James Fenimore Cooper,* Vol. II, 139.

69 *Cooper had been reading aloud:* Cooper, *Correspondence of James Fenimore Cooper,* Vol. I, 38.

70 *he was expelled at age sixteen:* Cooper, *Letters and Journals of James Fenimore Cooper,* Vol. I, 5.

70 *Finding he liked the sailor's life:* Franklin, *James Fenimore Cooper: The Early Years,* 109, 111.

70 *"By persuasion of Mrs. Cooper":* Cooper, *Letters and Journals of James Fenimore Cooper,* Vol. I, 44, 43.

71 *The house he had built burned:* Ibid., 84.

71 *Cooper had written* The Last of the Mohicans*:* Franklin, *The New World of James Fenimore Cooper,* 240.

71   *"I think* Pioneers, Mohicans": Cooper, *Letters and Journals of James Fenimore Cooper,* Vol. I, 168.

72   *He was hailed as the American Walter Scott:* Ibid., Vol. II, 84.

72   *"the mere butterflies":* Ibid., Vol. I, 15.

72   *"The fear of losing their butterfly distinctions":* Ibid., 16.

72   *"It is a weary path, indeed":* Cooper, *The Prairie* (Penguin), 23.

72   *"a point of honor":* Cooper, *Letters and Journals of James Fenimore Cooper,* Vol. II, 61.

72   *"gaining ground daily":* Ibid., Vol. I, 165.

73   *"more than anyone":* Ashbel Smith to W. Hall, February 25, 1832, Center for American History, University of Texas at Austin.

73   *"a very* distingué *part of the town":* Susan Cooper to her sister Caroline, April 26, n.d. (probably 1833), James Fenimore Cooper Papers, Beinecke Library, Yale University.

73   *The salon is near thirty feet:* Cooper, *Gleanings in Europe: France,* Vol. I, 83. The building in which the Coopers lived at 59 rue Saint-Dominique is still there.

73   *"adjoining Mr. Cooper's library":* Susan Cooper to her sister Caroline, April 26, n.d. (probably 1833), James Fenimore Cooper Papers, Beinecke Library, Yale University.

73   *"prattle like natives":* Cooper, *Letters and Journals of James Fenimore Cooper,* Vol. I, 223.

73   *"We [are] . . . very retired":* Susan Cooper to her sister Martha, January 26–27, 1831, James Fenimore Cooper Papers, Beinecke Library, Yale University.

74   *"Instead of seeking society":* Cooper, *Gleanings in Europe: France,* Vol. I, xx.

74   *"The people seem to think":* Cooper, *Letters and Journals of James Fenimore Cooper,* Vol. I, 209.

74   *Willis would describe:* Ibid., Vol. II, 122.

74   *"Some of the best hours":* Willard, *Journal and Letters, from France and Great Britain,* 90.

74   *"our worthy friend, Mr. Morse":* Susan Cooper to her sister Caroline, January 26, 1832(?), James Fenimore Cooper Papers, Beinecke Library, Yale University.

74   *"an excellent man":* Silverman, *Lightning Man,* 113.

75   *"daily . . . almost hourly":* Morse, *Samuel F. B. Morse: His Letters and Journals,* Vol. II, 314.

75   *"gentlemen in all republican simplicity":* Franklin, *James Fenimore Cooper: The Early Years,* 382.

75   *"understood the look of a gentleman":* Dowling, *Oliver Wendell Holmes in Paris,* 119.

75   *"genius in land speculation":* Cunningham, ed., *James Fenimore Cooper: A Re-Appraisal,* 374.

75   *"my noble-looking":* Cooper, *Correspondence of James Fenimore Cooper,* Vol. I, 340.

76   *"Geography"* Morse: Morse, *Samuel F. B. Morse: His Letters and Journals,* Vol. I, 15; Silverman, *Lightning Man,* 10.

76   *"very steady and good scholars":* Morse, *Samuel F. B. Morse: His Letters and Journals,* Vol. I, 21.

76   *"I was made for a painter":* Ibid.

76   *"unsteady":* Ibid., 11.

76   "Attend to one thing at a time": Ibid., 4.

76   *"steady and undissipated":* Ibid., 5.

76   *"one object":* Silverman, *Lightning Man,* 12.

76 *"Your mama and I"*: Morse, *Samuel F. B. Morse: His Letters and Journals,* Vol. I, 22.

77 *"no use of Segars"*: Silverman, *Lightning Man,* 11.

77 *"The main business of life"*: Morse, *Samuel F. B. Morse: His Letters and Journals,* Vol. I, 8.

77 *study under Washington Allston:* Ibid., 21, 32.

77 *His parents had designed:* Ibid., 31–32.

78 *desire to "shine":* Ibid., 177.

78 *"mortifying":* Ibid., 74–75.

78 *"and that really to improve":* Ibid., 75.

78 *"Oh, he is an angel":* Silverman, *Lightning Man,* 22.

79 *Morse was amazed to learn:* Morse, *Samuel F. B. Morse: His Letters and Journals,* Vol. I, 45.

79 *"appeared very zealous":* Prime, *The Life of Samuel F. B. Morse,* 36.

79 *"Paint large!":* Ibid., 103.

79 *"Mr. West . . . told me":* Morse, *Samuel F. B. Morse: His Letters and Journals,* Vol. I, 102.

79 *"These are necessary to a painter":* Ibid.

79 *"You mention being acquainted":* Ibid., 118.

79 *"quarrelsome companions":* Ibid., 180.

80 *"no nice dinners":* Silverman, *Lightning Man,* 27.

80 *"mere portrait painter":* Ibid., 132.

80 *I need not tell you:* Ibid.

80 *"I long to bury myself":* Ibid., 152.

81 *"She is very beautiful":* Ibid., 204.

81 *"Is she acquainted with domestic affairs":* Ibid., 207.

81 $2,000 to $3,000: Morse, *Samuel F. B. Morse: His Letters and Journals,* Vol. I, 209.

81 *he developed a flexible (leather) piston:* Ibid., 211.

81 *machine for carving marble:* Ibid., 245, 247.

81 *Reverend Morse was asked to leave the pulpit:* Ibid., 223–24.

82 *"fully employed":* Ibid., 257.

82 *"a nine days' wonder":* Ibid., 258.

82 *"You will rejoice with me":* Ibid., 259.

82 *"My feelings were almost too powerful for me":* Ibid., 262.

82 *"not good":* Ibid.

82 *"noble" countenance:* Ibid., 261.

82 *"accordance between the face and the character":* Ibid., 262.

83 *"There was a great crowd":* Ibid.

83 *"I have but little room":* Ibid., 264.

83 *"My affectionately beloved son":* Ibid., 265.

83 *"My whole soul seemed wrapped":* Ibid., 269.

83 *To my friends here:* Ibid., 270.

84 *"a life of severe and perpetual toil":* New York *Evening Post,* May 4, 1827.

84 *Reverend Jedidiah Morse died:* Morse, *Samuel F. B. Morse: His Letters and Journals,* Vol. I, 288.

84 *In 1828 she, too, died:* Ibid., 293.

85 *The sun is just disappearing:* Willis, *Pencillings by the Way,* 112.

85 *"exotic production":* Delaporte, *Disease and Civilization,* 17.

85 *The first word of cholera in Paris:* New York *Evening Post,* May 1, 1832.

85 *"in the presence of thirty-eight medical men":* Ibid.

86 *"Her eyes were started from their sockets":* Willis, *Pencillings by the Way,* 126.

86 *Stomach contained a quart of reddish fluid:* James Jackson, Jr., to James Jackson, Sr., March 20, 1832, Jackson Family Papers, Countway Library, Harvard Medical School.

86 *"Vast numbers of people":* New York Evening Post, May 7, 1832.

86 *"a disease of the most frightful nature":* James Jackson, Jr., to James Jackson, Sr., April 1, 1832, Jackson Family Papers, Countway Library, Harvard Medical School.

86 *"It is almost like walking through an autopsy room":* Ibid.

86 *The official bulletin of the morning:* Journal of Ashbel Smith, April 3, 1832, Center for American History, University of Texas.

86 *"But if, as I think it highly possible":* James Jackson, Jr., to James Jackson, Sr., November 25, 1831, Jackson Family Papers, Countway Library, Harvard Medical School.

87 *We are bound as men:* James Jackson, Jr., to James Jackson, Sr., April 1, 1832, Jackson Family Papers, Countway Library, Harvard Medical School.

87 *The common understanding:* See, generally, Delaporte, *Disease and Civilization,* 199–200.

87 *Wild rumors spread: New-York Mirror,* May 19, 1832; *New York Evening Post,* May 18, 1832.

88 *"We have had pestilence":* Susan Cooper to her sister, April 1832, James Fenimore Cooper Papers, Beinecke Library, Yale University.

88 *"in the doctor's hands":* Cooper, *Letters and Journals of James Fenimore Cooper,* Vol. II, 242.

88 *"bilious attack":* Ibid.

88 *"It is spreading rapidly all over France":* Susan Cooper to her sister, April 1832, James Fenimore Cooper Papers, Beinecke Library, Yale University.

88 *"Samuel was nervous even unto flight":* Cooper, *Letters and Journals of James Fenimore Cooper,* Vol. II, 245.

88 *"The churches are all hung in black":* Willis, *Pencillings by the Way,* 120.

88 *A young French woman, Amandine-Aurore-Lucie Dupin:* Harlan, *George Sand,* 141.

89 *There was a* cholera-waltz: Willis, *Pencillings by the Way,* 122.

89 *I walk by the riverside:* James Jackson, Jr., to James Jackson, Sr., April 5, 1832, Jackson Family Papers, Countway Library, Harvard Medical School.

89 *"bent on bringing some especial thing":* Memorial of James Fenimore Cooper, 18.

90 *"My anxiety to finish my picture":* Morse, *Samuel F. B. Morse: His Letters and Journals,* Vol. I, 422.

90 *The thirty-eight pictures in his painting:* See, generally, David Tatham, "Samuel F. B. Morse's Gallery of the Louvre: The Figures in the Foreground," *American Art Journal,* Vol. XIII, No. 4 (Autumn 1981), 38–48.

92 *"total want of all the usual courtesies":* Trollope, *Domestic Manners of the Americans,* 20.

92 *"I do not like their principles":* Ibid., vii.

92 *Nathaniel Willis had observed:* Willis, *Pencillings by the Way,* 110.

92 *"He has a bold, original, independent mind":* Morse, *Samuel F. B. Morse: His Letters and Journals,* Vol. I, 426–28.

93 *"without feeling every day":* Willis, *Pencillings by the Way,* 164.

93 *"Paris is a home to me":* Ibid., 165.

93 *Even Alexander von Humboldt:* Silverman, *Lightning Man,* 117.

93 *"took pains to find me out":* Ibid.

94 *Probably 12,000 people:* Arnold, *Memoir of Jonathan Mason Warren, M.D.,* 54.

94 *By summer's end:* Ibid.

94 *In New York the epidemic: New York Times,* April 15, 2008.

94 *Fourth of July:* Morse, *Samuel F. B. Morse: His Letters and Journals,* Vol. I, 423–25.

94 *"like the buoys upon tide-water":* Ibid., 425.

95 *"a splendid and valuable" work:* Silverman, *Lightning Man,* 117.

95 *In the completed painting:* See, generally, Tatham, "Samuel F. B. Morse's Gallery of the Louvre: The Figures in the Foreground," *American Art Journal,* Vol. XIII, No. 4 (Autumn 1981), 38–48.

97 *By rendering Sue Cooper as he did:* Ibid., 41, 44–45.

97 *"dissipating their time in gambling":* Mabee, *American Leonardo,* 129.

97 *"disfiguring the landscape":* Ibid.

97 *"numberless bowings":* Ibid.

97 *"If it were a mere civility":* Ibid., 130.

97 *Once, on a street in Rome:* Silverman, *Lightning Man,* 105.

98 *"He is with me":* Morse, *Samuel F. B. Morse: His Letters and Journals,* Vol. I, 426.

98 *more than 200 people a day were dying: New York Evening Post,* September 3, 1832.

98 *His work at the Louvre at an end:* Morse, *Samuel F. B. Morse: His Letters and Journals,* Vol. I, 432.

99 *"the manner, the place, and the moment":* Silverman, *Lightning Man,* 153–54.

99 *"I confess I thought the notion":* Morse, *Samuel F. B. Morse: His Letters and Journals,* Vol. I, 419.

99 *I recollect also:* Ibid., 418.

100 *"My picture, c'est fini":* Cooper, *Correspondence of James Fenimore Cooper,* Vol. I, 320.

100 *It went on public view: New York Evening Post,* October 14, 1833.

100 *We do not know which most to admire: New-York Mirror,* November 2, 1833.

100 *Eventually it was bought:* Silverman, *Lightning Man,* 129–30.

100 *Morse had hoped to get:* Ibid., 129.

101 *That The Gallery: New York Times,* July 30, 1982.

4. The Medicals

The wealth of material in the letters of the American medical students in Paris is extraordinary, and again one is struck by how extremely well written they are, even though the young men writing them (with the exception of Oliver Wendell Holmes) did not aspire to be writers or to write "writing." Those by Mason Warren, for example, are exemplary in their thoroughness and clarity. But then it was a day and age when young people were expected to write letters to their families and to use the English language properly. Holmes's letters are notable for their wit and his consistent, irrepressible love of learning.

Of books written at the time, *Old Wine in New Bottles* by Augustus Kinsley Gardener is particularly good on student life in Paris, and John Harley Warner's excellent *Against the Spirit of System: The French Impulse in Nineteenth-Century American Medicine* (1998) has also been of great value in understanding the long-range effect of the Paris training.

PAGE

103 It is no trifle: Morse, *Life and Letters of Oliver Wendell Holmes*, Vol. I, 86.

104 *Largest of the hospitals:* Warren, *The Parisian Education of an American Surgeon*, 13.

104 *This one hospital:* Ibid., 13–14.

104 *Second in size:* Ibid., 14.

104 *The Hôpital des Enfants Malades:* Ibid., 15.

105 *In the single year of 1833:* Ibid., 13.

105 *In Boston, by comparison:* Ibid.

105 *Velpeau, as everyone knew:* Ibid., 29.

106 *Compared to the hospitals:* Stewart, *Eminent French Surgeons*, 129.

106 *Its central amphitheater for lectures:* The École de Médecine's central amphitheater is still much as it was and still in use.

106 *Further, for foreign students:* Warren, *The Parisian Education of an American Surgeon*, 3.

106 *There were still, in the 1830s:* Jones, "American Doctors and the Parisian Medical World, 1830–1840," *Bulletin of the History of Medicine*, January–February 1973, 50.

106 *[At about age eighteen] the lad:* Cooper, *The Pioneers*, 72–73.

107 *Enrollment was as high as:* Jones, "American Doctors and the Parisian Medical World, 1830–1840," 50.

107 *The American students:* Ibid., 47.

107 *"attachment":* Ashbel Smith to Eugene Rousseau, January 1, 1832, Center for American History, University of Texas.

107 *"I dislike to fix":* Ashbel Smith to Daniel Seymour, February 6, 1832, Center for American History, University of Texas.

108 *"The glory of the week":* James Jackson, Jr., to James Jackson, Sr., November 1, 1832, Jackson Papers, Countway Library, Harvard Medical School.

108 *"perfect ignoramus":* Bowditch, *Life and Correspondence of Henry Ingersoll Bowditch*, Vol. II, 128.

108 *"quite overwhelmed":* Warren, *The Parisian Education of an American Surgeon*, 158.

108 *"very nice":* Oliver Wendell Holmes to his parents, May 31, 1833, Holmes Papers, Houghton Library, Harvard University.

108 *A "little extra":* Ibid.

108 *Holmes found he could make it:* Though the house where Holmes lived is no longer there on the rue Monsieur-le-Prince, the walk to the École can still be made in under four minutes, even by one more than three times his age.

108 *I commonly rise:* Warren, *The Parisian Education of an American Surgeon*, 100.

109 *"No one ever heard":* Arnold, *Memoir of Jonathan Mason Warren, M.D.*, 269.

109 *he "never for a moment":* Ibid., 119.

109 *In a pencil drawing:* See Warren, *The Parisian Education of an American Surgeon*, 10.

109 *"He was, in truth":* Arnold, *Memoir of Jonathan Mason Warren, M.D.*, 171–72.

110 *"in regard to the necessities":* Warren, *The Parisian Education of an American Surgeon*, 70.

110 *"Observe operations":* Arnold, *Memoir of Jonathan Mason Warren, M.D.*, 306.

110 *"Send me without delay":* Ibid., 309.

111 *"There is a face":* Jackson, *Memoir of James Jackson, Jr., M.D.*, 212.

111 *In the United States:* Jones, "American Doctors and the Parisian Medical World, 1830–1840," 50.

111 *"a French head"*: James Jackson, Jr., to James Jackson, Sr., July 27, 1831, Jackson Papers, Countway Library, Harvard Medical School.

112 *"shake them off from his broad shoulders"*: Morse, *Life and Letters of Oliver Wendell Holmes*, Vol. I, 93.

112 *Holmes had from the start*: See ibid., 102.

112 *Dupuytren, one of the medical giants*: See ibid., 93.

112 *"a lesser kind of deity"*: Ibid.

112 *"make a show"*: Warren, *The Parisian Education of an American Surgeon*, 89.

112 *"His operations are always brilliant"*: Arnold, *Memoir of Jonathan Mason Warren, M.D.*, 84.

112 *"He is always endeavoring"*: Warren, *The Parisian Education of an American Surgeon*, 108.

112 *"very neat and rapid"*: Ibid., 167.

113 *"kind of off-hand way"*: Ibid.

113 *"a great drawer of blood"*: Morse, *Life and Letters of Oliver Wendell Holmes*, Vol. I, 92.

113 *"Without it he would probably"*: Warren, *The Parisian Education of an American Surgeon*, 205.

114 *If his orders*: Ibid., 108.

114 *"In his lectures"*: Ibid., 116.

114 *"le brigand"*: Warren, *The Parisian Education of an American Surgeon*, 84.

115 *"a good sound head"*: Holmes, "Some of My Early Teachers," in *Medical Essays, 1842–1882*, 429.

115 *"The French woman"*: Gardener, *Old Wine in New Bottles*, 161.

115 *The second great difference*: Truax, *The Doctors Warren of Boston*, 153.

116 *In the South*: Shafer, *The American Medical Profession, 1783–1850*, 62.

116 *"living a kind of student's life"*: Sanderson, *The American in Paris*, Vol. I, 184.

116 *"cut him into inch pieces"*: Warren, *The Parisian Education of an American Surgeon*, 51.

116 *Here the assiduous student*: Gardener, *Old Wine in New Bottles*, 68–69.

117 *I never was so busy*: Morse, *Life and Letters of Oliver Wendell Holmes*, Vol. I, 89.

117 *By comparison, the library*: Shafer, *The American Medical Profession: 1783–1850*, 73.

117 *"What a feast"*: Warner, *Against the Spirit of System*, 110.

118 *"By the blessing of God"*: Bowditch, *Life and Correspondence of Henry Ingersoll Bowditch*, Vol. I, 20.

118 *"devotes himself"*: Ibid., 28.

119 *"The days are so much occupied"*: Warren, *The Parisian Education of an American Surgeon*, 221.

119 *"an entire new field"*: Ibid., 191–92.

119 *Madame Marie-Louise LaChapelle*: Ibid.

119 *Bowditch was to say*: Arnold, *Memoir of Jonathan Mason Warren, M.D.*, 205 n.

119 *To Wendell Holmes*: Morse, *Life and Letters of Oliver Wendell Holmes*, Vol. I, 186.

119 *"I send you by ship"*: Warren, *The Parisian Education of an American Surgeon*, 107.

120 *Trois Frères*: Ibid., 59.

120 *"sad on finding himself"*: Ibid., 111.

120 *There is no doubt*: Ibid.

121 *"There is a notion"*: Morse, *Life and Letters of Oliver Wendell Holmes*, Vol. I, 106.

121 *The King is caricatured*: Ibid.

121 *"sober revolution":* Ibid.
121 *"impulsive, ardent":* Bowditch, *Life and Correspondence of Henry Ingersoll Bowditch*, Vol. I, 84–85.
121 *Olivia Yardley:* Ibid.
121 *"La Grisette":* Arnold, *Memoir of Jonathan Mason Warren, M.D.*, 112.
122 *"with his* grisette": Frazee, *The Medical Student in Europe*, 116.
122 *In the 1840s young Philip Claiborne Gooch:* Warner, *Against the Spirit of System*, 119. See also Gooch's journal at the Virginia Historical Society, Richmond, Virginia.
122 *I uncork the bottle:* Ibid., 125.
123 *"At 6 A.M. I go to the hospital":* Jones, "American Doctors and the Parisian Medical World, 1830–1840," 76.
123 *"the love of truth":* Holmes, "Some of My Early Teachers," in *Medical Essays, 1842–1882*, 436.
124 *"You are working, sir":* Morse, *Life and Letters of Oliver Wendell Holmes*, Vol. I, 107.
124 *"almost a novelty":* Ibid., 183.
124 *"The mind of this gentleman":* Bowditch, *Life and Correspondence of Henry Ingersoll Bowditch*, Vol. I, 37.
124 *"serene and grave aspect":* Morse, *Life and Letters of Oliver Wendell Holmes*, Vol. I, 91.
125 *"In very truth":* James Jackson to his father, January 16, 1833, Jackson Family Papers, Countway Library, Harvard Medical School.
126 *"We are a business":* Jackson, *Memoir of James Jackson, Jr., M.D.*, 80.
126 *"In two hours":* James Jackson to his father, July 13, 1833, Jackson Family Papers, Countway Library, Harvard Medical School.
126 *"Thrice happy":* Bowditch, *Life and Correspondence of Henry Ingersoll Bowditch*, Vol. I, 64.
126 *because the young man:* Morse, *Life and Letters of Oliver Wendell Holmes*, Vol. I, 108–9.
127 *"I am more and more attached":* Ibid., 89.
127 *My aim has been to qualify:* Oliver Wendell Holmes to his parents, April 30, 1834, Holmes Papers, Houghton Library, Harvard University.
127 *"I tell you that it is not throwing away money":* Morse, *Life and Letters of Oliver Wendell Holmes*, Vol. I, 123.
127 *"one poor fellow":* Warren, *The Parisian Education of an American Surgeon*, 195.
128 *"Many of the dead":* Ibid., 196.
128 *"No one could excite":* Morse, *Life and Letters of Oliver Wendell Holmes*, Vol. I, 122.
128 *"I have seldom seen":* Arnold, *Memoir of Jonathan Mason Warren, M.D.*, 178.
128 *Our autumnal fever:* Jackson, *Memoir of James Jackson, Jr., M.D.*, 58.
128 *"What shall I say of his ambition?":* Ibid., 65.
129 *"They buried the old patriot":* Willis, *Pencillings by the Way*, 459.
130 *"great crowd":* Warren, *The Parisian Education of an American Surgeon*, 243.
130 *George Shattuck:* See Warner, *Against the Spirit of System*, 76–77.
130 *"every kind of hurt":* Pierce, *Memoir and Letters of Charles Sumner*, Vol. I, 249.
130 *"Blessed be science":* Oliver Wendell Holmes to his parents, December 28, 1834, Holmes Papers, Houghton Library, Harvard University.
131 *"He had quite a large audience":* Pierce, *Memoir and Letters of Charles Sumner*, Vol. I, 241.
131 *They were standing in the midst:* Ibid., 241.

131 *"They appear to be nothing more"*: Ibid., 113.

132 *"a thousand things undone"*: Ibid., 294.

132 *"medical mecca"*: Warren, *The Parisian Education of an American Surgeon*, 2.

132 *nearly seven hundred Americans*: Ibid., 2.

132 *"Apart from all other considerations"*: Arnold, *Memoir of Jonathan Mason Warren, M.D.*, 216.

132 *"modern scientific medicine"*: Warner, *Against the Spirit of System*, 363.

133 *John Collins Warren, at age seventy*: Warren, *The Parisian Education of an American Surgeon*, 64.

133 *A month later, on November 12, 1846*: Ibid.

134 *"He was never tired"*: Morse, *Life and Letters of Oliver Wendell Holmes*, Vol. I, 1, 77.

134 *"He had that quality"*: Holmes, "Some of My Early Teachers," in *Medical Essays, 1842–1882*, 532–33.

135 *"that I gave myself"*: Ibid., 433.

135 *"the best of all"*: Holmes, "Scholastic and Bedside Teaching," in *Medical Essays, 1842–1882*, 305.

135 *"He never allowed his interests"*: Bowditch, *Life and Correspondence of Henry Ingersoll Bowditch*, Vol. I, 262.

136 *While medicine is your chief aim*: Ibid., 262–63.

136 *"I suspect that my ear-drums"*: Arnold, *Memoir of Jonathan Mason Warren, M.D.*, 254.

136 *"Found my old garçon, John"*: Bowditch, *Life and Correspondence of Henry Ingersoll Bowditch*, Vol. I, 318.

136 *"as beautiful in his old age"*: Ibid., 144.

5. American Sensations

The advantage of the English language newspaper *Galignani's Messenger* as a window on American life in Paris can hardly be overstated. Founded in 1814, it became a daily paper that covered virtually all aspects of political, business, cultural, social, and international news and with a degree of objectivity rare for a Paris paper. For following events surrounding *les sensations américaines*, it has been of immense help.

S. Frederick Starr's *Louis Moreau Gottschalk* is a superb biography of the brilliant pianist, and best by far on George Catlin and his show are Catlin's own writings in *The Adventures of the Ojibbeway and Ioway Indians*.

PAGE

139 *We were met on the steps*: Catlin, *The Adventures of the Ojibbeway and Ioway Indians*, Vol. II, 211.

139 *"the most beautiful"*: Gernsheim and Gernsheim, *L. J. M. Daguerre: The History of the Diorama and the Daguerreotype*, 89.

139 *the paddle steamer Sirius*: See *New York Herald* articles, May 2–June 21, 1838.

140 *"Little Healy"*: Healy, *Reminiscences of a Portrait Painter*, 25.

140 *Arriving in Paris at age twenty-one*: Ibid., 34–35.

141 *"Perhaps many a young and audacious"*: Ibid., 108.

141 *"went to work with a will"*: Ibid., 36.

141 *He coolly turned over my sheet*: Ibid., 78.

141 *"There was in Couture's"*: Ibid., 80.

142 *"a saddened and almost despairing"*: Ibid., 37.

142 "Gros est un homme": Ibid., 38.
142 "He had outlived his popularity": Ibid., 39.
142 My life at this time was a life: Ibid.
142 His physical appearance: De Mare, G. P. A. Healy, American Artist, 28.
142 He was seldom still: Healy, Reminiscences of a Portrait Painter, 109, 40.
143 General Lewis Cass, asked Healy: Ibid., 116, 52.
143 In June of 1838: Ibid., 204, 167.
143 Audubon was in London: Ibid., 205.
143 "enough to fix my destinies": Ibid., 43.
143 In the spring of 1839: Ibid., 45.
143 "not a penny": Ibid., 47.
143 General Cass, who was on excellent terms: Ibid., 116.
144 Before beginning the portrait: Ibid., 117–18.
144 Healy found Louis-Philippe easy to talk to: Ibid., 118.
144 The concierge kept the place clean: Ibid., 48.
144 They began entertaining: Ibid., 44–45.
145 "perfectly charming": Ibid., 177.
145 "cold": Ibid., 175, 179.
146 "Healy is an excellent fellow": Appleton, Life and Letters of Thomas Gold Appleton, 243–44.
146 "a rather better place": Healy, Reminiscences of a Portrait Painter, 50.
146 In 1842, at the request of the king: Ibid., 121.
146 When the king and others: De Mare, G. P. A. Healy, American Artist, 111.
146 "a magnificent-looking man": Healy, Reminiscences of a Portrait Painter, 163.
146 In the spring of 1845: Ibid., 139.
147 "Can't sit, sir": Ibid.
147 The visitor from Paris: Ibid., 141, 144, 145.
147 From Tennessee: Ibid., 145.
147 It seemed odd: Ibid., 153–54.
147 "Brush them off on one side": Ibid., 156.
148 "I was but a small boy then": Ibid., 154.
148 "In those far-away days": Ibid., 160.
148 "Having been delayed": Prime, The Life of Samuel F. B. Morse, 358.
148 "The beauty of the Seine": New York Herald, September 18, 1838.
148 Morse thought their hotel: Prime, The Life of Samuel F. B. Morse, 359.
149 "You cannot know the depth": Ibid., 361.
149 He welcomed the prospect: Silverman, Lightning Man, 129–32.
149 Moreover, to his extreme embarrassment: Ibid., 122.
149 A new position as professor: Ibid., 124.
149 carrying in his groceries after dark: Morse, Samuel F. B. Morse: His Letters and Journals, Vol. II, 43.
149 For a long time: Cooper, Letters and Journals of James Fenimore Cooper, Vol. I, 80, 143–44.
149 "historical edifice": Ibid., 80.
149 Morse had joined in the Nativist movement: Silverman, Lightning Man, 139.
150 "The serpent has already commenced": Ibid., 135.
150 Mr. Morse is a scholar and a gentleman: New York Commercial Advertiser, April 19, 1836.
150 But when word reached Morse: Silverman, Lightning Man, 144–45.
150 "Dismiss it then from your mind": Prime, The Life of Samuel F. B. Morse, 290.
151 He "staggered under the blow": Silverman, Lightning Man, 145.

151 *"quite ill":* Cooper, *Letters and Journals of James Fenimore Cooper,* Vol. III, 259.

151 *"divine authorization":* Silverman, *Lightning Man,* 145.

151 *"Painting has been a smiling mistress":* Morse, *Samuel F. B. Morse: His Letters and Journals,* Vol. II, 31.

151 *He must attend to one thing:* Ibid., Vol. I, 3.

151 *The apparatus he had devised:* Ibid., Vol. II, 38–39.

151 *"so rude":* Ibid., 42.

151 *His chief problem:* Ibid., 54–55.

151 *By increasing the power:* Silverman, *Lightning Man,* 160.

152 *A physician from Boston:* Ibid., 153, 156.

152 *"mutual discovery":* Ibid., 156.

152 *"I cannot conceive of":* Prime, *The Life of Samuel F. B. Morse,* 380.

152 *And for this reason:* Cooper, *Letters and Journals of James Fenimore Cooper,* Vol. VI, 43.

152 *Morse sent a preliminary request:* Silverman, *Lightning Man,* 159, 161, 163, 164.

152 *In a larger space:* Ibid., 165–66.

152 *"write at a distance":* Prime, *The Life of Samuel F. B. Morse,* 337.

152 *They set up their apparatus:* Silverman, *Lightning Man,* 168, 169.

153 *The wonder of Morse's invention:* Ibid., 169.

153 *Yet Morse felt he must have government support:* Morse, *Samuel F. B. Morse: His Letters and Journals,* Vol. II, 92.

153 *"The ground of objection":* Prime, *The Life of Samuel F. B. Morse,* 358.

153 *Paris was to treat him better:* Ibid., 360.

153 *For the sake of economy:* Ibid., 362.

153 *"great inventors who are generally permitted":* Morse, *Samuel F. B. Morse: His Letters and Journals,* Vol. II, 107.

153 *"levee day":* Ibid., 107.

154 *"the grand exhibitor":* Prime, *The Life of Samuel F. B. Morse,* 362.

154 *I explained the principles:* Ibid., 362.

154 *"So you want to be an artist?":* Healy, *Reminiscences of a Portrait Painter,* 34–35.

155 *"wonderful discovery":* Silverman, *Lightning Man,* 188.

155 *"He gave it a thorough examination":* Prime, *The Life of Samuel F. B. Morse,* 363.

155 *"My present instrument":* Ibid., 363.

155 *The savants of the Académie convened:* Silverman, *Lightning Man,* 179.

155 *"in the midst of the most celebrated":* Prime, *The Life of Samuel F. B. Morse,* 365.

155 *There was not a familiar face:* Ibid., 364–65.

155 *"A buzz of admiration":* Ibid., 365.

155 *The event was acclaimed in the Paris:* Silverman, *Lightning Man,* 179.

155 Comptes Rendus: Prime, *The Life of Samuel F. B. Morse,* 366.

156 *"transcends all yet made known":* Ibid., 368.

156 *"another revolution is at hand":* Ibid., 369.

156 *I do not doubt:* Ibid.

156 *"In being abroad":* Ibid., 368.

156 *"most flattering":* Ibid., 370.

156 *"Everything moves at a snail's pace":* Ibid., 371.

156 *"Dilatoriness":* Ibid., 374.

157 *"There is more of the 'go-ahead' ":* Ibid., 377.

157 *By March:* Silverman, *Lightning Man,* 189.

157 *paid a visit to Monsieur Louis Daguerre:* Prime, *The Life of Samuel F. B. Morse,* 389–90.

157 *"I am told every hour":* Ibid., 388.

157 *Skilled in theatrical lighting:* Ibid., 15–17.

157 *"flocking":* Ibid., 18.

158 *"We cannot sufficiently urge":* Ibid.

158 *Years before:* Silverman, *Lightning Man,* 189.

158 *"one of the most beautiful discoveries":* Morse, *Samuel F. B. Morse: His Letters and Journals,* Vol. II, 129.

158 *They are produced on a metallic:* Gernsheim and Gernsheim, *L. J. M. Daguerre: The History of the Diorama and the Daguerreotype,* 89.

158 *Morse stayed:* Ibid., 90.

159 *Morse's account of his visit:* Ibid., 129.

159 *Once Morse arrived back in New York:* Prime, *The Life of Samuel F. B. Morse,* 394.

159 *"throughout the United States your name":* Gernsheim and Gernsheim, *L. J. M. Daguerre: The History of the Diorama and the Daguerreotype,* 129.

159 *With help from a professor of chemistry:* Ibid., 132.

159 *Four years later, in July of 1844:* Galignani's Messenger, July 12, 1844.

159 *"What hath God wrought!":* Morse, *Samuel F. B. Morse: His Letters and Journals,* Vol. II, 222.

160 *Democratic National Convention:* Prime, *The Life of Samuel F. B. Morse,* 497.

160 *"This is indeed the annihilation":* Galignani's Messenger, July 12, 1844.

160 *Coinciding with all this excitement:* Starr, *Louis Moreau Gottschalk,* 59.

160 *With a genius for publicity:* Saxon, *P. T. Barnum: The Legend and the Man,* 9.

161 *"The people like to be humbugged":* New York Times, November 9, 2007.

161 *a child from Bridgeport, Connecticut:* Saxon, *P. T. Barnum: The Legend and the Man,* 123–24.

161 *He was perfectly formed:* Barnum, *Struggles and Triumphs of Forty Years' Recollections of P. T. Barnum,* 16.

161 *"for the opportunity":* Ibid., 135.

161 *He paid the boy's parents:* Ibid., 163.

161 *"to test the curiosity":* Ibid., 165.

161 *"decided hit":* Ibid., 173.

161 *before Her Majesty Queen Victoria:* Ibid., 176–77.

161 *"The French are exceedingly impressionable":* Ibid., 192.

161 *He settled Tom:* Ibid., 188–89.

162 *Yet Tom Thumb:* Ibid., 193.

162 *Tom came attired:* New York Commercial Advertiser, April 26, 1845.

162 *"apt pupil":* Barnum, *Struggles and Triumphs of Forty Years' Recollections of P. T. Barnum,* 164.

162 *When a lady:* New York Commercial Advertiser, April 26, 1845.

162 *The king asked:* Ibid., April 16, 1845.

162 *Tom performed an original dance:* Ibid., April 26, 1845.

163 *Reportedly the wardrobe:* Ibid.

163 *"FOR A SHORT TIME ONLY":* Galignani's Messenger, March 24, 1845.

163 *The grace, readiness:* Ibid., March 27, 1845.

163 *Shop windows:* Barnum, *Struggles and Triumphs of Forty Years' Recollections of P. T. Barnum,* 193.

163 *So great was the attendance:* Ibid., 193.

163 *The pale, slender:* Starr, *Louis Moreau Gottschalk,* 59–60.

164 *The boy had been born:* Ibid., 15, 24, 21, 29, 33, 45.

164 *One immensely wealthy young woman:* Ulrich Leben and Robert McDonald Parker, *The American Ambassador's Residence in Paris,* Special Issue of *Connaissance des Arts* (Paris: SFPA, 2007), 10–11.

164 *Young Moreau was enrolled:* Starr, *Louis Moreau Gottschalk,* 46.

165 *"This child is surprising":* Ibid., 48, 49.

165 *Moreau had been in Paris three years:* Ibid., 59.

165 *According to one study:* Ibid., 50.

165 *Chopin outshone them all:* Ibid., 55.

165 *His debut at the Salle Pleyel:* Ibid., 59.

166 *"Good, my child":* Ibid., 60.

166 *"the neatness and elegance of his playing":* Le Courrier de la Louisiane, May 17, 1845.

166 *"chiefly to the upper ranks":* Ibid.

166 *Midway into April:* Galignani's Messenger, April 17, 1845.

166 *Besides the more than five hundred paintings:* Catlin, *The Adventures of the Ojibbeway and Ioway Indians,* Vol. II, 211.

166 *Catlin's story:* See generally, Obituary, *New York Times,* December 24, 1872, and William Dunlap, "Mr. Catlin's Lectures," *New-York Mirror,* October 14, 1837.

166 *"a whole lifetime of enthusiasm":* Gurney and Heyman, eds., *George Catlin and His Indian Gallery,* 30.

167 *"a vast country of green fields":* Ibid., 40.

167 *"the proud and heroic elegance":* Ibid., 28.

167 *"rescue from oblivion":* Catlin, *The Adventures of the Ojibbeway and Ioway Indians,* Vol. I, 217.

167 *In 1839 he offered:* Gurney and Heyman, eds., *George Catlin and His Indian Gallery,* 63.

167 *The paintings went on display:* Ibid., 65–66, 69.

168 *The servants in the house:* Ibid., 206.

168 *"There was a great outcry":* Ibid., 207.

168 *"My father":* Ibid., 208.

168 *Others in the delegation included:* Galignani's Messenger, April 17, 1845.

168 *"of fine stature":* Ibid.

169 *While the Indians continued their sightseeing:* Catlin, *The Adventures of the Ojibbeway and Ioway Indians,* 205.

169 *"No tragedian ever trod the stage":* Gurney and Heyman, eds., *George Catlin and His Indian Gallery,* 157.

170 *all with their wampum:* Catlin, *The Adventures of the Ojibbeway and Ioway Indians,* Vol. II, 211.

170 *"in the most free and familiar manner":* Ibid.

170 *"Tell these good fellows":* Ibid., 212.

170 *In the winter of 1797–98:* Dippie, *Catlin and His Contemporaries: The Politics of Patronage,* 120.

170 *"This," wrote Catlin:* Catlin, *The Adventures of the Ojibbeway and Ioway Indians,* 212.

171 *With ceremony befitting a head of state:* Ibid., 212–14.

171 *"and sounding the frightful war-whoop":* Ibid., 215.

172 *"the most magnificent place God ever prepared":* Tocqueville, *Democracy in America,* Vol. I, 24.

172 *"energy of character and skill":* Catlin, *The Adventures of the Ojibbeway and Ioway Indians*, 319.

172 *In the midst of such reflections:* Ibid., 320.

173 *"crowds of savants":* Galignani's Messenger, May 24, 1845.

173 *"drawing full and fashionable":* Ibid., May 30, 1845.

173 *"wild America"* and *"natural man":* Sand, "Relation d'un Voyage Chez les Sauvages de Paris," *Le Diable à Paris: Paris et Les Parisiens*, 205–207.

173 *Delacroix was among:* Gurney and Heyman, eds., *George Catlin and His Indian Gallery*, 75.

173 *At first, I felt:* Sand, *Le Diable à Paris: Paris et Les Parisiens*, 205.

174 *The carefree Parisian audience:* Ibid.

174 *"the proud, free character":* Gurney and Heyman, eds., *George Catlin and His Indian Gallery*, 235.

174 *"one of the most curious collections":* Constitutionnel, June 22, 1845.

175 *Seeing the collection:* Observateur, October 9, 1845.

175 *"remarkable power":* Moniteur Industriel, November 16, 1845.

175 *Little Wolf, shattered, "heartbroken":* Catlin, *The Adventures of the Ojibbeway and Ioway Indians*, 272.

175 *Chopin mentioned her in a letter:* Chopin, *Chopin's Letters*, 287.

175 *"her feeble form wasted away":* Catlin, *The Adventures of the Ojibbeway and Ioway Indians*, 276.

175 *In the midst of his grief:* Ibid., 277–80.

176 *Still more acclaim followed:* Ibid., 285, 293.

176 *Ever the showman:* Saxon, *P. T. Barnum: The Legend and the Man*, 143.

176 *Moreau Gottschalk, who grew:* Dictionary of American Biography, Vol. IV, 442.

176 *"retired":* Catlin, *The Adventures of the Ojibbeway and Ioway Indians*, 311.

176 *"I thus painted on":* Ibid., 312.

176 *Catlin's Indian exhibition:* Dippie, *Catlin and His Contemporaries: The Politics of Patronage*, 125.

177 *Before leaving Paris:* Truettner, *The Natural Man Observed: A Study of Catlin's Indian Gallery*, 53.

177 *"My occupation was changed":* Catlin, *The Adventures of the Ojibbeway and Ioway Indians*, 323.

177 *By the time Healy returned:* Healy, *Reminiscences of a Portrait Painter*, 165–66.

6. Change at Hand

The correspondence of a diplomat serving abroad is necessarily of two kinds, official and private. In the case of Richard Rush, his extensive correspondence, all in his own hand, is divided. The official communications with Washington are at the National Archives, his private or personal letters at the Library of Congress.

PAGE

179 How then can strangers: Rush, *Occasional Productions, Political, Diplomatic, and Miscellaneous*, 462.

179 *"increased a hundred fold":* Willson, *America's Ambassadors to France (1777–1927)*, 218.

179 *"daily fire":* Ibid.

179 *In a long career in public service:* Dictionary of American Biography, Vol. III, pt. 2, 231–33.

180 *was still impressively handsome:* See Sparks, "Political Portraits with Pen and Pencil: Richard Rush," *United States Magazine,* Vol. VII (1840).

180 *On the afternoon of July 31:* Rush, *Occasional Productions, Political, Diplomatic, and Miscellaneous,* 303.

180 *"sufficiently grand":* Richard Rush to his sons, September 20, 1847, Richard Rush Papers, Library of Congress, Washington, D.C.

180 *I am representing a great nation:* Richard Rush to his son, October 6, 1847, Richard Rush Papers, Library of Congress, Washington, D.C.

181 *Last night we were at Mr. Walsh's:* Rush, *Occasional Productions, Political, Diplomatic, and Miscellaneous,* 336–37.

181 *"the appearance of things":* Richard Rush to James Buchanan, September 24, 1847, National Archives, Washington, D.C.

182 *"loose thoughts":* Ibid.

182 *"They are thrown out":* Ibid.

182 *"decamp":* Cooper, *Letters and Journals of James Fenimore Cooper,* Vol. V, 313.

182 *"serious troubles":* Ibid., 240.

182 *"profound and universal":* *Galignani's Messenger,* January 6, 1848.

182 *"Notwithstanding all the reform banquets":* Richard Rush to James Buchanan, January 22, 1848, National Archives, Washington, D.C.

182 *"We are sleeping on a volcano":* Mansel, *Paris Between Empires: Monarchy and Revolution, 1814–1852,* 397.

182 *"formidable":* Richard Rush to his sons, February 20, 1848, Richard Rush Papers, Library of Congress, Washington, D.C.

183 *We were too near to be pleasant:* Baker, *Richard Morris Hunt,* 41.

183 *"I have seen enough blood":* Howarth, *Citizen King: The Life of Louis-Philippe,* 319.

183 *The poor King and his government:* Ibid., 334.

184 *"general confusion [and] uncertainty":* Richard Rush to James Buchanan, February 24, 1848, National Archives, Washington, D.C.

184 *"moderation and magnanimity":* Richard Rush to James Buchanan, March 4, 1848, National Archives, Washington, D.C.

184 *"The responsibilities of my public station":* Rush, *Occasional Productions, Political, Diplomatic, and Miscellaneous,* 366.

184 *"But the French people were themselves":* Ibid., 367.

185 *"Was it for me to be backward when France":* Ibid., 368.

185 *As representative of the United States:* *Galignani's Messenger,* March 1, 1848.

185 *"full and unqualified approbation":* Message from the President of the United States, April 3, 1848, Executive No. 32, U.S. Senate, 30th Cong., 1st sess.

185 *"wonderfully, miraculously tranquil":* Richard Rush to George Bancroft, March 24, 1848, National Archives, Washington, D.C.

186 *"very civil and good tempered":* Emerson, *The Journals and Miscellaneous Notebooks of Ralph Waldo Emerson,* ed. Sealts, Vol. X, 270–71.

186 *"criminal excesses":* *Galignani's New Paris Guide,* 15th edition, 1827.

186 *They did not and could not employ:* Richard Rush to James Buchanan, July 3, 1848, National Archives, Washington, D.C.

187 *"On his way he passed my door":* Ibid.

187 *"So vast and horrible a desolation":* *New York Daily Tribune,* July 13, 1848.

187 *"beautiful revolution":* Saul K. Padover, *Karl Marx: An Intimate Biography* (New York: McGraw-Hill, 1978), 252.

187 *"battlefield":* Rush, *Occasional Productions, Political, Diplomatic, and Miscellaneous,* 449.

187 *"Scattered wisps of hay":* Ibid., 450.

187 *None can understand a country:* Ibid., 461–62.

188 *Of the more than seven million votes cast:* Mansel, *Paris Between Empires: Monarchy and Revolution, 1814–1852,* 414.

188 *"species":* Fuller, *At Home and Abroad,* 250.

188 *He comes abroad:* Ibid., 250–51.

189 *"instinctively bustling":* Ibid.

189 *"thinking American":* Ibid., 252.

189 *[He] recognized the immense advantage:* Ibid.

189 *"passably pretty ladies with excessively":* Fuller, *New York Tribune,* May 12, 1847.

189 *The air, half military, half dandy:* Ibid.

190 *I saw them and touched them:* Ibid.

190 *"takes rank in society like a man":* Fuller, *The Letters of Margaret Fuller,* Vol. IV, 256.

190 *"brilliant shows":* Ibid., 259.

190 *"It is too plain that you should conquer":* Ibid.

191 *"If that is a painting":* See biographical sketch of "William Morris Hunt" in *American National Biography,* ed. Garraty and Carnes (New York: Charles Scribner's Sons, 1964), 397.

191 *shared a bright, fifth-floor apartment:* The building where the Hunt brothers lived at 1 rue Jacob still stands.

191 *"Mr. William Hunt is our most":* Thomas Gold Appleton to his father, December 22, 1852, Massachusetts Historical Society.

191 *"with a very slender purse":* Blackwell, *Pioneer Work in Opening the Medical Profession to Women,* 2.

192 *"either mad or bad":* See biographical sketch of Elizabeth Blackwell in *Dictionary of National Biography,* Vol. I, 320.

192 *"not constituted":* Blackwell, *Pioneer Work in Opening the Medical Profession to Women.* See Introduction by Amy Sue Bix, 24.

192 *"the aspect of a great moral":* Ibid., 76.

192 *She was twenty-eight:* Passport application, National Archives, Washington, D.C.

193 *"sage-femme-in-chief":* Blackwell, *Pioneer Work in Opening the Medical Profession to Women,* 161.

193 *"So send a welcome greeting":* Ibid., 165.

193 *Imagine a large square of old:* Ibid.

193 *"all pretty and pleasant":* Ibid., 163.

193 *"eaten in haste":* Ibid., 167.

193 *"a little deformed woman, elderly":* Ibid., 161.

194 "en service": Ibid., 168.

194 *"If they answer promptly and well":* Ibid.

194 *Alternately satirical and furious:* Ibid., 169.

194 *"seeing all that was remarkable":* Ibid., 180.

194 *"How kind everybody was!":* Ibid., 188.

194 *"Yet the medical experience was":* Ibid., 186.

195 *"I am a native of the state of Kentucky":* Farrison, *William Wells Brown: Author and Reformer,* 140.

195 *"we shall break . . . in pieces every yoke":* Ibid., 150.

196 *"freely"*: Ibid.
196 *Curious to know more about him*: Ibid., 151.
196 *"It is with great concern"*: Alexis de Tocqueville to Richard Rush, Paris, June 27, 1849, National Archives, Washington, D.C.
197 *"Liberty and Union, now and forever"*: De Mare, *G. P. A. Healy, American Artist*, 169.
197 *According to a pamphlet*: Voss, "Webster Replying to Hayne: George Healy and the Economics of History Painting," *American Art*, Vol. XV, no. 3 (Fall 2001), 40.
197 *"my big picture"*: Healy, *Reminiscences of a Portrait Painter*, 166.
198 *Healy put the final touches*: *Webster's Reply to Hayne* still hangs in the place of honor at Faneuil Hall.
198 *"It was a proud moment that"*: *Boston Transcript*, September 22, 1851.
198 *The countenance—an admirable likeness*: *New York Times*, October 13, 1851.
198 *"We must answer decidedly"*: Voss, "Webster Replying to Hayne: George Healy and the Economics of History Painting," 48.
199 *"However onerous to an artist"*: Healy, *Reminiscences of a Portrait Painter*, 166.
199 *"a very castle of a man"*: *Memorial of James Fenimore Cooper*, 7.
199 *Irving was one of those notables*: Ibid., 12.
199 *"I never met with a more"*: Ibid., 36.

7. A City Transformed

Often it is the secondary characters in events of the past, like secondary characters in the theater, who have the most pertinent or entertaining observations to contribute. This is certainly the case with the brother of Harriet Beecher Stowe and what he wrote about their time together in Paris. *Harriet Beecher Stowe in Europe, The Journal of Charles Beecher*, is pure delight and certainly confirms that she was not the only one in the family with talent. Likewise, the chronicle of Napoleon III and his Empress would not be the same absent all that is unfolded by their American dentist Thomas W. Evans in his book *The Second French Empire*.

PAGE
201 At last I have come: Stowe, *Sunny Memories of Foreign Lands*, Vol. II, 158.
201 *"sleepwalker"*: Horne, *The Fall of Paris: The Siege and the Commune, 1870–1871*, 21.
201 *Victor Hugo, on the other hand*: Ridley, *Napoleon III and Eugénie*, 225.
201 *The British ambassador was "charmed"*: Gooch, *The Second Empire*, 17.
201 *Richard Rush found the president*: Rush, *Occasional Productions, Political, Diplomatic, and Miscellaneous*, 514.
201 *William C. Rives of Virginia*: William Rives to Secretary of State Clayton, November 14, 1849, Library of Congress.
202 *"He was very much better"*: Gooch, *The Second Empire*, 305.
202 *As a private person*: Ibid., 305.
202 *"His vulgar pleasures"*: Ibid.
202 *To Evans, the president*: Evans, *Memoirs of Dr. Thomas W. Evans: The Second French Empire*, 3.
202 *"extraordinary self-control"*: Ibid., 7.
202 *"My power is in an immortal name"*: Gooch, *The Second Empire*, 12.
203 *Like Louis-Philippe*: Evans, *Memoirs of Dr. Thomas W. Evans: The Second French Empire*, 3, 7.

203 *"Do you forget my years of study"*: Gooch, *The Second Empire*, 11.

203 *Then in 1846 he shaved off*: Ibid., 71.

203 *"It stands for order"*: Ibid., 15.

204 *The air was "soft and hazy"*: New York Times, November 6, 1851.

204 *They eat, drink*: Ibid.

204 *There were, however, Evans later wrote*: Evans, *Memoirs of Dr. Thomas W. Evans*, 6.

204 *At a formal reception*: Ibid.

204 *"Rubicon"*: Ridley, *Napoleon III and Eugénie*, 295.

205 *In a matter of hours*: Carson, *The Dentist and the Empress: The Adventures of Dr. Tom Evans in Gas-Lit Paris*, 20–21.

205 *The American minister, William Rives*: Secretary of State Daniel Webster to William Rives, January 12, 1852, Webster, *The Papers of Daniel Webster, Diplomatic Papers*, Vol. 2, 1850–1852, 186.

205 *"Napoleon the Little"*: Gooch, *The Second Empire*, 2.

205 *The author of this crime*: Ibid., 284.

206 *To a large part of the nation*: Carmona, *Haussmann: His Life and Times, and the Making of Modern Paris*, 179–80.

206 *He put a new prefect of the Seine*: Gooch, *The Second Empire*, 200.

206 *"according to their degree of urgency"*: Carmona, *Haussmann: His Life and Times, and the Making of Modern Paris*, 9.

206 *"demolition artist"*: Jones, *Paris: The Biography of a City*, 305.

207 *"I could never forget"*: Carmona, *Haussmann*, 298.

207 *Haussmann was vigorous*: Jordan, *Transforming Paris: The Life and Labors of Baron Haussmann*, 50.

207 *With its population now more than a million*: Jones, *Paris: The Biography of a City*, 297.

207 *The plan was to improve public health*: Ibid., 301.

208 *Streets and boulevards would be lined*: Ibid., 313.

208 *The emperor directed*: Ibid.; Horne, *The Fall of Paris*, 23.

208 *"At every step is visible"*: Levenstein, *Seductive Journey: American Tourists in France from Jefferson to the Jazz Age*, 87.

208 *Les Halles, a great new central market*: Jones, *Paris: The Biography of a City*, 316.

209 *"Is there not something"*: Lytton, *The Parisians*, 107.

209 *In the twists and curves*: Ibid., 107.

209 *By 1869 some 2.5 billion*: Korn, *History Builds the Town*, 62.

209 *"When building flourishes"*: Shapiro, *Housing the Poor of Paris: 1850–1902*, 33.

209 *Acting on "inside" information*: Carson, *The Dentist and the Empress*, 69–75.

210 *"floating palaces"*: New York Times, October 12, 1854.

210 *The Arctic*: Shaw, *The Sea Shall Embrace Them: The Tragic Story of the Steamship Arctic*, 25.

210 *"God grant the time"*: New York Times, October 12, 1854.

211 *Two years later, in the spring of 1853*: Hedrick, *Harriet Beecher Stowe: A Life*, 233.

211 *Over half a million British women*: Ibid., 244.

212 *"a saint"*: Fields, *Life and Letters of Harriet Beecher Stowe*, 154.

212 *They crossed on the steamship Canada*: Hedrick, *Harriet Beecher Stowe: A Life*, 233.

212 *"At last I have come into a dreamland"*: Stowe, *Sunny Memories of Foreign Lands*, Vol. II, 158.

212 *"a little bit of a woman"*: Hedrick, *Harriet Beecher Stowe: A Life*, 244.

212 *Hatty was a natural "observer"*: Beecher, *Harriet Beecher Stowe in Europe: The Journal of Charles Beecher*, 163.

213 *"My spirits always rise"*: Stowe, *Sunny Memories of Foreign Lands*, Vol. II, 164.

213 *Whole families come, locking up their door*: Ibid., 153.

213 *There were grayheaded old men*: Ibid.

214 *"All is vivacity"*: Ibid., 147.

214 *Seeing the emperor*: Ibid., 182.

214 *"talked away, right and left"*: Beecher, *Harriet Beecher Stowe in Europe*, 155.

214 *"Poor Hatty!"*: Ibid., 156–57.

214 *"very touching"*: Ibid., 165.

214 *Surely the "life artery"*: Stowe, *Sunny Memories of Foreign Lands*, Vol. II, 149.

214 *"And there is no scene"*: Ibid.

215 *As the instinct*: Ibid.

215 *"sublimity"*: Ibid., 150.

215 *"rules of painting"*: Ibid., 157.

215 *He chooses simple*: Ibid., 161.

215 *"the great, joyous"*: Ibid.

215 *Like Shakespeare*: Ibid., 163.

216 *"glorious enough"*: Ibid., 160.

216 *"painted with dry eyes"*: Ibid.

216 *"driest imitation"*: Ibid., 165.

216 *that passion for the outward*: Ibid., 167.

217 *I gazed until all surrounding*: Ibid., 152.

217 *"who had not seen human life"*: Ibid., 166.

217 *"With all New England's earnestness"*: Ibid., 392.

218 *"One in whom"*: Ibid.

218 *"The splendor of Paris"*: Hawthorne, *The French and Italian Notebooks*, ed. Woodson, 13.

218 *The emperor deserved great credit*: Ibid., 15.

219 *"Perhaps never before"*: *New York Times*, October 29, 1855.

219 *When Queen Victoria*: Ibid., September 14, 1855.

220 *American visitors, however, were delighted*: *New York Tribune*, August 23, 1855.

220 *Of the 796 French artists*: *The Crayon*, September 12, 1855.

220 *Among them were William Morris Hunt*: Ibid., November 5, 1855.

220 *William B. Ogden*: Healy, *Reminiscences of a Portrait Painter*, 57.

220 *I had often thought of returning*: Ibid., 57–88.

221 *He was small*: Walker, *James Abbott McNeill Whistler*, 24.

221 *Much of his boyhood*: Weintraub, *Whistler: A Biography*, 4–10.

221 *At sixteen, like his father*: Ibid., 16.

221 *The only course*: Ibid., 17, 19.

221 *"Had silicon been a gas"*: Ibid., 24.

221 *Nor would his "peculiar" hat*: Pennell and Pennell, *Life of James McNeill Whistler*, Vol. I, 5.

222 *He did, however, take up with*: Weintraub, *Whistler: A Biography*, 52.

222 *"the universal harmonizer"*: Walker, *James Abbott McNeill Whistler*, 95.

222 *"I don't think he stayed long"*: Pennell and Pennell, *Life of James McNeill Whistler*, Vol. I, 51.

222 *"His genius, however"*: Ibid., 52.

222 *"Everything he enjoyed"*: Ibid., 69.

222 *He left owing Monsieur Lalouette*: Weintraub, *Whistler: A Biography*, 58.

223 *"For heaven's sake"*: Thomas Appleton to his father, October 31, 1846, Massachusetts Historical Society.

223 *"I think slavery a sin"*: Donald, *Charles Sumner and the Coming of the Civil War*, 112.

223 *The first news of the savage physical attack: Galignani's Messenger*, June 9, 1856.

223 *The assault had taken place*: Donald, *Charles Sumner and the Coming of the Civil War*, 292–97.

223 *"The Crime against Kansas"*: Ibid., 283.

223 *Like Webster's reply to Hayne*: Ibid.

224 *"harlot slavery"*: Ibid., 285.

224 *An incensed congressman*: Ibid., 289–90.

224 *He chose the cane*: Ibid., 291.

224 *"wrest"*: Ibid.

224 *It was early afternoon*: Ibid., 291–97.

224 *"Mr. Sumner"*: Ibid., 294.

224 *Sumner's desk*: Ibid., 294–95. The fact that the desk would have been screwed to the floor was verified by the Senate Curator's Office in Washington, D.C.

225 *"thirty first-rate"*: Ibid., 295.

225 *"I wore my cane out"*: Ibid.

225 *"an oppressive sense of weight"*: White, "Was Charles Sumner Shamming, 1856–1869?" *New England Quarterly*, Vol. 33, No. 3 (September 1960), 307.

225 *Sumner departed New York*: Pierce, *Memoir and Letters of Charles Sumner*, Vol. III, 520.

226 *To look at Mr. Sumner now: New York Tribune*, April 11 and 13, 1857.

226 *"The sea air, or seasickness"*: Pierce, *Memoir and Letters of Charles Sumner*, Vol. III, 530.

226 *"Civilization seemed to abound"*: Ibid., 530.

226 *"sallied forth"*: Ibid.

226 *"The improvements are prodigious"*: Ibid.

227 *From his "beautiful apartment"*: Ibid.

227 *"He did not disguise"*: Ibid., 531.

227 *"With a people so changeable"*: Ibid., 538.

227 *"He speaks of the emperor"*: Ibid., 535.

228 *"they call it* la grippe": Ibid., 525.

228 *"very gay and beautiful"*: Ibid., 526.

228 *"I tremble for Kansas"*: Ibid.

228 *Young Henry James*: Donald, *Charles Sumner and the Coming of the Civil War*, 347.

228 *At one evening affair*: Pierce, *Memoir and Letters of Charles Sumner*, Vol. III, 539.

228 *At two other gatherings*: Ibid., 538–39.

228 *He visited the Imperial Library*: Ibid., 539.

228 *He made a return visit*: Ibid., 540.

228 *"I dine out very often"*: Thomas Appleton to his father, December 22, 1852, Massachusetts Historical Society.

229 *One evening it was an American naval officer*: Pierce, *Memoir and Letters of Charles Sumner*, Vol. III, 540.

229 *"although apparently functionally sound"*: Donald, *Charles Sumner and the Coming of the Civil War*, 275.

229 *"vileness and vulgarity"*: Ibid., 276.

230 *When several doctors advised:* Ibid., 561.

230 *Charles Edward Brown-Séquard:* Ibid., 336–37.

230 *"a bold experimenter":* Pierce, *Memoir and Letters of Charles Sumner,* Vol. III, 563.

230 *The cure the doctor recommended:* Ibid., 338.

230 *"The doctor is clear":* Ibid., 565.

231 *"baseless theory":* Donald, *Charles Sumner and the Coming of the Civil War,* 340.

231 *From what is known:* See ibid., 336–42.

231 *"cruel treatment":* Pierce, *Memoir and Letters of Charles Sumner,* Vol. III, 565.

231 *When in August:* Galignani's Messenger, August 22, 1858.

231 *"At this moment my system":* Prime, *The Life of Samuel F. B. Morse,* 600.

232 *"the utmost enthusiasm":* New York Times, September 9, 1858.

232 *Of the eighty gentlemen:* Galignani's Messenger, August 22, 1858.

232 *"Every figure of rhetoric":* Silverman, *Lightning Man,* 376.

232 *"benefactor of mankind":* Report on the Dinner Given by Americans in Paris, August 17th at the "Trois Frères" to Professor S. F. B. Morse in Honor of His Invention of the Telegraph and on the Occasion of Its Completion Under the Atlantic Ocean, 40.

232 *He was to be awarded:* Silverman, *Lightning Man,* 376.

233 *I seize the moment:* Sumner, *Works of Charles Sumner,* Vol. IV, 410.

233 *"no great cause for despondency":* Galignani's Messenger, September 11, 1858.

233 *He was determined:* Pierce, *Memoir and Letters of Charles Sumner,* Vol. III, 570.

233 *"If anybody cares to know":* Ibid., 591.

233 *In the last few days:* Ibid., 592.

234 *"dear old Sumner":* Donald, *Charles Sumner and the Coming of the Civil War,* 288.

234 *He walks on those great long legs:* Ibid.

234 *"sat to the artist":* Eliot, *Abraham Lincoln: An Illustrated Biography,* 99.

234 *"She complains of my ugliness":* Healy, *Reminiscences of a Portrait Painter,* 69.

234 *"to hide my horrible":* Ibid., 70.

235 *"a Northern man":* Ibid., 68.

235 *"heart and soul":* Donald, *Charles Sumner and the Coming of the Civil War,* 323.

235 *In Paris the April weather:* Galignani's Messenger, April 5, April 20, April 23, 1861.

235 *Wagner's* Tannhäuser: Galignani's Messenger, March 15 and 27, 1861.

235 *Longfellow's* Hiawatha: New York Tribune, April 1, 1861.

236 *With great military pageantry:* Galignani's Messenger, April 4, 1861.

236 *"deep mourning":* Ibid.

236 *Demolition for the "prolongation":* Ibid., April 16, 1861.

236 *"telegraphic dispatches":* Ibid., April 27, 1862.

236 *"THE CIVIL WAR IN THE STATES":* Ibid., April 28, 1861.

236 *"in a frantic state of excitement":* Ibid.

236 *We who are residing:* New York World, April 28, 1861.

8. Bound to Succeed

The most valuable account of the life of Augustus Saint-Gaudens is his own autobiography, his *Reminiscences* in two volumes, compiled in the last years of his life with the help of his son Homer. Virtually all that he had to relate was either dictated to Homer or recorded by phonograph. Much that he did not cover, or that needed editorial explanation, Homer supplied. There is admirable candor and absence of pretension throughout, as characteristic of the man, and much that is particularly appealing concerns his student years in New York and Paris, along with generous samplings from the reminiscences of such lifelong friends as Alfred Garnier and Paul Bion.

Two subsequent biographies are *Saint-Gaudens and the Gilded Era* by Louise Hall Tharp (1969) and *Uncommon Clay: The Life and Works of Augustus Saint-Gaudens* by Burke Wilkinson (1985).

As an illustrated guide to the life and works, nothing surpasses *August Saint-Gaudens, 1848–1907, A Master of American Sculpture*, published by the Musée des Augustins, Toulouse, and the Musée National de la Coopération Franco-Américain, Château de Blérancourt. Its detailed chronology is a resource to be found nowhere else.

PAGE

239 I was chiefly impressed: Saint-Gaudens, *The Reminiscences of Augustus Saint-Gaudens*, Vol. I, 87.

239 *Augustus Saint-Gaudens came to Paris:* Ibid., 52.

239 *He was nineteen years old:* Ibid., 61.

239 *I walked with my heavy carpet bag:* Ibid., 62.

240 *His French father:* Ibid., 37.

240 *"sicker than a regiment":* Ibid., 61–62.

240 *Gus, as he was known:* Ibid., 9.

240 *In New York, after a struggle:* Ibid., 12.

240 *The sign read* FRENCH LADIES' BOOTS: Ibid., 16.

240 *At home the father addressed:* Ibid.

240 *"sweet Irish brogue":* Ibid., 18.

240 *"picturesque personality":* Ibid., 16.

240 *"typical long":* Ibid., 11.

241 *"heroic charges":* Ibid., 20.

241 *"through my fault":* Ibid.

241 *"one long imprisonment":* Ibid., 22.

241 *"the delights" of* Robinson Crusoe: Ibid., 24.

241 *His father apprenticed him:* Ibid., 32, 38.

241 *"a miserable slavery":* Ibid., 28–39.

241 *"When he was not scolding me":* Ibid., 38.

241 *"Sculptured heads": Scientific American*, November 6, 1847.

242 *The success of a cameo:* Saint-Gaudens, *The Reminiscences of Augustus Saint-Gaudens*, Vol. I, 37.

242 *The apprenticeship with Avet:* Ibid., 43.

242 *The boy refused:* Ibid.

242 *He later spoke:* Ibid.

242 *He went to work for another:* Ibid., 44.

242 *"I became a terrific worker":* Ibid., 45.

242 *Indeed, I became so exhausted:* Ibid., 45–46.

243 *Once, from an open window:* Ibid., 41.

243 *"Grant himself":* Ibid., 42.

243 *"entirely out of proportion":* Ibid.

243 *One day during the Draft Riots:* Ibid., 50.

243 *Like many parents, Eakins's father:* Kirkpatrick, *Revenge of Thomas Eakins*, 49.

244 *an "interminable" line:* Saint-Gaudens, *The Reminiscences of Augustus Saint-Gaudens*, Vol. I, 51.

244 *"full sympathy with the Rebellion":* Washburne, *Recollections of a Minister to France,* Vol. II, 248.

244 *That was well known:* Ibid.

244 *A Confederate mission:* Carson, *The Dentist and the Empress: The Adventures of Dr. Tom Evans in Gas-Lit Paris,* 83.

244 *The one time when the "excitement":* Galignani's Messenger, June 21, 1864.

245 *The painter Édouard Manet:* See Sloane, "Manet and History," *Art Quarterly,* Vol. XIV, no. 2 (Summer 1951), 93–95.

245 *According to one journal: Galignani's Messenger,* June 23, 1864.

245 *"In his spare but strong-knit":* Wilkinson, *Uncommon Clay: The Life and Works of Augustus Saint-Gaudens,* 373.

245 *"took long walks":* Saint-Gaudens, *The Reminiscences of Augustus Saint-Gaudens,* Vol. I, 60–61.

246 *"always the* triste *undertone":* Ibid., 129.

246 *Before leaving for Paris:* Ibid., 361.

246 *He considered a pencil portrait:* Ibid., 25.

246 *"bad straits":* Ibid., 62.

246 *"cheaper to cheaper":* Ibid., 63.

246 *"miserably poor":* Ibid.

246 *"dwell on the ugly side":* Ibid., 62.

246 *We worked in a stuffy:* Ibid., 69.

247 *The theme was "objects for the improvement":* King, *The Judgment of Paris: The Revolutionary Decade That Gave the World Impressionism,* 194.

247 *At the time of the official opening: Galignani's Messenger,* April 2, 1867.

247 *People were calling it: New York Times,* May 10, 1867.

247 *"At the Grand Hôtel they were":* Ibid., June 17, 1867.

248 *"Paris is now the great center":* Morse, *Samuel F. B. Morse: His Letters and Journals,* Vol. II, 454.

248 *The favorite American import:* Kirkpatrick, *The Revenge of Thomas Eakins,* 98.

248 *Travel was a "wild novelty":* Twain, *Innocents Abroad,* 645.

248 *They "deceive and defraud":* Ibid., 123.

248 *"I knew by their looks":* Ibid., 151.

249 *The idea of it is to dance:* Ibid., 136.

249 *"the beautiful city":* Ibid., 151.

249 *The most admiring crowds:* See Blake, ed., *Report of the U.S. Commissioners to the Paris Exposition, 1867,* Vol. I, 12; FitzWilliam Sargent to his mother, June 12, 1867, Archives of American Art.

249 *"M. Homer ought not":* Simpson, *Winslow Homer: Paintings of the Civil War,* 258.

250 *"I am working hard":* Cikovsky and Kelly, *Winslow Homer,* 191.

250 *A painting by Homer:* Adler, *Americans in Paris, 1860–1900,* 245.

250 *It was a small bronze, a standing figure:* Saint-Gaudens, *The Reminiscences of Augustus Saint-Gaudens,* Vol. II, 184.

251 *Further, on July 2, word reached: Galignani's Messenger,* July 2, 1867.

251 *The great majority:* Ibid.

251 *"The United States, having astonished":* Washburne, *Recollections of a Minister to France,* Vol. I, 35.

252 *The famous couturier:* Latour, *Kings of Fashion,* 83.

252 *Bringing one lady:* McCullough, *The Great Bridge,* 166.

252 *"waiting for ladies' dresses":* Adams, *The Letters of Henry Adams,* ed. J. C. Levenson, Vol. I, 546.

252 *"hordes of low Germans":* Ibid., 547.

252 *Dr. Thomas Evans regularly supplied:* Carson, *The Dentist and the Empress,* 77.

252 *One resident American in Paris:* Ibid., 78–79.

253 *I was obliged:* De Hegermann-Lindencrone, *In the Courts of Memory, 1858–1875,* 96.

253 *"The American flag is freely displayed":* FitzWilliam Sargent to his mother, June 12, 1867, Archives of American Art.

253 *"Lincoln's portrait":* Ibid.

253 *"He sketches quite nicely":* Mary Sargent to her mother from Nice, October 20, 1867.

254 *When a formal notification:* Saint-Gaudens, *The Reminiscences of Augustus Saint-Gaudens,* Vol. I, 73–74.

254 *"the triumphant one":* Ibid., 74.

254 *"with little, intelligent black eyes":* Ibid.

254 *But Jouffroy's compliments:* Ibid., 77.

254 *At a student party:* Ibid., 77–78.

254 *"I was finally admitted":* Ibid., 78.

254 *"amorous adventure":* Ibid., 63.

254 *"keep company":* Ibid.

255 *But so "soaring":* Ibid., 79.

255 *"Spartan-like superiority":* Ibid.

255 *"possessing so strongly":* Ibid., 87.

255 *"the most joyous creature":* Ibid.

255 *"crazy about wrestling":* Ibid., 84.

255 *"Five minutes after we reached":* Ibid., 88.

255 *"Nobody got his money's worth":* Ibid.

256 *"singing and whistling":* Ibid., 61.

256 *Conceive an idea:* Saint-Gaudens, *The Reminiscences of Augustus Saint-Gaudens,* Vol. II, 19.

256 *You can do anything you please:* Ibid., Vol. I, 166–67.

256 *"There was a real Egyptian sky":* McCullough, *The Path Between the Seas: The Creation of the Panama Canal, 1870–1914,* 54.

257 *"keeping up with the Joneses":* Singley, ed., *Edith Wharton: The House of Mirth: A Casebook,* 4.

257 *"deepest scorn":* Saint-Gaudens, *The Reminiscences of Augustus Saint-Gaudens,* Vol. I, 79.

257 *"Then," remembered Alfred Garnier:* Ibid., 93.

257 *The audience poured out:* Ibid.; Wilkinson, *Uncommon Clay: The Life and Works of Augustus Saint-Gaudens,* 37.

258 *"No language can measure":* Elihu Washburne to U. S. Grant, July 20 and 27, 1870, Grant, *The Papers of U. S. Grant,* ed. John Y. Simon, Vol. XX, 255.

259 *"as fine as I ever saw":* Sheridan, *The Personal Memoirs of Philip Henry Sheridan, General, United States,* Vol. II, 450.

259 *"No person not in Paris":* Washburne, *Recollections of a Minister to France,* Vol. I, 65.

259 *"covered it all over":* Ibid., 58.

259 *On September 2 came the ultimate:* Horne, *The Fall of Paris: The Siege and the Commune, 1870–1871,* 324; Elihu Washburne Diary, September 3, 1870, Library of Congress.

259 *More than 104,000 of the emperor's troops:* Horne, *The Fall of Paris,* 52.

260 *"Louis Napoleon Bonaparte and his dynasty"*: Marzials, *Life of Léon Gambetta*, 67.

260 *"I am rejoiced beyond expression"*: Elihu Washburne to his brother William, September 7, 1870, Library of Congress.

260 *"So perishes a harlequin"*: Jacobi, *Life and Letters of Mary Putnam Jacobi*, 258.

260 *France, or at least Paris:* Ibid.

260 *"I yield to force"*: Carson, *The Dentist and the Empress*, 117.

261 *She hurried down the long Grande Galerie:* Ibid., 118.

261 *"smiles everywhere, people dressed"*: Higonnet, *Paris: Capital of the World*, 289.

261 *The house he and his wife, Agnes:* Carson, *The Dentist and the Empress*, 73.

262 *He wasted no time:* Ibid., 107.

262 *On a flat stretch of open land:* Ibid., 108.

262 *"We were thoroughly impressed"*: Evans, *Memoirs of Dr. Thomas W. Evans*, 305.

263 *At five o'clock he knocked:* Carson, *The Dentist and the Empress*, 122.

263 *Evans appealed to an English yachtsman:* Ibid., 127.

263 *"I am heart and soul"*: Augustus Saint-Gaudens to Mrs. Whittlesey, September 17, 1870, Dartmouth College Special Collections, Hanover, N.H.

263 *"in utter confusion and dust"*: Saint-Gaudens, *The Reminiscences of Augustus Saint-Gaudens*, Vol. I, 101.

263 *"They seemed to me like so many"*: Augustus Saint-Gaudens to Mrs. Whittlesey, September 17, 1870, Dartmouth College Special Collections, Hanover, N.H.

264 *"in terrible grief"*: Wilkinson, *Uncommon Clay*, 40.

264 "Je suis persuadé": Saint-Gaudens, *The Reminiscences of Augustus Saint-Gaudens*, Vol. I, 94.

264 *"But they are getting old"*: Ibid., 99.

9. Under Siege

Elihu Washburne's extraordinary Paris diary has until now been overlooked beyond the Washburne family for the reason that its daily entries were written on separate sheets of paper from which letterpress copies were made; and these were later mixed in among his regular correspondence in the bound volumes deposited in 1946 at the Library of Congress.

It was the discovery of these entries during work on this book, as well as locating the original handwritten entries, bound separately as a diary, among the Washburne family collection at Livermore, Maine, that have made possible the account given in Chapters 9 and 10.

It is only in the nearly 200 diary entries (68 pages in typescript) that the full drama and detail of what Washburne experienced on the scene are to be found.

In addition, his own two-volume *Recollections of a Minister to France* (1887) remains a major source.

Of great value also are the contemporary accounts by three other Americans in Wickham Hoffman's *Camp, Court, and Siege: A Narrative of Personal Adventure and Observation During Two Wars* (1877); *Shut Up in Paris* (1871) by Nathan Sheppard; and the experiences of the Moulton family in Lillie de Hegermann-Lindencrone's *In the Courts of Memory, 1858–1875* (1912).

Excellent historical studies are provided in *The Siege of Paris, 1870–1871: A Political and Social History* (1971) by Melvin Kranzberg; and *From Appomattox to Montmartre* by Philip Katz (1998).

PAGE

267 I shall deem it my duty: Elihu Washburne to Secretary of State Hamilton Fish, July 19, 1870, Washburne, *Franco-German War and the Insurrection of the Commune, Correspondence of E. B. Washburne*, 1.

267 *There are no carriages:* Elihu Washburne Diary, September 19, 1870, Library of Congress.

267 *"Has the world ever witnessed":* Ibid.

268 *The Tuileries Garden:* Kranzberg, *The Siege of Paris, 1870–1871: A Political and Social History*, 24.

268 *"And it seems odd":* Elihu Washburne Diary, September 19, 1870, Library of Congress.

268 *"It is in Paris":* Kranzberg, *The Siege of Paris, 1870–1871*, 9–10.

268 *"Paris, pushed to extremities":* Ibid.

268 *A French tutor:* Frank Moore to Mr. Ostermann, September 27, 1869, Papers of Frank Moore, New-York Historical Society.

269 *Daughter Marie would remember:* Fowler, *Reminiscences: My Mother and I*, 28.

269 *"most agreeable":* Elihu Washburne to Mr. Plummer, March 5, 1870, Library of Congress.

269 *"Her tact, her grace":* Elihu Washburne to Edward Hempstead, July 14, 1870, Library of Congress.

269 *At the start of summer:* Elihu Washburne to C. C. Washburne, June 23, 1870, Library of Congress.

269 *"picked up their hats":* Washburne, *Recollections of a Minister to France, 1869–1877*, Vol. I, 127.

269 *All the rest "ran away":* Elihu Washburne Diary, September 23, 1870, Library of Congress.

269 *"I thought it would be, on all accounts":* Washburne, *A Biography of Elihu Benjamin Washburne: Congressman, Secretary of State, Envoy Extraordinary*, Vol. IV, 379.

270 *"However anxious I might be":* Elihu Washburne to Hamilton Fish, October 3, 1870, Washburne, *Franco-German War and the Insurrection of the Commune, Correspondence of E. B. Washburne*, 76.

270 *Numbers of Germans were being arrested:* Kranzberg, *The Siege of Paris, 1870–1871*, 9–10.

271 *"Employers discharged":* Hoffman, *Camp, Court, and Siege: A Narrative of Personal Adventure and Observation During Two Wars: 1861–1865; 1870–1871*, 153.

271 *The suffering, both moral and physical:* Ibid.

271 *As an assistant secretary named Frank Moore:* Frank Moore to his wife, Laura, September 7, 1870, Frank Moore Papers, New-York Historical Society.

271 *The American Legation:* Washburne, *A Biography of Elihu Benjamin Washburne*, Vol. IV, 13.

271 *One day a child:* Elihu Washburne Diary, November 11, 1870, Library of Congress.

272 *"I am depressed":* Elihu Washburne to Adele Washburne, September 2, 1870, Library of Congress.

272 *Yesterday forenoon:* Ibid.

272 *"Everything that energy":* Hoffman, *Camp, Court, and Siege*, 154.

272 *"And here let me remark":* Ibid., 154–55.

273 *Raised on a farm in Maine:* Hunt, *Israel, Elihu, and Cadwallader Washburn: A Chapter in American Biography*, 155.

273 *A judgment expressed by* The Nation: Hess, "An American in Paris," *American Heritage*, February 1967, 18.

273 *The* New York World *had called him:* New York World, December 12, 1868.

274 *"coarse, uncultivated":* Welles, *Diary of Gideon Welles*, Vol. III, 551.

274 *"enlarged views":* Ibid., 543.

274 *"He may represent":* Ibid., 551.

274 *"Our family was very, very poor":* Hunt, *Israel, Elihu, and Cadwallader Washburn*, 158.

274 *He had been born on September 23, 1816:* Ibid., 155.

274 *The family struggled to survive:* Kelsey, *Remarkable Americans: The Washburn Family*, 8.

274 *It would be said of the Washburn children:* Hunt, *Israel, Elihu, and Cadwallader Washburn*, 300.

275 *her mind was "quick":* Ibid., 158.

275 *"The foundation that is layed":* Martha Benjamin Washburn to Elihu Washburne from Livermore, Maine, March 21, 1846, Washburn-Norlands Living History Center, Livermore, Maine.

275 *When I think of her labors:* Hunt, *Israel, Elihu, and Cadwallader Washburn*, 158.

275 *As one of the founders of General Mills:* Grossman and Jennings, *Building a Business Through Good Times and Bad: Lessons From 15 Companies, Each with a Century of Dividends*, 45.

275 *"I dug up stumps":* Hunt, *Israel, Elihu, and Cadwallader Washburn*, 159.

275 *"more congenial":* Ibid., 160.

276 *"There is no humbug":* Ibid., 163.

276 *In 1839, after another two years:* Ibid., 166.

276 *He arrived by stern-wheeler:* Elihu Washburne Diary, April 1, 1871, Library of Congress.

276 *"knee deep":* Ibid.

276 *"a litigious set":* Hunt, *Israel, Elihu, and Cadwallader Washburn*, 172.

276 *In less than a month:* Ibid., 173.

276 *In a rough, wide-open town:* Ibid.

276 *He liked the life:* Ibid., 172.

277 *In 1845, at twenty-nine:* Ibid., 178.

277 *"He was not under the influence":* Ibid., 179.

277 *In little time:* Ibid., 183.

277 *He was praised:* Ibid., 183, 193.

277 *An Ohio newspaperman:* Ibid., 192–93.

277 *"blow off like a steam engine":* Ibid., 192.

277 *As chairman of the Committee on Appropriations:* Ibid., 183.

277 *It was Israel Washburn:* Ibid., 32–33.

277 *It happened at about two in the morning:* New York Herald, February 6, 1858; New York Times, February 8, 1858; New York Tribune, February 6, 8, 1858; Chicago Tribune, February 8, 1858.

277 *"Mr. Washburne of Illinois":* New York Herald, February 6, 1858.

278 *In 1860, when Lincoln ran for president:* Hess, "An American in Paris," 21.

278 *On the day Lincoln stepped:* Hunt, *Israel, Elihu, and Cadwallader Washburn*, 229–30; Hess, "An American in Paris," 21.

278 *"Without doing any injustice":* Hunt, *Israel, Elihu, and Cadwallader Washburn*, 220.

278 *The confidence Washburne placed in Grant:* Ibid., 243.

279 *"His life was despaired of"*: Fowler, *Reminiscences: My Mother and I*, 23.

279 *"quiet and repose"*: Elihu Washburne to his sister, October 12, 1870, Library of Congress.

279 *In its long history:* Sibbet, *Siege of Paris*, 169.

279 *"The weather is charming"*: Elihu Washburne to Adele Washburne, September 28, 1870, Library of Congress.

279 *The formal exchange:* Undated news article in Elihu Washburne scrapbooks, Library of Congress.

280 *On September 21, a daring balloonist:* Kranzberg, *The Siege of Paris, 1870–1871*, 38.

280 *Eventually some sixty-five balloons:* Ibid.

280 *"I have never before so much"*: Elihu Washburne to Adele Washburne, September 28, 1870, Library of Congress.

280 *To his brother Israel in Maine:* Elihu Washburne to Israel Washburn, October 21, 1870, Library of Congress.

281 *"great courage and spirit"*: Elihu Washburne Diary, September 30, 1870, Library of Congress.

281 *In early October:* Transcript of recollections by Charles William May of his balloon trip out of Paris, Manuscript Collection, Boston Athenaeum, 3.

281 *But when, on the morning of October 7:* Horne, *The Fall of Paris: The Siege and the Commune, 1870–1871*, 85.

281 *It was another perfect day:* Transcript of recollections by Charles William May of his balloon trip out of Paris, Manuscript Collection, Boston Athenaeum, 7.

281 *The air was clear:* Ibid., 7–8.

282 *So we opened the sand bag:* Ibid., 8.

282 *"There was no sense of motion"*: Ibid.

282 *"The days go and"*: Washburne, *Recollections of a Minister to France, 1869–1877*, Vol. I, 189.

282 *"laid by" his own sufficient stock:* Ibid., 133.

282 *"Were it not for Mr. Washburne"*: Labouchère, *Diary of a Besieged Resident in Paris*, 24.

282 *"cheerily shaking everyone"*: Ibid., 70.

283 *"The world cannot fail to admire"*: *Chicago Journal*, no date, Elihu Washburne scrapbooks, Library of Congress.

283 *"suffering . . . so sore I can hardly move"*: Elihu Washburne Diary, October 15, 1870, Library of Congress.

283 *Many people called:* Ibid., October 17, 1870, Library of Congress.

283 *"But Washburne"*: Hoffman, *Camp, Court, and Siege*, 203.

283 *"interminable gabble"*: Washburne, *Recollections of a Minister to France, 1869–1877*, Vol. I, 201.

283 *"a little depression"*: Elihu Washburne to Israel Washburn, October 27, 1870, Library of Congress.

283 *"We drove to the French"*: Hoffman, *Camp, Court, and Siege*, 204.

283 *While we waited:* Ibid., 205.

284 *On October 31, Trochu's army:* Kranzberg, *The Siege of Paris, 1870–1871*, 54–55.

284 *That same day:* Elihu Washburne Diary, October 31, 1870, Library of Congress.

284 *"marched with gigantic strides"*: Ibid.

284 *"People, and people"*: Sheppard, *Shut Up in Paris*, 120.

284 *Women with big feet:* Ibid., 120.

285 *A tall well-bred-looking:* Ibid., 122–23.

285 *"They all seemed to regard"*: Elihu Washburne Diary, October 31, 1870, Library of Congress.

286 *"What a city!"*: Washburne, *Recollections of a Minister to France, 1869–1877*, Vol. I, 211.

286 *"One moment revolution"*: Ibid.

286 *"perfectly raving"*: Ibid., 219.

286 *But by this time Bismarck*: Ibid., 219–20.

286 *"a prodigy of strength"*: Elihu Washburne Diary, November 7, 1870, Library of Congress.

286 *"Indeed, the defenses all round the city"*: Ibid.

286 *"I do not see for the life of me"*: Ibid., October 30, 1870, Library of Congress.

287 *At the Louvre, where Trochu*: Becker, ed., *Paris Under Siege, 1870–1871: From the Goncourt Journal*, 81.

287 *Reportedly 50,000 horses*: See estimates in Kranzberg, *The Siege of Paris, 1870–1871*, 46, *and* Washburne, *Recollections of a Minister to France, 1869–1877*, Vol. I, 153.

287 *"The situation here is dreadful"*: Elihu Washburne Diary, November 12, 1870, Library of Congress.

287 *"The Prussians can't get into"*: Ibid.

287 *"Nothing of interest today"*: Ibid., November 22, 1870.

287 *"too sober"*: Ibid., November 23, 1870.

287 *"Oh, for an opportunity"*: Sheppard, *Shut Up in Paris*, 140.

287 *"One felt an intense"*: Ibid., 3.

288 *"furtive glances"*: Ibid., 4.

288 *It is the intolerable tension*: Ibid., 133.

288 *Anything more dreary*: Labouchère, *Diary of a Besieged Resident in Paris*, 70.

288 *An American physician*: Sibbet, *Siege of Paris*, 262.

288 *The worst of it*: Ibid.

288 *The American medical student Mary Putnam*: Bittel, *Mary Putnam Jacobi and the Politics of Medicine in Nineteenth-Century America*, 79.

288 *Nor had she any desire*: Letter of Mary Putnam to Elihu Washburne, February 2, 1871, Library of Congress; Jacobi, *Life and Letters of Mary Putnam Jacobi*, 275.

289 *Her chosen topic*: Bittel, *Mary Putnam Jacobi and the Politics of Medicine in Nineteenth-Century America*, 83.

289 *"It is not at all probable"*: Jacobi, *Life and Letters of Mary Putnam Jacobi*, 271.

289 *And what a class*: Elihu Washburne Diary, November 18, 1870, Library of Congress.

289 *"The sun was just warm enough"*: Sheppard, *Shut Up in Paris*, 154.

290 *On the contrary*: Ibid.

290 *Shoes were polished*: Ibid., 155.

290 *"They are arriving"*: Elihu Washburne Diary, November 20, 1870, Library of Congress.

290 *"With an improvised"*: Ibid., November 27, 1870, Library of Congress.

290 *The American Ambulance*: Carson, *The Dentist and the Empress*, 108–9.

291 *"Here were order"*: Hoffman, *Camp, Court, and Siege*, 222.

291 *"I have known"*: Ibid., 225.

291 *"Is it necessary"*: Evans, *History of the American Ambulance Corps: Established in Paris During the Siege of 1870–71*, 44.

291 *The surgeon general*: Washburne, *Recollections of a Minister to France, 1869–1877*, Vol. I, 144.

291 *Numbering the days of the siege:* See daily notations in Elihu Washburne Diary, Library of Congress.

293 *As he explained in a letter:* Kelsey, *Remarkable Americans: The Washburn Family,* 218.

293 *"Too much cannot be said":* New York Times, January 15, 1871.

293 *Never did any population:* Ibid.

293 *"There is universal approbation":* Secretary of State Hamilton Fish to Elihu Washburne, December 8, 1870, Library of Congress.

294 *Lines formed as early as four:* Galignani's Messenger, December 27, 1870.

294 *As firewood began running out:* Ibid.

294 *"the climax of the forlorn":* Sheppard, *Shut Up in Paris,* 203.

294 *"Never has a sadder Christmas":* Elihu Washburne Diary, December 25, 1870, Library of Congress.

294 *The government is seizing:* Ibid.

294 *The bill-of-fare:* Elihu Washburne Diary, December 26, 1870, Library of Congress.

295 *"The French knew nothing":* Hoffman, *Camp, Court, and Siege,* 208.

295 *The large square:* Elihu Washburne Diary, December 26, 1870, Library of Congress; Elihu Washburne to his brother, December 26, 1870, Library of Congress.

295 *"These people cannot freeze":* Elihu Washburne Diary, December 26, 1870, Library of Congress.

295 *"The situation becomes more and more critical":* Ibid., December 28, 1870.

296 *I am unfitted:* Ibid.

296 *"sawdust, mud, and potato skins":* Sheppard, *Shut Up in Paris,* 220.

296 *"downright good eating":* Ibid., 219.

296 *By the second half of December:* Galignani's Messenger, December 31, 1870.

296 *A rat, Sheppard was surprised to find:* Sheppard, *Shut Up in Paris,* 165.

296 *"The worst of it is":* Ibid., 197.

296 *With little or nothing to feed:* Galignani's Messenger, December 18, 1870.

297 *"But bah!!!":* Jacobi, *Life and Letters of Mary Putnam Jacobi,* 277.

297 *The death toll in the city:* See Horne, *The Fall of Paris,* 221 for figure of 4,444 during the week of January 14–21.

297 *"Great discontent":* Elihu Washburne to Secretary of State Hamilton Fish, January 2, 1871, Washburne, *Franco-German War and the Insurrection of the Commune, Correspondence of E. B. Washburne,* 118.

297 *With the ground frozen:* Galignani's Messenger had ceased publication on September 19, 1870, during the siege. They resumed publication on March 10, 1871, with a day-by-day news chronology of events from September 20, 1870, to date. The entry from the weather on this day was for December 23, 1870.

298 *In fact, Bismarck:* Horne, *The Fall of Paris,* 203.

298 *"At 2 p.m. I walked":* Elihu Washburne Diary, January 5, 1871, Library of Congress.

298 *"Sometimes they would strike":* Olin Warner to his parents, February 20, 1871. Archives of American Art.

298 *An American student from Louisville, Kentucky:* Horne, *The Fall of Paris,* 213.

298 *They carry with them:* Sibbet, *Siege of Paris,* 335.

298 *"It was singularly dramatic":* Jacobi, *Life and Letters of Mary Putnam Jacobi,* 277.

299 *"Nearly twelve days of furious bombardment":* Elihu Washburne Diary, January 16, 1871, Library of Congress.

299 *"The bombardment so far":* Elihu Washburne to Secretary of State Hamilton

Fish, January 16, 1871, Washburne, *Franco-German War and the Insurrection of the Commune, Correspondence of E. B. Washburne*, 123.

299 *The total number of those killed:* Horne, *The Fall of Paris*, 217.

299 *"I am more and more convinced":* Elihu Washburne Diary, January 18, 1871, Library of Congress.

299 *"The ambulances have all been notified":* Ibid.

299 *The French novelist Edmond de Goncourt:* Horne, *The Fall of Paris*, 230.

300 *One hundred thousand men:* Ibid.

300 *They had brought in sixty-five:* Elihu Washburne Diary, January 19, 1871, Library of Congress.

300 *"whole country was literally covered":* Ibid.

300 *"All Paris is on the* qui-vive": Ibid.

300 *"trouble in the city":* Ibid., January 21, 1871.

300 *"And then such a scatteration":* Ibid., January 23, 1871.

301 *"'Mischief afoot'":* Ibid., January 22, 1871.

301 *"The city is on its last legs":* Ibid., January 24, 1871.

301 *"'Hail mighty day!'":* Ibid., January 27, 1871.

10. Madness

Alistair Horne's *The Fall of Paris: The Siege and the Commune, 1870–1871*, published in 1966, remains much the most thorough and well-written history of the Commune.

303 In the madness: Elihu Washburne to Secretary of State Hamilton Fish, May 2, 1871, Washburne, *Franco-German War and the Insurrection of the Commune, Correspondence of E. B. Washburne*, 193.

303 *The terms of the surrender:* Horne, *The Fall of Paris: The Siege and the Commune, 1870–1871*, 243.

303 *The cost to France:* Ibid., 244.

303 *By the terms of the surrender:* Wawro, *The Franco-Prussian War: The German Conquest of France in 1870–1871*, 310.

304 *"The enemy is the first to render":* Horne, *The Fall of Paris*, 242.

304 *"France is dead!":* Ibid.

304 *"Paris is trembling":* Ibid.

304 *Olin Warner spoke for nearly:* Olin Warner to his parents, June 6, 1871, Archives of American Art.

304 *"We are all furious":* Jacobi, *Life and Letters of Mary Putnam Jacobi*, 274.

304 *"quite Parisian":* Elihu Washburne to General Read, February 25, 1871, Library of Congress.

304 *"Oh, I was only a post-office":* Horne, *The Fall of Paris*, 171.

305 *The conduct of Mr. Washburne: New York Tribune*, undated news article, Elihu Washburne scrapbooks, Library of Congress.

305 *"No Minister":* Secretary of State Hamilton Fish to Elihu Washburne, February 20, 1871, Library of Congress.

305 *The German army marched: Galignani's Messenger*, March 10, 15, 1871.

305 *The first of the conquerors:* Ibid.

306 *At first the troops:* Washburne, *Recollections of a Minister to France, 1869–1877*, Vol. II, 11.

306 *The gas was not yet lighted:* Ibid., 13.

306 *"At 3 o'clock in the afternoon":* Ibid., 19.

306 *Gaslights burned once more:* See *Galignani's Messenger,* March 5, 7, 1871.

307 *In a surprise move:* Ibid., March 10, 1871.

307 *In an improvised mock trial:* Horne, *The Fall of Paris,* 272.

307 *The Commune, as often mistakenly assumed:* Ibid., 291.

308 *"culmination of every horror":* Elihu Washburne to Secretary of State Hamilton Fish, March 19, 1871, Library of Congress.

308 *With the official government now at Versailles:* Elihu Washburne to Peter [illegible], March 23, 1871, Library of Congress.

308 *He was gravely worried:* Elihu Washburne to his brother, March 21, 1871, Library of Congress.

308 *"no law, no protection":* Elihu Washburne to Benjamin Shaw, March 30, 1871, Library of Congress.

308 *On March 28, with great to-do:* Elihu Washburne to Secretary of State Hamilton Fish, March 30, 1871, Washburne, *Franco-German War and the Insurrection of the Commune, Correspondence of E. B. Washburne,* 171–72; Horne, *The Fall of Paris,* 288.

309 *At the same time:* Elihu Washburne to Secretary of State Hamilton Fish, March 30, 1871, Washburne, *Franco-German War and the Insurrection of the Commune, Correspondence of E. B. Washburne,* 173.

309 *Such a system of "denunciation":* Ibid.

309 *His private secretary:* Ibid.

309 *"He is mistaken":* Elihu Washburne Diary, March 28, 1871, Library of Congress.

309 *"The Commune is looming":* Ibid., March 31, 1871.

310 *The morning of that same day:* Horne, *The Fall of Paris,* 334–35.

310 *"a horrid place":* Elihu Washburne Diary, April 23, 1871, Library of Congress.

310 *"What mysteries":* Ibid.

310 *"I want sexual promiscuity":* Horne, *The Fall of Paris,* 334.

310 *Lillie Moulton described him:* Ibid., 335.

310 *"hideous" figures in history:* Washburne, *Recollections of a Minister to France, 1869–1877,* Vol. II, 192.

310 *Lillie was admitted to Rigault's office:* Horne, *The Fall of Paris,* 335.

311 *"No Elsa ever welcomed":* De Hegermann-Lindencrone, *In the Courts of Memory, 1858–1875,* 222.

311 *On April 4, the Commune formally impeached:* *Galignani's Messenger,* April 7, 1871.

312 *At first M. Darboy:* Ibid.

312 *"Big firing this morning":* Elihu Washburne Diary, April 10, 1871, Library of Congress.

312 *The firing is going on all the time:* Ibid., April 17, 1871, Library of Congress.

312 *All is one great shipwreck:* Ibid., April 19, 1871, Library of Congress.

313 *When the pope's nuncio:* Elihu Washburne Diary, April 23, 1871, Library of Congress.

313 *On the morning of Sunday, April 23:* Ibid.

313 *"So we all started off":* Ibid.

314 *With his slender:* Washburne, *Recollections of a Minister to France, 1869–1877,* Vol. II, 169.

314 *He seemed to appreciate his critical situation:* Elihu Washburne to Secretary of State Hamilton Fish, April 23, 1871, Washburne, *Franco-German War and the Insurrection of the Commune, Correspondence of E. B. Washburne,* 188.

314 *He was confined:* Elihu Washburne Diary, April 23, 1871, Library of Congress.

314 *When Washburne offered him any assistance:* Ibid.

315 *Two days later he was back:* Ibid., April 25, 1871, Library of Congress.

315 *"It is a little French village":* Elihu Washburne to [unknown] in Galena, Illinois, May 4, 1871, Library of Congress.

315 *"I have been so run down":* Ibid.

315 *Back in Paris an incident:* De Hegermann-Lindencrone, *In the Courts of Memory, 1858–1875,* 235.

316 *Mr. Moulton took the paper:* Ibid., 236.

316 *The Commune issued a decree:* See Horne, *The Fall of Paris,* 349–51.

316 *Hundreds of laborers:* Ibid., 350.

317 *The engineers had cut through:* Ibid.

317 *"I did not see it fall":* Elihu Washburne Diary, May 16, 1871, Library of Congress.

317 *Writing in his diary the next day:* Becker, ed., *Paris Under Siege, 1870–1871: From the Goncourt Journal,* 292.

318 *"Today they threaten to destroy":* Elihu Washburne Diary, May 19, 1871, Library of Congress.

318 *"a very delicate piece of business":* Washburne, *Recollections of a Minister to France, 1869–1877,* Vol. II, 175.

318 *On another visit to the Mazas Prison:* Elihu Washburne Diary, May 19, 1871, Library of Congress.

318 *"everything in a vastly different state":* Ibid., May 28, 1871.

319 *"He had lost his cheerfulness":* Elihu Washburne to Dr. Henry James Anderson, January 31, 1873, Library of Congress.

319 *He and Gratiot both dressed at once:* Elihu Washburne Diary, May 22, 1871, Library of Congress.

320 *"Everyone passing was forced":* Galignani's Messenger, June 1, 1871.

320 *"thick and fast":* Elihu Washburne to an unknown friend in Galena, Illinois, May 4, 1871, Library of Congress.

320 *"5:45 P.M. Have just taken a long ride":* Elihu Washburne Diary, May 22, 1871, Library of Congress.

320 *Washburne, for his part:* Ibid., May 23, 1871.

321 *"He [MacMahon] hopes they will":* Ibid.

321 *"Tremendous [cannon] firing":* Ibid., May 24, 1871.

321 *"Every woman carrying a bottle":* Hoffman, *Camp, Court, and Siege: A Narrative of Personal Adventure and Observation During Two Wars: 1861–1865; 1870–1871,* 282.

321 *All the fighting in all the revolutions:* Elihu Washburne Diary, May 24, 1871, Library of Congress.

322 *Nor was it yet generally known:* Horne, *The Fall of Paris,* 397.

323 *That afternoon on the avenue d'Antin:* Ibid., 392.

323 *The insurgents fought on "like fiends":* Gibson, *Paris During the Commune, 1871,* 37.

323 *"They are as they were when caught":* Becker, ed., *Paris Under Siege, 1870–1871,* 306.

323 *There are men of the common people:* Ibid.

323 *On Friday, 50 prisoners:* Horne, *The Fall of Paris,* 409.

323 *On Sunday, May 28:* Ibid., 413.

324 *One of the most infamous:* Ibid., 414.

324　*"There has been nothing but general butchery":* Elihu Washburne Diary, May 29, 1871, Library of Congress.

324　*"The vandalism of the dark ages":* Elihu Washburne to Secretary of State Hamilton Fish, May 31, 1871, Library of Congress.

324　*The incredible enormities:* Ibid.

325　*Although estimates of the total carnage:* Horne, *The Fall of Paris,* 418.

325　*Olin Warner, like Washburne:* "Olin Levi Warner Defense of the Paris Commune," Archives of American Art.

325　*"I hope it will never be my lot":* Olin Warner to his parents, June 6, 1871, Archives of American Art.

325　*The body of the archbishop: Galignani's Messenger,* June 9, 1871.

325　*one of "the most emotional and imposing" services:* Washburne, *Recollections of a Minister to France, 1869–1877,* Vol. II, 185–86.

326　*"Paris, the Paris of civilization": Galignani's Messenger,* June 3, 1871.

326　*Cook's Tours of London:* Horne, *The Fall of Paris,* 421.

326　*By July the Tuileries Garden: Galignani's Messenger,* July 1, 1871.

326　*The Venus de Milo:* Ibid., June 30, August 27, 1871.

327　*Everyone leaned forward:* Ibid., August 27, 1871.

327　*Lillie Moulton ordered several fine dresses:* De Hegermann-Lindencrone, *In the Courts of Memory, 1858–1875,* 246.

327　*Her engagement, too:* Jacobi, *Life and Letters of Mary Putnam Jacobi,* 281.

327　*"I have passed my last examination":* Ibid., 286.

327　*That a woman had acquired the legal right:* Ibid., 290.

328　*Tributes were to be published:* See various newspaper articles, editorials, and tributes in the Washburne Family Scrapbooks, Library of Congress.

328　*"Speaking of diplomacy":* Diary entry of Frank Moore, Paris, September 30, 1871, Frank Moore Papers, New-York Historical Society.

11. Paris Again

The wealth of Cassatt and Sargent family correspondence, in two collections at the Archives of American Art at the Smithsonian Institution and the Philadelphia Museum of Art, adds enormously to an understanding of the formative years in the lives of both Mary Cassatt and John Singer Sargent. Dr. FitzWilliam Sargent's letters are particularly important, given that his son John wrote so little about himself.

The best books about Mary Cassatt are those by Nancy Mowll Mathews: *Cassatt and Her Circle; Selected Letters* (1984); *Mary Cassatt* (1987); *Mary Cassatt: A Life* (1994); and *Cassatt: A Retrospective* (1996).

For Sargent, the two essential biographies are *John Sargent* by Evan Charteris, published in 1927, two years after Sargent's death, and the engagingly written *John Singer Sargent: His Portrait* by Stanley Olson (1986). Of particular appeal, too, are the Sargent vignettes in the letters and reminiscences of his friends Will Low and James Carroll Beckwith (as cited below).

Sargent's early work is magnificently reproduced and documented in two monumental books by Richard Ormond and Elaine Kilmurray, *John Sargent: The Early Portraits* (1998), and *John Singer Sargent: Figures and Landscapes, 1874–1882.*

For a comprehensive study of American students and their atelier masters, nothing equals H. Barbara Weinberg's *The Lure of Paris: Nineteenth-Century American Painters and Their French Teachers* (1991).

PAGE

331 I began to live: Mathews, ed., *Cassatt and Her Circle: Selected Letters*, 132.

331 *"I have never seen"*: James, *Parisian Sketches: Letters to the New York Tribune, 1875–1876*, 39.

331 *To help meet expenses:* Ibid., xiii.

331 *"sense of Parisian things"*: Ibid., 3.

332 *"decidedly the most"*: Ibid., 21.

332 *"looked and looked again"*: Lewis, *The Jameses: A Family Narrative*, 86.

332 *Called* The American: James, *The American*, 33.

332 *The street was relatively quiet:* Rue de Luxembourg is now rue Cambon. Author's visit to the street and location of James's apartment. See also James, *Henry James Letters*, Vol. II, 3.

332 *"If you were to see me"*: Ibid., 6.

332 *"Considering how nice"*: Ibid.

333 *"taken a desperate plunge"*: Ibid., 20.

333 *"I am waiting anxiously"*: Ibid., 17.

333 *"Love to all in superabundance"*: James, *Henry James Letters*, Vol. II, ed. Edel, 47.

333 *He was in Paris to work:* Ibid., 23.

333 *"I want the biggest kind of entertainment"*: James, *The American*, 58.

333 *"What shall I tell you?"*: James, *Henry James Letters*, Vol. II, ed. Edel, 35.

333 *"The spring is now quite settled"*: Ibid., 41.

333 *Since the brutal catastrophes:* Galignani's Messenger, October 5, 1872.

333 *In a single week:* Ibid., September 21, 1872.

334 *"the recipient of much attention"*: Ibid., October 21, 1872.

334 *It is generally acknowledged:* Galignani's Messenger, January 6, 1872.

335 *Will Low, an art student:* Low, *A Painter's Progress: Six Discourses Forming the Fifth Annual Series of the Scammon Lectures, Delivered Before the Art Institute of Chicago, April, 1910*, 146.

335 *George Healy, with his wife:* See George P. A. Healy to Henry Wadsworth Longfellow, November 11, 1874, and Henry Wadsworth Longfellow to George P. A. Healy, October 19, 1874, Houghton Library, Harvard University.

335 *"We can give garden parties"*: De Mare, *G. P. A. Healy, American Artist*, 270.

335 *The Healys had been among:* George P. A. Healy to Henry Wadsworth Longfellow, November 5, 1872, Houghton Library, Harvard University.

336 *"Healy is strong in portraits"*: Thomas Gold Appleton to Henry Wadsworth Longfellow, June 3, 1875, Houghton Library, Harvard University.

336 *"This will be an historical picture"*: "Souvenir of the Exhibition Entitled Healy's Sitters or a Portrait Panorama of the Victorian Age," Virginia Museum of Fine Arts, 1950, 54.

336 *"I go every morning"*: Excerpt from the Diary of Edith Healy, Rome, October 9, 1868, Archives of American Art.

337 *Mary Cassatt, too, had been hard hit:* Mathews, *Mary Cassatt: A Life*, 75.

337 *In 1866, at twenty-one:* Ibid., 29.

337 *I think she has a great deal of talent:* Eliza Haldeman to Mrs. Samuel Haldeman, May 15, 1867, Mathews, ed., *Cassatt and Her Circle: Selected Letters*, 46.

337 *"It is much pleasanter"*: Ibid., 54.

338 *"She is only an amateur"*: Mary Cassatt to Lois Cassatt, August 1, 1869, Philadelphia Museum of Art.

338 *"Oh how wild I am"*: Mathews, ed., *Cassatt and Her Circle: Selected Letters*, 77.

338 *"The Hôtel de Ville"*: Ibid., 80.

338 *"Don't be disheartened":* Emily Sartain to her father, February 26, 1872, Moore College of Art.

338 *On one excursion:* Ibid., August 4, 1872.

339 *I must candidly confess: Galignani's Messenger,* June 22, 1872.

339 *"Velázquez oh!":* Mathews, ed., *Cassatt and Her Circle: Selected Letters,* 103.

339 *"She astonished me":* Ibid., 124.

339 *Mary Cassatt had been born:* Sweet, *Miss Mary Cassatt: Impressionist from Pennsylvania,* 7.

339 *Her father, Robert Simpson Cassatt:* Ibid.

340 *But the mother and father:* Ibid., 18.

340 *At sixteen Mary:* Mathews, *Mary Cassatt: A Life,* 14.

340 *When, at twenty:* Ibid., 26.

340 *The summer of 1874:* Ibid., 92.

341 *"Miss Cassatt's tall figure":* Mathews, *Cassatt: A Retrospective,* 86.

341 *Once having seen her:* Ibid.

341 *"I felt that Miss Cassatt":* Mathews, *Mary Cassatt: A Life,* 101.

341 *"Miss C. is a tremendous talker":* Emily Sartain to her father, May 25, 1875, Moore College of Art.

341 *Emily went home:* See Mathews, ed., *Cassatt and Her Circle: Selected Letters,* 70, n. 1.

342 *"I would go there":* Mathews, *Mary Cassatt: A Life,* 114.

342 *She took Louisine:* Hale, *Mary Cassatt,* 54.

342 *The price was 500 francs:* Ibid.

343 *To learn to paint:* Mathews, *Cassatt: A Retrospective,* 195.

343 *"happy American youths":* Weinberg, *The Lure of Paris: Nineteenth-Century American Painters and Their French Teachers,* 199.

344 *Years later, recalling the "advent" of Sargent:* Mathews, *Cassatt: A Retrospective,* 205.

344 *I had a place:* "Sargent and his Painting," *Century Monthly Magazine,* Vol. 52 (June 1896), 72.

344 *The master studied these:* Mathews, *Cassatt: A Retrospective,* 205.

345 *The spring comes:* FitzWilliam Sargent to his mother from Florence, Italy, October 10, 1870, Archives of American Art.

345 *She also suffered spells:* Olson, *John Singer Sargent: His Portrait,* 1.

346 *"Mary's income":* Letter of FitzWilliam Sargent, November 24, 1869, Archives of American Art.

346 *His first memory:* Olson, *John Singer Sargent,* 8.

346 *"Drawing seems to be his favorite":* FitzWilliam Sargent to his father from Florence, Italy, March 1, 1870, Archives of American Art.

346 *"He is a good boy":* Ibid.

346 *"I see myself":* FitzWilliam Sargent to his father from Dresden, November 11, 1871, Archives of American Art.

347 *"We hear that the French":* FitzWilliam Sargent to his father from Paris, May 19, 1874, Archives of American Art.

347 *"So," explained FitzWilliam:* Ibid., May 30, 1874, Archives of American Art.

347 *"works with great patience":* Ibid.

348 *"one of the most talented":* Young, *The Life and Letters of J. Alden Weir,* 50.

348 *"makes me shake":* Diary of J. Carroll Beckwith, October 13, 1874, National Academy of Design.

348 *One must look for the middle-tone:* Olson, *John Singer Sargent,* 39.

348 *"If you begin with the middle-tone"*: Ibid.

348 *we cleared the studio*: Davis, *Strapless: John Singer Sargent and the Fall of Madame X*, 72.

349 *"Of course, we are dealing"*: Low, *A Painter's Progress*, 90.

349 *"There were no difficulties for him"*: Gay, *Memoirs of Walter Gay*, 40.

349 *"the most highly educated"*: Olson, *John Singer Sargent*, 47.

349 *"very sensible and beautiful"*: Young, *Life and Letters of J. Alden Weir*, 55.

349 *"The society of the Sargents"*: Diary of J. Carroll Beckwith, March 16, 1875, National Academy of Design.

349 *In the spring of 1876*: FitzWilliam Sargent to his sister, January 7, 1876, and to his brother Tom, April 13, 1876, Archives of American Art.

350 *Yet curiously nothing is known*: See FitzWilliam Sargent to his brother, May 13, 1876, Archives of American Art.

350 *His Philadelphia cousin, Mary Hale*: Olson, *John Singer Sargent*, 52.

350 *The three touring Sargents*: Ibid., 51–52.

350 *In spring, John's friend Will Low*: Low, *A Chronicle of Friendships, 1873–1900*, 52.

350 *In the spring of 1877*: *American Register*, April 28, 1877.

351 *Pedestrian traffic on the Pont Neuf*: Ibid., May 5, 1877.

351 *"Among our American portrait painters"*: Ibid., April 28, 1877.

351 *Another of Healy's subjects*: The portrait of Dr. Thomas Evans is at the University of Pennsylvania School of Dental Medicine, Philadelphia, Pennsylvania.

352 *"I accepted with joy"*: Hale, *Mary Cassatt*, 61.

352 *"Finally I could work"*: Ibid.

352 *He dressed always*: Ibid., 59.

352 *His mother was an American*: Ibid., 62.

352 *The American art student Walter Gay*: Gay, *Memoirs of Walter Gay*, 44.

352 *"Oh, my dear, he is dreadful!"*: Mathews, *Cassatt: A Retrospective*, 112.

352 *"Oh," Mary answered*: Mathews, *Mary Cassatt: A Life*, 149.

353 *"You know we live up very high"*: Katherine Cassatt to her granddaughter, July 2, 1878, Philadelphia Museum of Art.

353 *Paris was "a wonder to behold"*: Robert Cassatt to Alexander Cassatt, October 4, 1878, Philadelphia Museum of Art.

353 *"interested in everything"*: Mathews, *Cassatt: A Retrospective*, 86.

354 *"It is pleasant to see how well"*: Ibid., 103.

354 *"Here there is but one opinion"*: Mathews, ed., *Cassatt and Her Circle: Selected Letters*, 138.

354 *"The doctor frightened us"*: Katherine Cassatt to Alexander Cassatt, n.d., Philadelphia Museum of Art.

354 *In this case Degas advised her*: Mathews, *Cassatt: A Retrospective*, 101.

355 *They lived "as usual"*: Katherine Cassatt to Alexander Cassatt, December 23, 1881, Philadelphia Museum of Art.

355 *"on fame and money"*: Mathews, *Mary Cassatt: A Life*, 189.

355 *After eight and a half years*: Washburne, *Recollections of a Minister to France, 1869–1877*, Vol. II, 353.

355 *He submitted his resignation*: Ibid., 352.

355 *"After a reasonably good passage"*: Ibid., 353.

356 *As expected, the arrival of General Grant*: *American Register*, November 3, 1877.

356 *"It has been a mystery to me"*: Grant, *Papers of Ulysses S. Grant, November 11, 1876–September 30, 1878*, Vol. XXVIII, 299.

356 *"The contrast between the two"*: Healy, *Reminiscences of a Portrait Painter*, 193.

12. The Farragut

The letters of Augusta Saint-Gaudens to her parents are exceptional in their quantity—nearly 150 in total—and in that they cover the entire time when she and Augustus were in Paris between 1877 and 1880. But they are also unique and of greatest value in that they are the observations of an American bride coping with the altogether new kind of life on the Left Bank.

Her letters are part of the large body of Saint-Gaudens papers at Dartmouth College, in the Rauner Special Collections Library.

The building at 3 rue Herschel is still there, a block from the Luxembourg Gardens, and with the diagram of the apartment that she drew in one of her letters, as well as the interior views she provided in two of her paintings, it is easy to picture the setting of their way of life.

The studio where the Farragut was created is gone, but the nearby building where John Singer Sargent and Carroll Beckwith shared a studio apartment is still there.

PAGE

357 His whole soul: Augusta Saint-Gaudens to her parents, January 25, 1874, Saint-Gaudens Papers, Dartmouth College.

357 "We have bought a Persian rug": Augusta Saint-Gaudens to her mother, July 22, 1877, Saint-Gaudens Papers, Dartmouth College.

357 "art current": Ibid., from Rome, n.d.

358 Winslow Homer was her first cousin: Tharp, Saint-Gaudens and the Gilded Era, 145.

358 Her father, Thomas Homer: Thomas Homer to his son, May 10, 1868, Saint-Gaudens Papers, Dartmouth College.

358 Since meeting her "Mr. Saint-Gaudens": Augusta Saint-Gaudens to her parents, December 26, 1873, Saint-Gaudens Papers, Dartmouth College.

358 Medium sized, neither short nor tall: Augusta Saint-Gaudens to her mother, from Rome, n.d., Saint-Gaudens Papers, Dartmouth College.

358 "Now I must tell you": Ibid., February 2, 1874.

359 His education in everything: Ibid.

359 "I am not dead in love": Ibid.

359 "I am very sure": Ibid., from Rome, n.d.

359 Years later, however, in an uncharacteristic: Wilkinson, Uncommon Clay: The Life and Works of Augustus Saint-Gaudens, 72.

359 "What I have is a splendid": Augustus Saint-Gaudens to Thomas Homer, March 1, 1874, Saint-Gaudens Papers, Dartmouth College.

360 If successful: Ibid.

360 He cut her a cameo engagement ring: Saint-Gaudens, ed., Reminiscences of Augustus Saint-Gaudens, Vol. I, 144.

360 "You'll have to get used to a Gus": Augusta Saint-Gaudens to her mother, n.d., but in July–December, 1873, file of Augusta Saint-Gaudens Correspondence, Saint-Gaudens Papers, Dartmouth College.

360 Once prosperous: Wilkinson, Uncommon Clay, 65.

360 "like a great fire": Ibid., 77.

360 He rented a shabby studio: Saint-Gaudens, ed., Reminiscences of Augustus Saint-Gaudens, Vol. I, 154.

360 Hearing from Gussie: Ibid., 174.

360 Soon after, Saint-Gaudens learned: See Saint-Gaudens, ed., Reminiscences of Augustus Saint-Gaudens, Vol. I, 162–72.

361 *A sum of $9,000:* See copy of contract between Saint-Gaudens and City of New York dated May 23, 1877, Saint-Gaudens Papers, Dartmouth College.

361 *"I have made two models":* Saint-Gaudens, ed., *Reminiscences of Augustus Saint-Gaudens,* Vol. I, 163.

361 *He and Gussie were married:* Ibid.

361 *Two days later:* Ibid.

362 *Gus said it was the wine:* Augusta Saint-Gaudens to her mother, August 14, 1877, Saint-Gaudens Papers, Dartmouth College.

362 *"I wish someone would invite":* Ibid., October 26, 1877.

362 *Only think there are twenty-four families:* Ibid., October 18, 1877.

362 *"Aug keeps wracking":* Ibid., no date, but written from 178 boulevard Pereire, Paris, France, Saint-Gaudens Papers, Dartmouth College.

362 *"While Gussie is wrestling":* Augustus Saint-Gaudens to Mr. and Mrs. Thomas Homer, September 26, 1877, Saint-Gaudens Papers, Dartmouth College.

362 *"She eats more, sleeps more":* Ibid.

363 *You write splendid letters:* Ibid.

363 *The following spring:* See letter of April 22, 1878, from Augusta Saint-Gaudens to her mother, Saint-Gaudens Papers, Dartmouth College. In the letter Gussie included a sketch of the apartment.

363 *"a beautiful Japanese matting":* Ibid., May 17, 1878.

363 *You have no idea:* Ibid., July 25, 1878.

364 *like "Cinderella":* Ibid., June 13, 1878.

364 *Gus was devoted:* See "Biography of Louis Saint-Gaudens—Handwritten in Pencil," Saint-Gaudens Papers, Dartmouth College; Wilkinson, *Uncommon Clay,* 9.

364 *"He is certainly the easiest person":* Augusta Saint-Gaudens to her mother, October 11 (no year), Saint-Gaudens Papers, Dartmouth College.

364 *However, I forgive you:* Bernard Saint-Gaudens to Augustus and Louis Saint-Gaudens, Drafts of the "Reminiscences of Augustus Saint-Gaudens," Saint-Gaudens Papers, Dartmouth College.

365 *Working as never before:* Saint-Gaudens, ed., *Reminiscences of Augustus Saint-Gaudens,* Vol. I, 211; Wilkinson, *Uncommon Clay,* 88.

365 *The new studio:* Wilkinson, *Uncommon Clay,* 88.

365 *"by the alternate waves of exaltation":* Armstrong, *Day Before Yesterday: Reminiscences of a Varied Life,* 266.

365 *For additional help on the Farragut:* Wilkinson, *Uncommon Clay,* 90.

365 *"He hasn't a cent":* Augusta Saint-Gaudens to Genie Emerson, September 6, 1877, Saint-Gaudens Papers, Dartmouth College.

366 *Before leaving New York:* Saint-Gaudens, ed., *Reminiscences of Augustus Saint-Gaudens,* Vol. I, 164–65.

366 *"a spur to higher endeavor":* Ibid., 161.

366 *He and Saint-Gaudens had met first:* Ibid., 159.

367 *"devouring love of ice cream":* Ibid., 160.

367 *Early in 1878, hearing that White:* Wilkinson, *Uncommon Clay,* 98.

367 *"When you come over":* Ibid.

367 *"I hope you will let me help you":* Ibid.

367 *"little of the adventurous swing of life":* Saint-Gaudens, ed., *Reminiscences of Augustus Saint-Gaudens,* Vol. I, 244.

367 *"It's really a business trip":* Augusta Saint-Gaudens to her mother, August 2, 1878, Saint-Gaudens Papers, Dartmouth College.

367 *Their route was from Paris:* See Saint-Gaudens, ed., *Reminiscences of Augustus Saint-Gaudens*, Vol. I, 248; Wilkinson, *Uncommon Clay*, 100–101.

368 *"[It] is 275 ft. long":* Baldwin, *Stanford White*, 79.

368 *"the sound of a Beethoven":* Saint-Gaudens, ed., *Reminiscences of Saint-Gaudens*, Vol. I, 247.

368 *Stanford White thought the portal:* Baldwin, *Stanford White*, 81.

368 *"We sat on the top row":* Ibid., 82.

368 *"struck an attitude":* Ibid.

368 *To commemorate the fellowship:* Baker, *Stanny: The Gilded Life of Stanford White*, 51.

369 *Gus had "a most successful trip":* Augusta Saint-Gaudens to her mother, August 16, 1878, Saint-Gaudens Papers, Dartmouth College.

369 *"He is one of the nicest fellows":* Ibid., no specific date but circa August 1878.

369 *"I hug S[ain]t-Gaudens like a bear":* Baker, *Stanny*, 53.

369 *She is very kind:* Ibid.

369 *One night, with another gregarious American:* Augusta Saint-Gaudens to her mother, January 31, 1879, Saint-Gaudens Papers, Dartmouth College.

370 *"I have just taken this paper":* Ibid., postscript written by Augustus Saint-Gaudens.

370 *"I am writing in the studio":* Ibid., February 12, 1879.

370 *The model has just come in:* Ibid.

370 *"Please don't say anything":* Ibid.

370 *"Do you want to know":* White, *Stanford White: Letters to His Family*, 76.

370 *Coffee, eggs, and oatmeal:* Ibid.

371 *"I am convinced":* Saint-Gaudens, ed., *Reminiscences of Augustus Saint-Gaudens*, Vol. II, 60.

371 *With her trouble hearing:* See letters from Augusta Saint-Gaudens to her mother, May 30, 1879, and January 8, 1870, Saint-Gaudens Papers, Dartmouth College.

371 *"We went to a dancing party":* Ibid., January 13, 1879.

371 *"Every time I go out":* Ibid., March 13, 1879.

372 *Twain would be remembered:* Baldwin, *Stanford White*, 95.

372 *"of making one 'see things' ":* Wilkinson, *Uncommon Clay*, 91.

372 *He, in all simplicity:* Ibid.

373 *"I have such respect":* Saint-Gaudens, ed., *Reminiscences of Augustus Saint-Gaudens*, Vol. I, 166.

373 *"It was all Mr. White":* Augusta Saint-Gaudens to her mother, March 31, 1879, Saint-Gaudens Papers, Dartmouth College.

373 *"You have no idea":* Ibid., April 4, 1879.

373 *His inspiration had been:* Gibson, "Augustus Saint-Gaudens and the American Monument," *New Criterion*, October 2009, 44.

373 *"Conceive an idea":* Saint-Gaudens, ed., *Reminiscences of Augustus Saint-Gaudens*, Vol. II, 19.

374 *"Don't leave any serious":* Ibid., 30.

374 *"I don't fully understand":* Ibid., Vol. I, 241.

375 *"all the while trying":* Ibid., 268.

375 *"A poor picture":* Ibid., Vol. II, 79.

375 *"Farragut's legs seem to be":* Augusta Saint-Gaudens to her mother, March 13, 1879, Saint-Gaudens Papers, Dartmouth College.

375 *"He has been very much bothered":* Ibid., March 21, 1879.

375 *"Am sorry to bother you":* Ibid., May 21, 1879.

375 *"He is very much bothered by visitors"*: Ibid., May 30, 1879.

376 *"Gus is working"*: Augusta Saint-Gaudens to her parents, May 8, 1879, Saint-Gaudens Papers, Dartmouth College.

376 *"Augustus . . . seems to be conquering"*: Augusta Saint-Gaudens to her mother, May 15, 1879, Saint-Gaudens Papers, Dartmouth College.

376 *"Farragut has two legs"*: Ibid., May 30, 1879.

376 *"It is strange how fascinating the life here"*: Ibid., June 13, 1879.

376 *She painted a portrait of a friend*: Ibid., June 13, 1879, and June 20, 1879.

376 *"[He] feels like a lion"*: Ibid., August 14, 1879.

376 *But something had gone wrong*: Baker, *Stanny*, 56.

376 *The nearest thing to an explanation*: Genie Emerson to Homer Saint-Gaudens, November 15 (no year), included in the "Drafts to the Reminiscences of Augustus Saint-Gaudens," Saint-Gaudens Papers, Dartmouth College.

377 *In early days*: Ibid.

377 *Food was the way White*: Ibid.

377 *Genie said, and recalled how*: Ibid.

377 *"feeling sorry for things"*: Baker, *Stanny*, 63.

377 *"If ever a man acted"*: Ibid.

378 *"If you stick to eight feet"*: White, *Stanford White: Letters to His Family*, 90.

378 *White thought Madison Square Park*: Ibid., 101.

378 *"a quiet and distinguished place"*: Ibid.

378 *"Go for Madison Square"*: Tharp, *Saint-Gaudens and the Gilded Era*, 136.

378 *"to break away from the regular"*: Baker, *Stanny*, 55.

378 *October 14, 1879*: Augusta Saint-Gaudens to her mother, October 14, 1879, Saint-Gaudens Papers, Dartmouth College.

379 *"purely mechanical thing"*: Ibid., November 21, 1879.

379 *Gus had acquired a flute*: Ibid., February 28, 1879, and March 6, 1879.

379 *Rental for both*: Ibid., November 21, 1879.

379 *In December came the coldest*: Ibid.

379 *The Seine froze over*: *American Register*, December 20, 1879.

379 *Two large coal stoves*: Augusta Saint-Gaudens to her mother, December 12, 1879, Saint-Gaudens Papers, Dartmouth College.

379 *"Poor Aug is driven"*: Augusta Saint-Gaudens to her parents, December 12, 1879, Saint-Gaudens Papers, Dartmouth College.

379 *"Louis sleeps there"*: Augusta Saint-Gaudens to her mother, December 19, 1879, Saint-Gaudens Papers, Dartmouth College.

379 *"All my brain can conceive"*: Saint-Gaudens, ed., *Reminiscences of Augustus Saint-Gaudens*, Vol. I, 257–58.

380 *"I haven't the faintest"*: Wilkinson, *Uncommon Clay*, 102.

380 *"One of Farragut's legs"*: Augusta Saint-Gaudens to her mother, January 23, 1880, Saint-Gaudens Papers, Dartmouth College.

380 *"There are nineteen"*: Ibid., February 6, 1880.

381 *"I have seen nothing finer"*: *New York World*, February 24, 1880.

381 *Only days later*: Augusta Saint-Gaudens to her mother, March 10, 1880, Saint-Gaudens Papers, Dartmouth College.

381 *"It was immensely heavy"*: Ibid.

381 *"Clear and cloudless"*: Ibid.

381 *Aug was "very well"*: Ibid.

381 *In April, Gussie discovered*: Ibid., May 12, 1880, and June 11, 1880; Wilkinson, *Uncommon Clay*, 165.

381 *"He felt very much pleased"*: Augusta Saint-Gaudens to her mother, April 30, 1880, Saint-Gaudens Papers, Dartmouth College.

381 *His entries were awarded:* Tharp, *Saint-Gaudens and the Gilded Era*, 142.

381 *"that initiative and boldness"*: Wilkinson, *Uncommon Clay*, 102.

382 *"the incarnation of the sailor"*: Gilder, "The Farragut Monument," *Scribner's*, Vol. XXII (June 1881), 166.

382 *The cost was substantial:* Augusta Saint-Gaudens to her mother, May 7, 1880, Saint-Gaudens Papers, Dartmouth College.

382 *"You know it is quite an exciting thing"*: Ibid., May 12, 1880.

382 *The baby, a boy:* Saint-Gaudens, ed., *Reminiscences of Augustus Saint-Gaudens*, Vol. I, 271.

383 *This entire composition:* Augustus Saint-Gaudens to Augusta Saint-Gaudens, n.d., but written from New York City, Saint-Gaudens Papers, Dartmouth College.

383 *"Yesterday I had a good long day's work"*: Ibid.

383 *"They have commenced cutting"*: Ibid.

383 *"Did I ever tell you"*: Ibid.

383 *How was the "Babby"*: Ibid.

384 *A BEAUTIFUL AND REMARKABLE WORK:* New York Times, May 26, 1881.

384 *"The faces are naturally"*: Ibid.

384 *The character of the indomitable:* New York Evening Post, undated review in the Saint-Gaudens Papers, Dartmouth College.

384 *"In modeling severe"*: Gilder, "The Farragut Monument," *Scribner's*, Vol. XXII (June 1881), 164.

384 *"The sight of such a thing"*: Saint-Gaudens, ed., *Reminiscences of Augustus Saint-Gaudens*, Vol. I, 265.

385 *"Haven't I got a right"*: Ibid., 263.

13. Genius in Abundance

All of Sargent's masterworks from this period are in collections in the United States: The *Portrait of Carolus-Duran* is at the Sterling and Francine Clark Art Institute at Williamstown, Massachusetts. His two paintings of evening in the Luxembourg Gardens are at the Philadelphia Museum of Art and the Minneapolis Institute of Arts. *El Jaleo* is at the Isabella Stewart Gardner Museum in Boston; *The Daughters of Edward Darley Boit* at the Museum of Fine Arts, Boston; and *Madame X* at the Metropolitan Museum in New York.

The works of Mary Cassatt, too, are to be seen in collections in museums throughout the United States, though her first portrait of her mother, *Reading Le Figaro*, is in a private collection. Two of sister Lydia, *The Cup of Tea* and *Lydia Crocheting in the Garden at Marly*, are at the Metropolitan Museum in New York. One of her finest 1889 mother-and-child paintings, called *Mother and Child*, is at the Wichita Art Museum in Kansas.

Americans in Paris, 1860–1900, the illustrated catalogue for a memorable 2006 exhibition with essays by Kathleen Adler, Erica E. Hirshler, and H. Barbara Weinberg, is a superb survey of the works of Cassatt, Sargent, and thirty-five other American artists who studied in Paris. Erica E. Hirshler's *Sargent's Daughters: The Biography of a Painting* is an engaging study of *The Daughters of Edward Darley Boit*.

Robert Henri, who was to become a leading American painter of the early twentieth century and one of the most inspiring of all American art teachers, also wrote a delightful book called *The Art Spirit*, with reflections on his time in Paris and much else.

PAGE

387 Paris! We are here!: Robert Henri Diary, September 22, 1888, Archives of American Art.

387 *in 1879:* Mathews, *Mary Cassatt: A Life*, 133–34.

387 *"The Woman Reading . . . is a miracle":* Ibid., 137.

388 *"There was always a little crowd":* FitzWilliam Sargent to Tom Sargent, August 15, 1879, Archives of American Art.

388 *"No American had ever painted":* Ormond and Kilmurray, *John Singer Sargent: The Early Portraits*, Vol. I, 44.

388 *May Alcott of Boston:* Mathews, *Mary Cassatt: A Life*, 102–3.

388 *If Mr. John Sargent be excepted:* Mathews, *Cassatt: A Retrospective*, 87.

389 *Most of the summer of 1877:* Ormond and Kilmurray, *John Singer Sargent: The Early Portraits*, Vol. I, xiii.

390 *It was seeing the portrait of Carolus-Duran:* Olson, *John Singer Sargent*, 75.

390 *Sargent's childhood playmates:* Ormond and Kilmurray, *John Singer Sargent: The Early Portraits*, Vol. I, 75.

390 *"I enjoyed it very much":* Ibid., 76.

390 *"mere dabs and blurs":* Ibid.

391 *"application to art of psychological research":* Charteris, *John Sargent*, 250.

391 *"In his eyes":* Ibid.

391 *"very poor and bohemian":* Ormond and Kilmurray, *John Singer Sargent: The Early Portraits*, Vol. I, 57.

391 *He concentrated on each detail:* Ibid.

392 *Fanny Watts, the subject of:* Ibid., 42.

392 *Later came even more talk:* Ibid., 64–65.

393 *"she has wonderful spirits":* Mrs. Robert Simpson Cassatt to Robbie Cassatt, May 21, 1882, Philadelphia Museum of Art.

394 *"Mame's success is certainly more marked":* Mathews, ed., *Cassatt and Her Circle: Selected Letters*, 160–61.

394 *"very ill":* Robert Simpson Cassatt to Alexander Cassatt, August 2, 1882, Philadelphia Museum of Art.

394 *"Mary being the worst kind of alarmist":* Ibid.

394 *"Poor dear!":* Mathews, *Mary Cassatt: A Life*, 162.

395 *"left alone in the world":* Ibid.

395 *"the most striking picture":* Charteris, *John Sargent*, 57.

396 *Edward Darley Boit:* Hirshler, *Sargent's Daughters*, 20.

396 *"brilliantly friendly":* Ibid., 21.

396 *The two oldest Boit daughters:* Ibid., 4.

397 *"I am persuaded that the individual":* Charteris, *John Sargent*, 236.

397 *"more felicitous and interesting":* Hirshler, *Sargent's Daughters*, 130.

397 *"the complete effect":* Ibid., 96.

397 *"the most talked-about painter in France":* Ratcliff, *John Singer Sargent*, 67.

398 *"especially attracted by the bizarre":* Charteris, *John Sargent*, 250–51.

398 *Born in New Orleans:* Ormond and Kilmurray, *John Singer Sargent: The Early Portraits*, Vol. I, 113.

398 *Pierre Gautreau:* Ibid.

399 *"thrilled by every movement":* Simmons, *From Seven to Seventy: Memories of a Painter and Yankee*, 127.

399 *"homage to her beauty"*: Charteris, *John Sargent*, 59.

399 *Do you object to people*: Ormond and Kilmurray, *John Singer Sargent: The Early Portraits*, Vol. I, 113.

399 *"still struggling with the unpaintable beauty"*: Charteris, *John Sargent*, 59.

399 *"They have painters who carry off our medals"*: Davis, *Strapless: John Singer Sargent and the Fall of Madame X*, 94.

400 *"His life is a pleasant life"*: FitzWilliam Sargent to Tom Sargent, November 16, 1883, Archives of American Art.

400 *"a horrid state of anxiety"*: Ormond and Kilmurray, *John Singer Sargent: The Early Portraits*, Vol. I, 113.

401 *When, during one sitting*: Davis, *Strapless*, 205.

401 *One day I was dissatisfied with it*: Charteris, *John Sargent*, 60.

401 *When Carolus-Duran came by for a look*: Ormond and Kilmurray, *John Singer Sargent: The Early Portraits*, Vol. I, 113.

401 *"The only Franco-American product of importance"*: James, *Henry James Letters*, Vol. III, ed. Edel, 32.

401 *"half-liked"*: Ibid., 43.

402 *Walked up the Champs-Élysées*: Charteris, *John Sargent*, 61.

403 *"I went home with him"*: Ibid.

403 *The reviews were essentially of three kinds*: Ibid., 63.

403 *a "caricature"*: New York Times, May 18, 1884.

403 *"in a person of this type"*: Sidlauskas, "Painting Skin," *American Art*, Vol. XV, no. 3 (Fall 2001), 20.

404 *Years later, when he sold*: Charteris, *John Sargent*, 65.

404 *Yet hard hit as he was*: Ibid., 63.

404 *He left Paris in late May 1884*: Ormond and Kilmurray, *John Singer Sargent: The Early Portraits*, Vol. I, xv.

404 *The first rivet of her skin of copper sheets*: Weisberger, *Statue of Liberty: The First Hundred Years*, 64–65.

405 *The disassembly began in December*: Ibid., 74.

405 *The pedestal on which Liberty*: Ibid., 82.

405 *It was to stand on the Champ de Mars*: Jonnes, *Eiffel's Tower*, 22.

405 *"a project," it was said*: Ibid., 23.

406 *In the fall of 1886*: Ibid., 23–34.

407 *We, writers, painters, sculptors, architects*: Ibid., 26.

407 *"the commercial nation of America"*: Ibid., 27.

408 *The chief problem to contend with*: Harriss, *The Tallest Tower*, 62.

408 *"a metal spider web"*: Huysmans, "Le Fer," *Certains*, 1889, excerpted from *L'Art Moderne/Certains*, 1975, 346–50. This was included in Cate, *The Eiffel Tower: A Tour de Force*, 34.

408 *"a work of disconcerting"*: Ibid.

408 *"coarseness"*: Ibid.

408 *A professor of mathematics predicted*: Harriss, *The Tallest Tower*, 69.

408 *By March 1889*: Ibid., 105–6.

409 *"You will remember always"*: Ibid., 107.

409 *"We both lost our hearts"*: Stevenson, *Selected Letters of Robert Louis Stevenson*, ed., Mehew, 273.

409 *"the most intense creature"*: Ormond and Kilmurray, *John Singer Sargent: The Early Portraits*, Vol. I, 179.

409 *"Anybody may have a 'portrait' "*: Ibid., 167.

409 *"Walking about and talking"*: Ibid., 141.

410 *"John thinks of nothing else"*: Olson, *John Singer Sargent*, 153–54.

410 *In September of 1887*: Ormond and Kilmurray, *John Singer Sargent: The Early Portraits*, Vol. I, xvi.

411 *A group of aspiring young Mormon painters*: Gibbs, *Harvesting the Light*, 18.

411 *"the highest possible development of talent"*: Ibid., 3.

411 *Anna Klumpke, a tiny young woman*: Dwyer, *Anna Klumpke*, 3–5.

411 *"Prepare yourselves to compete"*: Ibid., 19.

411 *"The immense value"*: Beaux, *Background with Figures: Autobiography of Cecilia Beaux*, 174.

412 *"I am painting sunlight"*: Weinberg, *Childe Hassam: American Impressionist*, 64.

412 *"To go about Paris"*: Ibid., 60.

412 *"The people I saw copying at the Louvre"*: Clara Belle Owen to her mother, November 12, 1880, Archives of American Art.

412 *"The day was so short"*: Ibid., December 20, 1880.

412 *"the privilege we have of working there"*: Ibid.

412 *"I am too busy for that"*: Letter of Clara Belle Owen, June 13, 1881, Archives of American Art.

412 *"Paris! We are here!"*: Robert Henri Diary, September 22, 1888, Archives of American Art.

413 *"Dust and dirt are everywhere"*: Ibid., September 26, 1888.

413 *"bungling attempts"*: Ibid., September 25, 1888.

413 *"a pretty woman"*: Ibid., November 5, 1888.

413 *"Made start—poor one"*: Ibid.

414 *Since I have been here*: Ibid., December 25, 1888.

414 *"Who would not be an art student in Paris?"*: Ibid., September 27, 1888.

414 *Flags everywhere*: Ibid., May 6, 1889.

414 *Some 150,000 Americans*: Jonnes, *Eiffel's Tower*, 266.

414 *"shed over Paris a shower of gold"*: Ibid., 265.

415 *Thousands of electric bulbs*: Harriss, *The Tallest Tower*, 137.

415 *The Palais des Machines*: Ibid., 129.

415 *One of the many new productions*: Kimes, *The Star and the Laurel: The Centennial History of Daimler, Mercedes, and Benz*, 48.

416 *"the unchecked brutality"*: Reports of the U.S. Commissioners to the Universal Exposition of 1889, 27.

416 *portrait by Rosa Bonheur*: Jonnes, *Eiffel's Tower*, 253.

416 *By the close of the fair*: Harriss, *The Tallest Tower*, 116.

417 *To the Americans who made the ascent*: Jonnes, *Eiffel's Tower*, 158.

417 *"The glory of Eiffel is in the magnitude"*: Ibid., 214.

417 *Among the wealthy, prominent New Yorkers*: Weitzenhoffer, *The Havemeyers*, 56.

417 *For Louisine a great part of the excitement*: Ibid., 58.

417 *"indelibly graven"*: Ibid., 262.

417 *"Her horse had slipped upon the pavement"*: Ibid., 60.

418 *"What a man Courbet was!"*: Ibid.

418 *With Mary on the "lookout"*: Ibid.

418 *Since the death of her sister*: Mathews, *Mary Cassatt*, 171.

418 *"Mame has got to work again"*: Mathews, ed., *Cassatt and Her Circle: Selected Letters*, 166.

418 *"lamentably deficient in good sense"*: Robert Cassatt to Alexander Cassatt, July 18, 1883, Archives of American Art.

418 *"She is dreadfully headstrong. . . ."*: Ibid., August 20, 1883, Archives of American Art.

419 *"and the constant anxiety"*: Mary Cassatt to Alexander Cassatt, January 5, 1884, Archives of American Art.

419 *In 1886, when the French art dealer:* Mathews, *Mary Cassatt*, 175–76.

419 *But it was then, in 1889:* Ibid., 190.

419 *"easily the most distinguished"*: Jonnes, *Eiffel's Tower*, 105.

420 *"had become a silent and broken old one"*: Charteris, *John Sargent*, 246.

420 *"I say!"*: Ibid., 101.

420 *"to enter a new world altogether"*: *The Times* (London), May 3, 1889.

14. *Au Revoir, Paris!*

While a great deal about Saint-Gaudens's struggle with depression is included in his *Reminiscences*, many important additional details are to be found among the miscellaneous notes in the collection at Dartmouth College. What little is known about Davida Clark and Louis, and the Frances Grimes interview, are also there, as well as financial records kept by Gussie and the recollections of James Fraser. The immense photographic collection at the Saint-Gaudens National Historic Site has also been a major source of information for this and previous chapters.

PAGE

423 But coming here: Saint-Gaudens, ed., *Reminiscences of Augustus Saint-Gaudens*, Vol. II, 191.

423 *No particular notice:* Holmes, *One Hundred Days in Europe*, 175.

423 *"not a soul"*: Ibid., 162.

424 *"Rip Van Winkle experiment"*: Ibid., 1.

424 *"But when I found them"*: Ibid., 170.

424 *"What would the shopkeeper"*: Ibid., 163–64.

424 *"sacred edifice"*: Ibid., 165.

424 *"I was thinking much more of Foucault's"*: Ibid.

424 *"I sent my card in"*: Ibid., 171.

425 *"Nothing looked more nearly the same"*: Ibid., 175.

425 *"But what to me"*: Ibid., 168.

425 *"desirous of returning in what measure"*: Saint-Gaudens, ed., *Reminiscences of Augustus Saint-Gaudens*, Vol. I, 324.

426 *"a little box of a room"*: Ibid.

426 *"monumental largeness"* and *"too complex"*: Ibid., 326.

426 *"an old chap"*: Ibid., 324.

426 *He trudged:* Ibid., 324.

426 *"the blue smoke"*: Ibid., 325.

426 *"deeply felt need"*: Ibid., 323.

427 *James Earle Fraser:* Obituary, *New York Times*, October 12, 1953.

427 *"discovered"*: Freundlich, *The Sculpture of James Earle Fraser*, 21.

427 *"Strange that after having been in Paris"*: Tanner, "The Story of An Artist's Life," Part II, *The World's Work*, 11770.

427 *In a café on the Left Bank:* Perlman, *Robert Henri: His Life and Art*, 20.

427 *"He's modest"*: Robert Henri Diary, January 27, 1891, Archives of American Art.

427 *Tanner's expenses:* Tanner, "The Story of an Artist's Life," Part I, *The World's Work*, 11666.

427 *His total expenses:* Ibid., II, 11772.

427 *Never were windows opened:* Ibid., 11770.

428 *"In the cheap restaurants":* Ibid., 11771.

428 *William Dean Howells:* Weintraub, *Whistler: A Biography,* 380.

428 *"Oh, you are young":* Ibid.

428 *Live all you can:* Lewis, *The Jameses,* 518.

428 The Ambassadors: James, *The Ambassadors,* 13.

429 *My grandson, Georges de Mare:* De Mare, *G. P. A. Healy, American Artist,* 291.

429 *"His love of France":* Ibid., 292.

429 *In 1892, Healy decided:* Ibid., 293–94.

429 *arrived in Paris again:* Hureaux, *Augustus Saint-Gaudens, 1848–1907: A Master of American Sculpture,* 211.

430 *he was America's preeminent:* Saint-Gaudens, ed., *Reminiscences of Augustus Saint-Gaudens,* Vol. II, 206.

430 *the only nude he ever rendered:* Ibid., Vol. I, 393.

431 *"Augustus Saint-Gaudens—a sculptor whose art":* Research materials from Harvard University Archives, HUC 6897, HIG 300, UAI 5.150.

431 *His inspiration for the building:* Granger, *Charles Follen McKim: A Study of His Life and Architecture,* 23–24.

431 *By the late 1890s:* Hureaux, *Augustus Saint-Gaudens, 1848–1907,* 211.

431 *"I suppose through overwork":* Saint-Gaudens, ed., *Reminiscences of Augustus Saint-Gaudens,* Vol. II, 86–87.

432 *Gussie had suffered a miscarriage:* Bond, *Augustus Saint-Gaudens: The Man and His Art,* 55; Hureaux, *Augustus Saint-Gaudens, 1848–1907,* 210–11.

432 *"aflame":* Saint-Gaudens, ed., *Reminiscences of Augustus Saint-Gaudens,* Vol. I, 373.

432 *"the high pressure tension":* "Biography—Louis Saint-Gaudens—in pencil," n.d., Saint-Gaudens Papers, Dartmouth College.

432 *"But I was sick":* Saint-Gaudens, ed., *Reminiscences of Augustus Saint-Gaudens,* Vol. II, 179.

432 *"deplorable mental condition":* Ibid., 138.

432 *"neurasthenia," its symptoms described as:* Beard, ed., *A Practical Treatise on Nervous Exhaustion (Neurasthenia), Its Symptoms, Nature, Sequences, Treatment,* 24–30.

432 A Feeling of Profound Exhaustion: Ibid., 66.

433 *"a syndrome marked":* See *Webster's Third New International Dictionary* (Springfield, Mass.: 1993), 1520.

433 *"a weary lion":* Hagans, "Saint-Gaudens, Zorn, and the Goddesslike Miss Anderson," *American Art,* 76.

433 *"crippled for the remainder of his life":* Saint-Gaudens, ed., *Reminiscences of Augustus Saint-Gaudens,* Vol. II, 122.

433 *Quite on the contrary:* Ibid.

433 *Swedish model:* Hureaux, *Augustus Saint-Gaudens, 1848–1907,* 210–11.

433 *the summer of 1889, she had a baby:* Ibid.

434 *"many affairs":* Recollections of Frances Grimes, Saint-Gaudens Papers, Dartmouth College.

435 *Sweetness and kindness:* Augustus Saint-Gaudens to Augusta Saint-Gaudens, undated handwritten letter, Saint-Gaudens Papers, Dartmouth College.

435 *"the great things":* Saint-Gaudens, ed., *Reminiscences of Augustus Saint-Gaudens,* Vol. II, 205.

435 *In October of 1897:* Hureaux, *Augustus Saint-Gaudens, 1848–1907,* 211.

435 *"maddening"*: Saint-Gaudens, ed., *Reminiscences of Augustus Saint-Gaudens*, Vol. II, 123.

435 *"out-of-the-way corners"*: Ibid.

436 *The young woman who posed for him:* Hagans, "Saint-Gaudens, Zorn, and the Goddesslike Miss Anderson," *American Art*, 81.

436 *"the handsomest model"*: Material from *"Draft of the Reminiscences of Saint-Gaudens,"* Saint-Gaudens Papers, Dartmouth College.

436 *For the horse:* Saint-Gaudens, ed., *Reminiscences of Augustus Saint-Gaudens*, Vol. II, 77.

437 *"state of turmoil"*: Saint-Gaudens, ed., *Reminiscences of Augustus Saint-Gaudens*, Vol. II, 133.

437 *"I make seventeen models"*: Hureaux, *Augustus Saint-Gaudens, 1848–1907*, 108.

437 *"dominating little character"*: Fraser, unpublished autobiography, n.d., Saint-Gaudens Papers, Dartmouth College.

437 *"He is a big fellow"*: Saint-Gaudens, ed., *Reminiscences of Augustus Saint-Gaudens*, Vol. II, 194.

438 *"blue fits"*: Ibid., 120.

438 *"I am feeling very well now"*: Augustus Saint-Gaudens to Augusta Saint-Gaudens, February 26, 1898, Saint-Gaudens Papers, Dartmouth College.

438 *"This Paris experience"*: Saint-Gaudens, ed., *Reminiscences of Augustus Saint-Gaudens*, Vol. II, 186.

438 *"magnificent voice"*: Fraser, unpublished autobiography, n.d., Saint-Gaudens Papers, Dartmouth College.

438 *"Dear old Fellow"*: Saint-Gaudens, ed., *Reminiscences of Augustus Saint-Gaudens*, Vol. II, 188–92.

438 *. . . the elevated road:* Ibid.

438 *"Up to my visit here"*: Ibid., 192.

439 *"a feeling of weariness"*: Ibid.

439 *"another of those fearful depressions"*: Augustus Saint-Gaudens to Augusta Saint-Gaudens, February 10, 1899, Saint-Gaudens Papers, Dartmouth College.

439 *"I had come to appreciate Paris"*: Saint-Gaudens, ed., *Reminiscences of Augustus Saint-Gaudens*, Vol. II, 178.

440 *"Your father . . . is beginning the Sherman cloak"*: Augusta Saint-Gaudens to Homer Saint-Gaudens, December 9, 1898, Saint-Gaudens Papers, Dartmouth College.

440 *Now the left hind leg:* Saint-Gaudens, ed., *Reminiscences of Augustus Saint-Gaudens*, Vol. II, 133.

440 *"insane asylum"*: Ibid., 136.

440 *"Eleven moulders"*: Ibid.

440 *"The Sherman is in the place of honor"*: Augustus Saint-Gaudens to Augusta Saint-Gaudens, May 1 (no year but appears to be 1900), Saint-Gaudens Papers, Dartmouth College.

440 *Feeling a need to get away:* Augusta Saint-Gaudens to Homer Saint-Gaudens, May 26, 1899, Saint-Gaudens Papers, Dartmouth College.

440 *It had been their mutual friend John La Farge:* O'Toole, *The Five of Hearts: An Intimate Portrait of Henry Adams and His Friends, 1880–1918*, 165, 157.

441 *"The whole meaning and feeling of the figure"*: Saint-Gaudens, ed., *Reminiscences of Augustus Saint-Gaudens*, Vol. I, 363.

441 *"Paris delights me"*: Adams, *Letters of Henry Adams, 1892–1918*, 235.

441 *"risked"*: Adams, *The Education of Henry Adams*, 366.

441 *"to draw him out for a stroll"*: Ibid.

441 *"very—very bald"*: O'Toole, *The Five of Hearts*, 6.

441 *"most inarticulate"*: Adams, *The Education of Henry Adams*, 366.

442 *All the others*: Ibid.

442 *"excessive"*: Ibid.

442 *"inane"*: Saint-Gaudens, ed., *Reminiscences of Augustus Saint-Gaudens*, Vol. II, 198.

442 *"Evidently I must"*: Ibid.

442 *in a letter to Will Low*: Ibid., 198–201.

442 *"very sick"*: Ibid., 202.

442 *"It is fearful"*: Ibid.

442 *From a surviving note in his hand*: Augustus Saint-Gaudens to Louis Saint-Gaudens, October 27, 1899, Saint-Gaudens Papers, Dartmouth College.

443 *Your father is about the same*: Augusta Saint-Gaudens to Homer Saint-Gaudens, November 16, 1899, Saint-Gaudens Papers, Dartmouth College.

443 *"Your father has been made a member"*: Augusta Saint-Gaudens to Homer Saint-Gaudens, December 1, 1899, Saint-Gaudens Papers, Dartmouth College.

443 *trouble with the horse's upraised left hind leg*: Saint-Gaudens, ed., *Reminiscences of Augustus Saint-Gaudens*, Vol. II, 133.

443 *"on the homestretch"*: Augustus Saint-Gaudens to Augusta Saint-Gaudens, July 8, 1899, Saint-Gaudens Papers, Dartmouth College.

444 *He was anti-Semitic*: O'Toole, *The Five of Hearts*, 70.

444 *"Porcupine Poeticus"*: Saint-Gaudens, ed., *Reminiscences of Augustus Saint-Gaudens*, Vol. II, 334.

444 *I must study politics and war*: McCullough, *John Adams*, 236–37.

445 *"Every day opens new horizons"*: O'Toole, *The Five of Hearts*, 322.

445 *The automobile, considered a curiosity*: Weber, *France: Fin de Siècle*, 206–7, and *Paris Daily Messenger*, May 5, 1900.

445 *Not until they found themselves*: Adams, *The Education of Henry Adams*, 367.

445 *"conventional as death"*: Adams, *Letters of Henry Adams, 1892–1918*, 245.

445 *"a quintessence of Boston"*: Adams, *The Education of Henry Adams*, 368.

446 *"channel of force"*: Ibid.

446 *"channel of taste"*: Ibid.

446 *"instinctively preferred the horse"*: Ibid.

446 *"a new life"*: Adams, *Letters of Henry Adams, 1892–1918*, 246.

446 *Exposition Universelle*: See coverage of the 1900 exposition in the *American Register, Paris Daily Messenger,* and *Paris Herald.*

447 FIRST CHICAGOAN: Rosenblum, Stevens, and Dumas, *1900: Art at the Crossroads*, 57.

447 *"All Americans are in Paris"*: Adams, *Letters of Henry Adams, 1892–1918*, 291.

447 *Adams, who could not stay away*: Adams, *The Education of Henry Adams*, 360.

447 *"air-ships"*: Ibid., 367.

447 *"His chief interest"*: Ibid., 361.

448 *"began to feel the forty-foot dynamo"*: Ibid.

448 *"pell-mell"*: Saint-Gaudens, ed., *Reminiscences of Augustus Saint-Gaudens*, Vol. II, 185.

448 *"arms, legs, faces"*: Ibid.

448 *Four of his own major works*: Hureaux, *Augustus Saint-Gaudens, 1848–1907: A Master of American Sculpture*, 211.

449 *Auguste Rodin was seen*: Wilkinson, *Uncommon Clay: The Life and Works of*

Augustus Saint-Gaudens, 309; Gibson, "Augustus Saint-Gaudens and the American Monument," *New Criterion*, October 2009, 44.

449 *"too much the effect of a guttering candle"*: Saint-Gaudens, ed., *Reminiscences of Augustus Saint-Gaudens*, Vol. II, 50.

449 *struck by severe stomach pains*: Augustus Saint-Gaudens to Louis Saint-Gaudens, August 2, 1900; Fraser, unpublished autobiography, Saint-Gaudens Papers, Dartmouth College; Saint-Gaudens, ed., *Reminiscences of Augustus Saint-Gaudens*, Vol. II, 222; Tharp, *Saint-Gaudens and the Gilded Era*, 307.

449 *Years later Fraser put down on paper*: Fraser, unpublished autobiography, n.d., Saint-Gaudens Papers, Dartmouth College.

451 *a few final instructions*: Ibid.

451 *Saint-Gaudens sailed for home*: Wilkinson, *Uncommon Clay*, 311–12.

451 *At the Opera, Gounod's* Faust: *New York Tribune*, May 5, 1901.

452 *"daily thronged"*: *Paris Herald*, April 10, 1901.

452 *"making her mark"*: *New York Herald*, May 12, 1901.

452 *"We had no money . . . but we wanted nothing"*: Duncan, *My Life*, 67.

Epilogue

Not only are the Saint-Gaudens home and its furnishings at Cornish just as they were and the view of Mount Ascutney as magnificent as ever, the Saint-Gaudens National Historic Site includes the greatest assembly of Saint-Gaudens works to be seen anywhere.

Saint-Gaudens's *Sherman and Victory*, like his *Farragut*, remain major public monuments at Fifth Avenue and 59th Street and in Madison Square Park in New York, seen by tens of thousands of people every day, most all of whom have little or no idea of the Civil War history represented, or the story behind how each came to be.

John Singer Sargent's painting of Theodore Roosevelt hangs prominently in the East Room of the White House, while at the other end of the house, over the mantel in the State Dining Room, is a portrait of Abraham Lincoln by George P. A. Healy. Six other portraits by Healy are part of the White House Collection and another seventeen are at the National Portrait Gallery.

PAGE

453 Gus put Fraser in charge: Freundlich, *The Sculpture of James Earle Fraser*, 23.

453 *Work on the Sherman*: Fraser, unpublished autobiography, n.d., Saint-Gaudens Papers, Dartmouth College; ibid., 21.

454 *"The sculptor took no part"*: *New York Times*, May 31, 1903; *New York Herald*, May 31, 1903.

454 *In 1904, a fire*: Freundlich, *The Sculpture of James Earle Fraser*, 23.

454 *In 1906, Gus's old friend*: See Baker, *Stanny: The Gilded Life of Stanford White*, 373–76; Augustus Saint-Gaudens to Alfred Garnier, July 6, 1906, Saint-Gaudens Papers, Dartmouth College.

454 *"We are not dead yet"*: Saint-Gaudens, ed., *Reminiscences of Augustus Saint-Gaudens*, Vol. II, 58.

454 *The last and one of the most spirited*: See Hureaux, *Augustus Saint-Gaudens, 1848–1907: A Master of American Sculpture*, 188–89.

455 *In late July, an assistant*: Bond, *Augustus Saint-Gaudens: The Man and His Art*, 211–12.

455 *Homer Saint-Gaudens, after a career:* See obituaries of Homer Saint-Gaudens in *New York Times*, December 9, 1958, and *Pittsburgh Press*, December 10, 1958.

456 *Informed that he was to be knighted:* Charteris, *John Sargent,* 220.

456 *His glasses had been pushed up:* Olson, *John Singer Sargent: His Portrait,* 268.

456 *He found her propped up in bed:* Biddle, *An American Artist's Story,* 218–19.

456 *She regretted missing lunch:* Ibid., 219.

456 *"Miss Cassatt as usual":* Ibid.

Bibliography

Manuscript Collections

Archives of American Art, Smithsonian Institution, Washington, D.C.
  Papers of Mary Cassatt and Family (film edition from Philadelphia Museum of Art)
  Papers of George P. A. Healy and Family
  Papers and Diary of Robert Henri
  Papers of FitzWilliam Sargent
  Papers of Emily Sartain (film edition from Moore College of Art)
  Papers and Research Materials of Frederick A. Sweet on Mary Cassatt and Family
  Papers of Olin Warner

Dartmouth College, Special Collections, Rauner Library, Hanover, New Hampshire
  Papers of Augustus and Augusta Saint-Gaudens

Harvard University, Cambridge, Massachusetts
  Papers of Oliver Wendell Holmes—Houghton Library
  Papers of James A. Jackson, Sr. and Jr.—Harvard Medical Library
  Papers of Mary Putnam Jacobi—Schlesinger Library, Radcliffe College

Library of Congress, Washington, D.C.
  Papers of Samuel F. B. Morse
  Papers of Augustus and Augusta Saint-Gaudens (microfilm edition)
  Papers of Elihu Washburne—Diary and Correspondence

Henry Wadsworth Longfellow House, Cambridge, Massachusetts
  Papers of Thomas Gold Appleton

Massachusetts Historical Society, Boston, Massachusetts
  Papers of Thomas Gold Appleton

National Archives, Washington, D.C.
  Passport Application Records

Papers of Richard Rush—Diplomatic Correspondence
Papers of Elihu Washburne—Diplomatic Correspondence

New-York Historical Society, New York, New York
Papers of Frank Moore

University of Pennsylvania, Archives, Philadelphia, Pennsylvania
Papers of Dr. Thomas W. Evans

University of Texas, Center for American History, Austin, Texas
Papers of Ashbel Smith—Journal and Correspondence

Virginia Historical Society, Richmond, Virginia
Papers of Philip Claiborne Gooch

Washburn-Norlands, Living History Center, Livermore, Maine
Papers and Journals of Elihu Washburne

Yale University, Beinecke Library, New Haven, Connecticut
Papers of James Fenimore Cooper and Family

Books

Adams, Henry. *Eakins Revealed: The Secret Life of an American Artist.* Oxford: Oxford University Press, 2005.

Adams, Henry. *The Education of Henry Adams.* New York: Penguin Books, 1995.

———. *Letters of Henry Adams, 1892–1918.* Edited by Worthington Chauncey Ford. New York: Kraus Reprint, 1969.

———. *The Letters of Henry Adams.* Vol. I, 1858–1868. Edited by J. C. Levenson. Cambridge, Mass.: Belknap Press of Harvard University Press, 1982.

———. *Mont-Saint Michel and Chartres.* New York: Penguin Books, 1986.

Adler, Kathleen, Erica E. Hirshler, and H. Barbara Weinberg. *Americans in Paris, 1860–1900.* London: National Gallery, 2006.

Alberts, Robert C. *Benjamin West: A Biography.* Boston: Houghton Mifflin Co., 1978.

Allin, Michael. *Zarafa: A Giraffe's True Story, from Deep in Africa to the Heart of Paris.* New York: Walker & Co., 1998.

Allington, Peter, and Basil Greenhill. *The First Atlantic Liners: Seamanship in the Age of Paddlewheel, Sail, and Screw.* London: Conway Maritime Press, 1997.

Allston, Washington. *The Correspondence of Washington Allston.* Edited by Nathalia Wright. Lexington: University Press of Kentucky, 1993.

American Daguerreotypes from the Matthew R. Isenburg Collection. New Haven: Yale University Art Gallery, 1989.

Anderson, Ronald, and Anne Koval. *James McNeill Whistler: Beyond the Myth.* New York: Carroll & Graf, 2002.

Appleton, Thomas Gold. *Life and Letters of Thomas Gold Appleton.* Edited by Susan Hale. New York: D. Appleton & Co., 1885.

Armstrong, Maitland. *Day Before Yesterday: Reminiscences of a Varied Life.* New York: Charles Scribner's Sons, 1920.

Arnold, Howard Payson. *Memoir of Jonathan Mason Warren, M.D.* Boston: University Press, John Wilson & Son, 1886.

Art in a Mirror: The Counterproofs of Mary Cassatt. New York: Adelson Galleries, 2004.

Ash, Russell, and Bernard Higton, eds. *Paris: Spirit of Place.* New York: Arcade Publishing, 1989.

Atwood, William G. *The Parisian Worlds of Frédéric Chopin.* New Haven: Yale University Press, 1999.

Auser, Cortland P. *Nathaniel P. Willis.* New York: Twayne Publishers, 1969.

Ayers, Andrew. *The Architecture of Paris: An Architectural Guide.* London: Edition Axel Menges, 2004.

Bacon, Henry. *Parisian Art and Artists.* Boston: James R. Osgood & Co., 1883.

Baker, Paul R. *Richard Morris Hunt.* Cambridge, Mass.: MIT Press, 1980.

———. *Stanny: The Gilded Life of Stanford White.* New York: Free Press, 1989.

Baldwin, Charles C. *Stanford White.* New York: Da Capo Press, 1976.

Balzac, Honoré de. *The Wild Ass's Skin.* Translated by Herbert J. Hunt. New York: Penguin Putnam, 1977.

———. *Works of Honoré de Balzac.* Vol. II. Translated by Catherine Prescott Wormeley. New York: Athenaeum Club, 1896.

Barclay, Steven, ed. *A Place in the World Called Paris.* San Francisco: Chronicle Books, 1994.

Barnum, P. T. *Struggles and Triumphs of Forty Years' Recollections of P. T. Barnum.* Buffalo, N.Y.: Warren, Johnson & Co., 1873.

Barthes, Roland. *The Eiffel Tower and Other Mythologies.* Translated by Richard Howard. New York: Hill & Wang, 1979.

Bartz, Gabriele, and Eberhard König. *The Louvre: Art and Architecture.* New York: Könemann, 2005.

Beard, George M., ed. *A Practical Treatise on Nervous Exhaustion (Neurasthenia), Its Symptoms, Nature, Sequences, Treatment.* New York: William Wood, 1880.

Beaumont-Maillet, Laure. *Atget Paris.* Corte Madera, Calif.: Gingko Press, 1992.

Beaux, Cecilia. *Background with Figures: Autobiography of Cecilia Beaux.* Boston: Houghton Mifflin Co., 1930.

Becker, George J., ed. *Paris Under Siege, 1870–1871: From the Goncourt Journal.* Ithaca, N.Y.: Cornell University Press, 1969.

Beecher, Charles. *Harriet Beecher Stowe in Europe: The Journal of Charles Beecher.* Edited by Joseph S. Van Why and Earl French. Hartford: Stowe-Day Foundation, 1986.

Beers, Henry A. *American Men of Letters: Nathaniel Parker Willis.* Edited by Charles Dudley Warner. Boston: Houghton Mifflin Co., 1885.

Berg, Scott W. *Grand Avenues.* New York: Pantheon Books, 2007.

Bernier, Olivier. *Lafayette: Hero of Two Worlds.* New York: E. P. Dutton, 1983.

Biddle, George. *An American Artist's Story.* Boston: Little, Brown & Co., 1939.

Bigot, Madame Charles. *Life of George P. A. Healy.* N.p., n.d.

Bittel, Carla. *Mary Putnam Jacobi and the Politics of Medicine in Nineteenth-Century America.* Chapel Hill: University of North Carolina Press, 2009.

Blackwell, Elizabeth. *Pioneer Work in Opening the Medical Profession to Women.* Amherst, N.Y.: Humanity Books, 2005.

Blake, William P., ed. *Report of the U.S. Commissioners to the Paris Exposition, 1867.* Vol. I. Washington, D.C.: U.S. Government Printing Office, 1870.

Bond, John W. *Augustus Saint-Gaudens: The Man and His Art.* Washington, D.C.: National Park Service, 1967.

Bonfante-Warren, Alexandra. *The Louvre.* Beaux Arts Editions and Hugh Lauter Levin Assoc., 2000.

———. *The Musée d'Orsay*. Beaux Arts Editions and Hugh Lauter Levin Assoc., 2000.

Bowditch, Vincent Y. *Life and Correspondence of Henry Ingersoll Bowditch*. Vols. I–II. Boston: Houghton Mifflin Co., 1902.

Boynton, Henry Walcott. *James Fenimore Cooper*. New York: Century Co., 1931.

Braham, Allan. *The Architecture of the French Enlightenment*. Berkeley: University of California Press, 1980.

Bresc-Bautier, Geneviève. *The Louvre, a Tale of a Palace*. Paris: Musée du Louvre Éditions, 1995.

Brettell, Richard R., and Joachim Pissarro. *The Impressionist and the City: Pissarro's Series Paintings*. Edited by MaryAnne Stevens. London: Royal Academy of Arts, 1992.

Briggs, Charles F., and Augustus Maverick. *The Story of the Telegraph and a History of the Great Atlantic Cable*. New York: Rudd & Carleton, 1858.

Brissot de Warville, J.-P. *New Travels in the United States of America, 1788*. Translated by Mara Soceanu Vamos and Durand Echeverria. Cambridge, Mass.: Belknap Press of Harvard University Press, 1964.

Brogan, Hugh. *Alexis de Tocqueville: A Life*. New Haven: Yale University Press, 2006.

Brown, William Wells. *Sketches of Places and People Abroad: The American Fugitive in Europe*. Freeport, N.Y.: Books for Libraries Press, 1970.

Burchell, S. C. *Imperial Masquerade: The Paris of Napoleon III*. New York: Atheneum Books, 1971.

Cachin, Françoise, and Charles S. Moffett. *Manet, 1832–1883*. New York: Metropolitan Museum of Art and Harry N. Abrams, 1983.

Calhoun, Charles C. *Longfellow: A Rediscovered Life*. Boston: Beacon Press, 2004.

Cardot, Jean. *The Flame of Liberty*. Paris: TTM Editions, 2008.

Carmona, Michel. *Haussmann: His Life and Times, and the Making of Modern Paris*. Chicago: Ivan R. Dee, 2002.

Carson, Gerald. *The Dentist and the Empress: The Adventures of Dr. Tom Evans in Gas-Lit Paris*. Boston: Houghton Mifflin Co., 1983.

Carter, Alice A. *Cecilia Beaux: A Modern Painter in the Gilded Age*. New York: Rizzoli International Publications, 2005.

Cate, Curtis. *George Sand: A Biography*. Boston: Houghton Mifflin Co., 1975.

Cate, Phillip Dennis. *The Eiffel Tower: A Tour de Force*. New York: Grolier Club, 1989.

Catlin, George. *The Adventures of the Ojibbeway and Ioway Indians*. Vols. I–II. London: Published by the author, 1852.

Chalfant, Edward. *Better in Darkness: A Biography of Henry Adams—His Second Life, 1862–1891*. North Haven, Conn.: Archon Books, 1994.

———. *Improvement of the World: A Biography of Henry Adams—His Last Life, 1891–1918*. North Haven, Conn.: Archon Books, 2001.

Champney, Benjamin. *Sixty Years' Memories of Art and Artists, 1817–1907*. Edited by H. Barbara Weinberg. New York: Garland Publishing, 1977.

Charteris, Evan. *John Sargent*. New York: Charles Scribner's Sons, 1927.

Chessman, Harriet Scott. *Lydia Cassatt Reading the Morning Paper*. New York: Plume, 2002.

Chopin, Frederic. *Chopin's Letters*. Mineola, N.Y.: Dover Publications, 1988.

Christiansen, Rupert. *Paris Babylon: Grandeur, Decadence, and Revolution, 1869–1875*. London: Pimlico Books, 2003.

Cikovsky, Nicolai, Jr., and Franklin Kelly. *Winslow Homer*. Washington, D.C.: National Gallery of Art, 1995.

Clayson, Hollis. *Paris in Despair: Art and Everyday Life Under Siege (1870–71)*. Chicago: University of Chicago Press, 2002.

Cobb, Richard. *Paris and Elsewhere.* New York: New York Review Books, 1998.

Cohen-Solal, Annie. *Painting American: The Rise of American Artists, Paris 1867– New York 1948.* New York: Alfred A. Knopf, 2001.

Colby, Virginia Reed, and James B. Atkinson. *Footprints of the Past: Images of Cornish, New Hampshire and the Cornish Colony.* Concord: New Hampshire Historical Society, 1996.

Cooper, Helen A. *John Trumbull: The Hand and Spirit of a Painter.* New Haven: Yale University Art Gallery, 1982.

Cooper, James Fenimore. *The Bravo.* New York: Co-Operative Publication Society, n.d.

———. *Correspondence of James Fenimore Cooper.* Vols. I–II. Edited by James Fenimore Cooper. New Haven: Yale University Press, 1922.

———. *Gleanings in Europe: France.* Vol. I. New York: Kraus Reprint, 1970.

———. *The Last of the Mohicans.* New York: Penguin Books, 1986.

———. *Letters and Journals of James Fenimore Cooper.* Vols. I–VI. Edited by James Franklin Beard. Cambridge, Mass.: Belknap Press of Harvard University Press, 1960–1968.

———. *The Pioneers.* New York: Penguin Books, 1988.

———. *The Prairie.* New York: Penguin Group, 1987.

———. *The Prairie.* Paris: Baudry's European Library, 1837.

———. *The Spy.* New York: Penguin Group, 1997.

Cooper, Susan Fenimore. *Rural Hours.* Edited by Rochelle Johnson and Daniel Patterson. Athens: University of Georgia Press, 1998.

Cortissoz, Royal. *Art and Common Sense.* New York: Charles Scribner's Sons, 1913.

Cranch Scott, Leonora. *The Life and Letters of Christopher Pearse Cranch.* Boston: Houghton Mifflin Co., 1917.

Crenshaw, Mary Mayo, ed. *An American Lady in Paris, 1828–1829: The Diary of Mrs. John Mayo.* Boston: Houghton Mifflin Co., 1927.

Cunningham, Mary E., ed. *James Fenimore Cooper: A Re-Appraisal.* Cooperstown, N.Y.: New York State Historical Assoc., 1954.

Davis, Deborah. *Strapless: John Singer Sargent and the Fall of Madame X.* New York: Penguin Books, 2003.

Davis, Richard Harding. *About Paris.* New York: Harper & Brothers, 1895.

De Hegermann-Lindencrone, Lillie. *In the Courts of Memory, 1858–1875.* LaVergne, Tenn.: BiblioBazaar, 2007 (orig. 1912).

Delacroix, Eugène. *The Journal of Eugène Delacroix.* Translated by Walter Pach. New York: Hacker Art Books, 1980.

Delaporte, François. *Disease and Civilization: The Cholera in Paris, 1832.* Translated by Arthur Goldhammer. Cambridge, Mass.: MIT Press, 1986.

De Mare, Marie. *G. P. A. Healy, American Artist.* New York: David McKay Co., 1954.

Dion-Tenenbaum, Anne. *Les Appartements Napoléon III.* Paris: Les Éditions Beaux Arts and Musée du Louvre, 2006.

Dippie, Brian W. *Catlin and His Contemporaries: The Politics of Patronage.* Lincoln: University of Nebraska Press, 1990.

Donald, David. *Charles Sumner and the Coming of the Civil War.* New York: Alfred A. Knopf, 1961.

———. *Charles Sumner and the Rights of Man.* New York: Alfred A. Knopf, 1970.

———. *Lincoln.* New York: Simon & Schuster, 1995.

———. *We Are Lincoln Men: Abraham Lincoln and His Friends.* New York: Simon & Schuster, 2003.

Dowling, William C. *Oliver Wendell Holmes in Paris.* Durham: University of New Hampshire Press, 2006.

Duffy, Henry J., and John H. Dryfhout. *Augustus Saint-Gaudens: American Sculptor of the Gilded Age.* Washington, D.C.: Trust for Museum Exhibitions, 2003.

Duncan, Isadora. *My Life.* New York: Boni & Liveright, 1907.

Dunlap, William. *A History of the Rise and Progress of the Arts of Design in the United States.* Boston: C. E. Goodspeed & Co., 1918.

Dwyer, Britta C. *Anna Klumpke: A Turn-of-the-Century Painter and Her World.* Boston: Northeastern University Press, 1999.

Eakins, Thomas. *The Paris Letters of Thomas Eakins.* Edited by William Innes Homer. Princeton: Princeton University Press, 2009.

Eisler, Benita. *Naked in the Marketplace: The Lives of George Sand.* New York: Counterpoint Press, 2006.

Eliot, Alexander. *Abraham Lincoln: An Illustrated Biography.* New York: Gallery Books, 1985.

Emerson, Ralph Waldo. *The Journals and Notebooks of Ralph Waldo Emerson.* Vol. IV, 1832–1834. Edited by Alfred R. Ferguson. Cambridge, Mass.: Belknap Press of Harvard University Press, 1964.

———. *The Journals and Miscellaneous Notebooks of Ralph Waldo Emerson.* Edited by Merton M. Sealts, Jr. Cambridge, Mass.: Belknap Press of Harvard University Press, 1973.

Esten, John. *Sargent: Painting Out-of-Doors.* New York: Universe Publishing, 2000.

Evans, Thomas W. *History of the American Ambulance Corps: Established in Paris During the Siege of 1870–71.* London: Chiswick Press, 1873.

———. *Memoirs of Dr. Thomas W. Evans: The Second French Empire.* Edited by Edward Crane. New York: D. Appleton & Co., 1905.

Fabre, Michel. *From Harlem to Paris: Black American Writers in France, 1840–1980.* Urbana and Chicago: University of Illinois Press, 1991.

Fairbrother, Trevor. *Sargent Portrait Drawing: 42 Works by John Singer Sargent.* New York: Dover Publications, 1983.

Farrison, William Edward. *William Wells Brown: Author and Reformer.* Chicago: University of Chicago Press, 1969.

Fields, Annie. *Life and Letters of Harriet Beecher Stowe.* Boston: Houghton Mifflin Co., 1897.

Fitch, Noel Riley. *Literary Cafés of Paris.* Washington, D.C.: Starrhill Press, 1989.

Flayhart, William H. *Perils of the Atlantic: Steamship Disasters, 1850 to the Present.* New York: W. W. Norton & Co., 2003.

Flexner, James Thomas. *America's Old Masters: Benjamin West, John Singleton Copley, Charles Willson Peale, and Gilbert Stuart.* New York: Dover Publications, 1967.

Ford, Worthington Chauncey, ed. *Letters of Henry Adams (1858–1891).* Boston: Houghton Mifflin Co., 1930.

———. *Letters of Henry Adams (1892–1918).* Boston: Houghton Mifflin Co., 1938.

Foster, Kathleen A., and Cheryl Leibold. *Writing About Eakins: The Manuscripts in Charles Bregler's Thomas Eakins Collection.* Philadelphia: University of Pennsylvania Press, 1989.

Fowler, Marie Washburne. *Reminiscences: My Mother and I.* Livermore, Maine: Norlands, the Washburne Historic Site, n.d.

Franchi, Pepi Marchetti, and Bruce Weber. *Intimate Revelations: The Art of Carroll Beckwith (1852–1917).* New York: Berry Hill Galleries, 1999.

Franklin, Wayne. *James Fenimore Cooper: The Early Years.* New Haven: Yale University Press, 2007.

———. *The New World of James Fenimore Cooper.* Chicago: University of Chicago Press, 1982.

Frazee, Louis Jacob. *The Medical Student in Europe.* Maysville, Ky.: R. H. Collins, 1849.

Freundlich, A. L. *The Sculpture of James Earle Fraser.* LaVergne, Tenn.: Universal Publishers, 2010.

Friedrich, Otto. *Clover.* New York: Simon & Schuster, 1979.

Fuller, Margaret. *The Letters of Margaret Fuller.* Vol. IV. Edited by Robert Hudspeth. Ithaca: Cornell University Press, 1987.

Fuller Ossoli, Margaret. *At Home and Abroad.* Boston: Crosby, Nichols & Co., 1856.

Furnas, J. C. *Voyage to Windward: The Life of Robert Louis Stevenson.* New York: William Sloane Assoc., 1951.

Gardener, Augustus Kinsley. *Old Wine in New Bottles: Spare Hours of a Student in Paris.* New York: C. S. Francis & Co., 1848.

Gay, Walter. *Memoirs of Walter Gay.* New York: Privately printed, 1930.

George Catlin and His Indian Gallery, Smithsonian American Art Museum. New York: W. W. Norton & Co., 2002.

Gerdts, William. *Lasting Impressions: American Painters in France, 1865–1915.* Evanston, Ill.: Terra Foundation for the Arts, 1992.

Gerdts, William H., and Theodore E. Stebbins, Jr. *A Man of Genius: The Art of Washington Allston, 1779–1843.* Boston: Museum of Fine Arts, 1979.

Gernsheim, Helmut, and Alison Gernsheim. *L. J. M. Daguerre: The History of the Diorama and the Daguerreotype.* New York: Dover Publications, 1968.

Gibbs, Linda Jones. *Harvesting the Light: The Paris Art Mission and Beginnings of Utah Impressionism.* Salt Lake City, Utah: Corporation of the President of the Church of Jesus Christ of Latter-day Saints, 1987.

Gibson, William. *Paris During the Commune, 1871.* New York: Haskell House, 1974.

———. *Rambles in Europe in 1839.* Philadelphia: Lea & Blanchard, 1841.

Gooch, G. P. *The Second Empire.* London: Longmans, Green & Co., 1960.

Goodrich, Lloyd. *Winslow Homer.* New York: Macmillan Co., 1945.

Gopnik, Adam, ed. *Americans in Paris: A Literary Anthology.* New York: Library of America, 2004.

Gordon, Robert, and Andrew Forge. *Degas.* New York: Harry N. Abrams, 1988.

Gottschalk, Louis Moreau. *Notes of a Pianist: The Chronicles of a New Orleans Music Legend.* Edited by Jeanne Behrend. Princeton: Princeton University Press, 2006.

Granger, Alfred Hoyt. *Charles Follen McKim: A Study of His Life and Architecture.* Boston: Houghton Mifflin Co., 1913.

Grant, Ulysses S. *The Papers of U. S. Grant.* Vol. XX, November 1, 1869–October 31, 1870. Edited by John Y. Simon. Carbondale: Southern Illinois University Press, 1995.

———. *The Papers of Ulysses S. Grant.* Vol. XXVIII, November 1, 1876–September 30, 1878. Edited by John Y. Simon. Carbondale: Southern Illinois University Press, 2005.

Greenough, Horatio. *Letters of Horatio Greenough: American Sculptor.* Edited by Nathalia Wright. Madison: University of Wisconsin Press, 1972.

Grossman, James. *James Fenimore Cooper: The American Men of Letters Series.* New York: William Sloane Assoc., 1949.

Grossman, Louis, and Marianne M. Jennings. *Building a Business Through Good Times and Bad: Lessons from 15 Companies, Each with a Century of Dividends.* Westport, Conn.: Quorum Books, 2002.

Gurney, George, and Therese Thau Heyman, eds. *George Catlin and His Indian Gallery.* New York: W. W. Norton & Co., 2002.

Hale, Nancy. *Mary Cassatt.* New York: Doubleday & Co., 1975.

Harlan, Elizabeth. *George Sand.* New Haven: Yale University Press, 2004.

Harriss, Joseph. *The Tallest Tower: Eiffel and the Belle Epoque.* Boston: Houghton Mifflin Co., 1975.

Havemeyer, Louisine W. *Sixteen to Sixty: Memoirs of a Collector.* New York: Ursus Press, 1993.

Hawthorne, Nathaniel. *The French and Italian Notebooks.* Edited by Thomas Woodson. Columbus: Ohio State University Press, 1980.

Hazan, Eric. *The Invention of Paris: A History in Footsteps.* Translated by David Fernbach. New York: Verso Books, 2010.

Healy, George P. A. *Reminiscences of a Portrait Painter.* Chicago: A. C. McClurg & Co., 1894.

Heartney, Eleanor. *A Capital Collection: Masterworks from the Corcoran Gallery of Art.* Washington, D.C.: Corcoran Gallery of Art, 2002.

Hedrick, Joan D. *Harriet Beecher Stowe: A Life.* New York: Oxford University Press, 1994.

Higonnet, Patrice. *Paris: Capital of the World.* Translated by Arthur Goldhammer. Cambridge, Mass.: Belknap Press of Harvard University Press, 2002.

Hirshler, Erica E. *Sargent's Daughters: The Biography of a Painting.* Boston: Museum of Fine Arts Publications, 2009.

Hoffman, Wickham. *Camp, Court, and Siege: A Narrative of Personal Adventure and Observation During Two Wars: 1861–1865; 1870–1871.* New York: Harper & Brothers, 1877.

Holmes, Oliver Wendell. *The Autocrat at the Breakfast Table.* New York: Cosimo Classics, 2005.

———. *The Breakfast-Table Series: The Autocrat of the Breakfast-Table, The Professor at the Breakfast-Table, The Poet at the Breakfast-Table.* London: George Routledge & Sons, 1882.

———. *Medical Essays, 1842–1882.* Boston: Houghton Mifflin Co., 1911.

———. *A Mortal Antipathy.* Boston: Houghton Mifflin Co., 1891.

———. *One Hundred Days in Europe: The Works of Oliver Wendell Holmes, Part Ten.* Boston: Houghton Mifflin Co., 1891.

Horne, Alistair. *The Fall of Paris: The Siege and the Commune, 1870–1871.* New York: St. Martin's Press, 1966.

———. *Seven Ages of Paris.* New York: Alfred A. Knopf, 2002.

Howarth, T. E. B. *Citizen-King: The Life of Louis-Philippe.* London: White Lion Publishers, 1961.

Hughes, Robert. *American Visions: The Epic History of Art in America.* New York: Alfred A. Knopf, 1997.

Hugo, Victor. *Notre-Dame of Paris.* New York: Penguin, 2004.

Hunt, Gaillard. *Israel, Elihu, and Cadwallader Washburn: A Chapter in American Biography.* New York: Macmillan Co., 1925.

Hureaux, Alain Daguerre. *Augustus Saint-Gaudens, 1848–1907: A Master of American Sculpture.* Paris: Somogy Éditions d'Art, 1999.

Hussey, Andrew. *Paris: The Secret History.* New York: Bloomsbury USA, 2007.

Irmscher, Christoph. *Longfellow Redux.* Urbana & Chicago: University of Illinois Press, 2006.

Jackson, James. *Letters to a Young Physician Just Entering Upon Practice.* Boston: Phillips, Sampson & Co., 1855.

———. *A Memoir of James Jackson, Jr., M.D., with Extracts from His Letters to His Father.* Boston: I. R. Butts, 1835.

———. *Memoir of James Jackson, Jr., M.D.: Written by His Father with Extracts from His Letters and Reminiscences of Him by a Fellow Student.* Boston: Hilliard, Gray & Co., 1836.

Jacobi, Mary Putnam. *Life and Letters of Mary Putnam Jacobi.* Edited by Ruth Putnam. New York: G. P. Putnam's Sons, 1925.

James, Henry. *The Ambassadors.* New York: Penguin, 2003.

———. *The American.* Edited by William Spengeman. New York: Penguin Group, 1981.

———. *Collected Travel Writings: Great Britain and America.* New York: Library of America, 1993.

———. *Henry James Letters.* Vol. II. Edited by Leon Edel. Cambridge, Mass.: Belknap Press of Harvard University Press, 1975.

———. *Henry James Letters.* Vol. III. Edited by Leon Edel. Cambridge, Mass.: Belknap Press of Harvard University Press, 1980.

———. *Parisian Sketches: Letters to the New York Tribune, 1875–1876.* Edited by Leon Edel and Ilse Dusoir Lind. London: Rupert Hart-Davis, 1958.

Janin, Jules Gabriel. *The American in Paris; or, Heath's Picturesque Annual for 1843.* London: Longman, Brown, Green & Longmans; New York: Appleton & Son, 1843.

Jardin, André. *Tocqueville: A Biography.* Translated by Lydia Davis. Baltimore, Md.: Johns Hopkins University Press, 1998.

John La Farge. Pittsburgh and Washington, D.C.: Carnegie Museum of Art and Smithsonian Institution, 1987.

Johns, Elizabeth. *Thomas Eakins: The Heroism of Modern Life.* Princeton: Princeton University Press, 1983.

Johnston, Roy. *Parisian Architecture of the Belle Epoque.* Chichester, Eng., and Hoboken, N.J.: Wiley-Academy, 2007.

Jones, Colin. *Paris: The Biography of a City.* New York: Penguin, 2004.

Jonnes, Jill. *Eiffel's Tower: And the World's Fair Where Buffalo Bill Beguiled Paris, the Artists Quarreled, and Thomas Edison Became a Count.* New York: Viking Penguin, 2009.

Jordan, David P. *Transforming Paris: The Life and Labors of Baron Haussmann.* New York: Free Press, 1995.

Jouve, Daniel. *Paris: Birthplace of the U.S.A.: A Walking Guide for the American Patriot.* Edited by Alice Jouve. Paris: Grund, 1997.

Kelsey, Kerck. *Remarkable Americans: The Washburn Family.* Gardiner, Maine: Tilbury House, 2008.

Kennedy, Elizabeth, and Oliver Meslay. *American Artists and the Louvre.* Paris: Terra Foundation for American Art and Musée du Louvre, 2006.

Kennedy, William Sloane. *Oliver Wendell Holmes: Poet, Litterateur, Scientist.* Boston: S. E. Cassino & Co., 1883.

Kimes, Beverly Rae. *The Star and the Laurel: The Centennial History of Daimler, Mercedes, and Benz.* Montvale, N.J.: Mercedes-Benz of North America, 1986.

King, Ross. *The Judgment of Paris: The Revolutionary Decade That Gave the World Impressionism.* New York: Walker & Co., 2006.

Kirkpatrick, Sidney. *The Revenge of Thomas Eakins.* New Haven: Yale University Press, 2006.

Kirwin, Liza. *More than Words: Illustrated Letters from the Smithsonian's Archives of American Art.* New York: Princeton Architectural Press, 2005.

Kloss, William. *Samuel F. B. Morse.* New York: Harry N. Abrams, 1988.

Klumpke, Anna Elizabeth. *Memoirs of an Artist.* Edited by Lilian Whiting. Boston: Wright & Potter Printing Co., 1940.

Knowlton, Helen M. *Art: Life of William Morris Hunt.* Boston: Little, Brown & Co., 1899.

Korn, Arthur. *History Builds the Town.* London: Lund Humphries, 1953.

Kramer, Lloyd. *Lafayette in Two Worlds: Public Cultures and Personal Identities in an Age of Revolutions.* Chapel Hill: University of North Carolina Press, 1996.

Kranzberg, Melvin. *The Siege of Paris, 1870–1871: A Political and Social History.* Ithaca: Cornell University Press, 1950.

Kurtz, Harold. *The Empress Eugénie, 1826–1920.* Boston: Houghton Mifflin Co., 1964.

Labouchère, Henry. *Diary of a Besieged Resident in Paris.* New York: Harper & Brothers, 1871.

Laclotte, Michele, Geneviève Lacambre, Anne Distel, and Claire Frèches-Thory. *Paintings in the Musée d'Orsay.* Paris: Éditions Scala, 1986.

Langland, Tuck. *From Clay to Bronze: A Studio Guide to Figurative Sculpture.* New York: Watson-Guptill Publications, 1999.

Larkin, Oliver W. *Samuel F. B. Morse and American Democratic Art.* Edited by Oscar Handlin. Boston: Little, Brown & Co., 1954.

Latour, Anny. *Kings of Fashion.* New York: Coward-McCann, 1958.

Leben, Ulrich, and Robert McDonald Parker. *The American Ambassador's Residence in Paris.* Special Issue of *Connaissance des Arts.* Paris: SFPA, 2007.

Lee, Hermione. *Edith Wharton.* New York: Alfred A. Knopf, 2007.

Levasseur, Auguste. *Lafayette in America in 1824 and 1825: Journal of a Voyage to the United States.* Translated by Alan P. Hoffman. Manchester, N.H.: Lafayette Press, 2006.

Levenstein, Harvey. *Seductive Journey: American Tourists in France from Jefferson to the Jazz Age.* Chicago: University of Chicago Press, 1998.

Levin, Miriam R. *When the Eiffel Tower Was New: French Visions of Progress at the Centennial of the Revolution.* South Hadley, Mass.: Mount Holyoke College Art Museum, 1989.

Lewis, R. W. B. *Edith Wharton: A Biography.* New York: Harper Colophon Books, 1977.

———. *The Jameses: A Family Narrative.* New York: Farrar, Straus & Giroux, 1991.

Little, Carl. *The Watercolors of John Singer Sargent.* Berkeley: University of California Press, 1998.

Longfellow, Henry Wadsworth. *Letters of Henry Wadsworth Longfellow.* Vol. I. Edited by Andrew Hilen. Cambridge, Mass.: Belknap Press of Harvard University Press, 1967.

Longfellow, Samuel, ed. *Life of Henry Wadsworth Longfellow with Extracts from His Journals and Correspondence.* Vols. I–III. Boston: Houghton Mifflin Co., 1891.

Lord, John. *The Life of Emma Willard.* New York: D. Appleton & Co., 1873.

Low, Will H. *A Chronicle of Friendships, 1873–1900.* New York: Charles Scribner's Sons, 1908.

———. *A Painter's Progress: Six Discourses Forming the Fifth Annual Series of the Scammon Lectures, Delivered Before the Art Institute of Chicago, April, 1910.* Milton Keynes, Eng.: Lightning Source, 2010.

Lowe, David Garrard. *Beaux Arts New York*. New York: Whitney Library of Design, 1998.

Lucas, George. *The Diary of George Lucas, An American Art Agent in Paris, 1857–1909*. Vols. I–II. Edited by Lilian M.C. Randall. Princeton: Princeton University Press, 1979.

Lutz, Alma. *Emma Willard: Pioneer Educator of American Women*. Westport, Conn.: Greenwood Press, 1983.

Luxembourg Palace. Paris: Beaux Arts Magazine, 1999.

Lytton, Edward Bulwer-. *The Parisians*. New York: United States Book Co., ca. 1872.

Mabee, Carleton. *The American Leonardo: Life of Samuel F. B. Morse*. Fleischmanns, N.Y.: Purple Mountain Press, 2000.

Mansel, Philip. *Paris Between Empires: Monarchy and Revolution, 1814–1852*. New York: St. Martin's Press, 2001.

Marchetti, Francesca Castria. *American Painting*. New York: Watson-Guptill Publications, 2002.

Marzials, Sir Frank Thomas. *Life of Léon Gambetta*. London: W. H. Allen & Co., 1890.

Masterpieces of the Metropolitan Museum of Art. New York: Metropolitan Museum of Art, 2006.

Mathews, Marcia M. *Henry Ossawa Tanner: American Artist*. Chicago: University of Chicago Press, 1969.

Mathews, Nancy Mowll. *Cassatt: A Retrospective*. Beaux Arts Editions, 1996.

———. *Mary Cassatt: A Life*. New York: Villard Books, 1994.

———, ed. *Cassatt and Her Circle: Selected Letters*. New York: Abbeville Press, 1984.

McCullough, David. *The Great Bridge: The Epic Story of the Building of the Brooklyn Bridge*. New York: Simon & Schuster, 2001.

———. *John Adams*. New York: Simon & Schuster, 2001.

———. *Mornings on Horseback*. New York: Simon & Schuster, 1981.

———. *The Path Between the Seas: The Creation of the Panama Canal, 1870–1914*. New York: Simon & Schuster, 1977.

McFeely, William S. *Portrait: The Life of Thomas Eakins*. New York: W. W. Norton & Co., 2007.

Memorial of James Fenimore Cooper. New York: Putnam, 1852.

The Metropolitan Museum of Art Bulletin, Vol. LXI, no. 4 (Spring 2009). New York: Metropolitan Museum of Art, 2009.

Miller, John J., and Mark Molesky. *Our Oldest Enemy: A History of America's Disastrous Relationship with France*. New York: Simon & Schuster, 2004.

Morgan, H. Wayne. *The Letters of Kenyon Cox, 1877–1882: An American Art Student in Paris*. Kent, Ohio: Kent State University Press, 1986.

Morris, R. J. *Cholera, 1832: Social Response to an Epidemic*. London: Croom Helm, 1976.

Morse, Edward Lind, ed. *Samuel F. B. Morse: His Letters and Journals*. Vols. I–II. Boston: Houghton Mifflin Co., 1914.

Morse Exhibition of Arts and Science. New York: National Academy of Design, Science Section, 1950.

Morse Exhibition of Arts and Science: 125th Anniversary of the National Academy of Design, 1825–1950. New York: National Academy of Design, 1950.

Morse, John T., Jr. *Life and Letters of Oliver Wendell Holmes*. Vols. I–II. New York: Chelsea House, 1980.

Morse, Samuel F. B. *Lectures on the Affinity of Painting with the Other Fine Arts*. Edited by Nicolai Cikovsky, Jr. Columbia: University of Missouri Press, 1983.

Moss, Richard J. *The Life of Jedidiah Morse: A Station of Peculiar Exposure*. Knoxville: University of Tennessee Press, 1995.

Motley, Warren. *The American Abraham: James Fenimore Cooper and the Frontier Patriarch*. Cambridge: Cambridge University Press, 1987.

Musée d'Orsay: Impressionist & Post-Impressionist Masterpieces. London: Thames & Hudson, 1986.

The New Painting: Impressionism, 1874–1886. San Francisco: Fine Arts Museums of San Francisco with the National Gallery of Art, 1986.

Nineteen Hundred and Seven—United States Gold Coinage: Augustus Saint-Gaudens. Cornish, N.H.: Eastern National, 2002.

Numbers, Ronald L. *The Education of American Physicians: Historical Essays*. Berkeley: University of California Press, 1980.

O'Gorman, James F., ed. *The Makers of Trinity Church in the City of Boston*. Amherst: University of Massachusetts Press, 2004.

Olson, Stanley. *John Singer Sargent: His Portrait*. New York: St. Martin's Press, 1986.

O'Neill, John P. *A Walk Through the American Wing*. New York: Metropolitan Museum of Art, 2001.

Ormond, Richard. *John Singer Sargent: Paintings, Drawings, Watercolors*. New York: Harper & Row, 1970.

Ormond, Richard, and Elaine Kilmurray. *John Singer Sargent: Figures and Landscapes, 1874–1882*. New Haven: Yale University Press, 2006.

O'Toole, Patricia. *The Five of Hearts: An Intimate Portrait of Henry Adams and His Friends, 1880–1918*. New York: Clarkson Potter, 1990.

Overmyer, Grace. *America's First Hamlet*. New York: New York University Press, 1957.

The Painters in Grez-sur-Loing. Japan: Yomiuri Shimbun/Japan Association of Art Museums, 2000.

The Papers of African American Artists. Washington, D.C.: Archives of American Art, Smithsonian Institution, 1992.

Payne, Darwin. *Owen Wister: Chronicler of the West, Gentleman of the East*. Dallas: Southern Methodist University Press, 1985.

Peck, James F. *In the Studios of Paris: William Bouguereau and His American Students*. Tulsa: Philbrook Museum of Art, 2006.

Pennell, Elizabeth Robins, and Joseph Pennell. *The Life of James McNeill Whistler*. Vols. I–II. Philadelphia: J. B. Lippincott Co., 1908.

———. *The Whistler Journal*. Philadelphia: J. B. Lippincott Co., 1921.

Percoco, James A. *Summers with Lincoln: Looking for the Man in the Monuments*. New York: Fordham University Press, 2008.

Philbrick, Thomas. *James Fenimore Cooper and the Development of American Sea Fiction*. Cambridge, Mass.: Harvard University Press, 1961.

Pierce, Edward L. *Memoir and Letters of Charles Sumner*. Vols. I–II. Boston: Roberts Brothers, 1878.

———. *Memoir and Letters of Charles Sumner*. Vols. III–IV. Boston: Roberts Brothers, 1893.

Pinkney, David H. *Napoleon III and the Rebuilding of Paris*. Princeton: Princeton University Press, 1958.

Pissarro: Camille Pissarro 1830–1903. London and Boston: Arts Council of Great Britain and Museum of Fine Arts, Boston, 1980.

Poisson, Michael. *Paris: Buildings and Monuments*. New York: Harry N. Abrams, 1999.

Portrait of a Nation: Highlights from the National Portrait Gallery, Smithsonian Institution. New York: Merrell Publishers, 2006.

Portraits/Visages, 1853–2003: Galerie de Photographie. Paris: Bibliothèque Nationale de France/Gallimard, 2003.

Powell, Jessica. *Literary Paris: A Guide*. New York: Little Book Room, 2006.

Prime, Samuel Irenaeus. *The Life of Samuel F. B. Morse*. New York: D. Appleton & Co., 1875.

Protter, Eric, ed. *Painters on Painting*. Mineola, N.Y.: Dover Publications, 1997.

Ratcliff, Carter. *John Singer Sargent*. New York: Artabras, 1982.

Renard, Vincent. *The Cathedral of Rouen*. Bretteville-sur-Odon: Éditions Le Goubey, 2008.

Report on the Dinner Given by Americans in Paris, August 17th, at the "Trois Frères" to Professor S. F. B. Morse in Honor of His Invention of the Telegraph and on the Occasion of Its Completion Under the Atlantic Ocean. Paris: E. Brière, 1858.

Reports of the U.S. Commissioners to the Universal Exposition of 1889. Washington, D.C.: U.S. Government Printing Office, 1890.

Rewald, John. *The History of Impressionism*. New York: Museum of Modern Art, 1973.

Reynolds, David S. *John Brown, Abolitionist: The Man Who Killed Slavery, Sparked the Civil War, and Seeded Civil Rights*. New York: Alfred A. Knopf, 2005.

Richardson, Edgar Preston. *Washington Allston: A Study of the Romantic Artist in America*. Chicago: University of Chicago Press, 1948.

Richardson, Joanna. *The Bohemians: La Vie de Bohème in Paris, 1830–1914*. Cranbury, N.J.: A. S. Barnes & Co., 1971.

Richardson, Robert D. *Emerson: The Mind on Fire*. Berkeley: University of California Press, 1995.

———. *William James: In the Maelstrom of American Modernism*. Boston: Houghton Mifflin Co., 2006.

Ridley, Jasper. *Napoleon III and Eugénie*. London: Constable, 1979.

Rieder, William. *A Charmed Couple: The Art and Life of Walter and Matilda Gay*. New York: Harry N. Abrams, 2000.

Robb, Graham. *The Discovery of France: A Historical Geography from the Revolution to the First World War*. New York: W. W. Norton & Co., 2007.

———. *Parisians: An Adventure History of Paris*. New York: W. W. Norton & Co., 2010.

———. *Victor Hugo*. New York: W. W. Norton & Co., 1998.

Roger, Philippe. *The American Enemy: The History of French Anti-Americanism*. Edited by Sharon Bowman. Chicago: University of Chicago Press, 2005.

Rosenblum, Robert, MaryAnne Stevens, and Ann Dumas. *1900: Art at the Crossroads*. New York: Harry N. Abrams, 2000.

Rush, Richard. *Occasional Productions, Political, Diplomatic, and Miscellaneous*. Philadelphia: J. B. Lippincott & Co., 1860.

Russell, John. *Paris*. New York: Harry N. Abrams, 1983.

Saarinen, Aline B. *The Proud Possessions: The Lives, Times, and Tastes of Some Adventurous American Art Collectors*. New York: Random House, 1958.

Saint-Gaudens, Homer, ed. *The Reminiscences of Augustus Saint-Gaudens*. Vols. I–II. New York: Century Co., 1913.

Sand, George. "Relation D'un Voyage. Chez Les Sauvages de Paris," *Le Diable à Paris: Paris et Les Parisiens*. Paris: Maresca et Compagnie, 1853.

Sanderson, John. *The American in Paris*. Vols. I–II. Philadelphia: Carey & Hart, 1847.

Sawtell, Clement C. *Across the North Atlantic in Sailing Packet Days*. Lincoln, Mass.: Sawtells of Somerset, 1973.

Saxon, A. H. *P. T. Barnum: The Legend and the Man*. New York: Columbia University Press, 1989.

Seigel, Jerrold. *Bohemian Paris: Culture, Politics, and the Boundaries of Bourgeois Life, 1830–1930*. Baltimore, Md.: Johns Hopkins Paperbacks, 1999.

Shafer, Henry Burnell. *The American Medical Profession: 1783–1850*. New York: Columbia University Press, 1936.

Shapiro, Ann-Louise. *Housing the Poor of Paris: 1850–1902*. Madison: University of Wisconsin Press, 1985.

Shattuck, Roger. *The Banquet Years: The Arts in France, 1885 to World War I*. Garden City, N.Y.: Anchor Books, Doubleday & Co., 1961.

Shaw, David. *The Sea Shall Embrace Them: The Tragic Story of the Steamship* Arctic. New York: Free Press, 2002.

The Shaw Memorial: A Celebration of an American Masterpiece. Conshohocken, Pa.: Eastern National, 1997.

Sheppard, Nathan. *Shut Up in Paris*. London: Richard Bentley & Son, 1871.

Sheridan, Philip Henry. *The Personal Memoirs of Philip Henry Sheridan, General, United States*. Vol. II. New York: D. Appleton & Co., 1902.

Shikes, Ralph E., and Paula Harper. *Pissarro: His Life and Work*. New York: Horizon Press, 1980.

Sibbet, Robert. *The Siege of Paris by an American Eyewitness*. Harrisburg, Pa.: Meyers Printing and Publishing House, 1892.

Silverman, Kenneth. *Lightning Man: The Accursed Life of Samuel F. B. Morse*. New York: Alfred A. Knopf, 2003.

Simmons, Edward. *From Seven to Seventy: Memories of a Painter and Yankee*. New York: Harper & Brothers, 1922.

Simpson, Marc. *Winslow Homer: Paintings of the Civil War*. San Francisco: Fine Arts Museums of San Francisco, 1988.

Singley, Carol, ed. *Edith Wharton: The House of Mirth: A Casebook*. New York: Oxford University Press, 2003.

Sizer, Theodore. *The Works of Colonel John Trumbull, Artist of the American Revolution*. New Haven: Yale University Press, 1967.

Slowick, Theresa J. *America's Art: Masterpieces from the Smithsonian American Art Museum*. New York: Harry N. Abrams, 2006.

Smart, Mary. *A Flight with Fame: The Life and Art of Frederick MacMonnies*. Madison, Conn.: Sound View Press, 1996.

Spang, Rebecca L. *The Invention of the Restaurant: Paris and Modern Gastronomic Culture*. Cambridge, Mass.: Harvard University Press, 2001.

The Spirit of Genius: Art at the Wadsworth Atheneum. New York: Hudson Hills Press, 1992.

Starr, S. Frederick. *Louis Moreau Gottschalk*. Chicago: University of Illinois Press, 2000.

Stebbins, Theodore E., Jr., Carol Troyon, and Trevor J. Fairbrother. *A New World: Masterpieces of American Painting, 1760–1910*. Boston: Museum of Fine Arts, 1983.

Steele, Valerie. *Paris Fashion: A Cultural History*. New York: Berg Publishers, 2006.

Stein, Susan R., ed. *The Architecture of Richard Morris Hunt*. Chicago: University of Chicago Press, 1986.

Sterne, Laurence. *A Sentimental Journey Through France and Italy*. New York: Penguin, 1967.

Stevenson, Robert Louis. *Selected Letters of Robert Louis Stevenson.* Edited by Ernest Mehew. New Haven: Yale University Press, 1997.

Stewart, F. Campbell. *Eminent French Surgeons: With a Historical and Statistical Account of the Hospitals of Paris.* Buffalo, N.Y.: A. Burke, Publisher, n.d.

Stowe, Harriet Beecher. *Sunny Memories of Foreign Lands.* Vols. I–II. Boston: Phillips, Sampson & Co., 1854.

Sumner, Charles. *Works of Charles Sumner.* Vol. IV. Boston: Lee & Shepard, 1871.

Sutcliffe, Anthony. *Paris: An Architectural History.* New Haven: Yale University Press, 1993.

Sweet, Frederick A. *Miss Mary Cassatt: Impressionist from Pennsylvania.* Norman: University of Oklahoma Press, 1967.

Symonds, Craig L. *Lincoln and His Admirals.* New York: Oxford University Press, 2008.

Tappert, Tara Leigh. *Cecilia Beaux and the Art of Portraiture.* Washington, D.C.: Smithsonian Institution Press, 1995.

Tharp, Louise Hall. *The Appletons of Beacon Hill.* Boston: Little, Brown & Co., 1973.

———. *Mrs. Jack: A Biography of Isabella Stewart Gardner.* Boston: Little, Brown & Co., 1965.

———. *Saint-Gaudens and the Gilded Era.* Boston: Little, Brown & Co., 1969.

Thomson, Belinda. *Impressionism: Origins, Practice, Reception.* London: Thames & Hudson, 2000.

Thoron, Ward, ed. *The Letters of Mrs. Henry Adams, 1865–1883.* Boston: Little, Brown & Co., 1936.

Thorp, Nigel, ed. *Whistler on Art: Selected Letters and Writings of James McNeill Whistler.* Washington, D.C.: Smithsonian Institution Press, 1994.

The Ties that Bind. Paris: U.S. Embassy, 2006.

Tilton, Eleanor M. *Amiable Autocrat: A Biography of Dr. Oliver Wendell Holmes.* New York: Henry Schuman, 1947.

Tocqueville, Alexis de. *Democracy in America.* New York: Library of America, 2004.

———. *The Recollections of Alexis de Tocqueville.* Translated by Alexander Teixeira de Mattos and edited by J. P. Mayer. New York: Columbia University Press, 1949.

Tolles, Thayer. *Augustus Saint-Gaudens in the Metropolitan Museum of Art.* New York: Metropolitan Museum of Art, 2009.

Trollope, Frances. *Domestic Manners of the Americans.* New York: Penguin, 1997.

———. *Paris and the Parisians in 1835.* Vol. I. London: Richard Bentley, 1836.

Truax, Rhoda. *The Doctors Warren of Boston: First Family of Surgeons.* Boston: Houghton Mifflin Co., 1968.

Truettner, William H. *The Natural Man Observed: A Study of Catlin's Indian Gallery.* Washington, D.C.: Smithsonian Institution Press, 1979.

Trumbull, John. *The Autobiography of Colonel John Trumbull: Patriot-Artist, 1756–1843.* Edited by Theodore Sizer. New Haven: Yale University Press, 1953.

Twain, Mark. *Innocents Abroad.* New York: Oxford University Press, 1996.

Twombly, Robert. *Louis Sullivan: His Life and Work.* New York: Viking Penguin, 1986.

Tyler, David Budlong. *Steam Conquers the Atlantic.* New York: D. Appleton-Century Co., 1939.

Vallois, Thirza. *Around and About Paris: New Horizons, Haussmann's Annexation.* London: Iliad Books, 1999.

Van Rensselaer, Mariana Griswold. *Henry Hobson Richardson and His Works.* New York: Dover Publications, 1969.

Vasari, Giorgio. *Lives of the Artists.* New York: Penguin Books, 1982.

Walker, John. *James Abbott McNeill Whistler.* New York: Harry N. Abrams, 1987.

Wangensteen, Owen H., and Sarah D. Wangensteen. *The Rise of Surgery: From Empiric Craft to Scientific Discipline.* Minneapolis: University of Minnesota Press, 1978.

Warner, Charles Dudley, ed. *American Men of Letters.* Boston: Houghton Mifflin Co., 1883.

Warner, John Harley. *Against the Spirit of System: The French Impulse in Nineteenth-Century American Medicine.* Princeton: Princeton University Press, 1998.

Warren, Jonathan Mason. *The Parisian Education of an American Surgeon: Letters of Jonathan Mason Warren (1832–1835).* Edited by Russell Jones. Philadelphia: American Philosophical Society, 1978.

Washburne, Elihu B. *Franco-German War and the Insurrection of the Commune. Correspondence of E. B. Washburne.* Washington, D.C.: U.S. Government Printing Office, 1878.

———. *Recollections of a Minister to France, 1869–1877.* Vols. I–II. New York: Charles Scribner's Sons, 1887.

Washburne, Mark. *A Biography of Elihu Benjamin Washburne: Congressman, Secretary of State, Envoy Extraordinary.* Vols. III–IV. Philadelphia: Xlibris, 2005, 2007.

Wawro, Geoffrey. *The Franco-Prussian War: The German Conquest of France in 1870–1871.* Cambridge: Cambridge University Press, 2003.

Weber, Eugen. *France: Fin de Siècle.* Cambridge, Mass.: Belknap Press of Harvard University Press, 1986.

———. *My France: Politics, Culture, Myth.* Cambridge, Mass.: Belknap Press of Harvard University Press, 1991.

———. *Peasants into Frenchmen: The Modernization of Rural France, 1870–1914.* Stanford, Calif.: Stanford University Press, 1976.

Webster, Daniel. *The Papers of Daniel Webster. Diplomatic Papers.* Vol. II, 1850–1852. Edited by Kenneth Shewmaker and Kenneth Stevens. Hanover, N.H.: Dartmouth College by the University Press of New England, 1987.

Webster, Sally. *William Morris Hunt.* New York: Cambridge University Press, 1991.

Weigley, Russell F., ed. *Philadelphia: A 300 Year History.* New York: W. W. Norton & Co., 1982.

Weinberg, H. Barbara. *Childe Hassam: American Impressionist.* New York: Metropolitan Museum of Art, 2004.

———. *The Lure of Paris: Nineteenth-Century American Painters and Their French Teachers.* New York: Abbeville Press, 1991.

Weintraub, Stanley. *Whistler: A Biography.* New York: Truman Talley Books, 1974.

Weisberger, Bernard A. *Statue of Liberty: The First Hundred Years.* New York: American Heritage, 1985.

Weitzenhoffer, Frances. *The Havemeyers: Impressionism Comes to America.* New York: Harry N. Abrams, 1986.

Welles, Gideon. *Diary of Gideon Welles.* Vol. III. Boston: Houghton Mifflin Co., 1911.

Wharton, Edith. *A Backward Glance: An Autobiography.* New York: Charles Scribner's Sons, 1964.

Wharton, Edith, and Ogden Codman, Jr. *The Decoration of Houses.* New York: W. W. Norton & Co., 1997.

White, Edmund. *The Flâneur: A Stroll Through the Paradoxes of Paris.* London: Bloomsbury Publishing, 2001.

White, Elizabeth Brett. *American Opinion of France from Lafayette to Poincaré.* New York: Alfred A. Knopf, 1927.

White, Stanford. *Stanford White: Letters to His Family.* Edited by Claire Nicolas White. New York: Rizzoli International Publications, 1997.

Wilkinson, Burke. *Uncommon Clay: The Life and Works of Augustus Saint-Gaudens.* New York: Harcourt Brace Jovanovich, 1985.

Willard, Emma. *Journal and Letters, from France and Great Britain.* Troy, N.Y.: N. Tuttle, Printer, 1833.

Williams, Ellen. *The Historic Restaurants of Paris.* New York: Little Book Room, n.d.

Willis, Nathaniel Parker. *Paul Fane; or, Parts of a Life Else Untold.* New York: Charles Scribner, 1857.

———. *Pencillings by the Way: Written During Some Years of Residence and Travel in Europe.* Auburn, N.Y.: Alden, Beardsley & Co., 1854.

Willson, Beckles. *America's Ambassadors to France (1777–1927).* London: John Murray, 1928.

Wilson, Forrest. *Crusader in Crinoline: The Life of Harriet Beecher Stowe.* Philadelphia: J. B. Lippincott Co., 1941.

Wright, Nathalia. *Horatio Greenough: The First American Sculptor.* Philadelphia: University of Pennsylvania Press, 1963.

Young, Dorothy Weir. *The Life and Letters of J. Alden Weir.* New York: Da Capo Press, 1971.

Young, Sylvia. *Cecilia Beaux: American Figure Painter.* Atlanta: High Museum of Art, 2007.

Zola, Émile. *The Debacle.* Translated by Leonard Tancock. New York: Penguin Group, 1972.

Articles

Gibson, Eric. "Augustus Saint-Gaudens and the American Monument." *New Criterion*, October 2009, 43–46.

Gilder, Richard Watson. "The Farragut Monument." *Scribner's*, Vol. XXII (June 1881), 164.

Hagans, William E. "Saint-Gaudens, Zorn, and the Goddesslike Miss Anderson." *American Art*, Vol. 16, no. 2 (Summer 2002).

Hess, Stephen. "An American in Paris." *American Heritage*, February 1967, 18–73.

Jones, Russell M. "American Doctors and the Parisian Medical World, 1830–1840." *Bulletin of the History of Medicine*, Vol. XLVII, no. 1 (January–February 1973).

———. "American Doctors and the Parisian Medical World, 1830–1840 (Concluded)." *Bulletin of the History of Medicine*, Vol. XLVII, no. 2 (March–April 1973).

———. "An American Medical Student in Paris, 1831–1833." *Harvard Library Bulletin*, Vol. XV, no. 1 (January 1967).

Sloane, Joseph C. "Manet and History." *Art Quarterly*, Vol. XIV, no. 2 (Summer 1951).

Sparks, Jared. "Political Portraits, with Pen and Pencil." *United States Magazine and Democratic Review*, Vol. VII (1840).

Tanner, Henry O. "The Story of an Artist's Life." Part II, *The World's Work* (July 1909), 11769–75.

Tatham, David. "Samuel F. B. Morse's Gallery of the Louvre: The Figures in the Foreground." *American Art Journal*, Vol. XIII, no. 4 (Autumn 1981).

Voss, Frederick. "Webster Replying to Hayne: George Healy and the Economics of History Painting." *American Art*, Vol. XV, no. 3 (Fall 2001).

Washburne, Elihu. "Abraham Lincoln in Illinois." *North American Review*, October 1885, 307–19.

White, Laura. "Was Charles Sumner Shamming, 1856–1869?" *New England Quarterly*, Vol. 33, no. 3 (September 1960).

General References

Baedeker, Karl. *Paris and Environs with Routes from London to Paris.* London: Dulau & Co., 1888.

———. *Paris and Environs with Routes from London to Paris.* London: Dulau & Co., 1904.

Baedeker's France. Englewood Cliffs, N.J.: Prentice-Hall, n.d.

Berkow, Robert, ed. *The Merck Manual of Diagnosis and Therapy.* 16th edition. Rahway, N.J.: Merck Research Laboratories, 1992.

Boucher, François. *20,000 Years of Fashion: The History of Costume and Personal Adornment.* New York: Harry N. Abrams, 1965.

Boyer, Paul S., ed. *The Oxford Companion to United States History.* Oxford: Oxford University Press, 2001.

Brogan, Hugh. *The Penguin History of the United States of America.* New York: Penguin Books, 1985.

Cole, Robert. *A Traveller's History of France.* 7th edition. New York: Interlink Books, 2005.

Dictionary of American Biography. Edited by Allen Johnson. New York: Charles Scribner's Sons, 1964.

Foner, Eric, and John A. Garraty, eds. *The Reader's Companion to American History.* Boston: Houghton Mifflin Co., 1991.

Galignani's New Paris Guide. Paris: A. & W. Galignani, 1827.

Galignani's New Paris Guide. Paris: A. & W. Galignani & Co., 1848.

Galignani's New Paris Guide. Paris: Galignani Library, 1883.

Gerrard, Mike. *Bloom's Literary Guide to Paris.* New York: Checkmark Books, 2007.

Gowing, Sir Lawrence, ed. *A Biographical Dictionary of Artists.* New York: Facts on File, 1995.

Grant, Susan. *Paris: A Guide to Archival Sources for American Art History.* Washington, D.C.: Archives of American Art, Smithsonian Institution, 1997.

Gray, Henry. *Anatomy: Descriptive and Surgical.* Edited by T. Pickering Pick and Robert Howden. New York: Gramercy Books, 1977.

Guterman, Norbert. *The Anchor Book of French Quotations.* New York: Anchor Books Editions, 1990.

The Houghton Mifflin Dictionary of Biography. Boston: Houghton Mifflin Co., 2003.

Kloss, William, and Diane K. Skvarla. *United States Senate Catalogue of Fine Art.* Washington, D.C.: U.S. Government Printing Office, 2002.

Kronenberger, Louis, ed. *Atlantic Brief Lives: A Biographical Companion to the Arts.* Boston: Little, Brown & Co., 1971.

Kullen, Allan S. *The Peopling of America: A Timeline of Events That Helped Shape Our Nation.* Beltsville, Md.: People of America Foundation, 1993.

Latham, Alison, ed. *The Oxford Companion to Music.* New York: Oxford University Press, 2003.

Lejeune, Anthony, ed. *Quote Unquote, French.* London: Stacey International, 2008.

Lyons, Albert S., and R. Joseph Petrucelli II. *Medicine: An Illustrated History.* New York: Abradale Press, 1987.

The Oxford Dictionary of Quotations. Revised 4th edition. Oxford: Oxford University Press, 1996.

Paris Plan. Paris: Pneu Michelin, 1987.

Paris Pratique: Par Arrondissement. Paris: Éditions L'Indispensable, 2005.

Paris Restaurants: 2007–08. Edited by Alexander Lobrano, Mary Deschamps, and Troy Segal. New York: Zagat Survey, 2007.

Ribeiro, Aileen. *The Art of Dress: Fashion in England and France, 1750 to 1820.* New York: National Academy of Design, 1982.

Rood, Karen Lane, ed. *Dictionary of Literary Biography: American Writers in Paris, 1920–1939.* Vol. IV. Detroit: Gale Research Company, 1980.

Shapiro, Fred R., ed. *The Yale Book of Quotations.* New Haven: Yale University Press, 2006.

Newspapers and Journals

American Register (Paris)
Antiques Magazine
Galignani's Messenger (Paris)
Harper's Weekly
New York Commercial Advertiser
New York Evening Post
New York Herald
New-York Mirror
New York Times
New York Tribune
Paris Daily Messenger
Paris Herald
The Times (London)

INDEX

Institute, Williamstown, MA / The Bridgeman Art Library, New York, NY: 71 • Tate Gallery, London / Art Resource, New York, NY: 72 • Terra Foundation for American Art, Chicago, IL / Art Resource, New York, NY, Samuel F. B. Morse, *Gallery of the Louvre*, Daniel J. Terra Collection, 1992.51: 11 • U.S. Dept. of Interior, National Park Service, Saint-Gaudens National Historic Site, Cornish NH: 49, 65, 67 (photograph by Dewitt Clinton Ward), 89, 91 (photograph by Kevin Daley) • Wellcome Library, London: 23 • Emma Willard School Archives, Troy, NY: 13.

Text Permissions. The author gratefully acknowledges permission from the following sources to use material in their control: Moore College of Art and Design Archives, Philadelphia, PA, for excerpts from the letters of Emily Sartain • National Academy Museum and School of Fine Arts, New York, NY, for excerpts from the Papers of James Carroll Beckwith • Philadelphia Museum of Art, Carl Zigrosser Collection, Philadelphia, PA, for excerpts from the Family Letters of Mary Cassatt • Harvard Medical School Library, Countway Building, Boston, MA, for excerpts from the Papers of James Jackson Sr. and Jr. (H MS c8.1 folders 1–9 and H MS c8.2 folders 1016).

Also by
DAVID McCULLOUGH

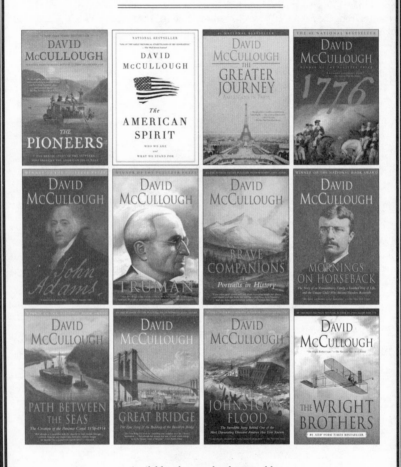

Available wherever books are sold
or at SimonandSchuster.com

SIMON &
SCHUSTER